Illustrated Series®

Microsoft® 365® & Office® Introductory

First Edition

David Beskeen
Carol Cram
Jennifer Duffy
Lynn Wermers
Robert S. Wilson

Australia • Brazil • Canada • Mexico • Singapore • United Kingdom • United States

Illustrated Series® Microsoft® 365® & Office® Introductory, First Edition

David Beskeen, Carol Cram, Jennifer Duffy, Lynn Wermers, Robert S. Wilson

SVP, Product Management: Cheryl Costantini

VP, Product Management & Marketing: Thais Alencar

Senior Product Director, Portfolio Product Management: Mark Santee

Portfolio Product Director: Rita Lombard

Senior Portfolio Product Manager: Amy Savino

Senior Product Assistant: Ciara Boynton

Learning Designer: Zenya Molnar

Senior Content Manager: Samantha Rundle

Digital Project Manager: Jim Vaughey

Developmental Editors: Barbara Clemens, MT Cozzola, Lisa Ruffolo, Michael Sanford

Senior Director, Product Marketing: Danae April

Senior Marketing Manager: Mackenzie Paine

Portfolio Specialist: Matt Schiesl

Content Acquisition Analyst: Callum Panno

Production Service: Lumina Datamatics Ltd.

Senior Designer: Erin Griffin

Cover Image Source: Novendi Prasetya/Shutterstock.com

Copyright © 2025 Cengage Learning, Inc. ALL RIGHTS RESERVED.

WCN: 01-100-496

No part of this work covered by the copyright herein may be reproduced or distributed in any form or by any means, except as permitted by U.S. copyright law, without the prior written permission of the copyright owner.

Unless otherwise noted, all content is Copyright © Cengage Learning, Inc.

Mac Users: If you're working through this product using a Mac, some of the steps may vary. Additional information for Mac users is included with the Data files for this product.

Disclaimer: This text is intended for instructional purposes only; data is fictional and does not belong to any real persons or companies.

Disclaimer: The material in this text was written using Microsoft Windows 11 and Office 365 Professional Plus and was Quality Assurance tested before the publication date. As Microsoft continually updates the Windows operating system and Office 365, your software experience may vary slightly from what is presented in the printed text.

Windows, Access, Excel, and PowerPoint are registered trademarks of Microsoft Corporation. Microsoft and the Office logo are either registered trademarks or trademarks of Microsoft Corporation in the United States and/or other countries. This product is an independent publication and is neither affiliated with, nor authorized, sponsored, or approved by, Microsoft Corporation.

The names of all products mentioned herein are used for identification purposes only and may be trademarks or registered trademarks of their respective owners. Cengage Learning disclaims any affiliation, association, connection with, sponsorship, or endorsement by such owners.

Previous edition(s): © 2023, © 2020, © 2017

> For product information and technology assistance, contact us at
> **Cengage Customer & Sales Support, 1-800-354-9706**
> or support.cengage.com.
>
> For permission to use material from this text or product, submit all requests online at **www.copyright.com**.

Library of Congress Control Number: 2024920337

Student Edition ISBN: 978-0-357-88256-6

Looseleaf ISBN: 978-0-357-88257-3

K12 Edition ISBN: 978-0-357-88258-0

Cengage
5191 Natorp Boulevard
Mason, OH 45040
USA

Cengage is a leading provider of customized learning solutions. Our employees reside in nearly 40 different countries and serve digital learners in 165 countries around the world. Find your local representative at **www.cengage.com**.

To learn more about Cengage platforms and services, register or access your online learning solution, or purchase materials for your course, visit **www.cengage.com**.

Notice to the Reader

Publisher does not warrant or guarantee any of the products described herein or perform any independent analysis in connection with any of the product information contained herein. Publisher does not assume, and expressly disclaims, any obligation to obtain and include information other than that provided to it by the manufacturer. The reader is expressly warned to consider and adopt all safety precautions that might be indicated by the activities described herein and to avoid all potential hazards. By following the instructions contained herein, the reader willingly assumes all risks in connection with such instructions. The publisher makes no representations or warranties of any kind, including but not limited to, the warranties of fitness for particular purpose or merchantability, nor are any such representations implied with respect to the material set forth herein, and the publisher takes no responsibility with respect to such material. The publisher shall not be liable for any special, consequential, or exemplary damages resulting, in whole or part, from the readers' use of, or reliance upon, this material.

Printed in the United States of America
Print Number: 03   Print Year: 2025

Brief Contents

Preface .... ILP-i

Getting to Know Microsoft Office Versions ... OFF-1

Using SAM Projects and Textbook Projects .. SAM-1

Word

Module 1: Creating Documents with Word .... WD 1-1

Module 2: Editing and Formatting Documents .... WD 2-1

Module 3: Formatting Text and Graphics .... WD 3-1

Excel

Module 1: Getting Started with Excel ...... EX 1-1

Module 2: Formatting a Worksheet .... EX 2-1

Module 3: Analyzing Data Using Formulas .... EX 3-1

Module 4: Working with Charts .... EX 4-1

Integration

Module 1: Integrating Word and Excel .. INT 1-1

Access

Module 1: Getting Started with Access ... AC 1-1

Module 2: Building Tables and Relationships .... AC 2-1

Module 3: Creating Queries .... AC 3-1

Module 4: Working with Forms and Reports .... AC 4-1

Integration

Module 2: Integrating Word, Excel, and Access .... INT 2-1

PowerPoint

Module 1: Creating a Presentation in PowerPoint .... PPT 1-1

Module 2: Modifying a Presentation ...... PPT 2-1

Module 3: Inserting Objects into a Presentation .... PPT 3-1

Integration

Module 3: Integrating Word, Excel, Access, and PowerPoint .... INT 3-1

Index Index-1

Contents

Preface .... ILP-i
Getting to Know Microsoft Office Versions ... OFF-1
Using SAM Projects and Textbook Projects ... SAM-1

Word

Module 1: Creating Documents with Word .... WD 1-1

Use Word-Processing Software .... WD 1-2
    Planning a document
Start Word .... WD 1-4
Enter and Revise Text .... WD 1-6
Save a Document .... WD 1-8
    Saving with AutoSave
Select Text .... WD 1-10
Format Text Using the Mini Toolbar and the Ribbon .... WD 1-12
View and Navigate a Document .... WD 1-14
    Using Word document views
Cut and Paste Text .... WD 1-16
    Highlighting text in a document
    Using the Undo, Redo, and Repeat commands
Copy and Paste Text .... WD 1-18
    Splitting the document window to copy and move items in a long document
    Copying and moving items between documents
Format with Fonts .... WD 1-20
    Applying shadows and other text effects to text
Set Document Margins .... WD 1-22
    Using keyboard shortcuts
    Changing orientation, margin settings, and paper size
Add Bullets and Numbering .... WD 1-24
Insert a Graphic .... WD 1-26
    Enhancing pictures with styles and effects
Apply a Theme .... WD 1-28
Practice .... WD 1-30

Module 2: Editing and Formatting Documents .... WD 2-1

Insert Comments .... WD 2-2
    Using modern comments in Word
    Inking comments in Word
Find and Replace Text .... WD 2-6
    Navigating a document using the Navigation pane and the Go to command
Check Spelling and Grammar .... WD 2-8
    Searching for information
    Inserting text with AutoCorrect
Proofread and Revise Text .... WD 2-10
    Reading a document aloud using Word
    Using an add-in for Word
Change Line Spacing and Indents .... WD 2-12
Apply Styles to Text .... WD 2-14
    Changing the Style set
Insert Page Numbers and Page Breaks .... WD 2-16
Add Headers and Footers .... WD 2-18
Add Footnotes and Endnotes .... WD 2-20
Insert Citations .... WD 2-22
Create a Bibliography .... WD 2-24
    Finding and citing sources with the Word Researcher
Inspect a Document .... WD 2-26
Practice .... WD 2-28

Module 3: Formatting Text and Graphics .... WD 3-1

Use the Format Painter .... WD 3-2
    Clearing formatting from text
Set and Modify Tabs .... WD 3-4
Add Borders and Shading .... WD 3-6
    Underlining text
Insert a Table .... WD 3-8
Insert and Delete Rows and Columns .... WD 3-10
Apply a Table Style .... WD 3-12
Insert Online Pictures .... WD 3-14
Size and Scale a Graphic .... WD 3-16

Draw and Format Shapes .... WD 3-18
    Correcting pictures, changing colors, and
    applying artistic effects
Adjust and Rotate Shapes .... WD 3-20
    Enhancing graphic objects with
    styles and effects
Arrange Graphic Objects .... WD 3-22
    Creating an illustration in a drawing canvas
Create SmartArt Graphics .... WD 3-24
Add Alt Text to Objects .... WD 3-26
Practice .... WD 3-28

Excel

Module 1: Getting Started with Excel ...... EX 1-1
Describe an Excel Workbook .... EX 1-2
    Navigating a worksheet
Enter Data .... EX 1-4
    Inserting and deleting selected cells
Edit Data .... EX 1-6
    Recovering unsaved changes to a
    workbook file
Copy and Move Cell Data .... EX 1-8
    Using Paste Options and
    Paste Preview
Enter Formulas .... EX 1-10
Enter a Formula with Multiple
Operators .... EX 1-12
Insert a Function .... EX 1-14
Change Worksheet Views .... EX 1-16
    Working with Sheet View options
Customize Print Options .... EX 1-18
    Setting a print area
    Scaling to fit
Practice .... EX 1-20

Module 2: Formatting a Worksheet .... EX 2-1
Format Values .... EX 2-2
    Working with online pictures,
    other images, and symbols
Change Font Attributes .... EX 2-4
    Modify, create, and merge styles
Modify Font Styles and Alignment .... EX 2-6
    Rotating and indenting cell entries

Adjust Column Width and Row Height ...... EX 2-8
    Changing row height
Insert and Delete Rows and Columns ..... EX 2-10
    Hiding and unhiding columns
    and rows
Modify Data Formatting
and Documentation .... EX 2-12
    Working with Microsoft Office
    color palettes
Apply Conditional Formatting .... EX 2-14
    Formatting data with icon sets
    Managing conditional formatting rules
Modify Worksheet Tabs .... EX 2-16
    Copying, adding, and deleting worksheets
Check Spelling and Find Text .... EX 2-18
    Translating text
    Using Find & Select features
Practice .... EX 2-20

Module 3: Analyzing Data Using
Formulas .... EX 3-1
Enter a Formula Using the Quick
Analysis Tool .... EX 3-2
Copy Formulas with Relative Cell
References .... EX 3-4
    Inserting functions into formulas
Build a Logical Formula with the
IF Function .... EX 3-6
    Nesting IF functions
Copy Formulas with Absolute Cell
References .... EX 3-8
    Using a mixed reference
Build a Logical Formula with the
AND Function .... EX 3-10
    Using the OR and NOT logical functions
Use a Function to Round a Value .... EX 3-12
    Using Excel rounding functions
Build a Statistical Formula with
the COUNTA Function .... EX 3-14
Enter a Date Function .... EX 3-16
Control Worksheet Calculations .... EX 3-18
    Showing and printing worksheet formulas
Practice .... EX 3-20

Module 4: Working with Charts .... EX 4-1
Identify Chart Features .... EX 4-2
Create a Chart with a Title .... EX 4-4
Position a Chart .... EX 4-6
Modify a Chart .... EX 4-8
   Creating a combo chart
Change the Chart Layout .... EX 4-10
   Working with chart axes
Format a Chart .... EX 4-12
   Working with WordArt
   Aligning charts
Create a Pie Chart .... EX 4-14
   Working with other chart types
Summarize Data with Sparklines .... EX 4-16
Identify Data Trends .... EX 4-18
   Choosing the right trendline options for your chart
Practice .... EX 4-20

Integration

Module 1: Integrating Word and Excel ... INT 1-1
Identify Integration Options Between Word and Excel .... INT 1-2
   Understanding object linking and embedding (OLE)
Copy Data from Excel to Word .... INT 1-4
Copy a Chart from Excel to Word .... INT 1-6
Insert Linked Objects .... INT 1-8
   Opening linked files and reestablishing links to charts
Embed a Word File in Excel .... INT 1-10
Practice .... INT 1-12

Access

Module 1: Getting Started with Access .... AC 1-1
Describe Relational Databases .... AC 1-2
Open and Explore a Database .... AC 1-4
Navigate and Enter Data .... AC 1-6
   Changing from Navigation mode to Edit mode
   Resizing and moving datasheet columns
Edit Existing Data .... AC 1-8
Create a Table .... AC 1-10
   Creating a table in Datasheet View
   Object views
Modify Fields .... AC 1-12
   Field properties
Create a Query .... AC 1-14
   Simple Query Wizard
Create a Form .... AC 1-16
Create a Report .... AC 1-18
   Changing page orientation
Save and Share a Database with OneDrive .... AC 1-20
   Cloud computing
   Access is a local application
Create a Database .... AC 1-22
Compact and Back Up a Database .... AC 1-24
Practice .... AC 1-25

Module 2: Building Tables and Relationships .... AC 2-1
Import Data from Excel .... AC 2-2
Modify Fields in Datasheet View .... AC 2-4
   Currency versus Number data type
Modify Number and Currency Fields ...... AC 2-6
Modify Short Text Fields .... AC 2-8
   Working with the Input Mask property
Modify Date/Time Fields .... AC 2-10
   Entering dates
   Using Action Tags
Create Primary Key Fields .... AC 2-12
Design Related Tables .... AC 2-14
Create One-to-Many Relationships .... AC 2-16
   Specifying the data type of the foreign key field
   Cascade options
Use Subdatasheets .... AC 2-18
Practice .... AC 2-20

Module 3: Creating Queries .... AC 3-1
Use Query Datasheet View .... AC 3-2
Use Query Design View .... AC 3-4
   Adding or deleting a table in Query Design View
   Linking tables in Query Design View

Use SQL View .... AC 3-6
Sort Data .... AC 3-8
Find and Replace Data .... AC 3-10
Filter Data .... AC 3-12
Enter and Save Criteria .... AC 3-14
Apply AND Criteria .... AC 3-16
   Searching for blank fields
Apply OR Criteria .... AC 3-18
   Using wildcard characters
Create Calculated Fields .... AC 3-20
Format a Datasheet .... AC 3-22
Practice .... AC 3-24

Module 4: Working with Forms and Reports .... AC 4-1
Use Form View .... AC 4-2
Use Form Layout View .... AC 4-4
Use Form Design View .... AC 4-6
   Bound versus unbound controls
Use Report Layout View .... AC 4-8
Use Report Design View .... AC 4-10
Add Conditional Formatting .... AC 4-12
Use the Format Painter and Themes .... AC 4-14
Practice .... AC 4-16

Integration

Module 2: Integrating Word, Excel, and Access .... INT 2-1
Identify Integration Options Among Word, Excel, and Access .... INT 2-2
Import an Excel Worksheet into Access .... INT 2-4
Copy a Word Table to Access .... INT 2-6
Link an Access Table to Excel and Word ... INT 2-8
Copy an Access Table to Word .... INT 2-10
   Opening linked files and enabling content
Practice .... INT 2-12

PowerPoint

Module 1: Creating a Presentation in PowerPoint .... PPT 1-1
Define Presentation Software .... PPT 1-2
   Using PowerPoint on a touchscreen
Plan an Effective Presentation .... PPT 1-4
   Understanding copyright
Examine the PowerPoint Window .... PPT 1-6
   Creating a presentation using a template
Add Text to a Slide .... PPT 1-8
   Aligning paragraph text
Add a New Slide .... PPT 1-10
   Viewing your presentation in grayscale or black and white
Format Text .... PPT 1-12
   Adding bullets to paragraphs
Apply a Design Theme .... PPT 1-14
   Changing theme colors
Compare Presentation Views .... PPT 1-16
Insert and Resize a Picture .... PPT 1-18
   Rehearse with the Speaker coach
Check Spelling .... PPT 1-20
   Checking spelling as you type
Print a PowerPoint Presentation .... PPT 1-22
   Office for the Web Apps
Practice .... PPT 1-24

Module 2: Modifying a Presentation ...... PPT 2-1
Convert Text to SmartArt .... PPT 2-2
   Entering and printing notes
Insert and Style Shapes .... PPT 2-4
   Using the Eyedropper to match colors
Rotate and Modify Shapes .... PPT 2-6
   Inking a slide
Rearrange and Modify Shapes .... PPT 2-8
   Changing the size and position of shapes
Edit and Duplicate Shapes .... PPT 2-10
   Editing points of a shape
Align and Group Objects .... PPT 2-12
   Distributing objects
Add Slide Footers .... PPT 2-14
   Creating superscript and subscript text
Set Slide Transitions and Timings .... PPT 2-16
   Inserting hyperlinks in a webpage
Practice .... PPT 2-18

Module 3: Inserting Objects into a Presentation ....PPT 3-1
Insert a Text Box................................... PPT 3-2
    Changing text box defaults
Revise and Crop a Picture .... PPT 3-4
    Inserting a screen recording
Insert a Chart....................................... PPT 3-6
Enter and Edit Chart Data .... PPT 3-8
    Adding a hyperlink to a chart
Insert Slides from Other Presentations .... PPT 3-10
    Working with multiple windows
Insert a Table .... PPT 3-12
    Setting permissions
Insert and Format WordArt .... PPT 3-14
    Coauthoring a presentation
Animate Objects .... PPT 3-16
    Attaching a sound to an animation
Insert and Edit Digital Video .... PPT 3-18
    Saving a presentation as a video
Practice... PPT 3-20

Integration

Module 3: Integrating Word, Excel, Access, and PowerPoint .... INT 3-1
Identify Integration Options among Word, Excel, Access, and PowerPoint ...... INT 3-2
Import a Word Outline into PowerPoint... INT 3-4
Embed an Excel Worksheet in PowerPoint .... INT 3-6
Link Access and Excel Objects to PowerPoint .... INT 3-8
Update and Break Links .... INT 3-10
Practice.. INT 3-12

Index Index-1

Preface: The Illustrated Series®: Microsoft® 365® and Office®

About the Authors

Access: Robert S. Wilson has a Computer Science degree from the University of Waterloo, holds numerous certifications from CompTIA, Microsoft, and Cisco, and has over 40 years of experience in the computing field. Rob has expertise in many areas including database development and administration. He has built complex applications using Microsoft® Access® as its foundation, including production control and project management systems. He is also the co-founder and chief technical officer of Got Your Six Cybersecurity Solutions, a cybersecurity firm offering services covering the entire cybersecurity spectrum.

Excel: Lynn Wermers is a professor in the Computer Science Department at North Shore Community College in Massachusetts, where she teaches IT, data management, data analysis, and web development courses. She also teaches part-time in the math department for the College of Professional Studies at Northeastern University. Professor Wermers has authored numerous leading Cengage books focusing on Excel.

PowerPoint: David W. Beskeen has authored or co-authored over 65 successful computer books since 1992 for Microsoft Press and other publishers, including more than 40 educational titles for Course Technology, Thomson Learning, and Cengage. Over the years he has guided readers in mastering PowerPoint®, Word®, Excel®, Internet Explorer, Outlook®, Windows®, LiveMotion, and other leading proprietary software packages. An expert in applied technology, Beskeen has extensive teaching and consulting experience in today's computer technology.

Integration and Word: Carol M. Cram is the author of more than 35 textbooks on computer applications, business communications, and Internet-related subjects. Ms. Cram was also a long-time faculty member at Capilano College in North Vancouver, where she served as the Convenor of the Executive Support Program and the Program Consultant for Business and Computers in Continuing Education as well as instructor of business and computer-related courses.

Word: Jennifer Duffy is the author of nine editions of Microsoft® Word® Illustrated and many other textbooks on computer applications for the popular Office series. An award-winning writer and educator, she has worked successfully in the business world as a content creator and communications consultant and in colleges and universities as an effective instructor of writing. She combines her expertise in Word with her strong business and teaching knowledge to create compelling learning tools for students.

Preface for the Instructor

The Illustrated series' concise, student-friendly approach uses a proven two-page layout that enables learners to focus on discrete Office skills as they complete module readings. Each module begins with a brief overview of the principles covered in the lesson while large, full-color screen images reflect what students see on their computers. Distinctive to *Illustrated*, Tips and Clues boxes are incorporated throughout the text, while Trouble elements help students troubleshoot or explain common errors to strengthen their confidence. Module learning objectives are mapped to Microsoft Office Specialist (MOS) certification objectives, preparing students to take the MOS exam, which they can leverage in their careers. In addition, MindTap and updated SAM (Skills Assessment Manager) online resources are available to guide additional studies and ensure successful results.

The Illustrated Series is designed for students at two- and four-year schools as well as in continuing education programs. Skill levels range from experienced—for those with a foundational understanding from prior exposure to technology—to introductory—for those using a computer or technology device for the first time. The Illustrated Series is comprised of three parts: introductory, intermediate, and advanced. The series offers a comprehensive title that includes the four main Microsoft applications (Word, Excel, PowerPoint, and Access) at the introductory level. The MindTap Collection includes additional module coverage, including Outlook, Operating Systems, and Teams.

Market research is conducted semi-annually with both current Cengage users and those who use other learning materials. The focus of our market research is to gain insights into the user experience and overall learner needs so we can continuously evolve our content to exceed user expectations. We survey hundreds of instructors to ensure we gather insights from a large and varied demographic.

New to This Edition

The Illustrated Series provides thoroughly updated coverage that reflects current Microsoft 365 features. Narrative content has been authored using Microsoft 365 Business Standard. Module projects incorporate career topics that apply diversity, equity, and inclusion principles and ensure accessibility. All projects, assignments, and lessons have been refreshed with authentic case scenarios that focus on practical skills and employability.

Access: New features in the Access content include an updated, real-world scenario from a leading industry that illustrates the relevance of Access databases in today's businesses. Completely updated projects use gapped Start and Solution files to ensure students use new, authentic files for each project from one module to the next.

Excel: With the thoroughly updated coverage in the Excel modules, students learn both long-standing Excel functions and tools as well as the most recent innovations. New Microsoft® Excel 365® features include dynamic arrays and related functions such as FILTER, RANDARRAY, SEQUENCE, SORT, SORTBY, TRANSPOSE, and UNIQUE. This edition also introduces new Excel data types and the Analyze Data feature for spotting trends and gaining insight into data. With co-authoring, threaded comments, and Notes, users can collaborate with colleagues on workbooks, annotate data, and have useful discussions about the data.

Integration: Along with understanding how to leverage Microsoft Word, Excel, PowerPoint, and Access individually, the Illustrated Series offers further opportunities for users to learn how these applications work together. This knowledge enables students to leverage the full potential of these applications and create comprehensive, professional, and visually appealing documents, spreadsheets, presentations, and databases. By integrating these tools, students can seamlessly transfer data between applications, analyze and visualize data in Excel, import charts and graphs into Word or PowerPoint, and create interactive databases in Access. This knowledge not only enhances their productivity and communication skills but also prepares them for real-world scenarios where the ability to work with these applications in an integrated manner is highly valued in academic and professional settings.

PowerPoint: The PowerPoint coverage introduces the new commenting experience, which lets users display comments in a contextual view or the Comments pane. The comment anchor helps reviewers identify specific slide elements with comments and place the comment bubble anywhere on the slide. With the revised search feature, users can enter a word or phrase in the Search box to find the definition. Microsoft Search also provides support articles to help perform tasks. Users can record and save a presentation that includes digital inking to capture text, drawings, and annotations, and then play back animated drawings. The Speaker Coach uses artificial intelligence (AI) to improve presentation skills by giving feedback on body language, the use of sensitive and filler words, and perceived mispronounced words.

Word: New features in the Word content include the enhanced Accessibility Checker, which identifies potential accessibility issues and presents suggestions to make documents more inclusive. The Word modules also introduce Focus mode, the updated collaboration experience, Microsoft's expanded search tool, and voice options. The Immersive Reader is covered, as is the ability to create a private document copy and use Word's screen reader.

Organization of the Text

The Illustrated Series: Microsoft 365 & Office, First Edition is a comprehensive introduction to Microsoft applications—Word, Excel, PowerPoint, and Access—and is intended for students in introductory computing courses. Each application is divided into modules within the three levels—introductory, intermediate, and advanced. Each module introduces a topic through a real-world case scenario and presents content that aligns directly with the learning objectives stated at the beginning of the module and the more specific learning objectives in each lesson. Skills are taught progressively in visually rich lessons to encourage student learning as they proceed through the modules.

To enable students to practice and apply skills learned and to assess their mastery of the learning objectives, each module ends with three types of exercises: Skills Review, Independent Challenge, and Visual Workshop. The Skills Review contains hands-on exercises that mirror the progression of the lesson material. Each step matches a lesson title or learning objective and provides practice in the skills learned in the module lessons. To encourage critical and creative thinking, modules include two Independent Challenges, with the second more challenging than the first. Each exercise uses a different case scenario based on a real-life application in a top industry. The Visual Workshop provides a figure or screenshot showing a completed document, worksheet, presentation, or part of a database and asks the student to recreate it independently, without following step-by-step instructions.

Features of the text

The features of the text, which are found consistently throughout all modules, are designed to aid the student in a specific way.

    The projects are centered around authentic case scenarios focused on employability and based on research and data to motivate students to perform the steps in the module.

Lesson titles organize topics within a module.

Numbered steps lead students through the process of completing a task while bullets in a Details section provide a planning lesson or, in the case of a challenging topic, a conceptual lesson.

Numbered steps include the following features:

QuickTips provide shortcuts and hints for using the app more effectively. A QuickTip points to a numbered step and is directly related to the corresponding action.

> **Quick Tip**
> You can also type a font size in the Font Size text box.
>
> ▶ 4. Click the **Font Size list arrow** in the Font group, drag the pointer slowly up and down the Font Size list, then click **18**
>
>   As you drag the pointer over a font size, a preview of the font size is applied to the selected text. Clicking 18 increases the font size of the selected text to 18 points.

Troubles are marginal elements that anticipate common errors or provide troubleshooting advice to fix problems that might occur while completing the steps. The troubleshooting advice is related to the numbered step to which it points.

> **Trouble**
> If the Mini toolbar disappears, right-click the selection to display it again.
>
> ▶ 1. Select **Fall Career Fair**
>
>   The Mini toolbar appears over the selected text, as shown in **Figure 1-9**. You click a formatting option on the Mini toolbar to apply it to the selected text. **Table 1-5** describes the function of the buttons on the Mini toolbar. Yours may differ. The buttons on the Mini toolbar are also available on the Ribbon.

Clues boxes provide information that either expands on one component of the lesson skill or describes an independent task related to the lesson skill.

> **Planning a document**
>
> Before you create a new document, it's a good idea to spend time planning it. Identify the audience for your document, the message you want to convey, and the elements, such as tables or charts, you want to include. You should also think about the tone and appearance of your document—are you writing a business letter, which should be written in a pleasant, but serious, tone and have a formal appearance, or are you creating a flyer that must be colorful, eye-catching, and fun to read? The purpose and audience for your document determine the appropriate design. Planning the layout and design of a document involves deciding how to organize the text, selecting the fonts to use, identifying the graphics to include, and selecting the formatting elements that will enhance the message and appeal of the document. For longer documents, such as newsletters, it can be useful to sketch the layout and design of each page before you begin.

Other in-text pedagogical elements include the following:

Tables provide a quick summary of features that relate to the lesson task, such as identifying pointer shapes and what they do.

Table 1-1: Common mouse pointers in Word

name	pointer	use to
I-beam pointer	I	Move the insertion point in a document or to select text
Click and Type pointers, including left-align and center-align		Move the insertion point to a blank area of a document in Print Layout or Web Layout view; double-clicking with a Click and Type pointer automatically applies the Paragraph formatting (alignment and indentation) required to position text or a graphic at that location in the document
Selection pointer		Click a button or other element of the Word program window; appears when you point to elements of the Word program window
Right-pointing arrow pointer		Select a line or lines of text; appears when you point to the left edge of a line of text in the document window
Hand pointer		Open a hyperlink; appears when you point to a hyperlink in a task pane or when you press CTRL and point to a hyperlink in a document
Hide white space pointer		Hide the white space in the top and bottom margins of a document in Print Layout view
Show white space pointer		Show the white space in the top and bottom margins of a document in Print Layout view

Icons are included throughout the steps to show students examples of what buttons look like within the app.

> 8. Click the **Save button** 🖫 on the Quick Access toolbar
>   Your change to the notice is saved. After you save a document for the first time, you must continue to save the changes you make to the document.

Key terms appear in blue and bold font. The bold text appears as a clickable link in MindTap.

> - The **title bar** displays the name of the document and the name of the program. Until you give a new document a different name, its temporary name is Document1. The left side of the title bar contains the **Quick Access toolbar**, which includes buttons for saving a document. The middle of the title bar contains the **Search box**, which you can use to find a command or access the Word Help system. The right side of the title bar contains the resizing buttons and the program Close button.

SAM Upload and Download Icons are for SAM users. A SAM download icon appears next to any step where students download a Data File to begin a SAM Project.

> 1. **sam↓** Start Word, then click **Blank document**
>   A blank document opens in the **Word program window**, as shown in **Figure 1-2**. The blinking vertical line in the document window is the **insertion point**. It indicates where text appears as you type.

A SAM upload icon appears next to any step where students submit a file to SAM for a completed SAM project.

> 9. **sam↑** Click the **File tab**, then click **Close**
>   The document closes, but the Word program window remains open.

Course Solutions

Online Learning Platform: MindTap with SAM

The Illustrated Series MindTap Collection, powered by *SAM* (Skills Assessment Manager), enables proficiency in Microsoft Office and computing concepts for your Introductory Computing courses. With a library of renowned course materials, including ready-to-assign, auto-graded learning modules, you can easily adapt your course to best prepare students for the evolving job market. In addition to an eReader that includes the full content of the printed book, the Illustrated Collection, First Edition MindTap course includes the following:

- SAM Textbook Projects: Follow the steps and scenarios outlined in the textbook readings; enable students to complete projects based on a real-world scenario live in Microsoft Office applications and submit them in SAM for automatic grading and feedback.
- SAM Training and Exam: Trainings teach students to complete specific skills in a simulated Microsoft application environment while exams allow students to demonstrate their proficiency (also in a simulated environment).
- SAM Projects: Students complete projects based on real-world scenarios live in Microsoft applications and submit the projects in SAM for automatic grading and feedback. SAM offers several types of projects, each with a unique purpose: 1A and 1B, critical thinking, end of module, capstone, and integration.

- Microsoft Office Specialist (MOS) resources: Training and exams are based on the Microsoft Office 365 Objective Domains for the MOS Exam and exam simulation that replicates the test-taking environment of the MOS exam for Word, Excel, Access, PowerPoint, and Outlook.

To learn more, go to https://www.cengage.com/mindtap-collections/

Ancillary Package

Additional instructor and student resources for this product are available online. Instructor assets include an Instructor Manual, an Educator Guide, PowerPoint® slides, a Guide to Teaching Online, Solution Files, a test bank powered by Cognero®, and a Transition Guide. Student assets include data files and a glossary. Sign up or sign in at www.cengage.com to search for and access this product and its online resources. The instructor and student companion sites contain ancillary material for the full New Perspectives Series Collection, along with instructions on how to find specific content within the companion site.

- Instructor Manual: This guide provides additional instructional material to assist in class preparation, including module objectives, module outline, discussion questions, and additional activities and assignments. Each outline corresponds directly with the content in each module and additional discussion questions and activities are aligned to headings in the book.
- Educator Guide: The MindTap Educator Guide contains a detailed outline of the corresponding MindTap course, including activity types and time on task. The SAM Educator Guide explains how to use SAM functionality to maximize your course.
- PowerPoint slides: The slides may be used to guide classroom presentations, to provide to students for module review, or to print as classroom handouts. The slides align closely with the book while activities and the self-assessment align with module learning objectives and supplement the content in the book.
- Guide to Teaching Online: This guide presents technological and pedagogical considerations and suggestions for teaching the Introductory Computing course when you can't be in the same room with students.
- Solution Files: These files provide solutions to all textbook projects for instructors to use to grade student work.
  - Instructors using SAM do not need solution files since projects are auto-graded within SAM.
  - Solution files are provided on the instructor companion site for instructors *not* using SAM.
- Data Files: These files are provided for students to complete the projects in each module. Students using SAM to complete the projects download the required data files directly from SAM.
  - Students who are *not* using SAM to complete the projects can find data files on the student companion site and within MindTap.
- Test banks: A comprehensive test bank, offered in Cognero, Word, Blackboard, Moodle, Desire2Learn, Canvas, and SAM formats, contains questions aligned with each module's learning objectives and are written by subject matter experts. Powered by Cognero, Cengage Testing is a flexible, online system that allows you to author, edit, and manage test bank content from multiple Cengage solutions and to create multiple test versions that you can deliver from your LMS, your classroom, or wherever you want.
- Transition Guide: This guide highlights all the changes in the text and the digital offerings from the previous edition to the current one so that instructors know what to expect.

Acknowledgments

Lynn Wermers: I am extremely grateful for the creative talent, good judgment, and editing savvy that Mary-Terese Cozzola brought to the development of this publication. MT, thank you for your support, guidance, good humor and always finding the right words for every situation. Thanks also to Samantha Rundle for bringing her outstanding management skills to this project. Zenya Molnar's comprehensive feedback and suggestions for bringing together the concepts with the best learning experience have improved this edition greatly. Thank you also to Amy Savino for getting this project going and supporting it throughout its duration.

David W. Beskeen: The content of this book has evolved significantly since the first edition was published in 1994 and I am proud to have been given the opportunity since then to write and revise this book for the benefit of students. I want to thank Cengage for the opportunity to write this latest edition and to the whole Cengage team for their hard work on this project. Finally, I want to acknowledge my editor Barbara Clemens for her fine work, her diligence to detail, and her patience with me.

Carol M. Cram: Thank you to the wonderful team at Cengage and my developmental editor Michael Sanford for their expertise, support, and dedication. And, as always, my deepest thanks to my husband Gregg and our daughter Julia who make everything I do possible.

Jennifer Duffy: It is always a pleasure to work with a talented team of professionals to create a book. Thank you to Michael Sanford for his careful editing, and to the Cengage team—Amy Savino, Samantha Rundle, Zenya Molnar, and all the others—for their expertise and guidance.

Getting to Know Microsoft Office Versions

Cengage is proud to bring you the next edition of Microsoft Office. This edition was designed to provide a robust learning experience that is not dependent upon a specific version of Office.

Microsoft supports several versions and editions of Office: (Refer to Table 1 below for more information)

- **Microsoft 365 (formerly known as Office 365):** A service that delivers the most up-to-date, feature-rich, modern Microsoft productivity applications direct to your device. There are several combinations of Microsoft 365 programs for business, educational, and personal use. Microsoft 365 is cloud-based, meaning it is stored, managed, and processed on a network of remote servers hosted on the Internet, rather than on local servers or personal computers. Microsoft 365 offers extra online storage and cloud-connected features, as well as updates with the latest features, fixes, and security updates. Microsoft 365 is purchased for a monthly subscription fee that keeps your software up to date with the latest features.

- **Office 2021:** The Microsoft "on-premises" version of the Office apps, available for both PCs and Macintosh computers, offered as a static, one-time purchase and outside of the subscription model. Unlike Microsoft 365, Office 2021 does not include online product updates with new features.

- **Microsoft 365 Online (formerly known as Office Online):** A free, simplified version of Microsoft web applications (Teams, Access, Word, Excel, PowerPoint, and OneNote) that lets users create and edit files collaboratively.

- **Office 365 Education:** A free subscription including Word, Excel, PowerPoint, OneNote, and now Microsoft Teams, plus additional classroom tools. Only available for students and educators at select institutions.

Table 1 Microsoft Office applications — uses and availability

Application	Use	Availability/Editions
Word	Create documents and improve your writing with intelligent assistance features.	Microsoft 365 Family, Home, Business, Office 2021, Office 365 Education
Excel	Simplify complex data into easy-to-read spreadsheets.	Microsoft 365 Personal, Home, Business, Office 2021, Office 365 Education
PowerPoint	Create presentations that stand out.	Home, Business, Office 2021, Office 365 Education
OneNote	A digital notebook for all your note-taking needs.	Home, Office 365 Education
OneDrive	Save and share your files and photos wherever you are.	Home, Business
Outlook	Manage your email, calendar, tasks, and contacts all in one place.	Home, Business
SharePoint	Create team sites to share information, files, and resources.	Business
Publisher	Create polished, professional layouts without the hassle.	Home, Business, Office 2021 (PC only)
Access	Create your own database apps easily in formats that serve your business best.	Home, Business, Office 2021 (PC only)
Teams	Bring everyone together in one place to meet, chat, call, and collaborate.	Business, Office 365 Education
Exchange	Business-class email and calendaring.	Business

Over time, the Microsoft 365 cloud interface will continuously update using its web connection, offering new application features and functions, while Office 2021 will remain static.

Because Microsoft 365 releases updates continuously, your onscreen experience may differ from what you see in this product. For example, the more advanced features and functionalities covered in this product may not be available in Microsoft 365 Online, may have updated from what you see in Office 2021, or may be from a post-publication update of Microsoft 365.

For up-to-date information on the differences between Microsoft 365, Office 2021, and Microsoft 365 Online, please visit the Microsoft Support website.

Cengage is committed to providing high-quality learning solutions for you to gain the knowledge and skills that will empower you throughout your educational and professional careers.

Thank you for using our product, and we look forward to exploring the future of Microsoft Office with you!

Using SAM Projects and Textbook Projects

SAM (Skills Assessment Manager) **Projects** allow you to actively apply the skills you learned in Microsoft Word, Excel, PowerPoint, or Access. You can also submit your work to SAM for online grading. You can use SAM Projects to become a more productive student and use these skills throughout your career.

To complete SAM Textbook Projects, please follow these steps:

SAM Textbook Projects allow you to complete a project as you follow along with the steps in the textbook. As you read the module, look for icons that indicate when you should download sam⬇ your SAM Start file(s) and when to upload sam⬆ your solution file to SAM for grading.

Everything you need to complete this project is provided within SAM. You can launch the eBook directly from SAM, which will allow you to take notes, highlight, and create a custom study guide, or you can use a print textbook or your mobile app. Download IOS or Download Android.

To get started, launch your SAM Project assignment from SAM, MindTap, or a link within your learning management system.

1. Step 1:
   Download Files
   - Click the "Download All" button or the individual links to download your **Start File** and **Support File(s)** (when available). You must use the SAM Start file.
   - Click the Instructions link to launch the eBook (or use the print textbook or mobile app).
   - Disregard any steps in the textbook that ask you to create a new file or to use a file from a location outside of SAM.
   - Look for the SAM Download icon sam⬇ to begin working with your start file.
   - Follow the module's step-by-step instructions until you reach the SAM Upload icon sam⬆.
   - Save and close the file.

2. **Step 2:**
   Save Work to SAM
   - Ensure you rename your project file to match the Expected File Name.
   - Upload your in-progress or completed file to SAM. You can download the file to continue working or submit it for grading in the next step.

3. **Step 3:**
   Submit for Grading
   - Upload your completed solution file to SAM for immediate feedback and to view the available Reports.
     - The **Graded Summary Report** provides a detailed list of project steps, your score, and feedback to aid you in revising and resubmitting the project.
     - The **Study Guide** provides your score for each project step and links to the associated training and textbook pages.
   - If additional attempts are allowed, use your reports to assist with revising and resubmitting your project.
   - To re-submit your project, download the file you saved in step 2.
   - Edit, save, and close the file, then re-upload and submit it again.

For all other SAM Projects, please follow these steps:

To get started, launch your SAM Project assignment from SAM, MindTap, or a link within your learning management system.

1. **Step 1:**
   Download Files
   - Click the "Download All" button or the individual links to download your **Instruction File**, **Start File**, and **Support File(s)** (when available). You must use the SAM Start file.
   - Open the Instruction file and follow the step-by-step instructions. Ensure you rename your project file to match the Expected File Name (change _1 to _2 at the end of the file name).

2. Step 2:
   Save Work to SAM
   - Upload your in-progress or completed file to SAM. You can download the file to continue working or submit it for grading in the next step.

3. Step 3:
   Submit for Grading
   - Upload the completed file to SAM for immediate feedback and to view available Reports.
     - The **Graded Summary Report** provides a detailed list of project steps, your score, and feedback to aid you in revising and resubmitting the project.
     - The **Study Guide** provides your score for each project step and links to the associated training and textbook pages.
   - If additional attempts are allowed, use your reports to assist with revising and resubmitting your project.
   - To re-submit the project, download the file saved in step 2.
   - Edit, save, and close the file, then re-upload and submit it again.

For additional tips to successfully complete your SAM Projects, please view our [SAM Video Tutorials](#).

Word Module 1

Creating Documents with Word

Case

You have been hired to work at Mountain Springs Institute of Technology, an institute of higher education that offers practical, applied education to both local and international students. Shortly after reporting to your new office, Prasad Anil, Director of Career Services, asks you to use Word to create a notice for students and an info sheet for job seekers.

Module Objectives

After completing this module, you will be able to:

- Use word-processing software
- Start Word
- Enter and revise text
- Save a document
- Select text
- Format text using the Mini toolbar and the Ribbon
- View and navigate a document
- Cut and paste text
- Copy and paste text
- Format with fonts
- Set document margins
- Add bullets and numbering
- Insert a graphic
- Apply a theme

Files You Will Need

IL_WD_1-1.docx
Support_WD_1-2.jpg
IL_WD_1-3.docx
Support_WD_1-4.jpg
IL_WD_1-5.docx
Support_WD_1-6.jpg

Module 1 Creating Documents with Word

Use Word-Processing Software

Case Before beginning your notice, you explore the editing and formatting features available in Word.

Objectives
- Identify the features of Word
- State the benefits of using a word-processing program

A **word-processing program** is a software program that includes tools for entering, editing, and formatting text and graphics. Microsoft Word is a powerful word-processing program that allows you to create and enhance a wide range of documents quickly and easily. **Figure 1-1** shows the first page of a report created using Word and illustrates some of the Word features you can use to enhance your documents. The electronic files you create using Word are called **documents**. One of the benefits of using Word is that document files can be stored on a hard disk, flash drive, or another physical storage device, or to OneDrive or another Cloud storage place, making them easy to transport, share, and revise.

Details

You can use Word to accomplish the following tasks:

- **Type and edit text**
  The Word editing tools make it simple to insert and delete text in a document. You can add text to the middle of an existing paragraph; replace text with other text; undo an editing change; and correct typing, spelling, and grammatical errors with ease.

- **Copy and move text from one location to another**
  Using the more advanced editing features of Word, you can copy or move text from one location and insert it in a different location in a document. You also can copy and move text between documents. This means you don't have to retype text that is already entered in a document.

- **Format text and paragraphs with fonts, colors, and other elements**
  The sophisticated formatting tools in Word allow you to make the text in your documents come alive. You can change the size, style, and color of text; add lines and shading to paragraphs; and enhance lists with bullets and numbers. Creatively formatting text helps to highlight important ideas in your documents.

- **Format and design pages**
  The page-formatting features in Word give you the power to design attractive newsletters, create powerful résumés, and produce documents such as research papers, business cards, brochures, and reports. You can change paper size, organize text in columns, and control the layout of text and graphics on each page of a document. For quick results, Word includes preformatted cover pages, pull quotes, and headers and footers, as well as galleries of coordinated text, table, and graphic styles. If you are writing a research paper, Word makes it easy to manage reference sources and create footnotes, endnotes, and bibliographies.

- **Enhance documents with tables, charts, graphics, screenshots, and videos**
  Using the powerful graphics tools in Word, you can spice up your documents with pictures, videos, photographs, screenshots, lines, preset quick shapes, and diagrams. You also can illustrate your documents with tables and charts to help convey your message in a visually interesting way.

- **Use Mail Merge to create form letters and mailing labels**
  The Word Mail Merge feature allows you to send personalized form letters to many different people. You can also use Mail Merge to create mailing labels, directories, email messages, and other types of documents.

- **Share documents securely**
  The security features in Word make it quick and easy to remove comments, tracked changes, and unwanted personal information from your files before you share them with others. You can also add a password or a digital signature to a document and convert a file to a format suitable for publishing on the web.

Figure 1-1: A report created using Word

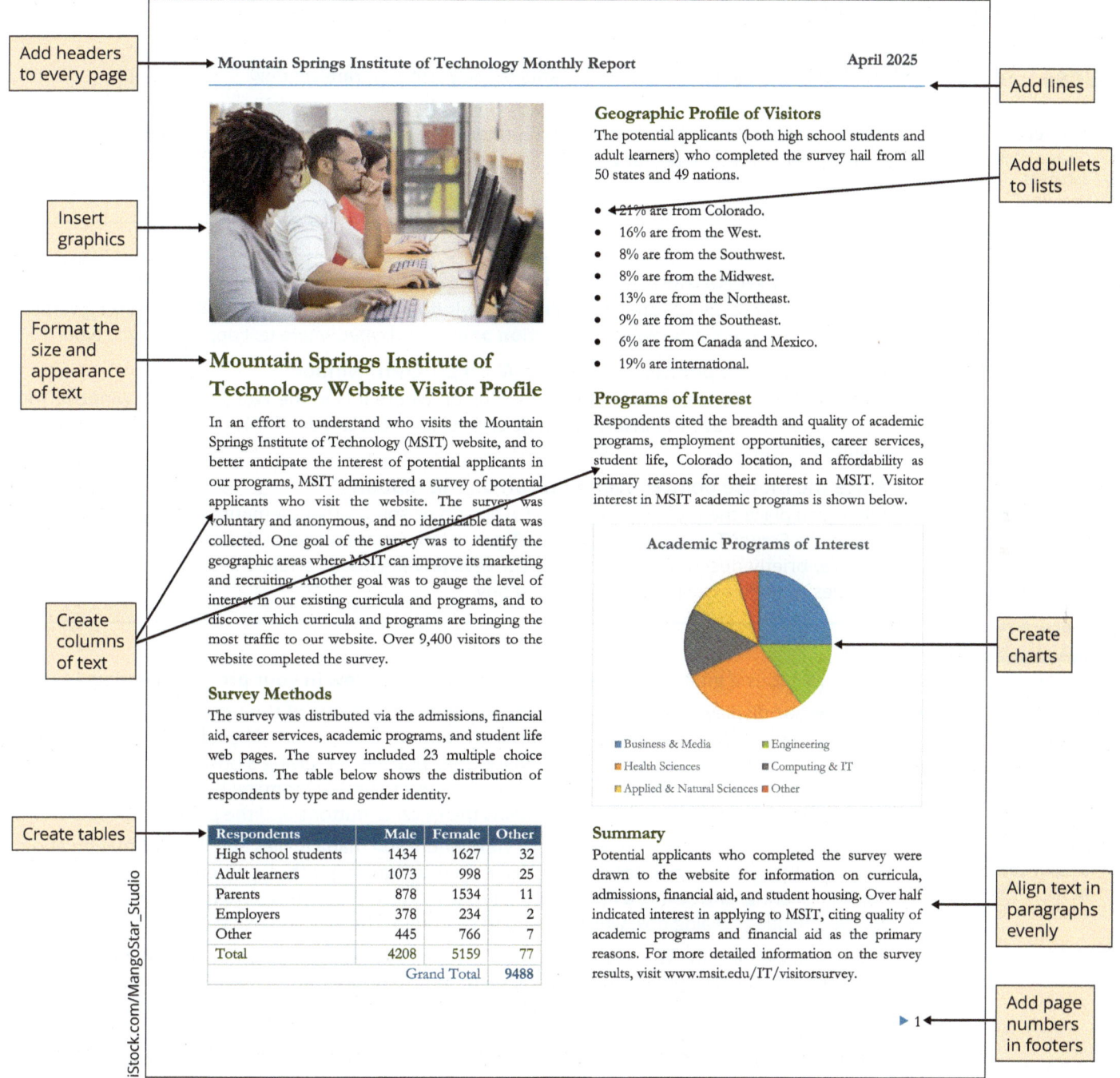

Planning a document

Before you create a new document, it's a good idea to spend time planning it. Identify the audience for your document, the message you want to convey, and the elements, such as tables or charts, you want to include. You should also think about the tone and appearance of your document—are you writing a business letter, which should be written in a pleasant, but serious, tone and have a formal appearance, or are you creating a flyer that must be colorful, eye-catching, and fun to read? The purpose and audience for your document determine the appropriate design. Planning the layout and design of a document involves deciding how to organize the text, selecting the fonts to use, identifying the graphics to include, and selecting the formatting elements that will enhance the message and appeal of the document. For longer documents, such as newsletters, it can be useful to sketch the layout and design of each page before you begin.

Start Word

Case You open a blank document and examine the elements of the Word program window.

Objectives
- Create a blank document
- Open Word

When you start Word, the Word start screen opens. It includes a list of recently opened documents and a gallery of templates for creating a new document.

Steps

1. **sam'** ⬇ Start Word, then click **Blank document**

   A blank document opens in the **Word program window**, as shown in **Figure 1-2**. The blinking vertical line in the document window is the **insertion point**. It indicates where text appears as you type.

2. **Move the mouse pointer around the Word program window**

   The mouse pointer changes shape depending on where it is in the Word program window. You use pointers to move the insertion point or to select text to edit. **Table 1-1** describes common pointers in Word.

   Trouble
   If the full Ribbon is hidden, click the Home tab, click the Ribbon Display Options button in the lower-right corner of the Ribbon, then click Always show Ribbon.

3. **Place the mouse pointer over a button on the Ribbon**

   When you place the mouse pointer over a button or some other elements of the Word program window, a ScreenTip appears. A **ScreenTip** is a label that identifies the name of the button or feature, briefly describes its function, conveys any keyboard shortcut for the command, and includes a link to associated help topics, if any.

Details

Quick Tip
The Quick Access toolbar can be customized. Yours might include additional buttons or be located below the ribbon.

Quick Tip
To display a different tab, you simply click its name on the Ribbon.

Using **Figure 1-2** as a guide, find the elements described below in your program window:

- The **title bar** displays the name of the document and the name of the program. Until you give a new document a different name, its temporary name is Document1. The left side of the title bar contains the **Quick Access toolbar**, which includes buttons for saving a document. The middle of the title bar contains the **Search box**, which you can use to find a command or access the Word Help system. The right side of the title bar contains the resizing buttons and the program Close button.

- The **File tab** provides access to **Backstage view** where you manage files and the information about them. Backstage view includes commands related to working with documents, such as opening, printing, sharing, and saving a document. The File tab also provides access to your account and to the Word Options dialog box, which is used to customize the way you use Word.

- The Ribbon contains the Word tabs. Each **tab** on the Ribbon includes buttons for commands related to editing and formatting documents. The commands are organized in **groups**. For example, the Home tab includes the Undo, Clipboard, Font, Paragraph, Styles, Editing, Voice, and Editor groups. The Ribbon also includes the **Comments button**, which you use to see comments, the Editing button, which is used to switch between editing, reviewing, and viewing modes, and the **Share button**, which you can use to save a document to the Cloud.

- The **document window** displays the current document. You enter text and format your document in the document window.

Trouble
Click the View tab, then click the Ruler check box in the Show group to display the rulers if they are not already displayed.

- The rulers appear in the document window in Print Layout view. The **horizontal ruler** displays left and right document margins as well as the tab settings and paragraph indents, if any, for the paragraph in which the insertion point is located. The **vertical ruler** displays the top and bottom document margins.

- The vertical and **horizontal scroll bars** are used to display different parts of the document in the document window. The scroll bars include **scroll boxes** and **scroll arrows**, which you use to scroll.

- The **status bar** displays the page number of the current page, the total number of pages and words in the document, and the Accessibility checker. It also includes the view buttons, the Zoom slider, and the Zoom level button. You can customize the status bar to display other information.

- The **view buttons** on the status bar allow you to display the document in Focus Mode, Read Mode, Print Layout, or Web Layout view. The **Zoom slider** and the **Zoom level button** provide quick ways to enlarge and decrease the size of the document in the document window, making it easy to zoom in on a detail of a document or to view the layout of the document as a whole.

Figure 1-2: Elements of the Word program window

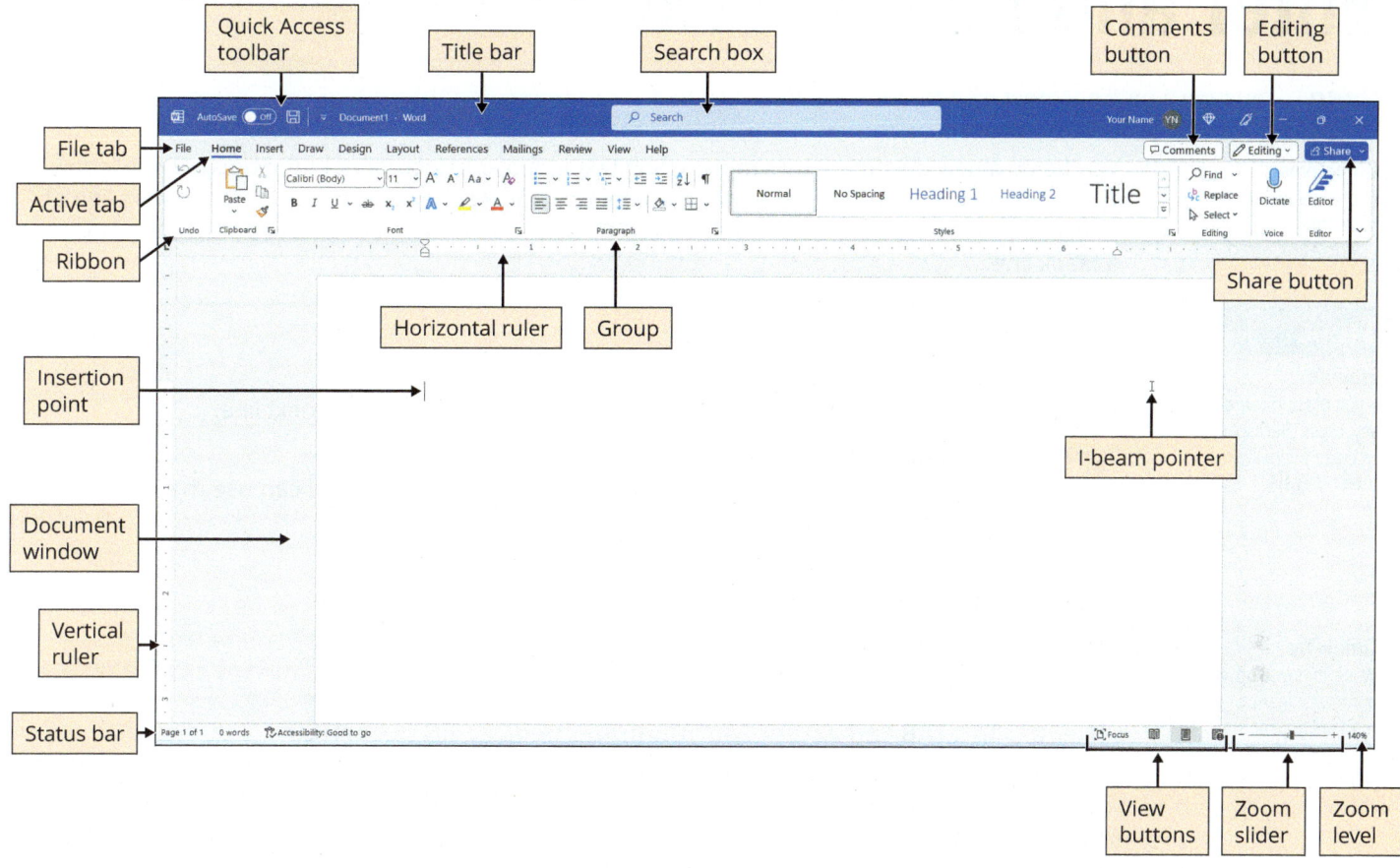

Table 1-1: Common mouse pointers in Word

name	pointer	use to
I-beam pointer	I	Move the insertion point in a document or to select text
Click and Type pointers, including left-align and center-align	I≡ I	Move the insertion point to a blank area of a document in Print Layout or Web Layout view; double-clicking with a Click and Type pointer automatically applies the Paragraph formatting (alignment and indentation) required to position text or a graphic at that location in the document
Selection pointer	⇖	Click a button or other element of the Word program window; appears when you point to elements of the Word program window
Right-pointing arrow pointer	⇗	Select a line or lines of text; appears when you point to the left edge of a line of text in the document window
Hand pointer	👆	Open a hyperlink; appears when you point to a hyperlink in a task pane or when you press CTRL and point to a hyperlink in a document
Hide white space pointer	↧↥	Hide the white space in the top and bottom margins of a document in Print Layout view
Show white space pointer	↧↥	Show the white space in the top and bottom margins of a document in Print Layout view

Enter and Revise Text

Case You type a notice to post on a bulletin board.

Objectives
- Correct spelling and grammar
- Undo AutoCorrect

You begin a new document by simply typing text in a blank document in the document window. Word uses **word wrap**, a feature that automatically moves the insertion point to the next line of the document as you type. You only press ENTER when you want to start a new paragraph or insert a blank line.

Steps

Trouble
If you press the wrong key, press [Backspace] to erase the mistake, then try again.

1. Type **Fall Career Fair**, then press **ENTER** twice
   Each time you press ENTER, the insertion point moves to the start of the next line.

2. Type **TO:**, then press **TAB** twice
   Pressing TAB moves the insertion point several spaces to the right. You can use the TAB key to align the text in a notice header or to indent the first line of a paragraph.

3. Type **Volunteers**, then press **ENTER**
   The insertion point moves to the start of the next line.

Quick Tip
Wavy lines and other automatic feature markers appear on the screen but do not print.

4. Type: **FROM:** TAB TAB **Prasad Anil** ENTER
   DATE: TAB TAB **June 4, 2025** ENTER
   RE: TAB TAB **Fall career fair planning meeting** ENTER ENTER
   Red wavy or blue double lines may appear under the words you typed, indicating a possible spelling or grammar error. Spelling and grammar checking is one of the many automatic features you will encounter as you type. **Table 1-2** describes several automatic features. You can correct any typing errors you make later.

Trouble
To reverse an AutoCorrect adjustment, immediately click the Undo button in the Undo group on the Home tab.

5. Type **A meeting for senior students interested in volunteering at the fall career fair will be held on the 17th of June at 4 p.m. in the conference room.** , then press **SPACEBAR**
   As you type, notice that the insertion point moves automatically to the next line of the document. You also might notice that Word automatically changed "17th" to "17th" in the notice. This feature is called **AutoCorrect**. AutoCorrect automatically makes typographical adjustments and detects and adjusts typing errors, certain misspelled words (such as "taht" for "that"), and incorrect capitalization as you type.

6. Type **Volunteering is an excellent opportunity to network with employers. The fall career fair is scheduled for September.**
   When you type the first few characters of "September" and certain other words, the Word text predictions feature displays a complete word in grey type. **Text predictions** suggests text to insert quickly into your documents. You can ignore text predictions for now. Your notice should resemble **Figure 1-3**.

Quick Tip
If you want uniform spacing between lines and paragraphs, apply the No Spacing style to the document by clicking the No Spacing button in the Styles group on the Home tab before you begin to type. Alternatively, select the text and then click the No Spacing button.

7. Press **ENTER**, then type **Over 100 employers from a wide range of industries will be in attendance. A list is available from Jacinda Zazgra. Employers will be recruiting MSIT talent from all academic programs for jobs, internships, and career opportunities.**
   When you press ENTER and type the new paragraph, notice that Word adds more space between the paragraphs than it does between the lines in each paragraph. This is part of the default style for paragraphs in Word, called the **Normal style**.

8. Position the I pointer after **for** (but before the space) in the last sentence of the first paragraph, then click to move the insertion point after **for**

9. Press **BACKSPACE** three times, then type **to take place in**
   Pressing BACKSPACE removes the character before the insertion point.

10. Move the insertion point before **senior** in the first sentence, then press **DELETE** seven times to remove the word "senior" and the space after it
    Pressing DELETE removes the character after the insertion point. **Figure 1-4** shows the revised notice.

Figure 1-3: Text in the document window

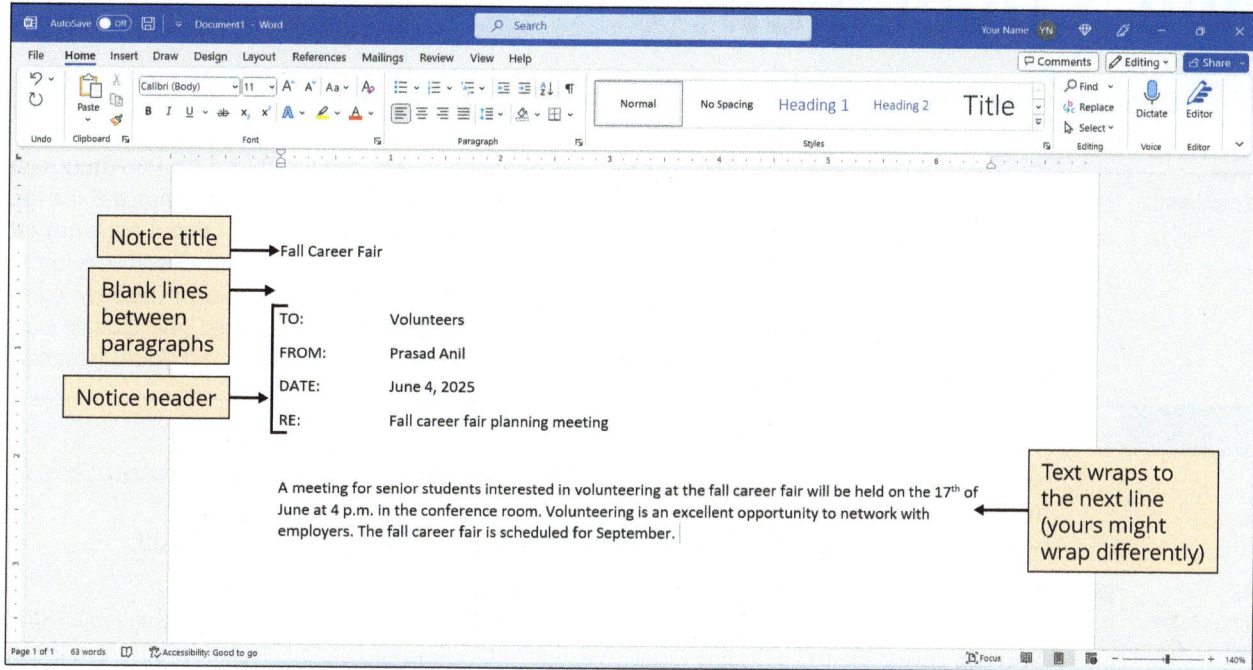

Figure 1-4: Edited document text

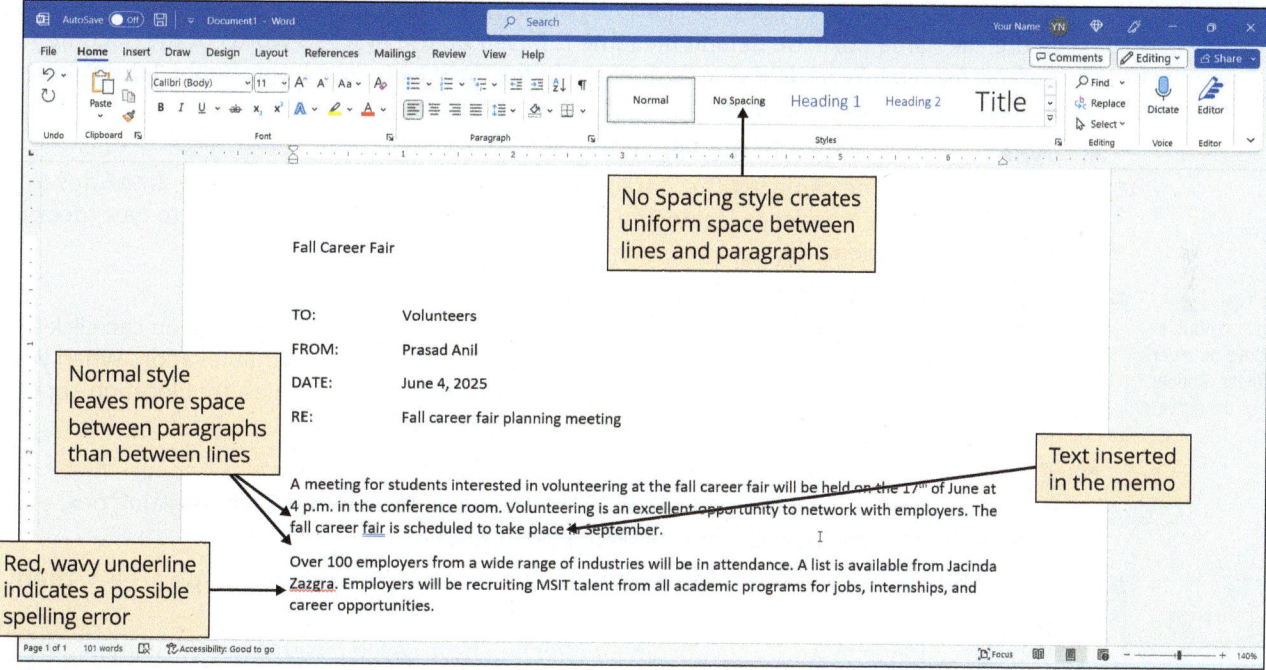

Table 1-2: Automatic features that appear as you type in Word

feature	what appears	to use
Text predications	Grey text suggesting text to insert appears as you type	Press TAB to insert the text suggested by text predictions; continue typing to reject the suggestion
AutoCorrect	A small blue box appears when you place the pointer over text corrected by AutoCorrect; an AutoCorrect Options button appears when you point to the blue box	Word automatically corrects typos, minor spelling errors, and capitalization, and adds typographical symbols (such as © and ™) as you type; to reverse an AutoCorrect adjustment, click the AutoCorrect Options arrow, then click the option that will undo the action
Spelling and Grammar	A red wavy line under a word indicates a possible misspelling or a repeated word; a blue double line under text indicates a possible grammar error	Right-click red- or blue-underlined text to display a shortcut menu of correction options; click a correction option to accept it and remove the colored underline, or click Ignore to leave the text as is

Module 1 Creating Documents with Word

Save a Document

Case You save the notice using a descriptive filename and the default file extension.

Objective
- Save a document

To store a document permanently so you can open it and edit it at another time, you must save it as a **file**. When you **save** a document, you give it a name, called a **filename**, and indicate the location where you want to store the file. Files created in the most recent version of Word are automatically assigned the .docx file extension to distinguish them from files created in other software programs. You can save a document using the Save button on the Quick Access toolbar or the Save command on the File tab. Once you have saved a document for the first time, you should save it again every few minutes and always before printing so that the saved file is updated to reflect your latest changes.

Steps

1. **Click the AutoSave toggle switch on the Quick Access toolbar to turn AutoSave off, if necessary**
   You use the AutoSave toggle switch to turn the AutoSave feature both on and off.

Trouble
If you don't see the extension .docx as part of the filename, the setting in Windows to display file extensions is not active.

2. **Click the File tab on the Ribbon, then click Save As**
   The first time you save a document, the Save As screen opens. The screen displays all the places you can save a file to, including OneDrive, your PC (identified as This PC), or a different location.

3. **Click Browse in the Save As screen**
   The Save As dialog box opens, similar to **Figure 1-5**. The default filename, Fall Career Fair, appears in the File name box. The default filename is based on the first few words of the document. The default file type, Word Document, appears in the Save as type list box. **Table 1-3** describes the functions of some of the buttons in the Save As dialog box.

4. **Type IL_WD_1_Notice in the File name box**
   The new filename replaces the default filename. Giving your documents brief descriptive filenames makes it easier to locate and organize them later. You do not need to type .docx when you type a new filename.

Quick Tip
You can also double-click a drive or folder in the folder window to change the active location.

5. **Navigate to the location where you store your Data Files**
   You can navigate to a different drive or folder in several ways. For example, you can click a drive or folder in the Address bar or the navigation pane to go directly to that location. When you are finished navigating to the drive or folder where you store your Data Files, that location appears in the Address bar. Your Save As dialog box should resemble **Figure 1-6**.

6. **Click Save**
   The document is saved to the drive and folder you specified in the Save As dialog box, and the title bar displays the new filename, IL_WD_1_Notice.docx.

Quick Tip
You also can press CTRL+S to save a document.

7. **Place the insertion point before conference in the first sentence, type green, then press SPACEBAR**
   You can continue to work on a document after you have saved it with a new filename.

8. **Click the Save button on the Quick Access toolbar**
   Your change to the notice is saved. After you save a document for the first time, you must continue to save the changes you make to the document.

Saving with AutoSave

The AutoSave feature saves a file automatically to OneDrive every few seconds for sharing, synching, or backup. AutoSave can be especially useful for live collaboration when multiple users are working on a shared document at once because it allows all users of the document to see the changes others are making in real time. To turn AutoSave on and off, simply click the AutoSave toggle switch on the Quick Access toolbar. AutoSave is enabled by default when a file is stored to OneDrive.

Figure 1-5: Save As dialog box

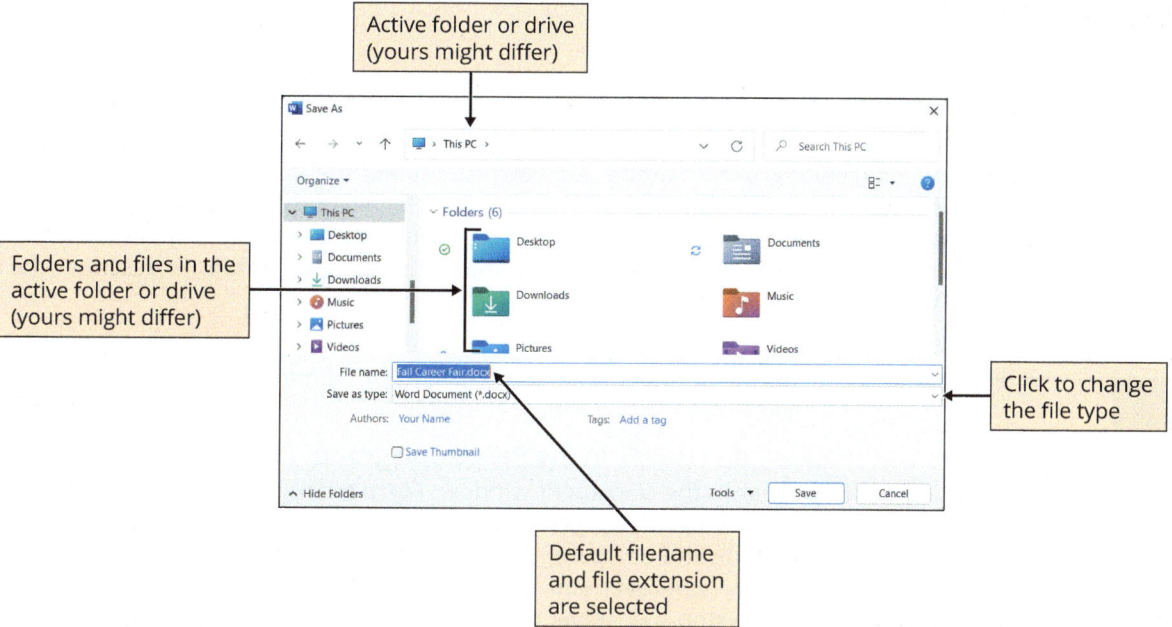

Figure 1-6: File to be saved in the Module 1 folder

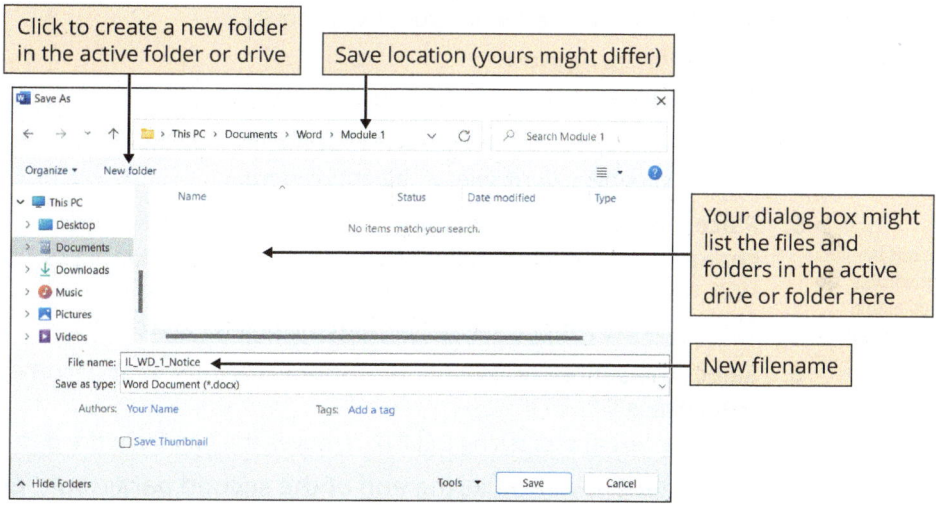

Table 1-3: Save As dialog box buttons

button	use to
Back	Navigate back to the last location shown in the Address bar
Forward	Navigate to the location that was previously shown in the Address bar
Up to	Navigate to the location above the current location in the folder hierarchy
Organize	Open a menu of commands related to organizing the selected file or folder, including Cut, Copy, Delete, Rename, and Properties
New folder	Create a new folder in the current folder or drive
Change your view	Change the way folder and file information is shown in the folder window in the Save As dialog box; click the Change your view button to toggle between views, or click the arrow to open a menu of view options

Select Text

Case You revise the notice by selecting text and replacing it with new text. You also remove a hyperlink from text.

Objectives
- Select text
- Show and hide formatting
- Undo and redo actions
- Remove hyperlinks

Before deleting, editing, or formatting text, you must **select** the text. Selecting text involves clicking and dragging the I-beam pointer across the text to highlight it. You can also select words and paragraphs by double-clicking or triple-clicking text, or you can click or double-click in the margin to the left of text with the pointer to select whole lines or paragraphs. **Table 1-4** describes the many ways to select text.

Steps

1. Click the **Show/Hide ¶ button** ¶ in the Paragraph group

   Formatting marks appear in the document window. **Formatting marks** are special characters that appear on your screen but do not print. Common formatting marks include the paragraph symbol (¶), which shows the end of a paragraph—wherever you press ENTER; the dot symbol (.), which represents a space—wherever you press SPACEBAR; and the arrow symbol (→), which shows the location of a tab stop—wherever you press TAB. Working with formatting marks turned on can help you to select, edit, and format text with precision.

   Quick Tip: You deselect text by clicking anywhere in the document window.

2. Click before **Volunteers**, then drag the pointer over the text to select it

   The words are selected, as shown in **Figure 1-7**. For now, you can ignore the floating Mini toolbar that appears over text when you first select it.

3. Type **MSIT Students**

   The text you type replaces the selected text.

4. Double-click **Prasad**, type your first name, double-click **Anil**, then type your last name

   Double-clicking a word selects the entire word.

   Trouble: If you delete text by mistake, immediately click the Undo button ↶ in the Undo group on the Home tab to restore the deleted text to the document.

5. Place the pointer in the margin to the left of the **RE: line** so that the pointer changes to ⇗, click to select the line, then type **RE:**, press **TAB**, press **TAB**, then type **Volunteering at the fall career fair**

   Clicking to the left of a line of text with the pointer selects the entire line.

6. Select the sentence **A list is available from Jacinda Zazgra.** in the second paragraph, then press **DELETE**

   Selecting text and pressing DELETE removes the text from the document.

7. Click after the period at the end of the second paragraph, press **SPACEBAR**, then type **See www.msit/careerfair.org for more information.**

   When you press SPACEBAR after typing the web address, Word automatically formats the web address as a hyperlink. A **hyperlink** is text that when clicked opens a webpage in a browser window. Text that is formatted as a hyperlink appears as colored, underlined text. You want to remove the hyperlink formatting.

8. Right-click **www.msit/careerfair.org**, then click **Remove Hyperlink**

   Removing a hyperlink removes the link, but the text remains.

   Quick Tip: Always save before and after editing text.

9. Click ¶, then click the **Save button** 💾 on the Quick Access toolbar

   Formatting marks are turned off, and your changes to the notice are saved. The Show/Hide ¶ button is a **toggle button**, which means you can use it to turn formatting marks on and off. The edited notice is shown in **Figure 1-8**.

Figure 1-7: Text selected in the document

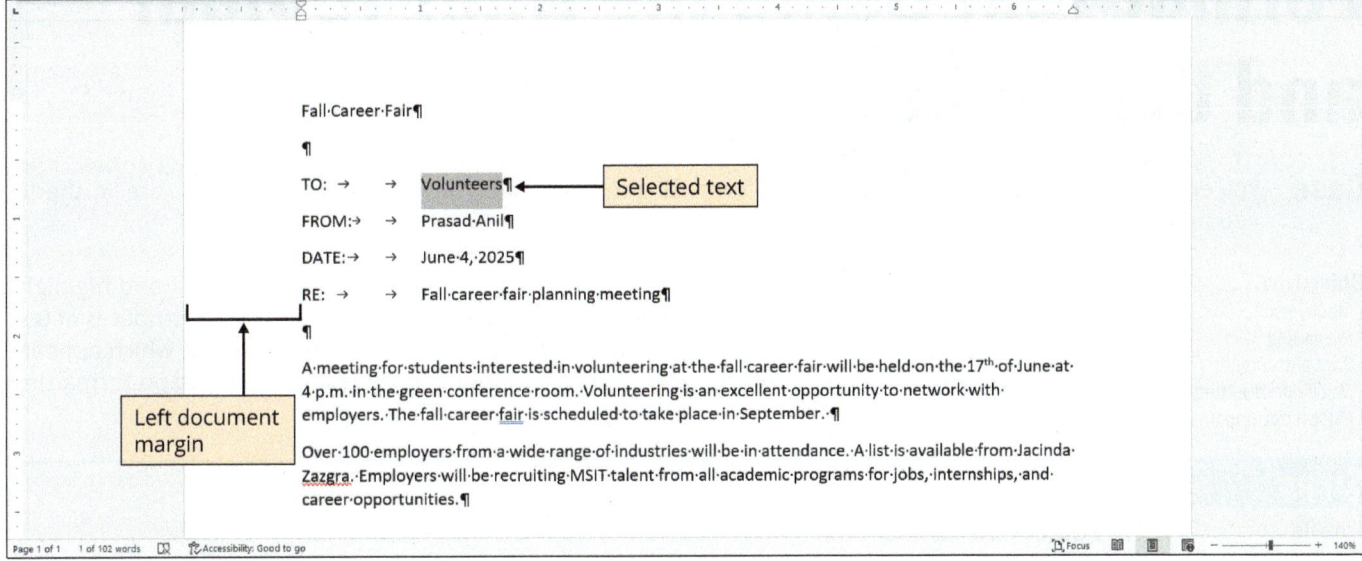

Figure 1-8: Edited document with replacement text

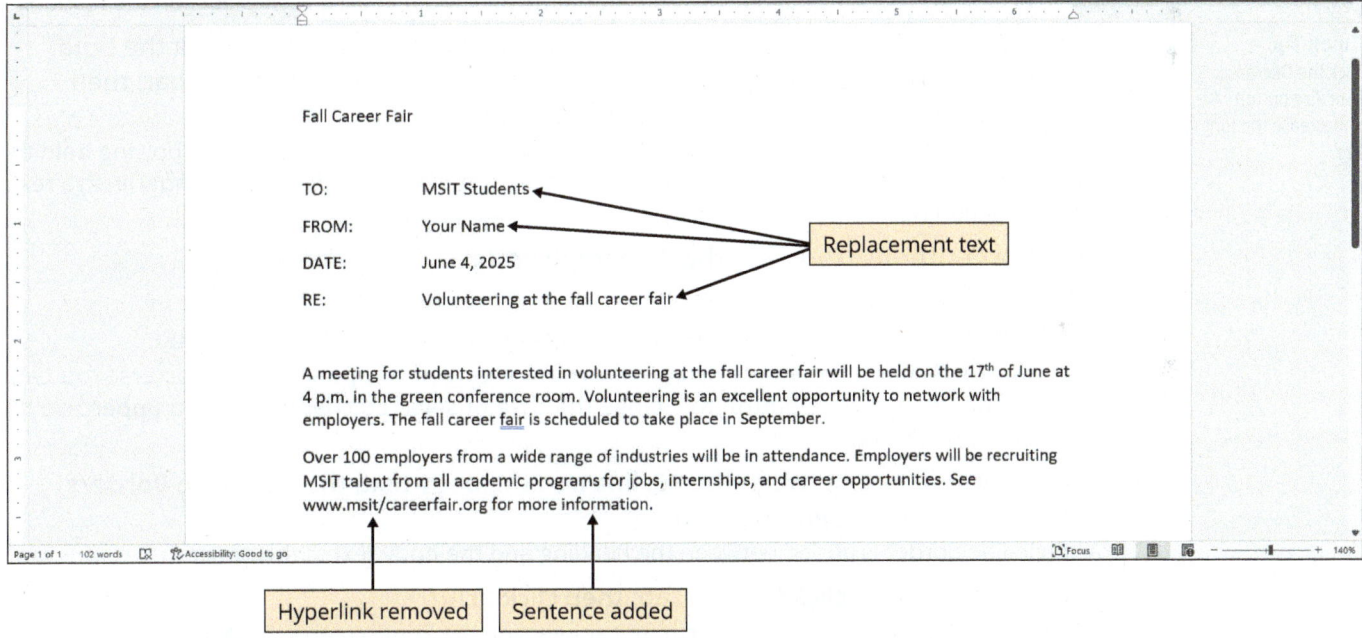

Table 1-4: Methods for selecting text

to select	use the pointer to
Any amount of text	Drag over the text
A word	Double-click the word
A line of text	Move the pointer to the left of the line, then click
A sentence	Press and hold CTRL, then click the sentence
A paragraph	Triple-click the paragraph or double-click with the pointer to the left of the paragraph
A large block of text	Click at the beginning of the selection, press and hold SHIFT, then click at the end of the selection
Multiple nonconsecutive selections	Select the first selection, then press and hold CTRL as you select each additional selection
An entire document	Triple-click with the pointer to the left of any text; press CTRL+A; or click the Select button in the Editing group on the Home tab, and then click Select All

Format Text Using the Mini Toolbar and the Ribbon

Case You enhance the appearance of the notice by formatting the text using the Mini toolbar. When you are finished, you preview the notice for errors and then print it.

Objectives
- Modify text formatting
- Print a document
- Modify print settings
- Close a document

Formatting text is a fast and fun way to improve the appearance of a document and highlight important information. You can easily change the font, color, size, style, and other attributes of text by selecting the text and clicking a command on the Home tab. The **Mini toolbar**, which appears above text when you first select it, also includes commonly used text and paragraph formatting commands.

Steps

Trouble
If the Mini toolbar disappears, right-click the selection to display it again.

Quick Tip
Click the Decrease Font Size button [A˅] to decrease the font size.

1. **Select Fall Career Fair**
   The Mini toolbar appears over the selected text, as shown in **Figure 1-9**. You click a formatting option on the Mini toolbar to apply it to the selected text. **Table 1-5** describes the function of the buttons on the Mini toolbar. Yours may differ. The buttons on the Mini toolbar are also available on the Ribbon.

2. **Click the Increase Font Size button [A˄] on the Mini toolbar six times, click the Bold button [B] on the Mini toolbar, click the Italic button [I] on the Mini toolbar, then click the Underline button [U] on the Mini toolbar**
   Each time you click the Increase Font Size button the selected text is enlarged. Applying bold to the text makes it thicker. Applying italic to text makes it slanted. Applying an underline to text adds an underline.

3. **Click the Center button [≡] in the Paragraph group on the Home tab**
   The selected text is centered between the left and right margins.

4. **Click the Change Case button [Aa˅] in the Font group, then click UPPERCASE**
   The lowercase characters in the selected text are changed to uppercase characters. You can also use the Change Case button to change the case of selected characters from uppercase to lowercase, and vice versa.

5. **Click the blank line between the RE: line and the body text, then click the Borders button [⊞] in the Paragraph group**
   A single-line border is added between the heading and the body text in the notice.

6. **Save the document, click the File tab, then click Print**
   Information related to printing the document appears on the Print screen in Backstage view. Options for printing the document appear on the left side of the Print screen and a preview of the document as it will look when printed appears on the right side, as shown in **Figure 1-10**. Before you print a document, it's a good habit to examine it closely so you can identify and correct any problems.

7. **Click the Zoom In button [+] on the status bar five times, then proofread your document carefully for errors**
   The document is enlarged in print preview. If you notice errors in your document, you need to correct them before you print. To do this, press ESC or click the Back button in Backstage view, correct any mistakes, save your changes, click the File tab, and then click the Print command again to be ready to print the document.

8. **Click the Print button on the Print screen**
   A copy of the notice prints using the default print settings. To change the current printer, change the number of copies to print, select which pages of a document to print, or modify another print setting, you simply change the appropriate setting on the Print screen before clicking the Print button.

9. **sam↑ Click the File tab, then click Close**
   The document closes, but the Word program window remains open.

Format Text Using the Mini Toolbar and the Ribbon   WD 1-13

Figure 1-9: Mini toolbar

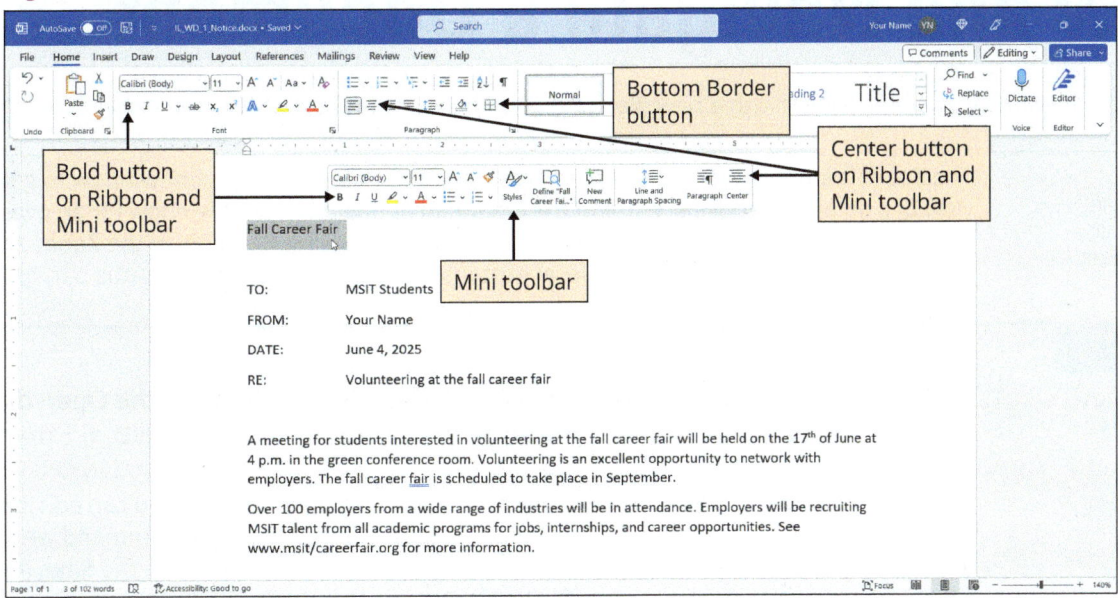

Figure 1-10: Preview of the completed document

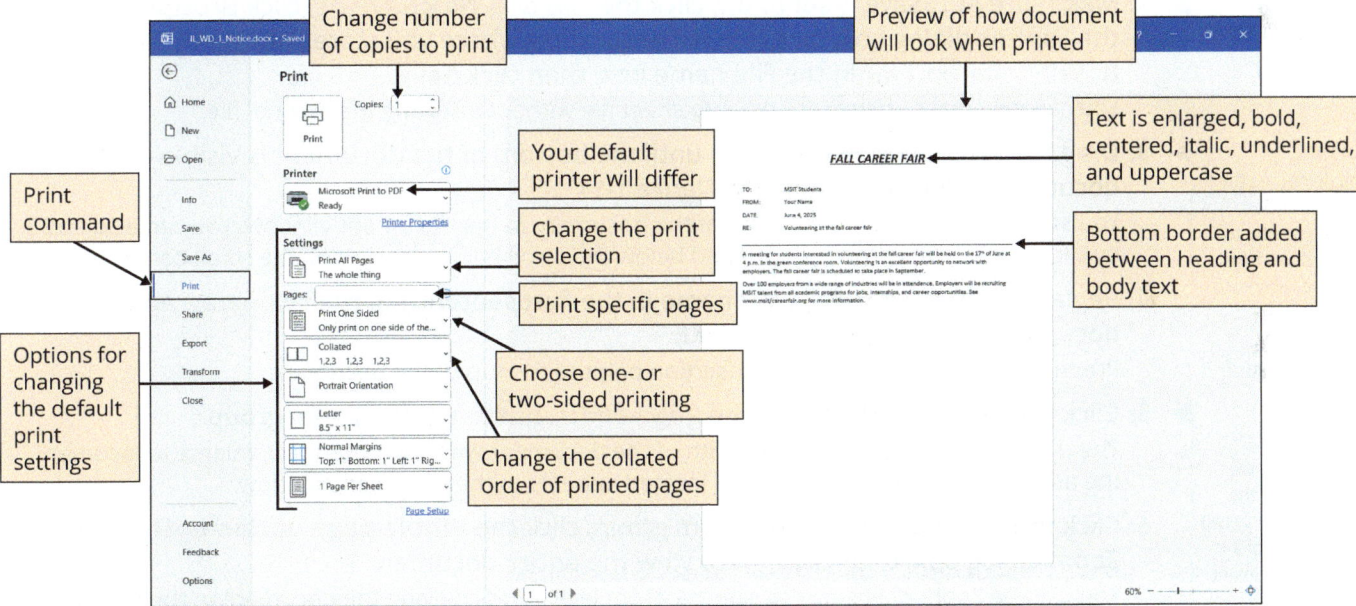

Table 1-5: Buttons on the Mini toolbar

button	use to	button	use to
Calibri (Body)	Change the font of text	B	Apply bold to text
11	Change the font size of text	I	Apply italic to text
A^	Make text larger	U	Apply an underline to text
A˅	Make text smaller	✏	Apply colored highlighting to text
🖌	Copy the formats applied to selected text to other text	A	Change the color of text
A	Apply a style to text	☷	Apply bullets to paragraphs
🔍	Look up the definition of a word	☷	Apply numbering to paragraphs
💬	Insert a new comment	‡☰	Change line and paragraph spacing
☰	Center text	☰	Align text with both margins

View and Navigate a Document

Case You open the info sheet, save it with a new filename, and then customize a document property for the file.

Objectives
- Open documents
- Zoom in and out
- Change document properties

The Zoom feature in Word lets you enlarge a document in the document window to get a close-up view of a detail, or reduce the size of the document in the document window for an overview of the layout as a whole. You zoom in and out on a document using the tools in the Zoom group on the View tab or you can use the Zoom level buttons and Zoom slider on the status bar.

Steps

1. **Click the File tab, click Open, click This PC, click Browse to open the Open dialog box, navigate to the location where you store your Data Files, click IL_WD_1-1.docx, then click Open**
   The document opens in Print Layout view. Once you have opened a file, you can edit it and use the Save or the Save As command to save your changes. You use the **Save** command when you want to save the changes you make to a file, overwriting the stored file. You use the **Save As** command when you want to leave the original file intact and create a duplicate file with a different filename, file extension, or location.

   Trouble
   Click the Enable Editing button if necessary.

2. **Make sure AutoSave is set to off, click the File tab, click Save As, click Browse to open the Save As dialog box, navigate to the location where you store your Data Files, type IL_WD_1_CareerFair in the File name box, then click Save**
   You can now make changes to the info sheet file without affecting the original file.

   Trouble
   If you do not see the vertical scroll box, move the pointer to the right side of the document window to display it.

3. **Drag the vertical scroll box down until the bottom of the document is visible in your document window, as shown in Figure 1-11**
   You **scroll** to display different parts of the document in the document window. You can also scroll by clicking the scroll arrows above and below the scroll bar, or by clicking the scroll bar.

4. **Replace Your Name with your name in the first sentence of the last paragraph in the document, then press CTRL+HOME**
   Pressing CTRL+HOME moves the insertion point to the top of the document.

   Quick Tip
   Click the Multiple Pages button in the Zoom group on the View tab to display two or more pages of a multi-page document in the document window.

5. **Click the View tab, then click the Page Width button in the Zoom group**
   The document is enlarged to the width of the document window. When you enlarge a document, the area where the insertion point is located appears in the document window.

6. **Click the Zoom button in the Zoom group, click the Whole page option button in the Zoom dialog box, then click OK to view the entire document**
   You use the Zoom dialog box to select a zoom level for displaying the document in the document window.

7. **Move the Zoom slider on the status bar to the right until the Zoom percentage is approximately 200%, then click the Zoom Out button until the zoom level is 140%**
   Dragging the Zoom slider enlarges or reduces a document in the document window. You can also click the Zoom Out and Zoom In buttons to change the zoom level.

8. **Click the File tab, then click Info**
   The right side of the Info screen in Backstage view shows the document properties for the file. **Document properties** are user-defined details about a file that describe its contents and origin, including the name of the author, the title of the document, and keywords that you can assign to help organize and search your files.

9. **Click the Add a title box in the Properties section of the Info screen, type Career Fair, then click outside the box**
   The new Title property for the document appears in Backstage view as shown in **Figure 1-12**.

10. **Click Back button to return to the Home tab, then save your changes**
    The document appears at 140% zoom in Print Layout view.

Figure 1-11: Zoom slider

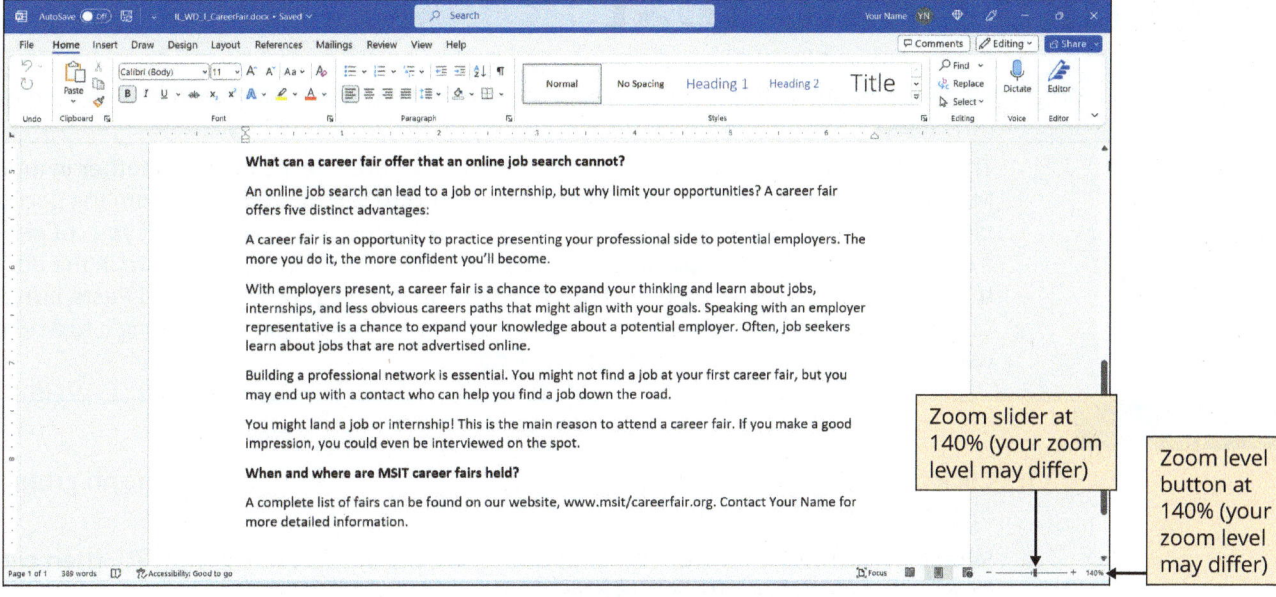

Figure 1-12: Document properties in Backstage view

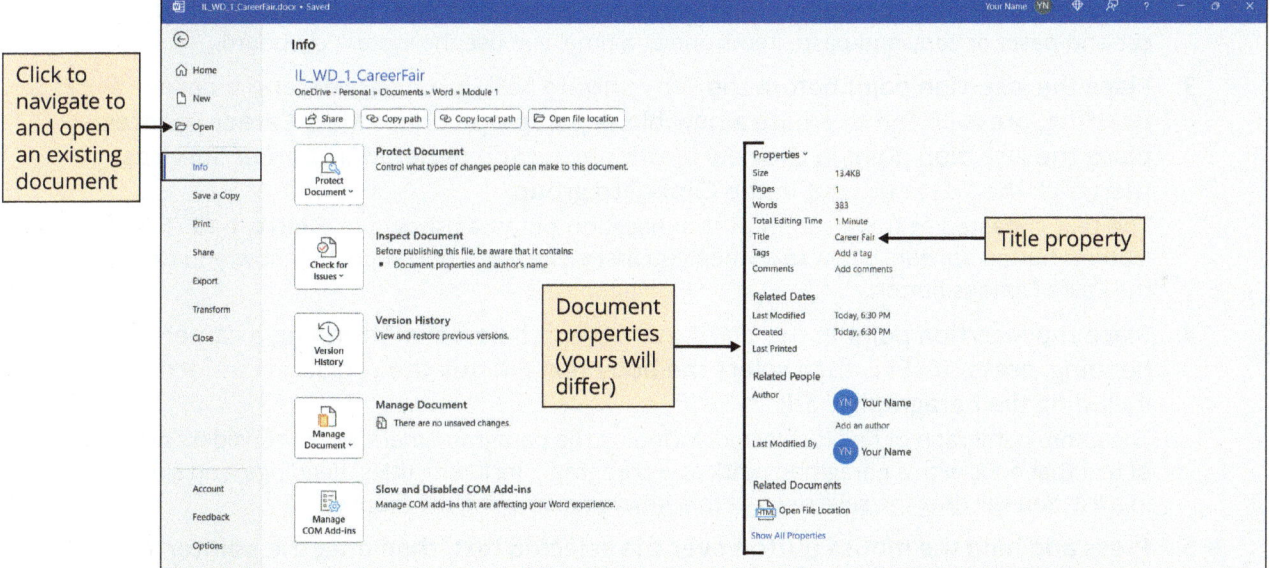

Using Word document views

Document views are different ways of displaying a document in the document window. Each Word view provides features that are useful for working on different types of documents. The default view, **Print Layout view**, displays a document as it will appear on a printed page. Print Layout view is helpful for formatting text and pages, including adjusting document margins, creating columns of text, inserting graphics, and formatting headers and footers. Also useful is **Read Mode view**, which displays document text so that it is easy to read on screen. Other Word views are helpful for performing specialized tasks. **Web Layout view** allows you to format web pages or documents that will be viewed on a computer screen. In Web Layout view, a document appears just as it will when viewed with a web browser. **Outline view** is useful for editing and formatting longer documents that include multiple headings. Outline view allows you to reorganize text by moving the headings. Finally, **Draft view** shows a simplified layout of a document, without margins, headers and footers, or graphics. When you want to quickly type and edit text, it's often easiest to work in Draft view. You switch between views by clicking the view buttons on the status bar or by using the commands on the View tab. Changing views does not affect how the printed document will appear. It simply changes the way you view the document in the document window.

Cut and Paste Text

Case You reorganize the information in the info sheet using the cut-and-paste and drag-and-drop methods.

Objectives
- Cut and paste text
- Undo and redo actions
- Highlight text

The editing features in Word allow you to move text from one location to another in a document. Moving text is often called **cut and paste**. When you **cut** text, it is removed from the document and placed on the **Clipboard**, a temporary storage area for text and graphics that you cut or copy from a document. You can then **paste**, or insert, text that is stored on the Clipboard in the document at the location of the insertion point. You cut and paste text using the Cut and Paste buttons in the Clipboard group on the Home tab. You can also move selected text by dragging it to a new location using the mouse. This is called **drag and drop**.

Steps

1. Click **Home tab**, then click the **Show/Hide ¶ button** ¶ in the Paragraph group to display formatting marks

2. Select **Attending a career fair** (including the paragraph mark after it), then click the **Cut button** in the Clipboard group

   The text is removed from the document and placed on the system clipboard. Word uses two different clipboards: the **system clipboard**, which holds just one item and is not visible, and the **Office Clipboard** (the Clipboard), which holds up to 24 items and can be displayed. When you cut-and-paste or copy-and-paste items one at a time, you use the system clipboard.

3. Place the insertion point before the **Why should MSIT students attend a career fair? heading**, press **ENTER** to create a new blank paragraph under MSIT Career Services, place the insertion point in the new **blank paragraph** under MSIT Career Services, then click the **Paste button** in the Clipboard group

   The text is pasted at the location of the insertion point, as shown in **Figure 1-13**. The Paste Options button appears below text when you first paste it in a document. For now, you can ignore the Paste Options button.

4. Place the insertion point in the **blank paragraph** below the Attending a career fair heading, press **DELETE**, then select the body text **Fill out the registration form.**, including the paragraph mark

   The entire paragraph of text is selected, including the paragraph mark. Word considers any string of text that ends with a paragraph mark as a paragraph, including titles, headings, and single lines in a list. You will drag the selected text to a new location using the mouse.

Quick Tip
As you drag, the pointer changes to ▯, and a black vertical line, which is the insertion point, moves with the pointer.

5. Press and hold the mouse button over the selected text, then drag the pointer's vertical line to the beginning of the **Wear professional clothing.** paragraph, as shown in **Figure 1-14**

   You drag the insertion point to where you want the text to be inserted when you release the mouse button.

Quick Tip
If you make a mistake, click the Undo button ↶ in the Undo group on the Home tab, then try again.

6. Release the mouse button, click to deselect the text, then save your changes

   The selected text is moved to the location of the insertion point. Text is not placed on the Clipboard when you drag and drop it.

Highlighting text in a document

The Highlight tool allows you to mark and find important text in a document. **Highlighting** is transparent color that is applied to text using the Highlight pointer ✎. To highlight text, click the Text Highlight Color arrow ✎▾ in the Font group on the Home tab, select a color, then use the I-beam part of the pointer to select the text you want to highlight. Click the Text Highlight Color button ✎▾ to turn off the Highlight pointer. To remove highlighting, select the highlighted text, click the Text Highlight Color arrow ✎▾ then click No Color. Highlighting prints, but it is used most effectively when a document is viewed on screen.

Figure 1-13: Moved text with Paste Options button

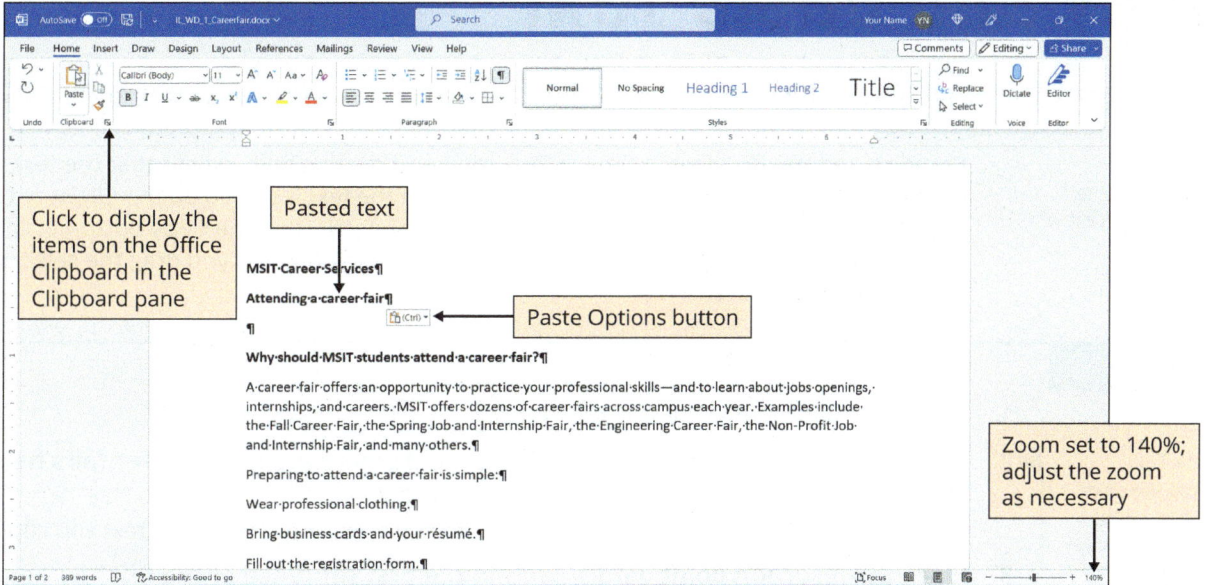

Figure 1-14: Dragging and dropping text in a new location

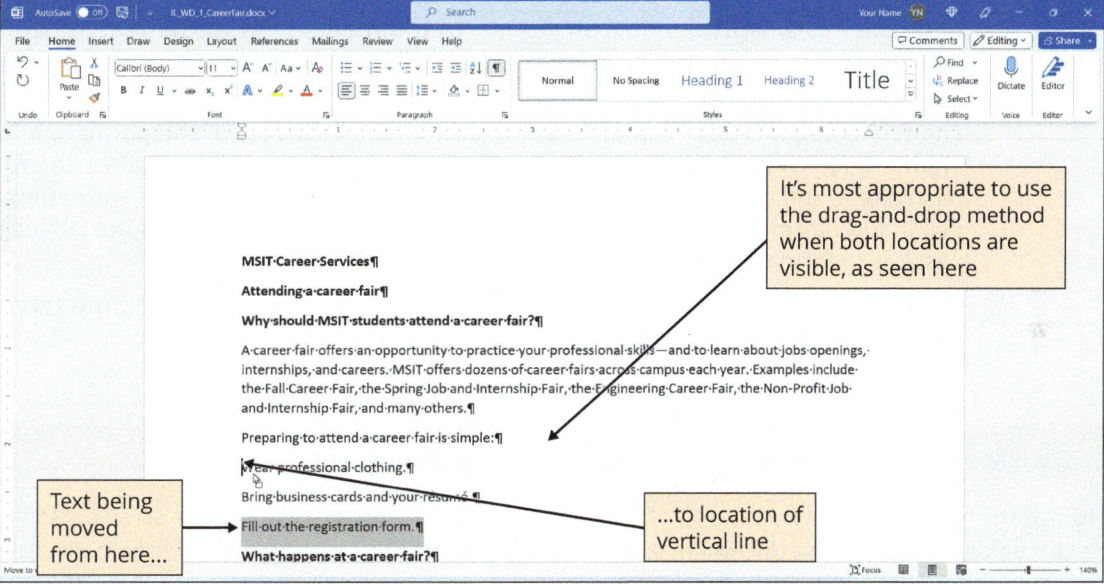

Using the Undo, Redo, and Repeat commands

Word remembers the editing and formatting changes you make so that you can easily reverse or repeat them. You can reverse the last action you took by clicking the Undo button in the Undo group on the Home tab or on the Quick Access toolbar, or you can undo a series of actions by clicking the Undo arrow and selecting the action you want to reverse. When you undo an action using the Undo arrow, you also undo all the actions above it in the list—that is, all actions that were performed after the action you selected. Similarly, you can keep the change you just reversed by using the Redo button in the Undo group on the Home tab or on the Quick Access toolbar. The Redo button appears only immediately after clicking the Undo button to undo a change.

If you want to repeat an action you just completed, you can use the Repeat button in the Undo group on the Home tab or on the Quick Access toolbar. For example, if you just typed "thank you," clicking inserts "thank you" at the location of the insertion point. If you just applied bold, clicking applies bold to the currently selected text. You also can repeat the last action you took by pressing F4.

Copy and Paste Text

Case You continue to edit the info sheet by copying text from one location to another using the copy-and-paste method.

Objectives
- Copy and paste text
- Split the document window
- Display multiple documents

Copying and pasting text is similar to cutting and pasting text, except that the text you **copy** is not removed from the document. Rather, a copy of the text is placed on the Clipboard, leaving the original text in place. You can copy text to the Clipboard using the Copy button in the Clipboard group on the Home tab, or you can copy text by pressing CTRL as you drag the selected text from one location to another.

Steps

Quick Tip
You can also cut or copy text by right-clicking the selected text, and then clicking the Cut or Copy command on the menu that opens.

1. Scroll to the bottom of the document

2. Select **MSIT career** in the heading When and where are MSIT career fairs held?, then click the **Copy button** in the Clipboard group

   A copy of the selected text is placed on the Clipboard, leaving the original text you copied in place.

3. Place the insertion point before **fairs** in the first sentence of the final paragraph, then click the **Paste button**

   The text "MSIT career" is inserted in the final paragraph, as shown in **Figure 1-15**. Notice that the pasted text is formatted differently than the paragraph in which it was inserted.

4. Click the **Paste Options button** (Ctrl) that appears next to the text, move the mouse over each button on the menu that opens to read its ScreenTip, then click the **Keep Text Only (T) button**

   The formatting of "MSIT career" is changed to match the rest of the paragraph, as shown in **Figure 1-16**. The buttons on the Paste Options menu allow you to change the formatting of pasted text. You can choose to keep the original formatting (Keep Source Formatting), match the destination formatting (Merge Formatting), paste the selection as a graphic object (Picture), or paste as unformatted text (Keep Text Only).

5. Click the **Show/Hide ¶ button** in the Paragraph group on the Home tab to turn off the display formatting marks, then save your changes.

Splitting the document window to copy and move items in a long document

If you want to copy or move items between parts of a long document, it can be useful to split the document window into two panes. This allows you to display the item you want to copy or move in one pane and the destination for the item in the other pane. To split a window, click the Split button in the Window group on the View tab, and then drag the horizontal split bar that appears to the location where you want to split the window. Once the document window is split into two panes, you can use the scroll bars in each pane to display different parts of the document. To copy or move an item from one pane to another, you can use the Cut, Copy, and Paste commands, or you can drag the item between the panes. When you are finished editing the document, double-click the split bar to restore the window to a single pane, or click the Remove Split button in the Window group on the View tab.

Figure 1-15: Text pasted in document

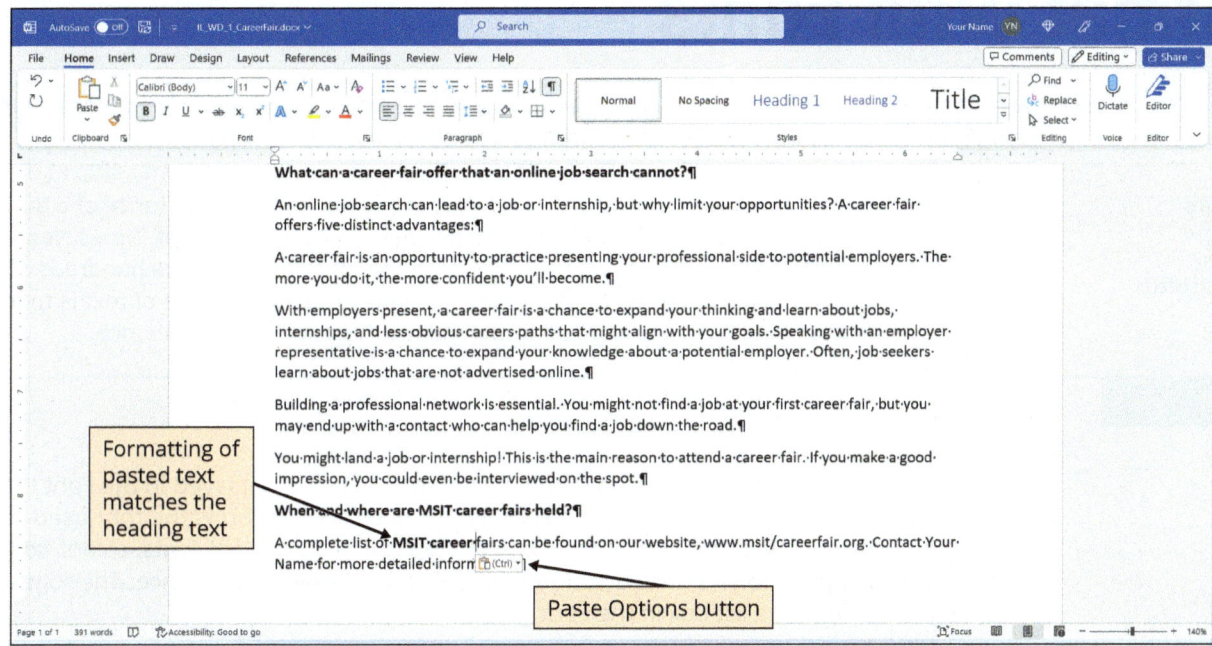

Figure 1-16: Copied text in document

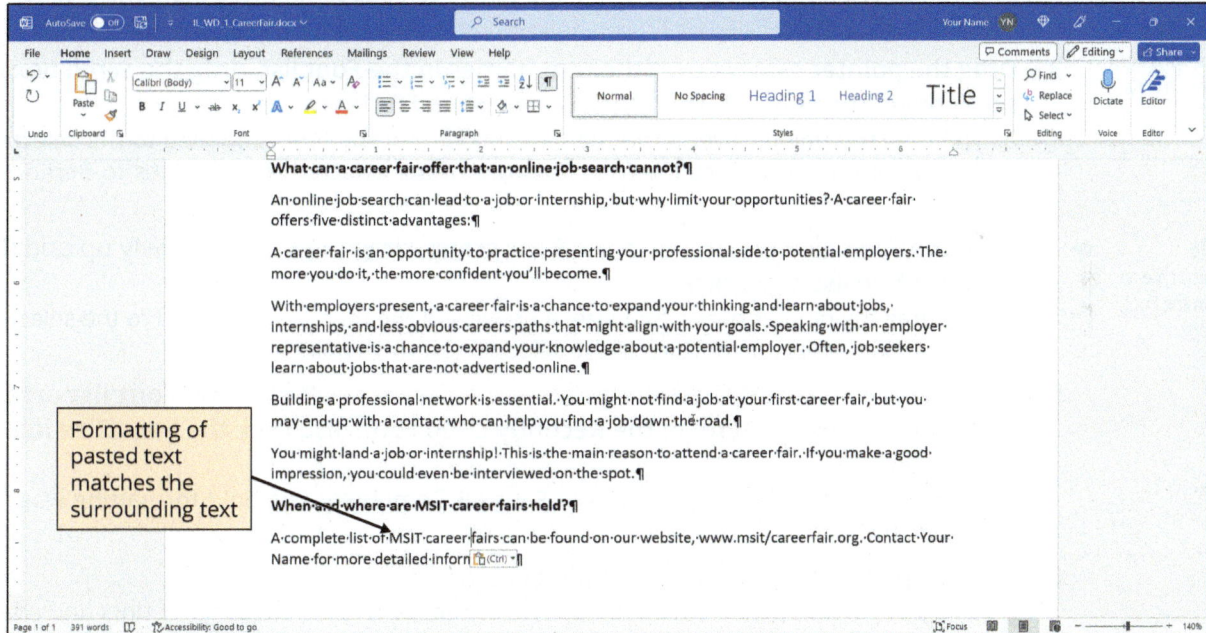

Copying and moving items between documents

You can also use the Clipboard to copy and move items between documents. To do this, open both documents and the Clipboard pane. With multiple documents open, copy or cut an item from one document and then switch to the other document and paste the item. To switch between open documents, point to the Word icon on the taskbar, and then click the document you want to appear in the document window. You can also display more than one document at the same time by clicking the Arrange All button or the View Side by Side button in the Window group on the View tab, or by pointing to the Maximize button on the title bar, and clicking a snap layout.

Format with Fonts

Case You change the font and font size of the headings in the info sheet. You select a font and font sizes that enhance the positive tone of the document and help to structure the info sheet visually for readers.

Objectives
- Modify text formatting
- Apply text effects

Formatting text with fonts is a quick and powerful way to enhance the appearance of a document. A **font** is a complete set of characters with the same typeface or design. Arial, Times New Roman, Courier, Tahoma, and Calibri are some of the more common fonts, but there are hundreds of others, each with a specific design and feel. Another way to change the appearance of text is to increase or decrease its **font size**. Font size is measured in points. A **point** is 1/72 of an inch.

Steps

1. Press **CTRL+HOME**
   Notice that the name of the font used in the document, Calibri, is displayed in the Font list box in the Font group. The word "(Body)" in the Font list box indicates Calibri is the font used for body text in the current theme, the default theme. A **theme** is a related set of fonts, colors, styles, and effects that is applied to an entire document to give it a cohesive appearance. The font size, 11, appears in the Font Size list box in the Font group.

   Quick Tip
   There are two types of fonts: **serif fonts** have a small stroke, called a serif, at the ends of characters; **sans serif fonts** do not have a serif.

2. Select **Attending a career fair**, then click the **Font list arrow** in the Font group
   The Font list, which shows the fonts available on your computer, opens as shown in **Figure 1-17**. The font names are formatted in the font. Font names can appear in more than one location on the Font list.

3. Drag the pointer slowly down the font names in the Font list, drag the scroll box to scroll down the Font list, then click **Berlin Sans FB Demi**
   As you drag the pointer over a font name, a preview of the font is applied to the selected text. Clicking a font name applies the font. The font of the selected text changes to Berlin Sans FB Demi.

   Quick Tip
   You can also type a font size in the Font Size text box.

4. Click the **Font Size list arrow** in the Font group, drag the pointer slowly up and down the Font Size list, then click **18**
   As you drag the pointer over a font size, a preview of the font size is applied to the selected text. Clicking 18 increases the font size of the selected text to 18 points.

5. Select **Why should MSIT students attend a career fair?**, click the **Font list arrow**, click **Berlin Sans FB Demi** in the Recently Used Fonts list, click the **Font Size list arrow**, click **22**
   The title is formatted in 22-point Berlin Sans FB Demi bold. The bold formatting was already applied to the text.

6. Click the **Font Color list arrow** in the Font group
   A gallery of colors opens. It includes the set of theme colors in a range of tints and shades as well as a set of standard colors. You can point to a color in the gallery to preview it applied to the selected text.

7. Click the **Green, Accent 6 color** as shown in **Figure 1-18**, then deselect the text
   The color of the title text changes to green. The active color on the Font Color button also changes to green.

   Trouble
   If the mini toolbar closes, select the text again.

8. Scroll down, select the heading **What happens at a career fair?**, then, using the Mini toolbar, click the **Font list arrow**, click **Berlin Sans FB Demi**, click the **Font Size list arrow**, click **14**, click ![A], then deselect the text
   The heading is formatted in 14-point Berlin Sans FB Demi bold with a green color.

9. Repeat step 8 to apply 14-point Berlin Sans FB Demi green to the **What can a career fair offer that an online job search cannot?** and **When and where are MSIT career fairs held?** headings, press **CTRL+HOME**, then save your changes
   Compare your document to **Figure 1-19**.

Figure 1-17: Font list

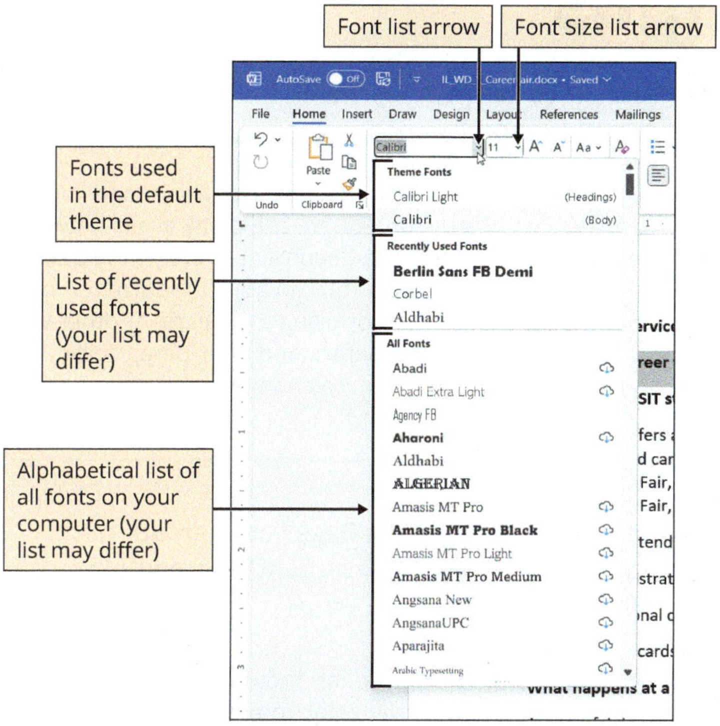

Figure 1-18: Font Color palette

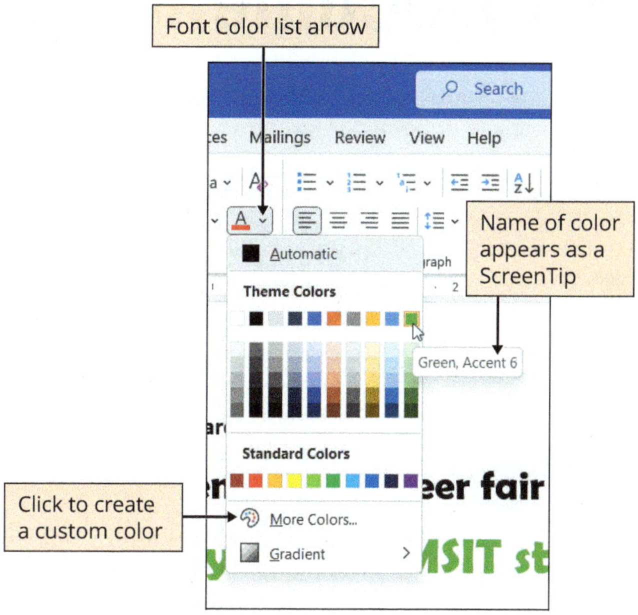

Figure 1-19: Document formatted with fonts

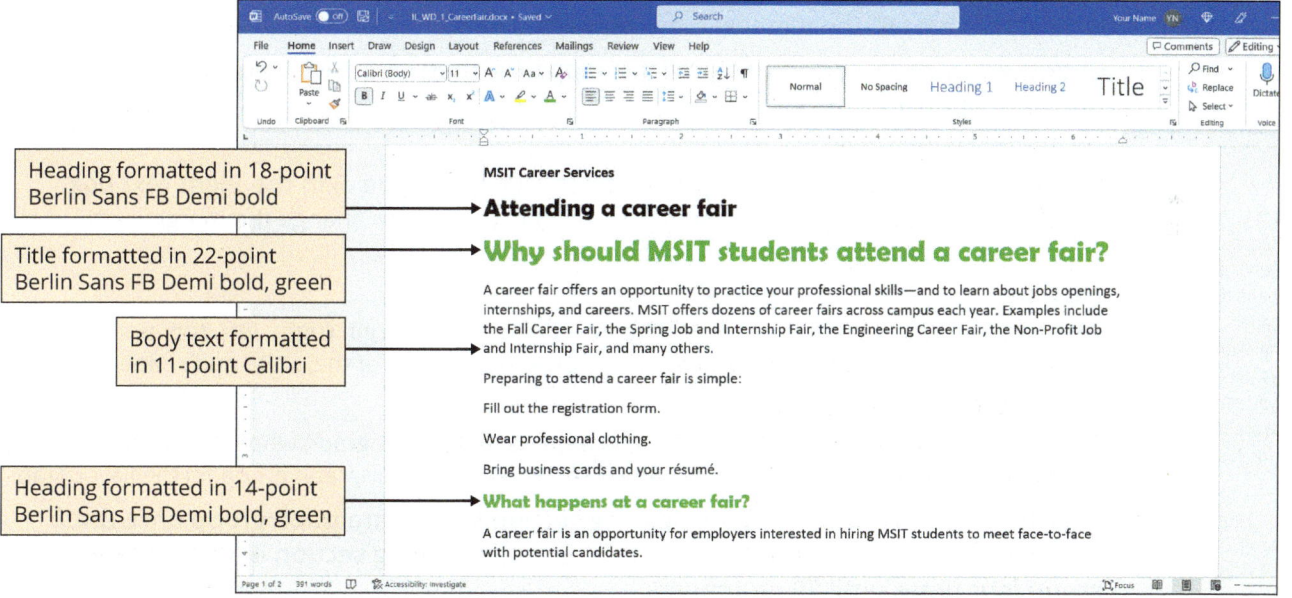

Applying shadows and other text effects to text

The Word Text Effects and Typography feature allows you to add visual appeal to your documents by adding special text effects to text, including outlines, shadows, reflections, and glows. The feature also includes a gallery of preformatted combined text effect styles, called **WordArt**, that you can apply to your text to format it quickly and easily. To apply a WordArt style to text, simply select the text, click the Text Effects and Typography button in the Font group on the Home tab, and select a WordArt style from the gallery. To apply an individual text effect style, such as a shadow, outline, reflection, or glow, select the text, click the Text Effects and Typography button, point to the type of text effect you want to apply, and then select a style from the gallery that opens. Experiment with combining text effect styles to give your text a striking appearance.

If you are unhappy with the way text is formatted, you can use the Clear All Formatting command to return the text to the default format settings—11-point Calibri. Select the text, then click the Clear All Formatting button in the Font group on the Home tab.

Set Document Margins

Case You reduce the size of the document margins in the info sheet so that more text fits on the page. You also add space under a paragraph.

Objectives
- Modify page setup
- Change paragraph spacing

Changing a document's margins is one way to change the appearance of a document and control the amount of text that fits on a page. The **margins** of a document are the blank areas between the edge of the text and the edge of the page. When you create a document in Word, the default margins are 1" at the top, bottom, left, and right sides of the page. You can adjust the size of a document's margins using the Margins command on the Layout tab or using the rulers. Another way to change the amount of open space on a page is to add space before and after paragraphs. You use the Spacing options in the Paragraph group on the Layout tab to change paragraph spacing. Paragraph spacing is measured in points.

Steps

1. **Click the Layout tab, then click the Margins button in the Page Setup group**
   The Margins menu opens. You can select predefined margin settings from this menu, or you can click Custom Margins to create different margin settings.

2. **Click Custom Margins**
   The Page Setup dialog box opens with the Margins tab displayed, as shown in **Figure 1-20**. You can use the Margins tab to change the top, bottom, left, or right document margin, to change the orientation of the pages from portrait to landscape, and to alter other page layout settings. **Portrait orientation** means a page is taller than it is wide; **landscape orientation** means a page is wider than it is tall. This info sheet uses portrait orientation.

3. **Click the Top down four times until 0.6" appears, then click the Bottom down arrow until 0.6" appears**
   The top and bottom margins of the info sheet will be .6".

4. **Press TAB, type .6 in the Left text box, press TAB, then type .6 in the Right text box**
   The left and right margins of the report will also be .6". You can change the margin settings by using the arrows or by typing a value in the appropriate text box.

5. **Click OK**
   The document margins change to .6". The location of each margin (right, left, top, and bottom) is shown on the horizontal and vertical rulers at the intersection of the white and shaded areas.

6. **Place the insertion point in Attending a career fair**
   The paragraph spacing settings for the active paragraph (the paragraph where the insertion point is located) are shown in the Before and After text boxes in the Paragraph group on the Layout tab.

7. **Click the Before up arrow in the Spacing section in the Paragraph group once until 6 pt appears, then click the After up arrow in the Spacing section in the Paragraph group four times until 30 pt appears**
   Six points of space are added before the Attending a career fair paragraph, and thirty points of space are added after, as shown in **Figure 1-21**.

Quick Tip
The minimum allowable margin settings depend on your printer and the size of the paper you are using. Word displays a warning message if you set margins that are too narrow for your printer.

Using keyboard shortcuts

A **shortcut key** is a function key, such as F1, or a combination of keys, such as CTRL+S, that you press to perform a command. For example, instead of using the Cut, Copy, and Paste commands on the Ribbon or the Mini toolbar, you can use the **keyboard shortcuts** CTRL+X to cut text, CTRL+C to copy text, and CTRL+V to paste text. You can also press CTRL+S to save changes to a document instead of clicking the Save button on the Quick Access toolbar. If a keyboard shortcut is available for a command, then it is listed in the ScreenTip for that command.

Set Document Margins

Figure 1-20: Margins tab in Page Setup dialog box

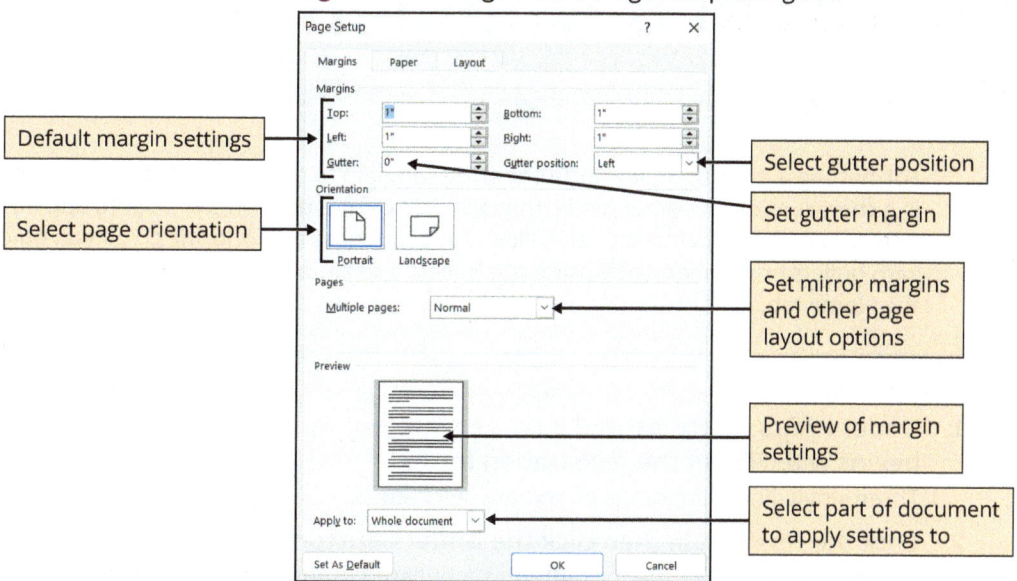

Figure 1-21: Info sheet with smaller margins and space after a paragraph

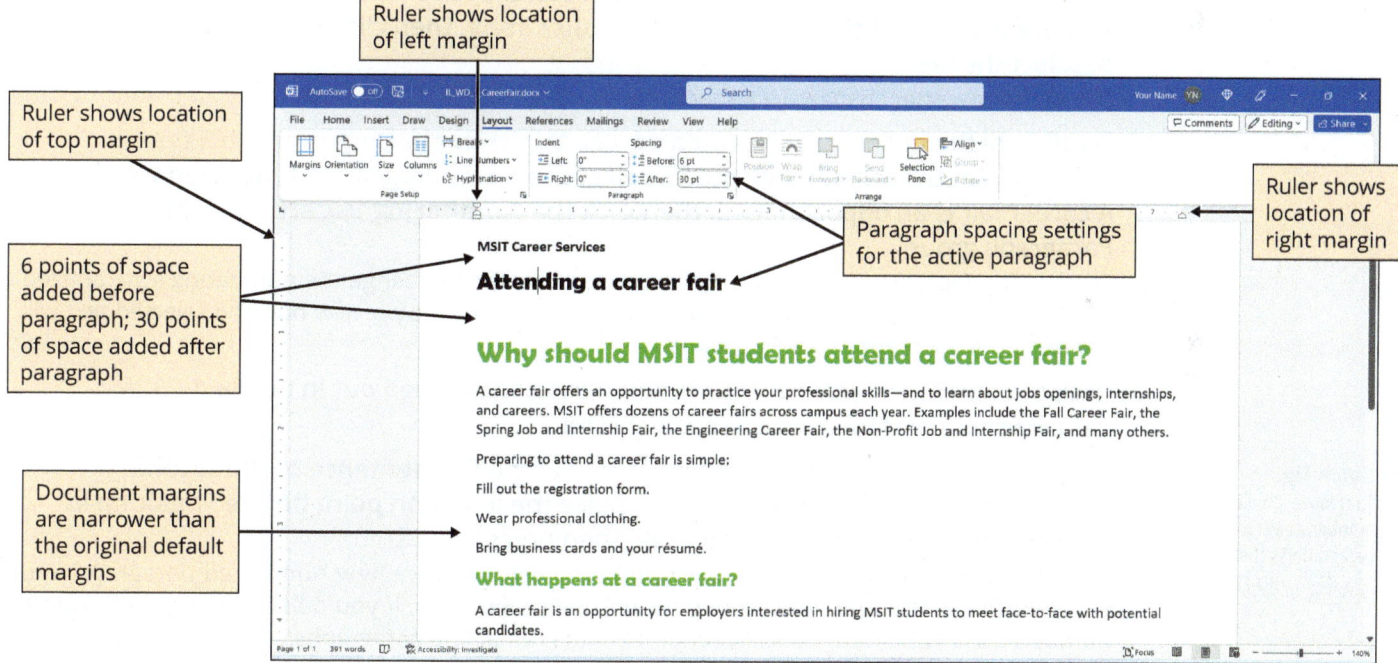

Changing orientation, margin settings, and paper size

By default, the documents you create in Word use an 8 ½" × 11" paper size in portrait orientation with the default margin settings. You can change the orientation, margin settings, and paper size to common settings using the Orientation, Margins, and Size buttons in the Page Setup group on the Layout tab. You can also adjust these settings and others in the Page Setup dialog box. For example, to change the layout of multiple pages, use the Multiple pages arrow on the Margins tab to create pages that use mirror margins, that include two pages per sheet of paper, or that are formatted using a book fold. **Mirror margins** are used in a document with facing pages, such as a magazine, where the margins on the left page of the document are a mirror image of the margins on the right page. Documents with mirror margins have inside and outside margins, rather than right and left margins. Another type of margin is a gutter margin, which is used in documents that are bound, such as books. A gutter adds extra space to the left, top, or inside margin to allow for the binding. Add a gutter to a document by adjusting the setting in the Gutter position box on the Margins tab. To change the size of the paper used, use the Paper size arrow on the Paper tab to select a standard paper size, or enter custom measurements in the Width and Height boxes.

Add Bullets and Numbering

Case You format the lists in your info sheet with numbers and bullets.

Objectives
- Create numbered and bulleted lists

Formatting a list with bullets or numbering can help to organize the ideas in a document. A **bullet** is a character, often a small circle, that appears before the items in a list to add emphasis. Formatting a list as a numbered list helps illustrate sequences and priorities. You can quickly format a list with bullets or numbering by using the Bullets and Numbering buttons in the Paragraph group on the Home tab.

Steps

1. Under **Preparing to attend a career fair is simple:**, select the **three-line list** that begins with Fill out the registration form.
   Three single-line paragraphs of text are selected.

2. Click the **Home tab,** then click the **Bullets button** in the Paragraph group
   The three paragraphs are formatted as a bulleted list using the most recently used bullet style as shown in **Figure 1-22**.

3. Click a **bullet** in the list to select all the bullets, click the **Bullets arrow** in the Paragraph group, click the **check mark bullet style**, then click the document to deselect the text
   The bullet character changes to a check mark.

4. Scroll until the heading **What can a career fair offer that an online job search cannot?** is at the top of your screen, select the **four paragraphs** that begin with A career fair is an opportunity..., then click the **Numbering list arrow** in the Paragraph group
   The Numbering Library opens. You use this list to choose or change the numbering style applied to a list. You can drag the pointer over the numbering styles to preview how the selected text will appear if the numbering style is applied.

5. Click the **Number alignment: Left** numbering style called out in **Figure 1-23**
   The paragraphs are formatted as a numbered list.

6. Place the insertion point before **employers** in the first sentence of the second numbered paragraph, type **dozens of**, place the insertion point before **Speaking** in the second sentence of the paragraph, then press **ENTER**
   Pressing ENTER in the middle of the numbered list creates a new numbered paragraph and automatically renumbers the remainder of the list. Similarly, if you delete a paragraph from a numbered list, Word automatically renumbers the remaining paragraphs.

7. Click **1** in the list
   Clicking a number in a list selects all the numbers, as shown in **Figure 1-24**.

8. Click the **Bold button** in the Font group then save your changes
   The numbers are all formatted in bold. Notice that the formatting of the items in the list does not change when you change the formatting of the numbers. You can also use this technique to change the formatting of bullets in a bulleted list.

Quick Tip
To remove a bullet or number, select the paragraph(s), then click or .

Figure 1-22: Bullets applied to list

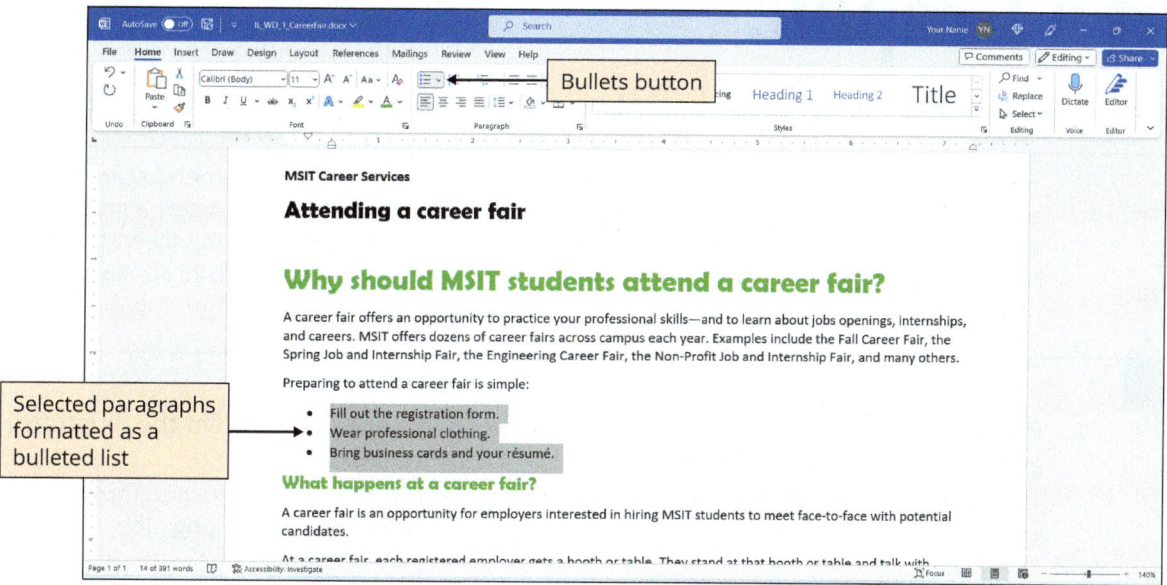

Figure 1-23: Numbering gallery

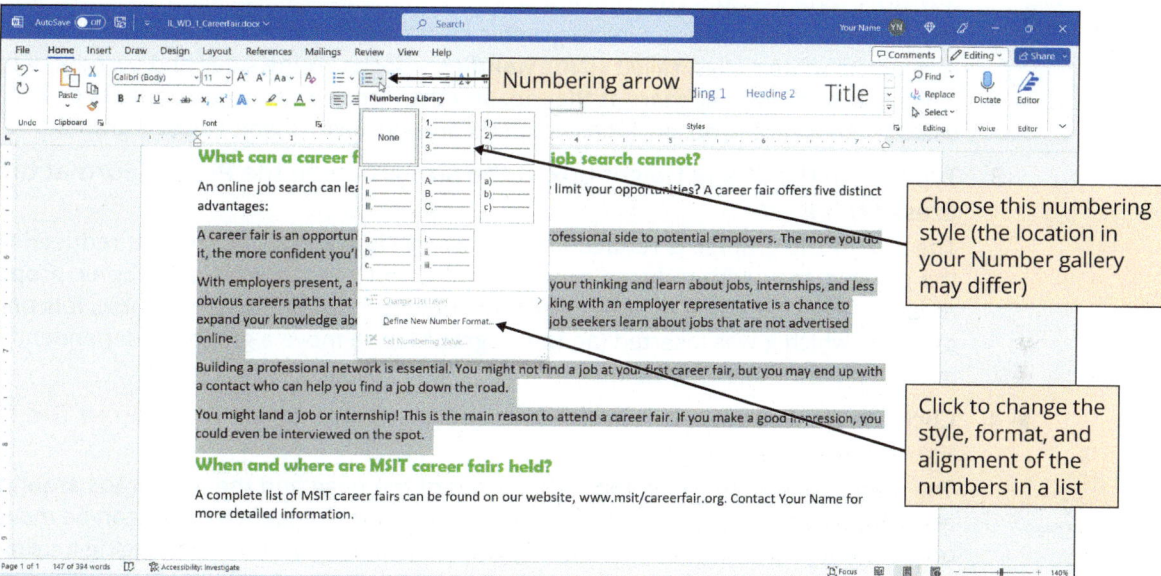

Figure 1-24: Numbered list

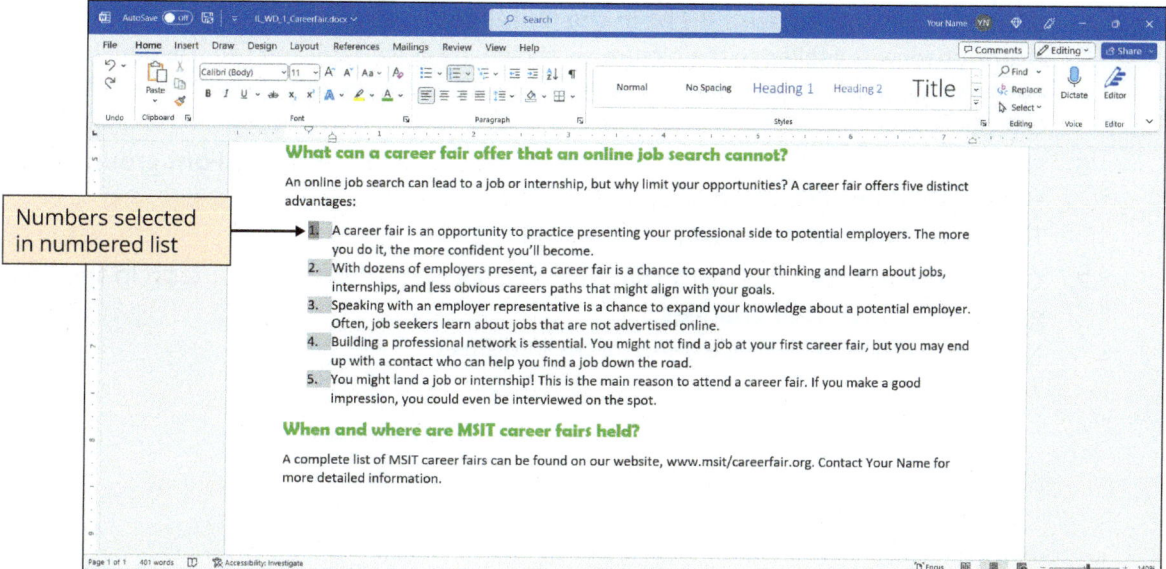

Insert a Graphic

Case You insert a picture in the document, resize it, position it, and then add a shadow.

Objectives
- Insert a picture
- Resize a picture
- Position a picture
- Apply picture styles and effects

You can insert graphic images, including photos taken with a digital camera, scanned art, and graphics created in other graphics programs, into a Word document. To insert a graphic file into a document, you use the Pictures command in the Illustrations group on the Insert tab. Once you insert a graphic, you can resize it and apply a Picture style to it to enhance its appearance.

Steps

1. **Press CTRL+HOME, click the Insert tab, click the Pictures button in the Illustrations group, then click This Device**
   The Insert Picture dialog box opens. You use this dialog box to locate and insert graphic files. Most graphic files are **bitmap graphics**, which are often saved with a .bmp, .png, .jpg, .tif, or .gif file extension.

2. **Navigate to the location where you store your Data Files, click the file Support_WD_1-2.jpg, then click Insert**
   The picture is inserted as an inline graphic at the location of the insertion point. When a graphic is selected, white circles, called **sizing handles**, appear on the sides and corners of the graphic, a white **rotate handle** appears at the top, and the Picture Format tab appears on the Ribbon. You use this tab to size, crop, position, wrap text around, format, and adjust a graphic.

3. **Type 2.1 in the Shape Height box in the Size group on the Picture Format tab, then press ENTER**
   The size of the graphic is reduced, as shown in **Figure 1-25**. When you reduced the height of the graphic, the width reduced proportionally. You can also resize a graphic proportionally by dragging a corner sizing handle. Until you apply text wrapping to a graphic, it is part of the line of text in which it was inserted (an **inline graphic**). To move a graphic independently of text, you must make it a **floating graphic**.

Quick Tip
Change a floating graphic to an inline graphic by changing the text-wrapping style to In Line with Text.

4. **Click the Position button in the Arrange group, then click Position in Top Right with Square Text Wrapping**
   The graphic is moved to the top-right corner of the page and the text wraps around it. Applying text wrapping to the graphic made it a floating graphic. A floating graphic can be moved anywhere on a page. You can also move a floating graphic to a new location by dragging it using the mouse.

5. **Click the Picture Effects button in the Picture Styles group, point to Shadow, move the pointer over the shadow styles in the gallery to preview them in the document, then click Offset: Bottom Right in the Outer section**
   A drop shadow is applied to the picture, as shown in **Figure 1-26**. You can use the Picture Effects button to apply other visual effects to a graphic, such as a glow, soft edge, reflection, bevel, or 3-D rotation.

6. **Select Attending a career fair, click the Font Color arrow in the Font group on the Home tab, then click Gray, Accent 3, Darker 25%**
   The text is formatted in dark gray.

7. **Click to deselect the text, click the View tab, click the One Page button in the Zoom group, then save your changes**
   Next, you will finalize the appearance of the info sheet.

Figure 1-25: Inline graphic in document

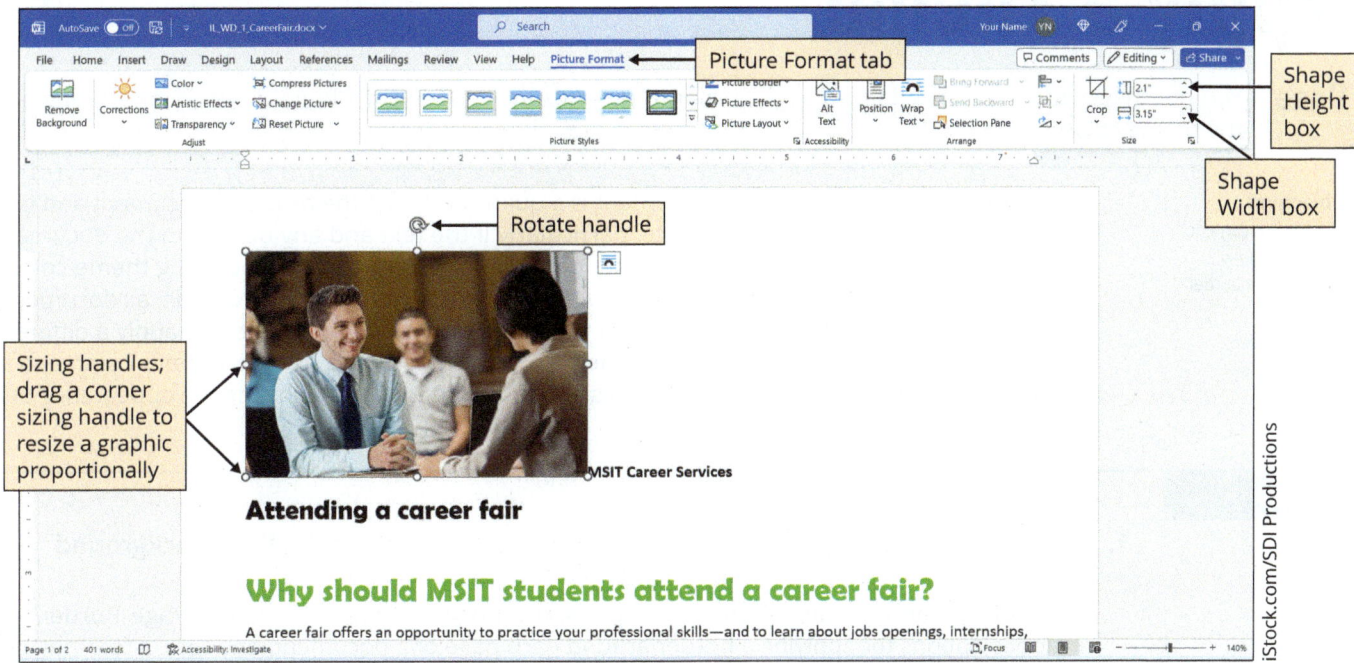

Figure 1-26: Floating graphic with shadow effect applied

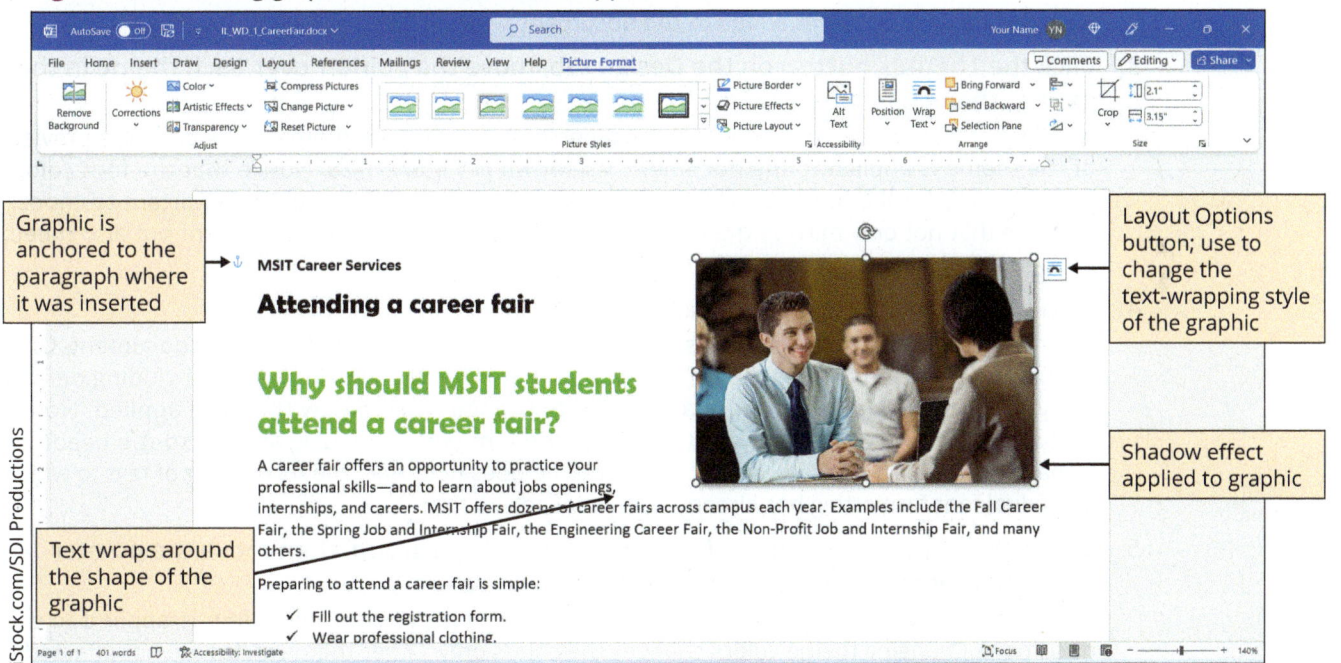

Enhancing pictures with styles and effects

A fun way to give a document personality and flair is to apply a style or an effect to a picture. To apply a style, select the picture and then choose from the style options in the Styles group on the Picture Format tab. Styles include a preset mixture of effects, such as shading, borders, shadows, and other settings. The Effects command in the Styles group on the Picture Format tab gives you the power to apply a customized variety of effects to an object, including a shadow, bevel, glow, reflection, soft edge, or 3-D rotation. To apply an effect, select the object, click the Picture Effects arrow, point to the type of effect you want to apply, and then select from the options in the gallery that opens. To further customize an effect, click the Options command for that type of effect at the bottom of the gallery to open the Format Picture pane. The best way to learn about styles and effects is to experiment by applying them to a picture and seeing what works. To return a picture to its original settings, click the Reset Picture button in the Adjust group on the Picture Format tab.

Apply a Theme

Case You polish the info sheet by adding a page border to the document, applying a built-in theme, and changing the theme colors.

Objectives
- Change document theme
- Add a page border

Changing the theme applied to a document is a quick way to set the tone of a document and give it a polished and cohesive appearance, particularly if the text and any objects in the document are formatted with styles. A **theme** is a set of unified design elements, including theme colors, theme fonts for body text and headings, and theme effects for graphics. By default, all documents that you create in Word are formatted with the Office theme, but you can easily apply a different built-in theme to a document. To apply a theme to a document, you use the Themes command in the Document Formatting group on the Design tab. Another way to enhance the appearance of a document is to apply a page border.

Steps

1. **Click the Design tab, then click the Page Borders button in the Page Background group**
   The Borders and Shading dialog box opens, as shown in **Figure 1-27**. The Page Border tab includes options for applying a border around each page of a document, and for customizing the appearance of borders.

2. **Click the Box button on the Page Border tab, then click OK**
   A single-line page border is added to the document.

3. **Click the Themes button on the Design tab, move the pointer over each theme in the gallery, then point to Organic**
   A gallery of built-in themes opens. When you point to the Organic theme in the gallery, a preview of the theme is applied to the document, as shown in **Figure 1-28**. Notice that the font colors and the fonts for the body text change when you preview each theme. It's important to choose a theme that not only mirrors the tone, content, and purpose of your document but also meets your goal for document length.

4. **Scroll down, then click Vapor Trail**
   A complete set of new theme colors, fonts, styles, and effects is applied to the document. Only document content that uses theme colors, text that is formatted with a style (including default body text), and table styles and graphic effects change when a new theme is applied. Notice that while the font of the body text changed, the font you previously applied to the headings remains the same. Changing the document theme does not affect the formatting of text to which individual font formatting has already been applied.

5. **Click the Colors button in the Document Formatting group, then move the pointer over each set of theme colors on the menu that opens**
   When you point to a theme color set in the gallery, a preview of the colors is applied to the document. Changing theme colors changes the colors only. Other theme styles are not affected.

6. **Click Blue Green**
   The Blue Green theme colors are applied to the document.

7. **Place the insertion point in What happens at a career fair? heading, click the Layout tab, click the Before up arrow in the Spacing section in the Paragraph group twice until 12 pt appears, then add 12 points of space before the What can a career fair offer that an online job search cannot? and When and where are MSIT career fairs held? headings**
   Twelve points of space are added before the three headings, as shown in **Figure 1-29**.

8. **sam↑ Save the document, submit the document to your instructor, close the file, then exit Word**

Apply a Theme WD 1-29

Figure 1-27: Page Border tab in Borders and Shading dialog box

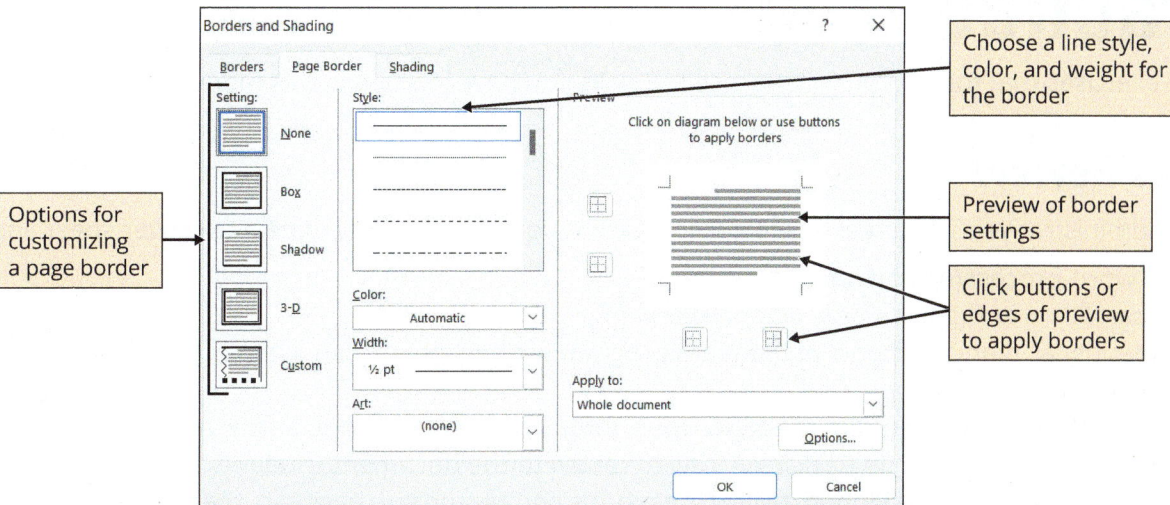

Figure 1-28: Organic theme previewed in document

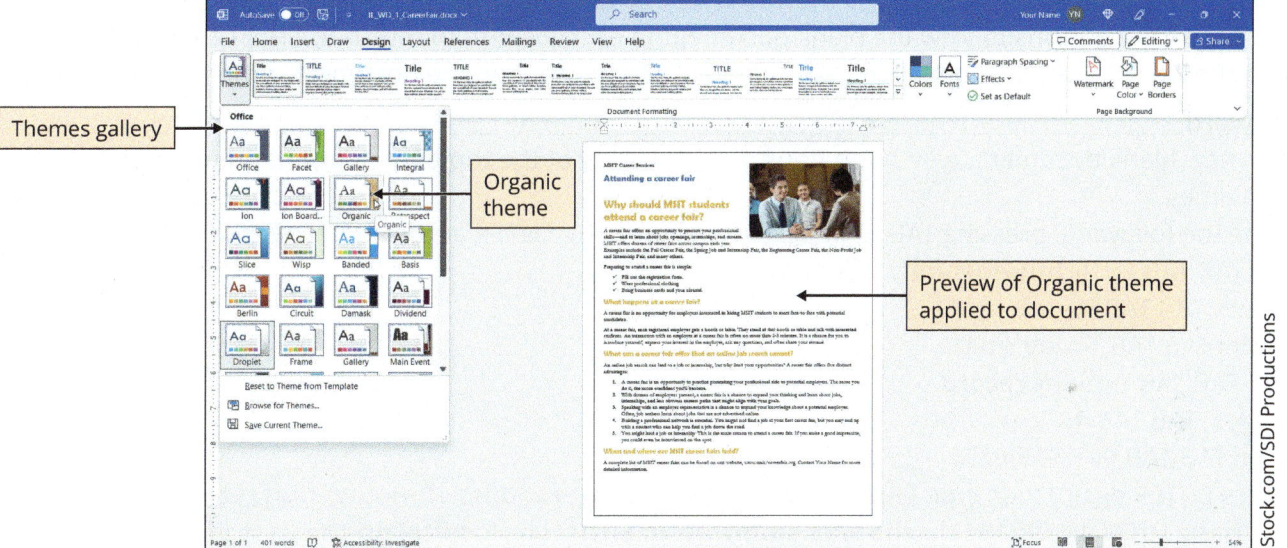

Figure 1-29: Vapor Trail theme and Blue Green theme colors applied to document

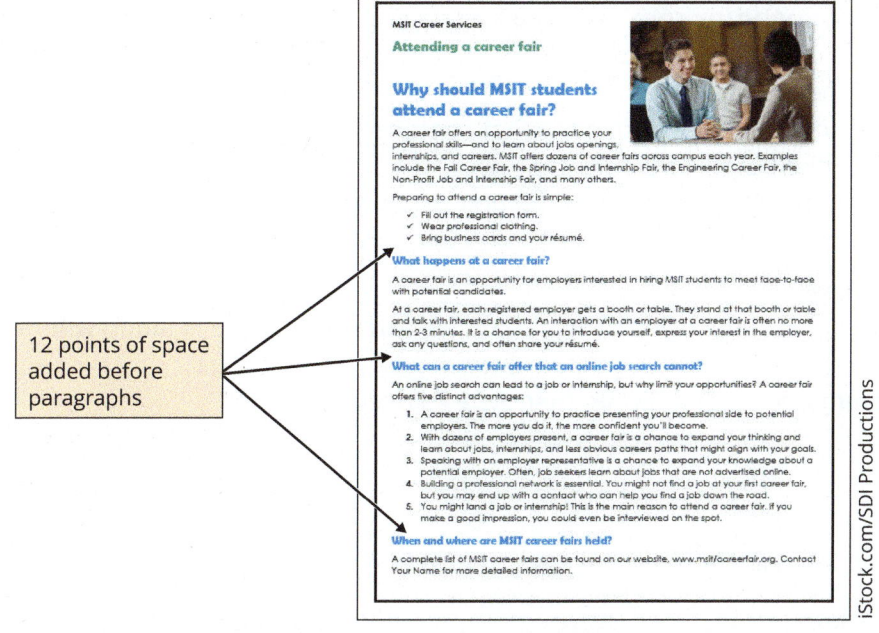

Practice

In the exercises that follow, you will practice the skills you have learned in this module.

Skills Review

As an administrative assistant at a senior living facility, you use Word to create a fax cover sheet and a flyer.

1. **Use word-processing software.**
   a. Start Word and open a new, blank document.
   b. Identify as many elements of the Word program window as you can without referring to the module material.
   c. Click the File tab, then click the New, Open, Info, Save, Save As, Print, Share, and Export commands.
   d. Click the Back button in Backstage view to return to the document window.
   e. Click each tab on the Ribbon, review the groups and buttons on each tab, then return to the Home tab.
   f. Point to each button on the Home tab and read its ScreenTip.
   g. Click the View tab and click the Ruler check box several times to hide and show the ruler. Show the ruler.
   h. Click the View buttons to view the blank document in each view, then return to Print Layout view.
   i. Use the Zoom slider to zoom all the way in and all the way out on the document, then return to 120%.

2. **Start Word.**
   a. In a new blank document, type **Loon Pond Senior Living** at the top of the page, then press ENTER two times.
   b. Type the following, pressing TAB as indicated and pressing ENTER at the end of each line:
      To: TAB TAB **Littleton Hospital**
      From: TAB TAB **Your Name**
      Date: TAB TAB **Today's date**
      Re: TAB TAB **Patient record**
      Pages: TAB TAB **1**
      Fax: TAB TAB **603-555-8476**
   c. Press ENTER again, then type **Thank you for your recent request of medication records for Li Zhang (DOB 12/08/1942), who was admitted to Littleton Hospital on the 31st of January. With Mr. Zhang's written permission, I am sending you his full medical record. This record includes clinical findings, diagnostic test results, and the patient's progress and prescribed medications.**
   d. Press ENTER, then type **For further information, please call Patient Records at 603-555-4343 or visit our website at www.loonpond/pr.com. All requests will be fulfilled within 24 hours. We are closed on weekends.**
   e. Insert **one of our residents,** before Li Zhang.
   f. Insert **South** before Littleton in the To: line and in the first sentence of the first paragraph.
   g. Use BACKSPACE to delete 1 in the Pages: line, then type **4**.
   h. Use DELETE to delete recent in the first sentence of the first paragraph.

3. **Save a document.**
   a. Click the File tab, then click Save.
   b. Save the document as **IL_WD_1_ZhangFax** with the default file extension to the location where you store your Data Files.
   c. After your name, type a comma, press SPACEBAR, then type **Patient Records**.
   d. Save the document.

4. **Select text.**
   a. Turn on formatting marks.
   b. Select the Re: line, then type **Re:** TAB TAB **Medical Records for Li Zhang**

c. Select prescribed in the third sentence, then type **current**.
d. Select 31st of January in the first sentence of the first paragraph, type **2nd of February**, select medication, then type **medical**.
e. Delete the sentence We are closed on weekends.
f. Turn off the display of formatting marks, then save the document.

5. **Format text using the Mini toolbar and the Ribbon.**
    a. Select Loon Pond Senior Living, click the Increase Font Size button on the Mini toolbar eight times, apply bold, then click the Decrease Font Size button on the Mini toolbar twice.
    b. Center Loon Pond Senior Living on the page.
    c. Change the case of Loon Pond Senior Living to uppercase.
    d. Apply a bottom border under Loon Pond Senior Living.
    e. Apply bold to the following words in the fax heading: To:, From:, Date:, Re:, Pages:, and Fax:.
    f. Apply yellow highlighting to 2nd of February.
    g. Use the Undo, Redo, and Repeat buttons to undo the highlighting, redo the highlighting, undo, repeat, then undo the highlighting again.
    h. Remove the hyperlink from the website address, then underline Li Zhang (DOB 12/08/1942) in the body of the fax.
    i. Italicize the last sentence of the second paragraph.
    j. Read the document using the Read Mode view.
    k. Return to Print Layout view, zoom in on the document, then proofread the fax.
    l. Correct any typing errors in your document, then save the document. Compare your document to **Figure 1-30**.
    m. Preview the document in Print Preview, identify each printing option available to you on the Print screen in Backstage view, then print the document only if required to do so by your instructor.

Figure 1-30

    n. Return to Print Layout view, save, submit the fax per your instructor's directions, then close the document.

6. **View and navigate a document.**
    a. Open the file IL_WD_1-3.docx from the location where you store your Data Files, then save it as **IL_WD_1_LoonPond** in the File name box.
    b. Switch to Page Width view, then scroll through the document to get a feel for its contents.
    c. Use the Zoom dialog box to view the Whole Page.
    d. Use the Zoom slider to set the Zoom percentage at approximately 120%.
    e. Read the document using the Read Mode view. (**Hint**: Press ESC to leave Read Mode view.)
    f. Return to Print Layout view, zoom in, scroll to the bottom of the document, then replace Your Name with your name in the final sentence.
    g. Add the Title property **CCRC** to the document properties in the file, return to Print Layout view, change the zoom level to 140%, then save your changes.

Skills Review (Continued)

7. **Cut and paste text.**
   a. Turn on the display of formatting marks.
   b. Select the first body paragraph that begins We have listened carefully... (including the paragraph mark after it), cut it to the clipboard, then paste the paragraph before the heading Choice in every aspect of life.
   c. In the list of housing options, move the Villa homes... paragraph after the Cottages... paragraph.
   d. Move the One- and two-bedroom apartments... paragraph after the Villa homes... paragraph.
   e. Move the Memory support... paragraph before the Skilled nursing... paragraph.
   f. Delete the heading Housing options, then save your changes.

8. **Copy and paste text.**
   a. Scroll to the bottom of the document, then remove the hyperlink in the final paragraph.
   b. Select the sentence Let the new chapter of your life begin., then copy the sentence to the clipboard.
   c. Scroll to the top of the page, add a blank paragraph under the Loon Pond Senior Living heading, then paste the sentence at the location of the blank paragraph.
   d. Use the Paste Options button to Keep Source formatting.
   e. Format the pasted sentence in italic, turn off formatting marks, then save your changes.

9. **Format with fonts.**
   a. Format the heading Loon Pond Senior Living in 20-point Calibri Light with an Orange, Accent 2, Darker 25% font color.
   b. Format the heading Living at Loon Pond is about choices, security, and lifestyle! in 14-point Calibri Light with a Green, Accent 6, Darker 25% font color.
   c. Format Choice in every aspect of life, Resident-centered care, and Healthy and active lifestyle options in 14-point Calibri Light with an Orange, Accent 2, Darker 25% font color.
   d. Apply bold formatting to the last paragraph in the document, change the font size to 12, then change the font color to Orange, Accent 2, Darker 25%.
   e. Scroll up, select Loon Pond Senior Living, click the Text Effects and Typography arrow, preview several WordArt styles applied to the text, then apply one of the styles.
   f. Click the Undo button, add an Offset: Bottom Right shadow to the title, then save your changes.

10. **Set document margins.**
    a. Change the left and right margins to 2".
    b. View the document in Multiple Pages view.
    c. Change the left and right margins to 1.5".
    d. Change all four document margins to .7".
    e. Change the zoom level to 120%, then add 12 points of space before the heading Living at Loon Pond is about choices, security, and lifestyle!
    f. Save your changes.

11. **Add bullets and numbering.**
    a. Select the six-line list of housing options that begins with Cottages and ends with Skilled nursing, then format it as a bulleted list using the circle bullet symbol.
    b. Change the font color of the bullets to Green, Accent 6, Darker 25%, then deselect the bullets.
    c. Press and hold CTRL to select the headings Choice in every aspect of life, Resident-centered care, and Healthy and active lifestyle options, then apply numbering.
    d. Click 1 in the list, then change the font color of the numbers to Green, Accent 6, Darker 25%.
    e. Save your changes.

12. **Insert a graphic.**
    a. Click in the first body paragraph to move the insertion point to the top of the document, then open the Insert Picture dialog box.
    b. Navigate to the location where you store Data Files, then insert the file **Support_ WD_1-4.jpg**.
    c. Change the height of the graphic to 1.2 using the Shape Height box in the Size group on the Picture Format tab.
    d. Use the Position command to wrap text around the graphic and position it in the Top Left with Square Text Wrapping.
    e. Apply the Double Frame, Black picture style to the graphic.
    f. Click the Reset Picture arrow in the Adjust Group on the Picture Format tab, reset the picture, then apply the Simple Frame, White picture style.
    g. Change the font size of Loon Pond Senior Living to 36 point, then change the font size of Let the new chapter of your life begin. to 14 point.
    h. Click before the Living at Loon Pond is about choices, security, and lifestyle! heading, press ENTER, change the font size of the heading to 20 point, then save your changes.

13. **Apply a theme.**
    a. Change the view to One Page, click the Design tab, click the Page Borders button, then apply a single-line box border to the page.
    b. Use the Themes feature to preview several different themes applied to the document. Apply a theme, zoom in and out on the document to evaluate its suitability, then apply another theme, zoom in and out, and so forth.
    c. Apply the View theme.
    d. Change all four document margins to .6" to better fit the text on the page.
    e. Zoom in on the bottom of the document, then add 24 points of space above the last paragraph.
    f. Change the theme colors to Green.
    g. Zoom in on the top of the document, then change the font color of the Let the new chapter... paragraph to Turquoise, Accent 6, Darker 25%.
    h. Change the font color of the Living at Loon Pond... heading to Lime, Accent 2, Darker 25% and the font color of the last paragraph to Turquoise, Accent 6, Darker 25%. Compare your document to **Figure 1-31**.
    i. Save your changes, preview the document, submit it per your instructor's directions, then close the document and exit Word.

Figure 1-31

Independent Challenge 1

You work at Pediatric Health Associates, a large community-based pediatric practice staffed by physicians, specialists, nurses, and other allied health professionals. Your boss has drafted an information sheet to educate parents about influenza and asks you to edit and format it so that it is eye-catching and attractive.

a. Open the file IL_WD_1-5.docx from the drive and folder where you store your Data Files, save it as **IL_WD_1_PediatricFlu**, then read the document to get a feel for the content. **Figure 1-32** shows how you will format the info sheet.

b. Show the rulers in your document window if they are not already visible.

c. Accept or ignore all suggested spelling and grammar changes in the document.

d. Insert the picture file Support_WD_1-6.jpg at the top of the document. Change the height of the image to 2", then position the image in the bottom right with square text wrapping. (**Hint**: Zoom in and out on the document as necessary. If an anchor symbol appears in the margin, you can ignore it.)

e. Center the first two lines of text in the document.

f. Change the font of Pediatric Health Associates to Arial Black. Change the font size to 18 point. Change the font color to Gray, Accent 3, Darker 25%.

g. Format Influenza (Flu) in Children in 28-point Arial Black with a Blue, Accent 1, Darker 25% font color. Apply an Offset: Bottom Left shadow text effect.

h. Apply italic to the first body paragraph.

i. Change all four document margins to .5", then reduce the font size of Pediatric Health Associates by 2 points.

j. Format the three-line list of who is at risk (beginning with Are around) as a bulleted list, then apply the Blue, Accent 1, Darker 25% font color to the bullets.

k. Format the Six-line list of common symptoms (beginning with Fever) as a numbered list. (**Hint**: If you make a mistake, click the Undo button and try again.)

l. Format the two-line list of medications (beginning with Acetaminophen) and the two-line list of other tips (beginning with Drinks) as bulleted lists.

m. Apply bold to the numbers in the numbered list, and change the font color of the numbers to Blue, Accent 1, Darker 25%.

n. In the numbered list, select paragraph 3 (Runny or stuffy nose), cut it, place the insertion point before Cough in the new paragraph 5, then paste the text.

o. Change the document theme to Facet, then change the theme colors to Red Violet.

p. Add a Box page border to the document.

q. Increase the font size of **Pediatric Health Associates** to 20, then add 12 points of space after **Influenza (Flu) in Children**.

r. Zoom in on the bottom of the document. Replace Your Name in the final line with your name, remove the hyperlink from www.pedhealthassoc.org, and add 24 points of space before the final line paragraph.

s. Zoom out, examine the document carefully for formatting errors, and make any necessary adjustments so that all the text fits on one page.

t. Save the document, submit it per your instructor's directions, then close the file and exit Word.

Figure 1-32

Independent Challenge 2

Yesterday you interviewed for a job as a virtual assistant at Valet Business Support Services. You interviewed in person and spoke with several people, including Sabrina Singh, director of human resources, whose business card is shown in **Figure 1-33**. Ms. Singh asked you to send her some physical samples of your work as evidence of your Word skills. You need to write a cover letter to Ms. Singh, thanking her for the interview and expressing your interest in the position.

a. Start Word and save a new blank document as **IL_WD_1_SinghLetter** to the location where you store your Data Files.

b. Begin the letter by clicking the No Spacing button in the Styles group. You use this button to apply the No Spacing style to the document so that your document does not include extra space between paragraphs.

c. Type a personal letterhead for the letter that includes your name, address, telephone number, email address, and webpage or LinkedIn address, if you have one. Remove any hyperlinks. Accept or undo any automatic corrections.
(Note: Format the letterhead after you finish typing the letter.)

d. Four lines below the bottom of the letterhead, type today's date.

e. Four lines below the date, type the inside address, referring to **Figure 1-33** for the information. Include the recipient's title, business name, and full mailing address.

f. Two lines below the inside address, type **Dear Ms. Singh:** for the salutation.

g. Two lines below the salutation, type the body of the letter, leaving a blank space between each paragraph, according to the following guidelines:

Figure 1-33

- In the first paragraph, thank her for the interview. Then restate your interest in the position and express your desire to work for the business. Add any specific details you think will enhance the power of your letter.
- In the second paragraph, note that you are enclosing three samples of your work, and explain something about the samples you are enclosing.
- Type a short final paragraph.

h. Two lines below the last body paragraph, type a closing, then four lines below the closing, type the signature block. Be sure to include your name in the signature block.

i. Two lines below the signature block, type an enclosure notation. (**Hint**: An enclosure notation usually includes the word "Enclosures" or the abbreviation "Enc." followed by the number of enclosures in parentheses.)

j. Edit your letter for clarity and precision. Move sentences if necessary, replace words with more precise words, and correct any spelling or grammar errors.

k. Change the font of the letter to a serif font, such as Times New Roman, Garamond, or something similar. Adjust the font size so the letter can be read easily.

l. Format the letterhead using fonts, font colors, text effects, borders, themes, paragraph spacing, paragraph alignment, change case, and other formatting features. Be sure the design of your letterhead reflects your personality and is suitable for a professional document.

m. Change the Title document property to **Letter**.

n. Save your changes, preview the letter, submit it per your instructor's directions, then close the document and exit Word.

Visual Workshop

Create the letter shown in **Figure 1-34**. Before beginning to type, click the No Spacing button in the Styles group on the Home tab. Type the letter before formatting the letterhead and applying the theme. To format the letterhead, change the font size of the first line of text to 30 point and apply the Fill: Black, Text Color 1; Outline: White, Background color 1; Hard Shadow: Blue, Accent color 5 WordArt style. Change the font color of the address line to Blue, Accent 5. Add the bottom border to the letterhead. When the letterhead is formatted, change the font size of the body text to 12 point, apply the Organic theme, then change the font color of the letterhead text to Red, Accent 4. Save the document as **IL_WD_1_KowalskiBaron** to the location where you store your Data Files, submit the letter to your instructor, then close the document and exit Word.

Figure 1-34

Kowalski-Baron Insurance Agency
3594 Cedar Avenue, Cleveland, OH 44115, www.kowalski-baron.com

August 12. 2025

Ms. Chandra Lakatos
85 Rouse Avenue
Cleveland, OH 44104

Dear Ms. Lakatos:

At Kowalski-Baron Insurance, we have all the protection you need for your home, auto, or business, and all the savings, too. As one of the largest independent, locally owned insurance agencies in the region, we take pride in the value, ease, and quality we offer our customers:

- We compare insurance rates from leading providers to present you with best offer.
- Choose from a range of payment plans, with the ability to pick your payment due date.
- File claims easily through our online system.

Looking for a specific type of coverage? Visit us on the web at www.kowalski-baron.com to explore our products and receive a free quote.

Sincerely,

Your Name
Account Manager

Word **Module 2**

Editing and Formatting Documents

Case
You have been asked to edit and format a research report on expanding the digital media degree program at MSIT. After editing the report and applying styles to format the text, you add page numbers, a header, footnotes, and a bibliography to the document. Finally, before distributing the report electronically, you strip the file of private information.

Module Objectives
After completing this module, you will be able to:

- Insert comments
- Find and replace text
- Check spelling and grammar
- Proofread and revise text
- Change line spacing and indents
- Apply styles to text
- Insert page numbers and page breaks
- Add headers and footers
- Add footnotes and endnotes
- Insert citations
- Create a bibliography
- Inspect a document

Files You Will Need

IL_WD_2-1.docx   IL_WD_2-3.docx
IL_WD_2-2.docx   IL_WD_2-4.docx

Insert Comments

Case Your colleague, Yolanda Ortiz, read the draft of the report and inserted comments. You open the report to review and respond to Yolanda's comments. You add and edit comments.

Objective
- Add comments

You can collaborate on documents with colleagues in different ways. One way is to insert comments into a document when you want to ask questions or provide information to other reviewers. A **comment** is text that appears in a comment box along the right side of a page in Print Layout view. Shading appears in the document at the point where you or another reviewer inserted a comment. A comment icon also appears in the margin to the right of the commented text to indicate the location of a comment. Each reviewer is assigned a unique color automatically, which appears in the comment box.

Steps

Quick Tip
To show all comments in the Comments pane, click the Comments button on the Ribbon.

1. **sam↓** Start **Word**, open the file **IL_WD_2-1.docx** from the location where you store your Data Files, save it as **IL_WD_2_DigitalMedia**, change the zoom level to **100%**, then click the **Review tab**

   Simple Markup is the default option in the Display for Review box in the Tracking group on the Review tab. A different markup option may be selected if another user was working on the computer before you. With the Simple Markup option, comments appear along the right side of the page. If you see comment icons and no comment wording, then click the Show Comments button in the Comments group. Alternatively, click a Go to comment icon to show the comments.

Quick Tip
When you click the reviewer's initials in the comment box, a person card for the reviewer appears; use this to communicate quickly with reviewers.

2. Click the **Display for Review arrow** in the Tracking group, then click **All Markup**

   In the first, third, and fourth body paragraphs, some of the text is shaded, indicating the text is associated with a comment.

3. Select the word **MSIT** in the title (the first line), then click the **New Comment button** in the Comments group

   The word "MSIT" is shaded with color, and a box for a comment appears to the right of the document. Your name or the name assigned to your computer appears in the comment box.

Trouble
If a Post comment button does not appear in your comment, click anywhere in the document text.

4. Type **This is the working title for the expanded program.**, then click the **Post comment button**

   Your comment appears as shown in **Figure 2-1**. To navigate between comments in a long document, use the Next and Previous buttons in the Comments group.

Trouble
If you don't see the Reply box, click the Reply button, type your reply, then click anywhere in the document text.

5. Click **Yolanda's first comment** (starts with "Is this..."), click the **Reply box** in the comment, type **I am researching other options.**, then click the **Post comment button**

   When you click in a comment box, it is outlined in color to indicate it is active. The reply you typed is indented under the original comment.

Figure 2-1: New comment in document

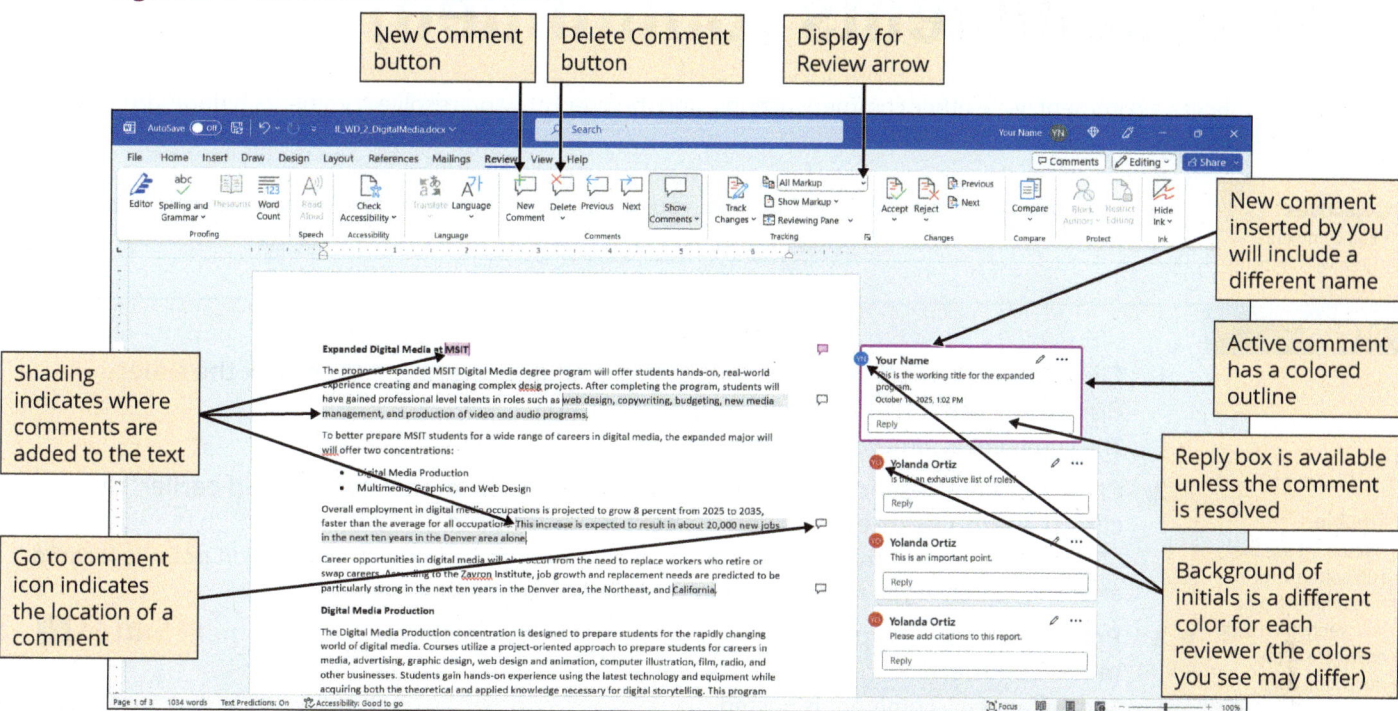

Using modern comments in Word

The "modern comment" experience in Word differs from the "legacy comment" experience. Modern comment boxes include a Post comment button that must be clicked for a comment to "post" or be committed. This allows users to finalize a comment before it becomes visible to collaborators on a shared document. By contrast, legacy comments do not include a Post comment button and are visible to collaborators as they are being typed. Modern comments also include an @mention feature that allows users working in a shared cloud environment to address a specific person in a comment or reply. Eventually, legacy comments will phase out and all Word users will experience modern comments. Until then, it is possible to switch between the modern and legacy comment experiences. To do so, click the File tab, click Options, click General in the Word Options dialog box, and then select or deselect the Enable modern comments check box.

Insert Comments (Continued)

Case You delete a comment, view other comment actions, and then reply to and resolve comments before formatting the document.

Objectives
- Edit comments
- Resolve comments

After inserting and editing comments, you can delete them, reply to them, and resolve them.

Steps

1. Click **Yolanda's second comment** ("This is an important..."), then click the **Delete Comment button** in the Comments group

   The comment is removed from the document.

2. Click the "I am researching other options." reply comment you inserted earlier, then click the **Edit comment button** next to your name

   Clicking the Edit comment button opens a comment for editing. The insertion point is located after the sentence you typed earlier in the Reply comment box.

   Trouble
   If you don't see the Edit button, click in the comment, type your reply, then click anywhere in the document text.

▶ 3. Press **[Spacebar]**, type **I will send you a list.**, then click the **Post comment button** in the comment

   The edited reply comment is posted.

▶ 4. Click **Yolanda's comment** containing the text "Please add citations...", click the **More thread actions button** in the comment, click **Resolve thread**, then click anywhere in the document text

   The comment is marked as resolved, as shown in **Figure 2-2**. You can reopen a comment that has been marked as resolved by clicking the Go to resolved comment icon in the document, and then clicking the Reopen button in the comment. You can also see resolved comments in the Comments pane.

   Trouble
   If you don't see the More thread actions button, click the Resolve button, then click anywhere in the document text.

▶ 5. Click **All Markup** in the Tracking group, click **No Markup**, then save your changes

   Selecting No Markup hides the comments. Hiding the comments does not remove them from the document. It simply hides them from view on the screen. You will keep the comments hidden while you format the document.

   Quick Tip
   To delete all comments in a document, click the Delete Comment arrow, then click Delete All Comments in Document.

Insert Comments   WD 2-5

Figure 2-2: Resolved comment in document

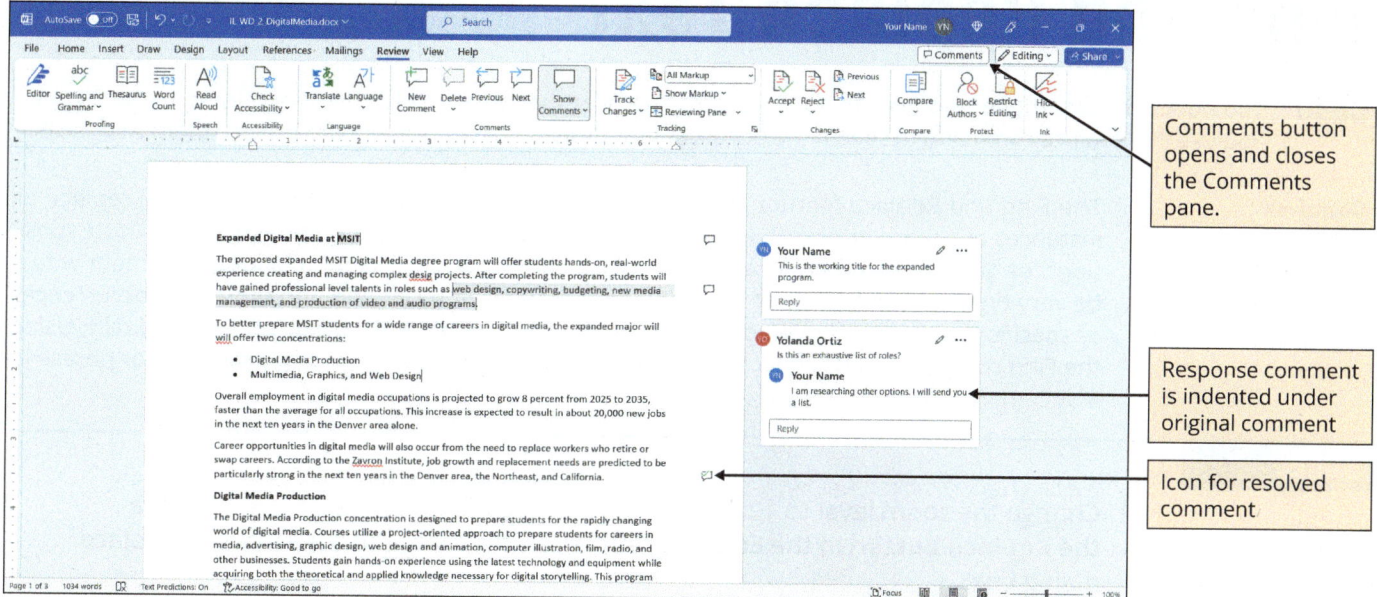

Inking comments in Word

If you are working in Touch mode on a touch-enabled device, you can draw or write comments using your finger, a digital pen, or a mouse. The type of inking features available to you will depend on your device. To begin, click the Draw tab on the Ribbon, click a pen in the Drawing Tools group to create an ink comment, and then use your finger, stylus, or mouse to draw or write in the document. On some devices, you can change the color and type of pen stroke to use for inking by using the Pen button in the Drawing Tools group. You can hide inked comments using the Hide Ink button in the Ink group on the Review tab. When you are finished inking a comment, click anywhere in the document. If you are on a touch-enabled device and want to switch your device to Touch mode and use the full range of inking features available in Word, you can add the Touch/Mouse Mode button to the Quick Access toolbar by clicking the Customize Quick Access Toolbar button on the Quick Access toolbar, and then clicking Touch/Mouse Mode. To use Touch mode, click the Touch/Mouse Mode button, and then click Touch.

Find and Replace Text

Case You notice the word "talent" is used to describe competencies that are actually skills, not talents, in the report. You use the Replace command to search the document for all instances of "talent" and replace them with "skill".

Objectives
- Find and replace text
- Search for text and formatting
- Move to a specific location in a document

The Find and Replace feature in Word allows you to automatically search for and replace all instances of a word or phrase in a document. For example, you might need to substitute "position" for "job". To manually locate and replace each instance of "job" in a long document would be very time-consuming. Using the Replace command, you can find and replace all occurrences of specific text at once, or you can choose to find and review each occurrence individually. Using the Find command, you can locate and highlight every occurrence of a specific word or phrase in a document.

Steps

1. **Change the zoom level to 120%, press CTRL+HOME, click the Home tab, click the Replace button in the Editing group, then click More in the Find and Replace dialog box**
   The Find and Replace dialog box opens and expands, as shown in **Figure 2-3**.

   Trouble
   If any Search Options check boxes are selected in your Find and Replace dialog box, deselect them. If Format appears under the Find what or Replace with box, click in the box, then click the No Formatting button.

2. **Type talent in the Find what box**
   The text "talent" is the text that will be replaced.

3. **Press TAB, then type skill in the Replace with box**
   The text "skill" will replace the text "talent".

4. **Click the Match case check box in the Search Options section to select it**
   Selecting the Match case check box tells Word to find only exact matches for the uppercase and lowercase characters you entered in the Find what text box. You want to replace all instances of "talent" in the body text of the report. You do not want to replace "Talent" in the proper name "Talent Match Program".

   Quick Tip
   To find, review, and replace each occurrence individually, click Find Next.

5. **Click Replace All**
   Clicking Replace All changes all occurrences of "talent" to "skill" in the report. A message box reports seven replacements were made.

6. **Click OK to close the message box, then click Close in the Find and Replace dialog box**
   Word replaced "talent" with "skill" in seven locations but did not replace "Talent" in the program name. To find or replace text that is formatted a certain way, click the Find arrow in the Editing group, click Advanced Find, click Format in the Find and Replace dialog box, and then select the appropriate format options. To find or replace special characters such as em dashes and paragraph marks, click Special in the Find and Replace dialog box.

7. **Click the Find button in the Editing group**
   Clicking the Find button opens the Navigation pane, which is used to browse a longer document by headings, pages, or specific text. The Find command allows you to quickly locate all instances of text in a document. You use it to verify that Word did not replace "Talent" in Talent Match Program.

8. **Type Talent in the search box in the Navigation pane**
   The word "Talent" is highlighted and selected in the document, as shown in **Figure 2-4**.

9. **Click the Close button in the Navigation pane**
   The highlighting is removed from the text when you close the Navigation pane.

10. **Press CTRL+HOME, then save the document**

Figure 2-3: Find and Replace dialog box

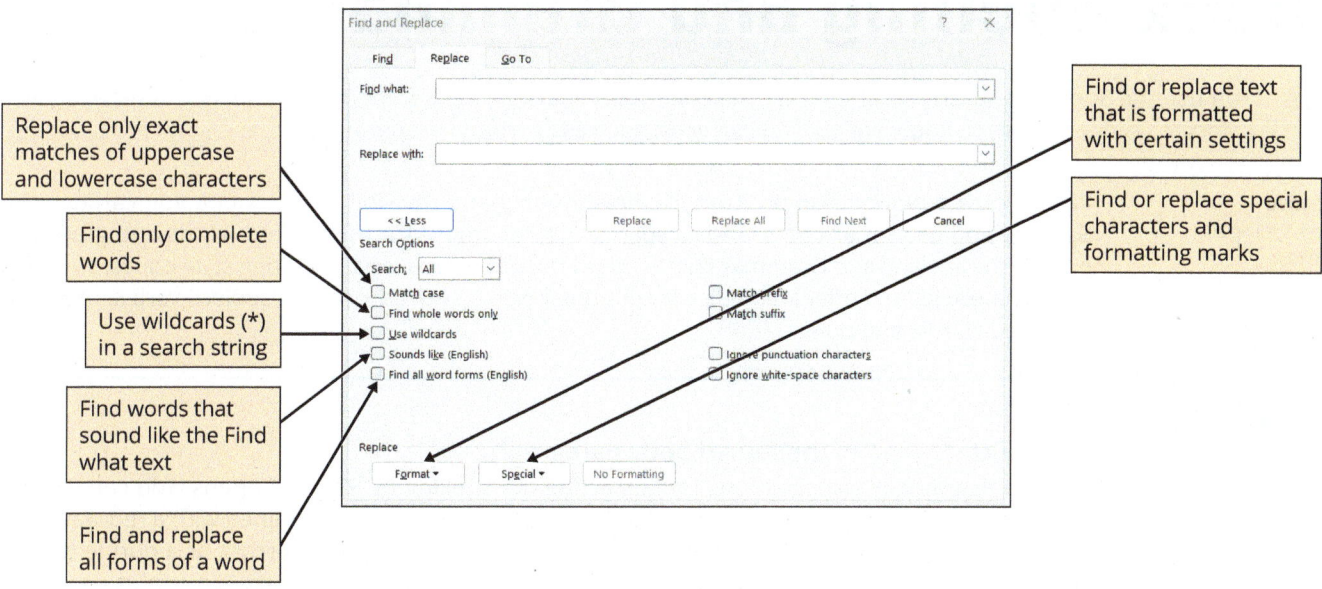

Figure 2-4: Found text highlighted in document

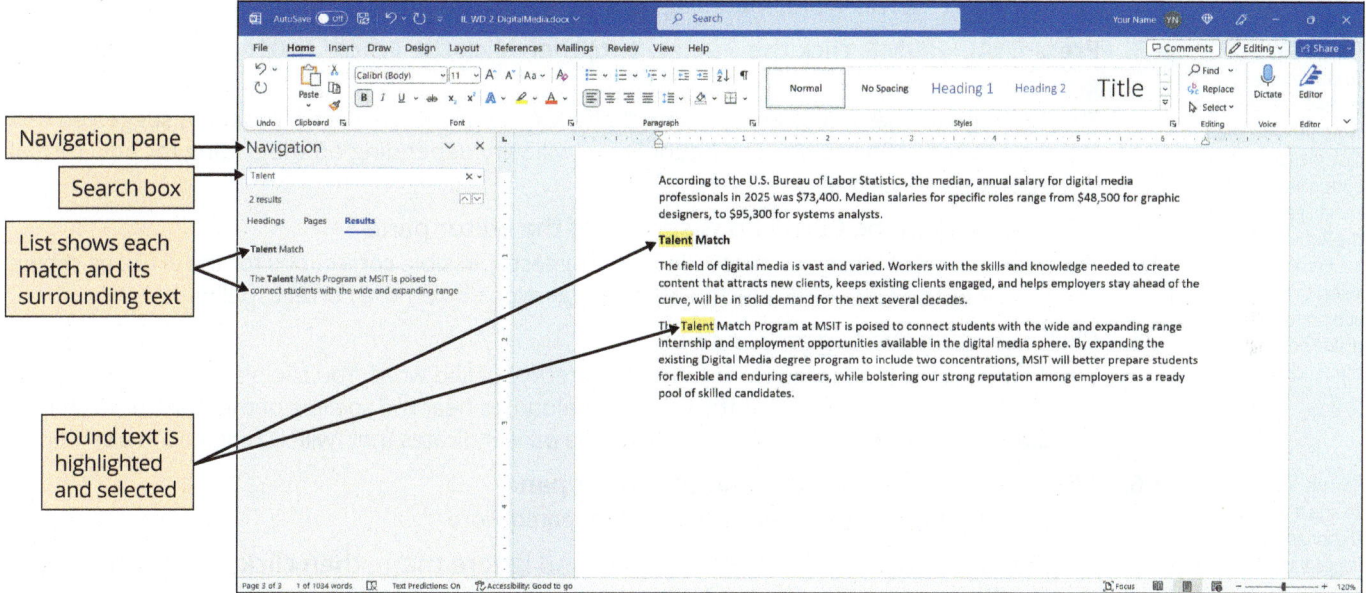

Navigating a document using the Navigation pane and the Go to command

Rather than scrolling to move to a different place in a longer document, you can use the Navigation pane to quickly move the insertion point to a specific page, heading, or text. To open the Navigation pane, click the Page number button on the status bar. In the Navigation pane, click the link for the type of item (headings or pages) you want to use to navigate the document. To navigate by specific text, type the text in the Search document text box, and then click the Results link.

To move to a specific page, section, line, table, graphic, or other item in a document, you use the Go To tab in the Find and Replace dialog box. On the Go To tab in the Find and Replace dialog box, select the type of item you want to find in the Go to what list, enter the relevant information about that item, and then click Next to move the insertion point to the item.

Check Spelling and Grammar

Case You use the Spelling and Grammar checker to search the report for errors. Before beginning the search, you select to ignore words you know are spelled correctly, such as Zavron, a proper noun.

Objective
- Check spelling and grammar

While you are working on or after you finish typing and revising a document, you can use the Spelling and Grammar command to search the document for misspelled words and grammar errors. The Spelling and Grammar checker flags possible mistakes and writing style issues, suggests correct spellings, and offers remedies for grammar errors such as incorrect subject–verb agreement, repeated words, and punctuation.

Steps

1. **Right-click Zavron in the fourth body paragraph**
   A menu that includes suggestions for correcting the spelling of "Zavron" opens. You can correct individual spelling and grammar errors by right-clicking text that is underlined with a red wavy line (a possible misspelling), a blue double underline (a possible grammar error), or a purple dotted line (a possible writing style issue), and then selecting a correction. Although "Zavron" is not in the Word dictionary, it is a proper name that is spelled correctly in the document.

   Trouble
   If Zavron is not flagged as misspelled, skip to Step 3.

2. **Click Ignore All**
   Clicking Ignore All tells Word not to flag "Zavron" as misspelled.

   Quick Tip
   To change the language used by the Word proofing tools, click the Language button in the Language group on the Review tab, click Set Proofing Language, select the language you prefer in the dialog box that opens, then click OK.

3. **Press CTRL+HOME, click the Review tab, then click the Editor button in the Proofing group**
   The Editor pane opens. It offers an Editor Score for the document that is based on suggested text corrections and refinements. The Editor Score will vary depending on the setting for how formal the writing is intended to be.

4. **Click Spelling in the Corrections section of the Editor pane**
   The pane identifies "desig" as misspelled and suggests possible corrections for the error, as shown in **Figure 2-5**. The first word selected in the Suggestions box is the correct spelling.

5. **Click design in the Suggestions box**
   Word replaces the misspelled word with the correctly spelled word. You can also use the arrow next to a suggested correction to hear the word read aloud, to hear the spelling of the word, or to change all instances of the error in a document. Next, the pane indicates that "will" is repeated in a sentence.

   Quick Tip
   To add a word to the Dictionary so it is not flagged as misspelled, click Add to Dictionary.

6. **Click Delete Repeated Word in the Editor pane**
   Word deletes the second occurrence of the repeated word.

7. **If additional errors are identified, review and ignore them, then click OK to complete the spelling and grammar check if necessary**
   The Editor identifies many common errors, but you cannot rely on it to find and correct all spelling and grammar errors in your documents, or to always suggest a valid correction. Always proofread your documents carefully.

8. **Click the Close button in the Editor pane, press CTRL+HOME, then save the document**

Searching for information

The Search feature on the References tab gives you quick access to information about document text, including definitions, images, and other material from online sources. For example, you might use Search to see the definition of a word used in a document or to hear the word pronounced. To use Search, select the text you want to look up in your document, right-click it, and then click Search. You can also select text, and then click the Search button in the Research group on the References tab. The Search pane opens and displays images and web links related to the selected text. Click the All button to display only web information, media, help articles files, or other data types.

Figure 2-5: Editor pane

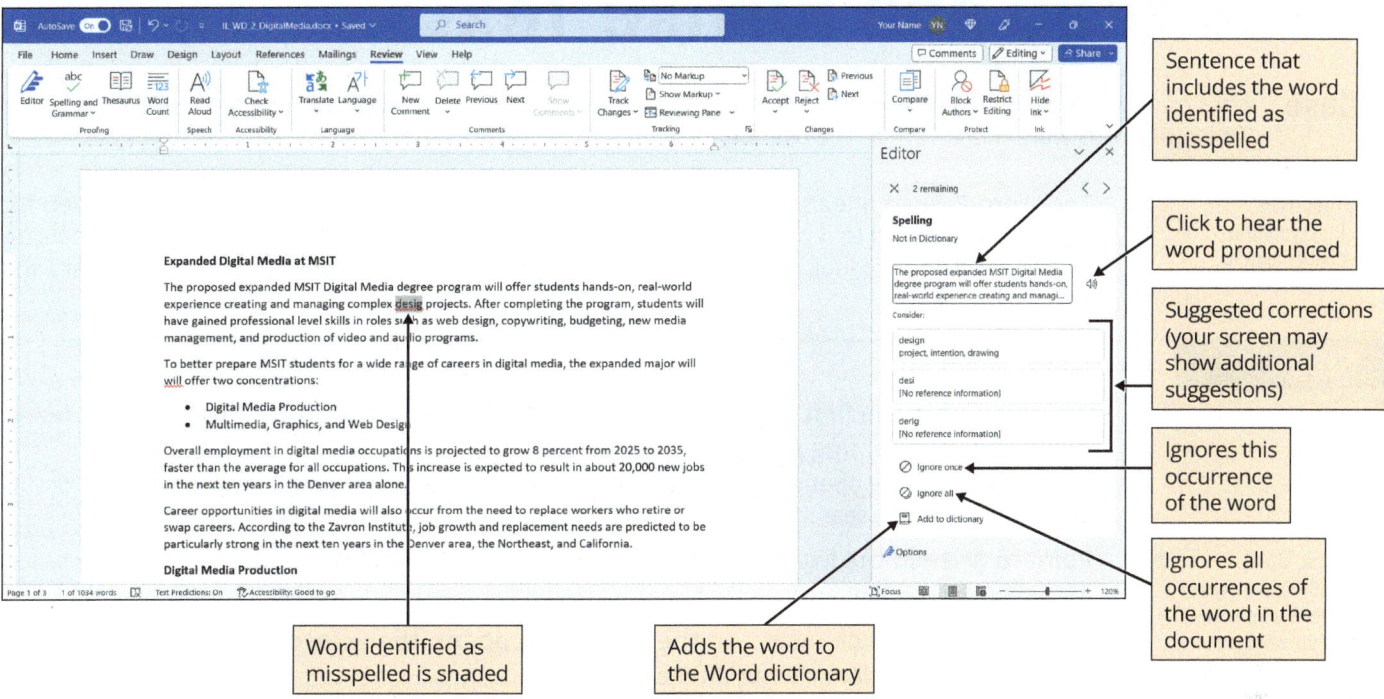

Inserting text with AutoCorrect

As you type, AutoCorrect automatically corrects many commonly misspelled words. By creating your own AutoCorrect entries, you can set Word to insert text that you type often, such as your name or contact information, or to correct words you misspell frequently. For example, you could create an AutoCorrect entry so that the name "Maria T. Weiss" is automatically inserted whenever you type "mtw" followed by a space. You create AutoCorrect entries and customize other AutoCorrect and AutoFormat options using the AutoCorrect dialog box. To open the AutoCorrect dialog box, click the File tab, click Options, click Proofing in the Word Options dialog box that opens, and then click AutoCorrect Options. On the AutoCorrect tab in the AutoCorrect dialog box, type the text you want to be corrected automatically in the Replace box (such as "mtw"), type the text you want to be inserted in its place automatically in the With box (such as "Maria T. Weiss"), and then click Add. The AutoCorrect entry is added to the list. Click OK to close the AutoCorrect dialog box, and then click OK to close the Word Options dialog box. Word inserts an AutoCorrect entry in a document when you press SPACEBAR or a punctuation mark after typing the text you want Word to correct. For example, Word inserts "Maria T. Weiss" when you type "mtw" followed by a space. If you want to remove an AutoCorrect entry, simply open the AutoCorrect dialog box, select the AutoCorrect entry you want to remove in the list, click Delete, click OK, and then click OK to close the Word Options dialog box.

Proofread and Revise Text

Case After proofreading your document for errors, you decide the report would read better for an academic audience if several words were more formal. You use the thesaurus to find synonyms.

Objectives
- Find synonyms
- Check the word count

The Word Research features allow you to quickly search reference sources and the web for information related to a word or phrase. Among the reference sources available is a thesaurus, which you can use to look up synonyms for awkward or repetitive words, as well as dictionary and translation sources.

Steps

1. **Select occur in the first line of the fourth body paragraph, then click the Thesaurus button in the Proofing group on the Review tab**
   The Thesaurus pane opens. "Occur" appears in the search box, and possible synonyms for "occur" are listed under the search box.

   Quick Tip
   To look up synonyms for a different word, type the word in the search box, then click the search button.

2. **Point to arise in the list of synonyms, as shown in Figure 2-6**
   A shaded box containing an arrow appears around the word.

3. **Click the arrow, click Insert on the menu that opens, then close the Thesaurus pane**
   The word "arise" replaces "occur" in the report.

4. **Right-click swap in the first line of the fourth body paragraph, point to Synonyms on the menu that opens, then click switch**
   The word "switch" replaces "swap" in the report.

5. **Select the four paragraphs of body text under the "Expanded Digital Media..." title (including the bulleted list), then click the Word Count button in the Proofing group**
   The Word Count dialog box opens, as shown in Figure 2-7. The dialog box lists the number of pages, words, characters, paragraphs, and lines included in the selected text. Notice that the status bar also displays the number of words included in the selected text and the total number of words in the entire document. If you want to view the page, character, paragraph, and line count for the entire document, make sure nothing is selected in your document, and then click Word Count in the Proofing group.

6. **Click Close, then save the document**

Reading a document aloud using Word

The Word Read Aloud feature reads a document aloud for you. Listening to a document read aloud can help you hear grammar errors, discover missing words, or notice other writing issues you might not notice when proofreading a document on screen. It can also be useful for multitasking or for increasing your reading comprehension and learning. To read a document aloud using Word, move the insertion point to the beginning of the document, and then click the Read Aloud button in the Speech group on the Review tab. A toolbar of playback controls opens at the top of the document window and Word begins to read aloud. As each word is pronounced, it is highlighted on the screen. You can use the Settings button on the playback controls to change the reading speed or the reading voice. The Previous, Next, Pause, and Play buttons allow you to pause and resume the reading, or to navigate through the document paragraph by paragraph. When you are finished reading the document aloud using Word, click the Stop button on the playback controls.

Figure 2-6: Thesaurus pane

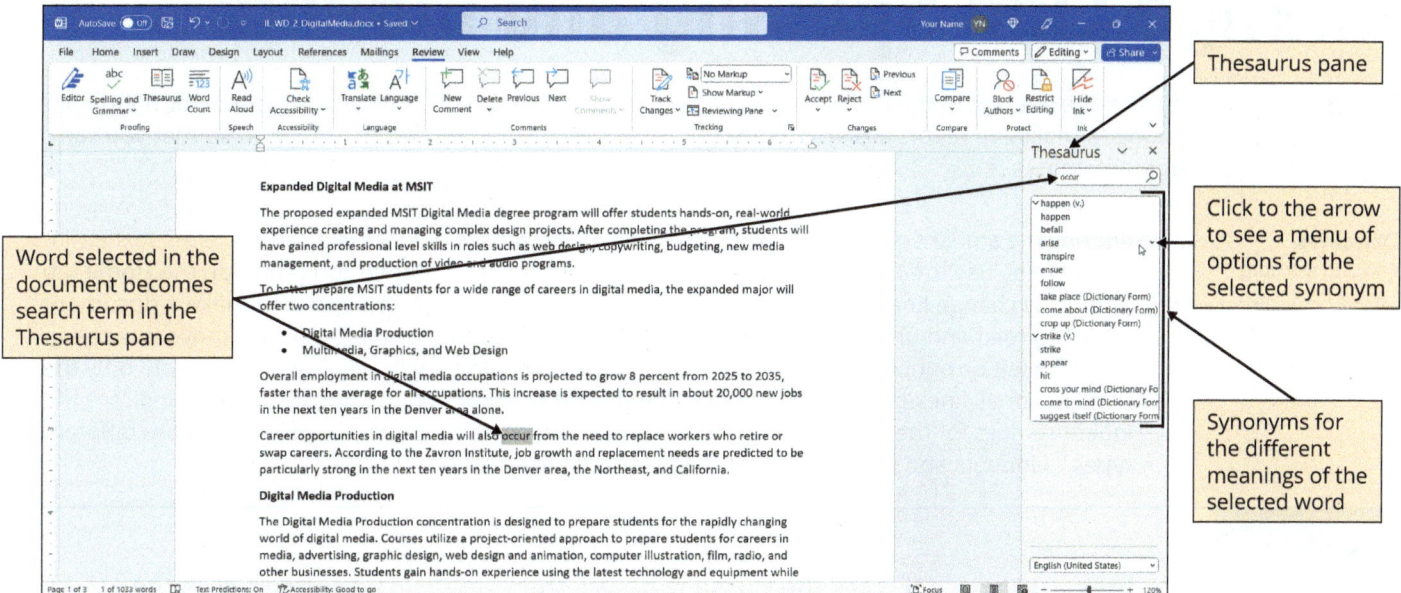

Figure 2-7: Word Count dialog box

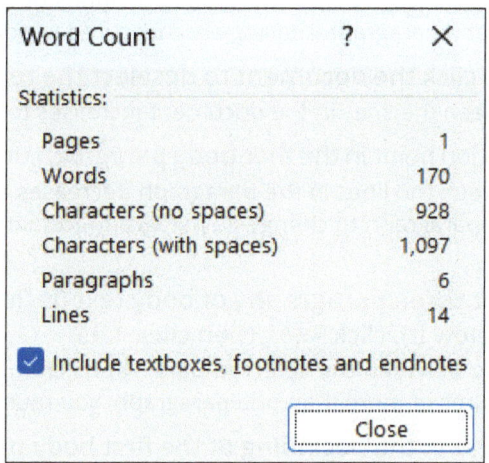

Using an add-in for Word

Add-ins are small programs embedded in Word that allow you to access information on the web without having to leave Word. For example, you can look up something on Wikipedia, insert an online map in one of your documents, or access dictionaries and other reference sources, all from within Word using an add-in. To find and install an add-in, click the Get Add-ins button in the Add-ins group on the Insert tab to open the Office Add-ins gallery. The Store tab in the Office Add-ins gallery includes a searchable list of the add-ins available to you, which you can also browse by category. Some add-ins are free, and some require purchase.

To install an add-in, click the Add button next to it on the Store tab. To use an add-in after you have installed it, click the My Add-ins button on the Insert tab to open the Office Add-ins gallery with the My Add-ins tab displayed. Select the Add-in you want to use on this tab, and then click Add. A new button for the add-in may be added to your ribbon. When you no longer need an add-in you have installed, you can remove it by right-clicking the add-in on the My Add-in tab in the Office Add-ins gallery, and then clicking Remove.

Change Line Spacing and Indents

Case You increase the line spacing of the report, remove space under a paragraph, and create indents for the body text paragraphs to make the report easier to read. You work with formatting marks turned on so that you can see the paragraph marks (¶).

Objectives
- Adjust line spacing
- Adjust indentation

Altering the amount of space between lines and paragraphs in a document can make the text easier to read. You use the Line and Paragraph Spacing button in the Paragraph group on the Home tab to quickly change line and paragraph spacing. Indenting paragraphs can also make a document easier to read and understand at a glance. When you **indent** a paragraph, you move its edge in from the left or right margin. You can indent the entire left or right edge of a paragraph, only the first line, or all lines except the first line. The **indent markers** on the horizontal ruler indicate the indent settings for the paragraph in which the insertion point is located. **Table 2-1** describes different types of indents and some of the methods for creating each.

Steps

1. Press **CTRL+HOME**, click the **Home tab**, click the **Show/Hide ¶ button** ¶ in the Paragraph group, press **CTRL+A** to select the entire document, then click the **Line and Paragraph Spacing button** in the Paragraph group

   The Line Spacing gallery opens. This gallery includes options for increasing the space between lines. Both line and paragraph spacing are measured in points.

2. Click **2.0**, then click the document to deselect the text

   The space between the lines in the document increases to 2.

   Quick Tip
   Word recognizes any string of text that ends with a paragraph mark as a paragraph, including titles, headings, and single lines in a list.

3. Place the insertion point in the **first body paragraph** under the title, click , then click **1.15**

   The space between the lines in the paragraph decreases to 1.15. Notice that you do not need to select an entire paragraph to change its paragraph formatting; simply place the insertion point in the paragraph.

4. Select the next **three paragraphs** of body text (including the bulleted list and the two paragraphs below it), click , then click **1.15**

   The line spacing between the selected paragraphs changes to 1.15. To change the paragraph-formatting features of more than one paragraph, you must select the paragraphs.

   Quick Tip
   If the rulers are not displayed, click the View tab, then click the Ruler check box.

5. Click before **The** at the beginning of the first body paragraph, then press **TAB**

   The first line of the paragraph is indented ½", as shown in **Figure 2-8**. Notice the First Line Indent marker is located at the ½" mark on the horizontal ruler. The ruler shows the indent settings for the paragraph in which the insertion point is located. Pressing TAB is a quick way to indent the first line of a paragraph ½".

   Trouble
   Take care to drag only the First Line Indent marker. If you make a mistake, click the Undo button , then try again.

6. Place the insertion point in the **second body paragraph (To better...)**, then drag the **First Line Indent marker** right to the ½" mark on the horizontal ruler

   Figure 2-9 shows the First Line Indent marker being dragged. The first line of the second body paragraph is indented 1/2". Dragging the First Line Indent marker indents only the first line of a paragraph.

7. Place the insertion point in the **third body paragraph (Overall...)**, then drag the **Hanging Indent marker** right to the ½" mark on the ruler

   Take care to drag the Hanging Indent marker and not the Left Indent marker. **Figure 2-10** depicts the Hanging Indent marker being dragged. The lines under the first line of the third body paragraph are indented ½". Dragging the Hanging Indent marker indents the subsequent lines of a paragraph more than the first line.

8. Place the insertion point in the **first body paragraph**, click , click **Remove Space After Paragraph**, then save your changes

   The space between the first and second body paragraphs is eliminated. Using the Line and Paragraph Spacing button is a quick way to add or remove space between paragraphs. You can also change the paragraph spacing settings for the active paragraph using the Spacing Before and After boxes in the Paragraph group on the Layout tab.

Figure 2-8: First line indent

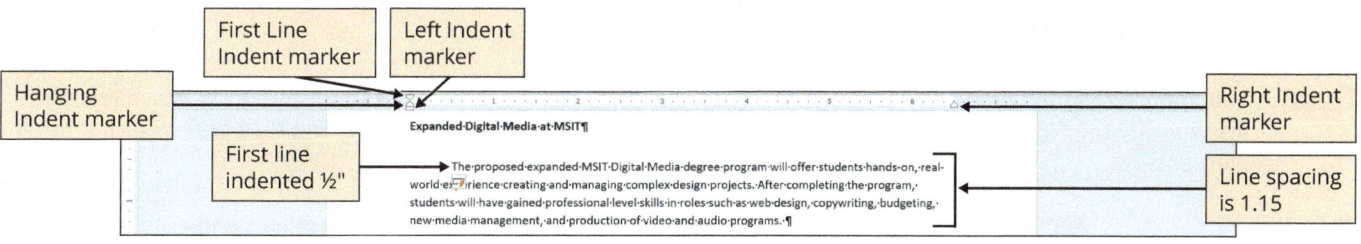

Figure 2-9: Dragging the First Line Indent marker

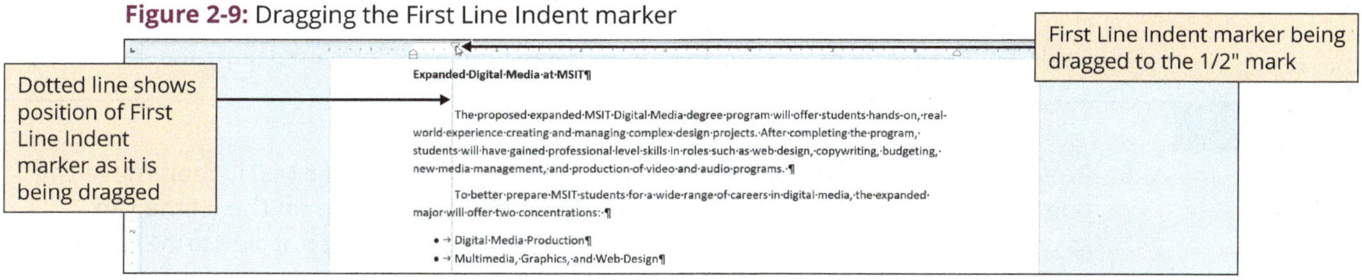

Figure 2-10: Dragging the Hanging Indent marker

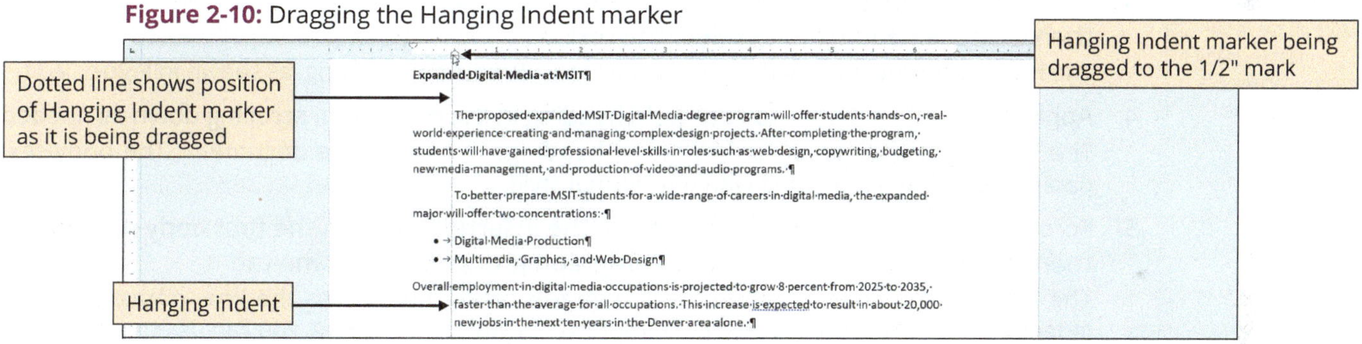

Table 2-1: Types of indents

indent type: description	to create
Left indent: left edge of a paragraph is moved in from the left margin	Drag the Left Indent marker □ on the ruler to the right to the position where you want the left edge of the paragraph to align; when you drag the left indent marker, all the indent markers move as one
Right indent: right edge of a paragraph is moved in from the right margin	Drag the Right Indent marker △ on the ruler to the left to the position where you want the right edge of the paragraph to align
First line indent: first line of a paragraph is indented more than the subsequent lines	Drag the First Line Indent marker ▽ on the ruler to the right to the position where you want the first line of the paragraph to begin; or activate the First Line Indent marker ▽ in the tab indicator, and then click the ruler at the position where you want the first line of the paragraph to begin
Hanging indent: subsequent lines of a paragraph are indented more than the first line	Drag the Hanging Indent marker △ on the ruler to the right to the position where you want the hanging indent to begin; or activate the Hanging Indent marker △ in the tab indicator, and then click the ruler at the position where you want the second and remaining lines of the paragraph to begin; when you drag the hanging indent marker, the left indent marker moves with it
Negative indent (or Outdent): left edge of a paragraph is moved to the left of the left margin	Drag the Left Indent marker □ on the ruler left to the position where you want the negative indent to begin; when you drag the left indent marker, all markers move as one

Apply Styles to Text

Case You apply title and heading styles to the report to make the report easier to read for people of all abilities. You also modify the Normal style that is applied by default to all body text to simplify the task of formatting other elements.

Objectives
- Apply built-in styles to text
- Modify existing styles

Applying a style to text allows you to apply multiple format settings to text in one easy step. A **style** is a set of format settings, such as font, font size, font color, paragraph spacing, and alignment, that are named and stored together. Word includes many **Style sets**—groups of related styles that share common fonts, colors, and formats, and are designed to be used together in a document to give it a polished and cohesive look. Each Style set includes styles for a title, subtitle, several heading levels, body text, and other text elements. By default, all text is formatted using the Normal style.

Steps

1. Press **CTRL+HOME**, select the title **Expanded Digital Media at MSIT**, then move the pointer over the styles in the Styles gallery in the Styles group on the Home tab
   As you move the pointer over a style in the gallery, a preview of that style is applied to the selected text.

Quick Tip
To change the active Style set, click the Design tab, click the More button in the Document Formatting group, then select a different style set.

2. Click the **More button** in the Style gallery, then click **Title**
   The Title style is applied to the selected text. All other paragraphs are formatted with the Normal style.

3. Select the heading **Digital Media Production**, click **Heading 1** in the Styles group, then click the heading to deselect the text
   The Heading 1 style is applied to the Digital Media Production heading, as shown in **Figure 2-11**.

4. Apply the **Heading 1** style to each bold heading in the document, scrolling down as needed
   The Heading 1 style is applied to seven headings in total in the document. The body text paragraphs are still formatted with the Normal style.

5. Scroll to the top of the document, place the insertion point in the first body paragraph, then click the **Launcher** in the Paragraph group on the Home tab
   The Indents and Spacing tab in the Paragraph dialog box shows the line, paragraph, and indentation settings for the active paragraph, as shown in **Figure 2-12**. You can use the Paragraph dialog box to check or change any paragraph setting.

6. Click **OK** to close the paragraph dialog box, then, with the insertion point in the first body paragraph, right-click **Normal** in the Styles group, then click **Update Normal to Match Selection**
   The format of each paragraph formatted with the Normal style in the document is changed to match the first body paragraph. The title and headings are indented now, too, because the Heading 1 and Title styles are based on the Normal style. When the Normal style changed, the styles based on the Normal style changed, too.

Trouble
If you apply the wrong style, click the Undo button on the Quick Access toolbar, then right-click the style name in the Styles group again.

7. Right-click **Heading 1** in the Styles group, click **Modify**, click the **Style based on arrow** in the Modify Style dialog box, click **(no style)**, then click **OK**
   The Heading 1 style is now based on no style and the indent is removed from the headings in the document. You can use the Modify Style dialog box to change any format setting in a style.

8. Right-click **Title** in the Styles group, click **Modify**, click the **Style based on arrow** in the Modify Style dialog box, click **(no style)**, then click **OK**
   The Title style is now based on no style and the indent is removed from the title in the document.

9. Select the **Expanded Digital... title**, click the **Increase Font Size button** in the Font group, click the **Font Color arrow**, click **Blue, Accent 1, Darker 25%**, click the **Line and Paragraph Spacing button** in the Paragraph group, click **Add Space After Paragraph**, deselect the title, then save your changes
   The font size of the title is increased, the font color changes to dark blue, and extra space is added after the title paragraph, as shown in **Figure 2-13**. You can modify the format of text to which a style has been applied without changing the style itself.

Figure 2-11: Styles applied to the report

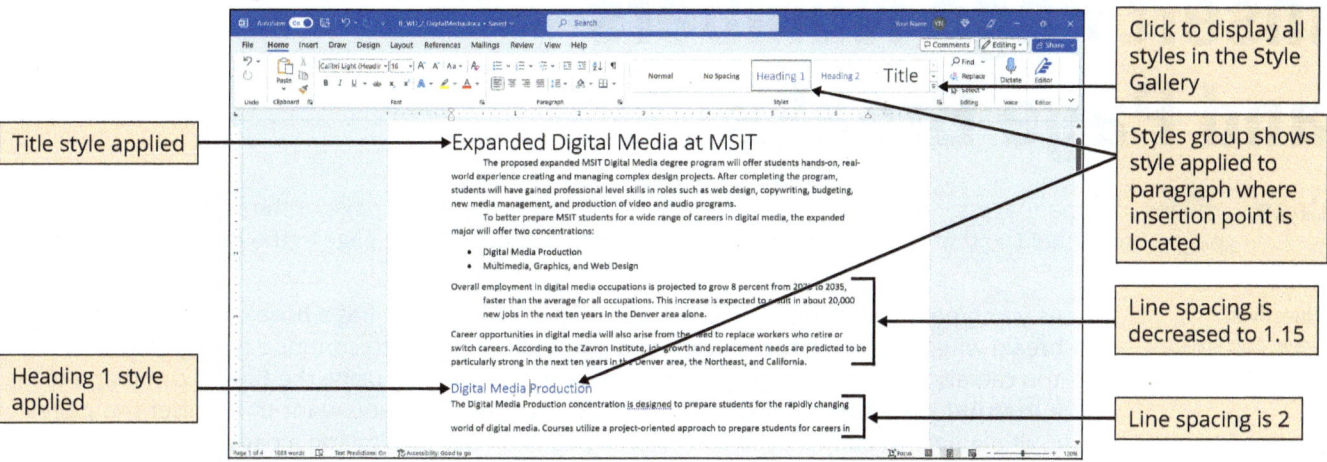

Figure 2-12: Indents and Spacing tab in Paragraph dialog box

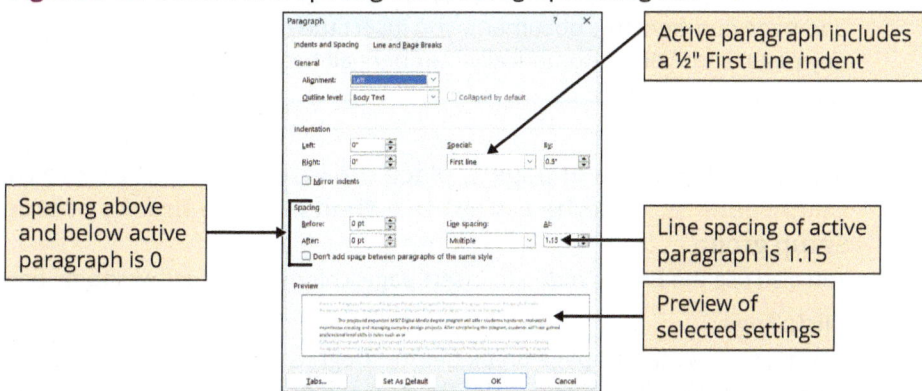

Figure 2-13: Modified styles applied to the document

Changing the Style set

Changing the Style set applied to a document is a quick way to give a document a different look and design. Style sets include font and paragraph settings for headings and body text. When you change the Style set, a complete set of new fonts and colors is applied to the entire document. All the body text and all the headings that have been formatted with a style change to the format settings for the active Style set. To change the Style set, you click one of the Style sets available in the Document Formatting group on the Design tab. You can also change the color scheme or font used in the active Style set by clicking the Colors or Fonts buttons in the Document Formatting group and then selecting from the available color schemes or font options.

You can also save a group of font and paragraph settings as a new Style set. To do this, click the More button in the Document Formatting group, and then click Save as a New Style Set. If you want to return a document to its original Style set, click the More button, and then click Reset to the Default Style Set.

Insert Page Numbers and Page Breaks

Case You insert a manual page break where you know you want to begin a new page of the report. You then add a page number field so that page numbers will appear at the bottom of each page in the document.

Objectives
- Insert page breaks
- Insert page numbers

As you type text in a document, Word inserts an **automatic page break** (also called a soft page break) when you reach the bottom of a page, allowing you to continue typing on the next page. You can also force text onto the next page of a document by using the Breaks command to insert a **manual page break** (also called a hard page break). If you want to number the pages of a multiple-page document, you can insert a page number field to add a page number to each page. A **field** is a code that serves as a placeholder for data that changes in a document, such as a page number or the current date. When you use the Page Number button on the Insert tab to add page numbers to a document, you insert the page number field at the top, bottom, or side of any page, and Word automatically numbers all the pages in the document for you.

Steps

Quick Tip
Pressing CTRL+ENTER is a fast way to insert a manual page break.

1. Scroll to the bottom of page 1, place the insertion point before the heading **Degree Requirements**, click the **Layout tab**, then click the **Breaks button** in the Page Setup group
   You also use the Breaks menu to insert page, column, and text-wrapping breaks. Refer to **Table 2-2**.

2. Click **Page**
   Word inserts a manual page break before "Degree Requirements" and moves all the text following the page break to the beginning of the next page, as shown in **Figure 2-14**.

Quick Tip
To delete a page break, select it and then press DELETE. Page breaks are only visible when formatting marks are turned on.

3. Scroll down, place the insertion point before the heading **Career Preparation and Outlook** on page 2, press and hold **CTRL**, then press **ENTER**
   The heading is forced to the top of the third page.

4. Press **CTRL+HOME**, click the **Insert tab**, then click the **Page Number button** in the Header & Footer group
   Use the Page Number menu to select the position for the page numbers. If you choose to add a page number field to the top, bottom, or side of a document, a page number will appear on every page in the document.

5. Point to **Bottom of Page**
   A gallery of formatting and alignment options for page numbers at the bottom of a page opens.

Quick Tip
To change the location or formatting of page numbers, click the Page Number button, point to a page number location, then select a format from the gallery.

6. Click **Plain Number 2** in the Simple section
   A page number field containing the number 1 is centered in the Footer area at the bottom of page 1 of the document, as shown in **Figure 2-15**. The document text is gray, or dimmed, because the Footer area is open. Text that is inserted in a Footer area appears at the bottom of every page in a document.

7. Double-click the **document text**
   The page number is now dimmed because it is located in the Footer area, which is no longer the active area. When the document is printed, the page numbers appear as normal text.

Quick Tip
To remove page numbers from a document, click the Page Number button, then click Remove Page Numbers.

8. Press **CTRL+HOME**, click the **View tab**, click the **Multiple Pages button** in the Zoom group, then save the document
   Word numbered each page of the report automatically, and each page number is centered at the bottom of the page, as shown in **Figure 2-16**.

Figure 2-14: Manual page break in document

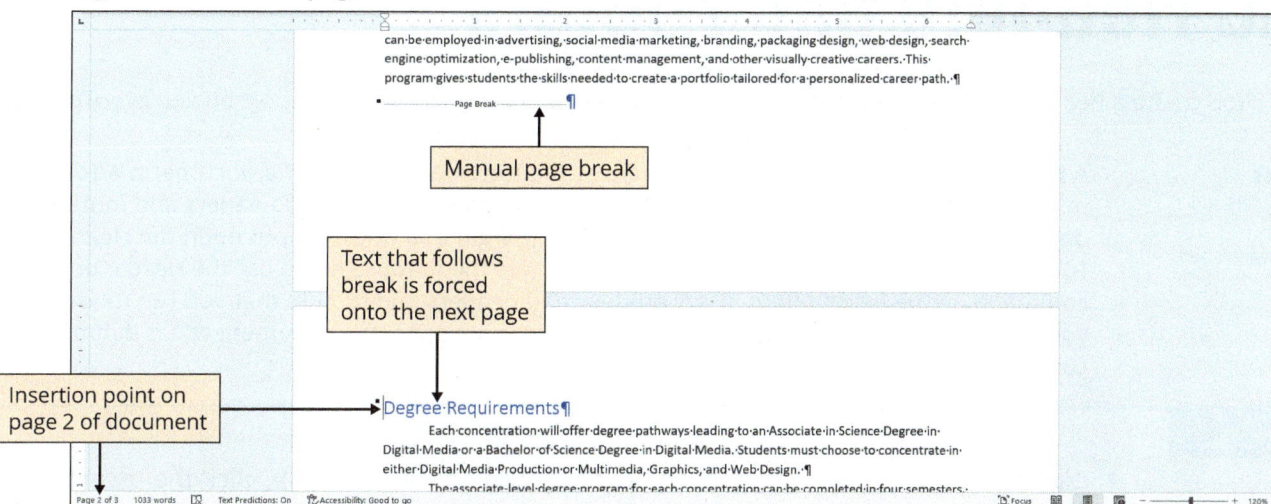

Figure 2-15: Page number in document

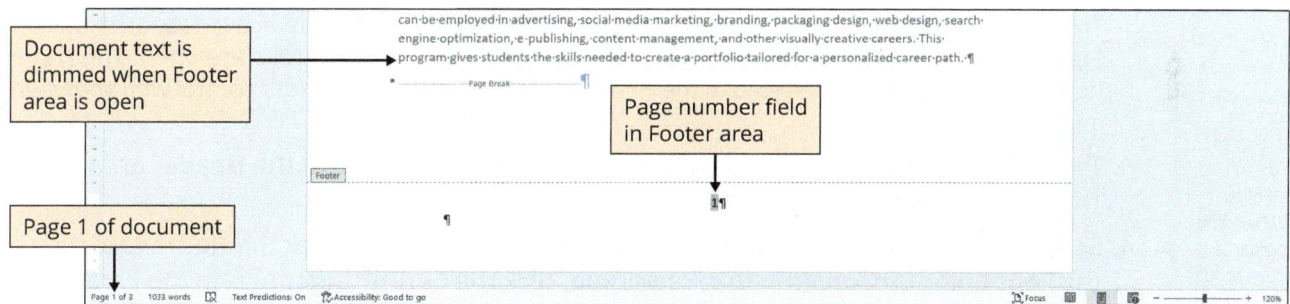

Figure 2-16: Pages 1, 2, and 3

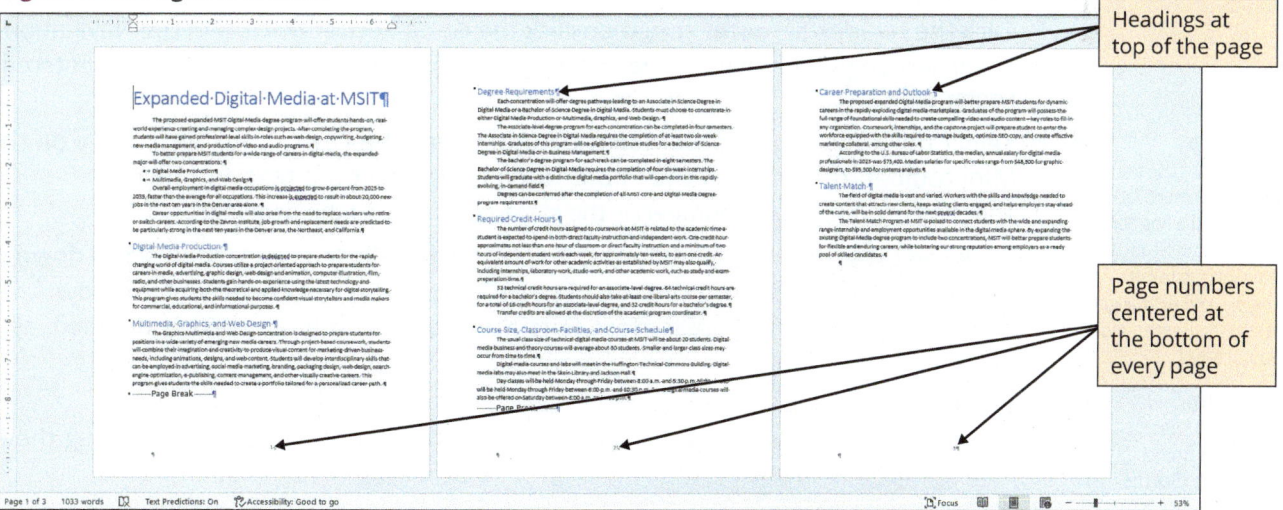

Table 2-2: Types of breaks

break	function
Page	Forces the text following the break to begin at the top of the next page
Column	Forces the text following the break to begin at the top of the next column
Text Wrapping	Forces the text following the break to begin at the beginning of the next line

Add Headers and Footers

Case You create a header that includes the title of the report so that readers can see the report title on every page.

Objectives
- Insert headers and footers
- Format headers and footers

A **header** is text or graphics that appears at the top of every page of a document. A **footer** is text or graphics that appears at the bottom of every page. You can add headers and footers to a document by double-clicking the top or bottom margin of a document to open the Header and Footer areas, and then inserting text and graphics into them. You can also use the Header or Footer command on the Insert tab to insert predesigned headers and footers that you can modify with your information. When the header and footer areas are open, the document text is dimmed and cannot be edited.

Steps

1. Click the **Page Width button** in the Zoom group on the **View tab**, click the **Insert tab**, then click the **Header button** in the Header & Footer group
   A gallery of built-in header designs opens.

2. Scroll down the gallery to view the header designs, scroll up the gallery, then click **Blank**
   The Header area opens and the Header & Footer tab opens and is the active tab, as shown in **Figure 2-17**. This tab is available whenever the Header and Footer areas are open. The [Type here] **content control** is selected in the Header area. You replace a content control with your own information.

Trouble
If blue is not your active color, click the Font Color arrow, click Blue, Accent 1, Darker 25%. If bottom border is not your active border setting, click the Border arrow, then click Bottom Border.

3. Type **Expanded Digital Media at MSIT** in the content control in the Header area
   This text will appear at the top of every page in the document.

4. Select the **header text** (but not the paragraph mark below it), click the **Home tab**, click the **Font Color button** in the Font group, click the **Center button** in the Paragraph group, click the **Borders button**, then click in the Header area to deselect the text
   The text is the same blue used in the document and is centered in the Header area with a bottom border.

5. Click the **Header & Footer tab**, then click the **Go to Footer button** in the Navigation group
   The insertion point moves to the Footer area, where a page number field is centered in the Footer area.

Quick Tip
You can also use the Insert Alignment Tab button in the Position group on the Header & Footer tab to left-, center-, and right-align text in the Header and Footer areas.

6. Select the **page number field** in the footer, click the **Font Color button** on the Mini toolbar, then click in the Footer area to deselect the text and field
   The footer text (the page number) is the same color blue as the headings.

7. Click the **Close Header and Footer button** in the Close group, then scroll down until the bottom of page 1 and the top of page 2 appear in the document window
   The Header and Footer areas close, and the header and footer text is dimmed, as shown in **Figure 2-18**.

Quick Tip
To remove headers or footers from a document, click the Header or Footer button, and then click Remove Header or Remove Footer.

8. Press **CTRL+HOME**
   The report already includes the report title at the top of the first page, making the header information redundant.

9. Position the pointer over the header text at the top of page 1, double-click the **header** to open the Header area, click the **Different First Page check box** in the Options group on the Header and Footer tab, then click the **Close Header and Footer button**
   The header and footer text is removed from the Header and Footer areas on the first page.

10. Click the **Show/Hide ¶ button** in the Paragraph group on the Home tab, click the **View tab**, click the **Multiple Pages button** in the Zoom group, then save your changes
    The headers and footers and all the pages in the document are shown in **Figure 2-19**.

Figure 2-17: Header area

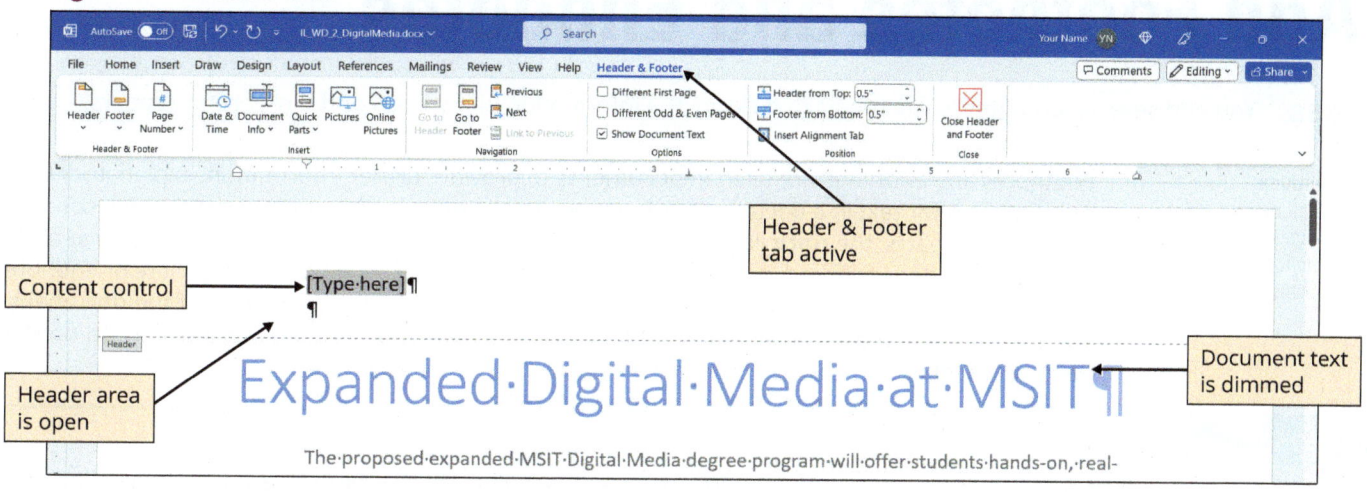

Figure 2-18: Header and footer in document

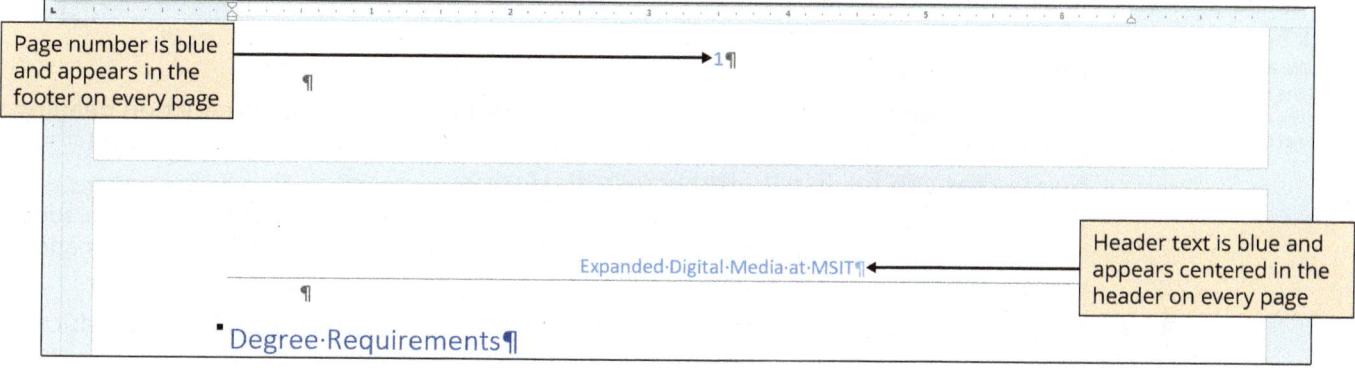

Figure 2-19: Header and footer on pages 2 and 3

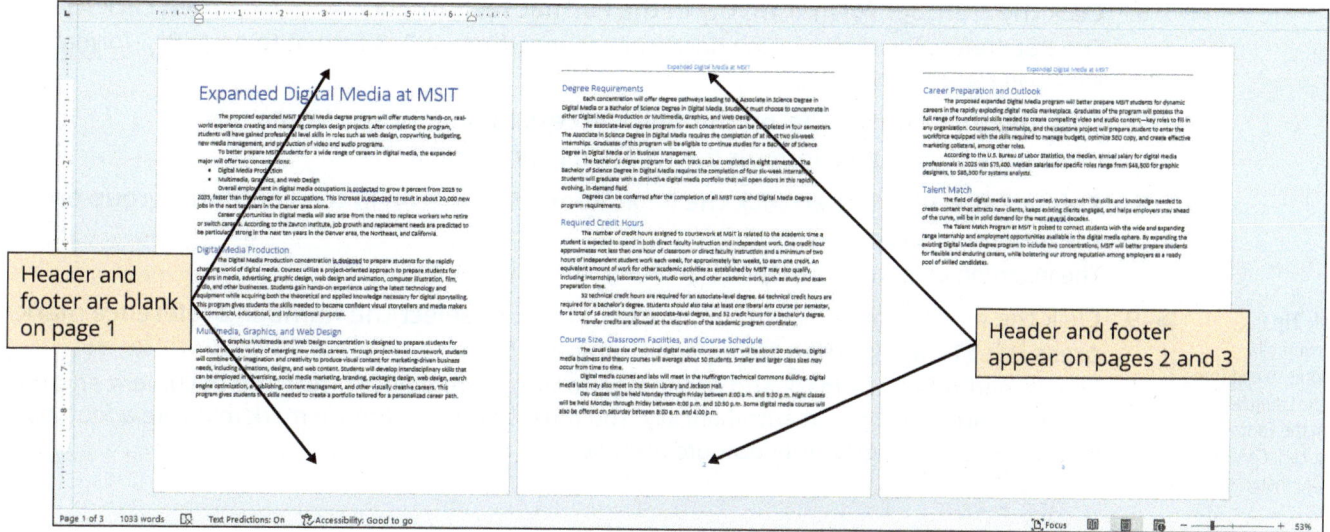

Add Footnotes and Endnotes

Case You add several footnotes to the report that clarify the information in the body of the report for readers.

Objectives
- Insert footnotes and endnotes
- Delete footnotes and endnotes

Footnotes and endnotes are used in documents to provide further information, explanatory text, or references for text in a document. A **footnote** or **endnote** is an explanatory note that consists of two linked parts: the **note reference mark** that appears next to the text to indicate that additional information is offered in a footnote or endnote, and the corresponding footnote or endnote text. Word places footnotes at the end of each page and endnotes at the end of the document. You insert and manage footnotes and endnotes using the tools in the Footnotes group on the References tab.

Steps

1. Click the **100% button** in the Zoom group, scroll until the Multimedia, Graphics, and Web Design heading is at the top of your screen, place the insertion point at the end of the last body paragraph (after "path."), click the **References tab**, then click the **Insert Footnote button** in the Footnotes group

   A note reference mark, in this case a superscript 1, appears after "path.", and the insertion point moves below a separator line at the bottom of the page. A note reference mark can be a number, a symbol, a character, or a combination of characters.

   Quick Tip
   To delete a footnote, select the note reference mark, then press DELETE.

2. Type **This concentration emphasizes technical skills.**

   The footnote text appears below the separator line at the bottom of page 1.

3. Scroll up, place the insertion point at the end of the Digital Media Production heading, click the **Insert Footnote button**, then type **Digital media refers to any visual media that can be distributed across platforms.**

   The footnote text appears at the bottom of the first page, above the first footnote you added. Notice that when you inserted a new footnote above an existing footnote, Word automatically renumbered the footnotes, as shown in **Figure 2-20**.

4. Place the insertion point at the end of the paragraph under the Digital Media Production heading, click the **Insert Footnote button**, then type **Students will specialize.**

   The footnote text appears between the text for footnotes 1 and 3 at the bottom of the page.

5. Click the **Launcher** in the Footnotes group

   The Footnote and Endnote dialog box opens. You can use this dialog box to change the location of footnote and endnote text, convert footnotes to endnotes, and change the formatting of the note reference marks.

6. Click the **Number format arrow** in the Format section, click **A, B, C,...**, then click **Apply**

   The note reference marks in the document change from 1, 2, 3 format to an A, B, C format, as shown in **Figure 2-21**.

7. Click the **Undo button** on the Quick Access toolbar or the Home tab

   Clicking the Undo button restores the 1,2,3 numbering format.

8. Press **CTRL+HOME**, then click the **Next Footnote button** in the Footnotes group on the References tab

   The insertion point moves to the "1" reference mark in the document.

   Quick Tip
   To convert all footnotes to endnotes, click the Launcher in the Footnotes group, click Convert, click OK, then click Close.

9. Click the **Next Footnote button**, press **DELETE** to select the number 2 reference mark, press **DELETE** again, then save your changes

   The second reference mark and associated footnote are deleted from the document and the footnotes are renumbered automatically. You must select a reference mark to delete a footnote; you cannot simply delete the footnote text itself.

Figure 2-20: Renumbered footnotes in the document

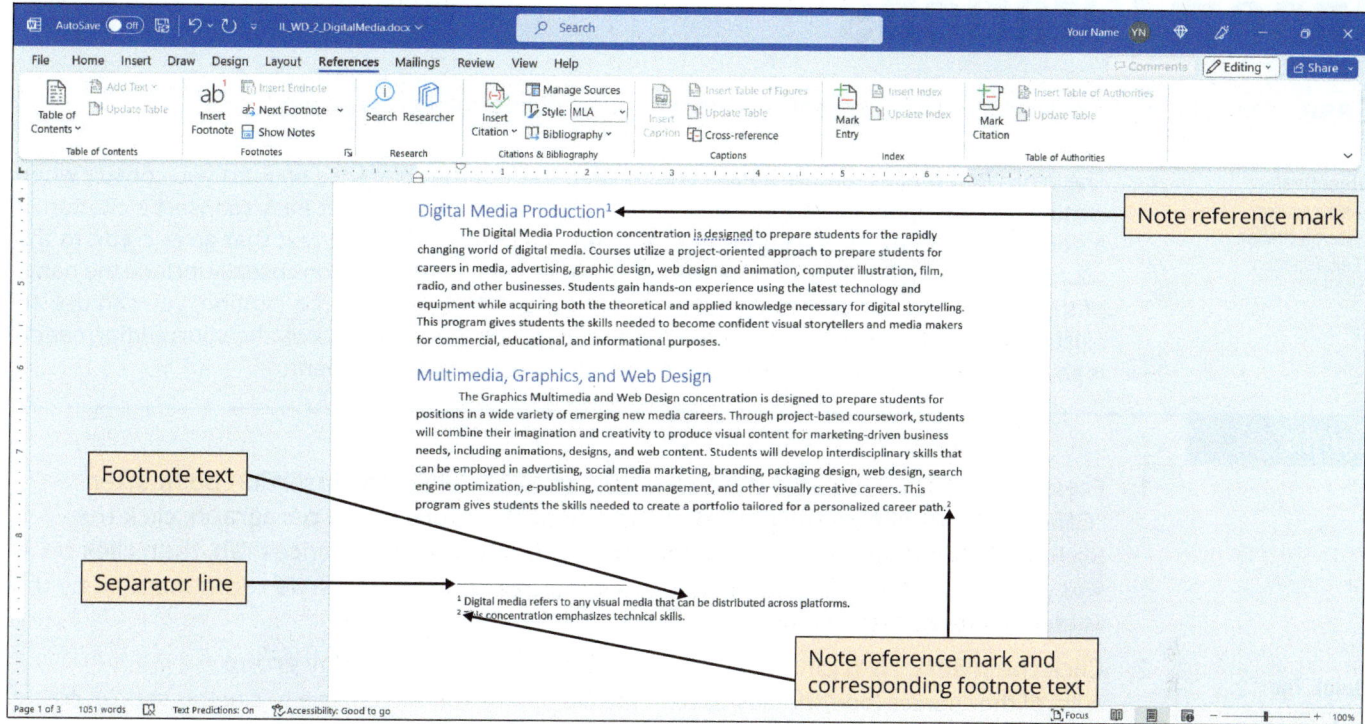

Figure 2-21: Note reference marks in new format

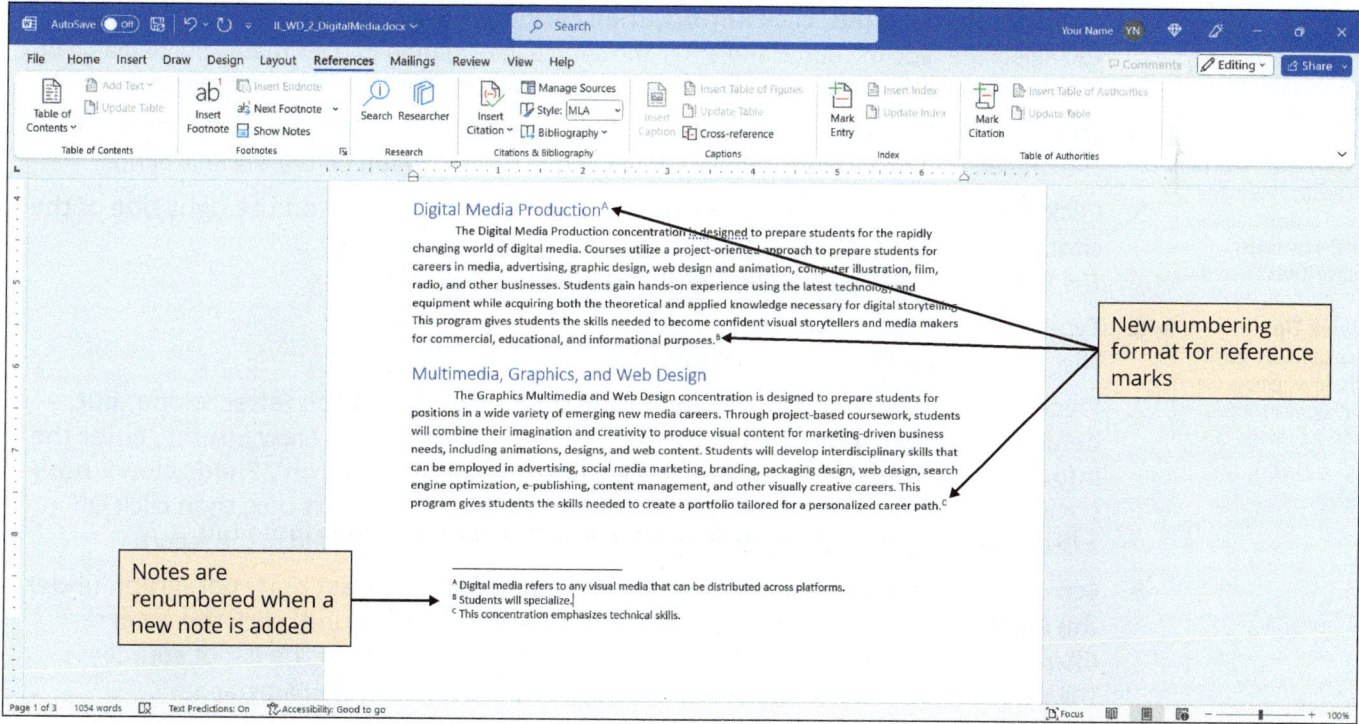

Insert Citations

Case You add several citations to the report that indicate the source of information to readers.

Objectives
- Add a source
- Insert a citation
- Edit a citation

The Word References feature allows you to keep track of the reference sources you consult when writing research papers, reports, and other documents, and makes it easy to insert a citation in a document. A **citation** is a parenthetical reference in the document text that gives credit to the source for a quotation, data, or other content used in a document. Citations usually include the name of the author and, for print sources, a page number. When you insert a citation, you can use an existing source or create a new source. Each time you create a new source, the source information is saved on your computer so that it is available for use in any document.

Steps

1. **Press CTRL+HOME**, change the zoom level to **120%**, place the insertion point after "California" but before the period at the end of the fourth body paragraph, click the **Style arrow** in the Citations & Bibliography group on the References tab, then click **MLA**
   You will format the sources and citations in the report using the style recommended by the Modern Language Association (MLA).

2. Click the **Insert Citation button** in the Citations & Bibliography group
   A list of the sources (one) already used in the file opens. You can choose to cite this source, create a new source, or add a placeholder for a source. When you add a new citation to a document, the source is added to the list of master sources stored on the computer. The new source is also associated with the document.

   Quick Tip
   When you create a new source for a document, it appears automatically in the bibliography when you generate it.

3. Click **Add New Source**, click the **Type of Source arrow**, scroll down to view the available source types, click **Report**, then click the **Corporate Author check box**
   You select the type of source and enter the source information in the Create Source dialog box. The fields available in the dialog box change, depending on the type of source selected.

   Quick Tip
   Only sources that you associate with a document stay with the document when you move it to another computer. The master list of sources remains on the computer where it was created.

4. Enter the data shown in **Figure 2-22** in the Create Source dialog box, then click **OK**
   The citation (Zavron Institute) appears at the end of the paragraph before the final period.

5. Click the citation to select it, click the **Citation Options arrow** on the right side of the citation, then click **Edit Citation**
   The Edit Citation dialog box opens, as shown in **Figure 2-23**.

   Quick Tip
   You can also choose to add or remove the author, year, or title from a citation.

6. Type **18** in the Pages box, then click **OK**
   The page number 18 is added to the citation.

7. Place the insertion point at the end of the third body paragraph (after "alone" but before the period), click the **Insert Citation button**, click **Add New Source**, enter the information shown in **Figure 2-24**, click the **Show all Bibliography Fields check box**, scroll down in the dialog box, type **www.bls.gov** in the URL text box, then click **OK**
   A citation for the Web publication that the data was taken from is added to the report.

8. Scroll to page 3, place the insertion point at the end of the last body paragraph under the Career Preparation and Outlook heading (before the period) click the **Insert Citation button**, then click **U.S. Bureau of Labor Statistics** in the list of sources
   The citation (U.S. Bureau of Labor Statistics) appears at the end of the paragraph.

9. Scroll down, place the insertion point at the end of the first body paragraph under the Talent Match heading (before the period) click the **Insert Citation button**, click **Add New Placeholder**, type **NYT**, click **OK**, then save your changes
   You added a citation placeholder for a source that you still need to add to the document.

Figure 2-22: Creating a report source

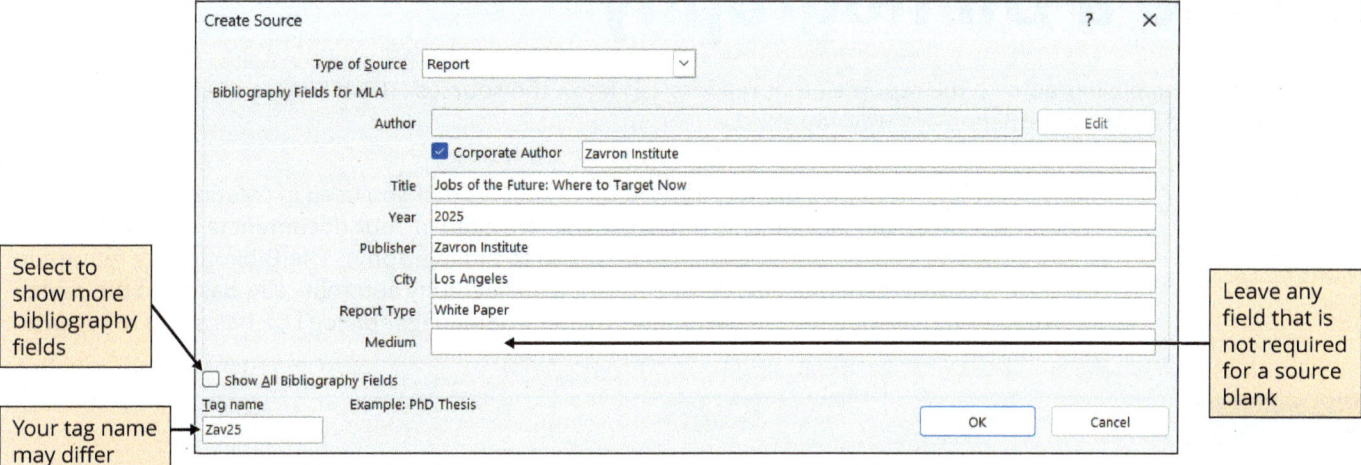

Figure 2-23: Edit Citation dialog box

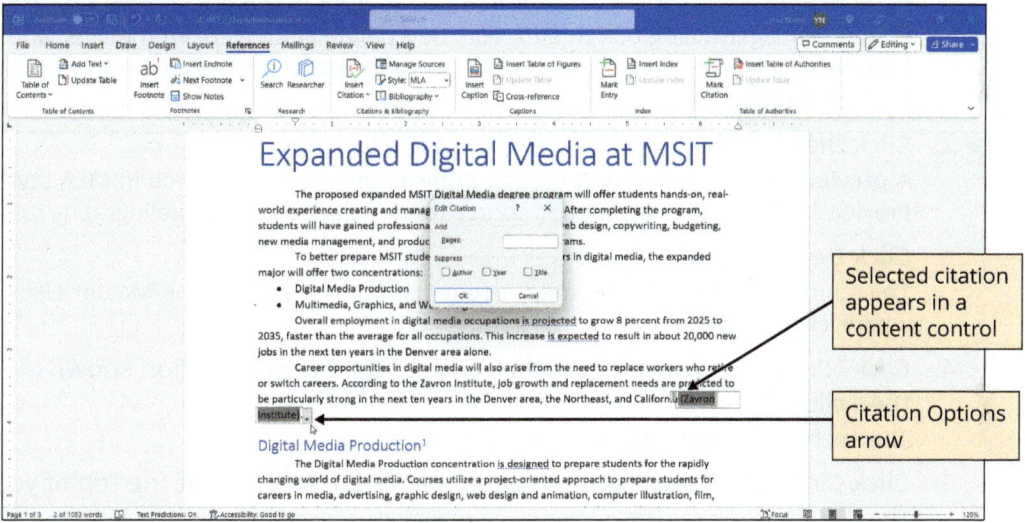

Figure 2-24: Adding a Web publication source

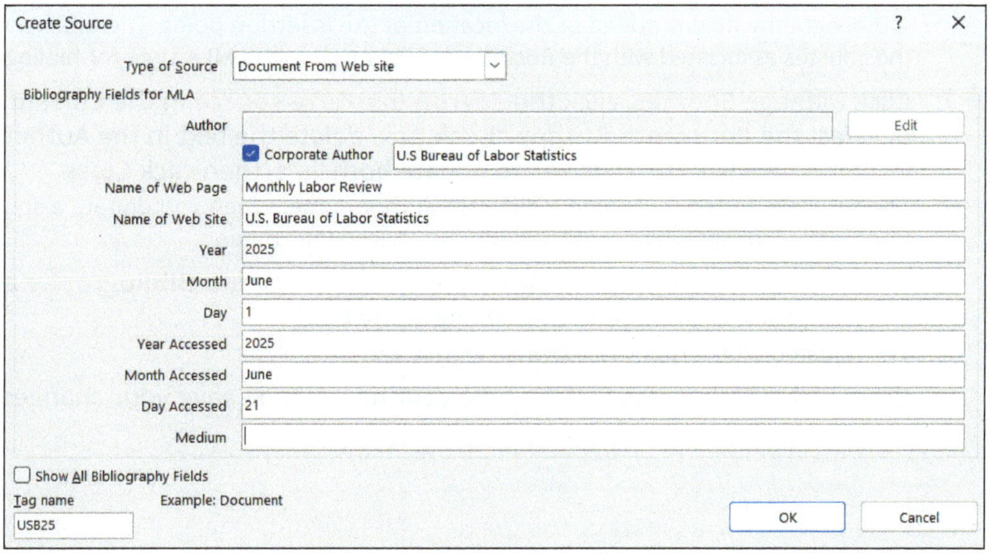

Create a Bibliography

Case You add a bibliography to the report so that readers can know the sources. The bibliography is inserted as a field and it can be formatted any way you choose.

Objectives
- Delete a source
- Edit a source
- Insert a bibliography field

Many documents require a **bibliography**, a list of sources that you used in creating the document. The list of sources can include only the works that are cited in your document (a **works cited** list) or both the works cited and the works consulted (a bibliography). The Bibliography feature in Word allows you to generate a works cited list or a bibliography automatically, based on the source information you provide for the document. The Source Manager dialog box helps you to organize your sources.

Steps

1. **Click the Manage Sources button in the Citations & Bibliography group**
   The Source Manager dialog box opens, as shown in **Figure 2-25**. The Master List shows the two sources you added and any other sources available on your computer. The Current List shows the sources available in the current document, as well as the NYT placeholder you added. A check mark next to a source indicates the source is cited in the document. You use the tools in the Source Manager dialog box to add, edit, and delete sources from the lists, and to copy sources between the Master and Current Lists. The sources that appear in the Current List will appear in the bibliography.

   Quick Tip
   You must copy sources from the Master List to the Current List for the sources to be available when you open the document on another computer.

2. **Click the Kirtida, Samantha source in the Current List**
   A preview of the citation and bibliographical entry for the source in MLA style appears in the Preview box. You do not want this source to be included in your bibliography for the report.

3. **Click Delete**
   The source is removed from the Current List but remains on the Master List on the computer where it originated.

4. **Click NYT in the Current List, click Edit, enter the information shown in Figure 2-26, then click OK**
   The Anzhela source is added to the Current List.

5. **Click Close, then scroll until the heading Talent Match is at the top of your screen**
   The NYT placeholder citation has been replaced with the information from the "Anzhela" source.

   Quick Tip
   Click References in the Built-in gallery to insert a References list. Click Works Cited in the Built-in gallery to insert a Works Cited list.

6. **Press CTRL+END to move the insertion point to the end of the document, click the Bibliography button in the Citations & Bibliography group, then click Bibliography in the Built-in gallery**
   A Bibliography field is added at the location of the insertion point. The bibliography includes all the sources associated with the document, formatted in the MLA style for bibliographies.

   Quick Tip
   To change the style used for citations and the bibliography, click the Style arrow in the Citations & Bibliography group, then select a different style.

7. **Click Manage Sources, click the Zavron Institute source in the Current List, click Edit, deselect the Corporate Author check box, delete the text in the Author text box, type Willa Perlie, click OK, click Yes to update both lists, then click Close**
   The source is edited to include a different author name. When you update a source, you need to update the Bibliography field to include the revised information.

8. **Click the Bibliography field, click Update Citations and Bibliography at the top of the field, then click outside the Bibliography field**
   The updated Bibliography is shown in **Figure 2-27**.

9. **Press CTRL+END, press ENTER, type your name, then save your changes**

Figure 2-25: Source Manager dialog box

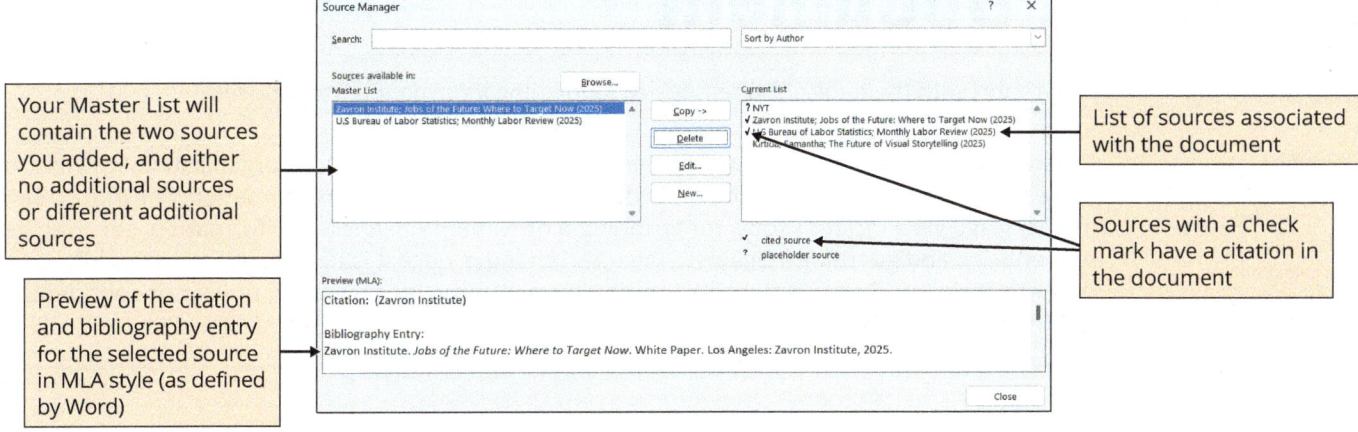

Your Master List will contain the two sources you added, and either no additional sources or different additional sources

Preview of the citation and bibliography entry for the selected source in MLA style (as defined by Word)

List of sources associated with the document

Sources with a check mark have a citation in the document

Figure 2-26: Adding a periodical source

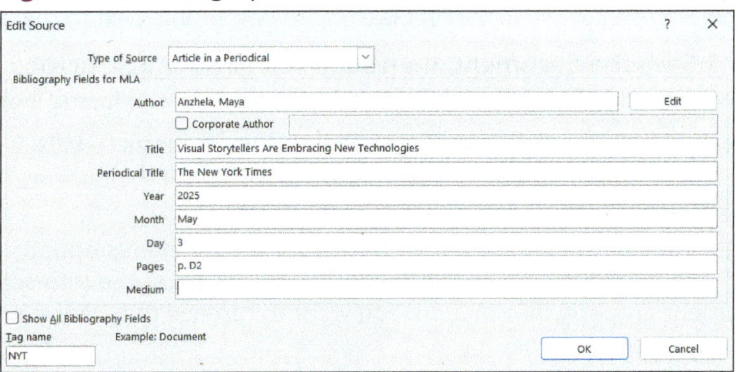

Figure 2-27: Bibliography field in document

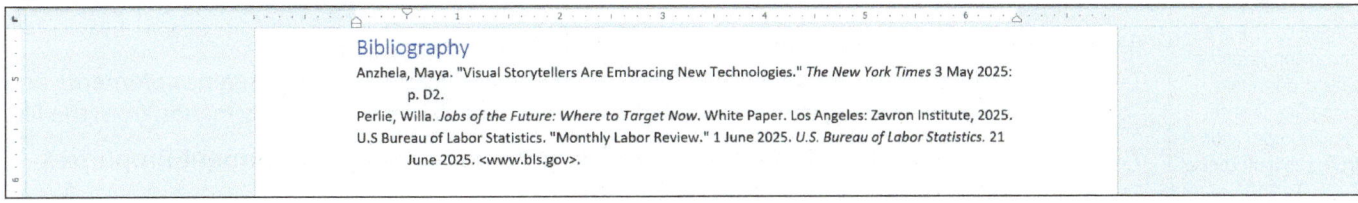

Finding and citing sources with the Word Researcher

The Word Researcher tool helps you find citable sources, quotations, images, and other material for a research paper. Using Researcher, you can search for journal articles and websites that relate to a topic, add information from those sources into a document, automatically create a citation for the source, and automatically create and update a bibliography—all without having to manually enter the source information. To begin, click the Researcher button in the Research group on the References tab to open the Researcher pane. Type a keyword for your topic in the search box, press ENTER, and then explore the list of sources related to your topic. When you find a source that is useful to you, you can select text (or an image) from it and add the selection to your document, choosing to add text only, or to add the text and a citation. When you add a citation, Word automatically creates a bibliography that is updated each time you add additional material to the document. To avoid plagiarism, be sure to paraphrase text that is not a quote, and always include citations giving credit for any content that is not your original work. Also, always verify that the bibliographies you create using Word are formatted in the most up-to-date MLA, APA, Chicago, or other style.

Inspect a Document

Case Before sharing the report with the public, you remove all identifying information from the file.

Objectives
- Inspect a document for embedded information
- Remove comments and document properties

Before you distribute a document electronically to people outside your organization, it's wise to make sure the file does not include embedded private or confidential information. The Info screen in Backstage view includes tools for stripping a document of sensitive information, securing its authenticity, and guarding it against unwanted changes once it is distributed to the public. One of these tools, the Document Inspector, detects and removes unwanted private or confidential information from a document.

Steps

1. Press **CTRL+HOME**, click the **View tab**, then click the **Multiple Pages button**
   The completed document is shown in **Figure 2-28**.

2. Click the **Review tab**, click **No Markup**, then click **All Markup**
   The comments you hid in the first lesson are now visible next to the document.

3. **sam↑** Save the document, then submit it to your instructor
   You will save the document with a new file name before stripping it of all identifying information.

Quick Tip
To recover unsaved changes to a file, click Manage Document on the Info screen, then click Recover Unsaved Documents.

4. Click the **File tab**, click **Save As**, save the document as **IL_WD_2_DigitalMedia_Inspected**, click the **File tab**, click **Info**, then click the **Show All Properties link** at the bottom of the Info screen
   The left side of the Info screen in Backstage view includes options related to stripping the file of private information. See **Table 2-3**. The right side of the Info screen displays the expanded document property information. You want to remove this information from the file before you distribute it electronically.

Quick Tip
A document property, such as author name, might appear automatically in a content control in a document. Stripping a file of document properties does not remove information from a content control.

5. Click the **Check for Issues button** on the Info screen, then click **Inspect Document**, clicking **Yes** if prompted to save changes
   The Document Inspector dialog box opens. You use this dialog box to indicate which private or identifying information you want to search for and remove from the document.

6. Make sure all the check boxes are selected, then click **Inspect**
   After a moment, the Document Inspector dialog box indicates the file contains comments and document properties, as shown in **Figure 2-29**. You want to remove this information from the file.

7. Click **Remove All** next to Comments, click **Remove All** next to Document Properties and Personal Information, then click **Close**
   The comments and document property information are removed from the report file, but the change will not be reflected on the Info screen until you reopen it.

8. Click the **Back button** on the Info screen, save your changes to the document, click the **File tab**, then click **Info**
   The comments have been removed from the file. The Info screen shows the document properties have been removed from the file.

9. Submit the document to your instructor, close the file, then exit Word

Figure 2-28: Formatted document

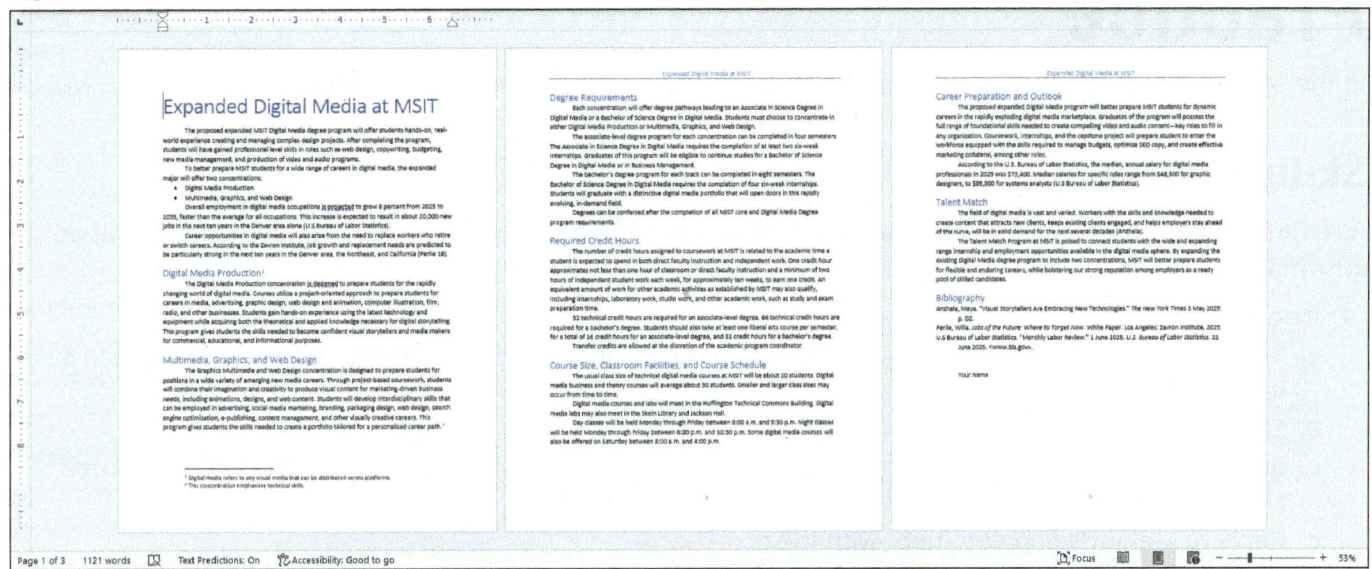

Figure 2-29: Results after inspecting document

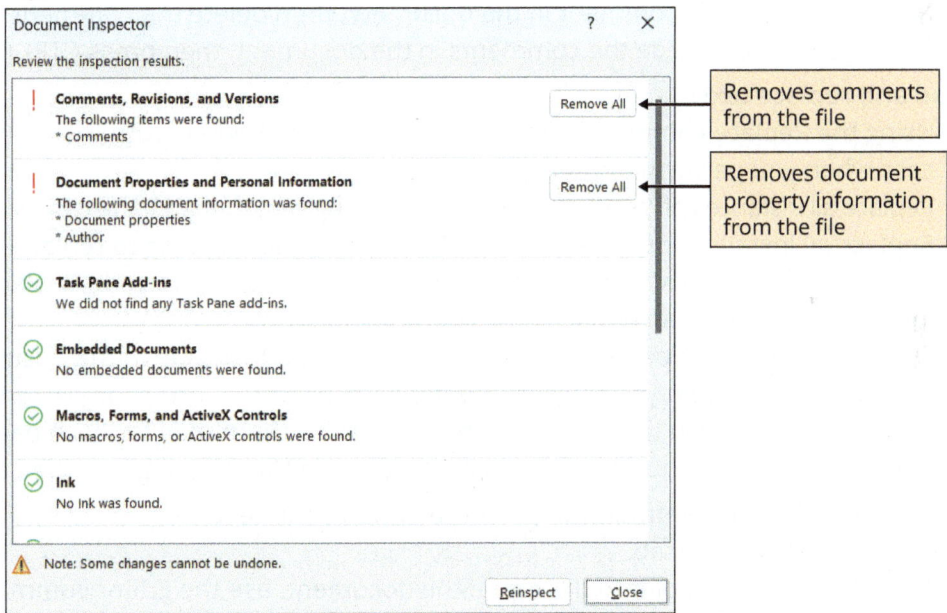

Table 2-3: Options on the Info screen

option	use to
Protect Document	Set a document to open as read-only so that users must opt into editing; encrypt a document so that a password is required to open it; restrict what kinds of changes can be made to a document and by whom; add a digital signature to a document to restrict access to editing, copying, and printing, and to verify its integrity; and mark a document as final so that it is read-only and cannot be edited
Check for Issues	Detect and remove unwanted information from a document, including document properties and comments; check for content that people with disabilities might find difficult to read; and check the document for features that are not supported by previous versions of Word
Version History	View and restore a previous version of a file stored on OneDrive
Manage Document	Browse and recover draft versions of unsaved files

Practice

In the exercises that follow, you will practice the skills you have learned in this module.

Skills Review

As a healthcare communications specialist, you have been hired by a wellness clinic to edit and format an informational report for clients, using Word.

1. **Insert comments.**
   a. Start Word, open the file IL_WD_2-2.docx from the location where you store your Data Files, then save it as **IL_WD_2_Lifestyle**.
   b. Show all the comments in the document, if necessary.
   c. Select Center in the title, then insert a new comment with the text **I will change this to "Institute" throughout.**
   d. Reply to Melody's first comment with the text **OK.**
   e. Navigate to Melody's next comment. Change 2022 to **2025** and 83 to **80** in the body text, and then mark the comment thread resolved.
   f. Navigate to the previous comment and edit your "OK." comment to add the sentence **I will add a footnote.**
   g. Navigate to the final comment in the document, then delete the comment thread.
   h. Save your changes, hide the comments in the document, then press CTRL+HOME.

2. **Find and replace text.**
   a. Using the Replace command, replace all instances of "Center" with **Institute**, taking care to match the case when you perform the search.
   b. Replace all instances of "medical" with **clinical**, taking care to match the case when you perform the replace.
   c. Replace all instances of "rehab" with **rehabilitation**, taking care to replace whole words only when you perform the replace. (**Hint**: Deselect Match case if it is selected.) Replace each instance of "rehab" individually rather than replacing all instances at once.
   d. Open the Navigation pane, then view all instances of "institute" in the document to make sure no errors occurred when you replaced Center with Institute. Correct any errors.
   e. Click the Pages link in the Navigation pane, click the thumbnail for each page to scroll through the document, click the thumbnail for page 1, close the Navigation pane, then save your changes.

3. **Check spelling and grammar and proofread and revise text.**
   a. Switch to the Review tab.
   b. Move the insertion point to the top of the document, use the Editor command to search for and correct spelling and grammar errors in the document, then close the Editor pane. (**Hint**: Ignore any suggested Refinements.)
   c. Use the Thesaurus to replace "enhance" in the first body paragraph with a different suitable word, then close the Thesaurus pane.
   d. Check the word count of the document.
   e. Proofread your document, correct any errors, then save your changes.

4. **Change line spacing and indents.**
   a. Change the line spacing of the entire document to 1.5.
   b. Change the line spacing of the first body paragraph to 1.15.
   c. Indent the first line of the first body paragraph .3". (**Hint**: Use the Paragraph dialog box.)
   d. Remove the paragraph space under the first body paragraph, then save your changes.

5. **Apply styles to text.**
   a. Apply the Title style to the title "North Coast Wellness Institute".
   b. Apply the Subtitle style to the subtitle "Lifestyle is Medicine".

c. Apply the Heading 1 style to each red heading in the document: "Jumpstart Health Living at North Coast Wellness Center" and "Clinical Services".
d. Apply the Heading 2 style to each blue heading in the document: "Lifestyle Medicine and Wellness", "Developing a Wellness Routine", "Staying Motivated", "Working with Our Medical Staff", "Rehabilitation", "Preventative Care", "Chronic Disease Management", and "Community Education".
e. With the insertion point in the first body paragraph, update the Normal style to match the first body paragraph.
f. Modify the Title style to be based on no style.
g. Modify the Subtitle, Heading 1, and Heading 2 styles to be based on no style.
h. Change the theme of the document to Gallery. (**Hint**: Use the Design tab.)
i. Select the title, change the font size to 36, then change the font color to Red, Accent 1, Darker 25%.
j. Select the subtitle, change the font size to 14, then add 24 points of space after the paragraph.
k. Select the heading "Jumpstart...", add 6 points of space after the paragraph, then update the Heading 1 style to match the selection
l. Select the heading "Lifestyle Medicine...", add 6 points of space before the paragraph, and 3 points of space after the paragraph, then update the Heading 2 style to match the selection.
m. Scroll to the bottom of page 1, click the first item in the bulleted list, add 6 points of space before the paragraph, then save your changes.

6. **Insert page numbers and page breaks.**
   a. Scroll to the bottom of page 2, then insert a manual page break before the heading "Clinical Services".
   b. Insert page numbers in the document at the bottom of the page.
   c. Close the Footer area, then scroll through the document to view the page number on each page.
   d. Turn on formatting marks, delete the manual page break at the bottom of page 2, then save your changes to the document.

7. **Add headers and footers.**
   a. Double-click the Footer area, then use the Go to Header button to move the insertion point to the Header area.
   b. Click the Header button, scroll down the gallery of built-in header designs, then select the Filigree header.
   c. Click the Document title content control in the header, then type **North Coast Wellness Institute**.
   d. Replace the text in the Author content control with your name, press END to move the insertion point out of the content control, then press SPACEBAR. (**Note**: If your name does not appear in the header, right-click the Author content control, click Remove Content Control, then type your name in the header.)
   e. Close headers and footers, then scroll to view the header and footer on each page.
   f. Open headers and footers, select the text in the Header area, including the paragraph mark after your name, change the alignment of the selected text to left, then remove the first line indent. (**Hint**: You can drag the indent marker on the ruler or use the Paragraph dialog box to remove the first line indent.)
   g. Remove the header and footer from the first page of the document, close headers and footers, then save your changes.

8. **Add footnotes and endnotes.**
   a. Press CTRL+HOME, scroll down, place the insertion point at the end of the first body paragraph, insert a footnote, then type **Healthcare resources include personnel, facilities, materials, and anything else that is used to provide medical care.**
   b. Place the insertion point at the end of the first paragraph under the Developing a Wellness Routine heading, insert a footnote, then type **Most wellness activities require only 30 minutes a day.**
   c. Place the insertion point at the end of the second paragraph under the Developing a Wellness Routine heading, insert a footnote, then type **Always consult a physician before beginning a new fitness program.**
   d. Change the number format of the footnotes to *, †, ‡ or another option, then save your changes.

Skills Review (Continued)

9. **Insert citations.**
   a. Place the insertion point at the end of the first paragraph under the Lifestyle Medicine and Wellness heading (after "poor lifestyle" but before the period), then be sure the style for citations and bibliography is set to MLA Seventh Edition.
   b. Insert a citation, add a new source, enter the source information shown in the Create Source dialog box in **Figure 2-30**, then click OK.
   c. Place the insertion point at the end of the second paragraph under the Developing a Wellness Routine heading, insert a citation, then select Chao, Brian from the list of sources.
   d. Edit the citation to include the page number **24**.
   e. Scroll to page 2, place the insertion point at the end of the "Schedule your wellness activity" paragraph in the bulleted list, but before the ending period, insert a citation for Hagen, then save your changes.

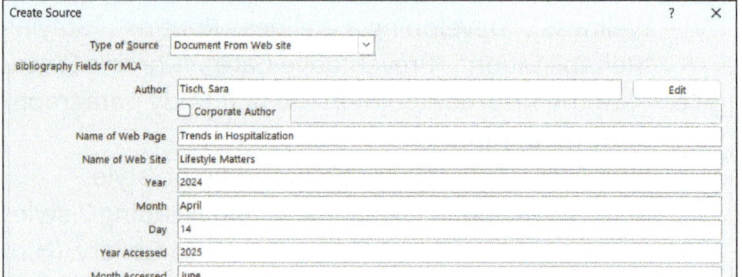

Figure 2-30

10. **Create a bibliography.**
    a. Press CTRL+END, then use the Bibliography command to insert a Works Cited list.
    b. Open the Source Manager dialog box.
    c. Delete the Mindfulness Institute source from the Current list.
    d. Select the source Tisch, Sara: ... in the Current List, click Edit, show all Bibliography fields, add the URL **www.lifestylematters.org** to the source, click OK, click Yes, then click Close.
    e. Update the bibliography field.
    f. With the bibliography field selected, click the Bibliographies button above the Bibliography field, then select References. Pages 1 and 3 of the formatted document are shown in **Figure 2-31**.
    g. Save your changes to the document, then submit it to your instructor without closing the document.

11. **Inspect a document.**
    a. Save a copy of the document as **IL_WD_2_Lifestyle_Inspected** to the drive and folder where you store your Data Files.
    b. Open the Navigation pane, click the Headings link, click the headings listed in the Navigation pane to scroll through the document, then close the Navigation pane.
    c. Use the Go To command to move the insertion point to the top of page 1.
    d. Use the Find and Replace dialog box to find all em dashes in the document, but do not replace the em dashes. (**Hint**: Scroll through the document using the Find Next button.)
    e. Use the Find and Replace dialog box to find text formatted with the Heading 2 style, but do not replace the text.
    f. Select a word in the document, look it up using the Search button on the References tab, then close the Search pane.
    g. Show the comments in the document, then, using the Review tab, delete all the comments in the document.
    h. Use the Check for Issues command to run the Document Inspector.
    i. Remove all document property and personal information data from the document, then save your changes.
    j. Submit a copy of the document to your instructor, close the document, then exit Word.

Figure 2-31

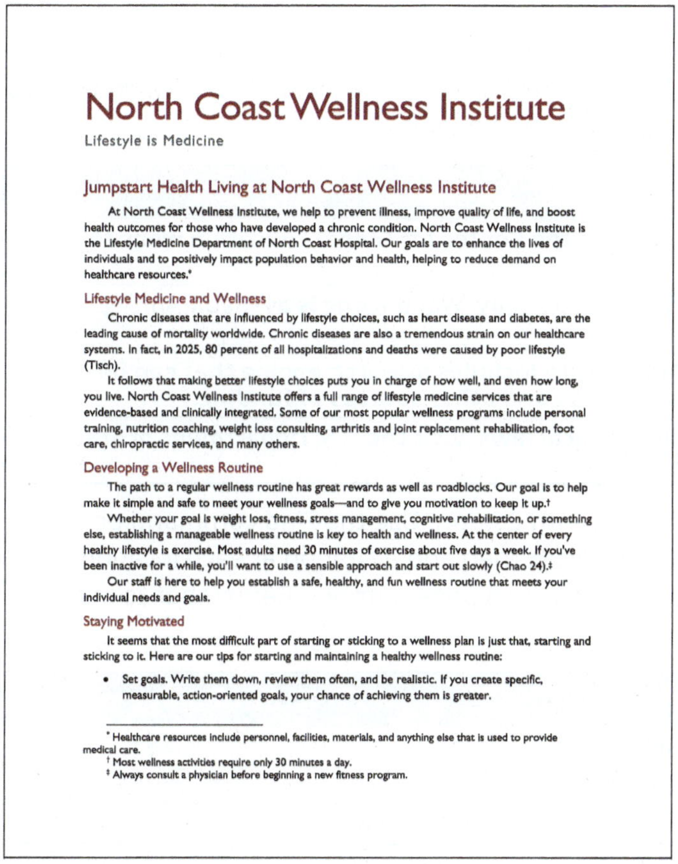

[Figure showing two pages of a North Coast Wellness Institute newsletter with headings: Jumpstart Health Living at North Coast Wellness Institute, Lifestyle Medicine and Wellness, Developing a Wellness Routine, Staying Motivated, Preventative Care, Chronic Disease Management, Community Education, References.]

Independent Challenge 1

The Center for Global Education at Coastal City College publishes a variety of newsletters and information reports related to work and study abroad opportunities for students. Your colleague has drafted the spring newsletter and forwarded the file to you. The file includes comments with instructions for finalizing the document. You need to add citations and footnotes and format the newsletter for distribution to patients.

   a. Start Word, open the file IL_WD_2-3.docx from the drive and folder where you store your Data Files, save it as **IL_WD_2_SpringNewsletter**, then read the document to get a feel for its contents.
   b. Show the comments in the document, scroll through the comments, reply to or resolve each comment, add a comment, then delete all comments from the document.
   c. Format the newsletter using styles. Apply the Title style to the purple text, the Heading 1 style to the blue text, the Heading 2 style to the green text, and the Heading 3 style to the dark orange text. (You will format the masthead after formatting the body of the document.)
   d. Apply a theme to the document. Choose a theme that suits the purpose and audience of the document. You can change the theme colors or style set if you wish.
   e. Change the font size of the title so that the title fits on one line, if necessary.
   f. Modify the Heading 1, Heading 2, and Heading 3 styles so that the font, font size, font color, and paragraph spacing of the headings gives the newsletter an attractive and cohesive appearance.
   g. Using styles, format the first three lines of the document as a masthead for the newsletter. The masthead for this document should not compete with the title of the document for attention. After applying styles, apply other formats, such as font size, font color, text effects, paragraph alignment, and borders to customize the look of the masthead.
   h. Add a header to the document using the Filigree header style. Type **Center for Global Education** in the Document title content control, then type your name in the Author content control. (**Hint**: If the Author content control shows different text, replace that text with your name.)
   i. Add a page number to the bottom of each page using the page number style of your choice.

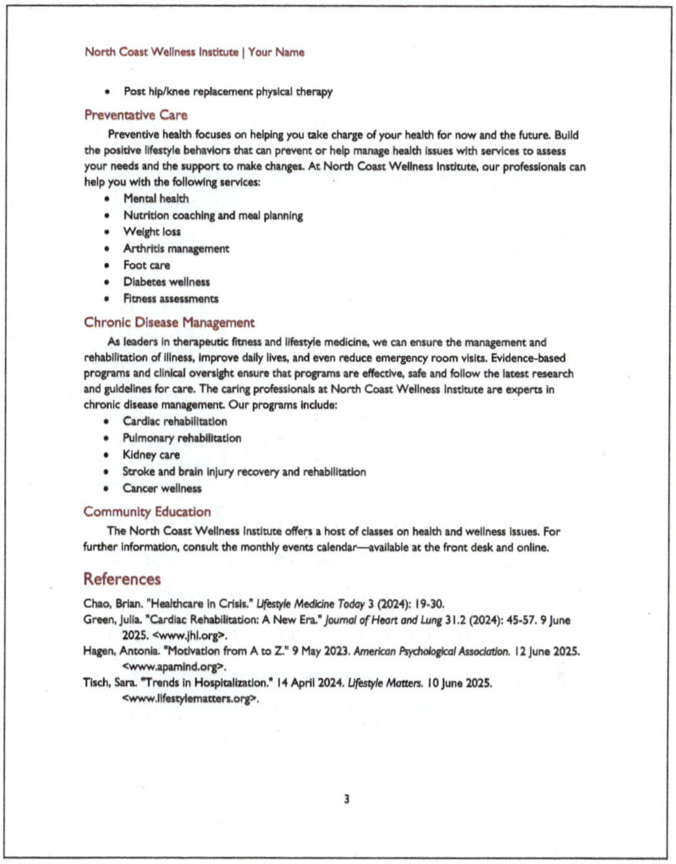

Independent Challenge 1 (Continued)

j. Remove headers and footers from the first page of the document.
k. Use the Find command or the Navigation pane to find the text specified in the table below, then add a footnote at each location, using the footnote text specified in the table.

Find text	Footnote text
best experiences of their lives	Testimonials are posted on the Center for Global Education website.
Australia (Perth, Wollongong)	Perth is available fall semester only. Wollongong is available spring semester only.
General Funding	The CCC Financial Aid website includes a search engine that can be used to identify scholarships and other sources of funding.
Laws and cultural attitudes in the host country	For more information on local laws, visit the U.S. Department of State and U.S. Embassy webpages.

l. Change the Citations and Bibliography style to MLA Seventh Edition. Use the Find command or the Navigation pane to find the text specified in the table below, then add a citation at each location, using the source specified in the table. Some citations include a page number. Remember to insert the citation before the period at the end of a sentence.

Find text	Citation source	Citation page number
study or work in another country	World Travel Institute	18
outcomes	World Health Organization	
public health concerns	Centers for Disease Control and Prevention	
Source:	Elliot, Margaret	132

m. Press CTRL+END, then add a bibliography to the newsletter.
n. Check the document for spelling and grammar errors, then use the thesaurus to replace a word with a synonym.
o. View the document in Multiple pages view, then make any formatting adjustments necessary so that the document flows smoothly between pages and is easy to read. **Figure 2-32** depicts a sample first page of the newsletter.
p. Save the document, submit a copy to your instructor, close the document, then exit Word.

Figure 2-32

Center for Global Education
Your student journey begins at CCC, but your path can take you across the globe.

Spring 2025 Newsletter

Internship and Study Abroad Opportunities

The Center for Global Education provides Coastal City College (CCC) students with off-campus study and internship experiences that foster an in-depth understanding of another culture, with the aim of encouraging students to develop the skills and understandings of global citizenship. Through our extensive range of program options, the Center for Global Education strives to provide CCC students with a transformative learning experience and marketable global skills.

Each year, roughly 25% of CCC students study abroad. Nationally, less than 3% of college and university students take advantage of the opportunity to study or work in another county (World Travel Institute 18). Most CCC students tell us that studying or working abroad was one of the best experiences of their lives.[1]

Global Study Programs
The Center for Global Education works with partner organizations and universities abroad to offer 120 study abroad programs in over 25 countries. A complete list of the study about programs available to students in the coming academic year is available on our website. Some of the destinations most popular with CCC students in recent years include the following:

- Australia (Perth, Wollongong)[2]
- Chile (Valparaiso)
- Hungary (Budapest)
- Japan (Matsumoto)
- Jordan (Amman)
- Kenya (Nairobi)
- Spain (Madrid)
- Vietnam (Hanoi)

Internships Abroad
CCC students can also apply for both part-time and full-time internship abroad opportunities. Part-time internships can be combined with study to create work and study experiences. A complete list of internship opportunities is available on the Center for Global Education website. Internships span a diversity of fields, including business, public policy, the arts, and others. An internship abroad is an excellent opportunity to develop your professional skills in a global context—giving you a distinct leg up when starting a career.

---

[1] Testimonials are posted on the Center for Global Education website.
[2] Perth is available for fall semester only. Wollongong is available for spring semester only.

Independent Challenge 2

As an administrative assistant at a research institute, you frequently format the research papers written by the researchers and policymakers of your department. The format recommended by the *MLA Handbook for Writers of Research Papers*, a style guide that includes information on preparing, writing, and formatting research papers, is the standard format used by many schools, colleges, and universities. In this independent challenge, you will research the MLA guidelines for formatting a research paper and use the guidelines you find to format the pages of a research report.

a. Use your favorite search engine to search the web for information on the MLA guidelines for formatting a research report. Use the keywords **MLA Style** and **research paper format** to conduct your search.

b. Look for information on the proper formatting for the following aspects of a research paper: paper size, margins, title page or first page of the report, line spacing, paragraph indentation, and page numbers. Also, find information on proper formatting for citations and a works cited page. Print the information you find.

c. Start Word, open the file IL_WD_2-4.docx from the drive and folder where you store your Data Files, then save it as **IL_WD_2_ResearchReport**. Using the information you learned, format this document as a research report.

d. Correct spelling and grammar errors in the document.

e. Adjust the margins, set the line spacing, and add page numbers to the document in the format recommended by the MLA. Use **The Affordable Housing Crisis: Challenges and Solutions** as the title for your sample report, use your name as the author name, and use the name of the course you are enrolled in currently as well as the instructor's name for that course. Make sure to format the title page exactly as the MLA style dictates.

Figure 2-33

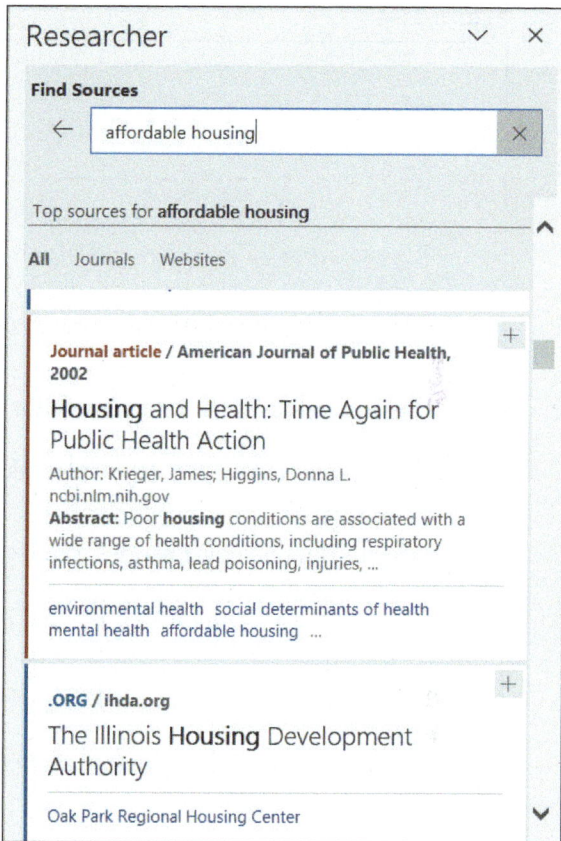

f. Format the remaining text as the body of the research report. Indent the first line of each paragraph rather than use quadruple spacing between paragraphs.

g. Create five sources and insert five citations in the document—including at least one journal article and one website. If possible, use the Researcher tool to add sources and citations. **Figure 2-33** depicts the Researcher pane with sample sources. You can also make up sources. (**Note**: For this practice document, you are allowed to make up sources. Never make up sources for real research papers.)

h. Add two citation placeholders to the document.

i. Create a works cited page, following MLA style. If necessary, edit the format of the citations and works cited page to conform to MLA format.

j. Save the document, submit a copy to your instructor, close the document, then exit Word.

Visual Workshop

Use a blank document to create the Works Cited page shown in **Figure 2-34**, then save the document as **IL_WD_2_GreenEnergyWorksCited**. Use 12-point Times New Roman for the text, double-space the lines in the document, and apply a hanging indent to the paragraphs in the list. Format "Works Cited" with the Heading 1 style and center the heading at the top of the document. Add your name and a page number to the header, then format the header text in 12-point Times New Roman. Correct spelling and grammar errors, remove the document property information from the file, then submit a copy to your instructor.

Figure 2-34

Your Name 1

Works Cited

Aran, Shea C. *Renewable Energy: Principles and Practices.* Sun Publishers, 2025.

Harris, Simon. "Renewable Power for Everyday Living." *Good Energy: Green from the Ground Up,* 18 Aug. 2024, www.goodenergy.com/article/renewable. Accessed 16 July 2025.

Hikari, Akira. "Solar Energy." *The Homeowner's Guide to Renewable Energy,* edited by Nuka Payne, Earth Press, 2025, pp. 209-17.

Roshni, Sushila. "Can Green Energy Replace Fossil Fuels?" *Green Energy Today,* www.greenenergytoday.org/replace-fossil-fuels.html. Accessed 14 July 2025.

Word Module 3

Formatting Text and Graphics

Case
You have been asked to finalize an event planning report for move-in week at MSIT that will be distributed to other departments. After formatting the headings in the report, you use tabs and create tables to organize the other information so that it is easy to understand. Finally, you illustrate the report with images, shapes, and SmartArt to help convey the friendly and welcoming tone of move-in week.

Module Objectives
After completing this module, you will be able to:

- Use the Format Painter
- Set and modify tabs
- Add borders and shading
- Insert a table
- Insert and delete rows and columns
- Apply a table style
- Insert online pictures
- Size and scale a graphic
- Draw and format shapes
- Adjust and rotate shapes
- Arrange graphic objects
- Create SmartArt graphics
- Add alt text to objects

Files You Will Need

IL_WD_3-1.docx
IL_WD_3-2.docx
IL_WD_3-3.docx
IL_WD_3-4.docx
IL_WD_3-5.docx

Use the Format Painter

Case You enhance the appearance of the title and headings in the report by applying different font styles and text effects. You also insert the date and a copyright symbol in the document to mark the planning stage and indicate the report content is proprietary.

Objectives
- Apply formatting
- Clear formatting
- Insert the date
- Insert special characters

You can dramatically change the appearance of text by applying different font styles, font effects, and character-spacing effects. When you are satisfied with the formatting of specific text, you can quickly apply the same formats to other text in the document using the Format Painter. The **Format Painter** is a powerful Word feature that allows you to copy all the format settings applied to selected text to other text that you want to format the same way.

Steps

1. **sam↓** Start **Word**, open the file **IL_WD_3-1.docx** from the location where you store your Data Files, then save it as **IL_WD_3_PlanningReport**

2. Select the title **Welcoming New Students to the MSIT Campus**, click the **Text Effects and Typography button** in the Font group on the Home tab, click the **Fill: Blue; Accent color 1; Shadow style** (the second WordArt style in the first row), click the **Font Size arrow**, click **24**, click the **Font Color arrow**, then click **Orange, Accent 2, Darker 25%**
   The title is formatted in a 24-point WordArt style, orange.

   Quick Tip: To change the WordArt style currently applied to text, select the text, click the Text Effects and Typography button, then select a different WordArt style from the gallery.

3. Select the heading **What Does the Move-in Team Do?** to display the Mini toolbar, click the **Font Size arrow**, click **14**, click the **Bold button** **B**, click the **Font Color arrow**, click the **Blue, Accent 1, Darker 25%** color in the theme colors, then deselect the text
   The heading is formatted in 14-point bold, dark blue.

4. Select **What Does the Move-in Team Do?**, then click the **Format Painter button** in the Clipboard group on the Home tab
   The pointer changes to a paintbrush icon.

   Trouble: Move the pointer over the document text to see the paintbrush.

5. Scroll down, drag to select the heading **Move-in Week Planning and Budgeting**, then deselect the text
   The heading is formatted in 14-point bold, and dark blue, as shown in **Figure 3-1**.

   Quick Tip: You can also click in the left margin to select the heading text.

6. Select **Move-in Week Planning and Budgeting** again, then double-click the **Format Painter button**
   Double-clicking the Format Painter button allows the Format Painter to remain active until you turn it off. By keeping the Format Painter active, you can apply formatting to multiple items.

7. Scroll down, select the headings **Recruiting Move-in Team Volunteers** and **Administrative Team for Move-in Week**, then click the **Format Painter button** to turn off the Format Painter
   The headings are formatted in 14-point bold, and dark blue.

   Quick Tip: You can also press ESC to turn off the Format Painter.

8. Press **CTRL+END**, type **Prepared by**, press **SPACEBAR** and type your name followed by a comma, press **SPACEBAR**, click the **Insert tab**, then click the **Date and Time button** in the Text group
   The Date and Time dialog box opens with available formats for inserting the date and time.

   Quick Tip: To insert the date as a field that is updated automatically, select the Update automatically check box.

9. Select the **third format** in the list, click **OK** to insert the current date at the insertion point, press **ENTER**, then click the **Symbol button** in the Symbols group
   A gallery of commonly used symbols opens similar to the one in **Figure 3-2**. You may see a different selection of symbols depending on which symbols you insert most frequently. You can insert a symbol from this gallery or click More Symbols to open a larger gallery of symbols.

10. Click the **copyright symbol ©** in the gallery, press **SPACEBAR**, type **Mountain Springs Institute of Technology**, click the **Home tab**, press **CTRL+HOME**, then save your changes
    The copyright symbol is inserted before Mountain Springs Institute of Technology.

    Trouble: If you do not see the copyright symbol, click More Symbols, select the code in the Character code box, type 00A9, click Insert, then click Close.

Figure 3-1: Formats copied and applied using the Format Painter

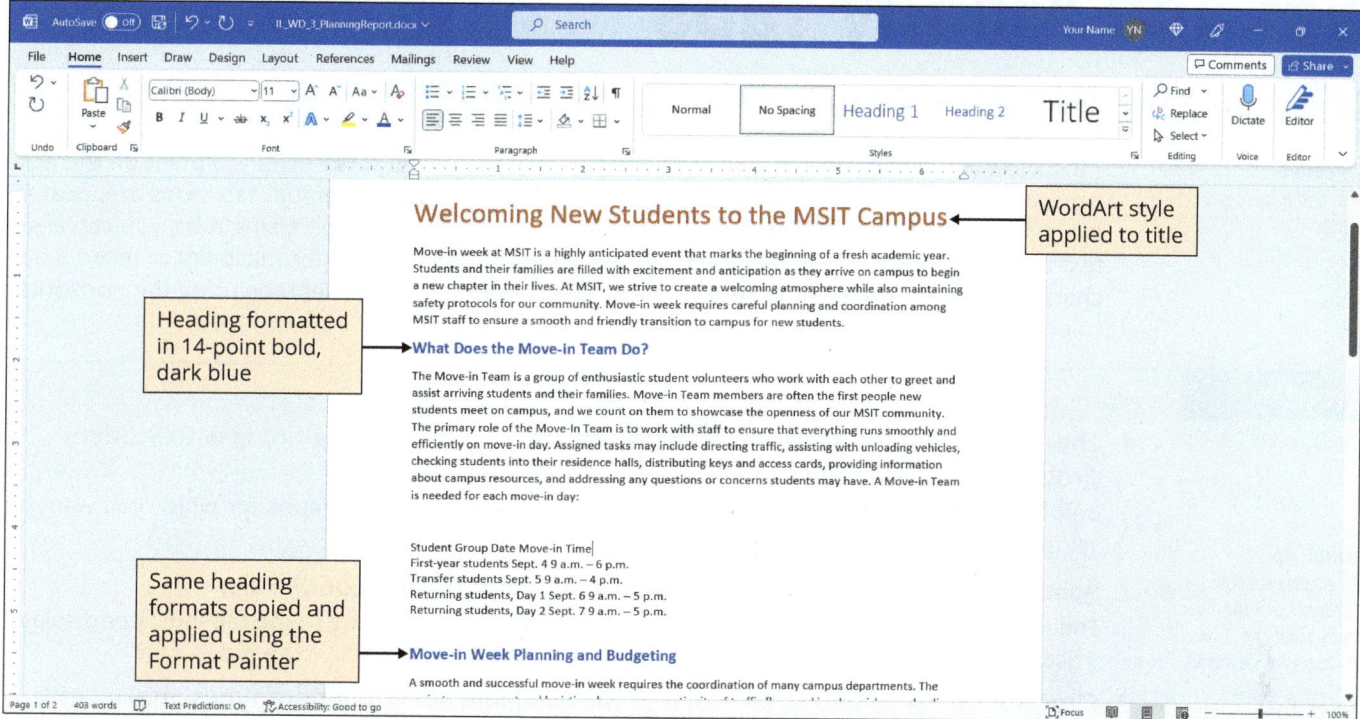

Figure 3-2: Symbol gallery

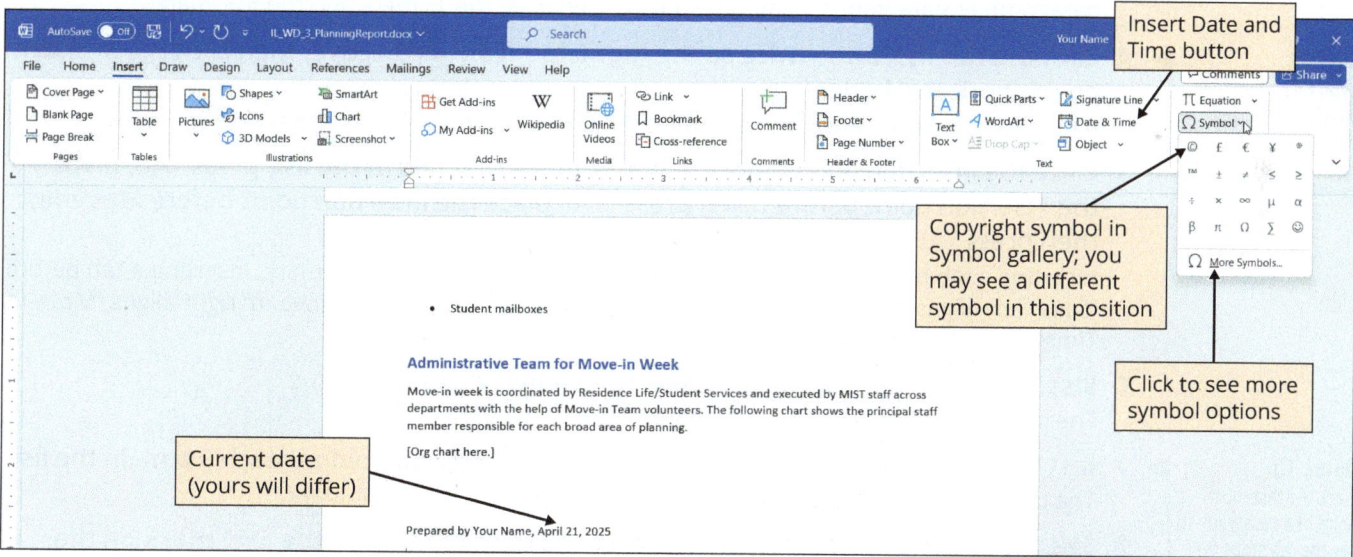

Clearing formatting from text

If you are unhappy with the way text is formatted, you can use the Clear All Formatting command to return the text to the default format settings. The default format includes font and paragraph formatting: text is formatted in 11-point Calibri, and paragraphs are left-aligned with 1.08 points of space between lines, 8 points of space after paragraphs, and no indents. To clear formatting from text and return it to the default format, select the text you want to clear, and then click the Clear All Formatting button in the Font group on the Home tab. If you prefer to return the text to the default font and remove all paragraph formatting, making the text 11-point Calibri, left-aligned, single-spaced, with no paragraph spacing or indents, select the text and then click the No Spacing button in the Styles group on the Home tab.

Set and Modify Tabs

Case You use tabs to format the move-in date and time information so that it is easy to read.

Objective
- Set and modify tab stops

Tabs allow you to align text at a specific location in a document. A **tab stop** is a point on the horizontal ruler that indicates the location at which to align text. By default, tab stops are located every ½" from the left margin, but you can also set custom tab stops. Using tabs, you can align text to the left, right, or center of a tab stop, or you can align text at a decimal point or insert a bar character. **Table 3-1** describes the different types of tab stops. You set tabs using the horizontal ruler or the Tabs dialog box.

Steps

1. **Change the zoom level to 140, then select the five-line list beginning with Student Group Date Move-in Time**
   Before you set tab stops for existing text, you must select the paragraphs for which you want to set tabs.

   Quick Tip
   If the rulers are not displayed, click the Ruler check box in the Show group on the View tab.

2. **Point to the tab indicator ⌐ at the far-left end of the horizontal ruler**
   The icon in the tab indicator indicates the active type of tab; pointing to the tab indicator displays a ScreenTip naming the active tab type. By default, left tab is the active tab type.

   Quick Tip
   To remove a tab stop, drag it off the ruler.

3. **Click the tab indicator to see each of the available tab and indent types, make Left Tab ⌐ the active tab type, click the 1" mark on the horizontal ruler, then click the 3¼" mark on the horizontal ruler**
   Clicking the horizontal ruler near the bottom inserts a tab stop of the active type for the selected paragraph or paragraphs. A left tab stop is inserted at the 1" mark and the 3¼" mark.

   Trouble
   If you click more than twice, keep clicking until the Right Tab icon again appears.

4. **Click the tab indicator twice so the Right Tab icon ⌐ is active, then click the 5" mark on the horizontal ruler**
   A right tab stop is inserted at the 5" mark on the horizontal ruler, as shown in **Figure 3-3**.

5. **Place the insertion point before Student in the first line in the list, press TAB, place the insertion point before Date, press TAB, place the insertion point before Move-in, then press TAB**
   Inserting a tab before "Student" left-aligns "Student Group" at the 1" mark, inserting a tab before "Date" left-aligns "Date" at the 3¼" mark, and inserting a tab before "Move-in" right-aligns "Move-in Time" at the 5" mark.

6. **Insert a tab at the beginning of each remaining line in the list**
   The paragraphs left-align at the 1" mark.

   Quick Tip
   Place the insertion point in a paragraph to see the tab stops for that paragraph on the horizontal ruler.

7. **Insert a tab before each Sept. in the list, then insert a tab before each 9 a.m. in the list**
   The dates left-align at the 3¼" mark. The times right-align at the 5" mark.

8. **Select the five lines of tabbed text, drag the right tab stop to the 5½" mark on the horizontal ruler, then deselect the text**
   Dragging the tab stop moves it to a new location. The times right-align at the 5½" mark.

   Quick Tip
   Double-click a tab stop on the ruler to open the Tabs dialog box.

9. **Select the last four lines of tabbed text, click the Launcher ⌐ in the Paragraph group, then click Tabs at the bottom of the Paragraph dialog box**
   The Tabs dialog box opens, as shown in **Figure 3-4**. You can use the Tabs dialog box to set tab stops, change the position or alignment of existing tab stops, clear tab stops, and apply tab leaders to tabs. **Tab leaders** are lines that appear in front of tabbed text.

   Quick Tip
   In the Tabs dialog box, click Set after changing the settings for each tab stop.

10. **Click 3.25" in the Tab stop position list box, click the 2 option button in the Leader section, click Set, click 5.5" in the Tab stop position list box, click the 2 option button in the Leader section, click Set, click OK, deselect the text, then save your changes**
    A dotted tab leader is added before each 3.25" and 5.5" tab stop in the last four lines of tabbed text, as shown in **Figure 3-5**.

Figure 3-3: Left and right tab stops on the horizontal ruler

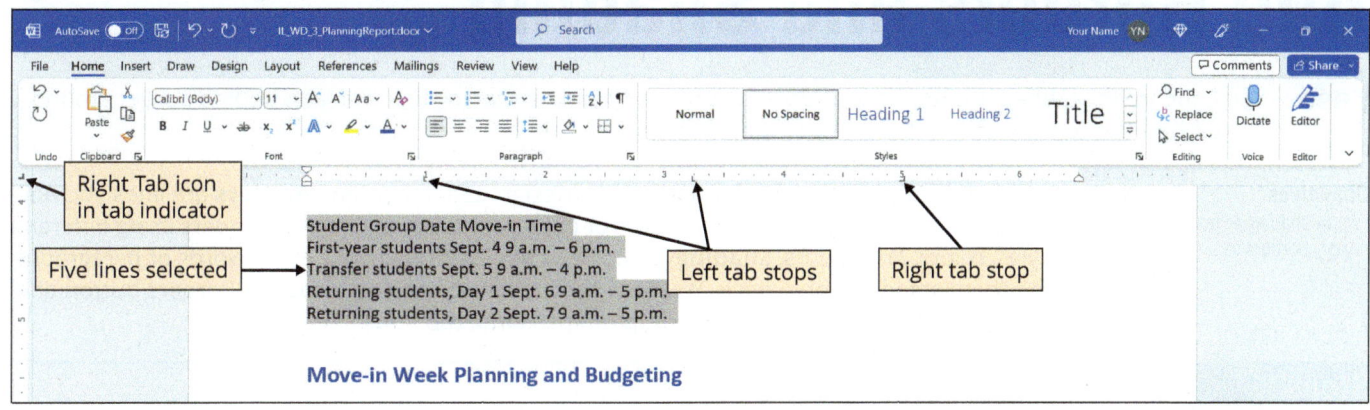

Figure 3-4: Tabs dialog box

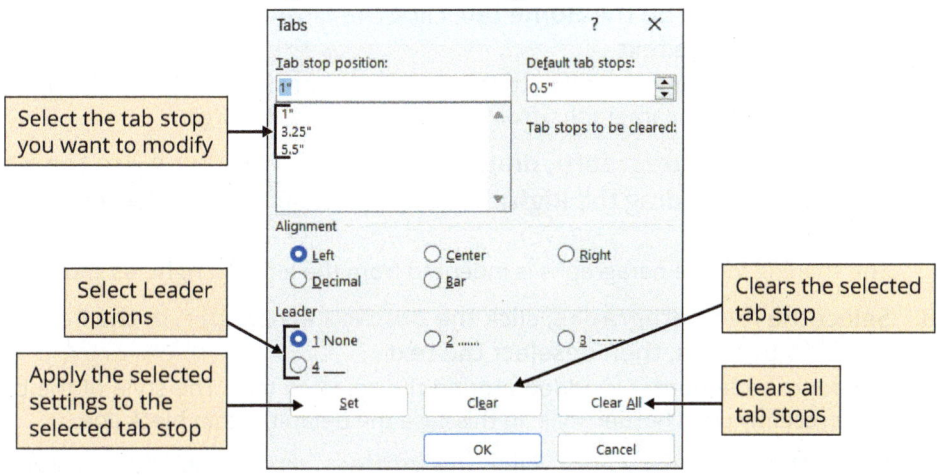

Figure 3-5: Tab leaders

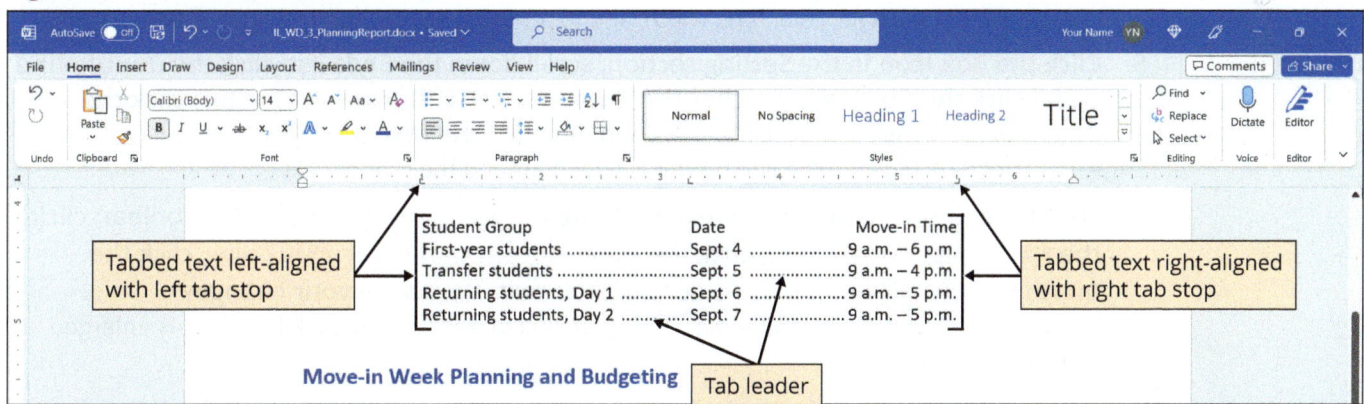

Table 3-1: Types of tabs

tab	use to
Left tab	Set the start position of text so that text runs to the right of the tab stop as you type
Center tab	Set the center align position of text so that text stays centered on the tab stop as you type
Right tab	Set the right or end position of text so that text moves to the left of the tab stop as you type
Decimal tab	Set the position of the decimal point so that numbers align around the decimal point as you type
Bar tab	Insert a vertical bar at the tab position

Add Borders and Shading

Case You enhance the tabbed text for move-in dates and times by adding shading to it. You also apply a border around the tabbed text to set it off from the rest of the document.

Objectives
- Apply shading to text
- Apply borders to text

Borders and shading can add color and artistic design to a document. **Borders** are lines you add above, below, to either side, or around words or paragraphs. You can format borders using different line styles, colors, and widths. **Shading** is a color or pattern you apply behind words or paragraphs to make them stand out on a page. You apply borders and shading using the Borders button and the Shading button in the Paragraph group on the Home tab.

Steps

1. Select the **five paragraphs** of tabbed text, click the **Shading arrow** in the Paragraph group on the Home tab, click the **Orange, Accent 2, Lighter 60% color**, then deselect the text
   Light orange shading is applied to the five paragraphs. Notice that the shading is applied to the entire width of the paragraphs, from the left to the right margin.

2. Select the **five paragraphs**, drag the **Left Indent marker** to the ¾" mark on the horizontal ruler, drag the **Right Indent marker** to the 5¾" mark, then deselect the text
   The shading for the paragraphs is indented from the left and right, as shown in **Figure 3-6**.

3. Select the **five paragraphs**, click the **Borders arrow** in the Paragraph group, click **Outside Borders**, then deselect the text
   A black outside border is added around the selected text. The style of the border added is the most recently used border style, in this case the default, a thin black line.

4. Select the **five paragraphs**, click the **Borders arrow**, click **No Border**, click the **Borders arrow**, then click **Borders and Shading**
   The Borders and Shading dialog box opens, as shown in **Figure 3-7**. You use the Borders tab to change the border style, color, and width, and to add boxes and lines to words or paragraphs.

5. Click the **Box icon** in the Setting section, scroll down the Style list, click the **double-line style**, click the **Color arrow**, click the **Blue, Accent 1, Darker 25% color**, click the **Width arrow**, click **1½ pt**, click **OK**, then deselect the text
   A 1½-point dark blue double-line border is added around the tabbed text.

6. Select the **first line** of tabbed text, click the **Bold button** on the Mini toolbar, click the **Font Color arrow**, click the **Blue, Accent 1, Darker 25% color**, click the **Increase Font Size button**, deselect the text, then save your changes
   The Student Group, Date, and Move-in Time text changes to bold dark blue and is enlarged, as shown in **Figure 3-8**.

Underlining text

Another way to call attention to text and enhance the appearance of a document is to apply an underline style to words you want to highlight. The Underline arrow in the Font group displays straight, dotted, wavy, dashed, and mixed underline styles, along with a gallery of colors to choose from. To apply an underline to text, select it, click the Underline arrow, and then select an underline style from the list. For a wider variety of underline styles, click More Underlines in the list, and then select an underline style in the Font dialog box. You can change the color of an underline at any time by selecting the underlined text, clicking the Underline arrow, pointing to Underline Color, and then choosing from the options in the color gallery. If you want to remove an underline from text, select the underlined text, and then click the Underline button.

Figure 3-6: Shading applied to the tabbed text

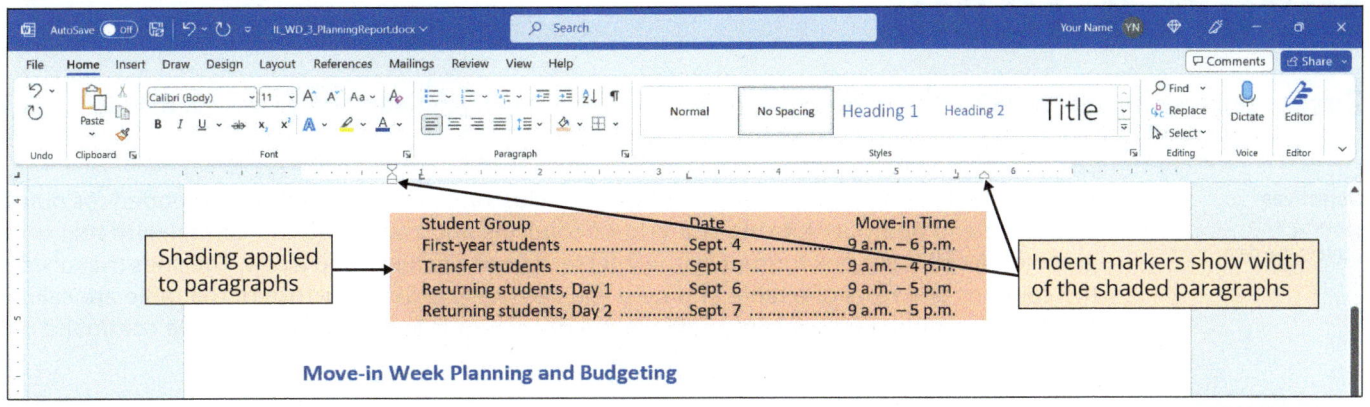

Figure 3-7: Borders tab in Borders and Shading dialog box

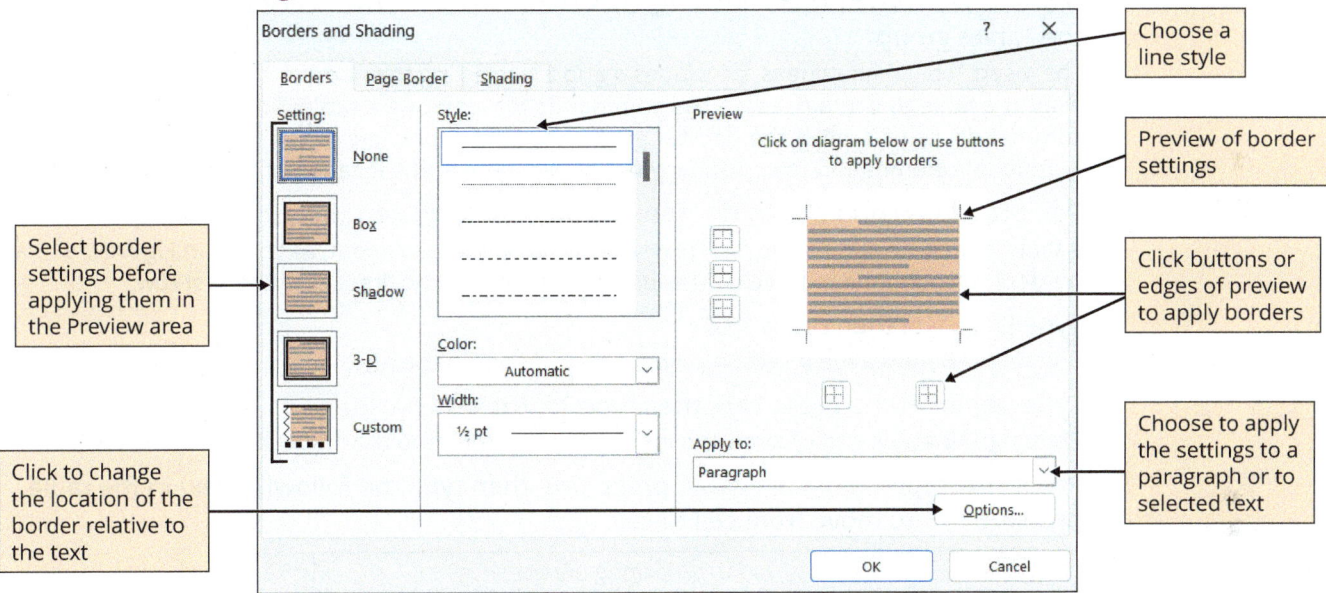

Figure 3-8: Borders and shading applied to the document

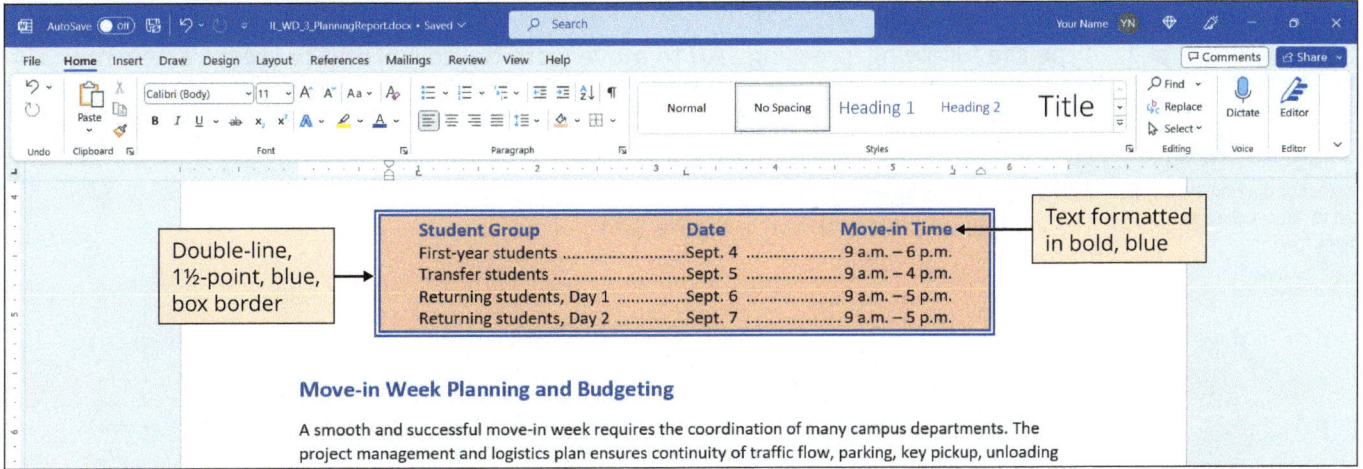

Module 3 Formatting Text and Graphics

Insert a Table

Case You need to add the budget for move-in week to the report. The budget data will be easiest to read if it is organized as a table, so you insert a blank table and add the data to it.

Objectives
- Insert a table
- Enter table data

Adding a table to a document is a useful way to illustrate information that is intended for quick reference and analysis. A **table** is a grid of columns and rows that you can fill with text and graphics. A **cell** is the box formed by the intersection of a column and a row. The lines that divide the columns and rows of a table and help you see the grid-like structure of the table are called **borders**. A simple way to insert a table into a document is to use the Insert Table command on the Insert tab.

Steps

1. Scroll down, place the insertion point in the **blank paragraph** above the Recruiting Move-in Team Volunteers heading, click the **Insert tab**, then click the **Table button** in the Tables group

   The Insert Table menu opens. It includes a grid for selecting the number of columns and rows you want the table to contain, as well as commands for inserting a table. **Table 3-2** describes these commands. As you move the pointer across the grid, a preview of the table with the specified number of columns and rows appears in the document at the location of the insertion point.

2. Point to the **second box in the fourth row** to select **2x4 Table**, then click

   A table with two columns and four rows is inserted in the document, as shown in **Figure 3-9**. Black borders surround the table cells. The insertion point is in the first cell in the first row.

3. Type **Expense**, then press **TAB**

   Pressing TAB moves the insertion point to the next cell in the row.

4. Type **Department**, press **TAB**, then type **Traffic and parking**

   Pressing TAB at the end of a row moves the insertion point to the first cell in the next row.

5. Press **TAB**, type **Transportation**, press **TAB**, then type the following text in the table, pressing **TAB** to move from cell to cell

Signage	Printing Services
Move-in staffing and information	Residence Life/Student Services

6. Press **TAB**

   Pressing TAB at the end of the last cell of a table creates a new row at the bottom of the table, as shown in **Figure 3-10**. The insertion point is located in the first cell in the new row.

Trouble
If you pressed TAB after the last row, click the Undo button on the Quick Access toolbar or the Home tab to remove the new blank row.

7. Type the following, pressing **TAB** to move from cell to cell and to create a new row

Technology	IT
Tents and moving equipment	Facilities

8. Save your changes

   The completed table is shown in **Figure 3-11**.

Figure 3-9: Blank table

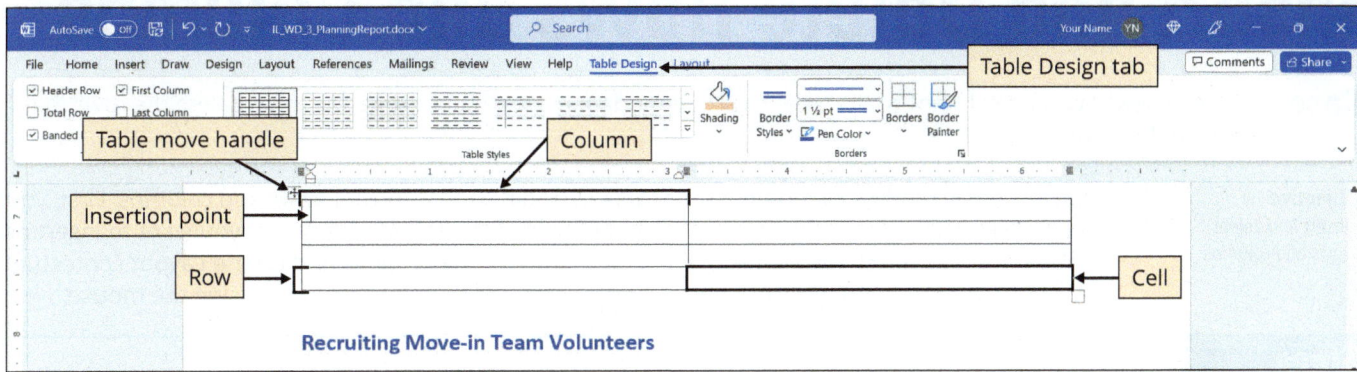

Figure 3-10: New row in table

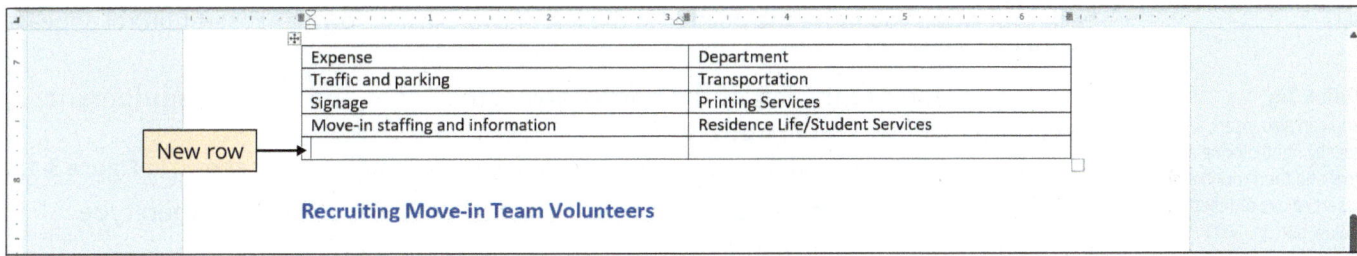

Figure 3-11: Text in the table

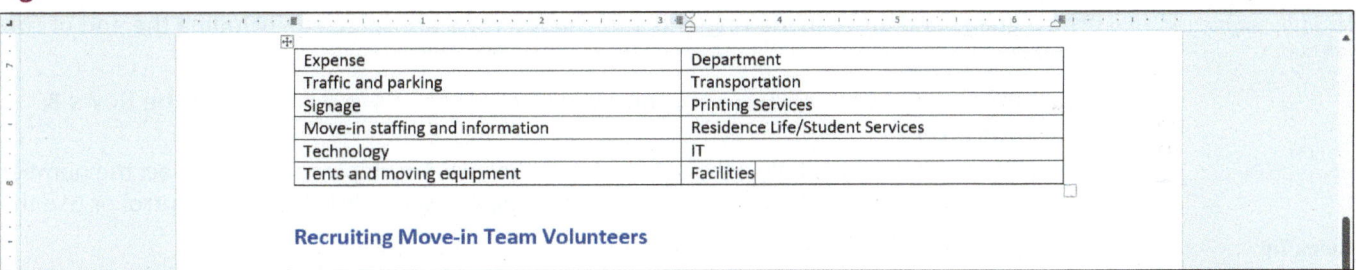

Table 3-2: Table menu commands

command	use to
Insert Table	Create a table with any number of columns and rows and select an AutoFit behavior
Draw Table	Create a complex table by drawing the table columns and rows
Convert Text to Table	Convert text that is separated by tabs, commas, or another separator character into a table
Excel Spreadsheet	Insert a blank Excel worksheet into the document as an embedded object
Quick Tables	Insert a preformatted table template and replace the placeholder data with your own data

Insert and Delete Rows and Columns

Case You add new rows and columns to the table to accommodate more expense data. You also delete the rows that prove to be unnecessary.

Objective
- Insert and delete rows and columns

You can easily modify the structure of a table by adding and removing rows and columns. First, you must click or select an existing row or column in the table to indicate where you want to insert or delete. You can select any element of a table using the Select command on the Layout contextual tab, but it is often more direct to select, add, and delete rows and columns using the mouse.

Steps

1. Click the **Home tab**, click the **Show/Hide ¶ button** ¶ in the Paragraph group to display formatting marks, then move the pointer up and down the left edge of the table

   An end of cell mark appears at the end of each cell, and an end of row mark appears at the end of each row. When you move the pointer to the left of two existing rows, an Insert Control appears outside the table.

   Quick Tip: You can also insert a row by right-clicking a row and then clicking Insert Above or Insert Below button.

2. Move the pointer to the left of the border above the **Tents and moving equipment row**, then click the **Insert Control**

   A new row is inserted directly above the Tents and moving equipment row, as shown in **Figure 3-12**.

3. Click the **first cell** of the new row, type **Water and first aid**, press **TAB**, then type **Environmental Health and Safety**

   Quick Tip: If the end of row mark is not selected, you have selected only the text in the row, not the row itself.

4. Place the pointer in the margin to the left of the **Signage row** until the pointer changes to ⬈, click to select the row, press and hold the mouse button, drag down to select the **Move-in staffing and information row**, then release the mouse button

   The Signage and Move-in staffing and information rows are selected, including the end of row marks.

5. Click the **Layout contextual tab**, then click the **Insert Below button** in the Rows & Columns group

   Two new rows are added below the selected rows. To insert multiple rows, you select the number of rows you want to insert before inserting the rows, and then click an Insert Control or use the buttons on the Ribbon.

   Quick Tip: If you select a row and press DELETE, you delete only the contents of the row, not the row itself.

6. Click the **Technology row**, click the **Delete button** in the Rows & Columns group, click **Delete Rows**, select the **two blank rows**, click the **Delete button** on the Mini toolbar, then click **Delete Rows**

   The Technology row and the two blank rows are deleted.

   Quick Tip: To select a cell, place the pointer near the left border of the cell, then click.

7. Place the pointer over the top border of the **Department column** until the pointer changes to ⬇, then click to select the entire column

8. Click the **Insert Right button** in the Rows & Columns group, then type **Code**

   A new column is inserted to the right of the Department column, as shown in **Figure 3-13**.

9. Place the pointer over the border between the **Department** and **Code columns** at the top of the table, click the **Insert Control**, then type **Budget** in the first cell of the new column

   A new column for Budget is added between the Department and Code columns.

   Quick Tip: You can use the arrow keys or press TAB to move the insertion point from cell to cell.

10. Press **DOWN ARROW** to move the insertion point to the next cell in the Budget column, click the **Home tab**, click ¶ to turn off the display of formatting marks, enter the text shown in **Figure 3-14** in each cell in the Budget and Code columns, then save your changes

    Compare your table to **Figure 3-14**.

Figure 3-12: Inserted row

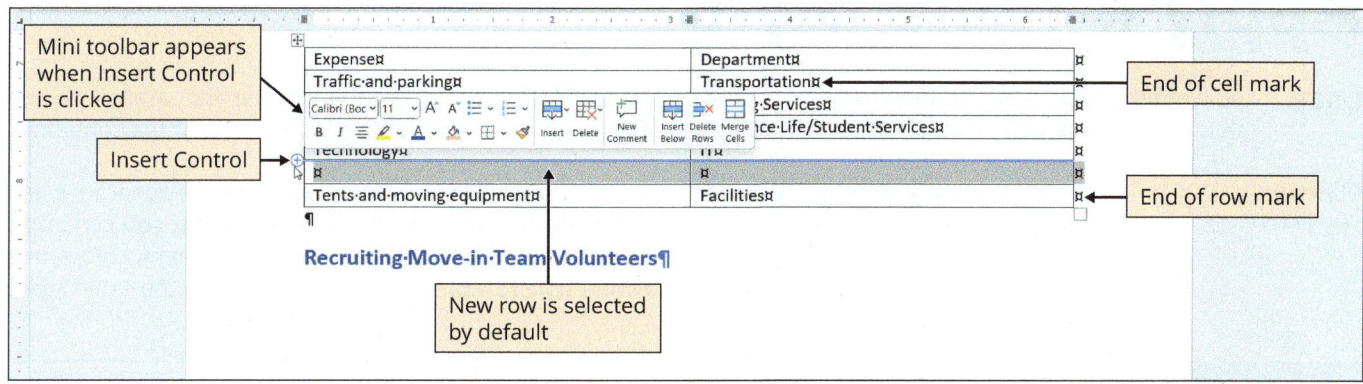

Figure 3-13: Inserted column

Expense¤	Department¤	Code¤
Traffic·and·parking¤	Transportation¤	¤
Signage¤	Printing·Services¤	¤
Move-in·staffing·and·information¤	Residence·Life/Student·Services¤	¤
Water·and·first·aid¤	Environmental·Health·and·Safety¤	¤
Tents·and·moving·equipment¤	Facilities¤	¤

Recruiting·Move-in·Team·Volunteers¶

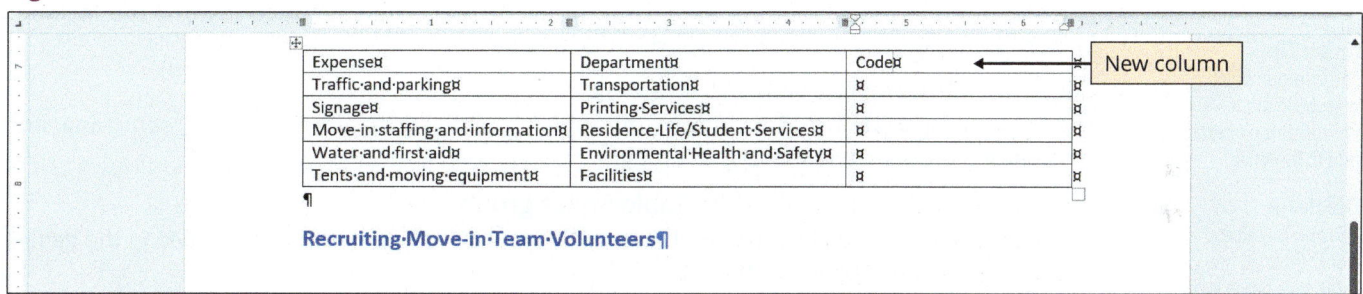

Figure 3-14: Text in Budget and Code columns

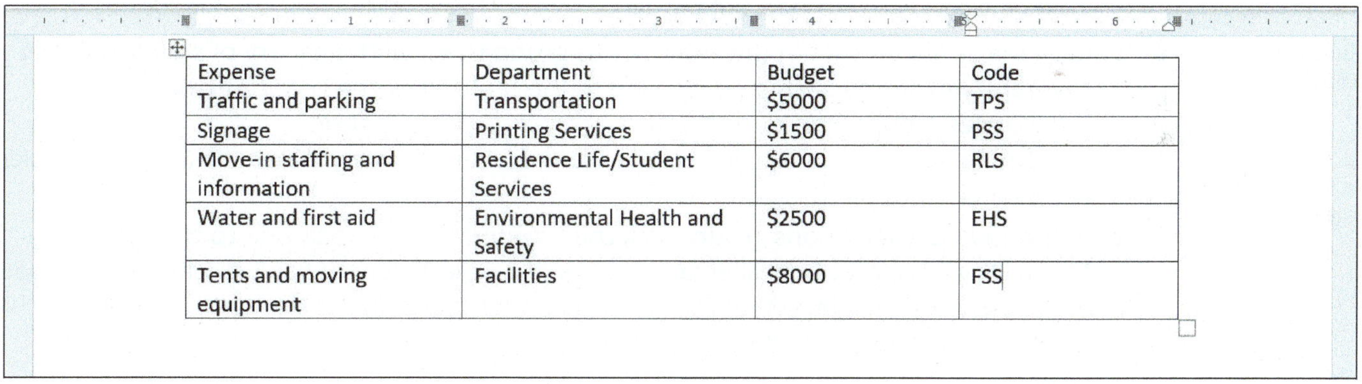

Expense	Department	Budget	Code
Traffic and parking	Transportation	$5000	TPS
Signage	Printing Services	$1500	PSS
Move-in staffing and information	Residence Life/Student Services	$6000	RLS
Water and first aid	Environmental Health and Safety	$2500	EHS
Tents and moving equipment	Facilities	$8000	FSS

Apply a Table Style

Case You want the budget information to stand out, so you apply a table style that enhances the appearance of the table and makes it easier to read. Before applying a style, you adjust the width of the columns to fit the contents.

Objective
- Apply a table style

Adding shading and other design elements to a table can help give it a polished appearance and make the data easier to read. Word includes predefined, built-in table styles that you can apply to a table to format it quickly. Table styles include borders, shading, fonts, alignment, colors, and other formatting effects. You can apply a table style to a table using the buttons in the Table Styles group on the Table Design tab.

Steps

1. **Click the Layout contextual tab, click the AutoFit button in the Cell Size group, then click AutoFit Contents**
   The width of the table columns is adjusted to fit the text. The Layout contextual tab includes buttons for modifying the structure and size of a table.

   > **Quick Tip**: The insertion point must be in the table for the table contextual tabs to be active.

2. **Click the Table Design tab**
   The Table Design tab includes buttons for applying table styles and for adding, removing, and customizing borders and shading in a table.

3. **Click the More button in the Table Styles group**
   The gallery of table styles opens, as shown in **Figure 3-15**. You point to a table style in the gallery to preview the style applied to the table.

   > **Quick Tip**: The number after the word "Table" in the Table style name is the row identifier in the gallery of table styles.

4. **Move the pointer over the styles in the gallery, then click the Grid Table 5 Dark - Accent 1 style**
   The Grid Table 5 Dark - Accent 1 style is applied to the table, as shown in **Figure 3-16**. This style makes the data easier to read, but the dark colors are heavy for the tone of your document.

5. **Click the scroll arrows in the Table Styles group to scroll the gallery of styles, point to several styles to see each style applied to the table, click the More button in the Table Styles group, then click the Grid Table 3 - Accent 3 style**
   The Grid Table 3 - Accent 3 style is applied to the table. This style makes the table data easier to read.

   > **Quick Tip**: Click Clear in the gallery of table styles to remove all borders, shading, and other style elements from a table.

6. **In the Table Style Options group, click the Banded Rows check box to clear it**
   The shading is removed from alternating rows in the table. When the banded columns or banded rows setting is active, the odd columns or rows are formatted differently from the even columns or rows to make the table data easier to read.

7. **Select the first column of the table, click the Font Color arrow on the Mini toolbar, click Orange, Accent 2, Darker 50%, select the first row of the table, click, then click Blue, Accent 1, Darker 25%**
   The text in the first column is dark orange and the text in the header row is blue.

8. **Select the Budget and Code columns, then click the Center button on the Mini toolbar**
   The text in the Budget and Code columns is center-aligned. You can also use the buttons in the Alignment group on the Layout contextual tab to change the alignment of text in cells.

9. **Click the table move handle, click the Home tab, click the Center button in the Paragraph group on the Ribbon, then deselect the table**
   Clicking the table move handle selects the entire table. Clicking the Center button with the entire table selected centered the table between the margins, as shown in **Figure 3-17**.

   > **Quick Tip**: You can also use the Select button in the Table group on the Layout contextual tab to select a table, row, column, or cell.

10. **Press CTRL+HOME, then save your changes**

Figure 3-15: Gallery of table styles

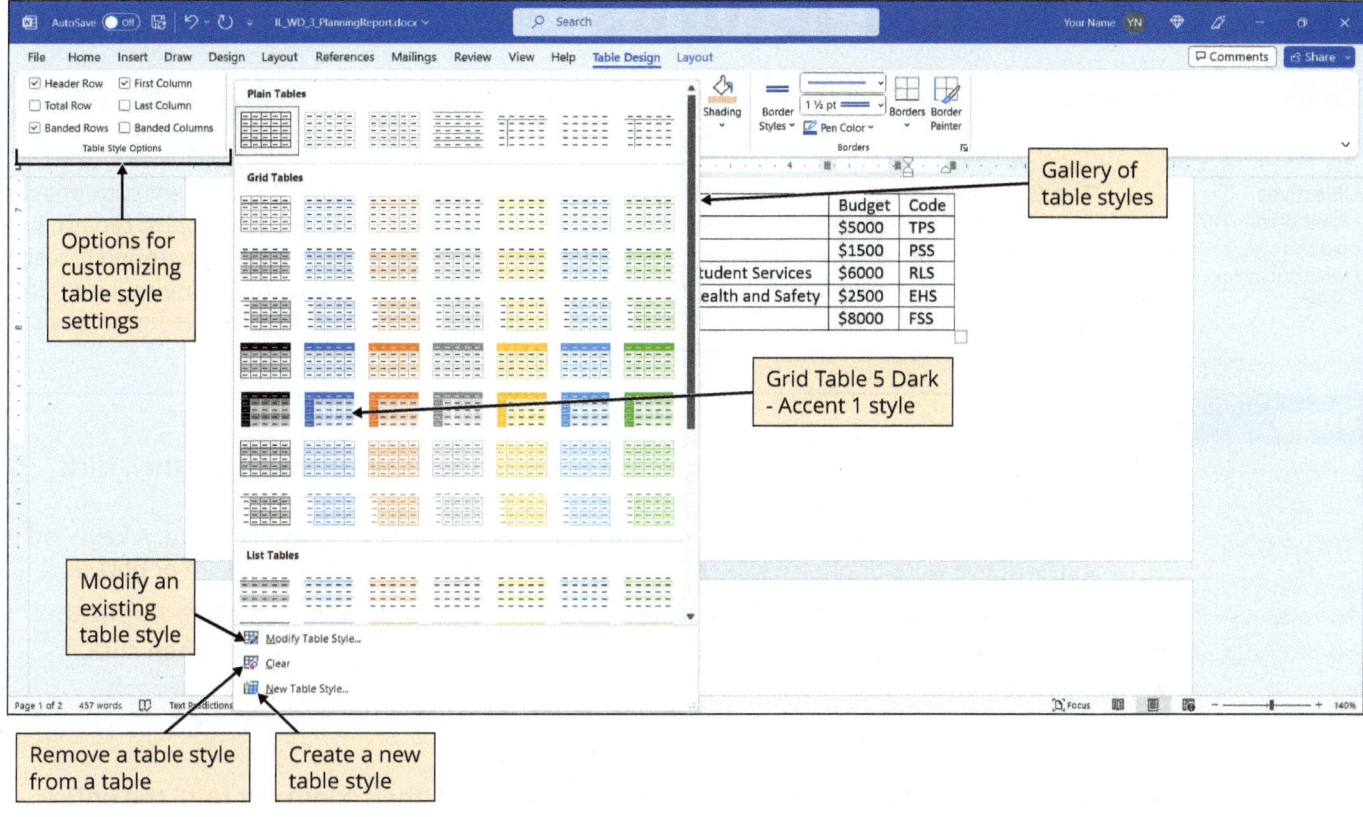

Figure 3-16: Grid Table 5 Dark - Accent 1 style applied to table

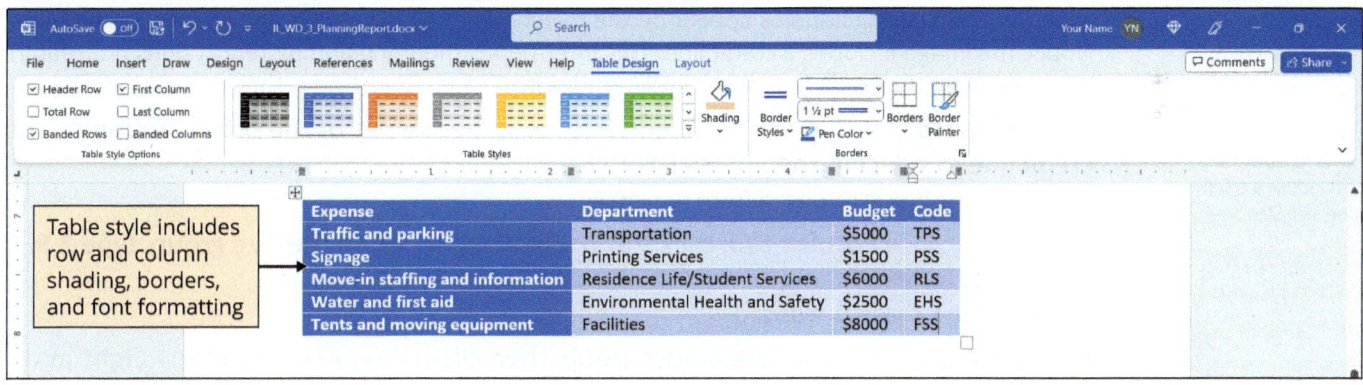

Figure 3-17: Completed table

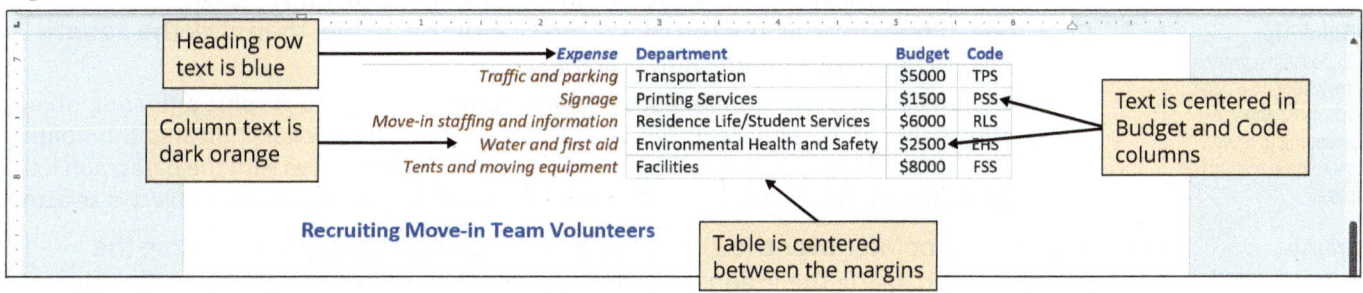

Insert Online Pictures

Case You illustrate the document with an online image that expresses the upbeat mood of move-in day. Note: To complete this lesson, your computer must be connected to the Internet.

Objectives
- Insert online pictures
- Wrap text around objects

The Online Pictures command on the Insert tab allows you to illustrate a document with images found online through Bing Image Search. These online pictures include photographs, clip art, line drawings, and other types of images. Once you insert an image, you can wrap text around it, resize it, enhance it, and move it to a different location. Always carefully review any license requirements for an image before you include it in a document. Images licensed under Creative Commons can be used by the public but carry copyright restrictions.

Steps

1. **Click the Insert tab, click the Pictures button in the Illustrations group, then click Online Pictures**
   The Online Pictures window opens. You can search for images related to a keyword. A **keyword** is a descriptive word or phrase you enter to obtain an image described by the word or phrase.

2. **Type college students in the search box, press ENTER, click the Creative Commons only check box if it is not already selected, click the Filter button, then click Clipart**
   Clip art images that have the keywords "college students" associated with them appear in the Online Pictures window, as shown in **Figure 3-18**.

   Trouble: Select a different image that has similar rectangular dimensions if the image shown in **Figure 3-18** is not available to you.

3. **Click the image called out in Figure 3-18, click Insert, then zoom out until the entire image is visible on your screen**
   The image is inserted as an inline graphic at the location of the insertion point, as shown in **Figure 3-19**. Until you apply text wrapping to an inline graphic, it is part of the line of text in which it was inserted. Sizing handles appear on the rectangular edges of the graphic when it is selected. Notice the image includes a credit line. This inter-departmental planning report does not require that you retain the credit line, so you will remove it.

   Trouble: If your graphic does not include a credit line, skip Step 5.

4. **Click the word Unknown in the credit line, click the border of the box surrounding the credit line to select it, then press DELETE**
   The credit line box is removed from the image.

5. **Click the Picture Format tab, click the Shape Height box in the Size group, type 2.5, then press Enter**
   The size of the image is reduced.

6. **Click the Color button in the Adjust group, then click Blue, Accent color 1 Light in the Recolor section**
   The color of the image changes from multi-colored to shades of blue. To move a graphic independently of the line of text in which it was inserted, you must make it a floating graphic.

   Quick Tip: To position a graphic anywhere on a page, you must apply text wrapping to it even if there is no text on the page.

7. **Click the Layout Options button on the side of the image, then click the Square button in the With Text Wrapping section**
   The text wraps around the square sides of the graphic, making the graphic a floating object. Notice the anchor that appears to the left of the graphic. The anchor indicates the floating graphic is **anchored** to the nearest paragraph so that the graphic moves with the paragraph if the paragraph is moved. The anchor is a nonprinting symbol that appears when an object is selected.

   Trouble: If green alignment guides do not appear, click the Align Objects button in the Arrange group, then click Use Alignment Guides.

8. **Position the pointer over the graphic, when the pointer changes to, drag the graphic down, using the green alignment guides that appear, so its top is directly under the document title and its left aligns with the left margin, as shown in Figure 3-20, then release the mouse button**
   The graphic is positioned below the title on the left side of the page.

9. **Deselect the graphic, then save your changes**

Figure 3-18: Online Pictures window

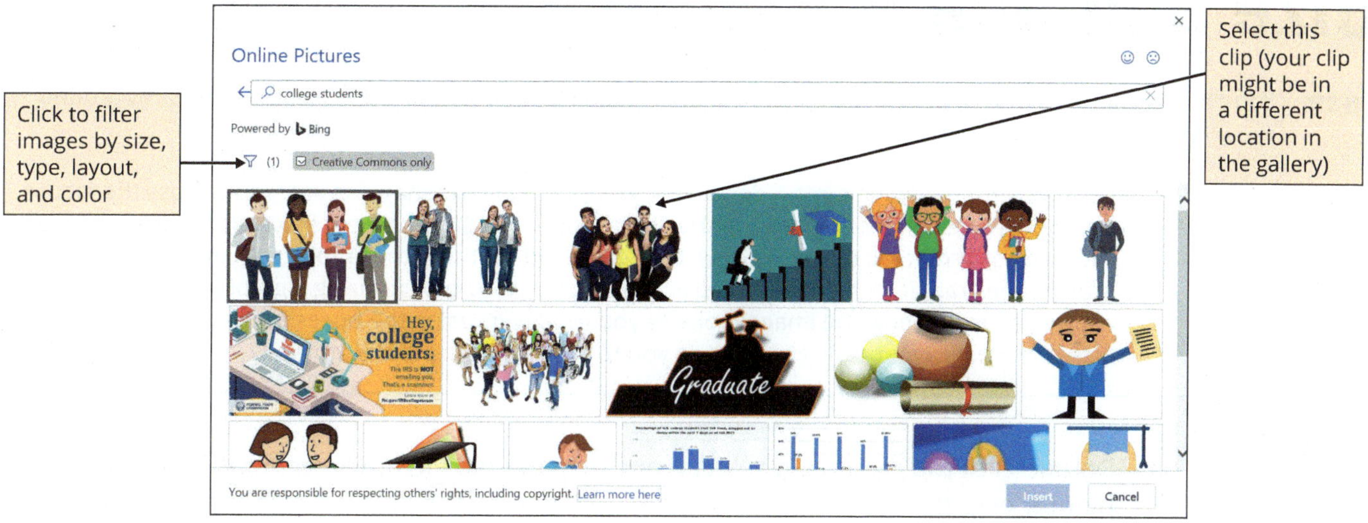

Figure 3-19: Inline graphic

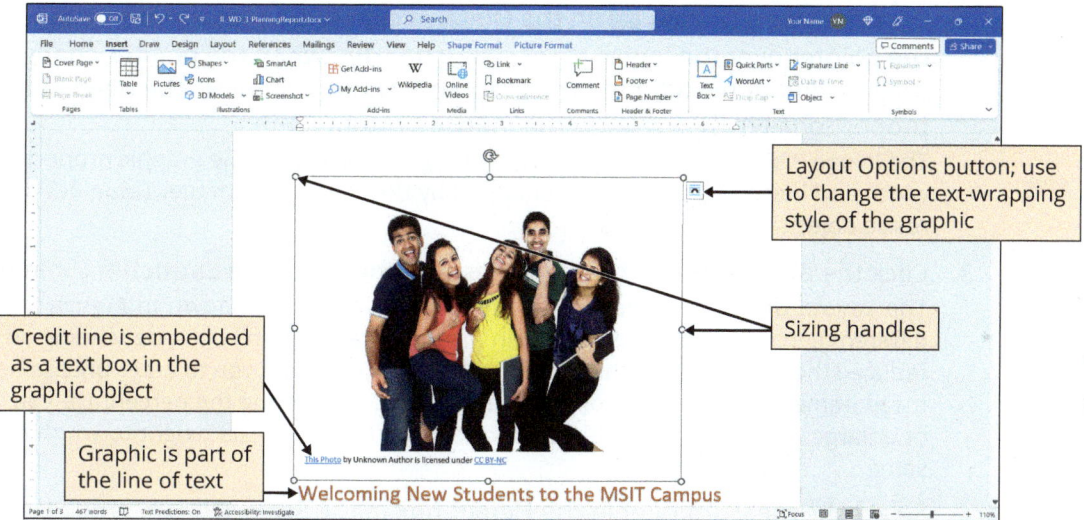

Figure 3-20: Graphic being moved to a new location

Size and Scale a Graphic

Case You reduce the size of the graphic and position it precisely on the page so that the text wraps smoothly around the graphic.

Objectives
- Resize a graphic
- Scale a graphic
- Position a graphic

Once you insert a graphic into a document, you can change its shape or size. You can use the mouse to drag a sizing handle, you can use the Shape Width and Shape Height boxes in the Size group on the Picture Format tab to specify an exact height and width for the graphic, or you can change the scale of the graphic using the Size tab in the Layout dialog box. Resizing a graphic with the mouse allows you to see how the image looks as you modify it. Using the boxes in the Size group or the Size tab in the Layout dialog box allows you to set precise measurements.

Steps

1. **Double-click the graphic to select it and activate the Picture Format tab, place the pointer over the middle-right sizing handle, when the pointer changes to ↔, drag to the left until the graphic is about 2" wide**
   Refer to the ruler as you drag. When you release the mouse button, the image is taller than it is wide. Dragging a side, top, or bottom sizing handle changes only the width or height of a graphic.

   Quick Tip
   As you drag the corner handle, refer to the measurements in the Size group on the Ribbon to best approximate the size of the image.

2. **Click the Undo button ↶ on the Quick Access toolbar or the Home tab, place the pointer over the lower-right sizing handle, when the pointer changes to ⤡, drag up and to the left until the graphic is about 2.5" wide (the height will adjust proportionally), then release the mouse button**
   The image is smaller. Dragging a corner sizing handle resizes the graphic proportionally so that its width and height are reduced or enlarged by the same percentage. **Table 3-3** describes ways to resize objects using the mouse.

3. **Click the Picture Format tab if necessary, then click the Launcher ⌐ in the Size group**
   The Layout dialog box opens with the Size tab active, as shown in **Figure 3-21**. Note that a different percentage may be entered in the Height and Width boxes, depending on how much you reduced the size of the graphic in Step 2. The Size tab allows you to enter precise height and width measurements for a graphic or to scale a graphic by entering the percentage you want to reduce or enlarge it by. When a graphic is sized to **scale** (or scaled), its height-to-width ratio remains the same.

   Quick Tip
   Deselect the Lock aspect ratio check box if you want to change a graphic's proportions.

4. **Select the measurement in the Height box in the Scale section, type 50, then click the Width box in the Scale section**
   The scale of the width changes to 50% and the Absolute measurements in the Height and Width sections decrease proportionally.

5. **Click OK**
   The height and width measurements are reduced to 50% of the height and width measurements in the Original size section of the dialog box.

6. **Type 1.5 in the Shape Height box in the Size group, then press ENTER**
   The image is enlarged to be 1.5" high, with the width changed in proportion.

7. **Click the Position button in the Arrange group, click Position in Top Right with Square Text Wrapping, click the Position button again, click More Layout Options, click the Absolute position button in the Vertical section, type .6 in the Absolute position box, then click OK**
   The graphic is positioned below the title on the right side of the page.

8. **Click the Dropped Shadow Rectangle style in the Picture Styles group, then save your changes**
   A style is applied to the image, as shown in **Figure 3-22**.

Size and Scale a Graphic   WD 3-17

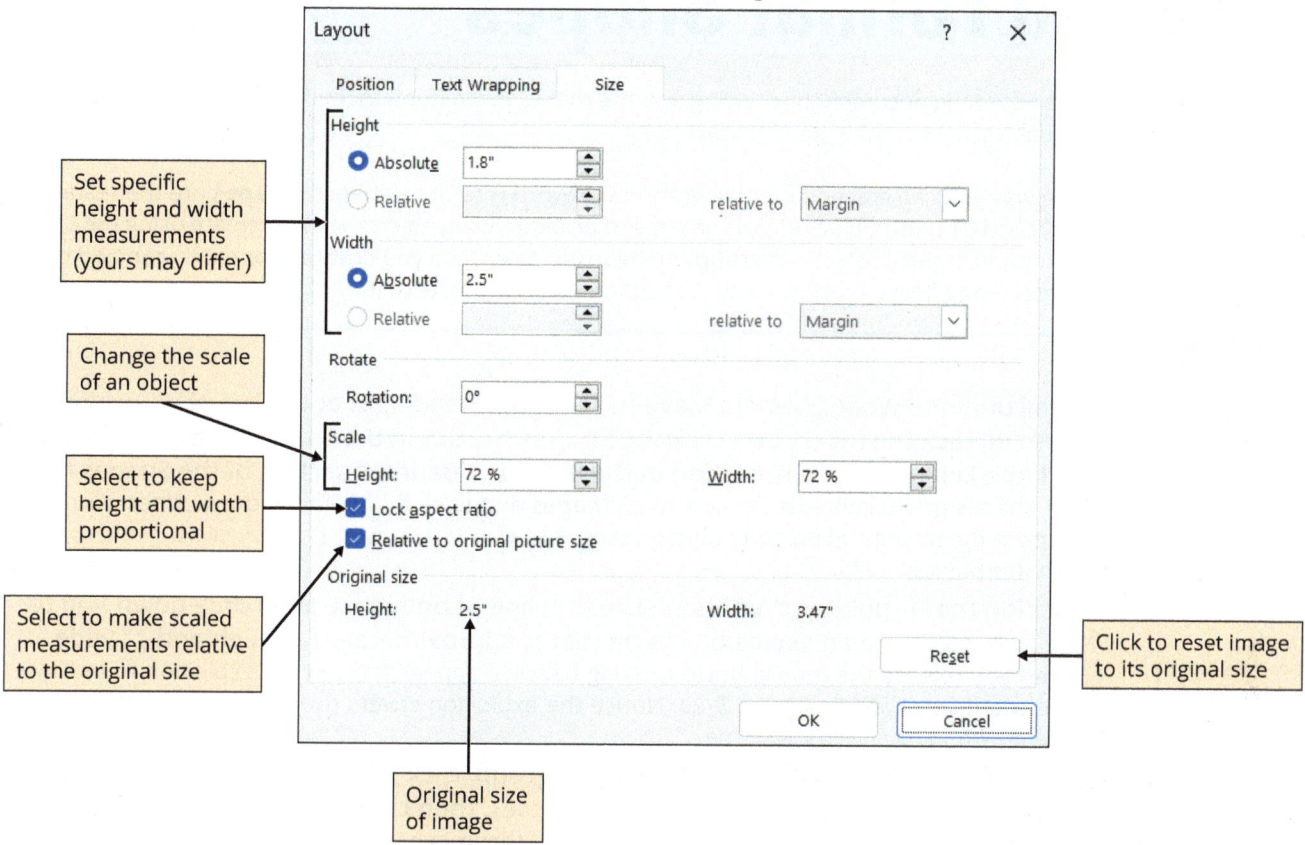

Figure 3-21: Size tab in the Layout dialog box

Figure 3-22: Style applied to resized image

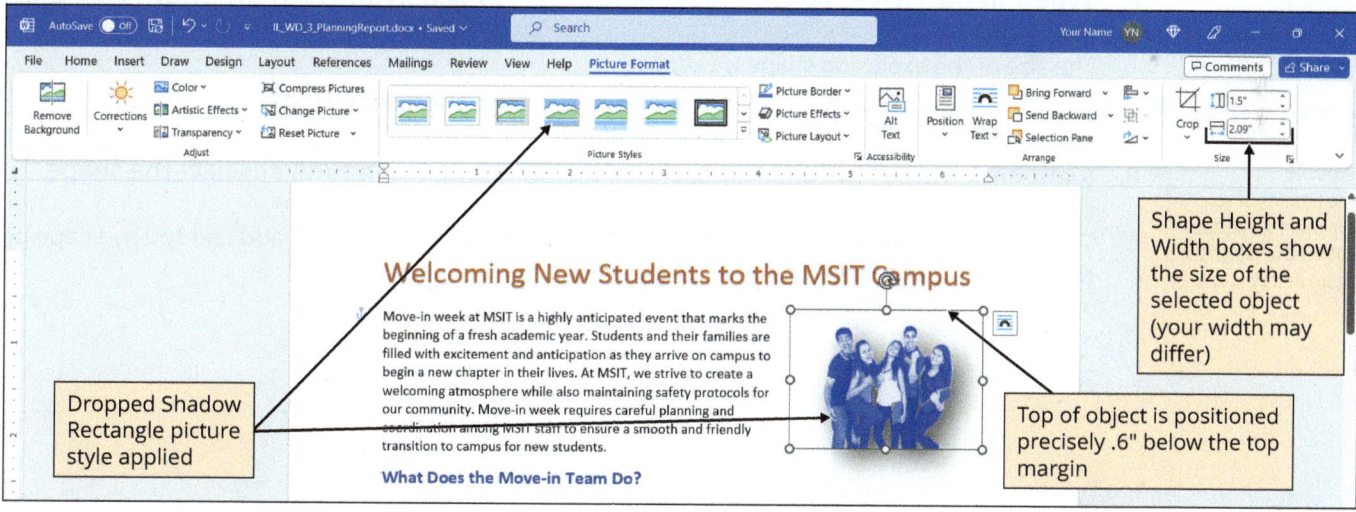

Table 3-3: Methods for resizing an object using the mouse

do this	to
Drag a corner sizing handle	Resize a clip art or bitmap graphic and maintain its proportions
Press SHIFT and drag a corner sizing handle	Resize any graphic object and maintain its proportions
Press CTRL and drag a side, top, or bottom sizing handle	Resize any graphic object vertically or horizontally while keeping the center position fixed
Press CTRL and drag a corner sizing handle	Resize any graphic object diagonally while keeping the center position fixed
Press SHIFT+CTRL and drag a corner sizing handle	Resize any graphic object while keeping the center position fixed and maintaining its proportions

Draw and Format Shapes

Case You add visual interest to the document by drawing a shape that calls attention to the Move-in Team information, and then you format, resize, arrange, and add text to it.

Objectives
- Insert a shape
- Apply styles to objects

One way you can create your own graphics in Word is to draw shapes. **Shapes** are the rectangles, ovals, lines, callouts, block arrows, stars, and other drawing objects you can create using the Shapes command in the Illustrations group on the Insert tab. Once you draw a shape, you can add colors, borders, fill effects, shadows, and three-dimensional effects to it.

Steps

1. Scroll until the What Does the Move-in Team Do? heading is at the top of your screen, zoom in, click the **Insert tab**, click the **Shapes button** in the Illustrations group, then click the **Explosion: 8 points icon** in the Stars and Banners section of the Shapes menu
   The Shapes menu contains categories of shapes and lines that you can draw. When you click a shape in the Shapes menu, the pointer changes to ┼. You draw a shape by clicking and dragging with this pointer.

   Quick Tip
   To draw a perfect square or circle, click the Rectangle or Oval shape on the menu, then press SHIFT while you drag with the pointer.

2. Position the ┼ pointer over **The** in the first line of body text, then drag down and to the right to create an explosion shape that is approximately **1.5"** high and **2"** wide
   When you release the mouse button, sizing handles appear around the explosion to indicate it is selected, as shown in **Figure 3-23**. Notice the explosion covers the text. In Front of Text is the default wrapping style for a shape.

3. Click the **More button** in the Shape Styles group, click **Subtle Effect - Blue Accent 1**, click the **Shape Effects button**, point to **Preset**, then click **Preset 1**
   The color of the shape changes to light blue and the image is formatted with a preset style that includes a shadow, bevel, and white contour.

   Quick Tip
   You can also use the Layout Options button to change the text wrapping style applied to an object.

4. Type **1** in the Height box in the Size group, press **TAB**, type **1.5** in the Width box, then press **ENTER**
   The size of the explosion shape is reduced.

5. Click the **Wrap Text button** in the Arrange group, then click **Tight**
   The text wraps to the jagged shape of the image.

   Trouble
   The position of your explosion shape does not need to match the figure exactly.

6. Right-click the **explosion shape**, click **Add Text**, type **Have fun!**, deselect the shape, then save your document
   Text is added to the explosion shape, as shown in **Figure 3-24**. You can add text to any shape by right-clicking it and then clicking Add Text or Edit Text.

Figure 3-23: Shape in document

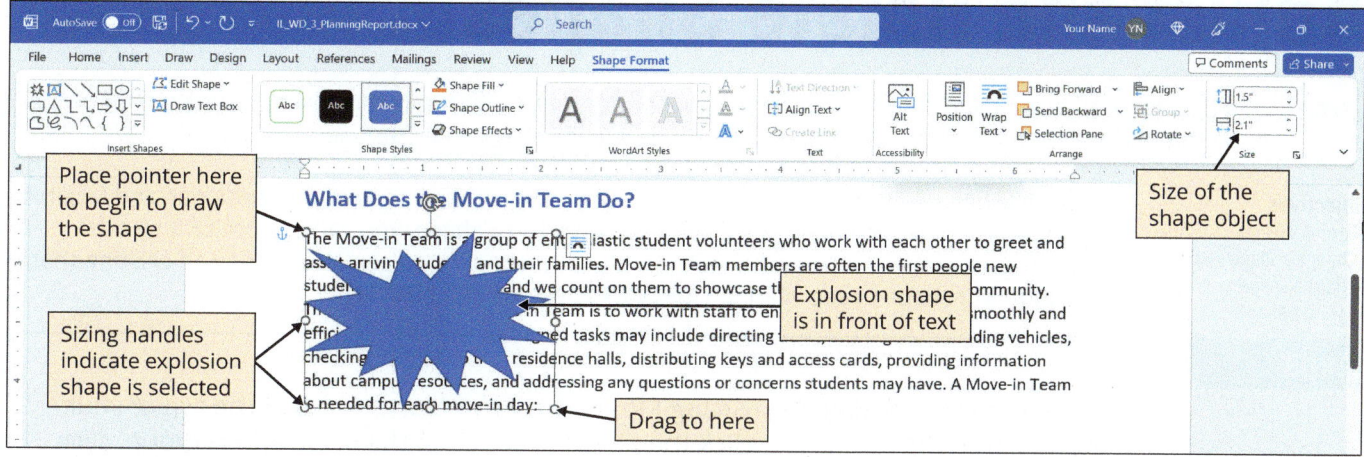

Figure 3-24: Text added to shape

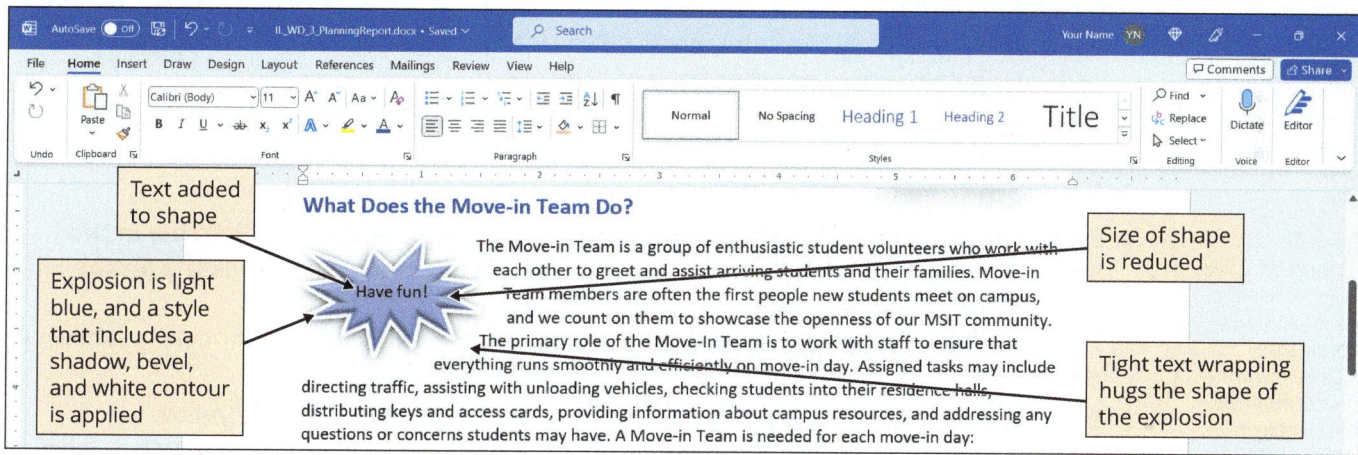

Correcting pictures, changing colors, and applying artistic effects

The Corrections command in the Adjust group on the Picture Format tab allows you to adjust a picture's relative lightness (**brightness**), alter the difference between its darkest and lightest areas (**contrast**), and change the sharpness of an image. To make these adjustments, select the image and then click the Corrections button to open a gallery of preset percentages applied to the selected picture. Point to an option in the gallery to preview it in the document; click an option in the gallery to apply it. You can also fine-tune brightness, contrast, or sharpness by clicking Picture Corrections Options in the Corrections gallery, and then using the sliders in the Picture Corrections section of the Format Picture pane to adjust the percentage.

The Color command in the Adjust group is used to change the vividness and intensity of color in an image (**color saturation**), and to change the "temperature" of a photo by bringing out the cooler blue tones or the warmer orange tones (**color tone**). The Color command is also used to recolor a picture to give it a stylized effect, such as sepia tone, grayscale, or duotone (using theme colors). To make changes to the colors in a picture, select it, click the Color button, and then select one of the color modes or variations in the gallery that opens, or click Picture Color Options to fine-tune color settings using the Format Picture pane.

The Artistic Effects command in the Adjust group allows you to make a photo look like a drawing, a painting, a photocopy, a sketch, or some other artistic medium. To experiment with applying an artistic effect, select a photo, click the Artistic Effects button, and then point to each effect to preview it applied to the photo.

After you adjust a picture, you can undo any changes by clicking the Reset Picture arrow in the Adjust group. This command discards all formatting changes made to a picture, including size, cropping, borders, and effects.

Module 3 Formatting Text and Graphics

Adjust and Rotate Shapes

Case You decide to illustrate page 2 of the document with shapes that suggest moving boxes. You start by drawing cube shapes, and then you format, adjust, and resize each cube shape to be unique.

Objectives
- Format objects
- Change a shape
- Adjust a shape
- Rotate a shape

Shapes, when used appropriately, can be used as visual cues to help present ideas and facilitate the message of a document. Once you have inserted a shape, you can customize it by adding fill, adjusting its interior proportions, resizing it, and rotating it. You can also change an existing shape to a different shape to see which shape works best for the document.

Steps

1. Scroll until the heading **Recruiting Move-in Team Volunteers** is at the top of your screen, click the **Insert tab**, click the **Shapes button** in the Illustrations group, click the **Cube icon** in the Basic Shapes section of the Shapes menu, then click a blank area of page 2

   A 1.33" cube shape is inserted in the document.

2. Press **CTRL+C** to copy the cube, press **CTRL+V** to paste a copy of the cube, then press **CTRL+V** again to paste another copy of the cube

   Two cubes are pasted for a total of three overlapping cubes. These pasted objects have the same text wrapping style as the source object—In Front of Text.

Quick Tip
To align shapes with each other, select two or more shapes, click the Align button in the Arrange group, then select an alignment option.

3. Drag each **cube** to position them in a non-overlapping horizontal line

Quick Tip
To change color, line weight, or line style of a shape outline, click the Shape Outline arrow in the Shape Styles group, then select from the options.

4. Select the first **cube**, click the **Shape Format tab**, click the **Shape Fill arrow** in the Shape Styles group, click **Orange, Accent 2**, select the **third cube**, click the **Shape Fill arrow**, then click **Blue, Accent 1, Lighter 40%**

   The first cube is orange, the second cube is blue, and the third cube is light blue, as shown in **Figure 3-25**.

5. Select the **orange cube** (the first cube), position the pointer over the yellow **adjustment handle**, drag the handle up about **1/8"**, then release the mouse button

   Dragging an adjustment handle changes the internal proportions of a shape. The orange cube becomes taller and shallower.

6. Select the **light blue cube** (the third cube), drag the yellow **adjustment handle** down about **1/2"**, then release the mouse button

   The light blue cube becomes shorter and deeper.

7. Select the **orange cube**, position the pointer over the **top right sizing handle**, drag down and left until the cube is approximately **.8"** high and **.9"** wide, select the **light blue cube**, position the pointer over the **top right sizing handle**, then drag down and right until the cube is approximately **1"** high and **2"** wide

   The cubes are resized to be unique from each other. The measurements don't have to be exact.

Quick Tip
To rotate a graphic object 90 degrees, click the Rotate Objects button in the Arrange group, then click Rotate Right or Rotate Left. To flip a graphic object, click the Rotate Objects button, then click Flip Vertical or Flip Horizontal.

8. Select the **orange cube**, press **CTRL+C**, press **CTRL+V**, drag the copied cube to a blank area, click the **Edit Shape button** in the Insert Shapes group, point to **Change Shape**, then click the **Star: 5 points icon** in the Stars and Banners section

   The rectangle changes to a star. Notice that changing the object shape does not change the format settings applied to the object.

9. Drag the yellow **adjustment handle** in the star down about **1/8"**

   The star becomes narrower.

10. Drag the **rotate handle** on the star right about **1/4"**, then save your changes

    The star is rotated right, as shown in **Figure 3-26**.

Figure 3-25: Cubes with fill color applied

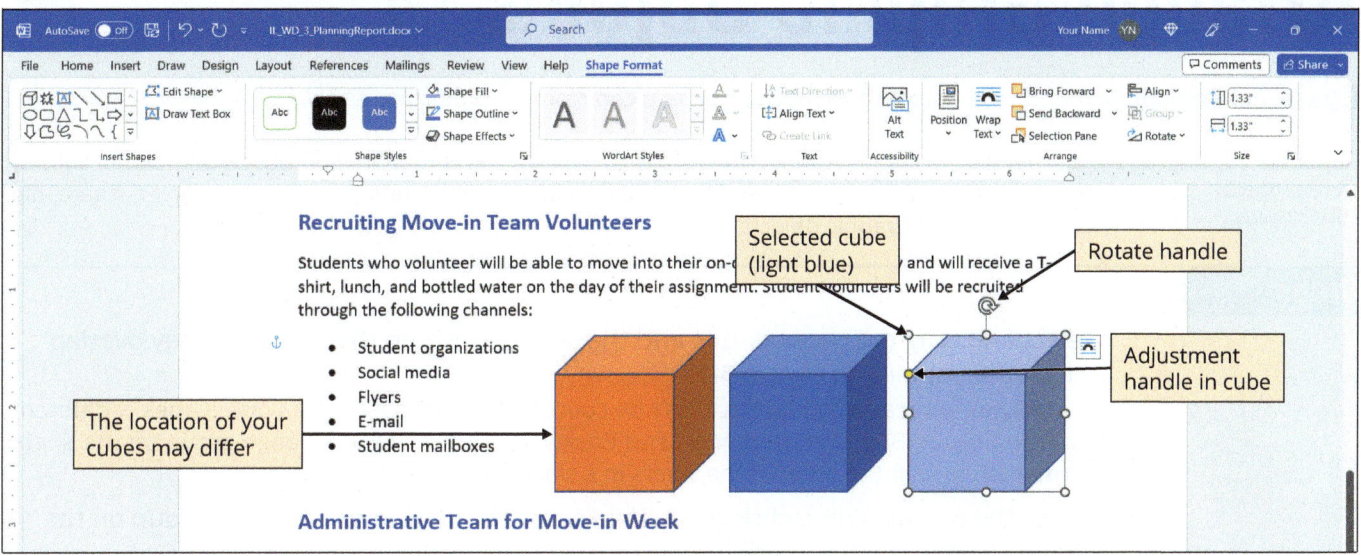

Figure 3-26: Cube shapes adjusted and resized, and star shape adjusted and rotated

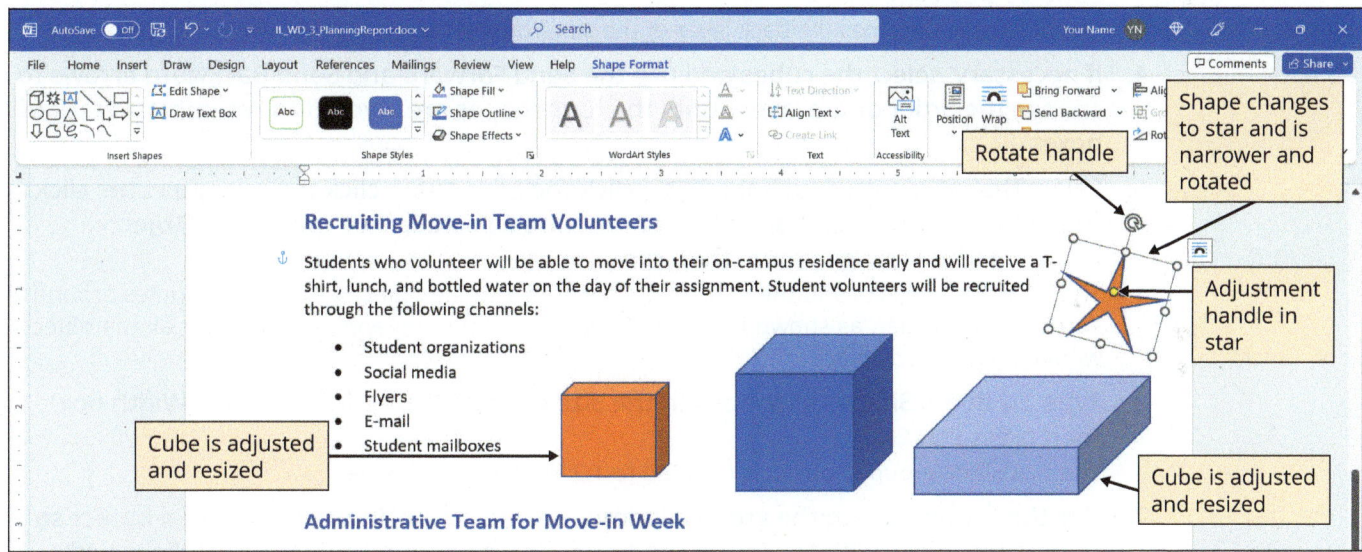

Enhancing graphic objects with styles and effects

Another way to make a document fun and visually appealing for the reader is to apply a style or an effect to a graphic object. To apply a style, select the object and then choose from the style options in the Styles group on the active Format tab for that type of object. Styles include a preset mixture of effects, such as shading, borders, shadows, and other settings. The Effects command in the Styles group on the active Format tab gives you the power to apply a customized variety of effects to an object, including a shadow, bevel, glow, reflection, soft edge, or 3-D rotation. To apply an effect, select the object, click the Effects command for that type of object, point to the type of effect you want to apply, and then select from the options in the gallery that opens. To further customize an effect, click the Options command for that type of effect at the bottom of the gallery to open the Format Shape pane. The best way to learn about styles and effects is to experiment by applying them to an object and seeing what works.

Arrange Graphic Objects

Case You group the four shapes into a single object that you can resize and position easily.

Objectives
- Arrange objects
- Group objects

Another way to create graphics in Word is to create objects that are composed of multiple shapes. The Arrange group on the Shape Format tab includes commands you can use to layer, rotate, flip, align, and group graphic objects.

Steps

1. Select and drag the **three cubes** and the **star** to position them so that they overlap each other, similar to **Figure 3-27**
   The shapes are stacked in layers. Don't be concerned if the layering of your shapes is different. You can use the Bring Forward and Send Backward arrows in the Arrange group on the Shape Format tab to shift the order of the layers in a stack of graphic objects.

2. Select the **orange cube**, click the **Bring Forward arrow** in the Arrange group on the Shape Format tab, then click **Bring to Front**
   The orange cube becomes the front layer of the stack of objects.

3. Select the **blue cube**, click the **Send Backward arrow** in the Arrange group, then click **Send to Back**
   The blue cube becomes the back layer of the stack of objects.

4. If necessary, select the cubes and use the Send Forward and Send Backward arrows to change the order of the layers until the four shapes are layered to resemble a stack of boxes

5. Select the **star**, press and hold **CTRL**, click the **blue cube**, click the **orange cube**, click the **light blue cube** so that all four shapes are selected, click the **Group Objects button** in the Arrange group, then click **Group**
   The four cube objects and the star object become a single object with sizing handles around a surrounding border, as shown in **Figure 3-28**. Any formatting applied will affect all the objects within the grouped object.

6. Type **1.2** in the Shape Height box in the Size group, type **1.6** in the Shape Width box, then press **ENTER**
   The size of the grouped object is reduced to 1.2" high and 1.6" wide.

7. Use the pointer and the green alignment guides to position the **grouped object** so that its top aligns with the top of the first bullet point and the right side aligns with the right margin, as shown in **Figure 3-29**, then release the mouse button
   The grouped object is positioned below the first body paragraph on the right side of the page.

8. Save your changes

Figure 3-27: Cubes layered in document

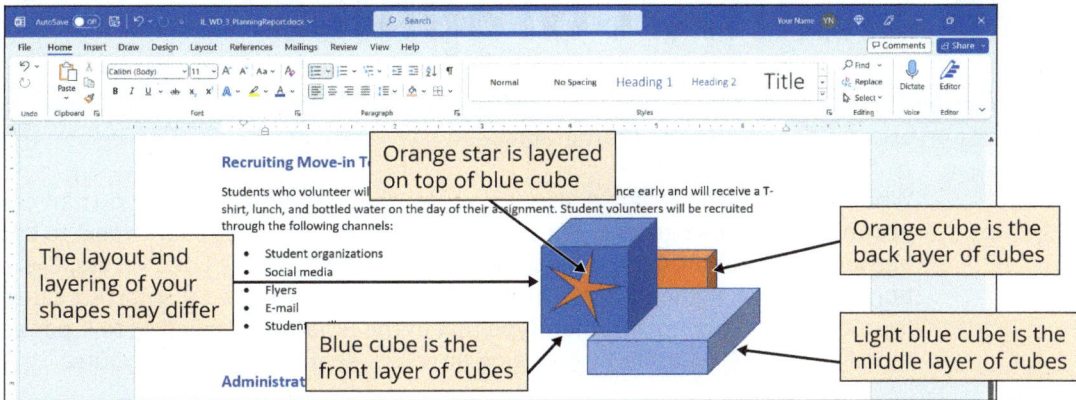

Figure 3-28: Grouped object

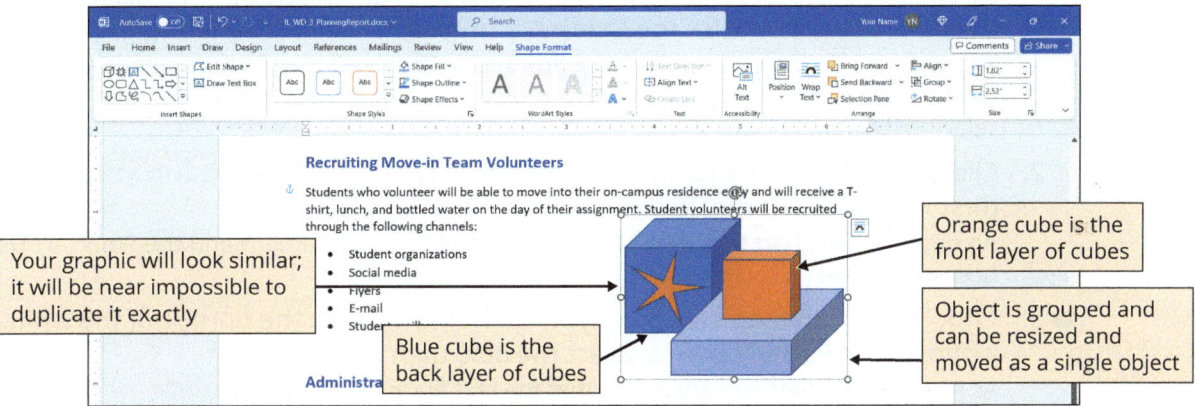

Figure 3-29: Positioning the grouped object

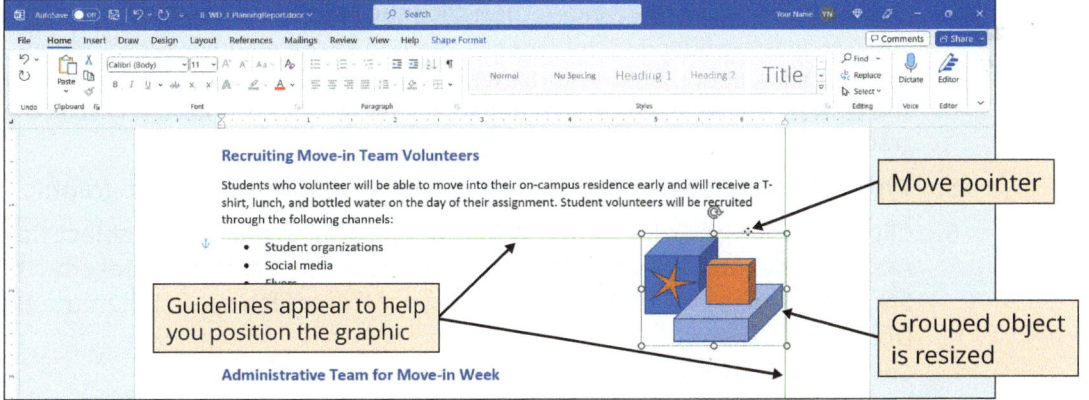

Creating an illustration in a drawing canvas

A **drawing canvas** is a workspace for creating your own graphics. It provides a frame-like boundary between an illustration and the rest of the document so that the illustration can be sized, formatted, and positioned like a single graphic object. If you are creating an illustration that includes multiple shapes, such as a flow chart, it is helpful to create the illustration in a drawing canvas. To draw shapes or lines in a drawing canvas, click the Shapes button in the Illustrations group on the Insert tab, click New Drawing Canvas to open a drawing canvas in the document, and then create and format your illustration in the drawing canvas. When you are finished, right-click the border of the drawing canvas and then click Fit to resize the drawing canvas to fit the illustration. You can then resize the illustration by dragging a border of the drawing canvas. Once you have resized a drawing canvas, you can wrap text around it and position it. By default, a drawing canvas has no border or background so that it is transparent in a document, but you can add fill and borders to it if you wish.

Create SmartArt Graphics

Case To help recipients of the planning document better understand the management structure for move-in week, you create an organizational chart SmartArt graphic.

Objectives
- Insert SmartArt
- Customize SmartArt

When you want to provide a visual representation of information, you can create a **SmartArt graphic**. A SmartArt graphic is a diagram that combines shapes with text to show relationships between information. Categories of SmartArt diagrams include List, Process, Cycle, Hierarchy, Relationship, Matrix, Pyramid, and Picture. Once you have selected a SmartArt category, you select a layout for the diagram and then type text in the SmartArt shapes or text pane. You can further modify a SmartArt graphic by changing fill colors, shape styles, and layouts.

Steps

1. Scroll down, select **[Org chart here.]** under the Administrative Team... heading, click the **Insert tab**, then click the **SmartArt button** in the Illustrations group
   The Choose a SmartArt Graphic dialog box opens. You use it to select the category of diagram you want to create and the layout and design for the diagram. The right pane shows a preview of the selected diagram layout.

2. Click **Hierarchy** in the left pane, select the **Name and Title Organization Chart style** (first row, third column) in the middle pane, then click **OK**
   An organization chart SmartArt object is inserted in the document and the SmartArt Design tab becomes active.

   Quick Tip
   You can type directly in the shapes, or you can use the text pane to enter the text.

3. Click **[Text]** in the top blue box, type **Rachel Tong**, click the **border** of the white box just beneath Rachel's box to select the box, then type **Director**
   As you type, the font size adjusts so that the text fits in each text box.

4. Click the **blue box** below and to the left to select it, press **DELETE**, click the **right-most blue box** in the bottom row to select it, click the **Add Shape arrow** in the Create Graphic group, click **Add Shape Below**, then click the **Add Shape button** again two times
   Three shapes are added to the graphic. The Add Shape menu provides options for adding more shapes below, above, before, and after to your SmartArt graphic. You can also add an Assistant shape. New shapes will be added depending on which box is currently selected in the SmartArt graphic.

5. Type the text shown in **Figure 3-30** in each box of the SmartArt graphic

6. Click the **Change Colors button** in the SmartArt Styles group, select **Colored Fill - Accent 2** (second selection in the Accent 2 section), click the **More button** in the SmartArt Styles group, then click **Intense Effect** (fifth selection in the Best Match for Document section)
   Color and a SmartArt style are applied to the organizational chart.

7. Click the **Olga McMahon box** to select it, click the **Format tab**, click the **Shape Fill arrow** in the Shape Styles section, then click **Blue, Accent 1**
   The orange box changes to blue. You can also format each element of a SmartArt graphic individually.

8. Click outside the object to deselect it, save your changes, click the **View tab**, then click **Multiple Pages** in the Zoom group
   The completed document layout is shown in **Figure 3-31**.

Figure 3-30: Organizational chart

Figure 3-31: Completed document layout

Welcoming New Students to the MSIT Campus

Move-in week at MSIT is a highly anticipated event that marks the beginning of a fresh academic year. Students and their families are filled with excitement and anticipation as they arrive on campus to begin a new chapter in their lives. At MSIT, we strive to create a welcoming atmosphere while also maintaining safety protocols for our community. Move-in week requires careful planning and coordination among MSIT staff to ensure a smooth and friendly transition to campus for new students.

What Does the Move-in Team Do?

Have fun!

The Move-in Team is a group of enthusiastic student volunteers who work with each other to greet and assist arriving students and their families. Move-in Team members are often the first people new students meet on campus, and we count on them to showcase the openness of our MSIT community. The primary role of the Move-in Team is to work with staff to ensure that everything runs smoothly and efficiently on move-in day. Assigned tasks may include directing traffic, assisting with unloading vehicles, checking students into their residence halls, distributing keys and access cards, providing information about campus resources, and addressing any questions or concerns students may have. A Move-in Team is needed for each move-in day:

Student Group	Date	Move-in Time
First-year students	Sept. 4	9 a.m. – 6 p.m.
Transfer students	Sept. 5	9 a.m. – 4 p.m.
Returning students, Day 1	Sept. 6	9 a.m. – 5 p.m.
Returning students, Day 2	Sept. 7	9 a.m. – 5 p.m.

Move-in Week Planning and Budgeting

A smooth and successful move-in week requires the coordination of many campus departments. The project management and logistics plan ensures continuity of traffic flow, parking, key pickup, unloading of vehicles, the efficient moving of belongings into residence halls, and a safe and secure campus environment. Following is a preliminary budget for move-in week.

Expense	Department	Budget	Code
Traffic and parking	Transportation	$5000	TPS
Signage	Printing Services	$1500	PSS
Move-in staffing and information	Residence Life/Student Services	$6000	RLS
Water and first aid	Environmental Health and Safety	$2500	EHS
Tents and moving equipment	Facilities	$8000	FSS

Recruiting Move-in Team Volunteers

Students who volunteer will be able to move into their on-campus residence early and will receive a T-shirt, lunch, and bottled water on the day of their assignment. Student volunteers will be recruited through the following channels:

- Student organizations
- Social media
- Flyers
- E-mail
- Student mailboxes

Administrative Team for Move-in Week

Move-in week is coordinated by Residence Life/Student Services and executed by MIST staff across departments with the help of Move-in Team volunteers. The following chart shows the principal staff member responsible for each broad area of planning.

Rachel Tong
Director
Eric Sze
Communications
Lian Gim
Security
Azar Birni
Logistics
Olga McMahon
Move-in Teams
Elna Pedersen
Traffic/Parking
Jordan Gupta
Facilities

Prepared by Your Name, April 21, 2025

© Mountain Springs Institute of Technology

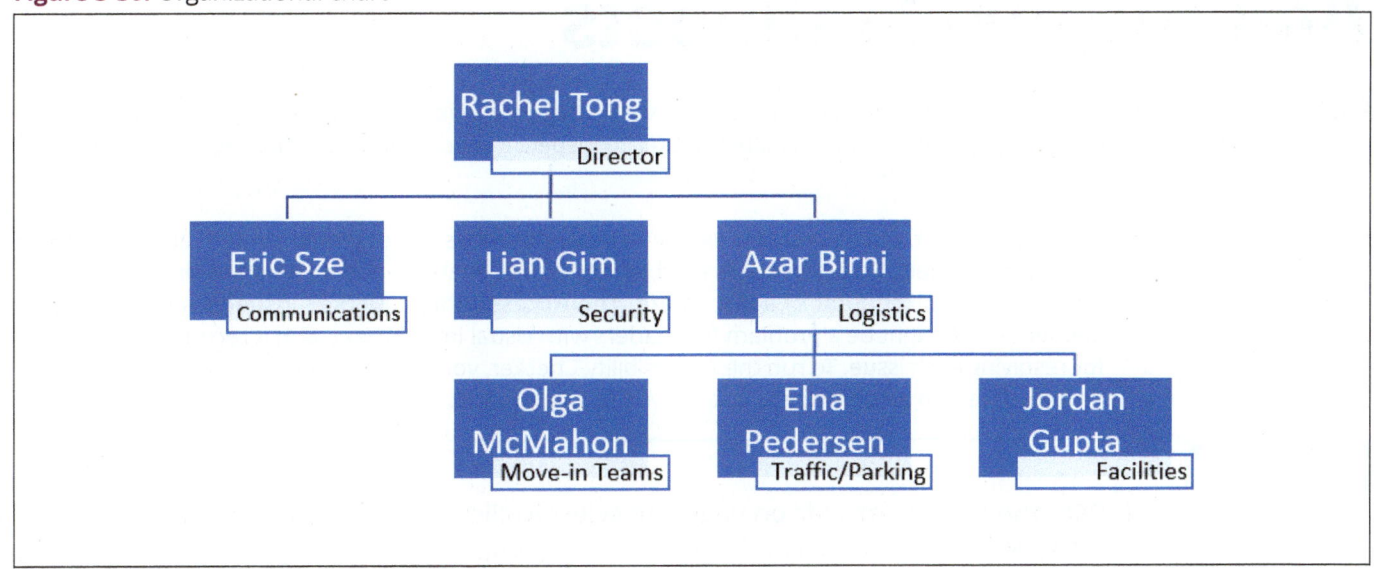

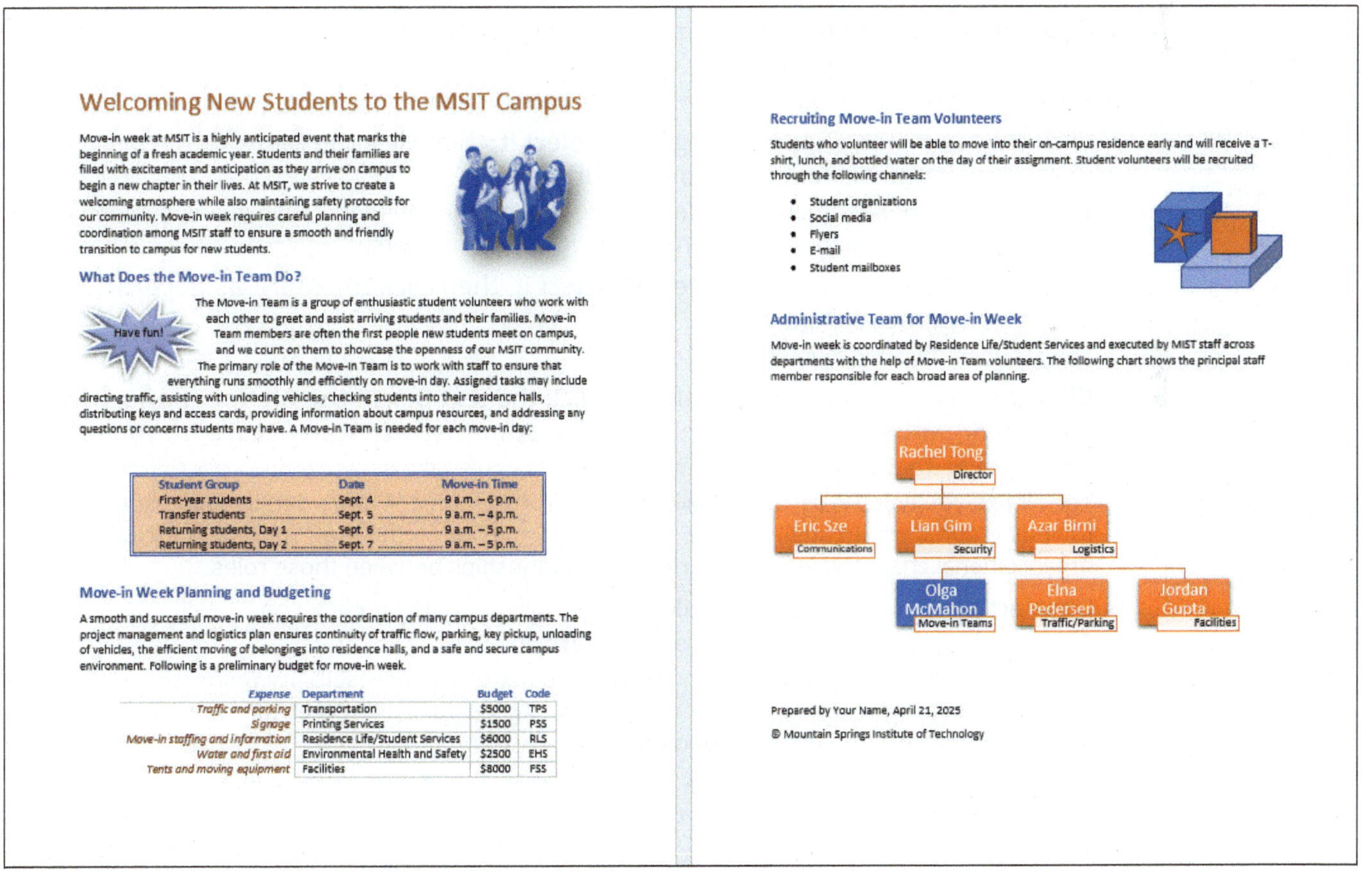

Add Alt Text to Objects

Case Before distributing the document, you add alt text to several images to make them accessible to people who use screen readers. Finally, you run the Accessibility Checker to inspect the document for other accessibility issues and resolve any accessibility errors.

Objectives
- Add alt text to images
- Check documents for accessibility

Alternative text, also called **alt text**, is text that describes the essential content and meaning of an image or object. Screen readers read alt text aloud, enabling people who are visually impaired to access the full content of a document. The **Accessibility Checker** inspects a document for elements that might be a problem for readers with visual impairment, and it recommends actions for resolving each issue. To run the Accessibility Checker, you use the Check Accessibility command. To add alt text to an object, you use the Alt Text command.

Steps

1. Click the **clip art graphic** on page 1 to select it, click the **Picture Format tab**, then click the **Alt Text button** in the Accessibility group

   The Alt Text pane opens, as shown in **Figure 3-32**. You use this pane to type alternative text for the selected object. The pane includes an option for generating automatic alt text. You can experiment with this option or write your own alt text.

   Quick Tip
   You can also add or edit alt text by right-clicking an object, clicking Edit Alt Text, and then typing the alt text in the Alt Text pane.

2. Click the **text box** in the Alt Text pane, then type **Five happy college students posing for a photo and laughing.**

   The alt text you typed is associated with the selected image.

3. Click the **explosion shape** on page 1 to select it, then click the **Mark as decorative check box** in the Alt Text pane to select it

   The explosion shape is marked as decorative. Objects that are decorative in a document are for visual interest only and do not require alt text for screen readers.

4. Click the **grouped object** on page 2 to select it, then click the **Mark as decorative check box** in the Alt Text pane

   The grouped object is marked as decorative.

5. Click the **SmartArt graphic** to select it, click the text box in the **Alt Text pane**, then type **An organizational chart showing the administrative structure for move-in week, with Rachel Tong as director.**

   The alt text you typed is associated with the SmartArt graphic. A more detailed alt-text description for this graphic would spell out the names and roles of all the staff members included in the organizational chart and would describe the relationships between those roles.

   Quick Tip
   To hear the document read aloud by a screen reader, click the View tab, click the Immersive Reader command in the Immersive group, then click Read Aloud.

6. Deselect the SmartArt graphic, click the **Review tab**, then click the **Check Accessibility button** in the Accessibility group

   The Accessibility pane opens. It shows the results of the accessibility inspection and offers suggestions for how to resolve each issue. The Accessibility Checker identifies one potential accessibility issue in the planning document.

7. Click **Image or object not inline** in the Accessibility pane, then click **Picture 1**

   Picture 1, the clip art graphic on page 1, is identified by the Accessibility Checker as a floating object—i.e., not part of a line of text ("inline"). The clip art graphic is selected in the document, as shown in **Figure 3-33**. Two actions for fixing the accessibility issue are recommended by the Accessibility Checker: convert the floating object to an inline object or mark it as decorative. Since the image is not essential to the meaning and purpose of the planning document, you mark the clip art graphic as decorative.

8. Click **Mark as decorative**

   The clip art graphic is marked as decorative, removing the alt text associated with it. The Accessibility pane now indicates the document is free of accessibility issues.

9. Close the Accessibility pane, close the Alt Text pane, deselect the clip art graphic, then save your changes

10. **sam↑** Submit the document to your instructor, close the file, then exit Word

Figure 3-32: Alt Text pane

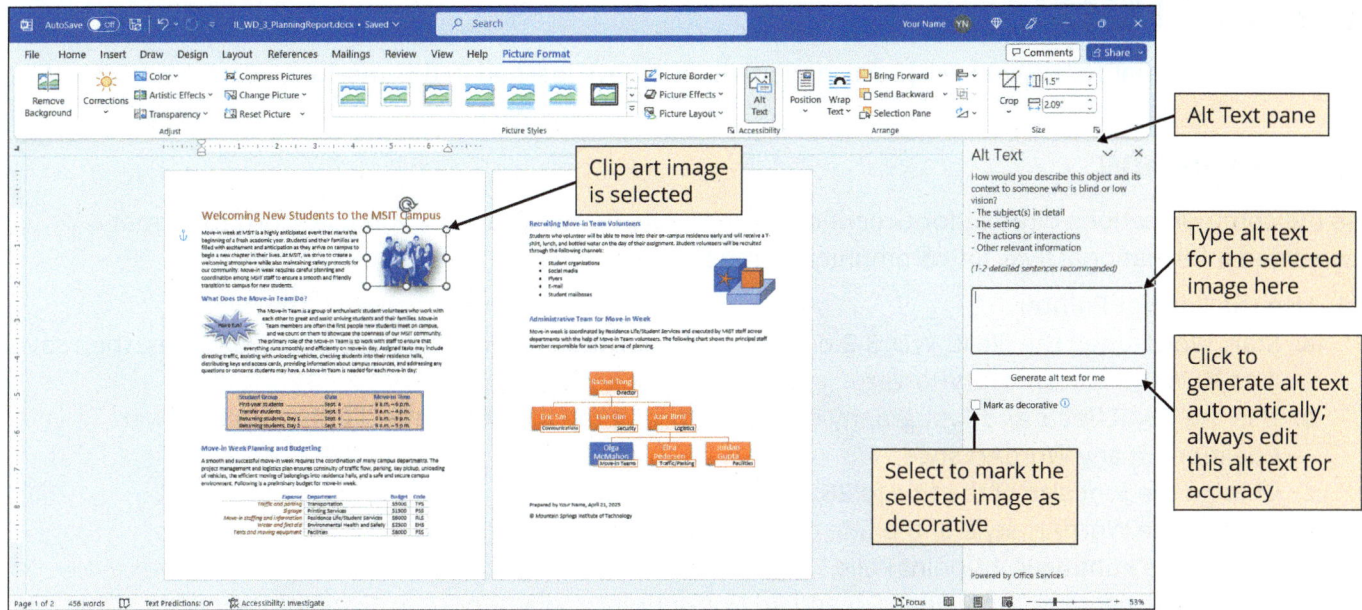

Figure 3-33: Accessibility pane

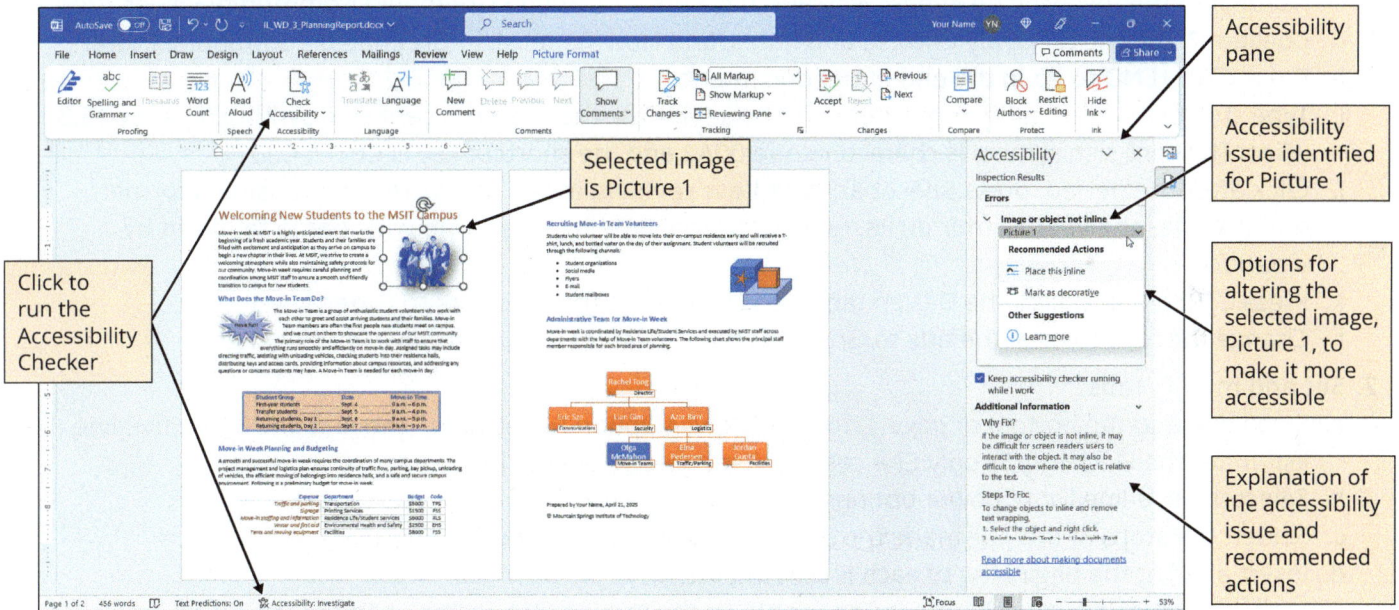

Practice

In the exercises that follow, you will practice the skills you have learned in this module.

Skills Review

As the communications director for Greenfield Community Power Coalition, you use Word to format a two-sided informational flyer for community members.

1. **Use the Format Painter.**
   a. Start Word, open the file IL_WD_3-2.docx from the location where you store your Data Files, then save it as **IL_WD_3_CommunityPower**.
   b. Use the Text Effects and Typography button to format the title "Greenfield Community Power Coalition" in any WordArt style.
   c. Change the font size of the title to 28.
   d. Change the WordArt style of the title to the third style in the third row.
   e. Format the subtitle in 14-point italic.
   f. Format the heading "How Does Greenfield Community Power Work?" in 14-point italic with a Blue, Accent 1, Darker 25% font color.
   g. Use the Format Painter to copy the format of the How Does Greenfield Community Power Work? heading to the following headings: Why Purchase Power through Greenfield Community Power Coalition?, Electricity Supply Choices and Rates, and How To Enroll in Greenfield Community Power.
   h. Press CTRL+END to go to the end of the document,
   i. Type **Our rates start at 15.5 per kilowatt-hour (kWh).**, then insert a cent sign symbol (¢) after 15.5. (Hint: The cent sign symbol is character code 00A2 and the shortcut key is Ctrl+/, C.)
   j. Click after the period, press Spacebar, type **Last revised**, insert the current date using a format that includes the year as four digits, type a comma, type **by**, then type your name followed by a period.
   k. Press CTRL+HOME, click the Design tab, then change the theme colors to Green.
   l. Change the font color of the title to Green, Accent 1, Darker 25%, then save your changes.

2. **Set and modify tabs.**
   a. Scroll down to the bottom of page 1, format "Power Option Renewable," the first line in the five-line list under the Electricity Supply Choices and Rates heading, in bold.
   b. Select the five-line list of power options.
   c. Set left tab stops at the 1½" mark, the 3¾" mark, and the 5" mark.
   d. Insert a tab at the beginning of each line in the list.
   e. In the first line, insert a tab before Renewable. In the second line, insert a tab before 22. In the remaining lines, insert a tab before 33, 50, and 100.
   f. Select the five lines of tabbed text, then drag the second tab stop to the 4" mark on the horizontal ruler.
   g. Drag the third tab stop at the 5" mark off the ruler to remove it.
   h. Select the five lines of tabbed text, open the Tabs dialog box, then change the alignment of the 4" tab stop to Center.
   i. Select the last four lines of tabbed text, open the Tabs dialog box, then apply a dotted line tab leader to the 4" tab stop.
   j. Save your changes to the document.

3. **Add borders and shading.**
   a. Select "Power Option," then apply an underline.
   b. Use the Underline arrow in the Font group to change the color of the underline to Green, Accent 1.
   c. Use the Format Painter to copy the underline formatting from "Power Option" to "Renewable."
   d. Click the heading Electricity Supply Choices and Rates, add 6 points of space after the paragraph, then open the Borders and Shading dialog box.
   e. Use the Borders tab to apply a ½-point width, Turquoise, Accent 6 colored border below the heading.
   f. Use the Format Painter to apply the same paragraph and border settings to the other headings in the report: How Does…, Why Purchase…, and How To Enroll…
   g. Scroll to the end of the document, click in the Our rates… paragraph, then center the paragraph.
   h. Apply Turquoise, Accent 6, Lighter 80% shading to the paragraph.
   i. Add a ½-point, Turquoise, Accent 6 box border around the paragraph.
   j. Save your changes.

4. **Insert a table.**
   a. Turn on formatting marks, click in the middle blank paragraph above the How To Enroll in Greenfield Community Power heading, then insert a table that contains three columns and three rows.
   b. Type the text shown below in the table, pressing TAB to add rows as necessary.

22%	Green Basic	$94/month
33%	Green Plus	$97/month
50%	Green Enhanced	$101/month
65%	Green Clean	$108/month
100%	Green Complete	$116/month
22%	PowerHub	$122/month

   c. Save your changes.

5. **Insert and delete rows and columns.**
   a. Insert a row above the top row, type **Renewable Content** in the first cell, type **Power Options** in the second cell, then type **Estimated Cost** in the third cell.
   b. Delete the 65% row.
   c. Insert a column to the left of the Estimated Cost column, then type **Rate/kWh** in the first cell.
   d. Type the following prices in the empty cells in the new column, starting at the top of the table: **15.5¢**, **16.2¢**, **16.9¢**, **19.3¢**, **20.3¢**. (Hint: Insert the cent sign symbol.)
   e. Save your changes.

6. **Apply a table style.**
   a. Select the table, then use the AutoFit command to fit the table to the contents.
   b. Click the Table Design tab, preview table styles applied to the table, and then apply an appropriate style.
   c. Apply the Grid Table 6 Colorful - Accent 1 style to the table, add the Header Row, Total Row, and First Column table style options, remove the Banded Rows, Banded Columns, and Last Column table style options, if necessary, then change the font color of the header row to Turquoise, Accent 6, Darker, 25%.
   d. Change the font color of the last row to black, remove the bold formatting from the last row, then apply bold to the 22% cell in the last row.
   e. Center the text in the Renewable Content and Rate/kWh columns.
   f. Center the table between the margins, then save your changes.

Skills Review (Continued)

7. **Insert online pictures.** (**Note**: To complete these steps, your computer must be connected to the Internet.)
   a. Press CTRL+HOME, then open the Online Pictures window.
   b. Search using Bing Image Search to find images related to the keyword **energy**. Click the Filter link in the Online Pictures window, select Clipart on the Filter menu to filter the search results, then verify the Creative Commons only check box is selected.
   c. Insert the renewable energy clip art image shown in **Figure 3-34**. (**Note**: Select a different image if this one is not available to you. It is best to select an image that is similar in shape to the image shown in **Figure 3-34**.)
   d. Scroll down. If the image includes a credit line, click the text in the credit line, select the box that surrounds the credit line, then delete the credit line box.
   e. Use the Shape Width box in the Size group on the Picture Format tab to change the width of the image to 3".
   f. Use the Position command to position the image in the top right with square text wrapping.
   g. Change the color of the image to Lime, Accent color 2 Dark.
   h. Use the Artistic Effects button to apply the Glow Edges artistic effect to the image (fifth row, third column).
   i. Use the Reset Picture arrow to reset the picture (but not the size), then save your changes.

8. **Size and scale a graphic.**
   a. Resize the image proportionally so that it is about **1"** high and **1.5"** wide.
   b. Drag the image so its top is aligned with the first line of body text and its left side is aligned with the left margin.
   c. Resize the image so that it is precisely **1.5"** high and **2.25"** wide. Deselect the Lock aspect ratio check box, if necessary.
   d. Position the image so its Horizontal absolute position is 0" to the right of the margin and its Vertical absolute position is 1" below the margin.
   e. Add ¾-point Turquoise, Accent 6 picture border around the image, then save your changes.

9. **Draw and format shapes.**
   a. Scroll until the Why Purchase Power… heading is at the top of your screen.
   b. Click the Shapes button, click the Cloud shape, then click in the numbered list below the Why Purchase… heading.
   c. Resize the shape to be **.8"** high and **.8"** wide.
   d. Fill the shape with Turquoise, Accent 6, then apply the Preset 3 shape effect.
   e. Change the shape of the object to Sun.
   f. Apply square text wrapping, then position the shape in the bottom left corner of the page.

10. **Adjust and rotate shapes.**
    a. Draw a teardrop shape in a blank space on the page, then resize it to **1"** high and **1"** wide.
    b. Select the sun shape, then use the Format Painter to copy the format of the sun shape to the teardrop shape.

Figure 3-34

c. Rotate the teardrop shape left about 45 degrees so that the yellow adjustment handle is at the top of the shape, then drag the yellow adjustment handle up about ¼".
d. Draw a lightning bolt shape near the teardrop shape, then resize it to be about **1"** high and **.4"** wide.
e. Fill the shape with Lime, Accent 3, then apply the Preset 3 shape effect.
f. Draw a sun shape near the teardrop shape, resize it to be about **.8"** high and **.8"** wide, then drag the adjustment handle right slightly.
g. Fill the sun shape with Orange from the Standard Colors section, apply the Preset 3 shape effect, then save your changes.

11. **Arrange graphic objects.**
    a. Position the lightning bolt shape on top of the teardrop shape.
    b. Position the orange sun so that it overlaps the teardrop slightly, then use the Send Backward arrow to send the orange sun to the back.
    c. Select the teardrop shape, press and hold CTRL, select the lightning bolt shape, select the orange sun shape, then group the shapes into a single object.
    d. Resize the grouped object to be **1"** high and **1"** wide, then apply square text wrapping to the object.
    e. Position the grouped object so it aligns with the right margin and the first line of body text under the Why Purchase... heading. (**Hint**: Make sure the object is under the border.)
    f. Select the turquoise sun shape, copy it, then paste a copy.
    g. Drag the pasted copy of the sun shape to a blank area of the page, adjust the sun shape, reduce the size of the sun shape, then rotate the sun shape.
    h. Position the rotated sun shape in the blank space to the right of the tabbed text.
    i. Change the fill color of the two turquoise suns to orange, then save your changes.

12. **Create SmartArt graphics.**
    a. Scroll to the end of the document, click in the middle blank paragraph above the Our rates... shaded paragraph, then click the SmartArt button.
    b. Select Process in the list of SmartArt types, select the Accent Process style, then click OK.
    c. Change the colors of the SmartArt object to the Colorful - Accent Colors style.
    d. Enter text in the SmartArt object so that the process diagram appears as shown in **Figure 3-35**.
    e. Resize the SmartArt object to be **3.2"** high, then save your changes.
    f. Adjust the size or position of objects as needed so that your document resembles the document shown in the figure. View your document in two-page view and compare it to the document shown in **Figure 3-36**.

Figure 3-35

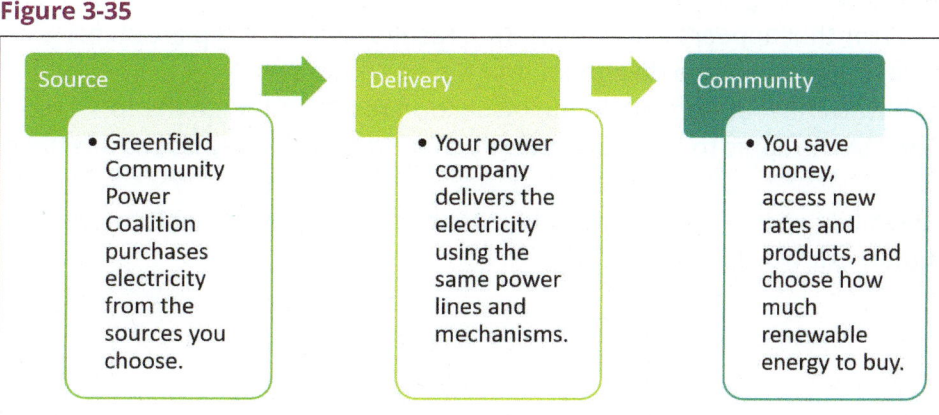

Skills Review (Continued)

Figure 3-36

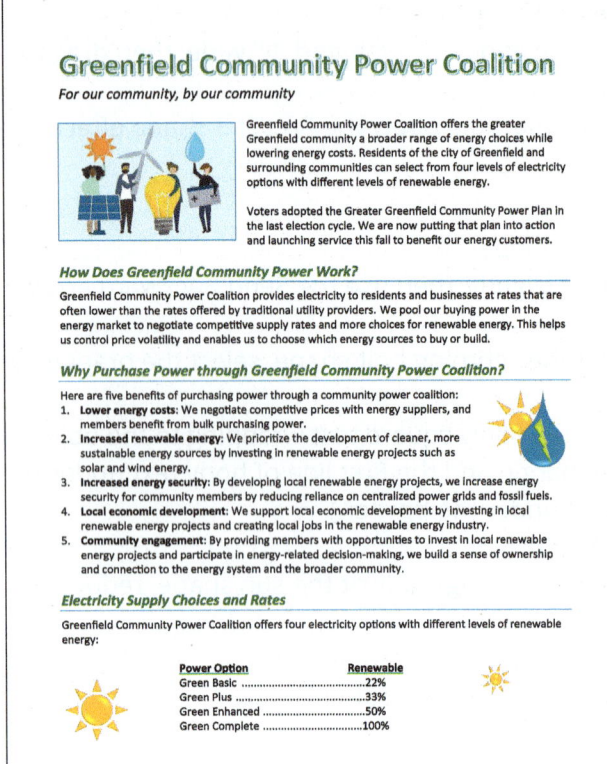 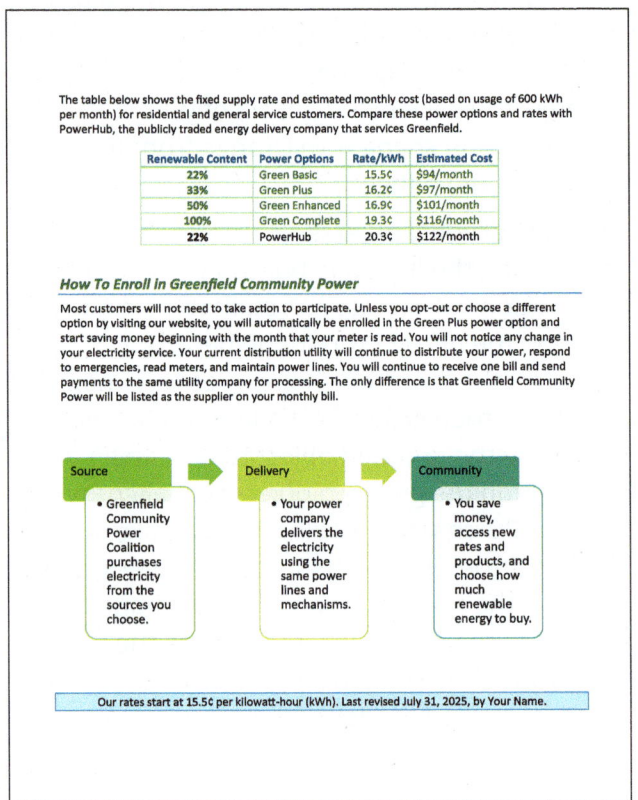

13. **Add alt text to objects.**
    a. Select the clip art graphic on page 1, use the Alt Text command to open the Alt Text pane, then type the following alt text: **A group of people holding solar panels, wind turbines, lightbulbs, and water, representing renewable energy sources.**
    b. Select the grouped object on page 1, mark it as decorative in the Alt Text pane, then select and mark the two sun shapes as decorative.
    c. Click the SmartArt graphic, then type the following alt text in the Alt Text pane: **A chart detailing the electricity source, delivery process, and community benefits for Greenfield Community Power customers.**
    d. Use the Check Accessibility command on the Review tab to run the Accessibility Checker.
    e. Resolve each error that appears in the inspection results. Since the clip art object is not essential to the meaning and purpose of the document, mark it as decorative.
    f. Consider each warning that appears in the inspection results. Change the font color of the white text in the SmartArt graphic to black, then verify that no accessibility issues are flagged in the document.
    g. Close the Accessibility pane, save your changes to the document, submit it to your instructor, close the file, and then exit Word.

Independent Challenge 1

The senior center where you work publishes a variety of helpful tips and information sheets related to health and safety issues for older adults. Your colleague has assembled a tip sheet on fall prevention and has asked you to format it so it highlights the important information. Design and formatting elements will make the document attractive to readers.

a. Start Word, open the file IL_WD_3-3.docx from the drive and folder where you store your Data Files, save it as **IL_WD_3_FallPrevention**, then read the document to get a basic understanding of its contents.
b. Select the entire document, then change the font to 10-point Arial.
c. Change all four document margins to Narrow 0.5".
d. Change the font size of the first line, "Healthy Aging", to 14, and apply italic.
e. Change the font size of the second line, the title "Fall Prevention...", to 20.
f. Change the font size of the heading "Discuss your medications with your healthcare provider" to 14, then add a single bottom border with the Blue, Accent 1 color, and a width of 1/2 pt.
g. Use the Format Painter to copy the format of the "Discuss your medications..." heading to the following headings in the tip sheet: Stay active and keep moving, Wear appropriate footwear, Improve lighting and remove home hazards, and Use assistive devices.
h. Insert an online picture that is a photograph. Select a photograph that is appropriate to the content. (**Hint**: Use the Filter link in the Online Pictures window to filter for photographs.)
i. Remove the credit line box from the image, if necessary.
j. Resize the image proportionally so that it is approximately 2.5" wide, wrap text around the image, then position the photograph above the "Discuss your medications..." heading. **Figure 3-37** shows a sample layout.
k. Change the theme colors to a theme color set that works with the photograph you selected. (**Hint**: Use the Theme Colors button on the Design tab.)
l. Enhance the photograph with corrections, colors, artistic effects, borders, or styles.
m. Using heart shapes, create an image similar to the one shown in the completed document in **Figure 3-37**. Apply a fill color to the larger heart and a different fill color to the smaller heart.
n. Use the adjustment handle to alter the shape of the hearts if necessary. Group the two heart shapes into a single object, then position the grouped object in the top-right corner of the page.
o. Apply font colors to the document that work with the photograph you selected, then adjust the color and style of the borders as necessary.
p. Add your name to the footer, then examine the document carefully for formatting errors and make any necessary adjustments. Adjust the size and placement of the photograph if necessary, so that all the text fits on a single page.
q. Check the document for accessibility, mark each image as decorative, and make any other necessary adjustments.
r. Save the tip sheet, submit it to your instructor, then close the file and exit Word.

Figure 3-37

Independent Challenge 2

The healthcare communications agency where you work has been contracted by City Health Clinic to redesign an info sheet on their supportive care services for expectant and new parents. The client would like the info sheet to include graphics, tables, and other elements that make the document visually interesting. The info sheet must also be accessible to people who are visually impaired and using a screen reader. You design the document to highlight the important information and add alt text so that readers of all abilities can access the content of the graphic images.

a. Start Word, open the file IL_WD_3-4.docx from the drive and folder where you store your Data Files, then save it as **IL_WD_3_SupportiveCare**.
b. Read the document to get a basic understanding of the contents, use CTRL+A to select all the text in the document, then clear all formatting from the text.
c. Determine the font and font sizes you will use for the body text, title, subtitle, and headings.
d. Select all the text again, change the style to No Spacing, then apply the font you intend to use for the body text to all the text in the report.
e. Format the title and subtitle using a font, font size, and font color of your choice.
f. Format the heading Mission and Goals using a font, font size, and font color of your choice, then, use the Format Painter to copy the formatting of the Mission and Goals heading to the Workshops and Support Groups and Advocacy Initiatives headings.
g. Format the subheading Emotional support using a font, font size, and font color of your choice, then use the Format Painter to copy the formatting of the Emotional support heading to the following headings: Education, Advocacy, Building community, Prenatal classes, Infant care classes, Breastfeeding support groups, Postpartum support groups, Prenatal yoga classes, Access to quality healthcare, Maternal and infant health, and Policy reform
h. Scroll down. Above the Advocacy Initiatives heading, insert a table with three columns and six rows, then enter the following text.

Class/Workshop	Day	Time
Prenatal	Tues., Thurs.	7–9 p.m.
Infant care	Mon., Wed.	6–7 p.m.
Breastfeeding	Mon., Wed., Fri.	10–11 a.m.
Postpartum	Tues., Thurs	10–11 a.m.
Yoga	Mon., Wed., Fri.	7–8 p.m.

i. Autofit the table to the content, apply an appropriate table style to the table, adjust the formatting, then center the table between the margins.
j. Scroll to the top of the document. Using shapes, create a graphic to illustrate the document. The graphic should be composed of two or more shapes. For example, you might draw an abstract design or something else you think will represent the content.
k. Format the shapes with fills, outlines, and effects. Use the adjustment and rotate handles to alter the shapes as necessary.
l. Position the shapes so that they overlap, use the Bring Forward and Send Backward buttons to adjust the layers, then group the shapes into a single object.
m. Resize the grouped object, wrap text around it, and position it in the document.

n. Create a SmartArt graphic similar to **Figure 3-38**. Use the Alternating Hexagons SmartArt style (List group), then format the SmartArt graphic using colors, styles, and effects.
o. Resize the SmartArt graphic and position it in the document.
p. Use the Multiple Pages button to view both pages of the document, then adjust the size and position of the graphics.
q. Select the shapes graphic you created in steps j–m, use the Alt Text button to open the Alt Text pane, then mark the shapes graphic as decorative.
r. Select the SmartArt graphic, then type a description of the SmartArt graphic in the Alt Text pane.
s. Use the Check Accessibility button on the Review tab to check the document for accessibility issues, and make any necessary adjustments.
t. Add your name to the footer, save your changes to the document, submit it to your instructor, close the file, and then exit Word.

Figure 3-38

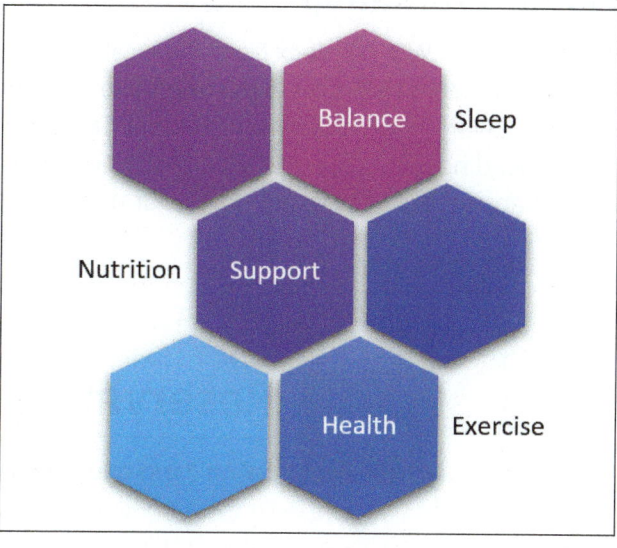

Visual Workshop

Open the file IL_WD_3-5.docx from the location where you store your Data Files, then save the document as **IL_WD_3_ReserveFAQ**. Create the one-page flyer shown in **Figure 3-39**. Change all four margins to .75". Use 12-point Calibri for the body text, 28-point Calibri for the title, 14-point Calibri for the subtitle, and 14-point Calibri for the headings. To create the SmartArt graphic object, use the Accent Process style from the Process group. Resolve any accessibility issues. Add your name to the footer, then submit a copy of the flyer to your instructor.

Figure 3-39

Reserving a Picnic Shelter

Salem Parks and Recreation

When can I reserve a picnic shelter?

- City of Salem residents may apply for a permit 12 months in advance of their event date.
- Nonresidents may apply 6 months in advance of their event date.
- Reservations need to be made a minimum of 14 days in advance.

How do I reserve a picnic shelter?

- Picnic shelters can be reserved online or by contacting the Park Permit Office at **626-555-6400** or **parkscustomerservice@parks.salem.us.gov**.
- Phone reservation hours are 7:30 a.m. – 4:30 p.m., Monday through Friday.
- Reservation calendars for picnic shelters can be viewed online.

How long is the rental session for a picnic shelter?

- Each day is divided into two sessions. If you would like to reserve the entire day, you are required to pay for two sessions.
- One session is 8 a.m. – 1:30 p.m. or 2:30 p.m. – 8:00 p.m.
- All day (two sessions) is 8:00 a.m. – 8:00 p.m.

Can a picnic shelter reservation be changed or cancelled?

- Changes to date, time, or location of a permit will be accepted up to 7 business days prior to the scheduled date of the event. A $25.00 fee will be charged each time a permit is changed.
- Refunds for cancellations require a 30-calendar day notice in advance of an event, otherwise the permit fee is not refundable.

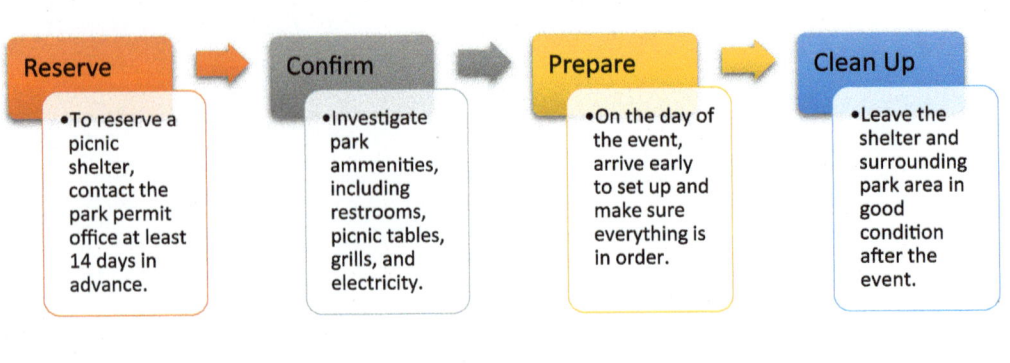

Your Name

Excel Module 1

Getting Started with Excel

Case

You have been hired as an Executive Assistant at Bayside Consulting, a company that provides IT services for small and medium-sized companies. You report to Jamia Arias, the CEO of the company. One of your responsibilities in this role is creating and analyzing worksheet data from various company offices to help Jamia make sound decisions on expansion, investments, and new recruiting opportunities.

Module Objectives

After completing this module, you will be able to:

- Describe an Excel workbook
- Enter data
- Edit data
- Copy and move cell data
- Enter formulas
- Enter a formula with multiple operators
- Insert a function
- Change worksheet views
- Customize print options

Files You Will Need

IL_EX_1-1.xlsx
IL_EX_1-2.xlsx
IL_EX_1-3.xlsx
IL_EX_1-4.xlsx
IL_EX_1-5.xlsx

Describe an Excel Workbook

Case Maria Lopez, Director of the IT Consulting Division, submitted preliminary data on consulting position postings and asked for your help in analyzing this data. You will begin by reviewing the postings in the southern region.

Objectives
- Define key spreadsheet terms
- Save an Excel file
- Identify Excel window elements

Microsoft Excel is an **electronic spreadsheet program**, a computer program used to perform calculations and analyze and present numeric data. An Excel file, a **workbook**, is a collection of related worksheets contained within a single file with the file extension xlsx. A workbook is made up of one or more worksheets. A **worksheet** contains a grid of columns and rows where you can enter and manipulate data, perform calculations with data, and analyze data.

Steps

Trouble
If the extension .xlsx doesn't appear after the filenames in the Save As dialog box, don't worry; Windows can be set up to display or not to display the file extensions.

1. **sam↓** Click the **Start button** on the Windows taskbar, type **Excel**, click **Excel**, click **Open**, navigate to the location where you store your Data Files, click **IL_EX_1-1.xlsx**, then click **Open**

Quick Tip
You can open a blank workbook by clicking Blank workbook rather than Open.

2. Click the **File tab**, click **Save As** on the navigation bar, click **Browse**, navigate to the location where you store your Data Files, if necessary, type **IL_EX_1_Postings** in the File name box, then click **Save**

   Referring to **Figure 1-1**, identify the following items:
   - The **Name box** is the box to the left of the formula bar that shows the cell reference or name of the active cell. "A1" appears in the Name box.
   - The **formula bar** is the area above the worksheet grid where you enter or edit data in the active cell.
   - The **worksheet window** is an area of the program window that displays part of the current worksheet, which can contain a total of 1,048,576 rows and 16,384 columns. The columns and rows intersect to form cells, where you can enter and manipulate text, numbers, formulas, or a combination of all three. Every cell has its own unique location or **cell address**, expressed by combining its column letter and row number such as A1.

Quick Tip
Depending on the installation of your software, the title bar may include a Quick Access Toolbar, which can be customized to provide easier access to the tools you use frequently. To display or hide it, click the Ribbon Display Options button ⌄, located in the lower-right of the ribbon, then click Show Quick Access Toolbar or Hide Quick Access Toolbar.

   - The **cell pointer** is a dark rectangle that outlines the active cell in a worksheet. In the figure, the cell pointer outlines cell A1, so A1 is the active cell.
   - By default, a workbook file contains one worksheet named Sheet1—but you can have as many sheets as your computer's memory allows in a workbook. The New sheet button to the right of Sheet1 allows you to add worksheets to a workbook. **Sheet tab scrolling buttons** are triangles that let you navigate to additional sheet tabs when available; they're located to the left of the sheet tabs.
   - The status bar provides a brief description of the active command or task in progress. The **mode indicator** on the left end of the status bar indicates the program's status, such as the Edit mode in Excel. You are in Edit mode any time you are entering or changing the contents of a cell. You can use the Zoom In and Zoom Out buttons on the status bar to increase or decrease the scale of the displayed worksheet.
   - You can use the **Search box** on the title bar to find a command or access the Excel Help system.
   - The AutoSave button on the title bar is on if you are working on a file saved on OneDrive. When AutoSave is on, your file will be automatically saved as you make changes.

3. Click cell **B4**

   Cell B4 becomes the active cell. To activate a different cell, you can click the cell or press the arrow keys on your keyboard to move to it.

Quick Tip
The button that opens in the bottom-right corner of a range is the Quick Analysis tool.

4. Click cell **B4**, press and hold the mouse button, drag the **pointer** to cell **E4**, then release the mouse button

   You selected a group of cells, and they are highlighted, as shown in **Figure 1-2**. A series of two or more adjacent cells in a column, row, or rectangular group of cells, notated using the cell address of its upper-left and lower-right corners, such as B4:B4, is called a **range**; you select a range when you want to perform an action on a group of cells at once, such as moving them or formatting them. When you select a range, the status bar displays the average, count (or number of items selected), and sum of the selected cells as a quick reference.

Describe an Excel Workbook   EX 1-3

Figure 1-1: Open workbook

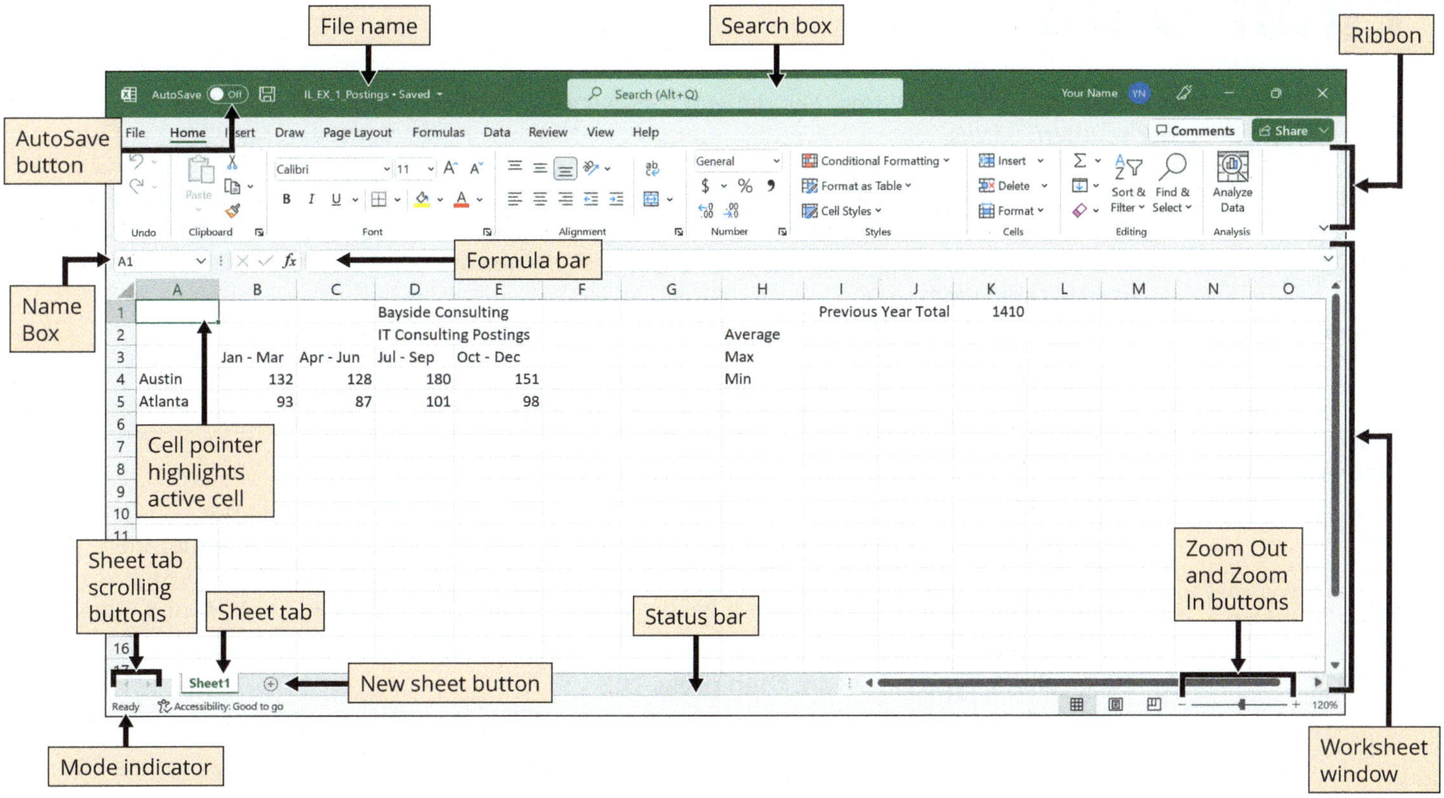

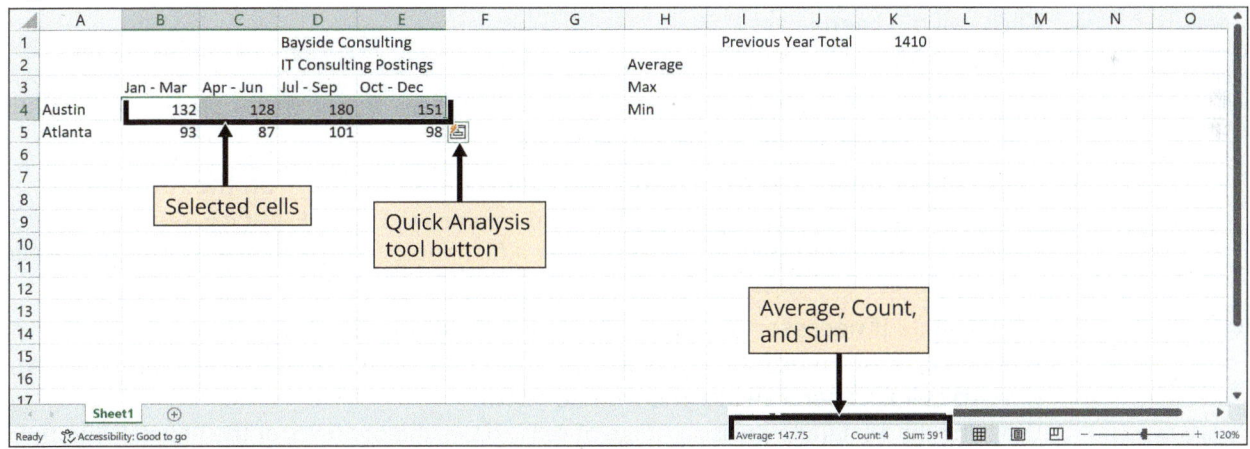

Figure 1-2: Selected range

Navigating a worksheet

With over a million cells available in a worksheet, it is important to know how to move around in, or navigate, a worksheet. You can use the arrow keys on the keyboard ↑, ↓, →, or ← to move one cell at a time, or press PAGE UP or PAGE DOWN to move one screen at a time. To move one screen to the left, press ALT+PAGE UP; to move one screen to the right, press ALT+PAGE DOWN. You can also use the mouse pointer to click the desired cell. If the desired cell is not visible in the worksheet window, use the scroll bars or use the Go To command by clicking the Find & Select button in the Editing group on the Home tab on the ribbon. To quickly jump to the first cell in a worksheet, press CTRL+HOME; to jump to the last cell, press CTRL+END.

Module 1 Getting Started with Excel

Enter Data

Case The Houston office was late in submitting their data for the year's four quarters. You need to add it to the data from the other southern offices.

Objectives
- Enter labels
- Enter values
- Enter a series of data with Auto Fill
- Copy data using the fill handle

To enter content in a cell, you can type in the formula bar or directly in the cell itself. **Labels** are descriptive text or other information that identifies data in rows, columns, or charts, not included in calculations, such as "2024 Sales" or "Expenses". **Values** are numbers, formulas, and functions used in calculations.

Steps

Quick Tip
If you change your mind and want to cancel an entry in the formula bar, click the Cancel button ✗ on the formula bar.

1. **Click cell F3, type Total, then click the Enter button ✓ on the formula bar**
   Clicking the Enter button accepts the entry without moving the cell pointer to a new location. The new text is left-aligned in the cell because labels are left-aligned by default. Excel recognizes an entry as a value if it is a number or it begins with one of these symbols: +, -, =, @, #, or $. When a cell contains both text and numbers, Excel recognizes it as a label.

2. **Click cell A6, type Houston, then press TAB**
   Pressing TAB accepts the entry and moves the active cell to the right, to cell B6.

3. **With B6 as the active cell, type 89, press TAB, type 132, press TAB, type 127, press TAB, type 125, then press TAB**
   The quarterly data is displayed for the Houston office, as shown in **Figure 1-3**. The numbers are right-aligned because values are right-aligned by default. You want to replace the monthly labels in row 3 with quarter labels.

Quick Tip
If you want to clear a cell's content, including its formatting, click the Clear button ◆ in the Editing group on the Home tab on the ribbon, then click Clear All.

4. **Click cell B3, then press DEL**
   You can delete each cell entry individually or delete a range of cells.

5. **Click cell C3, press and hold the mouse button, drag the Normal pointer ✛ to cell E3, release the mouse button, then press DEL**

6. **Click cell B3, type Quarter 1, then click the Enter button ✓ on the formula bar**
   You could continue to type quarter labels into columns C, D, and E, but it is easier to use Auto Fill to enter these labels. **Auto Fill** lets you drag a fill handle to copy a cell's contents or continue a selected series into adjacent cells.

Trouble
On your screen, column widths may differ slightly from the figures, depending on your screen resolution and display settings.

7. **Click cell B3 if necessary, position the Normal pointer on the lower-right corner of the cell (the fill handle) so that the pointer changes to the fill handle pointer ✚, drag to cell E3, then release the mouse button**
   Dragging the fill handle across a range of cells copies the contents of the first cell into the other cells in the range or completes a data series. In this case, since Excel detected a data pattern in the selected cells, it filled the remaining selected cells with a series of annual quarters.

8. **Click the Auto Fill Options button**
   Options for filling the selected range include Fill Series, which is selected, as shown in **Figure 1-4**. The other available options allow you to change to copying cells, fill the cells with formatting only, or fill the cells without formatting.

9. **Save your work**

Figure 1-3: Houston data entered

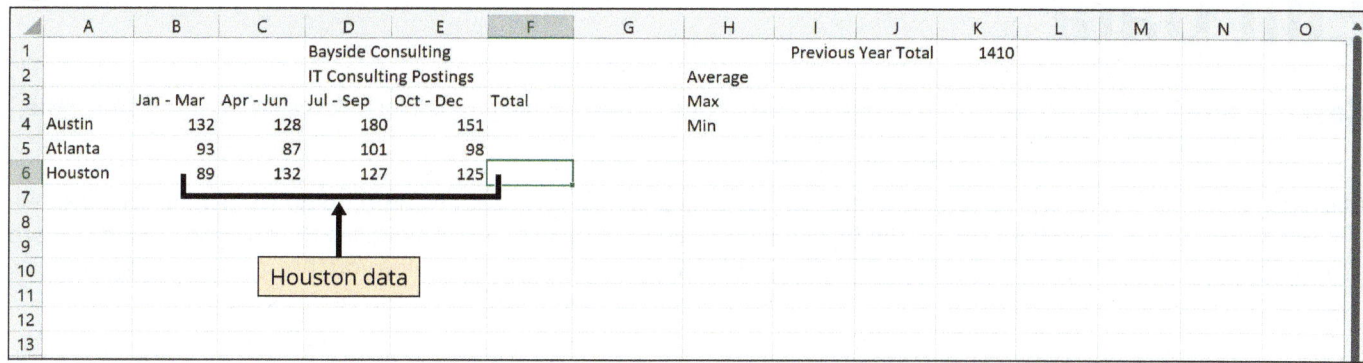

Figure 1-4: Auto Fill options

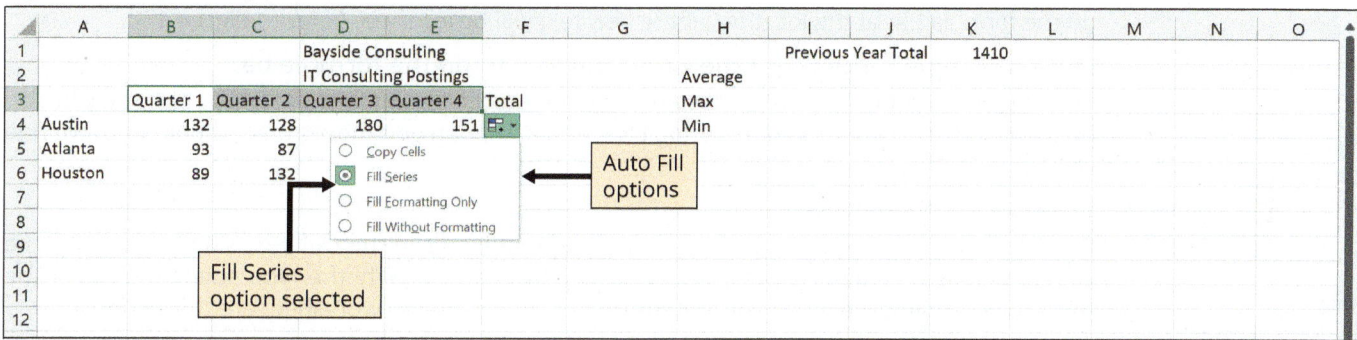

Inserting and deleting selected cells

As you add formulas to your workbook, you may need to insert or delete cells. To insert cells, click the Insert arrow in the Cells group on the Home tab on the ribbon, then click Insert Cells. The Insert dialog box opens, asking if you want to insert a cell and move the current active cell down or to the right of the new one. To delete one or more selected cells, click the Delete arrow in the Cells group, click Delete Cells, and in the Delete dialog box, indicate which way you want to move the adjacent cells. When using this option, be careful not to disturb row or column alignment that may be necessary to maintain the accuracy of cell references on the worksheet. You can also click the Insert button or Delete button in the Cells group to insert or delete a single cell. Excel automatically adjusts cell references within the formulas of any moved cells to reflect their new locations.

EX 1-6   Module 1 Getting Started with Excel

Edit Data

Case In reviewing the worksheet, you noticed a few input errors you need to correct. You also want to change the wording of two labels.

Objectives
- Edit cell entries in the formula bar
- Edit cell entries in the cell

You can change, or edit, the contents of an active cell at any time. To do so, double-click the cell, and then click in the formula bar or just start typing. Excel switches to Edit mode when you are making cell entries. Different pointers, shown in **Table 1-1**, guide you through the editing process.

Steps

1. **Click cell B4, then click to the left of 2 in the formula bar**
   As soon as you click in the formula bar, a blinking vertical line called the **insertion point** appears on the formula bar at the location where new text will be inserted. Refer to **Figure 1-5**.

2. **Press DEL, type 7, then click the Enter button ✓ on the formula bar**
   Clicking the Enter button accepts the edit, and the Austin first quarter posting is 137. You can also press ENTER to accept an edit. Pressing ENTER to accept an edit moves the cell pointer down one cell.

   Quick Tip
   On some keyboards, you might need to press F-LOCK to enable the function keys.

3. **Click cell B6, then press F2**
   Excel switches to Edit mode, and the insertion point blinks in the cell. Pressing F2 activates the cell for editing directly in the cell instead of the formula bar. Whether you edit in the cell or the formula bar is simply a matter of preference; the results on the worksheet are the same.

   Quick Tip
   If you notice a mistake *after* confirming a cell entry, click the Undo button ↶ in the Undo group on the Home tab. The Undo button allows you to reverse up to 100 previous actions, one at a time. If you mistakenly undo an action, you can click the Redo button ↷ in the Undo group on the Home tab.

4. **Press BACKSPACE, type 5, then press ENTER**
   The value in the cell changes from 89 to 85, and cell B7 becomes the active cell.

5. **Click cell H3, then double-click the word Max in the formula bar**
   Double-clicking a word in a cell selects it. When you selected the word, the Mini toolbar automatically opened.

6. **Type Maximum, then press ENTER**
   When text is selected, typing deletes it and replaces it with the new text.

7. **Double-click cell H4, click to the right of n, type imum, then click the Enter button ✓**
   Double-clicking a cell activates it for editing directly in the cell. Compare your screen to **Figure 1-6**.

8. **Save your work**

Recovering unsaved changes to a workbook file

You can use Excel's AutoRecover feature to automatically save your work as often as you want. This means that if you suddenly lose power or if Excel closes unexpectedly while you're working, you can recover all or some of the changes you made since you saved it last. (This is added insurance and not a substitute for regularly saving your work.) To customize the AutoRecover settings, click the File tab, click More, click Options, then click Save. AutoRecover lets you decide how often and into which location it should save files. When you restart Excel after an unexpected close, a Recovered files section may open above the listing of recent files. You can click Show Recovered Files to access the saved versions of files that were open when Excel closed.

Figure 1-5: Worksheet in Edit mode

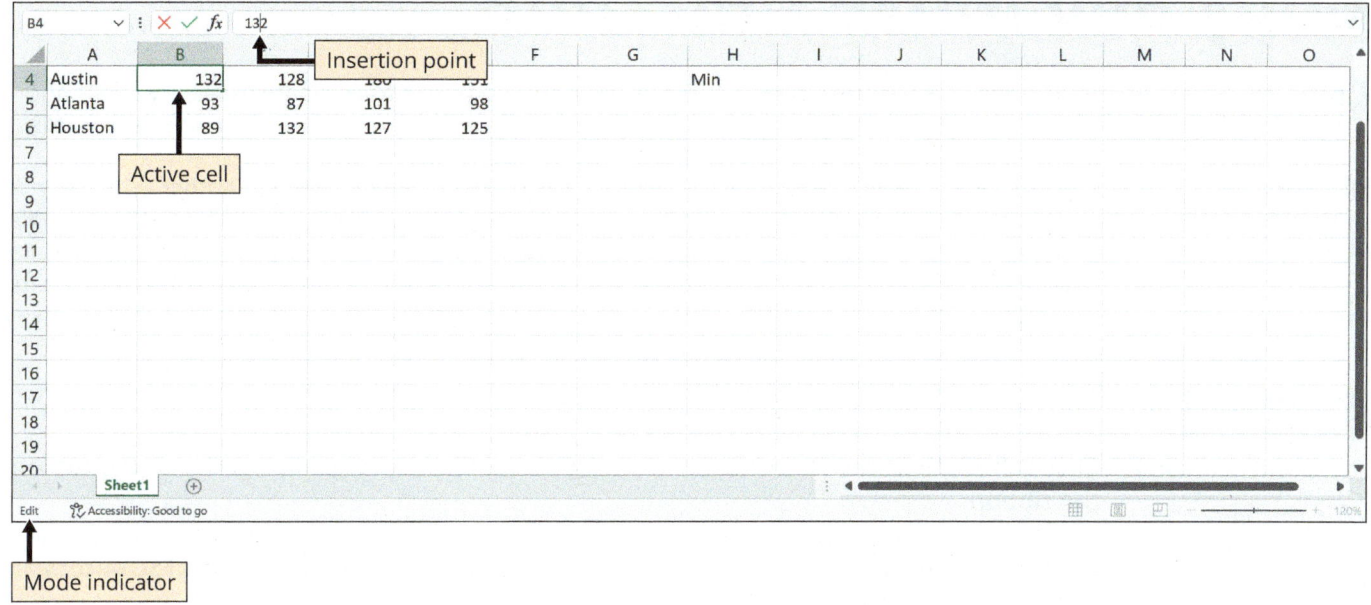

Figure 1-6: Edited worksheet

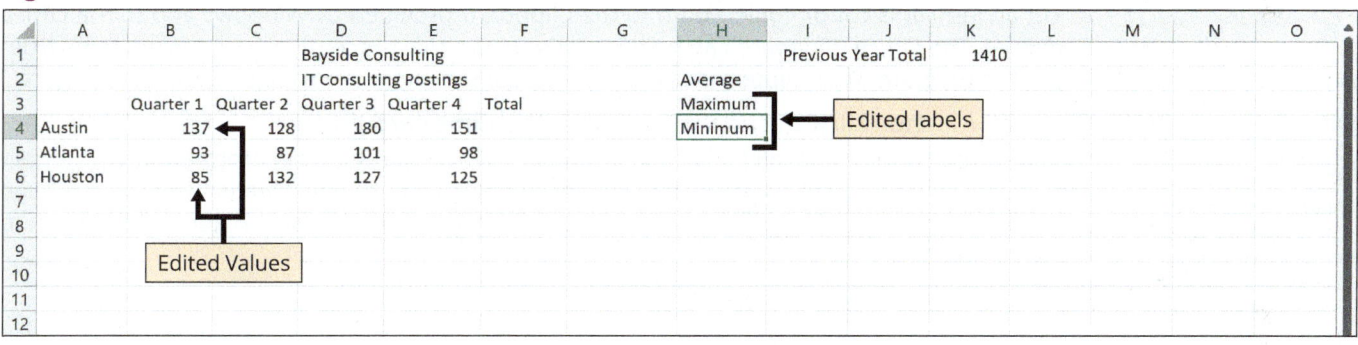

Table 1-1: Common pointers in Excel

name	pointer	use to	visible over the
Normal	✛	Select a cell or range; indicates Ready mode	Active worksheet
Fill handle	+	Copy cell contents or series to adjacent cells	Lower-right corner of the active cell or range
I-beam	I	Edit cell contents in active cell or formula bar	Active cell in Edit mode or over the formula bar
Move	✥	Change the location of the selected cell(s)	Perimeter of the active cell(s)
Copy	▷⁺	Create a duplicate of the selected cell(s)	Perimeter of the active cell(s) when CTRL is pressed
Column resize	↔	Change the width of a column	Border between column heading indicators

Copy and Move Cell Data

Case To evaluate open posting in the southern region of the company, you want to compare quarterly totals and statistical information. You will speed up this task by copying and moving existing worksheet labels to selected cells.

Objectives
- Copy cell data to the Clipboard
- Paste a Clipboard entry
- Move a range

You can copy or move the contents of cells and ranges from one location to another using several methods, including the Cut, Copy, and Paste buttons on the Home tab on the ribbon, the fill handle of the active cell or range, or the drag-and-drop feature. When you copy cells, the original data remains in its original location; when you cut or move cells, the original data is deleted from its original location. You can copy and move cells or ranges within a worksheet or from one worksheet to another.

Steps

Quick Tip
To cut or copy selected cell contents, activate the cell, then select the characters within the cell that you want to cut or copy.

1. **Click cell F3, then click the Copy button in the Clipboard group on the Home tab on the ribbon**
   The cell data is copied to the **Clipboard**, a temporary Windows storage area that holds the selections you copy or cut. A moving border surrounds the selected cell until you press ESC or copy an additional item to the Clipboard.

2. **Click the dialog box launcher in the Clipboard group**
   The Office Clipboard opens in the Clipboard task pane, as shown in **Figure 1-7**. When you copy or cut an item, it is cut or copied both to the Clipboard provided by Windows and to the Office Clipboard. The Office Clipboard can hold up to 24 of the most recently cut or copied items from any Office program. Your Clipboard task pane may contain more items than shown in the figure.

Quick Tip
You can have multiple items in the Clipboard resulting from multiple copy operations. You can paste these items individually or all the items at the same time by clicking the Paste All button.

3. **Click cell A7, then click the Paste button in the Clipboard group**
   A copy of the contents of cell F3 is pasted into cell A7. Notice that the information you copied remains in the original cell F3; if you had cut instead of copied, the information would have been deleted from its original location once it was pasted. You can also paste an item by clicking it in the Office Clipboard.

4. **Click the Paste Options button (Ctrl)**
   The Paste Options open, as shown in **Figure 1-8**. These options allow you to determine what you want pasted and how you want the pasted data to appear on the worksheet. Review the three categories, Paste, Paste Values, and Other Paste Options. The current pasted data doesn't need any change in formatting.

5. **Press ESC twice, then click the Close button on the Clipboard task pane**

6. **Select the range H2:H4, point to any edge of the selected range until the Normal pointer changes to the Move pointer, drag the range to cell A9, then release the mouse button**
   The move pointer displays an outline of the range you are dragging. When you release the mouse button, you "drop" the selection to the range A9:A11. When pasting an item from the Clipboard, you only need to specify the upper-left cell of the range where you want to paste the selection. If you press and hold CTRL while dragging and dropping, the information is copied instead of moved. The Quick Analysis tool to the right of the copied content offers some useful tools in Excel.

7. **Save your work**

Figure 1-7: Copied data in Office Clipboard

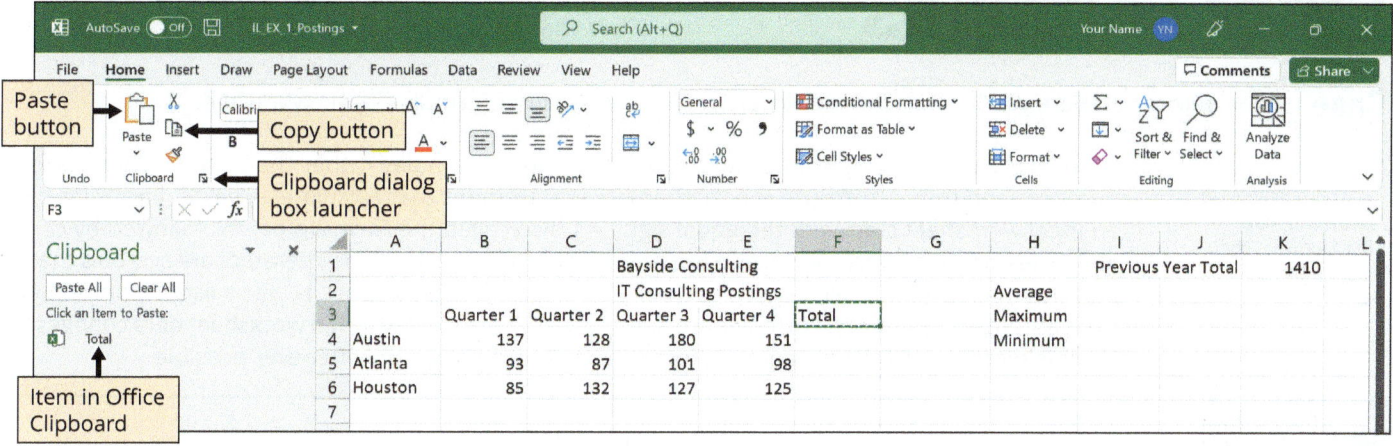

Figure 1-8: Paste options

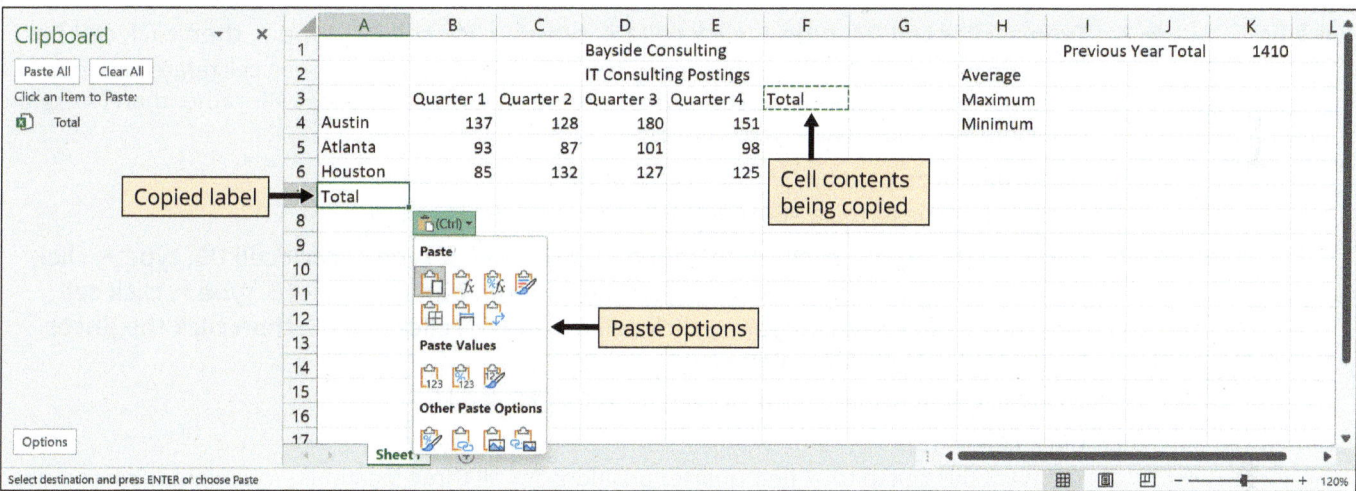

Using Paste Options and Paste Preview

You can selectively paste copied or cut formulas, values, or other data by using the Paste Options button that opens on the worksheet after you paste data or clicking the Paste arrow in the Clipboard. The Paste Preview feature shows how the current selection will look when pasted. When you click the Paste Options button (or simply press [Ctrl] or the Paste arrow, a gallery of paste option icons opens, organized by category. The Paste category includes pasting formulas, pasting formulas and number formatting, pasting using the source formatting, pasting with no borders (to remove any borders around pasted cells), pasting with the source column widths, and pasting transposed data so that column data appears in rows and row data appears in columns. The Paste Values category includes pasting values only (without formatting), pasting values and number formatting, and pasting values with source formatting. The Other Paste Options category includes pasting formatting, links, pictures, and linked pictures. Clicking Paste Link in this category creates a link to the source data so that in the future, changes to the copied data update the pasted data. Clicking Picture in this category pastes the data as a picture where the picture tools can be used to format it, resize it, or move it.

Module 1 Getting Started with Excel

Enter Formulas

Case To be able to compare yearly totals for each location you need to enter formulas in the worksheet.

Objectives
- Use cell references to create a formula
- Build formulas and use the AutoSum function

Excel is a powerful program because cells can contain formulas rather than simply values like numbers and text. A **formula** is a mathematical statement that calculates a value. Formulas in an Excel worksheet start with the equal sign (=), also called the **formula prefix**, followed by cell addresses, range names, values, and **arithmetic operators**. Arithmetic operators are symbols that perform mathematical calculations such as +, -, *, and /. Refer to **Table 1-2** for a list of commonly used arithmetic operators. Formulas are automatically recalculated when worksheet data changes. For this reason, use cell references in formulas, rather than values, whenever possible.

Steps

1. **Click cell F4**
   This is the first cell where you want to insert a formula. To calculate the yearly total for the Austin location, you need to add the quarterly totals.

Quick Tip
You can reference a cell in a formula either by typing the cell reference or clicking the cell on the worksheet; when you click a cell to add a reference, the Mode indicator changes to "Point."

2. **Type =, click cell B4, type +, click cell C4, type +, click cell D4, type +, then click cell E4**
   Compare your formula bar to **Figure 1-9**. The blue, red, purple, and green cell references in cell F4 correspond to the color of the cells. When entering a formula, clicking cells rather than typing the cell addresses helps avoid typing errors.

3. **Click the Enter button ✓ on the formula bar**
   The result of the formula =B4+C4+D4+E4, 596, appears in cell F4.

4. **Click cell F5, type =, click cell B5, type +, click cell C5, type +, click cell D5, type +, click cell E5, click the Enter button ✓ on the formula bar, click cell F6, type =, click cell B6, type +, click cell C6, type +, click cell D6, type +, click cell E6, then click the Enter button ✓ on the formula bar**
   The results of these two formulas appear in cells F5 and F6.

5. **Click cell B7**
   You want this cell to total first-quarter positions for all three locations. You might think you need to create a formula that looks like this: =B4+B5+B6. However, there's an easier way to achieve this result.

Trouble
Your button may only be displaying the Sum ScreenTip. Not all display devices show the AutoSum label.

6. **On the ribbon, click the AutoSum button Σ in the Editing group on the Home tab**
   The SUM function is inserted in the cell, and a suggested range appears in parentheses. A **function** is a predefined procedure that returns a value; it includes the **arguments** (the information necessary to calculate an answer) as well as cell references and other unique information. Clicking the AutoSum button sums the adjacent range (that is, the cells next to the active cell) above or to the left, although you can adjust the range if necessary by selecting a different range before accepting the cell entry. Using the SUM function is quicker than entering a formula, and using the range B4:B6 is more efficient than entering individual cell references.

7. **Click the Enter button ✓ on the formula bar**
   Excel calculates the total contained in cells B4:B6 and displays the result, 315, in cell B7. The cell actually contains the formula =SUM(B4:B6), but it displays the result.

8. **Click cell C7, click the AutoSum button Σ, click the Enter button ✓, click cell D7, click the AutoSum button Σ, click the Enter button ✓, click cell E7, click the AutoSum button Σ, click the Enter button ✓, click cell F7, click the AutoSum button Σ, click the Enter button ✓, compare your screen to Figure 1-10, then save your work**

Enter Formulas EX 1-11

Figure 1-9: Entering a formula

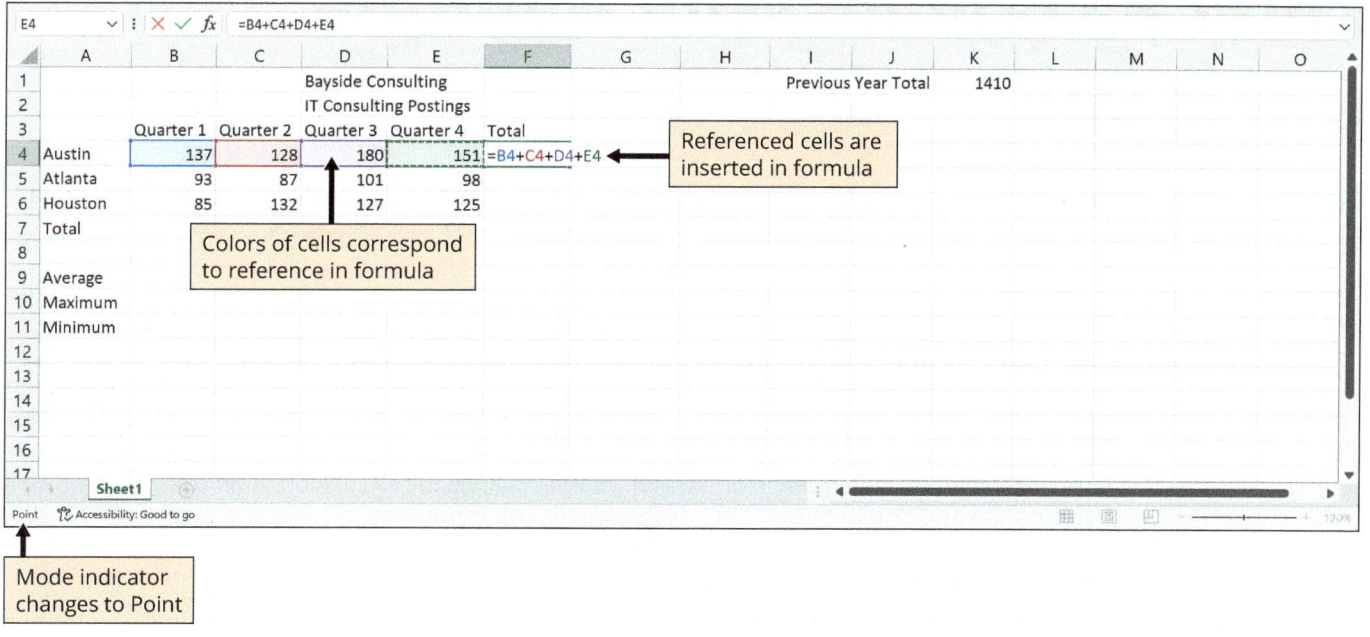

Figure 1-10: SUM functions in a worksheet

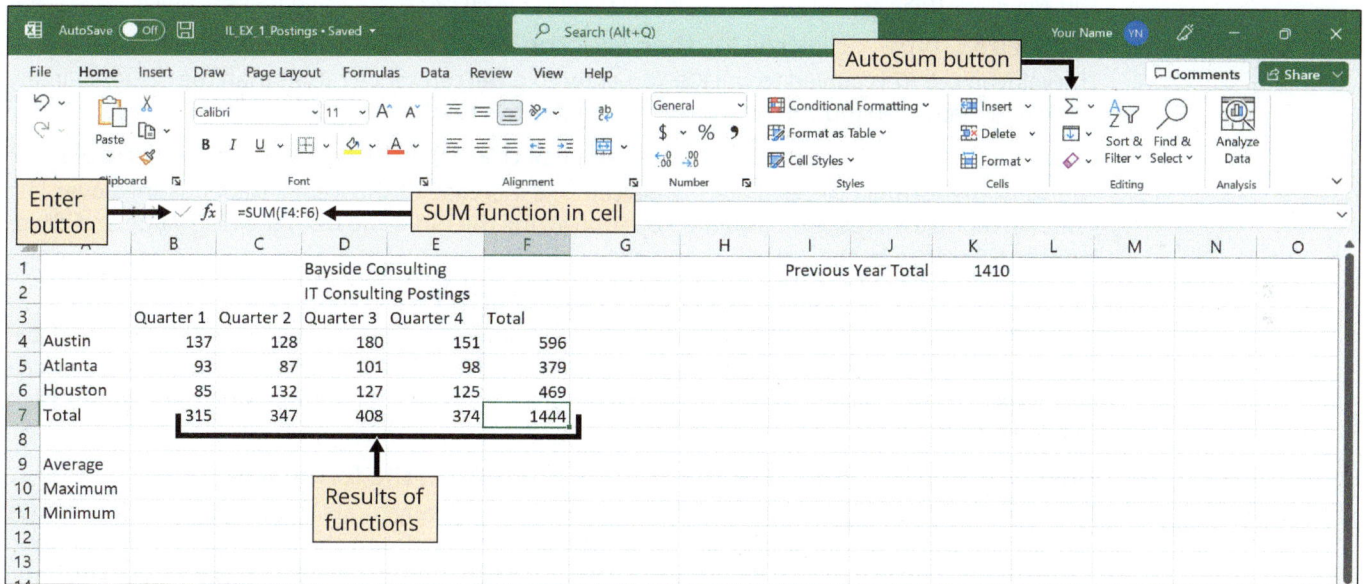

Table 1-2: Excel arithmetic operators

operator	purpose	example
+	Addition	=A5+A7
-	Subtraction or negation	=A5-10
*	Multiplication	=A5*A7
/	Division	=A5/A7
%	Percent	=35%
^ (caret)	Exponent	=6^2 (same as 6^2)

Enter a Formula with Multiple Operators

Case To compare this year's postings with last year's you need to calculate the percentage increase of this year's total from last year's total.

Objectives
- Apply the order of operations
- Create a formula with multiple operators

Formulas often contain more than one arithmetic operator. In these formulas, Excel follows the **order of operations**, the sequence in which operators are applied in a mathematical calculation. Instead of calculating simply from left to right, this order calls for calculations in parentheses to be performed first, exponent calculations second, then multiplication and division, and finally addition and subtraction. If there are multiple occurrences of an operation, such as two multiplication operations, they are calculated from left to right. If your formula requires addition or subtraction to be calculated before multiplication or division, you can change the calculation order using parentheses around the addition or subtraction. For example, the formula to average the numbers 100, 200, and 300 is (100+200+300)/3 to make sure the numbers are totaled before the division operation. **Table 1-3** shows more examples of how calculations are performed in Excel.

Steps

1. **Click cell J3, type This Year, then click the Enter button ✓ on the formula bar**
   You will enter this year's total using the calculation in cell F7.

2. **Click cell K3, type =, click cell F7, then click the Enter button ✓ on the formula bar**
   The value in cell F7 is copied to cell K3. You entered a cell reference rather than the value, so if any worksheet data is edited you won't have to reenter this total.

3. **Click cell J5, type Percent Increase, then click the Enter button ✓ on the formula bar**
   You want the formula to calculate the percentage increase of this year's total postings over last year. Percentage increase is calculated by subtracting the old value from the new value and dividing that difference by the old value, or (new − old)/old.

4. **Click cell K5, type =, type (, click cell K3, type -, click cell K1, then type)**
   In this first part of the formula, you are finding the difference in totals between this year and last year. You enclosed this calculation with parentheses so it will be performed before any other calculations, because calculations in parentheses are always calculated first. Compare your screen to **Figure 1-11**.

5. **Type /, click cell K1, then click the Enter button ✓ on the formula bar**
   The second part of this formula divides the difference in yearly totals by the total for the previous year to find the percentage of the growth. Because you enclosed the subtraction calculation in parentheses, it was calculated before the division calculation. The value in cell K5 is in decimal format. You want to display this value as a percentage with two decimal places.

6. **Click the Percent Style button % in the Number group on the Home tab, then click the Increase Decimal button in the Number group twice**
   The percentage increase in cell K5 is 2.41%, as shown in **Figure 1-12**.

7. **Save your work**

Figure 1-11: Formula with parentheses

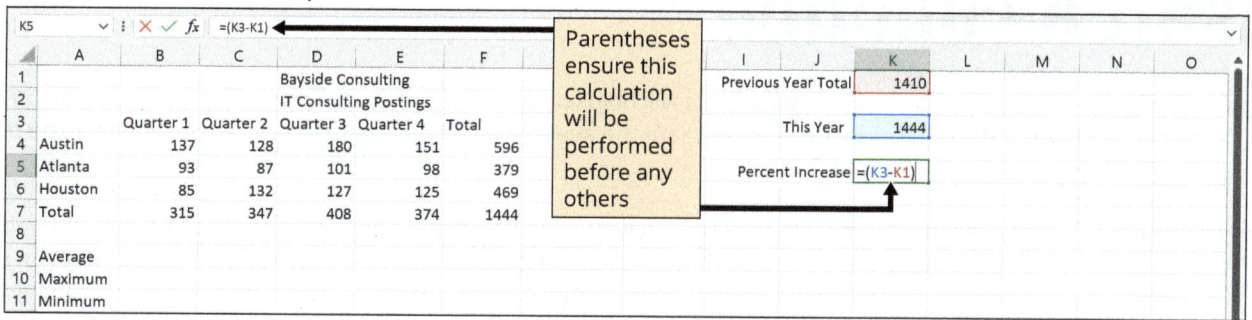

Figure 1-12: Formula with percentage increase

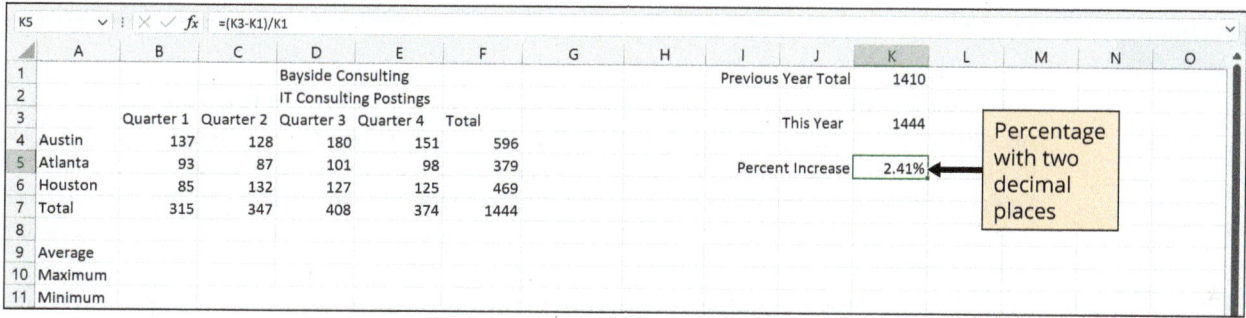

Table 1-3: Calculation results in Excel formulas

formula	result
10+20+40/2	50
(10+20+40)/2	35
10+5*2	20
(10+5)*2	30
20-10/2	15
(20-10)/2	5

Insert a Function

Case Adding a statistical analysis of the annual totals will help you evaluate the postings in the southern region offices. To help with this you will use functions to calculate the average, maximum, and minimum postings for the totals for the locations.

Objectives
- Use the Insert Function dialog box
- Insert a function manually

You can insert functions in several ways. So far, you have used the AutoSum button on the ribbon to add the SUM function. To choose from all available functions you can use the Insert Function dialog box. This is especially valuable if you're not sure of the name of the function you need, because functions are organized into categories, such as Financial, Date & Time, and Statistical, and you are guided through the process. Other ways to insert a function include manually typing it in a cell and using the AutoSum arrow to insert commonly used functions.

Steps

1. **Click cell B9, then click the Insert Function button f_x on the formula bar**
   An equal sign (=) is inserted in the active cell, and the Insert Function dialog box opens, as shown in **Figure 1-13**. In this dialog box, you specify the function you want to use by clicking it in the Select a function list of recently used functions, clicking the Or select a category arrow to choose a desired function category, or typing the function name, or its description, in the Search for a function field.

   Trouble
   If AVERAGE is not in the function list, type AVERAGE in the Search for a function box, then click Go.

2. **Click AVERAGE in the Select a function list if necessary, read the information that appears under the list, then click OK**
   The Function Arguments dialog box opens, as shown in **Figure 1-14**.

3. **Click the Collapse button ⬆ in the Number1 field of the Function Arguments dialog box, select the range F4:F6 on the worksheet, then click the Expand button ⬇ in the Function Arguments dialog box**
   Clicking the Collapse button minimizes the dialog box so that you can select cells on the worksheet. When you click the Expand button, the dialog box is restored. You can also begin dragging on the worksheet to automatically minimize the dialog box; after you select the desired range, the dialog box is restored.

4. **Click OK**
   The Function Arguments dialog box closes, and the calculated value is displayed in cell B9. The average number of postings for the year is 481.3333.

5. **Click cell B10, type =, then type m**
   Because you are manually typing this function, you must manually type the opening equal sign (=). Once you type an equal sign in a cell, each letter you type acts as a trigger to activate the Excel **Formula AutoComplete**, a feature that automatically suggests text, numbers, or dates to insert based on previous entries. Because you entered the letter *m*, this feature suggests a list of function names beginning with "M."

   Quick Tip
   In the AutoComplete list, if you click a function instead of double-clicking, a ScreenTip displays more detailed information about the function.

6. **Double-click MAX in the list, select the range F4:F6, then click the Enter button ✓ on the formula bar**
   The result, 596, appears in cell B10. When you completed the entry, the closing parenthesis was automatically added to the formula.

7. **Click cell B11, type =, type m, double-click MIN in the list of function names, select the range F4:F6, then press ENTER**
   The result, 379, appears in cell B11.

8. **Click cell A8, type Annual Statistics, press ENTER, then save your work**
   Compare your worksheet to **Figure 1-15**.

Figure 1-13: Insert Function dialog box

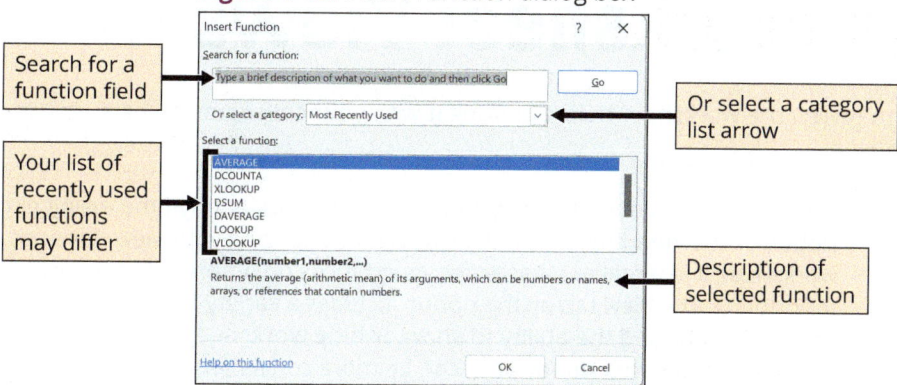

Figure 1-14: Function Arguments dialog box

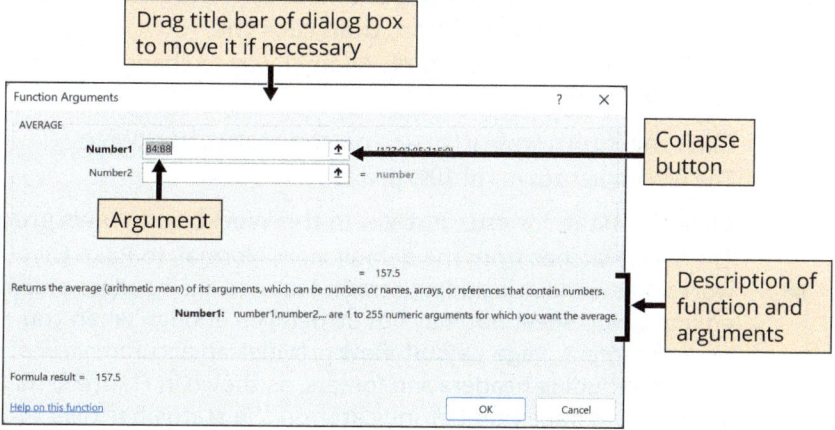

Figure 1-15: Worksheet with annual statistics

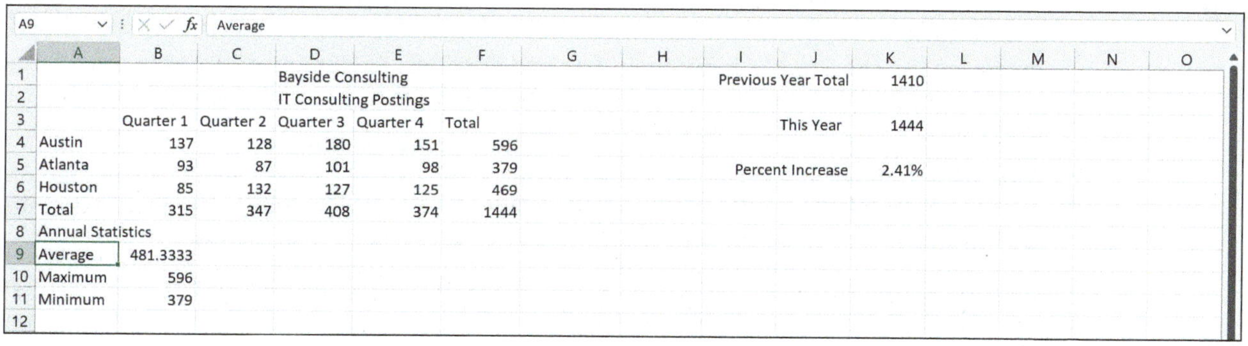

	A	B	C	D	E	F	G	H	I	J	K	L	M	N	O
1				Bayside Consulting					Previous Year Total		1410				
2				IT Consulting Postings											
3		Quarter 1	Quarter 2	Quarter 3	Quarter 4	Total			This Year		1444				
4	Austin	137	128	180	151	596									
5	Atlanta	93	87	101	98	379			Percent Increase		2.41%				
6	Houston	85	132	127	125	469									
7	Total	315	347	408	374	1444									
8	Annual Statistics														
9	Average	481.3333													
10	Maximum	596													
11	Minimum	379													
12															

Change Worksheet Views

Case You want to review the worksheet before sharing it with your colleagues to be sure it is easy for them to view the information.

Objectives
- Use the Zoom option on a worksheet
- Change worksheet views
- Adjust page breaks in a worksheet

You can change your view of the worksheet window at any time, using either the View tab on the ribbon or the View buttons on the status bar. Changing your view does not affect the contents of a worksheet; it just makes it easier for you to focus on different tasks, such as preparing a worksheet for printing. The View tab on the ribbon includes a variety of viewing options, such as View buttons, zoom controls, and the ability to show or hide worksheet elements such as gridlines. The status bar offers fewer view options but can be more convenient to use.

Steps

Quick Tip
You can use the Zoom button to select the worksheet magnification level or the Zoom to Selection button to zoom into the cell or range that is selected on the worksheet.

1. **Click cell A1, verify that the zoom level in the Zoom area of the status bar is 120%, click the View tab on the ribbon, then click the 100% button in the Zoom group**
   The worksheet zooms to 100%. Another way to change the zoom level is to use the Zoom slider on the status bar.

2. **Click the Zoom in button + on the status bar twice**
   The worksheet zooms in 10% at a time, to 120%.

3. **Click the Page Layout button in the Workbook Views group on the View tab**
   The view switches from the default view, Normal, to Page Layout view. **Normal view** shows the worksheet without including certain features like headers and footers; it's ideal for creating and editing a worksheet but may not be detailed enough when you want to put the finishing touches on a document. **Page Layout view** provides an accurate view of how a worksheet will look when printed, including headers and footers, as shown in **Figure 1-16**. Above and to the left of the page are rulers. A page number indicator on the status bar tells you the current page and the total number of pages in this worksheet.

Quick Tip
Although a worksheet can contain more than a million rows and thousands of columns, the current document contains only as many pages as necessary for the current project.

4. **Click the Ruler check box in the Show group on the View tab to remove the checkmark, then click the Gridlines check box in the Show group to remove the checkmark**
   Removing the checkmarks hides the rulers and gridlines. By default, gridlines in a worksheet do not print, so hiding them gives you a more accurate image of your final document.

5. **Click the Page Break Preview button on the status bar**
   Your view changes to Page Break Preview, which displays a reduced view of each page of your worksheet, along with page break indicators that you can drag to include more or less information on a page.

6. **Drag the Page Break Preview pointer ↕ from the bottom page break indicator to the bottom of row 15, as shown in Figure 1-17**
   When you're working on a large worksheet with multiple pages, sometimes you need to adjust where pages break; in this worksheet, however, the information all fits comfortably on one page.

Quick Tip
Once you view a worksheet in Page Break Preview, the page break indicators appear as lines after you switch back to Normal view or Page Layout view.

7. **Click the Page Layout button in the Workbook Views group, click the Ruler box in the Show group, then click the Gridlines box in the Show group**
   Adding checkmarks to the check boxes displays the rulers and gridlines. You can show or hide View tab items in any view.

8. **Click the Normal button in the Workbook Views group, then save your work**

Change Worksheet Views EX 1-17

Figure 1-16: Page Layout view

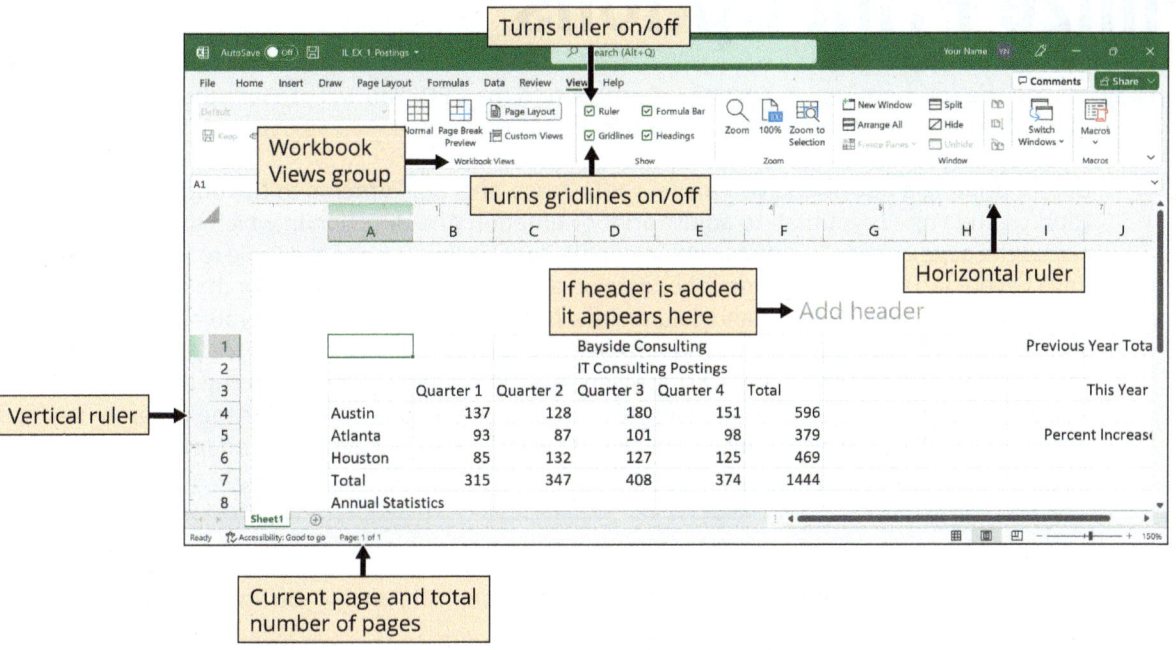

Figure 1-17: Page Break Preview

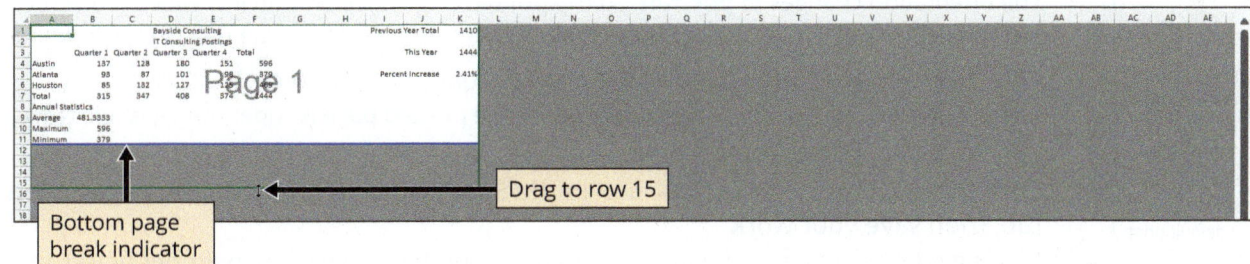

Working with Sheet View options

If you are collaborating with others on a worksheet containing a large amount of data, you can use a Sheet View to view and work with only the columns and rows you need. A Sheet View allows you to work with the data you need without being interrupted by others changing their view of the worksheet. Any changes you make to the worksheet will automatically be saved with the workbook.

The New button is available in the Sheet View group of the View tab on the ribbon when a workbook is saved on OneDrive, as shown in Figure 1-18. To create a Sheet View, click the View tab, click the New button in the Sheet View group, then click Exit guide if necessary. Your new view is named Temporary View because it hasn't been saved yet. You can save a Sheet View by selecting the name Temporary View, entering a new name, then pressing ENTER. An eye symbol is displayed next to the worksheet tab name; hovering over this will display the name of the Sheet View. You can delete a Sheet View by selecting it in the Sheet View group, clicking the Options button in the Sheet View group, clicking Delete, then clicking Delete again to confirm the action.

Figure 1-18: Sheet View options

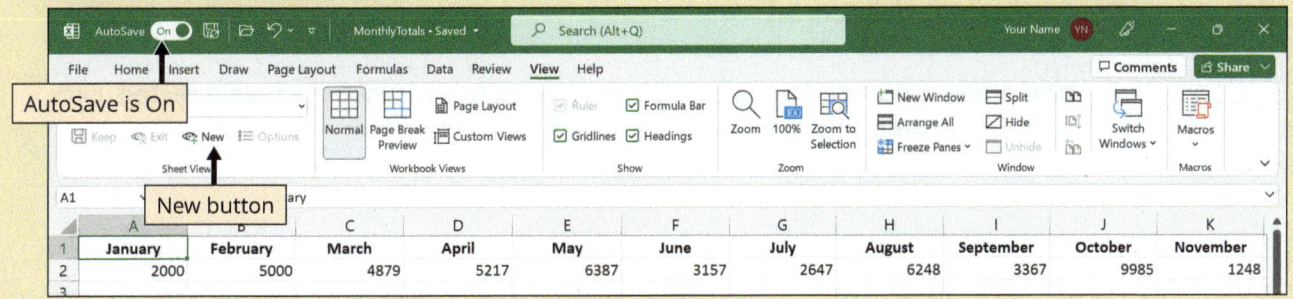

Customize Print Options

Case You are ready to send the southern region posting information to the CEO. You will prepare the worksheet for printing so Jamia has the option of viewing a hard copy of this information.

Objectives
- Change the page orientation
- Change print options for gridlines
- Change the Page Setup options for a worksheet
- Print a worksheet

Before printing a document, you may want to make final adjustments to the output. You can use tools on the Page Layout tab to adjust print orientation (the direction in which the content prints across the page), paper size, and location of page breaks. You can use the Scale to Fit options on the Page Layout tab to fit a large amount of data on a single page without making changes to individual margins, and to turn gridlines and column/row headings on and off. When you are ready to print, you can set print options such as the number of copies to print and the correct printer, and you can preview your document in Backstage view. **Backstage view**, accessed using the File tab of the ribbon, contains commands that allow you to manage files and options for the program such as print settings. You can also adjust page layout settings in Backstage view and immediately check the results in the document preview.

Steps

Quick Tip
If you choose to display the Quick Access Toolbar, you can add a Quick Print button to the toolbar by clicking the Customize Quick Access Toolbar button and choosing the Quick Print item from the menu. The worksheet will print using the default print settings.

1. Click cell **A13**, type your name, then click the **Enter button** ✓ on the formula bar
2. Click the **Page Layout tab** on the ribbon, click the **Orientation button** in the Page Setup group, then click **Portrait**

   The orientation changes to **portrait**, so the printed page is taller than it is wide. The vertical dotted line, indicating a page break, shows that all columns don't fit on one page in this orientation.

3. Click the **Orientation button** in the Page Setup group, then click **Landscape**

   The paper orientation returns to **landscape**, so the printed page is wider than it is tall. Now all the content fits on one page.

4. Click the **Gridlines Print check box** in the Sheet Options group on the Page Layout tab, then save your work

   Printing gridlines makes the data easier to read, but the gridlines will not print unless the Gridlines Print check box contains a checkmark. You can also print row numbers and column letters by clicking the Headings Print box. If you don't want to print gridlines or headings, make sure these boxes do not contain checkmarks.

Quick Tip
You can choose to print an entire workbook or a selected area of the worksheet by clicking the Print Active Sheets button in the Settings list, then clicking Print Entire Workbook or Print Selection.

5. Click the **File tab**, in Backstage view click **Print** on the navigation bar, then select an active printer if necessary

   The Print screen in Backstage view displays a preview of your worksheet exactly as it will look when it is printed. To the left of the preview, you can also change several document settings and print options. Compare your screen to **Figure 1-19**. You can print from this view by clicking Print, or you can return to the worksheet without printing by clicking the Back button ⬅.

6. Click the **Page Setup link** in the Settings list, click the **Margins tab** in the Page Setup dialog box, click the **Horizontally check box** in the Center on page section, click the **Vertically check box** in the Center on page section, then compare your screen to **Figure 1-20**

   The printed worksheet will be centered on the page.

Quick Tip
You can change the number of printed pages of your worksheet by clicking the Page Layout tab, then clicking the Width and Height arrows in the Scale to Fit group.

7. Click **OK**, then click **Print**

   One copy of the worksheet prints.

8. sam↑ Save your workbook, submit your work to your instructor as directed, click **File**, click **Close**, then click the **Close button** ✕ on the title bar

Customize Print Options   EX 1-19

Figure 1-19: Worksheet in Backstage view

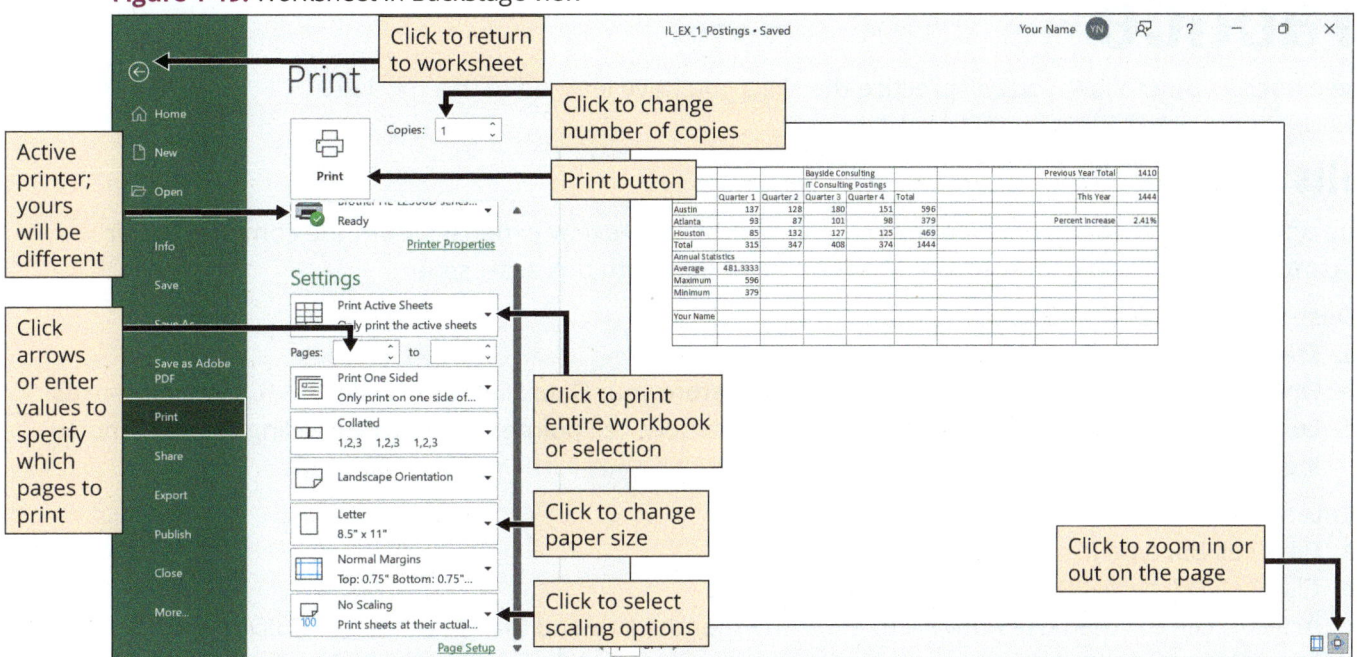

Figure 1-20: Page Setup dialog box

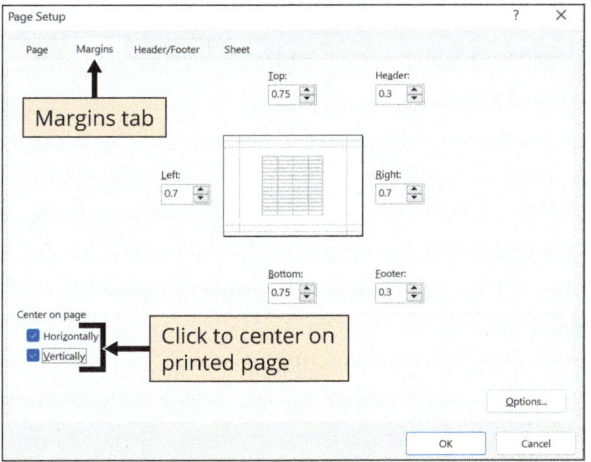

Setting a print area

If you want to print a selected worksheet area repeatedly, it's best to define a **print area**, so that the Quick Print feature prints only that portion of the worksheet area. To define a print area, select the range you want to print on the worksheet, click the Page Layout tab on the ribbon, click the Print Area button in the Page Setup group, then click Set Print Area. A print area can consist of one contiguous range of cells or multiple ranges in different parts of a worksheet. To clear a print area, click the Page Layout tab on the ribbon, click the Print Area button in the Page Setup group, then click Clear Print Area.

Scaling to fit

If you have a large amount of data that you want to fit onto a single sheet of paper, you can control how much of your work to print on a single sheet by clicking the No Scaling arrow in the Settings list in the Print screen in Backstage view, then clicking Fit Sheet on One Page, Fit All Columns on One Page, or Fit All Rows on One Page. Another method for fitting worksheet content onto one page is to click the Page Layout tab on the ribbon, then change the Width and Height settings in the Scale to Fit group to 1 page each. You can also click the Page Setup link in the Print tab in Backstage view, click the Page tab if necessary in the Page Setup dialog box, click the Fit to option button, then enter 1 in the page(s) wide by and tall fields.

Practice

In the exercises that follow, you will practice the skills you have learned in this module.

Skills Review

As the office manager for an engineering consulting firm, you review expenses from the company's four offices. You will use Excel features from this module to help with this assessment.

1. **Describe an Excel workbook.**
   a. Start Excel.
   b. Open IL_EX_1-2.xlsx from the location where you store your Data Files, then save it as **IL_EX_1_Expenses**.
   c. Locate the Name box, formula bar, worksheet window, cell pointer, sheet tab scrolling buttons, mode indicator, and Search box.

2. **Enter data.**
   a. Click cell B3, type **Jan**, then confirm the entry.
   b. Click cell D7, type **302497**, then confirm the entry.
   c. Activate cell B3, then use Auto Fill to enter the months **Feb** and **Mar** in the range C3:D3.
   d. Save your changes to the file.

3. **Edit data.**
   a. Use the F2 function key to correct the spelling of Seatle in cell A5 (the correct spelling is Seattle).
   b. Click cell C6, then use the formula bar to change the value to **288610**.
   c. Click cell A14, then enter your name.
   d. Save your changes.

4. **Copy and move cell data.**
   a. Select the range G4:G6.
   b. Copy the selection to the Clipboard.
   c. Open the Clipboard task pane, then paste the selection to cell A10.
   d. Delete the labels in the range G4:G6.
   e. Close the Clipboard task pane, then activate cell A8.
   f. Use the drag-and-drop method to copy the contents of cell A8 to cell E3. (**Hint**: Press and hold CTRL while dragging.)
   g. Save your work.

5. **Enter formulas.**
   a. Activate cell E4, then enter a formula that adds cells B4, C4, and D4.
   b. Activate cell E5, then enter a formula that adds cells B5, C5, and D5.
   c. Activate cell E6, then enter a formula that adds cells B6, C6, and D6.
   d. Activate cell E7, then enter a formula that adds cells B7, C7, and D7.
   e. Use AutoSum to enter the total expenses for the month of January in cell B8.
   f. Use AutoSum to enter the total expenses for the month of February in cell C8.
   g. Use AutoSum to enter the total expenses for the month of March in cell D8.
   h. Save your changes.

6. **Enter a formula with multiple operators.**
   a. Enter a formula in cell B10 that calculates the average office expenses for the month of January. Use a formula that contains cell references and not a function. (**Hint**: The formula is =(B4+B5+B6+B7)/4.)
   b. Enter a formula in cell C10 that calculates the average office expenses for the month of February. Use a formula that contains cell references and not a function.

c. Enter a formula in cell D10 that calculates the average office expenses for the month of March. Use a formula that contains cell references and not a function.
d. Review the use of the parentheses in the formulas.
e. Save your work.

7. **Insert a function.**
   a. Use the Insert Function button to enter a function in cell B11 that calculates the maximum office expense for January.
   b. Use the Insert Function button to enter a function in cell C11 that calculates the maximum office expense for February.
   c. Use the Insert Function button to enter a function in cell D11 that calculates the maximum office expense for March.
   d. In cell B12, enter a function to calculate the minimum office expenses for January.
   e. In cell C12, enter a function to calculate the minimum office expenses for February.
   f. In cell D12, enter a function to calculate the minimum office expenses for March.
   g. Save your work.

8. **Change worksheet views.**
   a. Click the View tab on the ribbon, then switch to Page Layout view.
   b. Verify that the Ruler and Gridlines check boxes contain checkmarks.
   c. Switch the view to Page Break Preview and adjust the page break so it comes at the bottom of row 16.
   d. Switch to Normal View, use a button in the Zoom group of the View tab to zoom the worksheet to 100%, then use the Zoom buttons on the status bar to zoom the worksheet back to 120%.
   e. Save your changes.

9. **Customize print options.**
   a. Use the Page Layout tab to change the orientation to Portrait.
   b. Turn on gridlines for printing using a check box in the Sheet Options group of the Page Layout tab.
   c. Preview the worksheet in Backstage view, then use the Page Setup dialog box to center the worksheet vertically and horizontally on the page. (*Hint*: The commands are located on the Margins tab.)
   d. Exit Backstage view. Compare your screen to **Figure 1-21**.
   e. Save your changes, submit your work to your instructor as directed, close the workbook, then exit Excel.

Figure 1-21

	A	B	C	D	E
1			Phan & Kader Engineering Services		
2			Office Expenses		
3		Jan	Feb	Mar	Total
4	Boston	357,845	348,625	366,341	1,072,811
5	Seattle	365,477	359,887	233,654	959,018
6	Atlanta	254,788	288,610	244,887	788,285
7	Dallas	298,774	352,188	302,497	953,459
8	Total	1,276,884	1,349,310	1,147,379	
9					
10	Average	319,221	337,328	286,845	
11	Maximum	365,477	359,887	366,341	
12	Minimum	254,788	288,610	233,654	
13					
14	Your Name				
15					
16					
17					

Independent Challenge 1

The manager at Westbank Urgent Care has hired you to help analyze departmental insurance reimbursements. The clinic management would like to review the quarterly totals and averages as well as check what each quarter's revenue would be with a 20% reimbursement increase. The worksheet provided by management is missing some of the data required for a complete analysis.

a. Open IL_EX_1-3.xlsx from the location where you store your Data Files, then save it as **IL_EX_1_Reimbursements**.
b. Enter the data shown in **Table 1-4** in the range E4:E11.
c. Type your name in cell A17.
d. Move the label in cell F2 to cell A15.
e. Use the Clipboard to copy and paste the label in cell F3 to cell A12, then delete the label in cell F3.

Independent Challenge 1 (Continued)

f. Use the formula bar to correct the spelling error in the label in cell A11. (**Hint**: The correct spelling is Immunizations.)
g. Edit cell A10 to change the cell entry from Pediatric to Pediatrics.
h. Type **Quarter 1** in cell B3, then use Auto Fill to enter Quarter 2, Quarter 3, and Quarter 4 in the range C3:E3.
i. Using AutoSum, enter a function in cell B12 that totals the reimbursements for Quarter 1.
j. Using AutoSum, enter a function in cell C12 that totals the second quarter reimbursements for all the departments.
k. Using AutoSum, enter a function in cell D12 that totals the third quarter reimbursements for all the departments.
l. Using AutoSum, enter a function in cell E12 that totals the fourth quarter reimbursements for all the departments.
m. Enter a formula in cell B14 to calculate a 20% increase in the first quarter reimbursement total in cell B12. (**Hint**: You need to add B12 to B12 multiplied by .20. Use parentheses if necessary to follow the order of operations.)
n. Enter formulas in cells C14, D14, and E14 that calculate a 20% increase in the second, third, and fourth quarters, respectively.
o. Enter a function, using the help of AutoComplete, in cell B15 that calculates the average first quarter reimbursement amount for the departments.
p. Use the Insert Function dialog box to enter functions in cells C15, D15, and E15 that calculate the average second, third, and fourth quarter reimbursements for the departments.
q. Switch the view to Page Break Preview and adjust the page break so it is the bottom of row 18.
r. Switch to Normal View, then zoom the worksheet to 130%.
s. Turn on gridlines for printing.
t. Change the page orientation to landscape.
u. Preview the worksheet in the Print pane of Backstage view, then use the Page Setup dialog box to center the worksheet horizontally and vertically on the page.
v. Exit Backstage view, then compare your screen to **Figure 1-22**.
w. Submit your work to your instructor as directed, close the workbook, then exit Excel.

Table 1-4:

cell address	value
E4	57854
E5	29874
E6	36874
E7	42157
E8	41859
E9	35241
E10	37548
E11	49847

Figure 1-22

	A	B	C	D	E	F
1		Westbank Urgent Care				
2		Insurance Reimbursements				
3		Quarter 1	Quarter 2	Quarter 3	Quarter 4	
4	Examinations	57,562.00	58,745.00	69,847.00	57,854.00	
5	Lab	41,587.00	39,584.00	42,327.00	29,874.00	
6	Cardiac	42,987.00	45,147.00	45,877.00	36,874.00	
7	Imaging	40,257.00	44,517.00	45,874.00	42,157.00	
8	Pharmacy	48,795.00	24,789.00	27,457.00	41,859.00	
9	Orthopedics	33,257.00	48,747.00	32,874.00	35,241.00	
10	Pediatrics	29,847.00	31,487.00	29,847.00	37,548.00	
11	Immunizations	68,457.00	67,201.00	32,147.00	49,847.00	
12	Total	362,749.00	360,217.00	326,250.00	331,254.00	
13						
14	20% increase	435,298.80	432,260.40	391,500.00	397,504.80	
15	Average	45,343.63	45,027.13	40,781.25	41,406.75	
16						
17	Your Name					
18						
19						

Independent Challenge 2

As the assistant to the Provost at North County College, it is your responsibility to review the budgets of the academic divisions to plan for the upcoming academic year. You've decided to use Excel formulas and functions to help with this analysis.

a. Open IL_EX_1-4.xlsx from the location where you store your Data Files, then save it as **IL_EX_1_Budgets**.
b. Move the labels in the range A6:A10 to the range A5:A9.
c. Enter **Total** in cell A10, then use AutoSum to calculate the total Year 1 budgeted amounts for all divisions in cell B10.
d. Use AutoSum to calculate the total Year 2 expenses in cell C10.
e. Enter **Average** in cell A11, then use the AutoSum arrow to enter a function in cell B11 that calculates the average Year 1 budgeted amount for all divisions. (**Hint**: Make sure you include only the division data and not the total.)
f. Enter a function in cell C11 that calculates the average Year 2 budgeted amount for all divisions.
g. Enter a formula in cell D2 that calculates the percentage increase in total expenses from Year 1 to Year 2. (**Hint**: The Year 1 total is in cell B10 and the Year 2 total is in cell C10.) Display the value in cell D2 as a percentage with two decimal places.
h. Using cell references, enter a formula in cell G2 that calculates the Projected Year 3 total, using the percent increase shown in cell D2 over the Year 2 total shown in cell C10. (**Hint**: Multiply the percentage in cell D2 by the Year 2 total expenses in cell C10, then add that amount to the Year 2 total shown in cell C10.)
i. Using cell references, enter a formula in cell J2 that calculates the Projected Year 3 average, using the percent increase shown in cell D2 over the Year 2 average shown in cell C11. (**Hint**: Multiply the percentage in cell D2 by the Year 2 average in cell C11, then add that amount to the Year 2 average shown in cell C11.)
j. Change the page orientation to landscape, then turn on gridlines for printing.
k. Enter your name in cell A13.
l. Preview the worksheet in Backstage view, exit Backstage view, then compare your screen to **Figure 1-23**.
m. Save your work, then submit the worksheet to your instructor as directed.
n. Close the workbook and exit Excel.

Figure 1-23

	A	B	C	D	E	F	G	H	I	J	K
1	North County College			% Increase Year 1 to Year 2			Year 3 Projected Total			Year 3 Projected Average	
2	Academic Affairs			31.32%			$1,430,871.04			$286,174.21	
3	Division Budgets										
4	Division	Year 1	Year 2								
5	STEM	$158,745.00	$167,475.00								
6	Humanities	$198,475.00	$205,874.00								
7	Business	$102,657.00	$135,627.00								
8	Health	$154,124.00	$215,247.00								
9	Graduate	$215,784.00	$365,417.00								
10	Total	$829,785.00	$1,089,640.00								
11	Average	$165,957.00	$217,928.00								
12											
13	Your Name										

Visual Workshop

Open IL_EX_1-5.xlsx from the location where you store your Data Files, then save it as **IL_EX_1_Sales**. Modify the content and view using the skills you learned in this module so that your worksheet and zoom level match **Figure 1-24**. Use functions in cells B8:B11 to calculate the values described in cells A8:A11. Enter formulas in cells C4:C8 to calculate the commissions. (**Hint**: Multiply each revenue in column B by the commission percentage in cell E2.) Enter your name in cell A14. Submit your work to your instructor as directed.

Figure 1-24

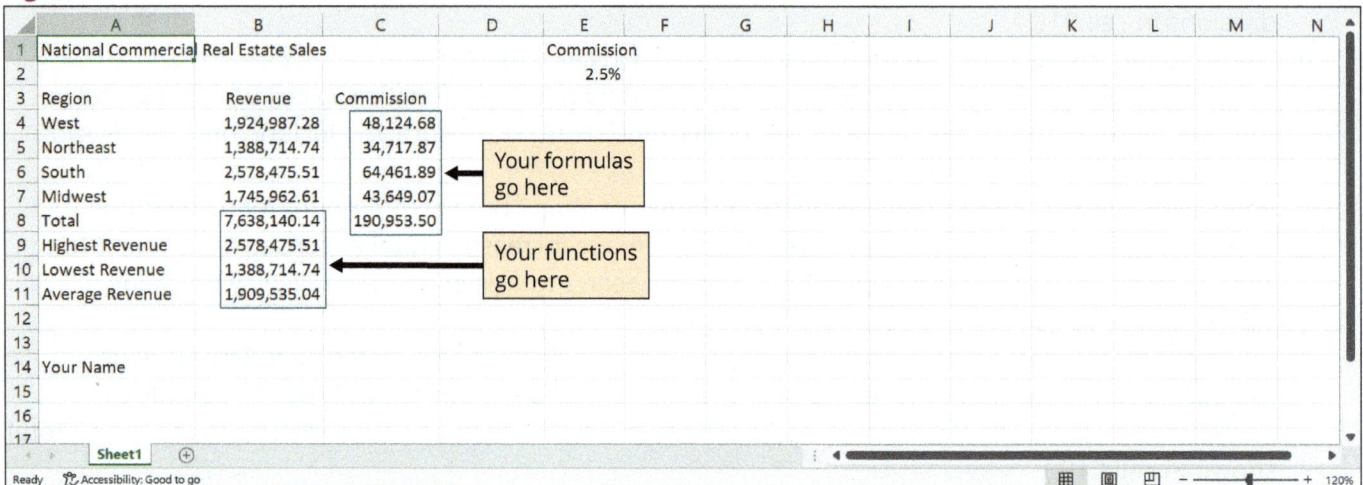

Formatting a Worksheet

Excel Module 2

Case

Luis Herrero, the manager of Bayside Consulting's Houston office, has gathered data on technology job postings for the first quarter of the year. Luis submitted this data to you in a worksheet. To make it easier to view and analyze the position postings, you will format the worksheet.

Module Objectives

After completing this module, you will be able to:

- Format values
- Change font attributes
- Modify font styles and alignment
- Adjust column width and row height
- Insert and delete rows and columns
- Modify data formatting and documentation
- Apply conditional formatting
- Modify worksheet tabs
- Check spelling and find text

Files You Will Need

IL_EX_2-1.xlsx
IL_EX_2-2.xlsx
IL_EX_2-3.xlsx
IL_EX_2-4.xlsx
IL_EX_2-5.xlsx

Format Values

Case Luis has provided you with a worksheet that details first-quarter postings. You decide to format several cells to reflect the type of values they contain, such as currency, percentages, and dates, so the worksheet is easier to understand.

Objectives
- Format a number
- Increase/decrease decimal places
- Format a date

When you **format** a cell, you enhance the appearance of information by changing its font, size, color, or alignment. Formatting changes only the appearance of a value or label; it does not alter the actual data in any way. To format a cell or range, first, you select it, then you apply the formatting using the ribbon, Mini toolbar, or a keyboard shortcut. You can apply formatting before or after you enter data in a cell or range.

Steps

Quick Tip
You can format values with a custom number format using format symbols. Right-click a cell range, click Format Cells on the shortcut menu, in the Category box of the Format Cells dialog box, click Custom, select the number format you want to use in the Type list, make changes to the format symbols in the Type box, then click OK.

1. **sam↓** Start Excel, open **IL_EX_2-1.xlsx** from the location where you store your Data Files, then save it as **IL_EX_2_Openings**

   This worksheet is difficult to interpret because all the information is crowded and looks the same. In some columns, the contents appear cut off because there is too much data to fit given the current column width. You decide not to widen the columns yet, because the other changes you plan to make might affect column width and row height.

2. Select the range **H3:H15**, then click the **Accounting Number Format button** $ in the Number group on the Home tab on the ribbon

   A **number format** is applied to values to express numeric concepts, such as currency, date, and percentage. The default Accounting number format adds dollar signs and two decimal places to the expense data, as shown in **Figure 2-1**.

3. Select the range **I3:I15**, then click the **Comma Style button** , in the Number group

   The values in column I display the Comma Style format, which does not include a dollar sign but can be useful for some types of accounting data.

Quick Tip
You can also apply formatting to a range of cells by clicking the Number Format arrow, then choosing the desired number format.

4. Select cell **B17**, click the **Percent Style button** % in the number group, then click the **Increase Decimal button** in the Number group

   The bonus rate is now formatted with a percent sign (%) and one decimal place. Each time you click the Increase Decimal button, you add one decimal place; clicking the button twice would add two decimal places.

5. Click the **Decrease Decimal button** in the Number group

   The decimal place is removed from the bonus value.

6. Select the range **C3:C15**, then click the **dialog box launcher** in the Number group

   The Format Cells dialog box opens.

Quick Tip
If you want numeric values to be treated as text, click Text in the Category list. Cells formatted in this way are treated as text even if they contain numeric data. You can also precede a number with an apostrophe to treat the value as text.

7. Click the Number tab if necessary, click **Date** in the Category list box, select the **3/14** format in the Type list box, as shown in **Figure 2-2**, then click **OK**

   The dates in column C appear in the 3/14 format.

8. Select the range **H3:I15**, right-click the range, click **Format Cells** on the shortcut menu, in the Category list of the Number tab in the Format Cells dialog box click **Currency**, in the Decimal places box type **2** if necessary, then click **OK**

   This number format looks similar to the Accounting format but aligns currency symbols and decimal points slightly differently. Compare your worksheet to **Figure 2-3**.

9. Click the **Decrease Decimal button** in the Number group twice, press **CTRL+HOME**, then save your work

   The cell values in this range now use a custom format that doesn't display decimal places. This format is applied to all cells in the selected range.

Format Values EX 2-3

Figure 2-1: Accounting number format applied to range

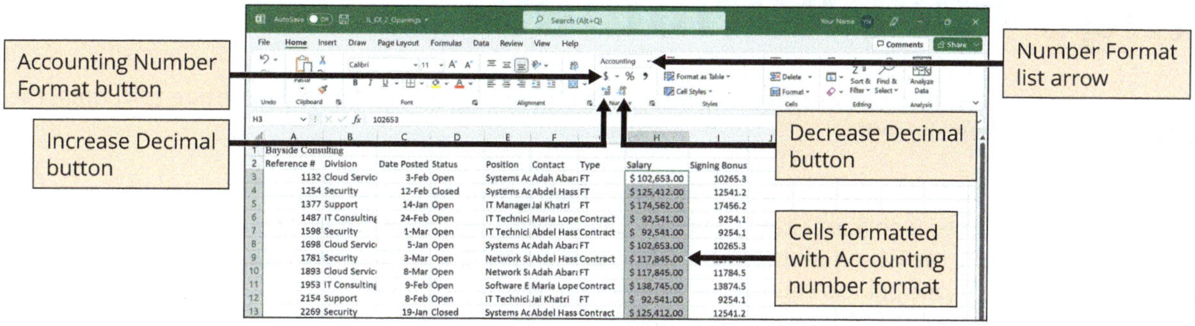

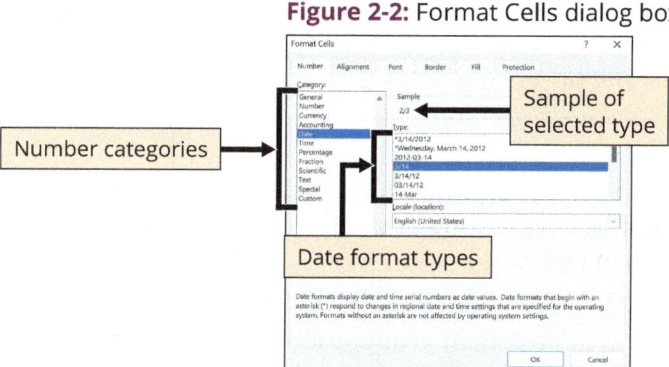

Figure 2-2: Format Cells dialog box

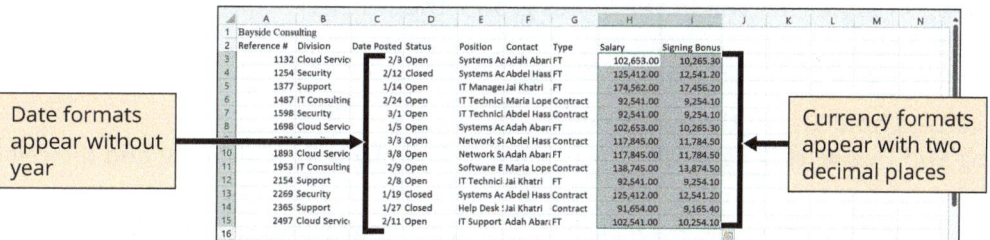

Figure 2-3: Worksheet with formatted values

Working with online pictures, other images, and symbols

You can illustrate your worksheets using online pictures and other images. To add a picture to a worksheet, click the Pictures button in the Illustrations group on the Insert tab on the ribbon, then choose the location of the picture. Clicking Online Pictures opens the Online Pictures dialog box where you can search for online pictures using the Bing search engine, as shown in **Figure 2-4**. To search, type one or more keywords in the search box, then press ENTER. When you double-click an image in the Search Results window, the image is inserted at the location of the active cell. Clicking an image selects it and adds resizing handles. To resize an image proportionally, drag any corner sizing handle. If you drag an edge sizing handle, the image will be resized non-proportionally. You can add alternative text to an image by right-clicking it, clicking Edit Alt Text on the shortcut menu, then entering the text in the Alt Text pane. To move an image, point inside the image until the pointer changes to the Move pointer, then drag it to a new location. To delete

Figure 2-4: Results of Online Picture search

a picture, select it, then press DEL. To work with an image, it must be selected. You can select an image, or any object, by clicking it. To work with multiple images at once, hold CTRL while clicking each image. You can insert a symbol in a worksheet by clicking the Insert tab, clicking the Symbols button in the Symbols group, Clicking Symbol, clicking a symbol from the Symbols tab in the Symbol dialog box, clicking Insert, then clicking Close to close the Symbol dialog box.

Module 2 Formatting a Worksheet

Change Font Attributes

Case You want the labels and worksheet title to stand out from other information, so you decide to change the font and font size of these elements.

Objectives
- Change a font
- Apply a cell style

A **font** is the appearance and shape of letters, numbers, and special characters and is usually designed with a font name, such as Calibri or Times New Roman. The **font size** is the size of characters, measured in units called points. A **point** is a unit of measure used for font size and row height; one point is equal to 1/72 of an inch. The default font and font size in Excel is 11-point Calibri. **Table 2-1** provides examples of several fonts in different font sizes. You can change the font and font size of any cell or range using the Font and Font Size arrows. The Font and Font Size arrows are located on the Home tab on the ribbon and on the Mini toolbar, which opens when you right-click a cell or range. To save time, you can also use a **cell style**, a predesigned combination of font, font size, and font color that you can apply to a cell.

Steps

1. Click the **Font arrow** in the Font group on the Home tab on the ribbon, scroll down in the Font list for an alphabetical listing of the fonts available on your computer, then click **Calibri**, as shown in **Figure 2-5**
    The font in cell A1 changes to Calibri to match the rest of the worksheet.

Quick Tip
You can also use the Increase Font Size button A^ to increase the font size by one point or the Decrease Font Size button A^ to decrease it by one point.

▶ 2. Click the **Font Size arrow** in the Font group, then click **20**
    The worksheet title is formatted in 20-point Calibri, and the Font and Font Size boxes on the Home tab display the new font and font size information.

3. Click the **Cell Styles button** in the Styles group, then click **Heading 1** under Titles and Headings
    The title is formatted in the Heading 1 cell style.

Quick Tip
Holding CTRL while selecting cells allows you to select multiple nonadjacent cells.

▶ 4. Click cell **A2**, hold **SHIFT**, then click cell **I2**
    Holding SHIFT while clicking a cell selects that cell and any cells between it and the cell first selected.

5. Click the **Cell Styles button**, then click **Heading 2** under Titles and Headings
    Notice that some of the column labels are now too wide to appear fully in the column. Excel does not automatically adjust column widths to accommodate cell formatting; these column widths must be adjusted manually. You'll learn to do this in a later lesson.

6. Click cell **A17**, click the **Cell Styles button**, then click **Heading 4** under Titles and Headings
    The worksheet's title and labels are formatted in different font sizes using consistent styles.

7. Compare your worksheet to **Figure 2-6**, then save your work

Table 2-1: Examples of fonts and font sizes

font name	12 point	24 point
Calibri	Excel	Excel
Playbill	Excel	Excel
Comic Sans MS	Excel	Excel
Times New Roman	Excel	Excel

Figure 2-5: Font list

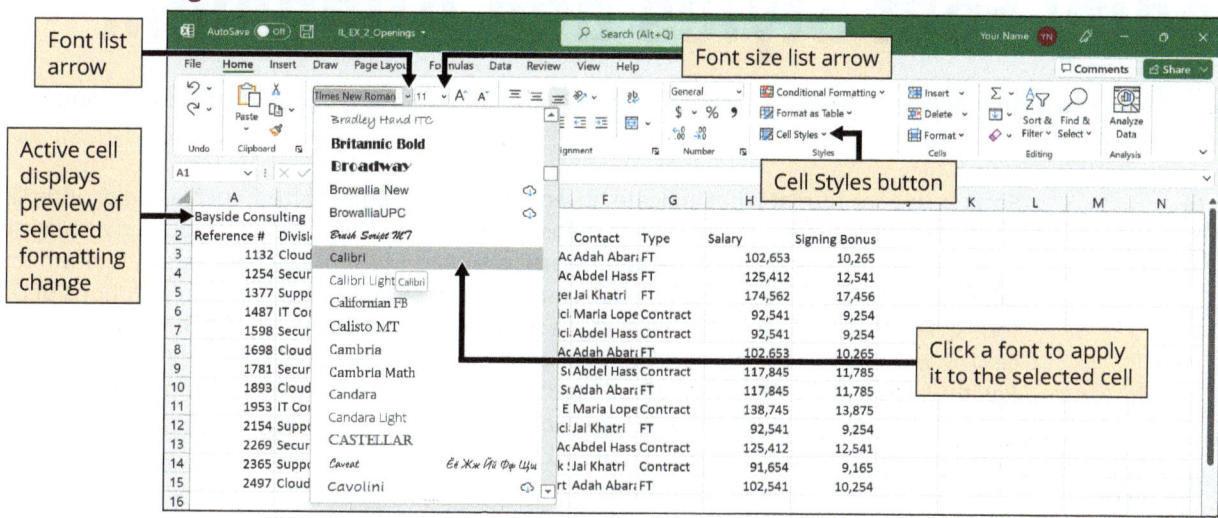

Figure 2-6: Worksheet with formatted headings and column labels

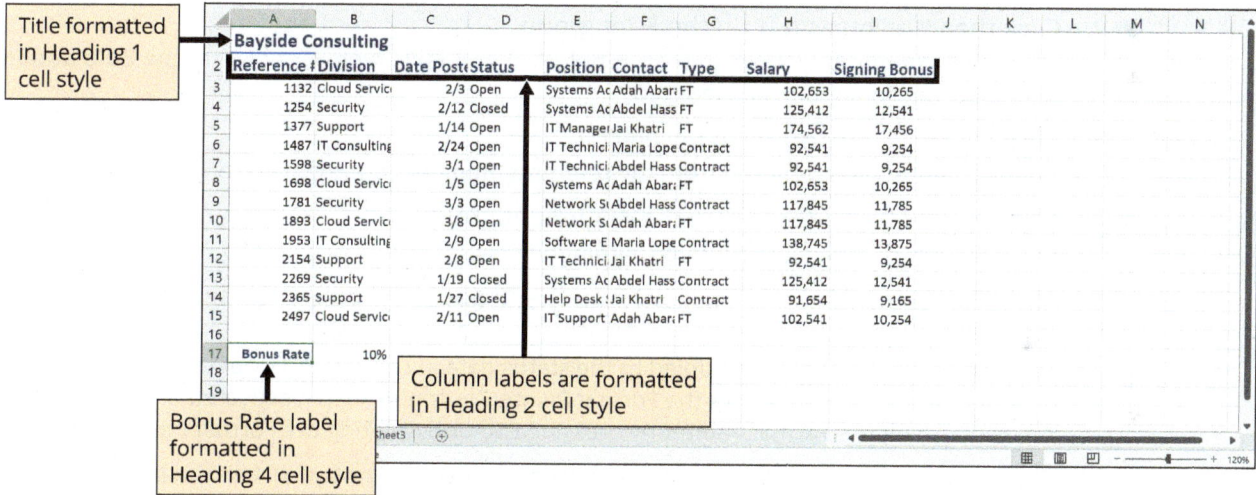

Modify, create, and merge styles

You can modify any style in the Cell Styles gallery. In the Cell Styles gallery, right-click the cell style that you want to modify, on the shortcut menu shown in **Figure 2-7**, click Modify, select the style options from the Style includes list in the Style dialog box, click the Format button to choose new customized formatting, then click OK twice. To create a new cell style, click New Cell Style at the bottom of the Cell Styles gallery, enter a name in the Style name box, select style options from the Style includes list, click the Format button to choose customized formatting for your style, then click OK twice. You can merge styles from a different workbook by opening the workbook that contains the cell styles that you want to copy, clicking Merge Styles at the bottom of the Cell Styles gallery, clicking the workbook in the Merge styles from list, then clicking OK. If styles in the workbooks have the same name, you will be asked if you want to merge those styles.

Figure 2-7: Shortcut menu in Cell Styles gallery

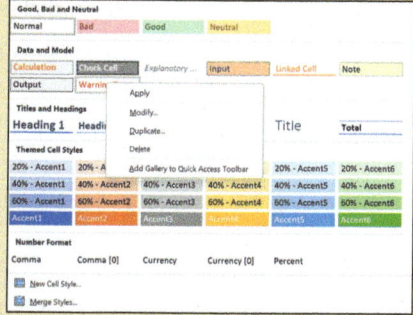

Module 2 Formatting a Worksheet

Modify Font Styles and Alignment

Case You want to further enhance the worksheet's appearance by adding bold and underline formatting and centering some of the labels.

Objectives
- Apply font styles
- Use the Format Painter
- Change cell alignment

Font styles are formats that indicate how characters are emphasized, such as bold, underline, and italic. You have applied multiple font styles at once using cell styles, and you can also apply them individually. You can change the **alignment**, the placement of cell contents in relation to a cell's edges such as left or centered, of labels and values in cells. **Table 2-2** lists descriptions of common font styles and alignment buttons that are available on the Home tab. Once you have formatted a cell the way you want it, you can "paint" or copy the cell's formats to other cells by using the Format Painter button in the Clipboard group on the Home tab. This is similar to using copy and paste, but instead of copying cell contents, it copies only the cell's formatting.

Steps

Quick Tip
You can use the Underline button U to underline cell contents. You can also use the Mini toolbar to format text by right-clicking selected cells.

1. **Select the range A3:A15, then click the Bold button** B **in the Font group on the Home tab on the ribbon**
   The reference numbers in column A appear in bold.

2. **Click the Italic button** I **in the Font group**
   The reference numbers now appear in boldface and italic type. Notice that the Bold and Italic buttons in the Font group are selected.

3. **Click the Italic button** I **to deselect it**
   The italic font style is removed from the reference numbers but the bold font style remains.

Quick Tip
To format a selected cell or range using keyboard shortcuts, you can press CTRL+B to bold, CTRL+I to italicize, and CTRL+U to underline.

4. **Click the Center button** ≡ **in the Alignment group**
   The reference numbers are centered within their cells.

5. **Click the Format Painter button** ✦ **in the Clipboard group, then select the range D3:D15**
   The formatting in column A is copied to the status data in column D. To paint the formats to more than one selection, double-click the Format Painter button to keep it activated until you turn it off. You can turn off the Format Painter by pressing ESC or by clicking the Format Painter button ✦.

Quick Tip
To clear all formatting from a selected range, click the Clear button ◇ in the Editing group on the Home tab, then click Clear Formats.

6. **Click cell A1, select the range A1:I1, then click the Merge & Center button** ▦ **in the Alignment group**
   The Merge & Center button creates one cell out of the nine cells across the row, then centers the text in that newly created, merged cell. The title "Bayside Consulting" is centered across the nine columns you selected. To split a merged cell into its original components, select the merged cell, then click the Merge & Center button ▦ to deselect it. Occasionally, you may find that you want cell contents to wrap within a cell. You can do this by selecting the cells containing the text you want to wrap, then clicking the Wrap Text button ab in the Alignment group on the Home tab.

7. **Compare your screen to Figure 2-8, then save your work**

Modify Font Styles and Alignment   EX 2-7

Figure 2-8: Worksheet with font styles and alignment applied

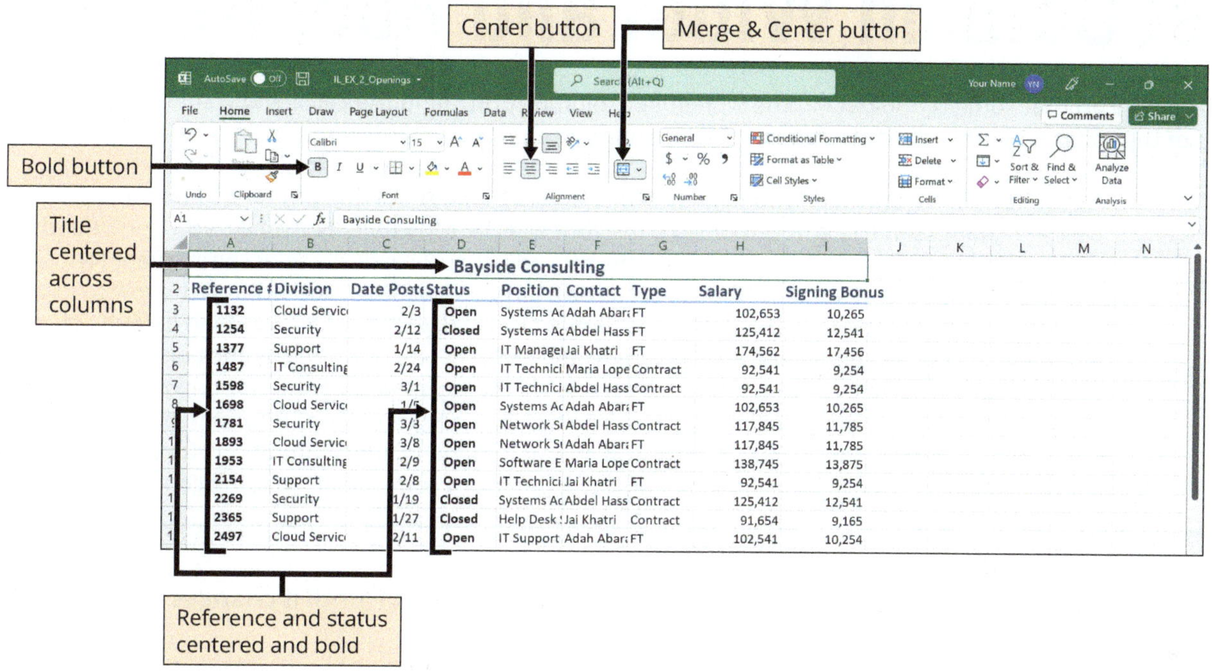

- Center button
- Merge & Center button
- Bold button
- Title centered across columns
- Reference and status centered and bold

Table 2-2: Common font style and alignment buttons

button	button name	description
B	Bold	Bolds cell content
I	Italic	Italicizes cell content
U	Underline	Underlines cell content
	Merge & Center	Centers content across columns; also merges two or more selected, adjacent cells into one cell; also unmerges previously merged cells
	Align Left	Aligns content at the left edge of the cell
	Center Align	Centers content horizontally within the cell
	Align Right	Aligns content at the right edge of the cell
	Wrap Text	Wraps long text into multiple lines to fit within a column
	Top Align	Aligns content at the top of a cell
	Bottom Align	Aligns content at the bottom of a cell
	Middle Align	Aligns content in the middle of a cell

Rotating and indenting cell entries

In addition to applying fonts and font styles, you can rotate or indent data within a cell. To rotate text within a cell, click the Home tab on the ribbon, select the cells you want to modify, then click the dialog box launcher in the Alignment group to open the Alignment tab of the Format Cells dialog box. Click a position in the Orientation box or type a number in the Degrees box to rotate text from its default horizontal orientation, then click OK. You can indent cell contents by clicking the Increase Indent button in the Alignment group, which moves cell contents to the right, or the Decrease Indent button, which moves cell contents to the left.

Module 2 Formatting a Worksheet

Adjust Column Width and Row Height

Case You have noticed that some of the data in the worksheet columns don't fit in the cells. You want to adjust the widths of the columns so that the data appear in their entirety.

Objectives
- Change a column width by dragging
- Resize a column with AutoFit
- Change the width of multiple columns

As you format a worksheet, you might need to adjust the width of one or more columns to accommodate changes in the amount of text, the font size, or font style. Normally, you don't need to adjust row height manually, because row heights adjust automatically to accommodate font size changes. If you format something in a row to be a larger point size, Excel adjusts the row to fit the largest point size in the row. The default row height is usually 12.75 points and the default column width is usually 8.43 characters. You can adjust the width of one or more columns or rows by using the mouse, the Format button in the Cells group on the Home tab on the ribbon, or the shortcut menu. Using the mouse, you can drag or double-click the right edge of a column heading or the lower edge of a row. The Format button and shortcut menu include commands for making more precise width and height adjustments. **Table 2-3** describes common formatting commands.

Steps

1. **Position the pointer on the line between columns E and F until it changes to the Column Resize pointer ↔ as shown in Figure 2-9**
   A **column heading** is a box that appears above each worksheet column and identifies it by a letter. You positioned the mouse pointer here because to adjust column width using the mouse, you need to position the pointer on the right edge of the column heading for the column you want to adjust.

2. **Double-click**
   Column E automatically widens to fit the widest entry. Double-clicking the right edge of a column heading activates **AutoFit**. This feature adjusts column width or row height to accommodate its widest or tallest entry.

   Trouble
   If you have difficulty dragging to the specified width, double-click the right edge of column B.

3. **Position the mouse pointer on the line between the column B and column C headings until it changes to the Column Resize pointer ↔**

4. ▶ **Click and drag the Column Resize pointer ↔ to the right slightly so there's room to fully display the names in the Division column (approximately 12.09 characters or 140 pixels)**
   Due to differences in Windows resolution and scaling from device to device, your measurements may vary slightly. As you change the column width, a ScreenTip opens displaying the column width.

   Quick Tip
   If "######" appears after you adjust a column of values, the column is too narrow to display the values completely; increase the column width until the values appear.

5. ▶ **Use AutoFit to resize columns A, C, and F**

6. **Position the mouse pointer in the column heading area for column H until it changes to the Column Select pointer ↓, then drag to select columns H and I**

7. **Click the Format button in the Cells group on the Home tab on the ribbon, then click Column Width**
   The Column Width dialog box opens. Column width measurement is based on the number of characters that will fit in the column when formatted in the Normal font and font size.

   Trouble
   In the last lesson of this module, you will fix spelling errors that may be now visible on the worksheet.

8. ▶ **Type 9 in the Column width box, then click OK**
   The widths of columns H and I change to reflect the new setting. You will format the label for column I for a better fit.

9. **Click cell I2, click the Wrap Text button in the Alignment group, click cell A1, compare your screen to Figure 2-10, then save your work**
   The height of row 2 automatically adjusts to accommodate the required size for the wrapped text.

Adjust Column Width and Row Height   EX 2-9

Figure 2-9: Preparing to change the column width

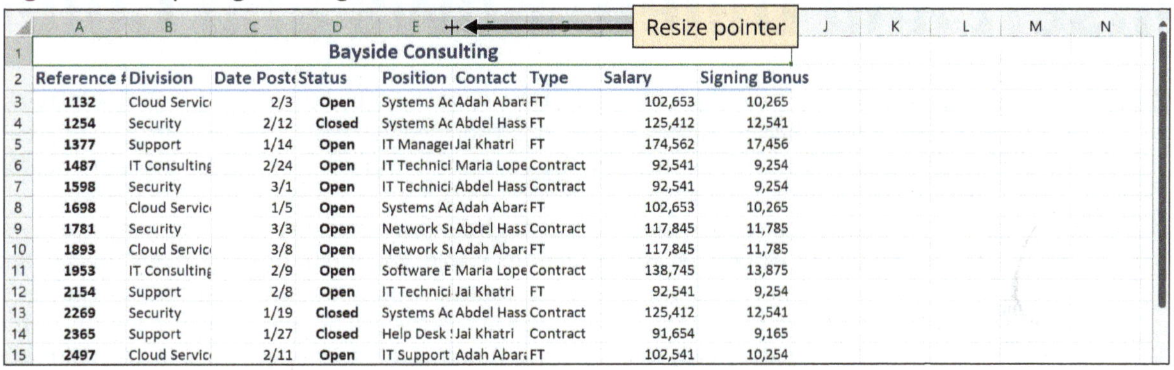

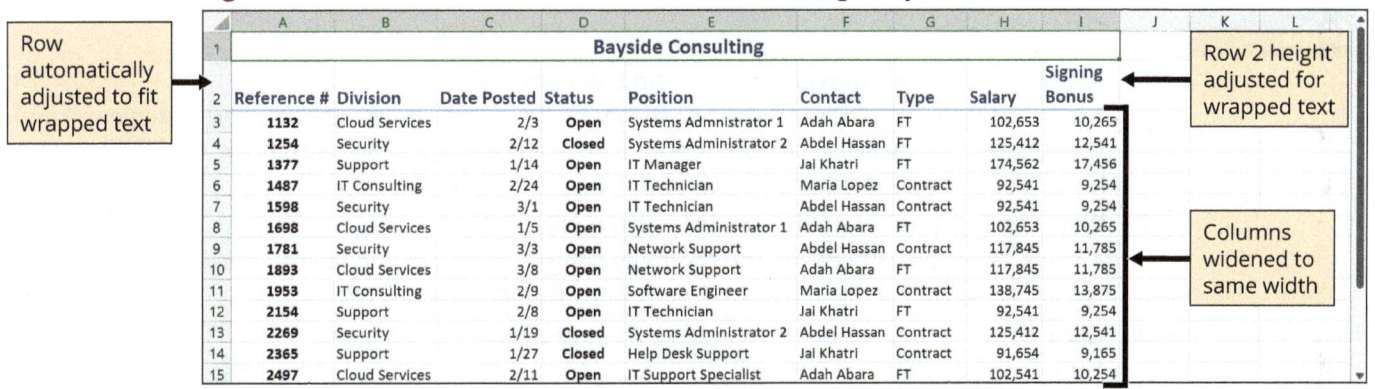

Figure 2-10: Worksheet with column widths and row height adjusted

Table 2-3: Common formatting commands

command	description	available using
Column Width	Sets the width to a specific number of characters	Format button; shortcut menu
Row Height	Sets the height to a specific number of points	Format button; shortcut menu
AutoFit Column Width	Fits to the widest entry in a column	Format button; mouse
AutoFit Row Height	Fits to the highest entry in a row	Format button; mouse
Hide & Unhide	Hides or displays selected column(s) or row(s)	Format button; shortcut menu
Default Width	Resets column to worksheet's default column width	Format button

Changing row height

You have just as many options for changing row height as you do column width. The row height must exceed the size of the font you are using to make a change. Using the mouse, you can place the ╪ pointer on the line dividing a row heading from the heading below it, and then drag to the desired height; double-clicking the line AutoFits the row height where necessary. You can also select one or more rows, right-click the selection, then use the Row Height command on the shortcut menu. Row height can also be changed by clicking the Format button on the Home tab on the ribbon, then clicking the Row Height or AutoFit Row Height command.

Insert and Delete Rows and Columns

Case You want to improve the overall appearance of the worksheet by inserting a blank row between the company name and the column labels. Additionally, Luis has informed you that the March 3rd posting is an error and that contact information should not be stored in the workbook. You will make these adjustments to the worksheet.

Objectives
- Use the Insert dialog box to insert a row
- Modify columns and rows using heading buttons

As you modify a worksheet, you might find it necessary to insert or delete rows and columns to keep your worksheet current. For example, you might need to insert rows to accommodate new inventory products or remove a column of yearly totals that are no longer necessary. When you insert a new row, the row is inserted above the cell pointer and the contents of the worksheet shift down from the newly inserted row. When you insert a new column, the column is inserted to the left of the cell pointer, and the contents of the worksheet shift to the right of the new column. To insert multiple rows, select the same number of row headings as you want to insert before using the Insert command.

Steps

1. **Right-click cell F2, then click Insert on the shortcut menu**
   The Insert dialog box opens as shown in **Figure 2-11**. You can choose to insert a single cell and shift the cells in the active column to the right, insert a single cell and shift the cells in the active row down, or insert an entire column or a row.

2. **Click the Entire row option button, then click OK**
   A blank row appears between the company name and the column labels, visually separating the worksheet data, and the Insert Options button opens next to cell F3.

Quick Tip
To insert a column, right-click the column heading to the right of where you want the new column, click Insert on the shortcut menu, then click the Entire column option button.

3. **Click the Insert Options button, then review your choices**
   This menu lets you format the inserted row in Format Same As Above (the default setting, already selected), Format Same As Below, or Clear Formatting.

4. **Click the Insert Options button to close the menu without making changes, then click the row 10 heading**
   All of row 10 is selected, as shown in **Figure 2-12**.

5. **Click the Delete button in the Cells group on the Home tab on the ribbon; do not click the Delete arrow**
   Excel deletes row 10, and all rows below it shift up one row, making Reference # 1893 the new row 10. You must use the Delete button or the Delete command on the shortcut menu to delete a row or column; pressing DEL on the keyboard removes only the *contents* of a selected row or column.

6. **Click the column F heading**
   The contact information is in this column and it is saved on a separate worksheet.

7. **Click the Delete button in the Cells group**
   Excel deletes column F. The remaining columns to the right shift left one column, and the Type column is now column F.

8. **Save your work**

Figure 2-11: Insert dialog box

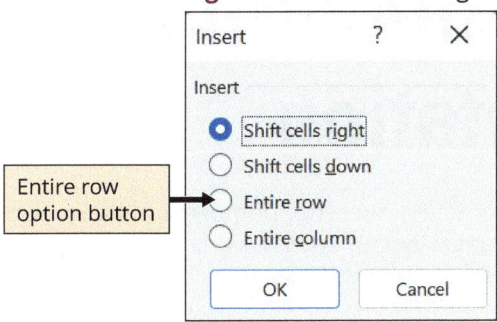

Figure 2-12: Worksheet with row 10 selected

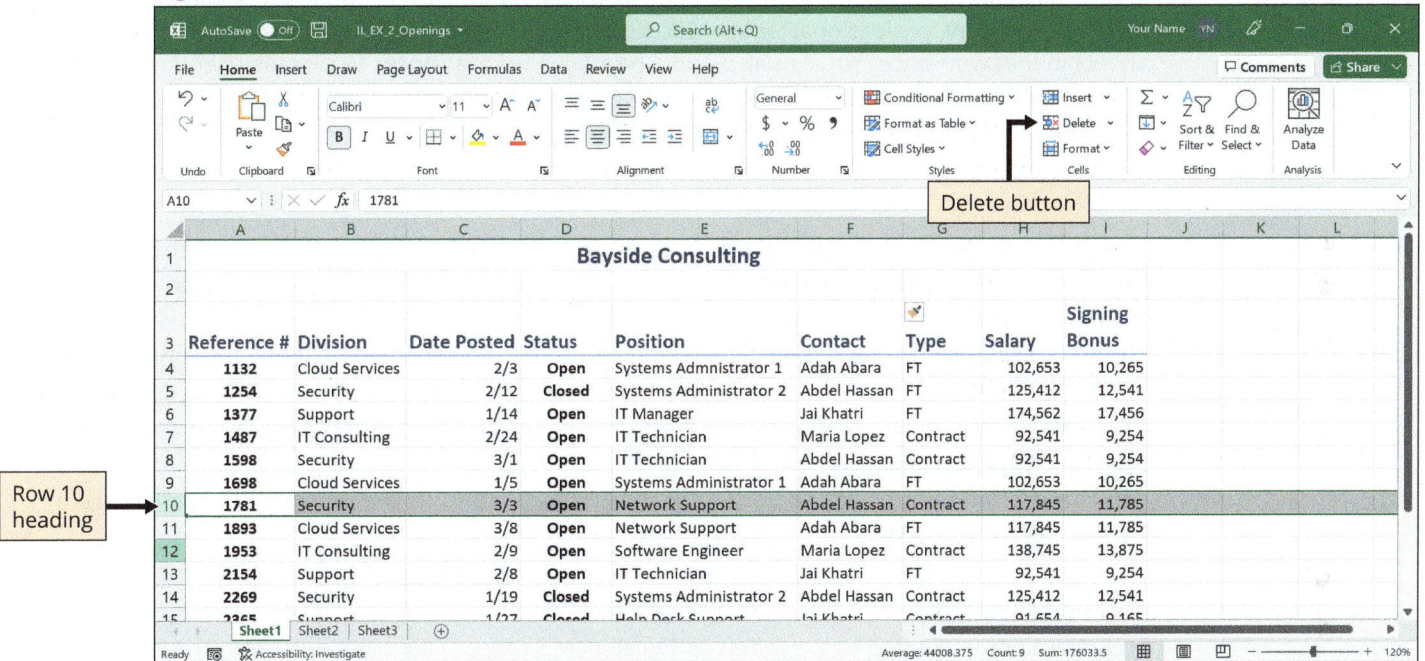

Hiding and unhiding columns and rows

When you don't want data in a column or row to be visible, but you don't want to delete it, you can hide the column or row. To hide a selected column, click the Format button in the Cells group on the Home tab on the ribbon, point to Hide & Unhide, then click Hide Columns. A hidden column is indicated by a dark green vertical line in its original position. This green line is removed when you click elsewhere on the worksheet, but a thin double line remains between the column heading to remind you that one or more columns are hidden. You can display a hidden column by selecting the column headings on either side of the hidden column, clicking the Format button in the Cells group, pointing to Hide & Unhide, then clicking Unhide Columns. (To hide or unhide one or more rows, substitute Hide Rows and Unhide Rows for the Hide Columns and Unhide Columns instructions.)

Modify Data Formatting and Documentation

Case You want to add a border and color to the reference numbers on the worksheet to make them stand out from the other information. You also want to document the worksheet by adding information about the worksheet in a header and footer.

Objectives
- Change text and fill color
- Apply a border to a cell
- Insert a worksheet header and footer

You have used cell styles to add predesigned formatting, including colors and borders to a worksheet. If a cell style doesn't capture the formatting you need for a worksheet, you can add this formatting individually. Color options are based on the worksheet theme. A **theme** is a predefined, coordinated set of colors, fonts, graphical effects, and other formats that can be applied to a spreadsheet to give it a consistent, professional look. In Excel, applying a theme to one sheet applies it to all other sheets in that workbook. You can also add a **header** and/or a **footer** to provide useful text, date, and other information, including a graphic, along the top or bottom of every page of a worksheet. A header prints above the top margin of the worksheet, and a footer prints below the bottom margin.

Steps

Trouble
If your device does not display the names of the colors in the palette, use the position of the theme color in the palette to select the correct color.

▶ 1. Select the range **A4:A15**, click the **Fill Color arrow** in the Font group on the Home tab on the ribbon, then click the **Blue-Gray, Text 2, Lighter 80%** color (second row, fourth column from the left)

The color is applied to the background (or fill) of this range. When you change fill or font color, the color on the Fill Color or Font Color button changes to the last color you selected.

2. Click the **Borders arrow** in the Font group, review the Borders menu, as shown in **Figure 2-13**, then click **Right Border**

You can use the options at the bottom of the Borders menu to draw a border or to change a border line color or style.

3. Click the **Font Color arrow** in the Font group, then click the **Blue-Gray, Text 2 color** (first row, fourth column from the left)

The new color is applied to the labels in the selected range. This color will make the reference numbers stand out.

Quick Tip
You can use the settings in the Options group on the Header & Footer tab to set a different header or footer for the first page of a worksheet. You can also use an option in this group to set different headers or footers for odd and even worksheet pages.

▶ 4. Click the **Insert tab** on the ribbon, click the **Text button**, then click the **Header & Footer button**

The header is divided into three sections, as shown in **Figure 2-14**, where you can enter or edit text. The Header & Footer tab includes elements and options for customizing the header or footer.

5. Click the **Sheet Name button** in the Header & Footer Elements group on the Header & Footer tab

The & [Tab] code is added, which will display the current sheet name in this location. Using codes instead of manually typing the information ensures this information is always up to date. In a later lesson, you will rename the worksheet to a more descriptive name.

6. Click the **Go to Footer button** in the Navigation group, enter your name in the center footer section, click **any cell** on the worksheet, click the **Normal button** on the status bar, then press **CTRL+HOME**

The header and footer are only visible in Page Layout view and Print Preview.

7. Click **File**, then click **Print**

Your header and footer will provide useful information to others viewing the worksheet.

8. Click the **Back button** to return to your worksheet, then save your work

Modify Data Formatting and Documentation   EX 2-13

Figure 2-13: Borders menu

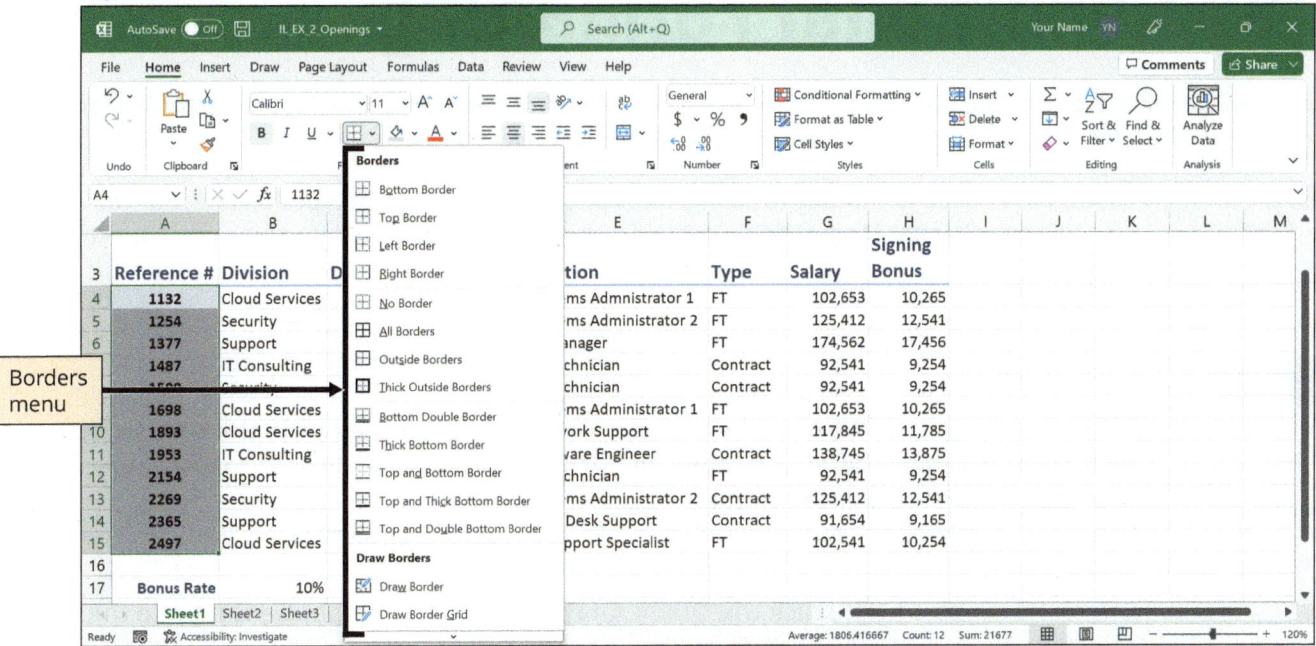

Figure 2-14: Header & Footer tab

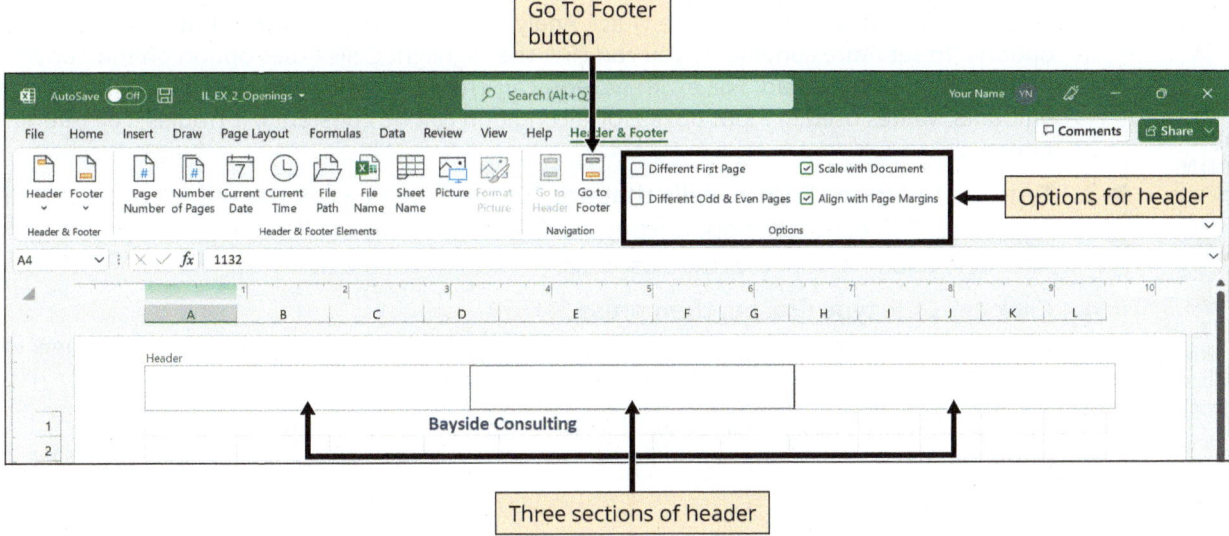

Working with Microsoft Office color palettes

Microsoft Office color palettes are divided into two main sections: Theme Colors and Standard Colors. The colors in the first row of theme colors each have a name, such as Blue or Green, and a description of their suggested use, such as Background 1, Text 1, or Accent 2. For most devices, this name is displayed when you hover over each color. The colors in the rows below the first row are shades of the theme colors. The first row of shades is the lightest with the colors labeled by percentage of intensity, such as Lighter 80% or Darker 5%. Each row gets progressively darker as you move down the palette and is named according to the intensity of shading, such as Lighter 60%. The last row in the palette displays the standard colors with names such as Light Blue and Orange. These colors are common to all themes but might vary according to factors such as color palette, screen resolution, and Office version. Screen resolution might also affect the location of the standard colors within the color palette.

Apply Conditional Formatting

Case Luis would like to highlight positions that are closed and you will use conditional formatting to help him identify these postings. You will also use conditional formatting to highlight salary patterns.

Objectives
- Create a Data Bars rule
- Create a Highlight Cells rule

So far, you've used formatting to change the appearance of different types of data, but you can also use **conditional formatting**, special formatting that is applied if values meet specified criteria.

Steps

Quick Tip
You can create a custom data bar rule by clicking the Conditional Formatting button, clicking New Rule, clicking the Format Style arrow, clicking Data Bar, adjusting the options in the New Formatting Rule dialog box, then clicking OK.

1. Select the range **H4:H15**, click the **Conditional Formatting button** in the Styles group on the Home tab on the ribbon, point to **Data Bars**, then click **Blue Data Bar** under Gradient Fill (first row, first column)

   Data bars are colored horizontal bars that visually illustrate differences between values in a range of cells.

2. Select the range **D4:D15**, click the **Quick Analysis button** that opens next to the selection, then click the **Equal To button** on the Formatting tab

   The Equal To dialog box opens, displaying an input box you can use to define the condition and a default format (Light Red Fill with Dark Red Text) selected for cells that meet that condition. You can define the condition using the input box and assigning the formatting you want to use for cells that meet that condition. The Quick Analysis tool offers a powerful but limited number of options. To set more conditions, you can click the Highlight Cells Rules option on the Conditional Formatting menu instead. For example, you can create a rule for values that are between two amounts. Values used in input boxes for a condition can be constants, formulas, cell references, or dates.

Quick Tip
You can highlight duplicate values in a selected range by clicking the Conditional Formatting button in the Styles group, pointing to Highlight Cells Rules, clicking Duplicate Values, then selecting a formatting option.

3. Type **Closed** in the Format cells that are EQUAL TO box, click the **with list arrow**, click **Light Red Fill**, compare your settings to **Figure 2-15**, then click **OK**

   All cells in column D with the text Closed appear with a light red fill.

4. Click cell **D15**, type **Closed**, then press **ENTER**

   Because of the rule you created, the appearance of cell D15 changes because the new value meets the condition you set. Compare your results to **Figure 2-16**.

5. Press **CTRL+HOME**, then save your work

Formatting data with icon sets

Icon sets are a conditional format in which different icons are displayed in a cell based on the cell's value. In one group of cells, for example, upward-pointing green arrows might represent the highest values, while downward-pointing red arrows represent the lower values. To add an icon set to a data range, select a data range, click the Conditional Formatting button in the Styles group, point to Icon Sets, then click an icon set. You can customize the values that are used as thresholds for an applied icon set by clicking the Conditional Formatting button in the Styles group, clicking Manage Rules, clicking the rule in the Conditional Formatting Rules Manager dialog box, clicking Edit Rule, entering new values, clicking OK, clicking Apply, then clicking OK to close the dialog box.

Figure 2-15: Equal To dialog box

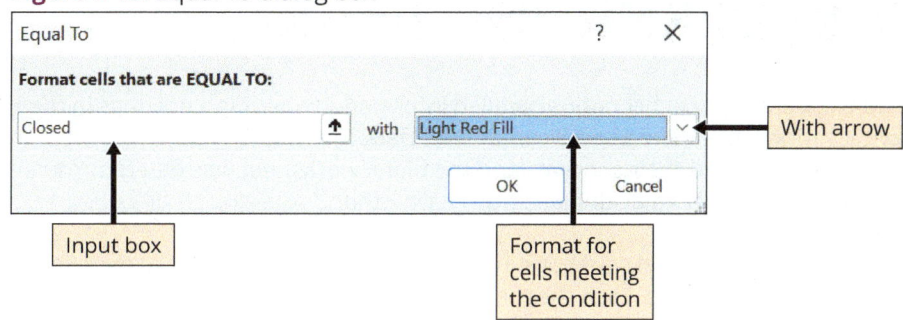

Figure 2-16: Worksheet with conditional formatting

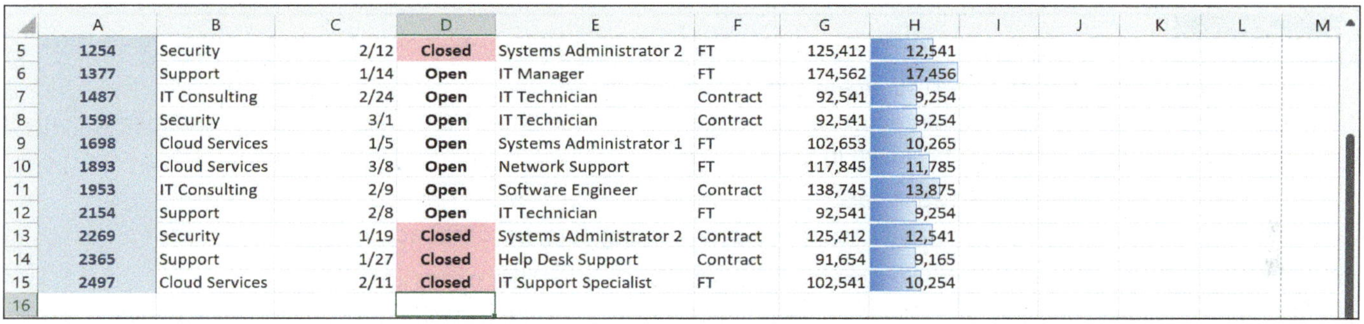

	A	B	C	D	E	F	G	H	I	J	K	L	M
5	1254	Security	2/12	Closed	Systems Administrator 2	FT	125,412	12,541					
6	1377	Support	1/14	Open	IT Manager	FT	174,562	17,456					
7	1487	IT Consulting	2/24	Open	IT Technician	Contract	92,541	9,254					
8	1598	Security	3/1	Open	IT Technician	Contract	92,541	9,254					
9	1698	Cloud Services	1/5	Open	Systems Administrator 1	FT	102,653	10,265					
10	1893	Cloud Services	3/8	Open	Network Support	FT	117,845	11,785					
11	1953	IT Consulting	2/9	Open	Software Engineer	Contract	138,745	13,875					
12	2154	Support	2/8	Open	IT Technician	FT	92,541	9,254					
13	2269	Security	1/19	Closed	Systems Administrator 2	Contract	125,412	12,541					
14	2365	Support	1/27	Closed	Help Desk Support	Contract	91,654	9,165					
15	2497	Cloud Services	2/11	Closed	IT Support Specialist	FT	102,541	10,254					
16													

Managing conditional formatting rules

If you create a conditional formatting rule and then want to change a condition, you don't need to create a new rule; instead, you can edit the rule using the Rules Manager. Select the cells containing the conditional formatting you want to change, click the Conditional Formatting button in the Styles group, then click Manage Rules. The Conditional Formatting Rules Manager dialog box opens where you can use the Show formatting rules for arrow to display rules for the current selection, the worksheet, or for other sheets in the workbook. Selecting This Worksheet displays the rules for the worksheet, as shown in **Figure 2-17.** Select the rule you want to edit, click Edit Rule, then modify the settings in the Edit the Rule Description area in the Edit Formatting Rule dialog box. To change the formatting for a rule, click the Format button in the Edit the Rule Description area, select the formatting styles you want the cells to have, then click OK three times to close the Format Cells dialog box, the Edit Formatting Rule dialog box, and the Conditional Formatting Rules Manager dialog box. To delete a rule, select the rule in the Conditional Formatting Rules Manager dialog box, click the Delete Rule button, then click OK. You can quickly clear conditional formatting rules by clicking the Conditional Formatting button in the Styles group, pointing to Clear Rules, then clicking Clear Rules from Selected Cells or Clear Rules from Entire Worksheet.

Figure 2-17: Conditional Formatting Rules Manager dialog box

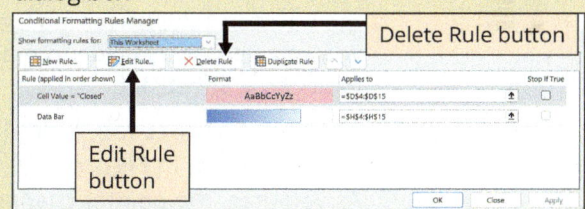

Modify Worksheet Tabs

Case In the current worksheet, Sheet1 contains detailed information about job postings in the Houston office. Sheet2 contains contact information, and Sheet3 contains no data. The worksheets would be more accessible and identifiable if the sheets reflected their contents and the blank worksheet was deleted. You also decide to add color to make the sheet tabs easier to distinguish from each other.

Objectives
- Rename a sheet
- Apply color to a sheet tab
- Reorder sheets in a workbook

By default, an Excel workbook initially contains one worksheet named Sheet1, although you can add sheets at any time. Each sheet name appears on a sheet tab at the bottom of the worksheet. Worksheets are initially given default names such as Sheet1. Renaming worksheet default names to more descriptive names can help people using screen readers to understand the worksheet contents. Worksheets are easier to identify if you add color to the tabs and organize them in a logical order. To move from sheet to sheet, you can click any sheet tab at the bottom of the worksheet window.

Steps

1. **Click the Sheet2 sheet tab**
   Sheet2 becomes active, appearing in front of the Sheet1 tab; this worksheet contains the contact information as shown in **Figure 2-18**.

2. **Click the Sheet1 tab**
   Sheet1, which contains the Houston posting data, becomes active again.

Quick Tip
If a workbook contains more sheet tabs than are visible, you can navigate between sheets by using the tab scrolling buttons to the left of the sheet tabs: the Previous Worksheet button ◄ and the Next Worksheet button ►.

3. **Double-click the Sheet2 tab, type Contact, then press ENTER**
   The new name for Sheet2 automatically replaces the default name on the tab. Worksheet names can have up to 31 characters, including spaces and punctuation.

4. **Right-click the Contact tab, point to Tab Color on the shortcut menu, then click the Blue, Accent 5, Darker 25% color** (fifth row, second column from the right), as shown in **Figure 2-19**

5. **Right-click the Sheet1 tab, click Rename on the shortcut menu, type Houston 1st Quarter, then press ENTER**
   Notice that the color of the Contact tab changes depending on whether it is the active tab; when the Houston 1st Quarter tab is active, the color of the Contact tab changes to the blue tab color you selected. You decide to rearrange the order of the sheets so that the Contact tab is to the right of the Sheet3 tab.

6. **Click the Contact tab, hold down the mouse button, drag it to the right of the Sheet3 tab**, as shown in **Figure 2-20**, then release the mouse button
   As you drag, the pointer changes to ▸, the Move sheet pointer, and a small black triangle just above the tabs shows the position where the moved sheet will be when you release the mouse button. The last sheet in the workbook is now the Contact sheet as shown in **Figure 2-21**. You can move multiple sheets by pressing and holding SHIFT while clicking the sheets you want to move, then dragging the sheets to their new location.

Quick Tip
To insert a worksheet, click the New sheet button ⊕ to the right of the sheet tabs.

7. **Right-click the Sheet3 tab, click Delete on the shortcut menu, press CTRL+HOME, then save your work**
   The sheet is deleted. With the sheet tabs renamed from their default to descriptive names, the Accessibility status on the status bar changes from Investigate to Good to go.

Modify Worksheet Tabs   EX 2-17

Figure 2-18: Sheet tabs in workbook

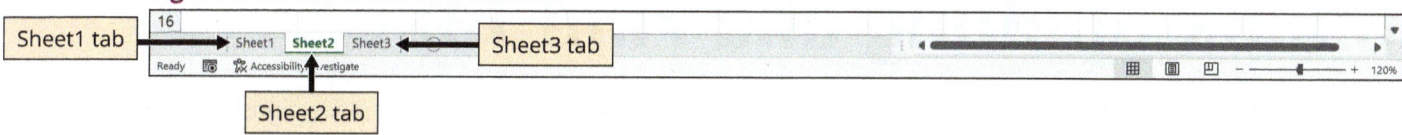

Figure 2-19: Tab Color palette

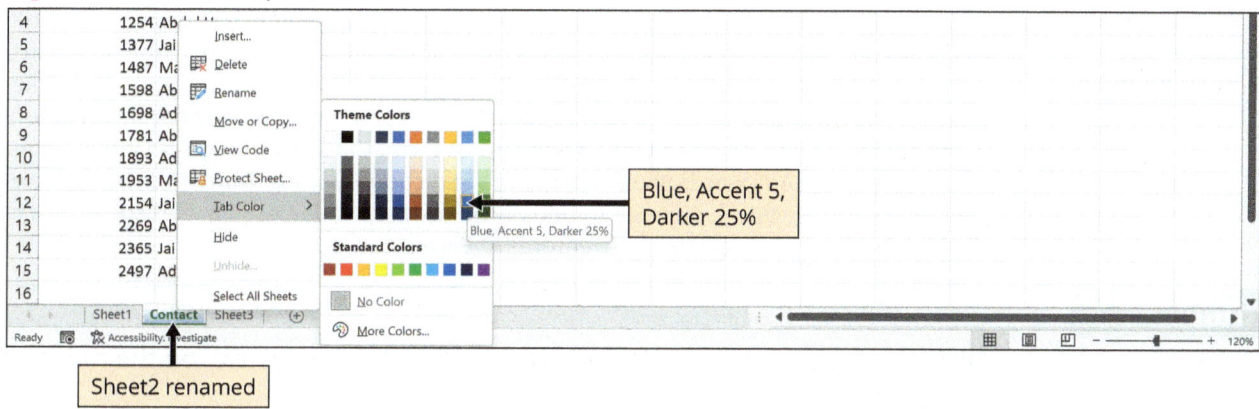

Figure 2-20: Moving the Contact sheet

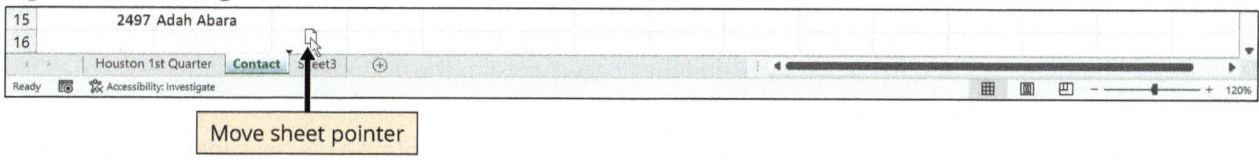

Figure 2-21: Reordered sheets

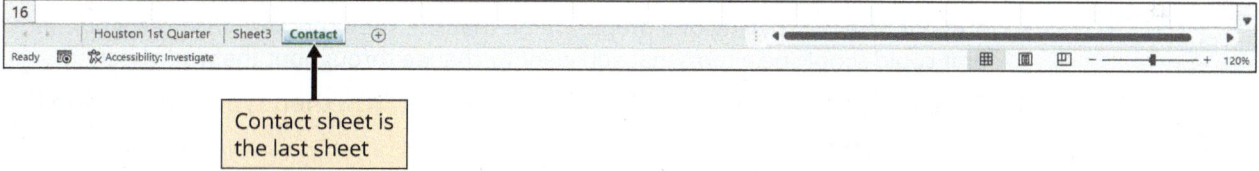

Copying, adding, and deleting worksheets

There are times when you may want to copy a worksheet. For example, a workbook might contain a sheet with Quarter 1 expenses, and you want to use that sheet as the basis for a sheet containing Quarter 2 expenses. To copy a sheet within the same workbook, press and hold CTRL, drag the sheet tab to the desired tab location, release the mouse button, then release CTRL. A duplicate sheet appears with the same name as the copied sheet followed by "(2)," indicating that it is a copy. You can then rename the sheet to a more meaningful name. To copy a sheet to a different workbook, both the source and destination workbooks must be open. Select the sheet to copy or move, right-click the sheet tab, click Move or Copy in the shortcut menu, then complete the information in the Move or Copy dialog box. Be sure to click the Create a copy check box if you want to copy rather than move the worksheet. Carefully check your calculation results whenever you move or copy a worksheet. You can add multiple worksheets quickly by pressing and holding SHIFT, clicking the number of existing worksheet tabs that correspond with the number of sheets you want to add, clicking the Insert arrow in the Cells group on the Home tab, then clicking Insert Sheet. You can delete multiple worksheets from a workbook by clicking the Home tab on the ribbon, pressing and holding SHIFT, clicking the sheet tabs of the worksheets you want to delete, clicking the Delete arrow in the Cells group, clicking Delete Sheet, then clicking Delete to confirm.

Check Spelling and Find Text

Case Before you share this workbook with Luis, you want to check the spelling and replace a position type in the worksheet.

Objectives
- Change spelling using a suggestion
- Replace text using Find & Select

Excel includes a spell checker to help you ensure that the words in your worksheet are spelled correctly. The spell checker scans your worksheet, displays words it doesn't find in its built-in dictionary, and suggests replacements when they are available. To check all the sheets in a multiple-sheet workbook, you need to display each sheet individually and run the spell checker for each one. You can also add words to the dictionary, such as your company name, an acronym, or an unusual technical term. Once you add a word or term, the spell checker no longer considers that word misspelled. Any words you've added to the dictionary using Word, Access, or PowerPoint are also available in Excel. If you need to find or replace text or values in a worksheet, you can quickly do this using the Find and Replace features in Excel.

Steps

Quick Tip
You can click the Thesaurus button in the Proofing group to open a Thesaurus pane with a list of synonyms for a selected word in a cell.

1. **Click the Houston 1st Quarter sheet tab, click the Review tab on the ribbon, then click the Spelling button in the Proofing group**
   The Spelling: English (United States) dialog box opens, as shown in **Figure 2-22**, with "Admnistrator" selected as the first misspelled word on the worksheet, and with "Administrator" selected in the Suggestions list as a possible replacement. For any word, you have the option to Ignore this case of the flagged word, Ignore All cases of the flagged word, Change the word to the selected suggestion, Change All instances of the flagged word to the selected suggestion, AutoCorrect the word, or Add to Dictionary to add the flagged word to the dictionary.

2. **Click Change**
   When no more incorrect words are found, Excel displays a message indicating that the spell check is complete.

3. **Click OK**

Quick Tip
If you want to find text, click Find & Select in the Editing group, then click Find.

4. **Click the Home tab, click Find & Select in the Editing group, then click Replace**
   The Find and Replace dialog box opens. You can use this dialog box to replace a word or phrase. It might be a misspelling of a proper name that the spell checker didn't recognize as misspelled, or it could simply be a term that you want to change throughout the worksheet.

5. **Type Contract in the Find what text box, press TAB, then type Temp in the Replace with text box**
   Compare your dialog box to **Figure 2-23**.

Quick Tip
You can find and replace cell formatting by clicking the Options button in the Find and Replace dialog box, then clicking the Format arrows to select the desired formatting.

6. **Click Replace All, click OK to close the Microsoft Excel dialog box, then click Close to close the Find and Replace dialog box**
   Excel made five replacements, changing each instance of "Contract" on the worksheet to "Temp."

7. **Compare your screen to Figure 2-24, save your workbook, then submit your work to your instructor as directed**

8. **sam↑ Close the workbook, then close Excel**

Translating text

You can translate text in a worksheet by clicking the Review tab, clicking the Translate button in the Language group, then, if necessary, clicking Turn on when asked if you want to use intelligent services. The Translator pane opens and allows you to select the From language and the To language from menus of world languages. The translated text appears in the To language box.

Figure 2-22: Spelling: English (United States) dialog box

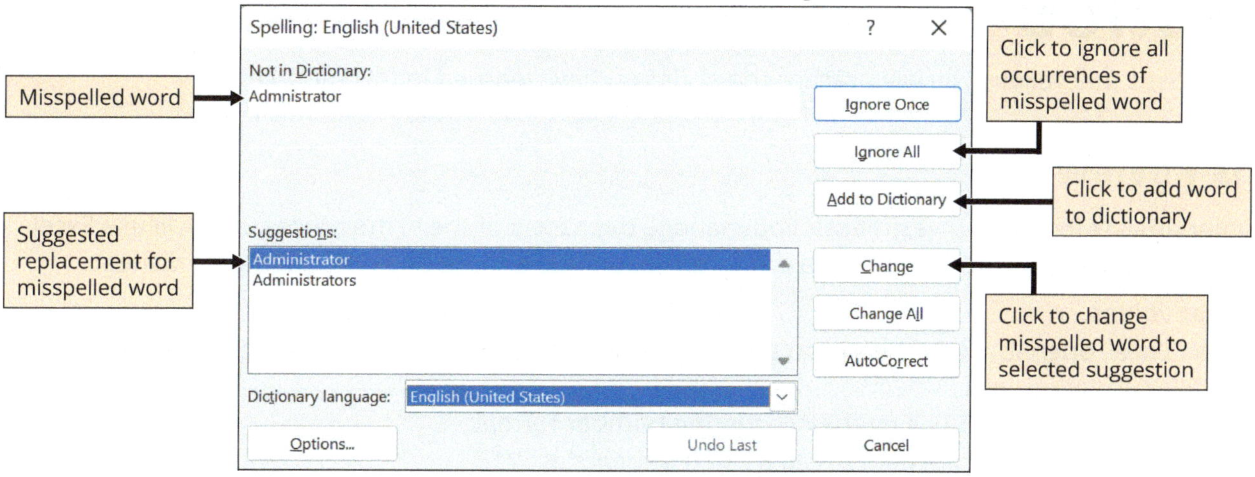

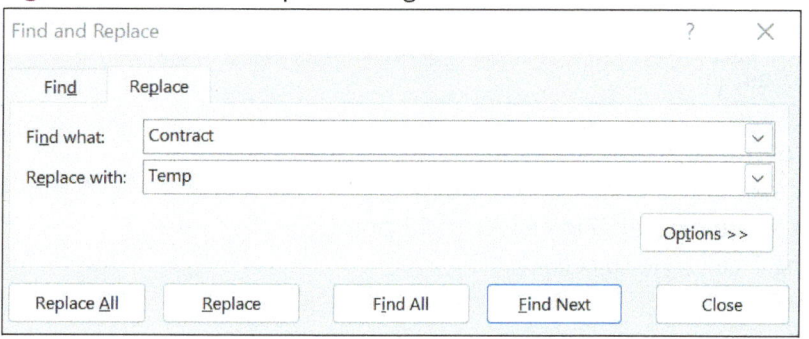

Figure 2-23: Find and Replace dialog box

Figure 2-24: Completed worksheet

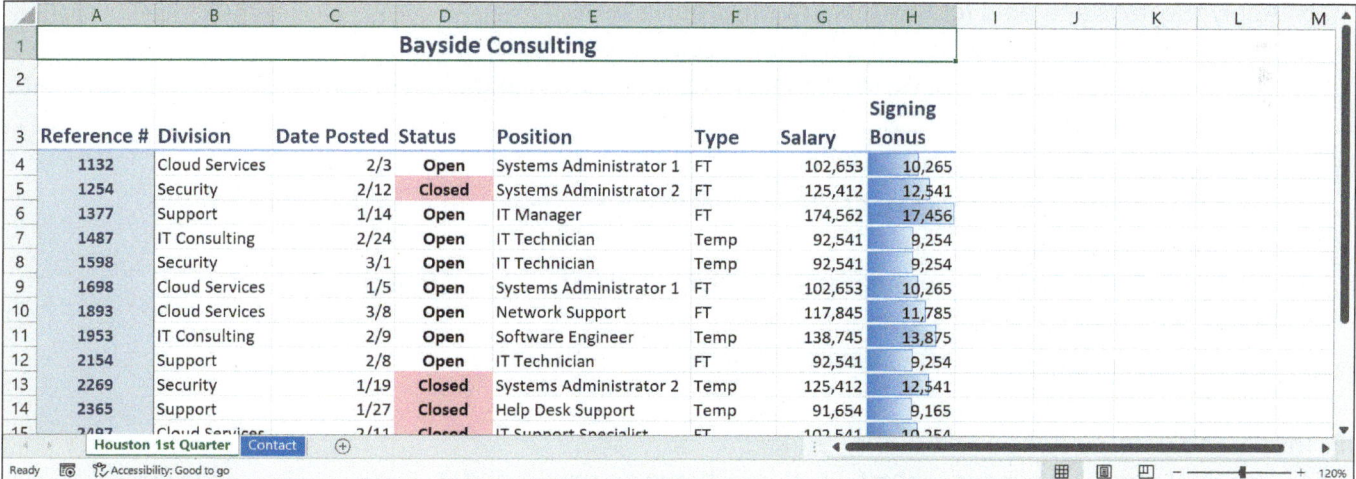

Using Find & Select features

You can navigate to a specific place in a workbook by clicking the Find & Select button in the Editing group on the Home tab, clicking Go To, typing a cell address, then clicking OK. Clicking the Find & Select button also allows you to quickly go to notes, formulas, constants, data validation, and conditional formatting in a worksheet. You can use the Go to Special dialog box to navigate to cells with special elements such as different types of formulas or objects. Some Go to Special commands also appear on the Find & Select menu. Using this Find & Select menu, you can also change the mouse pointer shape to the Select Objects pointer so you can quickly select drawing objects when necessary. To return to the standard Excel pointer, press ESC.

Practice

In the exercises that follow, you will practice the skills you have learned in this module.

Skills Review

As a junior analyst for GWW Investments, you manage the assets of the firm's offices. You will use Excel features from this module to format the asset information into a more understandable worksheet.

1. **Format values.**
   a. Start Excel, open IL_EX_2-2.xlsx from the location where you store your Data Files, then save it as **IL_EX_2_Investments**.
   b. Format the range B3:B7 using the Accounting number format.
   c. Change the format of the date in cell B9 so it appears as 7/1.
   d. Increase the number of decimals in cell D1 to 1, using a button in the Number group on the Home tab on the ribbon.
   e. Save your work.

2. **Change font attributes.**
   a. Select the range A3:A7.
   b. Change the font of the selection to Calibri.
   c. Increase the font size of the selection to 11 point.
   d. Increase the font size of the label in cell A1 to 11 point.
   e. Apply the Heading 2 cell style to cell A1.
   f. Save your changes.

3. **Modify font styles and alignment.**
   a. Use the Merge & Center button to center the label in cell A1 over columns A and B.
   b. Apply the italic and bold font formats to the label in cell C1.
   c. Use the Format Painter to copy the format in cell C1 to the label in cell A9.
   d. Change the alignment of cell B2 to Align Right using a button in the Alignment group on the Home tab.
   e. Save your changes.

4. **Adjust column width and row height.**
   a. Resize column C to a width of 20.55 characters. If you are unable to drag the column border, use AutoFit to resize the column.
   b. Use the AutoFit feature to automatically resize both columns A and B at the same time.
   c. Change the text in cell B2 to **Managed Assets**.
   d. Adjust the width of column B to display all of the content in cell B2.
   e. Save your changes.

5. **Insert and delete rows and columns.**
   a. Use the Insert dialog box to insert a new row between rows 1 and 2.
   b. Use a column heading to insert a new column between columns B and C.
   c. Type **Fee** in cell C3 and center the label in the cell.
   d. Use a row heading to delete the Philadelphia row from the worksheet.
   e. Create a formula in cell C4 that calculates the fee for the New York office by multiplying the total managed assets in cell B4 by the annual fee percentage in cell E1. (**Hint**: Use the correct type of cell reference for the annual fee percentage that will enable you to copy the formula.)
   f. Insert formulas in cells C5, C6, and C7 to calculate the fees for the Los Angeles, Miami, and Chicago offices.
   g. Save your changes.

Skills Review

6. **Modify data formatting and documentation.**
   a. Add an outside border around the range A3:C7.
   b. Apply the Green, Accent 6, Lighter 80% fill color (second row, last column under Theme Colors) to the range D1:E1.
   c. Change the color of the font in the range A9:B9 to Green, Accent 6, Darker 50% (last row, last column under Theme Colors).
   d. Add a header in the center section of the worksheet that contains the sheet name.
   e. Enter your name in the center section of the worksheet footer, then return to Normal view.
   f. Save your changes.

7. **Apply conditional formatting.**
   a. Select the range C4:C7, then create a Highlight Cells rule that changes cell contents to green fill with dark green text if the value is greater than 75000.
   b. Select the range B4:B7, then apply Gradient Fill green data bars. (**Hint**: Click Green Data Bar in the Gradient Fill section.)
   c. Open the Conditional Formatting Rules Manager dialog box and view the conditional formatting rules for the worksheet. (**Hint**: Click Manage Rules on the Conditional Formatting menu, then click the Show formatting rules for arrow.)
   d. Review the rules for the worksheet, making sure your rules are correct, then close the dialog box.
   e. Save your changes.

8. **Modify worksheet tabs.**
   a. Rename the Sheet1 tab to **Active Management** and rename the Sheet2 tab to **Passive Management**.
   b. Add a sheet to the workbook, then name the new sheet **Total Fees**.
   c. Change the Active Management tab color to Green, Accent 6, Darker 50% (last row, last column under Theme Colors).
   d. Change the Passive Management tab color to Blue, Accent 5, Darker 50% (last row, second to last column under Theme Colors).
   e. Reorder the sheets so that the Total Fees sheet comes before (to the left of) the Active Management sheet.
   f. Delete the Total Fees sheet.
   g. Activate the Active Management sheet, then save your work.

9. **Check spelling and find text.**
   a. Move the cell pointer to cell A1.
   b. Use the Find & Select feature to replace the word "New York" with **Boston**.
   c. Use the Spelling tool to check the spelling on the worksheet and correct any spelling errors, using suggestions as appropriate. (**Hint**: The label in cell A9 should be Report date.)
   d. Save your changes, then compare your Active Management sheet to **Figure 2-25**.
   e. Preview the Active Management sheet in Backstage view, submit your work to your instructor as directed, close the workbook, then close Excel.

Figure 2-25

	A	B	C	D	E	F
1		GWW		Annual Fee Percentage	1.1%	
2						
3	Office	Managed Assets	Fee			
4	Boston	$ 7,842,634.35	$ 86,268.98			
5	Los Angeles	$ 6,695,714.77	$ 73,652.86			
6	Miami	$ 4,815,981.19	$ 52,975.79			
7	Chicago	$ 7,713,257.23	$ 84,845.83			
8						
9	*Report date:*		7/1			
10						

Independent Challenge 1

As an accountant for Albuquerque Urgent Care, you have been asked to review the expenses for the facility. You have organized the data in an Excel workbook, and now you want to format the data to improve its readability and highlight trends in expenses.

a. Start Excel, open IL_EX_2-3.xlsx from the location where you store your Data Files, then save it as **IL_EX_2_Expenses**.
b. Format the values in the Total column in the Accounting number format.
c. Format the value in cell I1 as Percent format with two decimal places.
d. Format the values in the Inv. Date column with the Date format 14-Mar.
e. Apply bold formatting to the column labels in row two and increase the font size of the labels to 12.
f. Italicize the Departments in column A.
g. Change the font of the Sales Tax label in cell H1 to Calibri.
h. Apply the Title cell style to cell A1.
i. Delete column G, then delete row 13.
j. Merge and center the title in cell A1 over columns A1:F1.
k. Resize column widths as necessary using AutoFit so that all columns are wide enough to display the data and labels.
l. Use the Format Painter to copy the date format in the Inv. Date column to the dates in the Inv. Due column.
m. Change the fill color of the sales tax information in the range G1:H1 to the Blue, Accent 1, Lighter 80% color (second row, fifth column from the left), and the font color to the Blue, Accent 1, Darker 50% color (last row under Theme colors, fifth column from the left).
n. Add a bottom border to the column labels in row 2.
o. Use conditional formatting to apply blue gradient data bars to the Total column data.
p. Rename Sheet3 to **Budget** and rename Sheet1 to **Actual**.
q. Change the tab color of the Budget sheet to Red in the Standard colors. Change the tab color of the Actual sheet to Purple in the Standard colors.
r. Move Sheet2 to the right of the Budget sheet.
s. Activate the Actual Sheet and spell check the worksheet. Correct any spelling errors.
t. Using Find & Select, replace all instances of X-ray on the worksheet with Imaging.
u. Delete Sheet2, enter the sheet name in the center section of the Actual worksheet header, enter your name in the center section of the worksheet footer, then save the file.
v. Activate cell A1, switch to Normal view, then compare your worksheet to **Figure 2-26**.
w. Submit your work to your instructor as directed, close the workbook, then close Excel.

Figure 2-26

	A	B	C	D	E	F	G	H	I
1			Albuquerque Urgent Care				Sales Tax	5.13%	
2	Departments	Inv. Date	Inv. Due	Inv. Amount	Sales Tax	Total			
3	Imaging	1-Jan	31-Jan	$ 187.82	$ 9.63	$ 197.45			
4	Respiratory	7-Jan	6-Feb	$ 270.00	$ 13.84	$ 283.84			
5	Testing	20-Jan	19-Feb	$ 79.50	$ 4.07	$ 83.57			
6	Orthopedics	1-Jan	31-Jan	$ 755.00	$ 38.69	$ 793.69			
7	Telemedicine	13-Jan	12-Feb	$ 65.00	$ 3.33	$ 68.33			
8	Physical Exams	7-Jan	6-Feb	$ 75.00	$ 3.84	$ 78.84			
9	Optical	5-Jan	4-Feb	$ 155.00	$ 7.94	$ 162.94			
10	Respiratory	15-Jan	14-Feb	$ 250.00	$ 12.81	$ 262.81			
11	Imaging	12-Jan	11-Feb	$ 111.87	$ 5.73	$ 117.60			
12	Imaging	25-Jan	24-Feb	$ 125.00	$ 6.41	$ 131.41			
13	Immunization	3-Feb	5-Mar	$ 85.00	$ 4.36	$ 89.36			
14	Orthopedics	1-Feb	3-Mar	$ 175.00	$ 8.97	$ 183.97			
15	Imaging	1-Mar	31-Mar	$ 155.00	$ 7.94	$ 162.94			
16	Telemedicine	28-Feb	30-Mar	$ 85.00	$ 4.36	$ 89.36			

Independent Challenge 2

You are assisting the head of business operations at CGS Merchant Services. You have been asked to format a worksheet showing the first-quarter business services for the company's five branches. As part of this effort, you want to illustrate trends among the branches.

a. Start Excel, open IL_EX_2-4.xlsx from the location where you store your Data Files, then save it as **IL_EX_2_Services**.
b. Apply the Title cell style to cell A1, apply the Heading 4 cell style to the column headings in row 2, and apply the Total cell style to the range A8:G8.
c. Merge and center the title in cell A1 across the range A1:G1.
d. Format the range B3:G8 using the Accounting number format. AutoFit the widths of all columns and format the range with no decimal places.
e. Format the date in cell B9 using the 14-Mar date format.
f. Rotate the label in cell A2 up by 45 degrees. Copy this rotated format to the other column headings in row two. Center the rotated labels in their cells.
g. Format the range A9:B9 with a Blue-Gray, Text 2, Lighter 60% fill (third row, fourth column from the left, under Theme Colors).
h. Format the range A9:B9 with a Blue, Accent 1, Darker 50% font color (last row, fifth column from the left, under Theme Colors).
i. Create a conditional format in the range G3:G7 so that entries less than 30,000,000 appear in light red fill with dark red text.
j. Create a conditional format in the range B8:F8 to add the 3 Stars Ratings icon set. Widen the columns as necessary to fully display the data and formatting.
k. Use the Spelling tool to check spelling in the sheet. Make all necessary spelling corrections.
l. Rename Sheet1 to **First Quarter**. Copy the First Quarter sheet and rename the copied sheet **Second Quarter**. Move the Second Quarter sheet if necessary so it is to the right of the First Quarter sheet.
m. On the Second Quarter sheet, delete the data in the range B3:F7 and delete the date in cell B9.
n. Activate the First Quarter sheet. Compare your worksheet to **Figure 2-27**.
o. Enter your name in the center header section, change the worksheet orientation to landscape, then save your work.
p. Preview the worksheet, make any final changes you think are necessary, then submit your work to your instructor as directed.
q. Close the workbook, then close Excel.

Figure 2-27

	A	B	C	D	E	F	G
1				CGS Merchant Services			
2	Service	Main	North	South	East	West	Total
3	Credit card processing	$ 7,587,684	$ 5,257,896	$ 6,569,810	$ 7,518,451	$ 8,352,140	$ 35,285,981
4	Reconciliation	$ 7,531,478	$ 5,256,873	$ 3,984,755	$ 4,895,474	$ 8,221,435	$ 29,890,015
5	Check collection	$ 8,598,745	$ 3,987,416	$ 8,258,972	$ 7,996,350	$ 5,302,141	$ 34,143,624
6	Payroll service	$ 10,578,421	$ 4,129,821	$ 3,963,351	$ 4,355,871	$ 8,321,430	$ 31,348,894
7	Deposit services	$ 8,848,752	$ 3,665,474	$ 3,784,173	$ 5,012,642	$ 6,662,145	$ 27,973,186
8	Total	★ $ 43,145,080	★ $ 22,297,480	★ $ 26,561,061	★ $ 29,778,788	★ $ 36,859,291	$ 158,641,700
9	Verified	31-Dec					
10							

Visual Workshop

Open IL_EX_2-5.xlsx from the location where you store your Data Files, then save it as **IL_EX_2_Northbridge**. Use the skills you learned in this module to modify the worksheet as necessary so the content and formatting matches **Figure 2-28**. (Note that cell A1 is selected in the figure.) Use the blue gradient fill for the data bars in the Total column. Use the Title cell style for the company name in cell A1, the Heading 1 cell style for the column labels in row 2, and the Total cell style for the total values in the last row. The font color for the service packages listed in column A is Blue in the standard colors and the font is formatted in bold. (**Hint**: A row has been deleted from the worksheet.) Enter your name in the upper-left section of the header, check the spelling on the worksheet, change the worksheet orientation to landscape, save your changes, then submit your work to your instructor as directed.

Figure 2-28

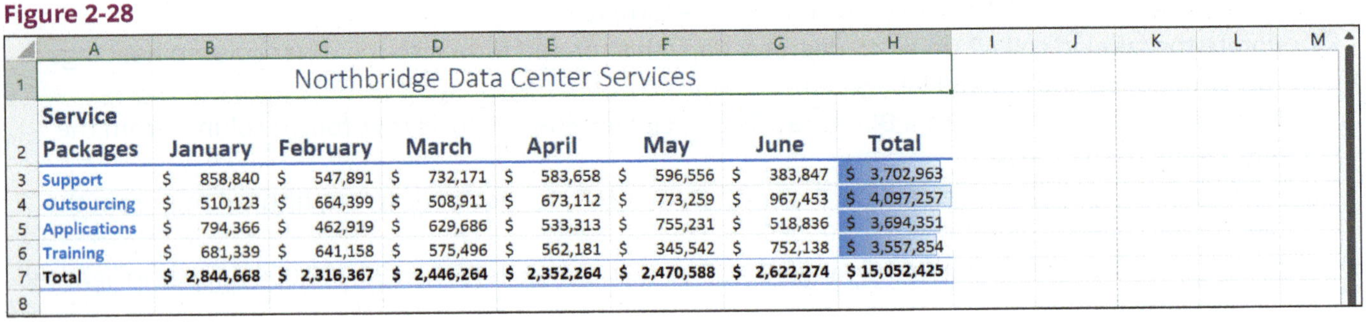

	A	B	C	D	E	F	G	H
1	Northbridge Data Center Services							
2	Service Packages	January	February	March	April	May	June	Total
3	Support	$ 858,840	$ 547,891	$ 732,171	$ 583,658	$ 596,556	$ 383,847	$ 3,702,963
4	Outsourcing	$ 510,123	$ 664,399	$ 508,911	$ 673,112	$ 773,259	$ 967,453	$ 4,097,257
5	Applications	$ 794,366	$ 462,919	$ 629,686	$ 533,313	$ 755,231	$ 518,836	$ 3,694,351
6	Training	$ 681,339	$ 641,158	$ 575,496	$ 562,181	$ 345,542	$ 752,138	$ 3,557,854
7	Total	$ 2,844,668	$ 2,316,367	$ 2,446,264	$ 2,352,264	$ 2,470,588	$ 2,622,274	$ 15,052,425

Excel Module 3

Analyzing Data Using Formulas

Case
Elena Fuentes, Vice President of Finance at Bayside Consulting, wants to know how U.S. revenues have performed compared to last year and relative to projected targets. She asks you to prepare a worksheet that summarizes and analyzes this revenue data.

Module Objectives

After completing this module, you will be able to:
- Enter a formula using the Quick Analysis tool
- Copy formulas with relative cell references
- Build a logical formula with the IF function
- Copy formulas with absolute cell references
- Build a logical formula with the AND function
- Use a function to round a value
- Build a statistical formula with the COUNTA function
- Enter a date function
- Control worksheet calculations

Files You Will Need

IL_EX_3-1.xlsx
IL_EX_3-2.xlsx
IL_EX_3-3.xlsx
IL_EX_3-4.xlsx
IL_EX_3-5.xlsx

Module 3 Analyzing Data Using Formulas

Enter a Formula Using the Quick Analysis Tool

Case To help Elena evaluate revenues at Bayside, you want to calculate yearly revenue totals for each U.S. office and compare the yearly performance of each office to the previous year.

Objectives
- Create a formula using the Quick Analysis tool
- Create a formula to find a percentage increase

So far, you have used the AutoSum button on the ribbon to quickly add simple formulas that sum and average selected data. You can also add formulas using the Quick Analysis tool, which opens when you select a range of cells. This tool allows you to quickly format, chart, or analyze data by calculating sums, averages, and other selected totals.

Steps

1. **sam↓** Start Excel, open **IL_EX_3-1.xlsx** from the location where you store your Data Files, then save it as **IL_EX_3_Revenue**

2. Select the range **B3:E11**, click the **Quick Analysis button** that appears below the selection, then click the **Totals tab**

   The Totals tab in the Quick Analysis tool displays commonly used functions, as shown in **Figure 3-1**. This tab includes two Sum buttons. The first Sum button, with displays a blue row, inserts the SUM function in a row beneath the selected range. The second button, which displays a gold column, inserts the SUM function in the column to the right of the range.

   Quick Tip
   Clicking the first Sum button enters totals in a row below a selected range.

3. Click the second **Sum button**, which displays the gold column

   The newly calculated totals are displayed in the column to the right of the selected range, in cells F3:F11.

4. Click cell **H3**, type **=(**, click cell **F3**, type **-**, click cell **G3**, then type **)**

   This first part of the formula finds the difference in total revenue from the previous year to this year. You enclosed this operation in parentheses to make sure this difference is calculated first.

5. Type **/**, then click cell **G3**

   The second part of this formula divides the difference in revenue by the total revenue for the previous year, to calculate the increase or decrease.

6. Click the **Enter button** on the formula bar

   The result, .82868268, appears in cell H3. The column isn't wide enough to fully display this value but the number of decimal places will be adjusted in the next formatting step.

7. Click the **Percent Style button** in the Number group on the Home tab on the ribbon, then click the **Increase Decimal button** in the Number group twice

   The formatted percentage, 82.87%, appears in cell H3, as shown in **Figure 3-2**.

8. Save the workbook

Figure 3-1: Quick Analysis tool

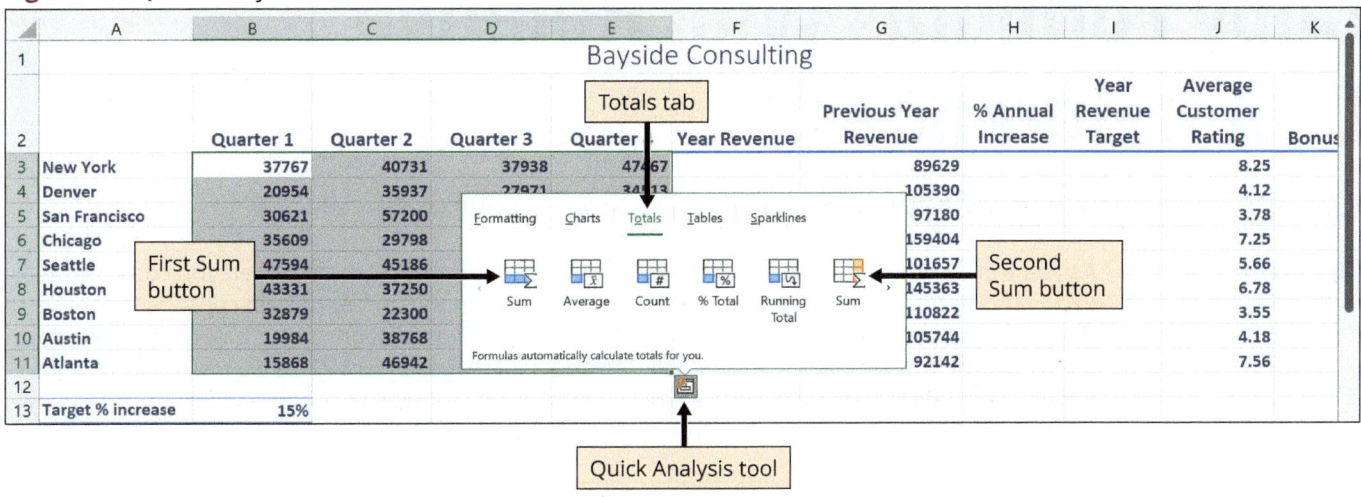

Figure 3-2: Formatted annual increase percentage

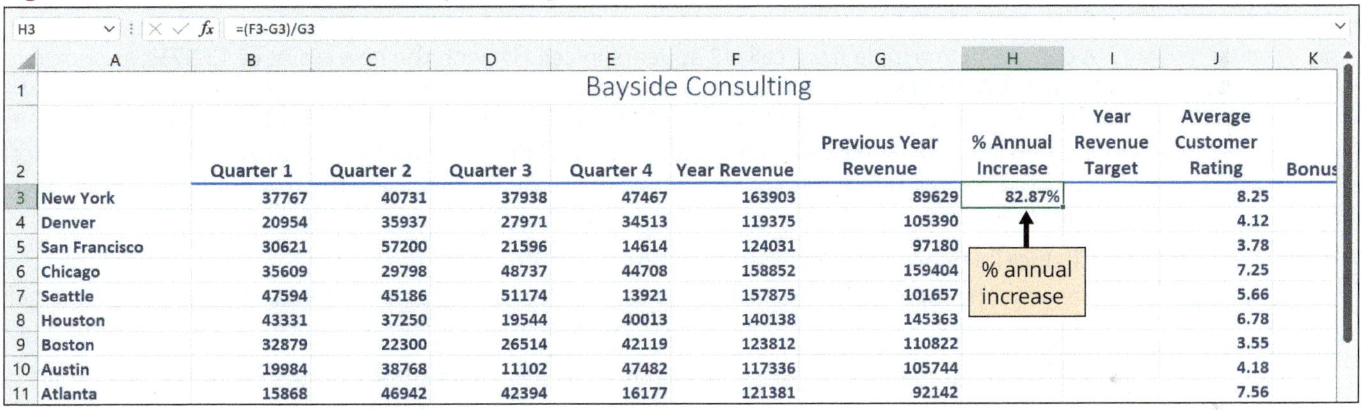

	A	B	C	D	E	F	G	H	I	J	K
H3		fx	=(F3-G3)/G3								
1					Bayside Consulting						
2		Quarter 1	Quarter 2	Quarter 3	Quarter 4	Year Revenue	Previous Year Revenue	% Annual Increase	Year Revenue Target	Average Customer Rating	Bonus
3	New York	37767	40731	37938	47467	163903	89629	82.87%		8.25	
4	Denver	20954	35937	27971	34513	119375	105390			4.12	
5	San Francisco	30621	57200	21596	14614	124031	97180			3.78	
6	Chicago	35609	29798	48737	44708	158852	159404			7.25	
7	Seattle	47594	45186	51174	13921	157875	101657			5.66	
8	Houston	43331	37250	19544	40013	140138	145363			6.78	
9	Boston	32879	22300	26514	42119	123812	110822			3.55	
10	Austin	19984	38768	11102	47482	117336	105744			4.18	
11	Atlanta	15868	46942	42394	16177	121381	92142			7.56	

Copy Formulas with Relative Cell References

Case It will save you a lot of time if you copy the annual increase formula rather than entering it for each office.

Objectives
- Copy formulas with relative cell references
- Use the fill handle to copy formulas

As you work in Excel, you may want to reuse formulas by copying them. When you copy formulas, Excel automatically adjusts any cell addresses in the formula so they remain consistent relative to the formula's new location. For example, if you copy a formula containing a cell reference down a column, the row number in each copied formula increases by one. This type of cell reference in a formula is called a **relative cell reference** because it changes to reflect the new formula's new location; it's the default type of addressing used in Excel worksheets.

Steps

1. **Click cell H3 if necessary, drag the fill handle from cell H3 down to cell H11**
   The formula for calculating the percentage increase is copied into the range H3:H11.

2. **Click cell H4**
   A copy of the formula from cell H3 appears in cell H4, with the new result of 13.27%, as shown in **Figure 3-3**. Notice in the formula bar that the cell references have changed so that cells in row 4 instead of those in row 3 are referenced. This formula contains relative cell references, which tells Excel to substitute new cell references within the copied formulas as necessary. In this case, Excel adjusted the cell references in the formula in cell H3 by increasing the row number references by one from 3 to 4.

3. **Click cell H5**
   Because the location of this cell is two rows below the original formula, Excel adjusted the cell references in the copied formula by increasing the row number references by two from 3 to 5.

4. **Click cell B12, click the AutoSum button Σ in the Editing group on the Home tab on the ribbon, then click the Enter button ✓ on the formula**

5. **Drag the fill handle to the right to cell E12**
   A formula similar to the one in cell B12 now appears in the range C12:E12.

6. **Click cell C12**
   In copying the formula one cell to the right, the cell references are adjusted by increasing the column letter references by one from B to C. Compare your worksheet to **Figure 3-4**.

7. **Save your work**

Copy Formulas with Relative Cell References   EX 3-5

Figure 3-3: Formula copied using the fill handle

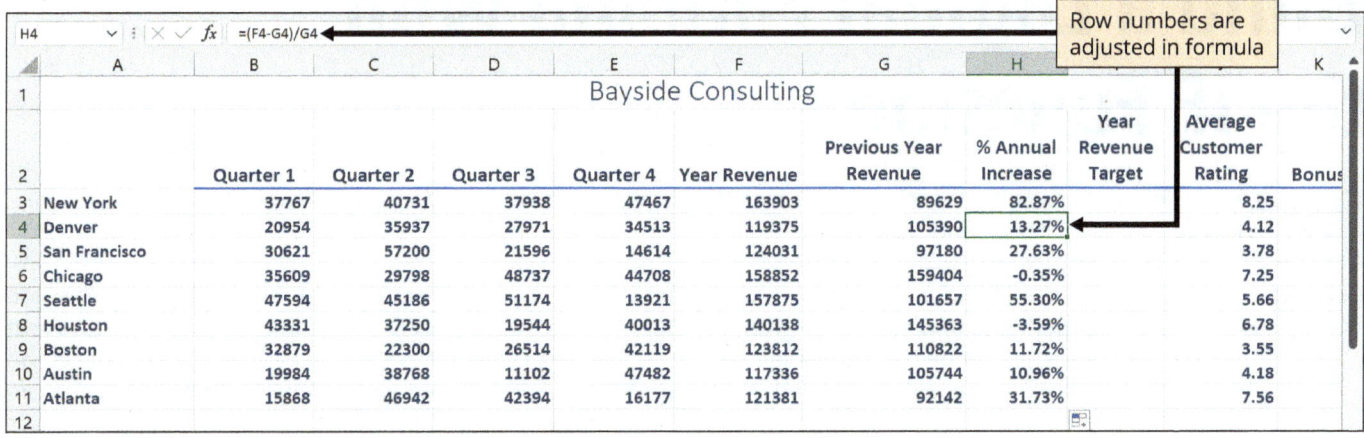

Figure 3-4: Formula column references changed

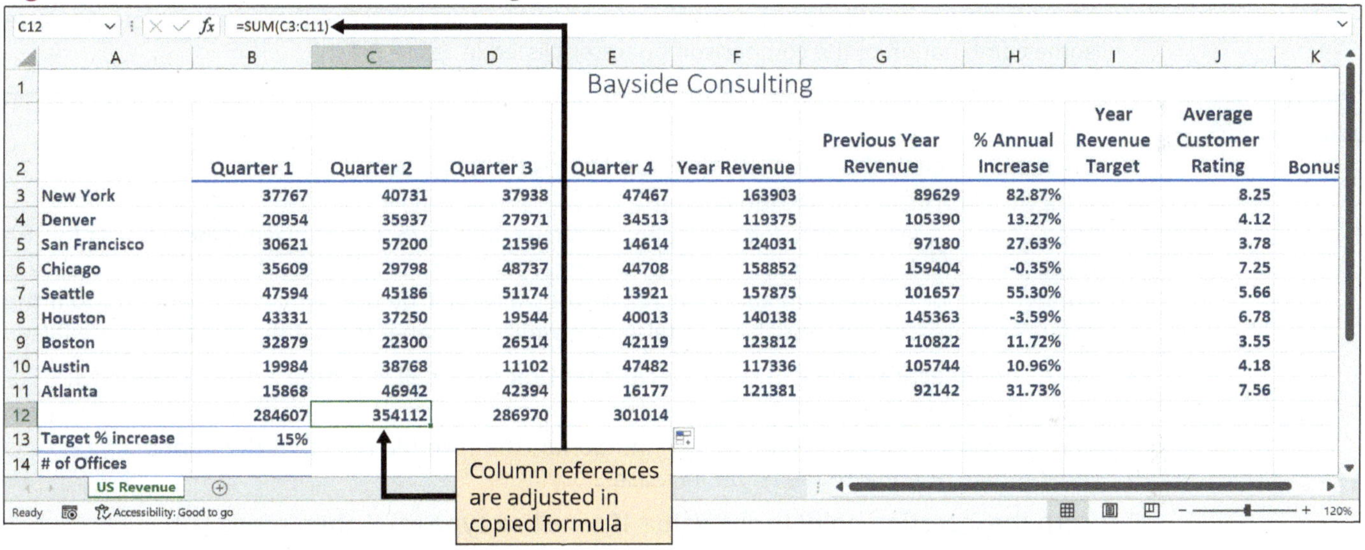

Inserting functions into formulas

You can insert a function on its own or as part of another formula. For example, you have used the SUM function on its own to sum a range of cells—for example, =SUM(B5:B9). You could also use the SUM function within a formula that adds a range of cells and then multiplies the total by a decimal—for example, =SUM(B5:B9)*.5.

Module 3 Analyzing Data Using Formulas

Build a Logical Formula with the IF Function

Case Elena asks you to calculate whether each office met or missed its revenue target for the year. An IF function will allow you to test for this condition.

Objectives
- Build a logical formula using the IF function
- Apply comparison operators in a logical test

You can build a formula in a worksheet using a **logical function** that returns a different value depending on whether the given condition is true or false. An **IF function** is a logical function that assigns a value to a cell based on a logical test. A **logical formula** makes calculations based on criteria that you create, called **stated conditions**. For example, you can build a formula to calculate bonuses based on a person's performance rating, where the stated condition is 5. If a person is rated a 5 on a scale of 1 to 5, they receive an additional 10% of their salary as a bonus; otherwise, there is no bonus. The IF function has three parts, including the **logical test**, which is the first part of the function. This test is a condition that can be answered with a true or false response. If the logical test is true, then the second part of the function is applied; if it is false, then the third part of the function is applied. When entering the logical test portion of an IF statement, you often use some combination of the comparison operators listed in **Table 3-1**.

Steps

1. **Click cell I3, click the Formulas tab on the ribbon, click the Logical button in the Function Library group, then click IF**
   The Function Arguments dialog box opens as shown in **Figure 3-5**, displaying three boxes for the three parts of a logical function: the Logical_test, which in this case tests if the annual increase is greater than or equal to the target increase; the Value_if_true box, which tells what to do if the test results are true; and the Value_if_false box, which tells what to do if the test results are false.

2. **With the insertion point in the Logical_test box click cell H3, type >=, click cell B13, then press TAB**
   The symbol (>) represents "greater than." So far, the formula reads, "If the annual increase is greater than or equal to the target increase…"

3. **With the insertion point in the Value_if_true box type MET, then press TAB**
   This part of the function tells Excel to display the text MET if the annual increase equals or exceeds the target increase of 15%. Quotation marks are automatically added around the text you entered.

4. **Type MISSED in the Value_if_false box, then click OK**
   This part tells Excel to display the text MISSED if the results of the logical test are false—that is, if the increase does not equal or exceed the target. The function is complete, and the result, MET, appears in cell I3, as shown in **Figure 3-6**.

5. **Click the Home tab, click the Center button in the Alignment group, then save the workbook**
   The status of the year revenue target in cell I3 is centered in the cell.

Figure 3-5: Function Arguments dialog box

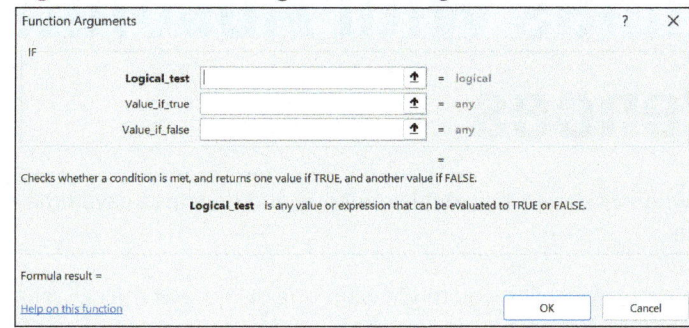

Figure 3-6: Worksheet with IF function

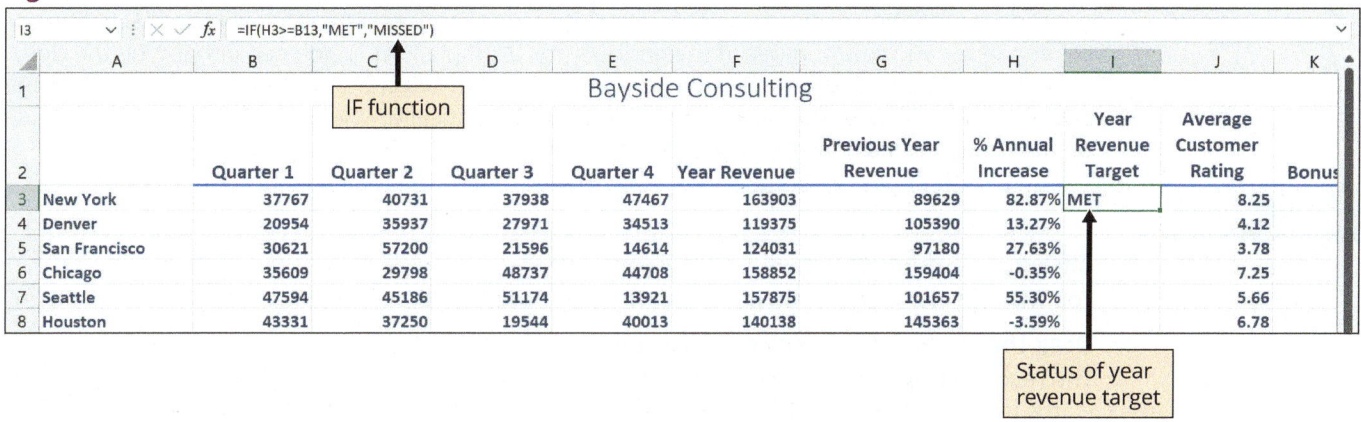

Table 3-1: Comparison operators

operator	meaning	operator	meaning
<	Less than	<=	Less than or equal to
>	Greater than	>=	Greater than or equal to
=	Equal to	<>	Not equal to

Nesting IF functions

You can nest IF functions to test several conditions in a formula. A **nested IF function** contains IF functions inside other IF functions to test these multiple conditions. To create a nested IF function, enter the second IF statement in the value_if_false argument of the first IF statement. For example, the nested statement =IF(H3<0%,"Warning",IF(H3<50%,"No Bonus","Bonus")) tests whether a warning should be issued based on the percentage increases for an office. Assuming the percentage increase of an office is in cell H3, the nested IF statement first evaluates whether the increase was less than 0. If that first test is true, the text "Warning" will display. If the first test is false, a second test will be performed to check to evaluate whether the increase is less than 50%. If that second test is true (values are less than 50%), the text "No Bonus" will display. If that second test is false, the text "Bonus" will display.

Copy Formulas with Absolute Cell References

Case You want to calculate whether each office met its revenue and decide to save time by copying the logical formula for the New York office.

Objectives
- Create an absolute cell reference
- Use the fill handle to copy absolute cell references

When copying formulas, you might want one or more of the cell references in the formula to remain unchanged. For example, you might have a price in a specific cell that you want to use in all the copied formulas, regardless of their location. If you used relative cell referencing, the formula results would be incorrect, because the formula would reference a different cell every time you copy it. In this situation, you need to use an **absolute cell reference**, which refers to a specific cell and does not change when you copy the formula. Absolute cell references display a dollar sign ($) before the column letter and row number of the address (for example, $A$1). You can either type the dollar sign when typing the cell address in a formula, or you can select a cell address on the formula bar and then press F4, and the dollar signs are added automatically. When copying a formula, absolute cell references remain fixed in the copied formulas.

Steps

1. **Click cell I3, if necessary**
   You will copy the logical formula for the New York office to the other offices.

2. **Drag the fill handle from cell I3 to cell I11**
   The revenue target values are displayed in the range I4:I11. However, you notice that the target status is incorrect for the Denver, Boston, and Austin offices where the annual increases are less than the target for the year.

   Quick Tip
   Before you copy or move a formula, always check whether you need to use an absolute cell reference.

3. **Click cell I4**
   Because you used relative cell addressing in the formula in cell I3, the copied formula adjusted so that the logical test in the formula in cell I4 is H4>=B14 because there is no value in cell B14, it has a value of zero. You need to use an absolute reference for cell B13 in the IF formula to keep the value in from adjusting in a relative way as the formula is copied. That way, the formula will always reference the target increase in cell B13.

   Quick Tip
   When changing a cell reference to an absolute reference, make sure the reference is selected or the insertion point is to the left of the reference you want to change before pressing F4.

4. **Click cell I3, press F2 to change to Edit mode, select B13 in the formula, then press F4**
   When you press F4, dollar signs are inserted in the B13 cell reference, making it an absolute reference as shown in **Figure 3-7**.

5. **Click the Enter button ✓, then drag the fill handle from cell I3 to cell I11**
   Because the formula correctly contains an absolute cell reference, the correct target status appears for each location in cells I4:I11. Compare your worksheet to **Figure 3-8**.

6. **Save your work**

Figure 3-7: Absolute reference created in formula

	A	B	C	D	E	F	G	H	I	J	K
1					Bayside Consulting						
2		Quarter 1	Quarter 2	Quarter 3	Quarter 4	Year Revenue	Previous Year Revenue	% Annual Increase	Year Revenue Target	Average Customer Rating	Bonus
3	New York	37767	40731	37938	47467	163903	89629	=IF(H3>=$B$13,"MET","MISSED")		5	
4	Denver	20954	35937	27971	34513	119375	105390	IF(logical_test, [value_if_true], [value_if_false])		4.12	
5	San Francisco	30621	57200	21596	14614	124031	97180	27.63%	MET	3.78	
6	Chicago	35609	29798	48737	44708	158852	159404	-0.35%	MISSED	7.25	
7	Seattle	47594	45186	51174	13921	157875	101657	55.30%	MET	5.66	
8	Houston	43331	37250	19544	40013	140138	145363	-3.59%	MISSED	6.78	
9	Boston	32879	22300	26514	42119	123812	110822	11.72%	MET	3.55	
10	Austin	19984	38768	11102	47482	117336	105744	10.96%	MET	4.18	
11	Atlanta	15868	46942	42394	16177	121381	92142	31.73%	MET	7.56	
12		284607	354112	286970	301014						
13	Target % increase	15%									
14	# of Offices										

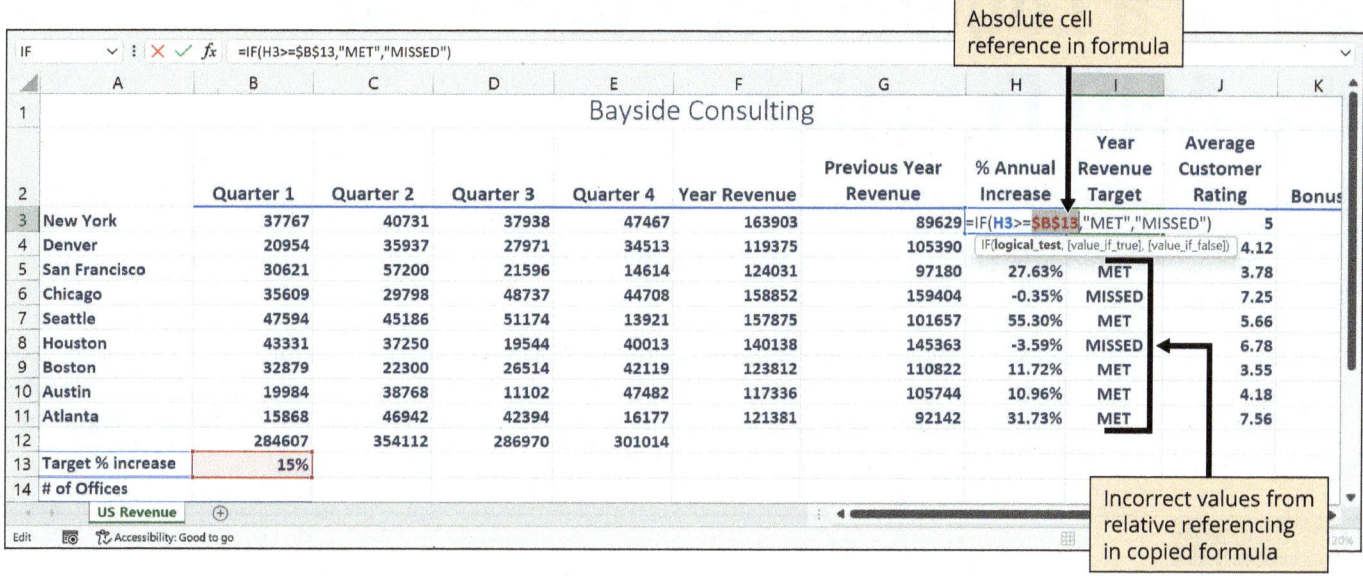

Figure 3-8: Correct percentages calculated

	A	B	C	D	E	F	G	H	I	J	K
1					Bayside Consulting						
2		Quarter 1	Quarter 2	Quarter 3	Quarter 4	Year Revenue	Previous Year Revenue	% Annual Increase	Year Revenue Target	Average Customer Rating	Bonus
3	New York	37767	40731	37938	47467	163903	89629	82.87%	MET	8.25	
4	Denver	20954	35937	27971	34513	119375	105390	13.27%	MISSED	4.12	
5	San Francisco	30621	57200	21596	14614	124031	97180	27.63%	MET	3.78	
6	Chicago	35609	29798	48737	44708	158852	159404	-0.35%	MISSED	7.25	
7	Seattle	47594	45186	51174	13921	157875	101657	55.30%	MET	5.66	
8	Houston	43331	37250	19544	40013	140138	145363	-3.59%	MISSED	6.78	
9	Boston	32879	22300	26514	42119	123812	110822	11.72%	MISSED	3.55	
10	Austin	19984	38768	11102	47482	117336	105744	10.96%	MISSED	4.18	
11	Atlanta	15868	46942	42394	16177	121381	92142	31.73%	MET	7.56	
12		284607	354112	286970	301014						
13	Target % increase	15%									
14	# of Offices										

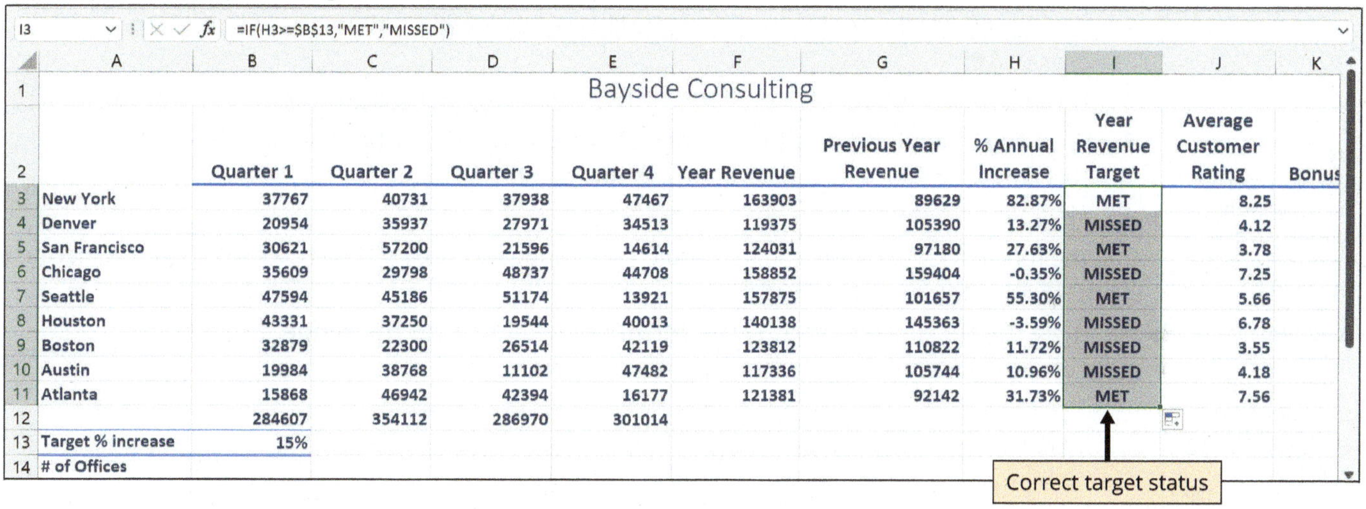

Using a mixed reference

Sometimes when you copy a formula, you want to change the row reference but keep the column reference the same. This type of cell referencing, where one factor remains constant and the other one varies, is a **mixed reference**. For example, when copied, a formula containing the mixed reference C$14 would change the column letter relative to its new location, but not the row number. In the mixed reference $C14, the column letter would not change, but the row number would be updated relative to its location. Like an absolute reference, a mixed reference can be created by pressing F4 with the cell reference selected. With each press of the F4 key, you cycle through all the possible combinations of relative, absolute, and mixed references (C14, $C$14, C$14, and $C14).

Build a Logical Formula with the AND Function

Case Bayside awards bonuses to offices that meet targets for both annual revenue and customer ratings. Now that you've determined which offices met their revenue target, you want to evaluate which offices are eligible for a bonus. You'll decide by building a formula that tests whether each office met both this target and the customer rating target.

Objectives
- Build a logical formula using the AND function
- Apply logical tests

You can also build a logical function using the AND function. The AND function evaluates all of its arguments and returns, or displays, TRUE if every logical test in the formula is true. The AND function returns a value of FALSE if one or more of its logical tests is false. The AND function arguments can include text, numbers, or cell references.

Steps

1. **Click cell K3, click the Formulas tab on the ribbon, click the Logical button in the Function Library group, then click AND**
   The Function Arguments dialog box opens.

2. **With the insertion point in the Logical1 box, click cell J3, type >=, type 6, then press TAB**
   This part of the formula reads, "If the average customer rating is greater than or equal to six..."

3. **With the insertion point in the Logical2 box, click cell I3, type = "MET"**
   This part of the formula reads, "If the revenue target was met..."

Trouble
If you get a formula error, check to be sure that you typed the quotation marks around MET.

4. **Click OK**
   The function is complete, and the result, TRUE, appears in cell K3, as shown in **Figure 3-9**, because both stated conditions were met.

Quick Tip
You can place one function, such as an AND function, inside a formula containing another function, such as an IF function. For example, you could replace the formulas in cell I3 and K3 with one formula in K3 that reads =IF(AND(H3>=$B$13, J3>=6),"TRUE", "FALSE").

5. **Drag the fill handle to copy the formula in cell K3 into the range K4:K11**
   Compare your results with **Figure 3-10**.

Using the OR and NOT logical functions

The **OR logical function** follows the same syntax as the AND function, but rather than returning TRUE if every argument is true, the OR function will return TRUE if any of its arguments are true. It will only return FALSE if all of its arguments are false. The **NOT logical function** reverses the value of its argument. For example, NOT(TRUE) reverses its argument of TRUE and returns FALSE. You might want to use this function in a worksheet to ensure that a cell is not equal to a particular value. **Table 3-2** lists examples of the AND, OR, and NOT functions.

Build a Logical Formula with the AND Function   EX 3-11

Figure 3-9: Worksheet with AND function

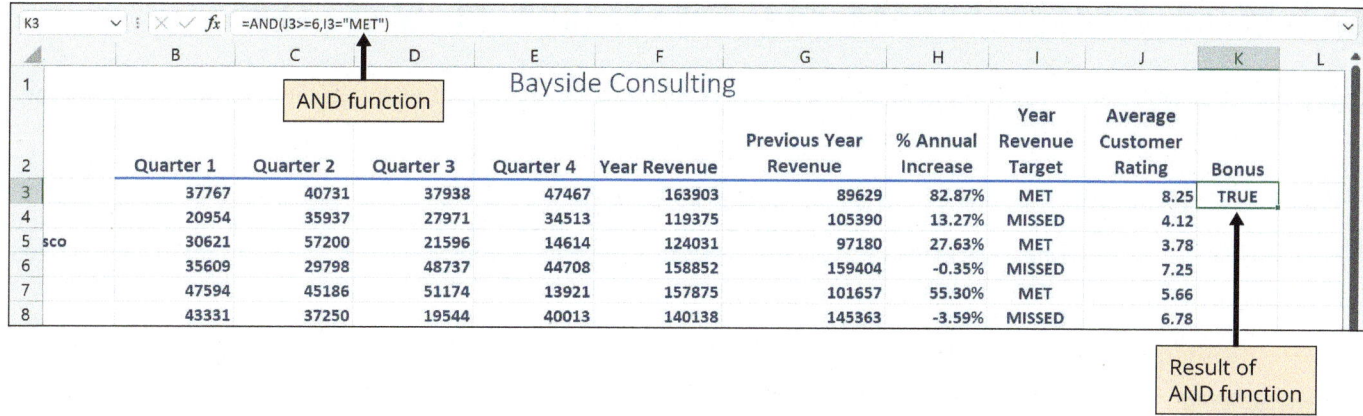

Figure 3-10: Worksheet with bonus status for all offices

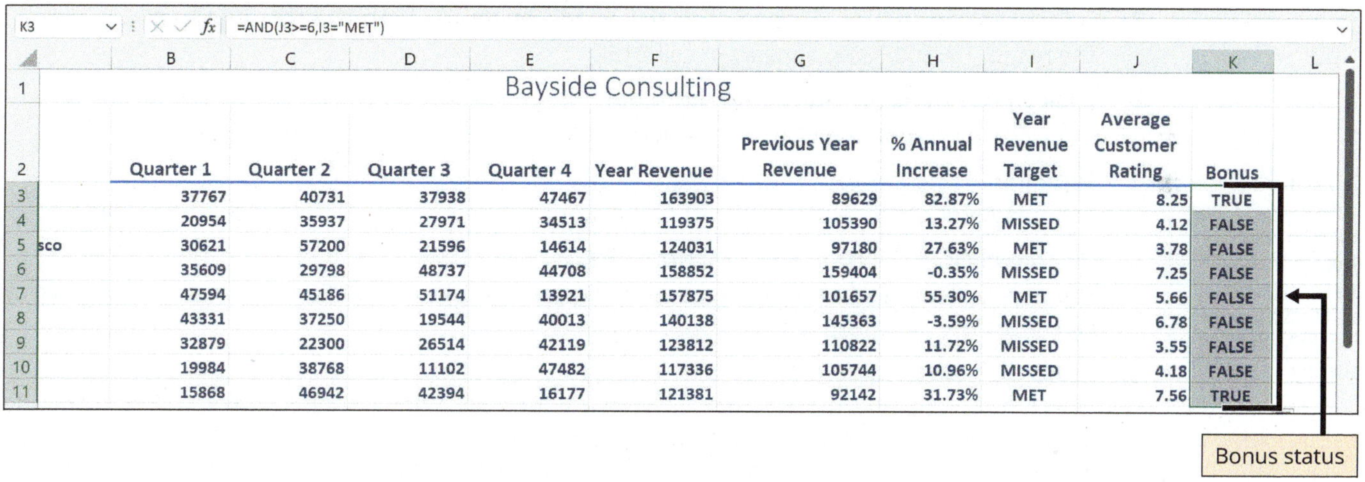

Table 3-2: Examples of AND, OR, and NOT functions with cell values A1=10 and B1=20

function	formula	result
AND	=AND(A1>5,B1>25)	FALSE
OR	=OR(A1>5,B1>25)	TRUE
NOT	=NOT(A1=0)	TRUE

Use a Function to Round a Value

Case In your worksheet, you want to find the average yearly revenue and round that calculated value to the nearest integer.

Objectives
- Build a formula using the ROUND function
- Use Formula AutoComplete to insert a function

You have used formatting to increase and decrease the decimal places of numbers displayed on a worksheet. In this case, only the formatting of these numbers changes. Their values, when used in future worksheet calculations, remain the same as they originally appeared on the worksheet. You can round a value or formula result to a specified number of decimal places by using the **ROUND function**; the resulting rounded value is then used instead of the original value in future worksheet calculations.

Steps

1. Click cell **B15**, if necessary click the Home tab on the ribbon, click the **AutoSum arrow** ∑· in the Editing group, then click **Average**

2. Select the range **F3:F11**, then click the **Enter button** ✓ on the formula bar
   The result, 136300.3333, appears in cell B15.

3. Click to the right of **=** in the formula bar
   You want to position the ROUND function here, at the beginning of the formula.

Quick Tip
In the Insert Function dialog box and Function Library on the Formulas tab, the ROUND function is in the Math & Trig category.

4. Type **RO**
   Formula AutoComplete displays a list of functions beginning with RO beneath the formula bar.

5. Double-click **ROUND** in the functions list
   The new function and an opening parenthesis are added to the AVERAGE function, as shown in **Figure 3-11**.

6. Press **END**, then type **,0)**
   The comma separates the arguments within the formula, and 0 indicates that you don't want any decimal places to appear in the calculated value. You may have also noticed that the parentheses at either end of the formula briefly became bold, indicating that you entered the correct number of open and closed parentheses so the formula is balanced. Rounding the average to zero decimal places changes the actual value in cell B15. On the other hand, using decimal place formatting would only affect the appearance of the value.

Trouble
If you have too many or too few parentheses, the extraneous parenthesis is displayed in red, or a warning dialog box opens with a suggested solution to the error.

7. Click the **Enter button** ✓ on the formula bar

8. Compare your worksheet to **Figure 3-12**, then save your work

Figure 3-11: ROUND function added to an existing function

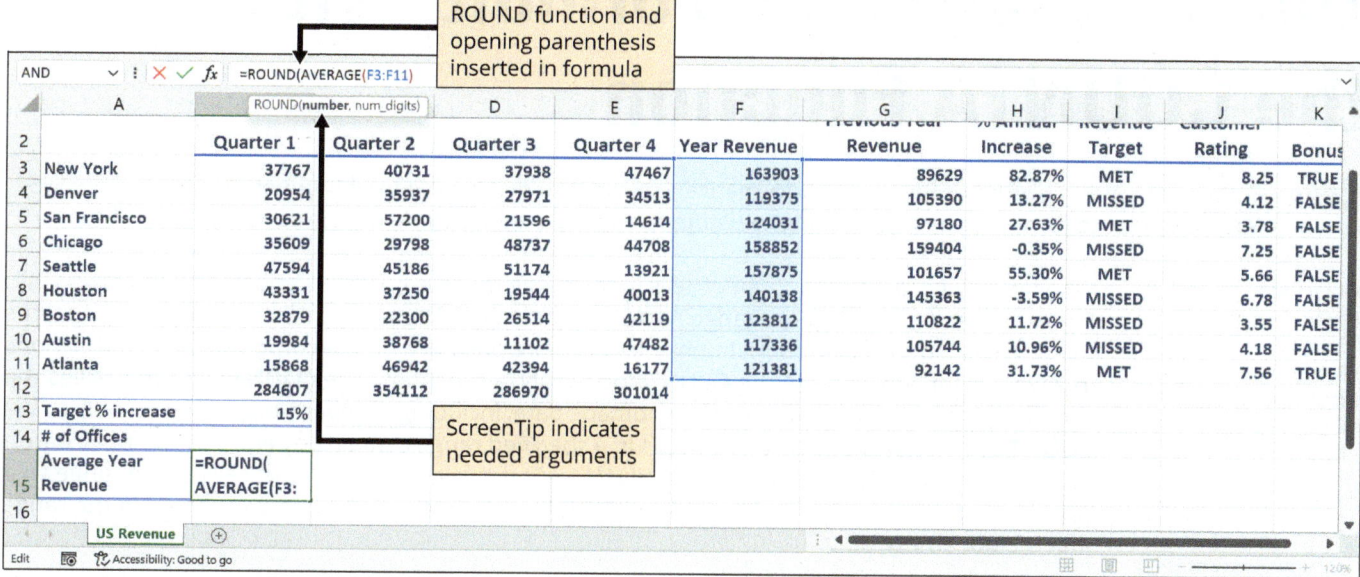

Figure 3-12: Rounded year average

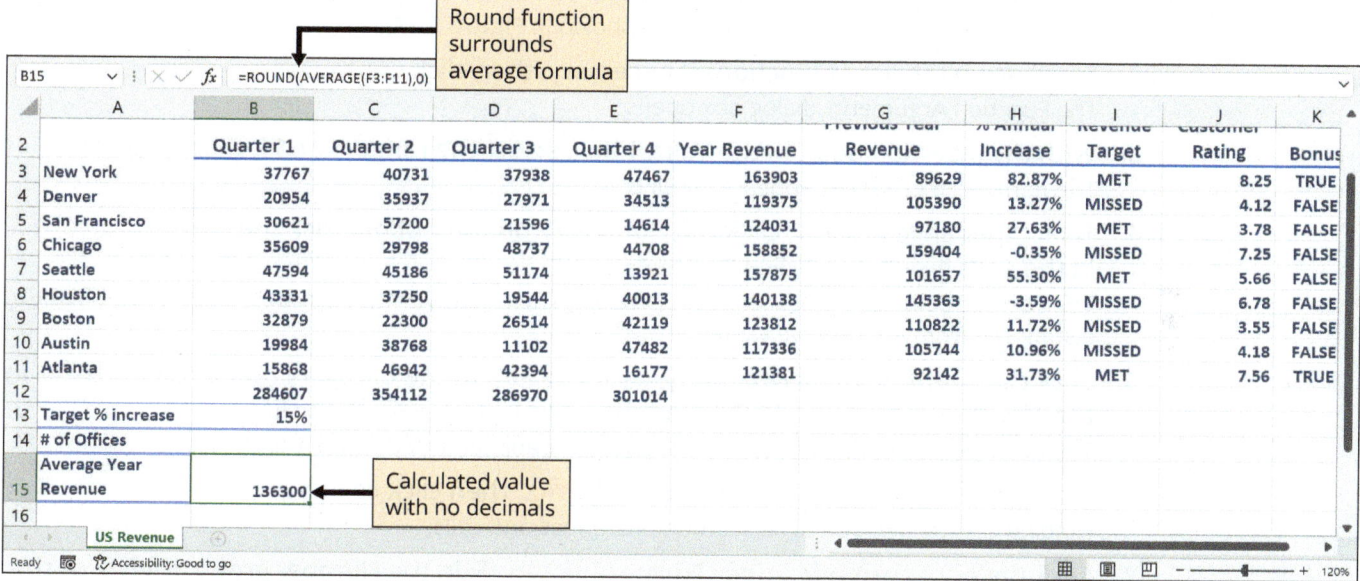

Using Excel rounding functions

You can use other rounding functions besides ROUND to fine-tune the rounding results you want to display. The **MROUND function** rounds a number to the nearest multiple of another number. The syntax is: MROUND(number, multiple). For example, MROUND(14,3) returns the value 15 because 15 is the nearest multiple of 3 to 14. The **ROUNDDOWN function** works like the ROUND function except that rather than rounding a number to the next closest value, it always rounds down. The syntax is ROUNDDOWN(number, num_digits). For example, =ROUNDDOWN(15.778, 2) returns a value of 15.77 because this is the nearest two-digit number below 15.778. The **ROUNDUP function** works similarly but rounds a number up. The syntax is ROUNDUP(number, num_digits). For example, =ROUNDUP(15.778, 2) returns a value of 15.78.

Build a Statistical Formula with the COUNTA Function

Case To provide a fuller picture of Bayside's performance, you want to display the total number of offices in the U.S. You also want to format some values using a custom format so that the worksheet is easier to read.

Objectives
- Insert a statistical function
- Build a formula using the COUNTA function
- Create a number format

When you select a range, a count of cells in the range that are not blank appears on the status bar. For example, if you select the range A1:A5 and only cells A1, A4, and A5 contain data, the status bar displays "Count: 3." To count nonblank cells more precisely, or to incorporate these calculations in a worksheet, you can use the COUNT and COUNTA functions. The **COUNT function** tallies the number of cells in a range that contain numeric data, including numbers, dates, and formulas. The **COUNTA function** tallies how many cells in a specified range contain any entries (numbers, dates, or text). For example, the formula =COUNT(A1:A5) returns the number of cells in the range that contain numeric data, and the formula =COUNTA(A1:A5) returns the number of cells in the range that are not empty.

Steps

1. Click cell **B14**, click the **Formulas tab** on the ribbon, click the **More Functions button** in the Function Library group, then point to **Statistical**
   A gallery of statistical functions opens, as shown in **Figure 3-13**.

2. Scroll down the list of functions if necessary, then click **COUNTA**
   The Function Arguments dialog box opens.

3. With the insertion point in the Value1 box, select the range **A3:A11**, then click **OK**
   The number of offices, 9, appears in cell B14.

4. Select the range **H3:H11**, click the **Home tab** on the ribbon, click the **Format button** in the Cells group, then click **Format Cells**
   The Format Cells dialog box opens. Currently, the negative values in this range are difficult to distinguish from the positive values.

5. Click the **Number tab** if necessary, click **Custom** in the Category menu, click after **%** in the Type box, type **;[Red](0.00%)** as shown in **Figure 3-14**, then click **OK**
   The negative percentages in cells H6 and H8 now appear in red with parentheses.

6. Select the range **B3:G11**, press and hold **CTRL**, then click cell **B15**
   Holding CTRL allows you to select multiple ranges and cells.

7. Click the **Accounting Number Format button** $ in the Number group, then click the **Decrease Decimal button** twice
   Formatting these revenue figures makes them easier to read. Compare your worksheet to **Figure 3-15**.

8. Save your work

Build a Statistical Formula with the COUNTA Function   EX 3-15

Figure 3-13: Statistical functions

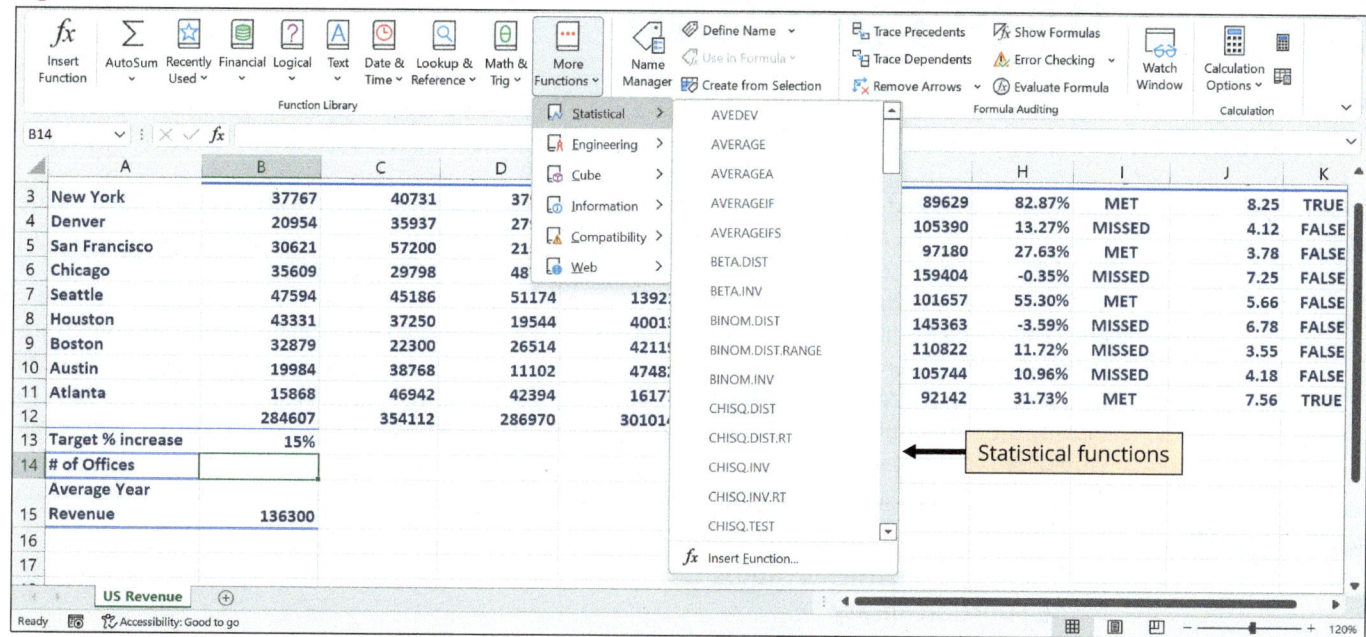

Figure 3-14: Custom number format

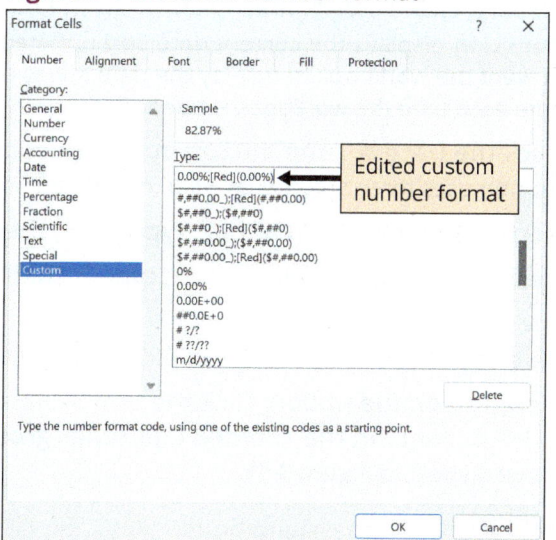

Figure 3-15: Formatted worksheet

	A	B	C	D	E	F	G	H	I	J	K
1					Bayside Consulting						
2		Quarter 1	Quarter 2	Quarter 3	Quarter 4	Year Revenue	Previous Year Revenue	% Annual Increase	Year Revenue Target	Average Customer Rating	Bonus
3	New York	$ 37,767	$ 40,731	$ 37,938	$ 47,467	$ 163,903	$ 89,629	82.87%	MET	8.25	TRUE
4	Denver	$ 20,954	$ 35,937	$ 27,971	$ 34,513	$ 119,375	$ 105,390	13.27%	MISSED	4.12	FALSE
5	San Francisco	$ 30,621	$ 57,200	$ 21,596	$ 14,614	$ 124,031	$ 97,180	27.63%	MET	3.78	FALSE
6	Chicago	$ 35,609	$ 29,798	$ 48,737	$ 44,708	$ 158,852	$ 159,404	(0.35%)	MISSED	7.25	FALSE
7	Seattle	$ 47,594	$ 45,186	$ 51,174	$ 13,921	$ 157,875	$ 101,657	55.30%	MET	5.66	FALSE
8	Houston	$ 43,331	$ 37,250	$ 19,544	$ 40,013	$ 140,138	$ 145,363	(3.59%)	MISSED	6.78	FALSE
9	Boston	$ 32,879	$ 22,300	$ 26,514	$ 42,119	$ 123,812	$ 110,822	11.72%	MISSED	3.55	FALSE
10	Austin	$ 19,984	$ 38,768	$ 11,102	$ 47,482	$ 117,336	$ 105,744	10.96%	MISSED	4.18	FALSE
11	Atlanta	$ 15,868	$ 46,942	$ 42,394	$ 16,177	$ 121,381	$ 92,142	31.73%	MET	7.56	TRUE
12		284607	354112	286970	301014						
13	Target % increase	15%									
14	# of Offices	9									
15	Average Year Revenue	$ 136,300									

Enter a Date Function

Case To accurately document this report, you want to use a date function that reflects the date the work was completed.

Objectives
- Enter a date using the TODAY function
- Enter a date using the DATE function

Excel includes date functions to make it easy to calculate date and time-related results, such as the current date or the time between events. **Table 3-3** lists some of the Date and Time functions in Excel. Note that although the results of all date and time functions appear by default in a worksheet in familiar-looking date and time formats, Excel actually stores them as sequential serial numbers and uses these numbers in calculations. January 1, 1900 is assigned serial number 1 and dates are represented as the number of days following that date. You can display the serial number of a date by using the **DATEVALUE function** or by applying the Number format to the cell. For example, to display the serial number of January 1, 2029 you would enter =DATEVALUE("1/1/2029"). The result would be serial number 47119.

Steps

1. Click cell **A2**, click the **Formulas tab** on the ribbon, then click the **Date & Time button** in the Function library
   A list of date and time functions opens, as shown in **Figure 3-16**.

2. Scroll if necessary, click **TODAY**, then click **OK** in the dialog box
   The **TODAY function** displays the current date and updates each time a worksheet is opened. However, you want the workbook to display the date it was completed, rather than adjusting for the current date each time the workbook is opened.

Quick Tip
To apply a format to a selection of time data, you can click the Format button in the Cells group, click Format Cells, click Time in the Category list, select the time format in the Type list, then click OK. For example, choosing the 13:30 type would display the time of 11:15 PM as 23:15.

3. Press **DEL**, click the **Date & Time button** in the Function Library, then click **DATE**
   The **DATE function** uses three arguments, year, month, and day, to enter a date.

4. With the insertion point in the Year box, type **2029**, then press **TAB**

5. With the insertion point in the Month box, type **2**, then press **TAB**

6. Type **24** in the Day box, then click **OK**
   The function is complete, and the result, 2/24/2029, appears in cell A2.

▶ 7. Click the **Home tab** on the ribbon, click the **Cell Styles button** in the Styles group, then click **20% - Accent1** in the Themed Cell Styles group
   Compare your worksheet to **Figure 3-17**.

8. Save the workbook

Figure 3-16: Date & Time functions

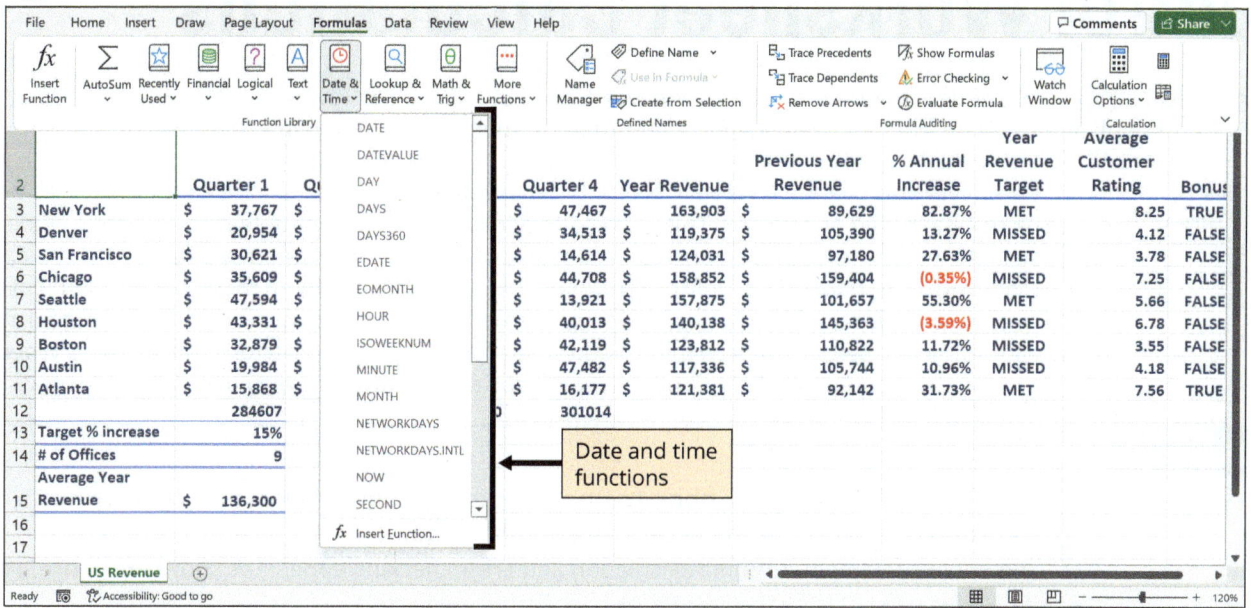

Figure 3-17: Formatted date

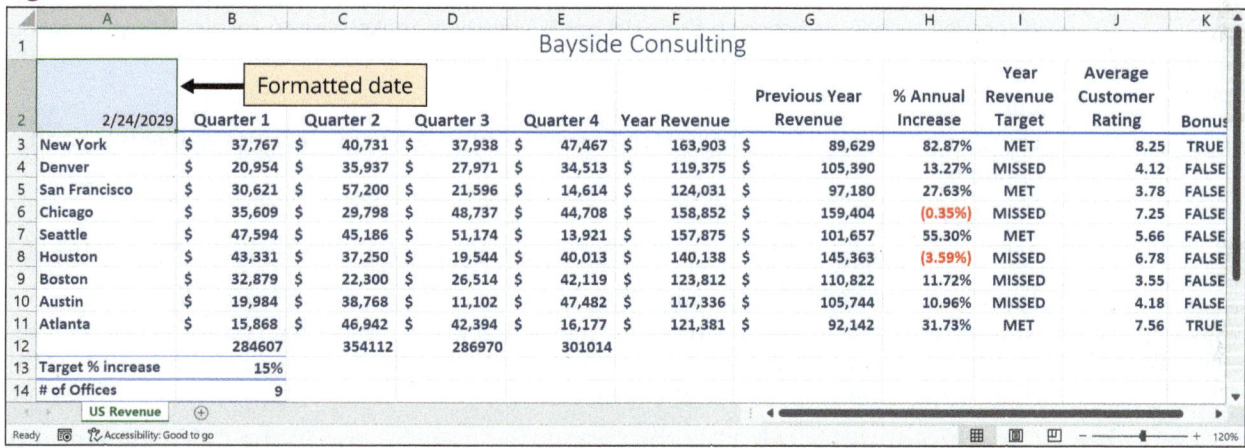

Table 3-3: Date and Time functions

function	calculates	example formula	example result
DAY	The day of the month using a date serial number	=DAY(47297)	28
NOW	The current date and time	=NOW()	1/1/2029 10:00
MONTH	The month number using a date serial number	=MONTH(47297)	6
TIME	A serial number in time format from hours, minutes, and seconds	=TIME(5,12,20)	0.216898
TIMEVALUE	A serial time in text format	=TIMEVALUE("5:15:24")	.219028
YEAR	The year portion of a date	=YEAR(47297)	2029
HOUR	The hour portion of a time	=HOUR("6:45:21 PM")	18
MINUTE	The minute portion of a time	=MINUTE("6:45:21 PM")	45
SECOND	The second portion of a time	=SECOND("6:45:21 PM")	21
WEEKDAY	The day of the week from a serial date (1 = Sunday, 2 = Monday...)	=WEEKDAY("6/21/2029")	5
WORKDAY	A serial number in date format after a certain number of working days	=WORKDAY(47297,5)	47304 (When formatted as a date: 1/8/2029)

Control Worksheet Calculations

Case Because you have added several formulas to the worksheet, you decide to review the formula settings in the workbook and evaluate whether changing from automatic to manual calculation improves performance.

Objectives
- Change formula calculation options
- Calculate worksheet formulas manually

Whenever you change a value in a cell, Excel automatically recalculates all the formulas on the worksheet based on that cell. This automatic calculation is efficient unless you create a worksheet so large that the recalculation process slows down data entry and screen updating. Worksheets with many formulas, data tables, or functions may also recalculate slowly. In these cases, you might want to apply the **manual calculation** option to turn off automatic calculation of worksheet formulas, allowing you to selectively determine if and when you want Excel to perform calculations. When you turn on the manual calculation option, Excel stops automatically recalculating all open worksheets.

Steps

1. Click the **File tab** on the ribbon to open Backstage view, click **More**, click **Options**, then click **Formulas** in the Excel Options dialog box
   The options related to formula calculation and error checking appear, as shown in **Figure 3-18**.

Quick Tip
You can also change the formula calculation to manual by clicking the Formulas tab, clicking the Calculation Options button in the Calculation group, then clicking Manual.

2. Under Calculation options, click the **Manual option button**
   When you select the Manual option, the Recalculate workbook before saving check box automatically becomes active and displays a check mark. Because the workbook will not recalculate until you save or close and reopen the workbook, you must make sure to recalculate your worksheet before you print it and after you finish making changes.

3. Click **OK**
   Elena informs you that the Quarter 1 revenue for the New York office is incorrect and needs updating.

4. Click cell **B3**
   Before proceeding, notice that in cell F3 the year revenue for the New York office is $163,903.

Quick Tip
The Calculate Now command in the Calculation group calculates the entire workbook, not just the worksheet. You can also manually recalculate a workbook by pressing F9. Pressing SHIFT+F9 recalculates only the current worksheet.

5. Type **36305** in cell B3, then click the **Enter button** ✓ on the formula bar
   Notice that the year revenue in cell F3 does not adjust to reflect the change in cell B3. The word "Calculate" appears on the status bar to indicate that a specific value on the worksheet did indeed change and to remind you that the worksheet must be recalculated.

6. Click the **Formulas tab**, click the **Calculate Sheet button** in the Calculation group, click cell **A1**, then save the workbook
   The year revenue in cell F3 is now $162,441. The other formulas on the worksheet affected by the value in cell B3 changed as well, as shown in **Figure 3-19**. Because this is a relatively small worksheet that recalculates quickly, you decide that the manual calculation option is not necessary.

Quick Tip
If your worksheet contains a table, such as a complex payment schedule, you may want to use manual recalculation just for the table. To do so, click the Automatic Except for Data Tables option in the list of calculation options.

7. Click the **Calculation Options button** in the Calculation group, then click **Automatic**
   Using the commands on the Calculation Options button is a quick alternative to opening the Options dialog box. Now any additional changes you make will automatically recalculate the worksheet formulas.

8. **sam↑** Enter your name in the center section of the worksheet footer, save your changes, activate cell **A1**, submit the workbook to your instructor as directed, close the workbook, then close Excel

Figure 3-18: Excel formula options

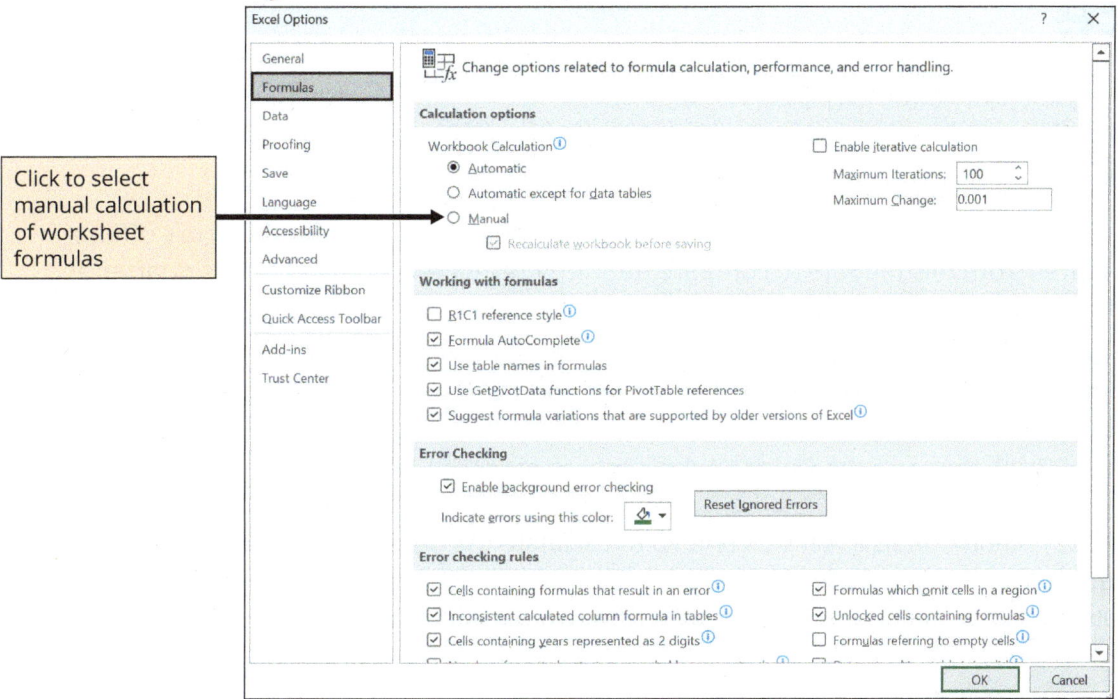

Click to select manual calculation of worksheet formulas

Figure 3-19: Worksheet with updated values

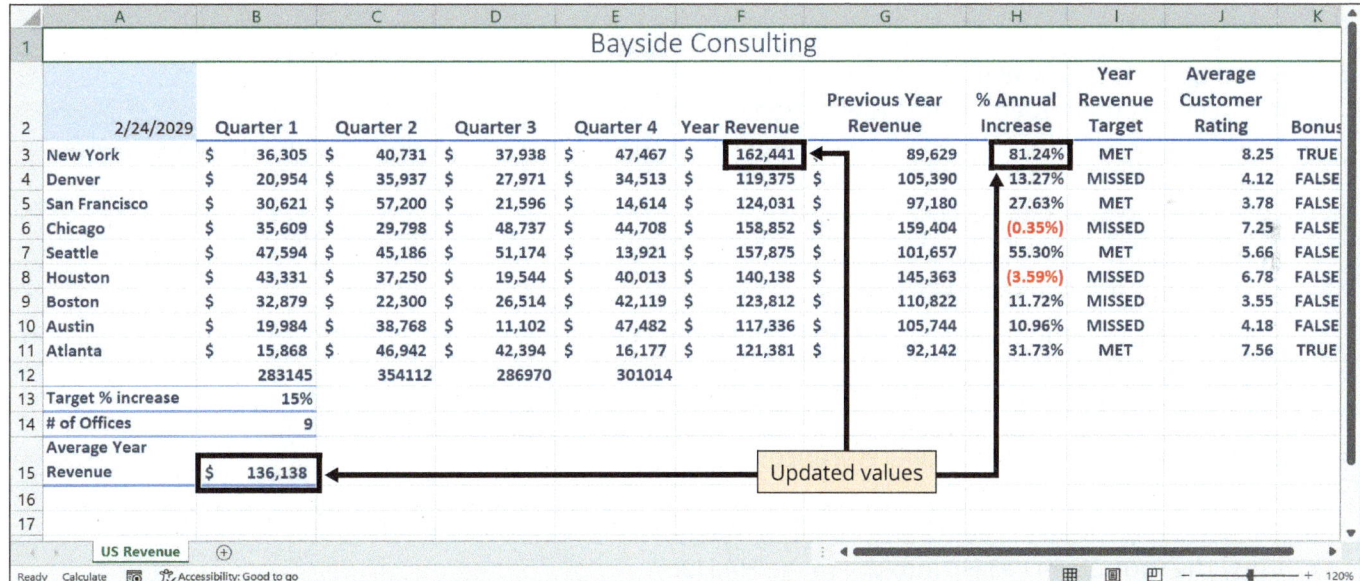

Updated values

Showing and printing worksheet formulas

Sometimes you need to display or keep a record of all the formulas in a worksheet. You might want to do this to display a complex calculation, so you can explain it to others. To display formulas rather than results in a worksheet, first, open the workbook. Click the Formulas tab on the ribbon, then click the Show Formulas button in the Formula Auditing group to select it. When the Show Formulas button is selected, formulas rather than resulting values are displayed on the worksheet, and any entered values appear without number formatting. You can print the worksheet to save a record of all the formulas. The Show Formulas button is a toggle: click it again to display the values, rather than the formulas, on the worksheet. You can also display a formula in a cell using the syntax =FORMULATEXT(Cell address). For example, entering =FORMULATEXT(A1) in a cell would display the text of the formula in cell A1.

Practice

In the exercises that follow, you will practice the skills you have learned in this module.

Skills Review

As a junior analyst for Enterprise Capital, you review the quarterly revenue reports for the firm's offices. You will use Excel features from this module to compare quarterly revenue with the previous quarter and determine if each office will receive a bonus.

1. **Enter a formula using the Quick Analysis tool.**
   a. Start Excel, open IL_EX_3-2.xlsx from the location where you store your Data Files, then save it as **IL_EX_3_Enterprise**.
   b. Select the range B3:D9, then use the Quick Analysis tool to enter the first quarter revenue totals in column E.
   c. In cell G3, use the revenue totals in cells E3 and F3 to calculate the percent increase in revenue from the previous quarter to the first quarter.
   d. Format the value in cell G3 using the percent style with two decimal places.
   e. Save your work.

2. **Copy formulas with relative cell references.**
   a. In cell G3, use the fill handle to copy the formula in cell G3 to the range G4:G9.
   b. Click cell G4 and review the copied formula making sure the cell references are correct.
   c. Save your work.

3. **Build a logical formula with the IF function.**
   a. Click cell H3, then open the Insert Function dialog box.
   b. Search for the IF function if necessary, then select the IF function to open the Function Arguments dialog box.
   c. In the Logical_test box, enter **G3 >= B11**.
   d. In the Value_if_true box, type **Met**.
   e. In the Value_if_false box, type **Missed**.
   f. Confirm the arguments are correct, then close the Function Arguments dialog, accepting the function argument entries.
   g. Save your work.

4. **Copy formulas with absolute cell references.**
   a. Activate cell H3, if necessary.
   b. Review the formula in cell H3 and edit it to make cell B11 an absolute cell address reference.
   c. Copy the formula in cell H3 into the range H4:H9.
   d. Center align the cells H3:H9.
   e. Save your work.

5. **Build a logical formula with the AND function.**
   a. In cell J3, use the Function Arguments dialog box to enter the formula **=AND(H3="Met",I3>=4)**.
   b. Copy the formula in cell J3 into the range J4:J9.
   c. Save your work.

6. **Round a value with a function.**
   a. In cell B13, use the AutoSum list arrow to enter a function to average the first quarter revenue values in column E.
   b. Use Formula AutoComplete to edit this formula to include the ROUND function showing zero decimal places.

c. Correct any errors in the formula.
d. Save your work.

7. **Build a statistical formula with the COUNTA function.**
   a. In cell B12, use a statistical formula to calculate the number of office locations in column A.
   b. Create a custom format for the percentages in column G so that the negative values appear in red with parentheses.
   c. Format the revenue values in the range B3:F9 and in cell B13 using the Accounting Number Format with no decimal places.
   d. Save your work.

8. **Enter a date function.**
   a. In cell D12, enter **Report Date**.
   b. In cell E12, use the TODAY function to enter today's date.
   c. Delete the TODAY function in cell E12, then use the DATE function to enter the date **4/3/2029**.
   d. Use the Cell Style Light Blue, 20% - Accent 1, (the first row and first column in the Themed Cell Styles group) to format the range D12:E12.
   e. Activate cell A1, then save your work.

9. **Control worksheet calculations.**
   a. Open the Formulas category of the Excel Options dialog box.
   b. Change the worksheet calculations to manual.
   c. Change the value in cell B3 to **70000**.
   d. Recalculate the worksheet manually.
   e. Change the worksheet calculation back to automatic using the Calculation Options button on the Formulas tab of the ribbon, then save the workbook.
   f. Compare your screen to **Figure 3-20**.
   g. Save your changes, enter your name in the center section of the footer for the First Quarter sheet, submit your work to your instructor as directed, close the workbook, then close Excel.

Figure 3-20

	A	B	C	D	E	F	G	H	I	J
1					Enterprise Capital					
2		January	February	March	First Quarter Revenue	Previous Quarter Revenue	% Increase	Quarter Revenue Target	Quality Rating	Bonus
3	Columbus	$ 70,000	$ 69,464	$ 57,485	$ 196,949	$ 192,571	2.27%	Missed	4	FALSE
4	Philadelphia	$ 68,966	$ 68,017	$ 55,409	$ 192,392	$ 163,545	17.64%	Met	5	TRUE
5	San Diego	$ 59,523	$ 52,965	$ 64,896	$ 177,384	$ 178,852	(0.82%)	Missed	2	FALSE
6	Detroit	$ 51,043	$ 68,523	$ 58,623	$ 178,189	$ 176,645	0.87%	Missed	3	FALSE
7	Austin	$ 57,323	$ 50,909	$ 54,087	$ 162,319	$ 134,587	20.61%	Met	5	TRUE
8	Portland	$ 67,228	$ 61,784	$ 74,202	$ 203,214	$ 185,421	9.60%	Met	4	TRUE
9	Charleston	$ 53,035	$ 65,943	$ 56,480	$ 175,458	$ 175,875	(0.24%)	Missed	4	FALSE
10										
11	Target % increase	8%								
12	# of Offices	7		Report Date	4/3/2029					
13	Average Revenue	$ 183,701								

Independent Challenge 1

As the manager at New England Insurance's Concord office, you analyze invoices for the billing department. You will calculate the average balance of accounts for the month of April and flag the overdue accounts.

a. Open IL_EX_3-3.xlsx from the location where you store your Data Files, then save it as **IL_EX_3_Accounts**.
b. Use the DATE function to return the date 5/8/2029 in cell B3.
c. Enter a formula in cell C5 that calculates the statement age by subtracting the statement date in cell B5 from the report date in cell B3. (**Hint**: The formula needs to use an absolute reference for the report date in cell B3 so this cell address doesn't change when copied.)
d. Copy the formula in cell C5 to the range C6:C11.
e. In cell F5, enter an IF function that calculates the balance using a logical test to evaluate whether the premium is greater than or equal to the payment. If the logical test is true, calculate the premium minus the payment; if the test is false, enter the word Credit in the cell.
f. Copy the IF function in cell F5 to the range F6:F11.
g. In cell G5, enter an AND function to find accounts that are past due. Accounts are past due if there is a balance and the statement age is over 30 days. (**Hint**: The Logical1 condition should evaluate whether the premium is greater than the payment and the Logical2 condition should check if the statement age is more than 30.)
h. Edit the formula in cell G5 to use the IF function to display a formula result of Yes or No rather than True or False. (**Hint**: The formula: IF(AND(D5>E5,C5>30),"Yes","No") should be in cell G5.)
i. Use the fill handle to copy the AND function in cell G5 into the range G6:G11.
j. In cell B13, enter a COUNTA function to calculate the number of accounts in column A.
k. In cell B14, enter a formula that averages the premium amounts in column D. (**Hint**: The formula includes a function.)
l. Use Formula AutoComplete to enter a formula to round the average in cell B14 to zero decimal places.
m. Enter your name in the center section of the footer.
n. Compare your screen to **Figure 3-21**.
o. Save your work, then submit the worksheet to your instructor as directed.
p. Close the workbook and Excel.

Figure 3-21

	A	B	C	D	E	F	G
1				NE Insurance			
2				April Accounts			
3	Report Date	5/8/2029					
4	Account	Statement Date	Statement Age	Premium Amount	Payment	Balance	Account Past Due
5	5102	4/2/2029	36	4045	4055	Credit	No
6	5103	4/3/2029	35	2404	1064	1340	Yes
7	5104	4/5/2029	33	3850	3350	500	Yes
8	5105	4/9/2029	29	1905	1905	0	No
9	5106	4/11/2029	27	4005	3850	155	No
10	5107	4/26/2029	12	3884	3284	600	No
11	5108	4/27/2029	11	2115	2215	Credit	No
12							
13	Total Accounts	7					
14	Average Balance	3173					

Independent Challenge 2

As the administrative assistant to the CEO of ERP, Educational Resources Place, an educational software company, one of your responsibilities is reviewing revenues to assist in budget planning. Your review includes providing statistics including total annual revenue amounts, average annual revenue, and revenue growth for the company's four offices. You need to prepare a report summarizing the annual revenue for an upcoming budget meeting.

a. Open IL_EX_3-4.xlsx from the location where you store your Data Files, then save it as **IL_EX_3_ERP**.
b. Use the TODAY function to enter today's date in cell B12. Verify today's date is displayed.
c. Delete the date in cell B12 and replace it with the date 12/31/2029 using the DATE function.
d. Use the Quick Analysis button to enter totals in the range F4:F7 and B8:E8. (**Hint**: You need to use two different buttons on the Totals tab to accomplish these tasks.)
e. Enter a formula in cell H4 to find the percentage increase for the total annual revenue in the Boston office, compared to the previous year. Format the percentage increase using the percent style with two decimal places.
f. Copy the percentage increase formula in cell H4 to the range H5:H7.
g. In cell J4, enter an AND function to determine whether the Boston office is eligible for a bonus. To be eligible, the percentage increase must be more than 5% and the customer survey ratings must be higher than 80%.
h. Use the fill handle to copy the AND function in cell J4 into the range J5:J7.
i. Format the revenue values in the ranges B4:G7 and B8:E8 using the Accounting Number Format with two decimals. Widen the columns as necessary to fully display all the worksheet data.
j. Enter a function in cell B10 that averages the total annual revenue amounts in column F, then round the average to one decimal place. (Note: Recall that rounding a result affects the actual value, whereas decimal place formatting affects only the appearance of the value.)
k. In cell B11, enter a function to calculate the number of offices in column A.
l. Create a custom format for the percentages in column H so that the negative values appear in red with parentheses.
m. Switch to manual calculation for formulas. Change the first quarter revenue for the Boston office in cell B4 to **2,006,300**. Calculate the worksheet formula manually. Turn on automatic calculation again. Compare your new Boston and First Quarter totals to **Figure 3-22**.
n. Autofit the width of columns A through J, then enter your name in the center footer section.
o. Save your work, then submit the worksheet to your instructor as directed.
p. Close the workbook and Excel.

Figure 3-22

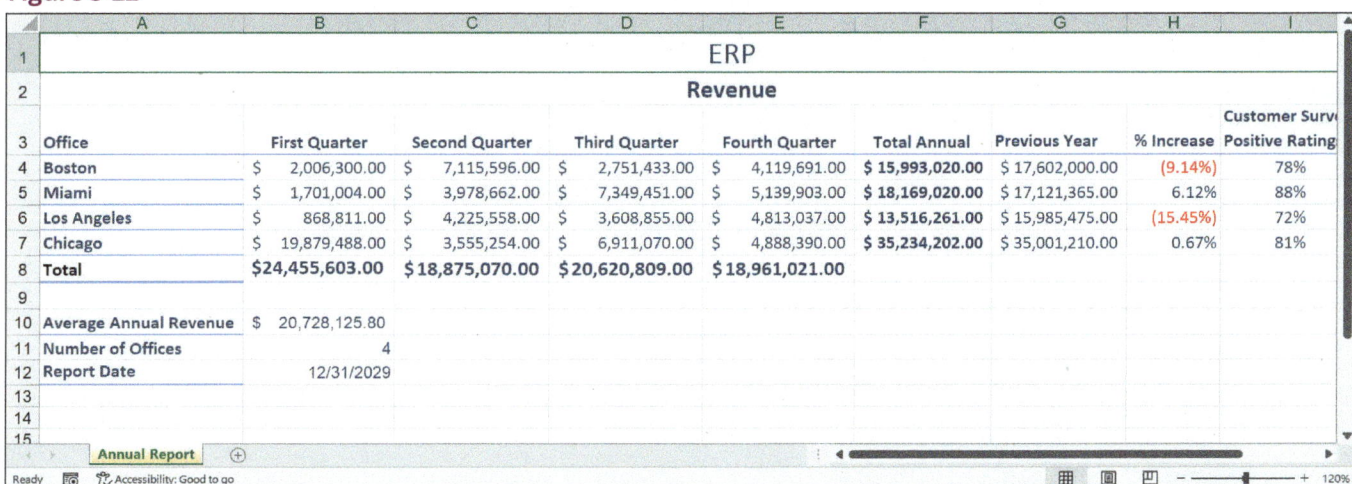

Visual Workshop

Open IL_EX_3-5.xlsx from the location where you store your Data Files, then save it as **IL_EX_3_Freight**. Use the skills you learned in this module to complete the worksheet so it looks like the one shown in **Figure 3-23**. To build the formulas in column G, calculate the percentage increase of the fourth quarter revenue over the third quarter revenue. (**Hint**: The percentage increases in column G must be calculated before calculating the average increase in cell B10.) To build the formulas in column I, issue a warning of TRUE if the percentage increase is less than the average increase shown in cell B10 AND the on-time delivery is less than 70%. (**Hint**: Remember to use an absolute cell reference where necessary.) When you are finished, enter your name in the center footer section, then submit your work to your instructor as directed.

Figure 3-23

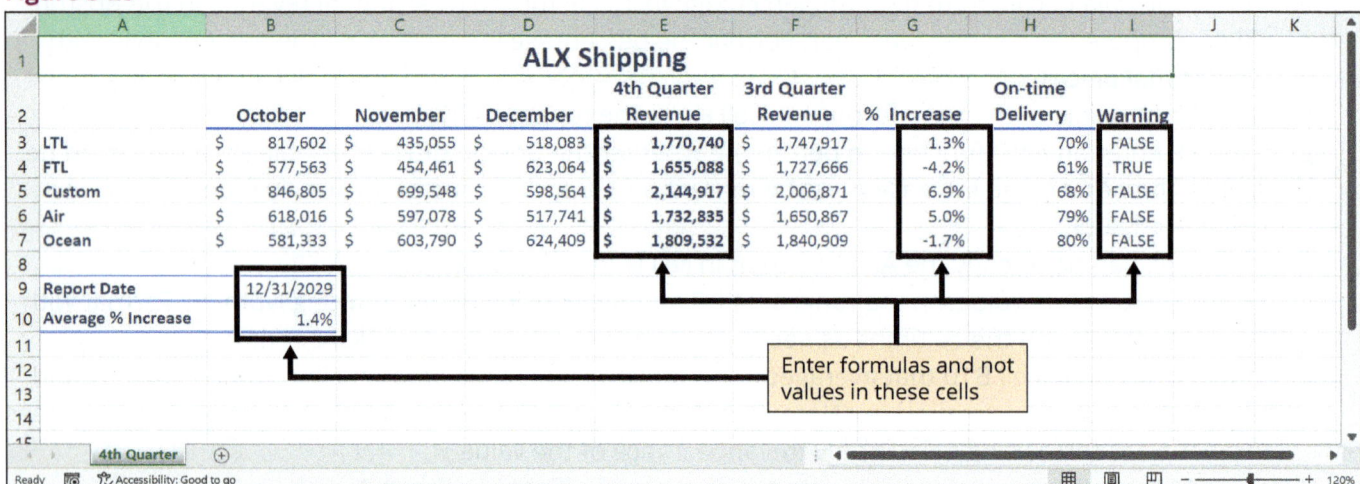

Excel Module 4

Working with Charts

Case

At the upcoming annual meeting, Elena Fuentes, vice president of finance, wants to review revenue at Bayside's U.S. offices. She asks you to create charts illustrating the revenue trends in these offices over the past four quarters.

Module Objectives

After completing this module, you will be able to:

- Identify chart features
- Create a chart with a title
- Position a chart
- Modify a chart
- Change the chart layout
- Format a chart
- Create a pie chart
- Summarize data with sparklines
- Identify data trends

Files You Will Need

IL_EX_4-1.xlsx
IL_EX_4-2.xlsx
IL_EX_4-3.xlsx
IL_EX_4-4.xlsx
IL_EX_4-5.xlsx

Identify Chart Features

Case In preparation for creating the charts for Elena's presentation, you review the purpose of the charts and decide how to organize the data to convey the information most effectively.

Objectives
- Identify chart elements
- Identify common chart types

The process of creating a chart involves deciding which data to use and what type of chart best highlights the trends or patterns that are most important, such as steady increases over time or stellar performance by one sales rep compared to others in the same division. Understanding the parts of a chart makes it easier to evaluate specific elements to make sure the chart effectively illustrates your data.

Details

Quick Tip
To display the available charts in Excel, select the worksheet data, click the Insert tab on the ribbon, click the Recommended Charts button in the Charts group, then click the All Charts tab.

Use the following guidelines to plan the chart:

- **Determine the purpose of the chart, and identify the data relationships you want to graphically communicate**

  You want to create a chart that displays quarterly revenue for Bayside's U.S. offices. You also want to illustrate whether the quarterly revenue for each office increased or decreased from quarter to quarter.

- **Determine the results you want to display, and decide which chart type is most appropriate**

  Different chart types display data in distinctive ways. For example, a pie chart compares parts of a whole, whereas a line chart is best for displaying trends over time. To choose the best chart type for your data, first decide how you want your data to be interpreted. **Figure 4-1** displays the available chart types in Excel, listed by category on the All Charts tab of the Insert Chart dialog box. **Table 4-1** describes the most frequently-used categories. Because you want to compare Bayside's revenue in multiple offices over a period of four quarters, you decide to use a column chart, which is ideal for comparing parts to each other.

- **Identify the worksheet data you want the chart to illustrate**

  Sometimes you use all the data in a worksheet to create a chart, while at other times you may need to select a range within the sheet. The worksheet from which you are creating your chart contains revenue data for each of the past four quarters and the totals for the past year. To create a column chart, you will need to use all the quarterly data except the quarterly totals.

- **Understand the elements of a chart**

  The chart displayed in **Figure 4-2** contains basic elements of a chart. In the figure, Bayside's offices are on the category axis and revenue dollar amounts are on the value axis. The **category axis**, also called the x-axis, is the horizontal axis in a chart, usually containing the names of data categories. The **value axis**, also called the vertical axis, contains numerical values. In a 2-dimensional chart, it is also known as the y-axis. (Three-dimensional charts contain a **z-axis**, for comparing data across both categories and values.) The area inside the horizontal and vertical axes that contains the graphical representation of the data series is the **plot area**. **Gridlines**, the horizontal and vertical lines, make a chart easier to read. Each piece of data plotted in a chart is a **data point**. In any chart, a **data marker** is a graphical representation of a data point, such as a bar or column. A set of values represented in a chart is a **data series**. In this chart, there are four data series: Quarter 1, Quarter 2, Quarter 3, and Quarter 4. Each is made up of columns of a different color. To differentiate each data series, information called a **legend** or a legend key identifies how the data is represented using colors and/or patterns.

Identify Chart Features EX 4-3

Figure 4-1: Insert Chart dialog box lists available charts by category

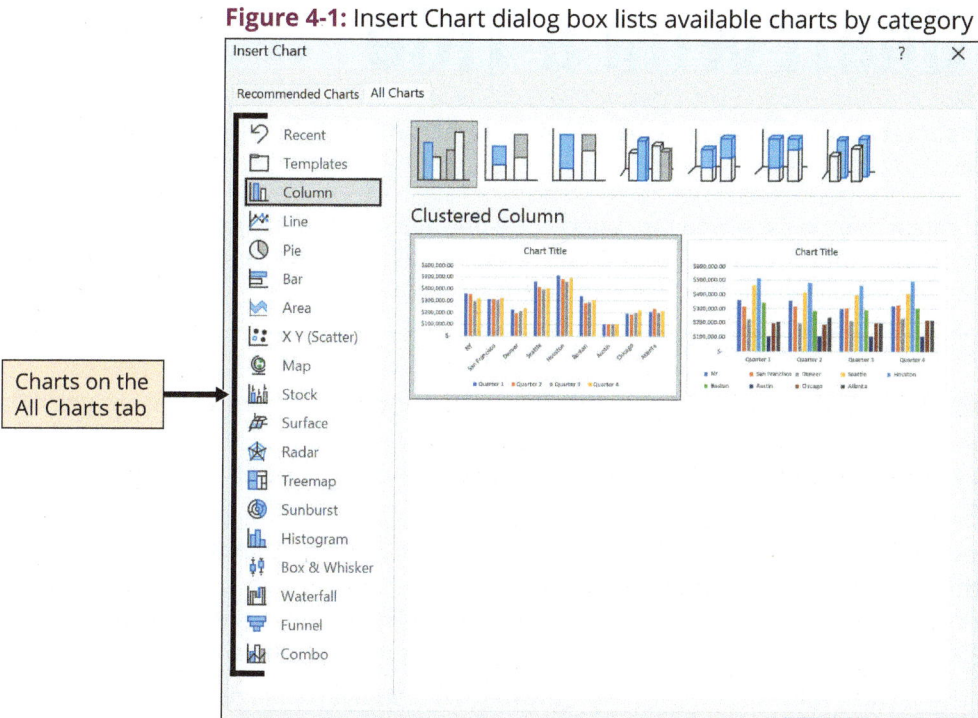

Figure 4-2: Chart elements

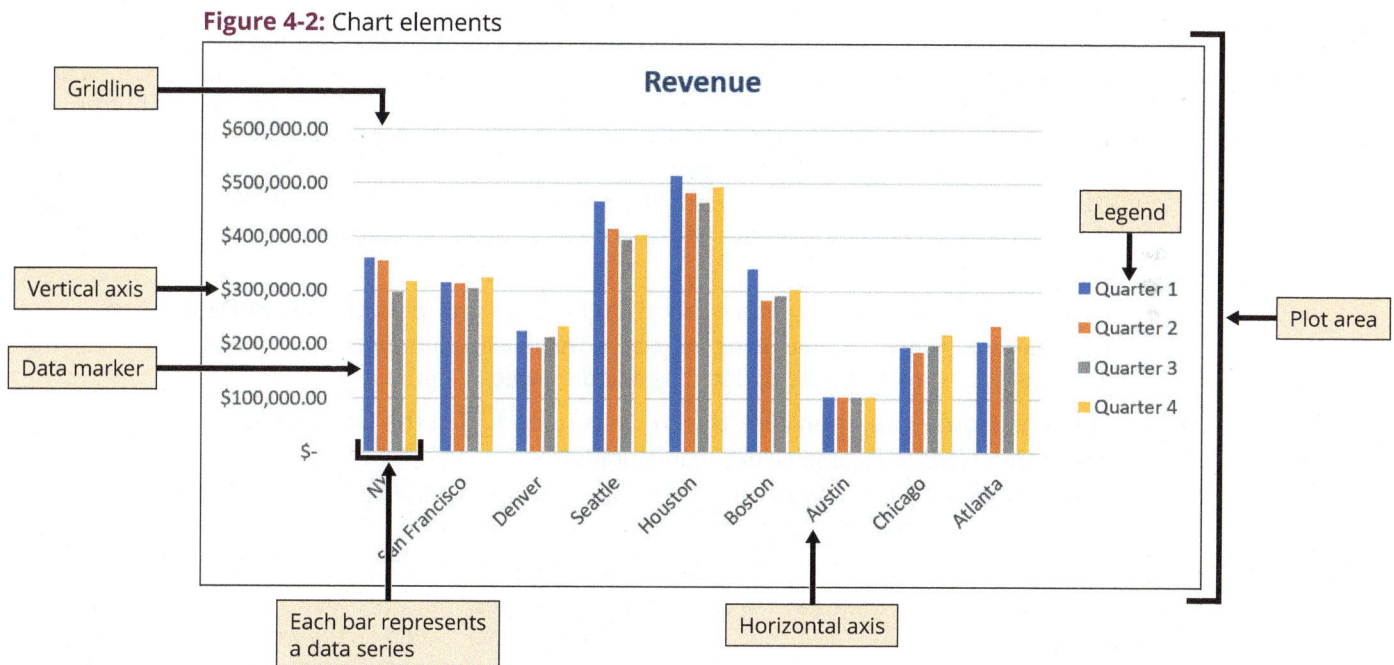

Table 4-1: Common chart types

type	description
Column	Displays data values as columns; column height represents its value
Line	Displays data as separate lines across categories
Pie	Is shaped in a circle and divided into slices like a pie, which displays data values as percentages of the whole
Bar	Displays data values in horizontal bars; the length of each bar represents its value
Area	Displays how individual volume changes over time in relation to total volume
Line with Markers	Compares trends over time by displaying data markers that represent worksheet data values

EX 4-4 Module 4 Working with Charts

Create a Chart with a Title

Case It is difficult to compare revenue data in worksheet format. A chart will make it easier to compare revenues across the U.S. offices.

Objectives
- Create a chart
- Add a title to a chart

To create a chart in Excel, you first select the worksheet range or ranges containing the data you want to chart. Once you've selected a range, you can use the Quick Analysis tool or the Insert tab on the ribbon to create a chart based on the data in that range.

Steps

1. **sam↓** Start Excel, open **IL_EX_4-1.xlsx** from the location where you store your Data Files, then save it as **IL_EX_4_USRevenue**

   You want the chart to include the quarterly revenue values, as well as the quarter and office labels, but not any totals.

2. Select the range **A3:E12**, click the **Quick Analysis button** in the lower-right corner of the range, then click the **Charts tab**

   The Charts tab on the Quick Analysis tool recommends commonly used chart types based on the range you have selected. It also includes a More Charts button for additional chart types.

   Trouble
   The Accessibility notice on the status bar has changed from Good to go to Investigate. You will investigate this notification in a later lesson.

3. On the Charts tab, click **Clustered Column**, as displayed in **Figure 4-3**

   A clustered column chart is inserted in the center of the worksheet. **Clustered column charts** display data values in side-by-side columns. Two contextual tabs, Chart Design and Format, become available on the ribbon. On the Chart Design tab, which is currently active, you can quickly change the chart layout and chart style, and you can swap how the columns and rows of data in the worksheet are represented in the chart or select a different data range for the chart. In Normal view, three tools open to the right of the chart: the Chart Elements button lets you add, remove, or change chart elements, the Chart Styles button lets you set a style and color scheme, and the Chart Filters button lets you filter the results displayed in a chart. Currently, the offices are charted along the horizontal x-axis, with the quarterly revenue dollar amounts charted along the vertical y-axis. This lets you easily compare the quarterly revenues for each office.

4. Click the **Switch Row/Column button** in the Data group on the Chart Design tab

   The quarters are now charted along the x-axis. The revenue amounts per office are charted along the y-axis, as indicated by the updated legend displayed in **Figure 4-4**.

   Quick Tip
   You can change either the data source or the legend by clicking the Select Data button on the Chart Design tab to open the Select Data Source dialog box. You can change the source data by editing the data range in the Chart data range box. Clicking Add, Edit, or Remove under Legend Entries (Series) allows you to change the legend labels. When you finish making changes, click OK to close the dialog box.

5. Click the **Home tab**, then click the **Undo button** in the Undo group

   The chart returns to its original data configuration.

6. Click the **Chart Title placeholder**, type **Bayside Quarterly Revenue**, then click anywhere in the chart to deselect the title

   Adding a title helps identify the chart. The border around the chart, along with the **sizing handles**, the small circles at the corners and the edges, indicates that the chart is selected as displayed in **Figure 4-5**. Your chart might be in a different location on the worksheet and may look slightly different; you will move and resize it in the next lesson. Any time a chart is selected, as it is now, a blue border surrounds the worksheet data range on which the chart is based, a purple border surrounds the cells containing the category axis labels, and a red border surrounds the cells containing the data series labels. This chart is known as an **embedded chart** because it is displayed as an object in the worksheet. Embedding a chart in the current sheet is the default selection when creating a chart, but you can also embed a chart on a different sheet in the workbook or a newly created chart sheet. A **chart sheet** is a separate sheet in a workbook that contains only a chart that is linked to the workbook data.

7. Save your work

Create a Chart with a Title   EX 4-5

Figure 4-3: Charts tab in Quick Analysis tool

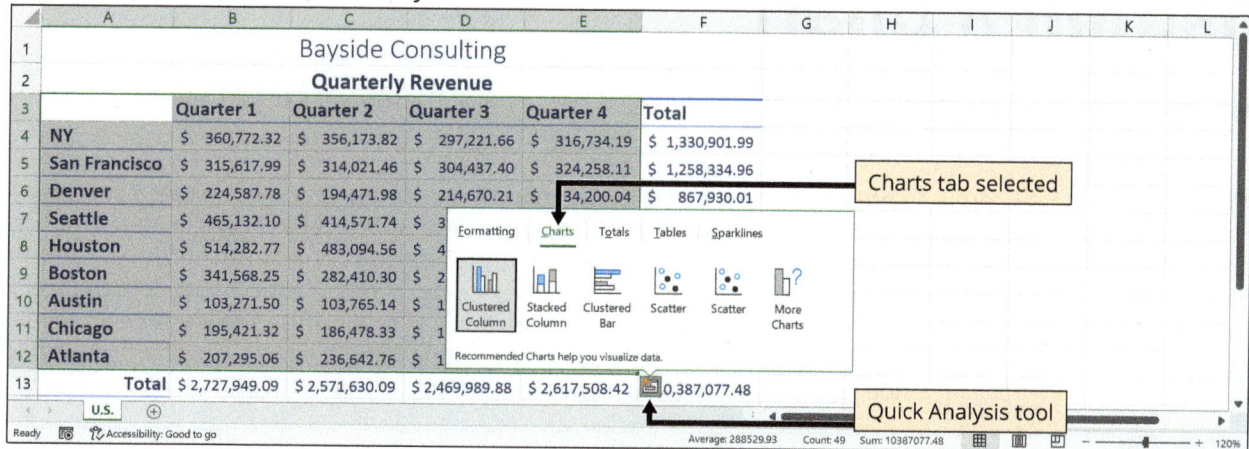

Figure 4-4: Clustered Column chart with different configuration of rows and columns

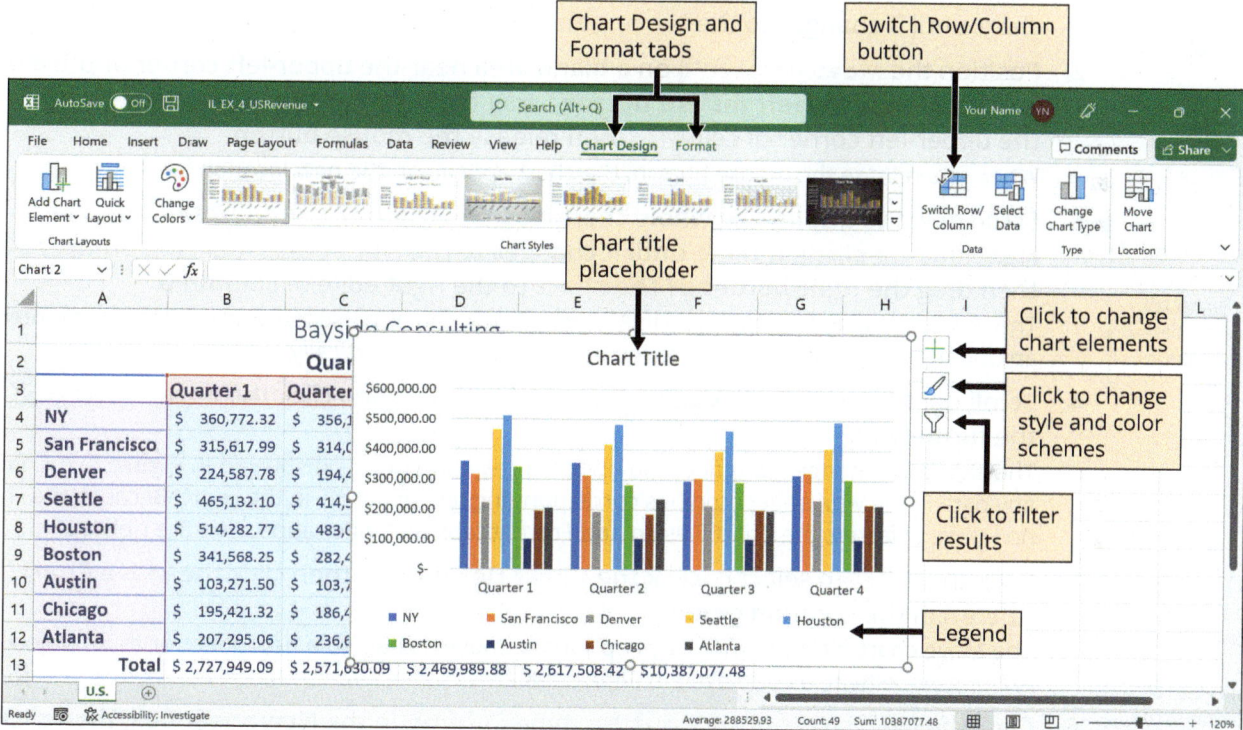

Figure 4-5: Chart with original configuration restored and title added

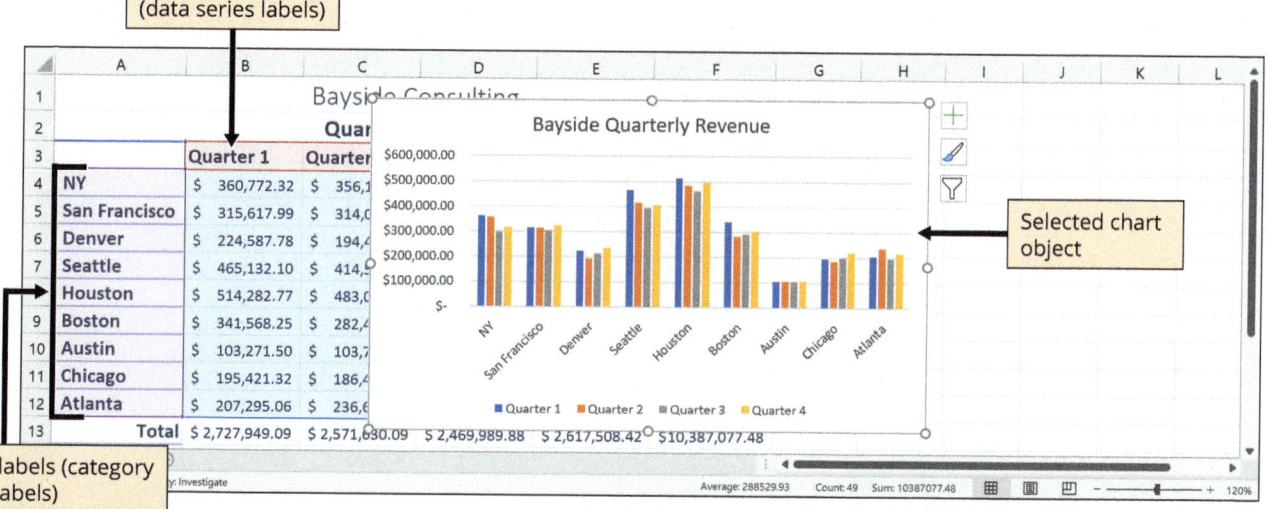

Position a Chart

Case You need to move the chart so it doesn't hide the worksheet data, and also want it to be bigger so it is easier for Elena to compare the revenue for the offices.

Objectives
- Reposition a chart
- Resize a chart

A chart is an **object**, an independent element on a worksheet that is not located in a specific cell or range and can be moved and resized. You can select an object by clicking it; the object displays sizing handles to indicate it is selected. You can move a selected chart anywhere on a worksheet or to another worksheet without affecting formulas or data in the worksheet. Any data changed in the worksheet is automatically updated in the chart. You can resize a chart to improve its appearance by dragging its sizing handles. Dragging a corner sizing handle resizes the chart proportionally. Dragging a side, top, or bottom handle resizes it horizontally or vertically.

Steps

Quick Tip
To delete a selected chart, press DEL.

1. Make sure the chart is still selected, then position the **Normal pointer** over the chart until it changes to the **Move pointer**

2. Position the **Move pointer** on a blank area near the upper-left corner of the chart, press and hold the **left mouse button**, drag the **chart** until its upper-left corner is at the upper-left corner of cell **A15**, then release the mouse button
   When you release the mouse button, the chart appears in the new location.

Quick Tip
To resize a selected chart to an exact size, click the Format tab, then enter the desired height and width in the Size group.

3. Scroll down to display the whole chart, position the **Normal pointer** on the **right-middle sizing handle** until it changes to the **Horizontal Resizing pointer**, then drag the **right border of the chart** to the right edge of column **G**
   The chart is widened as displayed in **Figure 4-6**. You can also use the Vertical Resizing pointer on an upper or lower sizing handle to increase the chart size vertically.

4. Scroll up if necessary, click cell **A4**, type **New York**, then click the **Enter button** on the formula bar
   The axis label changes to reflect the updated cell contents, as displayed in **Figure 4-7**. Changing any data in the worksheet modifies corresponding text or values in the chart. Because the chart is no longer selected, the Chart Design and Format tabs no longer appear on the ribbon.

Quick Tip
You can also use the Copy and Paste buttons in the Clipboard group of the Home tab to copy a selected chart and paste it on a different worksheet.

5. Click the **chart** to select it, click the **Chart Design tab**, then click the **Move Chart button** in the Location group
   The Move chart dialog box displays options to move a chart to a new sheet or as an object in an existing worksheet, as displayed in **Figure 4-8**.

6. Click the **New sheet option button**, type **Column** in the New sheet box, then click **OK**
   The chart is placed on its own chart sheet, named Column.

Position a Chart EX 4-7

Figure 4-6: Moved and resized chart

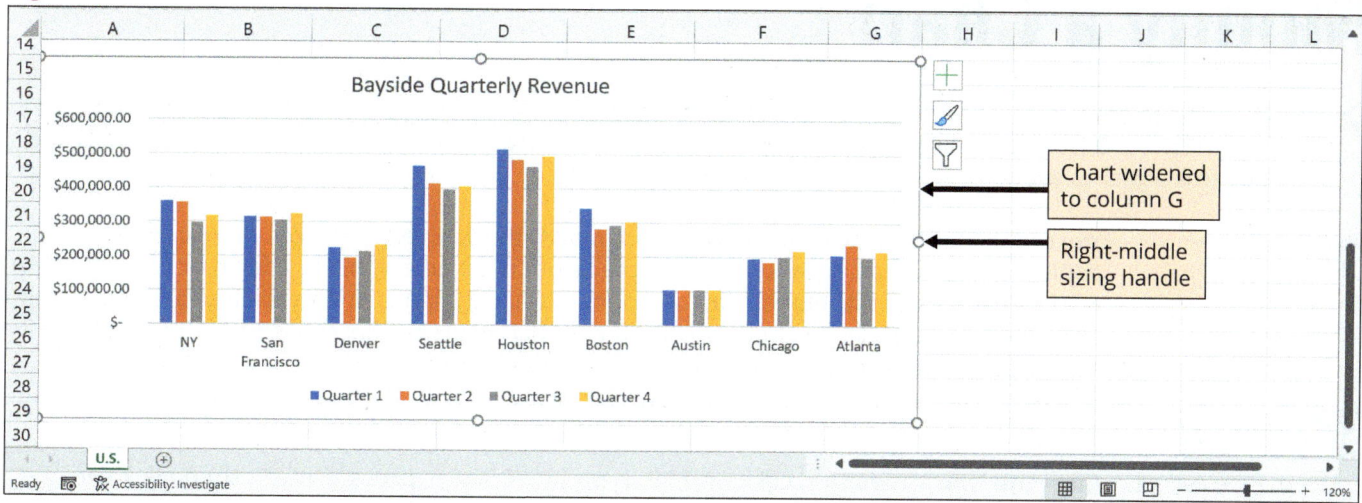

Figure 4-7: Worksheet with modified label

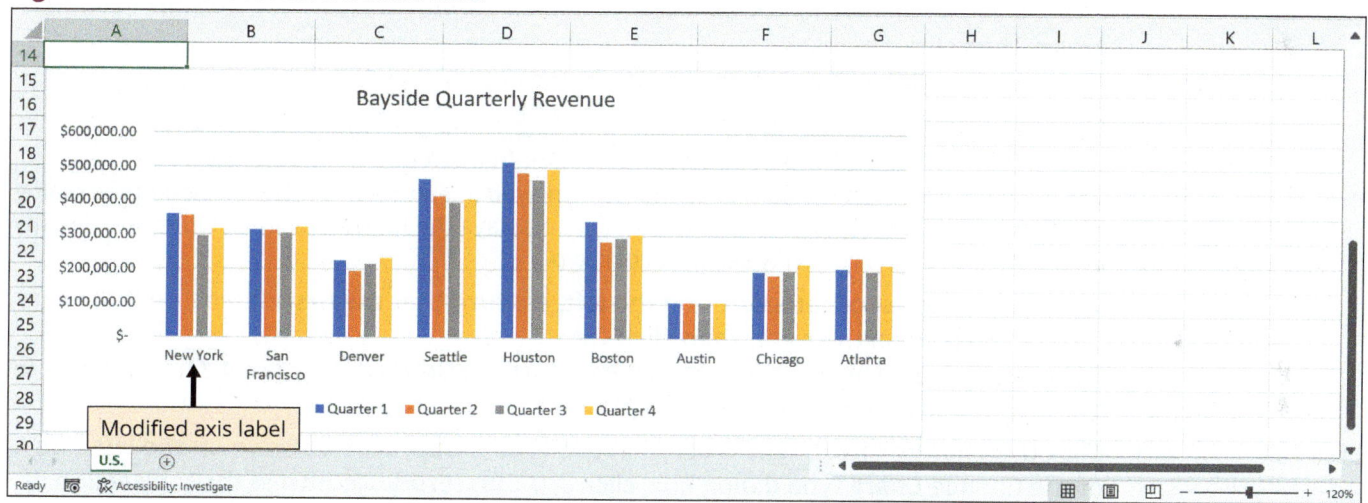

Figure 4-8: Move Chart dialog box

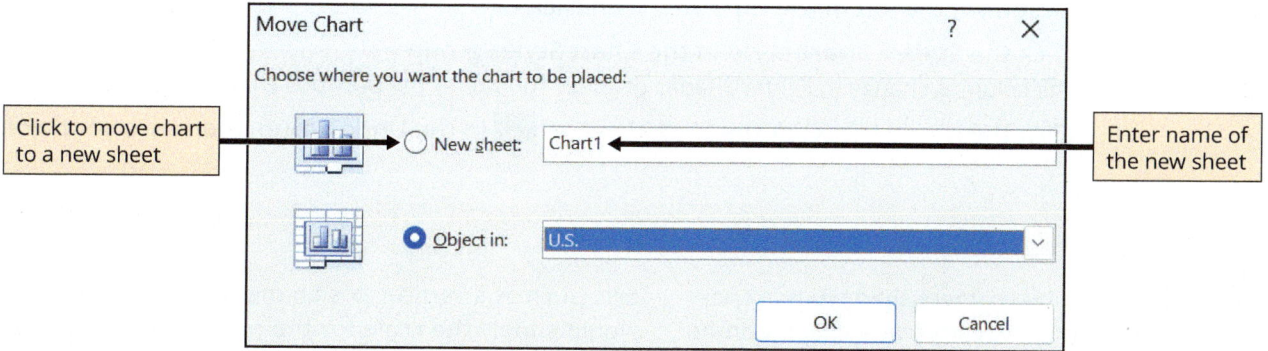

EX 4-8 Module 4 Working with Charts

Modify a Chart

Case You've been notified by the manager of the Boston office that there is a correction to the fourth quarter's revenue. You will make this correction and assess whether using different chart types and layouts makes the trends and patterns easier to spot.

Objectives
- Modify chart data
- Change the chart type
- Apply a chart style

You can change the type of an existing chart, modify the data range and column/row configuration, apply a different chart style, and change the layout of objects within it. The Chart Layouts group on the Chart Design tab lets you add or modify individual chart elements, such as a legend or title, using the Add Chart Element button, using the Quick Layouts button; choosing one of these layouts is a quick alternative to manually changing each object one at a time.

Steps

1. Click the **U.S. sheet tab**, click **cell E9**, type **302,800.05**, press **ENTER**, then click the **Column sheet tab**
   In the chart, the Quarter 4 data marker for Boston reflects the adjusted revenue figure, as displayed in **Figure 4-9**.

2. Select the **chart**, if necessary, by clicking a blank area within the chart border, click the **Chart Design tab** on the ribbon, click the **Quick Layout button** in the Chart Layouts group, then click **Layout 3**
   The chart columns are slightly wider. You prefer the original layout.

3. Click the **Home tab**, click the **Undo button** in the Undo group, click the **Chart Design tab**, then click the **Change Chart Type button** in the Type group
   The Change Chart Type dialog box opens, as displayed in **Figure 4-10**. The left side of the dialog box lists available categories and the right side displays the individual chart types. A pale gray border surrounds the currently selected chart type.

4. Click **Bar** in the list of categories on the left, confirm that the first **Clustered Bar chart type** is selected on the right, then click **OK**
   The column chart changes to a Clustered Bar chart as displayed in **Figure 4-11**. You decide to chart the data in a 3-D column chart.

Quick Tip
You can add a 3-D effect to a three-dimensional chart by selecting the chart, clicking the Format tab, clicking the Shape Effects button in the Shape Styles group, clicking 3-D Rotation, then selecting the desired effect.

5. Click the **Change Chart Type button** in the Type group, click **Column** on the left side of the Change Chart Type dialog box, click **3-D Clustered Column** in the top section of the dialog box, verify that the leftmost 3-D chart is selected, then click **OK**
   A three-dimensional column chart appears. You notice that the three-dimensional column format gives you a sense of volume, but it is more crowded than the two-dimensional column format.

6. Click the **Change Chart Type button** in the Type group, click **Clustered Column** (first from the left in the top row), then click **OK**

7. Click the **Style 3 chart style** in the Chart Styles group
   The columns change to lighter shades of color. You prefer the previous chart style's color scheme.

8. Click the **Home tab**, click the **Undo button** in the Undo group, then save your work

Creating a combo chart

A **combo chart** presents two or more chart types in one— for example, a column chart with a line chart. Combo charts are useful when charting dissimilar but related data. For example, you can create a clustered column–line combination chart based on both home price and home size data, displaying home prices in a Clustered Column chart and related home sizes in a line chart. Here, a secondary axis (such as a vertical axis on the right side of the chart) would supply the scale for the home sizes. To create a combo chart, select all the data you want to plot, click the Insert Combo chart button in the Charts group on the Insert tab, click a suggested type or Create Custom Combo Chart, supply additional series information if necessary, then click OK.

Modify a Chart   EX 4-9

Figure 4-9: Chart with modified data

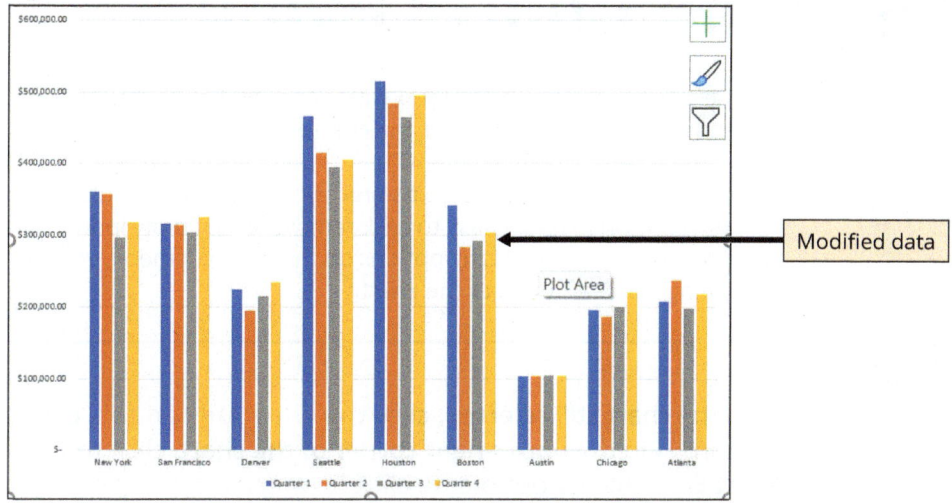

Figure 4-10: Change Chart Type dialog box

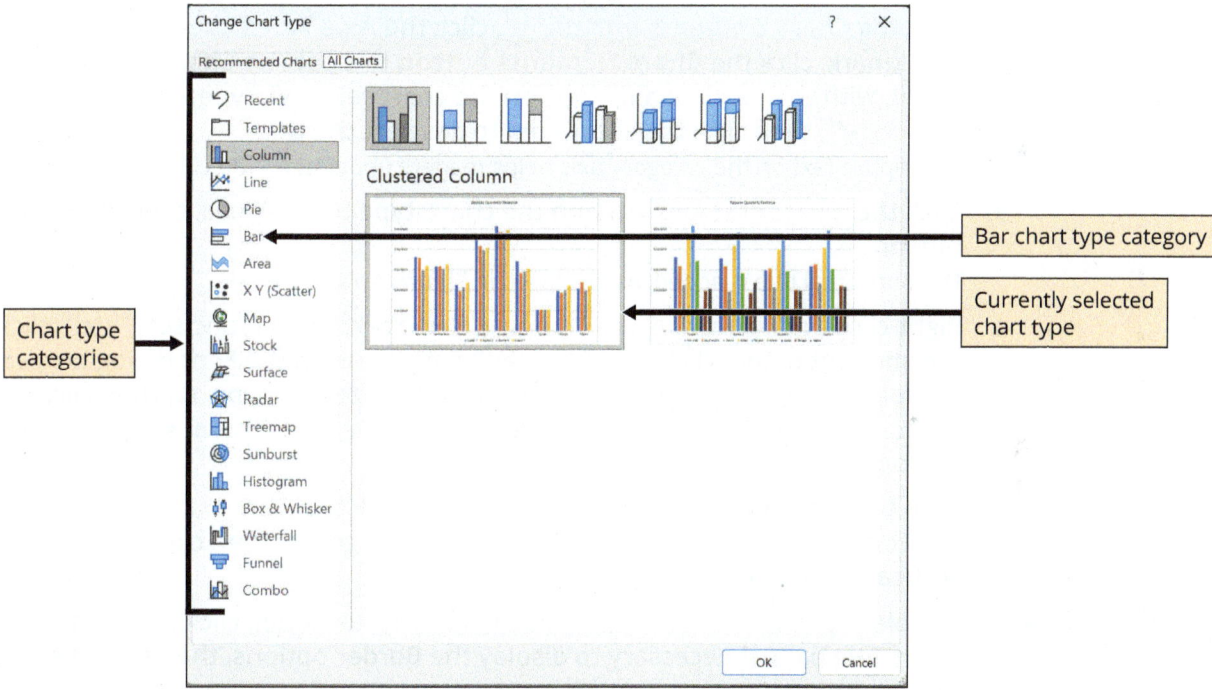

Figure 4-11: Column chart changed to bar chart

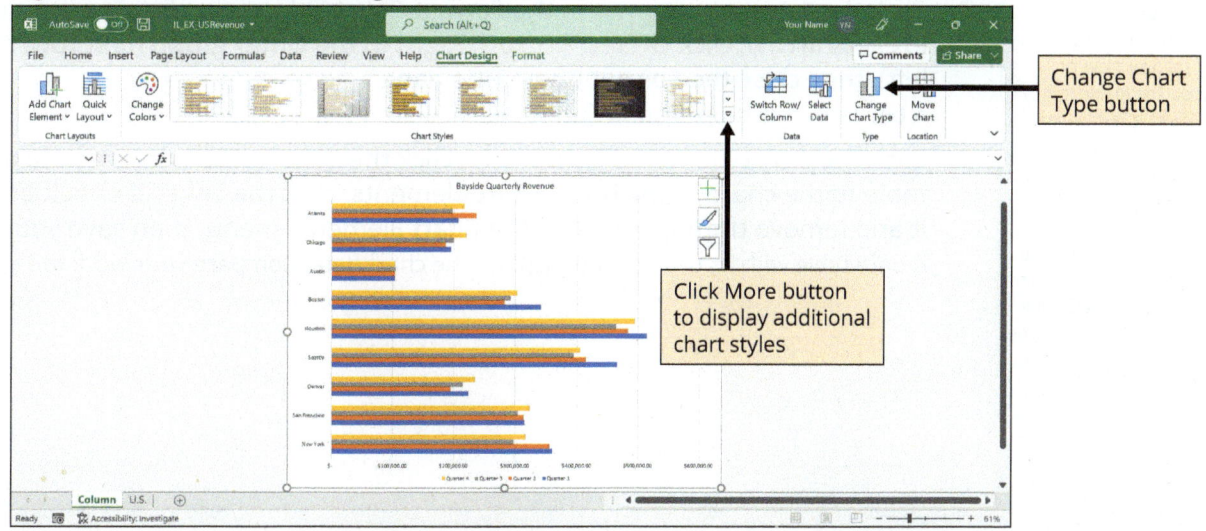

Module 4 Working with Charts

Change the Chart Layout

Case You want to make the chart easier to understand with horizontal and vertical axes titles. You also want to add a data table to provide more information about the charted data.

Objectives
- Change the gridlines display
- Add axis titles
- Add a data table

While the Chart Design tab contains preconfigured chart layouts you can apply to a chart, the Chart Elements button makes it easy to add, remove, and modify individual chart objects such as a chart title, gridlines, or legend. Using options on this shortcut menu, you can also add a **data table**, a grid containing the chart data, to the chart.

Steps

1. With the chart still selected, click the **Chart Design tab**, click the **Chart Elements button** in the upper-right corner of the chart, click the **Gridlines arrow** on the Chart Elements fly-out menu, click **Primary Major Horizontal** to deselect it, then click the **Chart Elements button** to close the menu
   The gridlines that extend across the chart's plot area are removed, as displayed in **Figure 4-12**.

2. Click the **Chart Elements button**, click the **Axis Titles check box** to add a checkmark, click the **Chart Elements button** to close the Chart Elements fly-out menu, with the **vertical axis title** on the chart selected, type **Revenue**, click the **Enter button**, then click the chart area to deselect the title
   Descriptive text on the category axis helps readers understand the chart.

3. Click the **horizontal axis title** on the chart, type **U.S. Offices**, then click **the Enter button**
   The horizontal title is added, as displayed in **Figure 4-13**.

4. Right-click the **horizontal axis labels** ("New York," "San Francisco," etc.), click **Font** on the shortcut menu, click the **Latin text font arrow** in the Font dialog box, scroll down the font list, click **Arial**, select the value in the Size box, type **12**, then click **OK**
   The font of the horizontal axis labels changes to Arial, and the font size increases, making the labels easier to read.

5. With the horizontal axis labels still selected, click the **Home tab** on the ribbon, click the **Format Painter button** in the Clipboard group, then click the area within the vertical axis labels

Quick Tip
You can also apply a border to a chart by double-clicking the Chart Area, clicking Border in the Format Chart Area pane, then selecting from the available border options.

6. Double-click the **chart title** (Bayside Quarterly Revenue), click **Border** in the Format Chart Title pane if necessary to display the Border options, then click the **Solid line option button**
   The default color (Blue, Accent 1) appears around the chart title.

Quick Tip
You can apply a shadow, glow, or outline to title text by clicking Text Options in the Format Chart Title pane. Clicking the Text Effects button allows you to select from the available shadow and glow options; clicking the Text Fill & Outline button displays outline options for chart text.

7. Click the **Effects button** in the Format Chart Title pane, click **Shadow**, click the **Presets arrow**, click **Offset: Bottom Right** in the Outer group (first row, first from the left), then close the Format Chart Title pane
   A border with a drop shadow surrounds the title.

8. Click the **Chart Elements button**, click the **Data Table check box** to add a data table to the chart, in the list of chart elements, click the **Legend check box** to deselect it and remove the legend, close the Chart Elements menu, then save your work
   A data table with its own legend displays the chart data. Compare your work to **Figure 4-14**.

Figure 4-12: Gridlines removed from chart

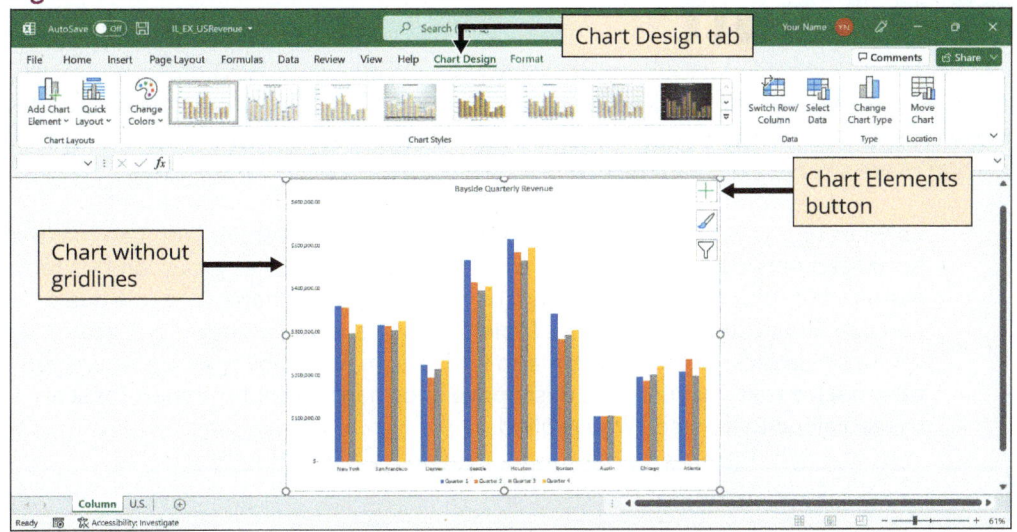

Figure 4-13: Axis titles added to chart

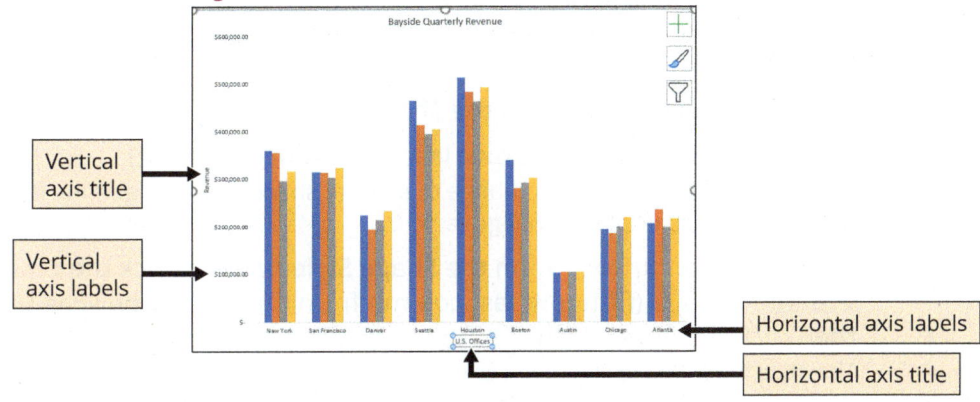

Figure 4-14: Enhanced chart

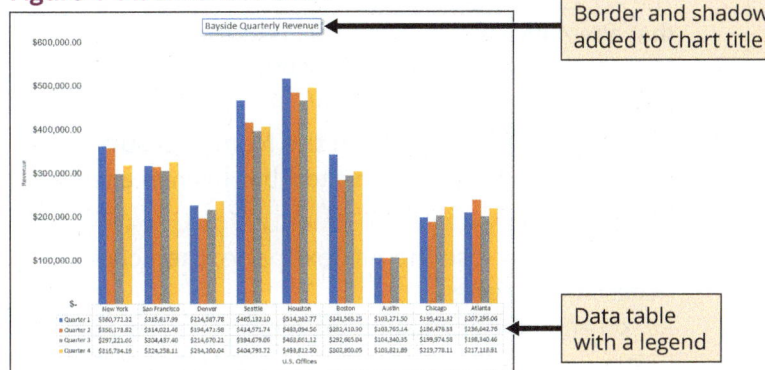

Working with chart axes

You can change both the number format and text formatting of a chart's axes. For example, you may want to change the starting and ending values of an axis. You can do this by double-clicking the axis, clicking Axis Options in the Format Axis pane if necessary, then entering new values in the Minimum and Maximum boxes under the Bounds headings. To change the number format of the values on an axis, scroll down in the Axis Options pane, click Number to display the options, if necessary, then select from the available number formats. In the Number area, you also can create a number format code by typing a custom code in the Format Code box, then clicking Add. In addition to these axis options, you can work with axis text by clicking the Text Options button at the top of the pane, then clicking the Text box button. The Text Box group includes options for changing the vertical alignment of the data labels on the axis and the text direction of axis data labels from horizontal to stacked or rotated.

Module 4 Working with Charts

Format a Chart

Case You want to enhance the look of the chart by formatting one of the data series. Elena has asked you to make sure the chart meets accessibility standards, so you also need to investigate the accessibility notification on the status bar and make any necessary adjustments.

Objectives
- Change the fill of a data series
- Apply a style to a data series

Formatting a chart can make it easier to read and understand. You can make many formatting enhancements using the Format tab. Using the Shape Styles group on this tab, you can change the fill color for a specific data series, or you can apply a shape style to a title or a data series. You can use Shape styles to apply multiple formats, such as an outline, fill color, and text color, all with a single click. The Format tab also includes an Accessibility group where you can add Alt Text, **alternative text**, that provides descriptive information about the chart for screen reader software to read aloud to a person who is blind.

Steps

Quick Tip
You can remove a data series from a chart by selecting the data series, then pressing DEL.

1. With the chart selected, click the **Format tab** on the ribbon, then click **any column** in the Quarter 3 data series
   Handles appear on each column in the Quarter 3 data series, indicating that the entire series is selected.

2. Click the **Shape Fill arrow** in the Shape Styles group

3. Click **Green, Accent 6** (first row, last column from the left)
   All the columns for the series change to a bright shade of green, and the legend changes to match the new color, as displayed in **Figure 4-15**.

Quick Tip
You can change the colors used in a chart by clicking the Chart Design tab, clicking the Change Colors button in the Chart Styles group, then clicking a color palette in the gallery.

4. Click the **More button** on the Shape Styles gallery, click the **Moderate Effect – Green, Accent 6** (fifth row, last column from the left) shape style under Theme Styles, then click **the Chart Area**
   The style is applied to the data series.

5. Click the **Accessibility checker** on the status bar
   The Accessibility tab is active and the Accessibility pane opens with the Inspection Results noting that alternative text is missing, as displayed in **Figure 4-16**. The Inspection Results include a link to more information on making worksheets accessible. It is important that the message "Good to go" is displayed on the status bar, to indicate the worksheet is accessible.

Quick Tip
You can also click the Alt Text button in the Accessibility group on the Format tab to open the Alt Text pane.

6. Click the **Alt Text button** in the Names group on the Accessibility pane
   The Alt Text pane opens with a text box to enter alternative text for the chart

7. Type **Bayside Quarterly Revenue for U.S. Offices** in the text box, click the **Close button** to close the Alt Text pane, then click the **Close button** to close the Accessibility pane
   As you enter the alternative text the accessibility notification on the status bar changes to Good to go.

8. Click the **Insert tab** on the ribbon, click the **Text button**, click the **Header & Footer button**, click **Custom Footer**, type your name in the center section, click **OK**, click **OK** again, then save your work

---

Working with WordArt

You can insert WordArt into a worksheet or a chart. To insert WordArt in a worksheet, click the Insert tab on the ribbon, click the Text button in the Text group, click WordArt, then select the WordArt style from the gallery. You can change a WordArt style by clicking the WordArt to select it, clicking the WordArt Styles More button on the Shape Format tab, then selecting a new WordArt style. You can change the fill color of the WordArt by clicking the Text Fill button in the WordArt Styles group and choosing a fill color, texture, gradient, or picture.

Format a Chart   EX 4-13

Figure 4-15: New shape fill applied to data series

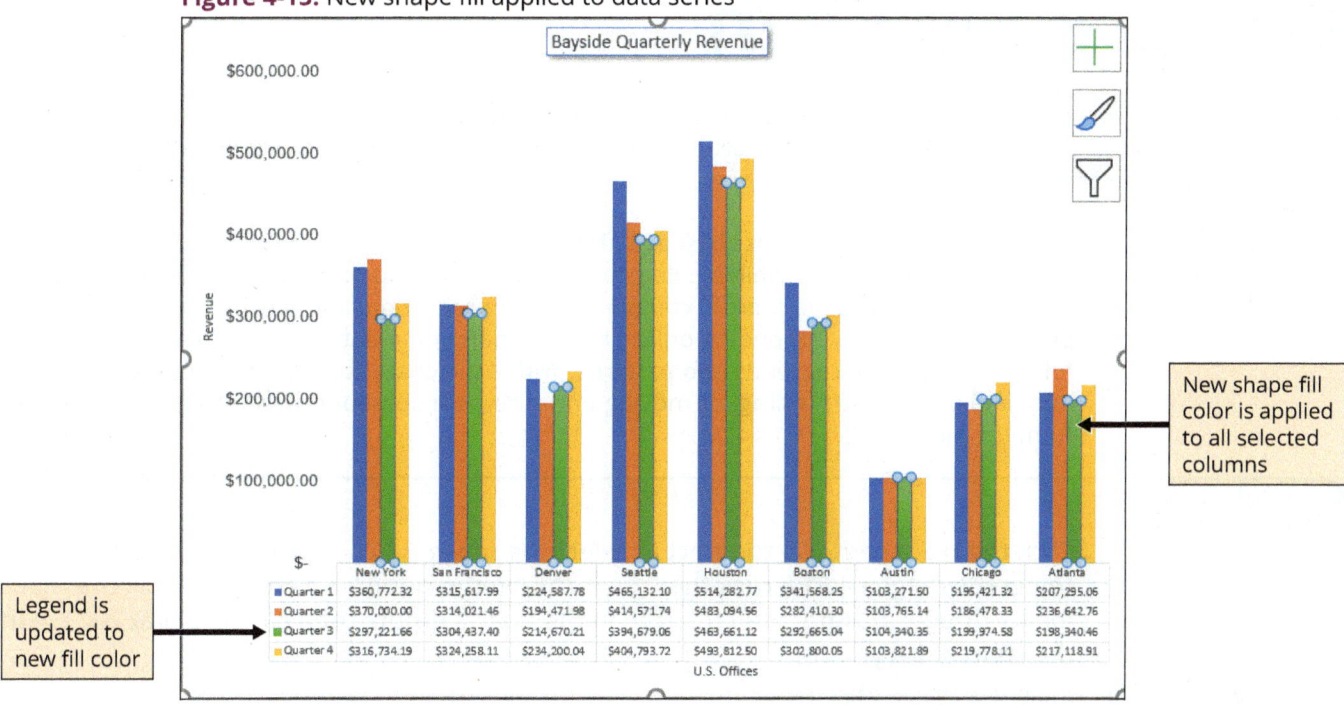

Figure 4-16: Accessibility pane

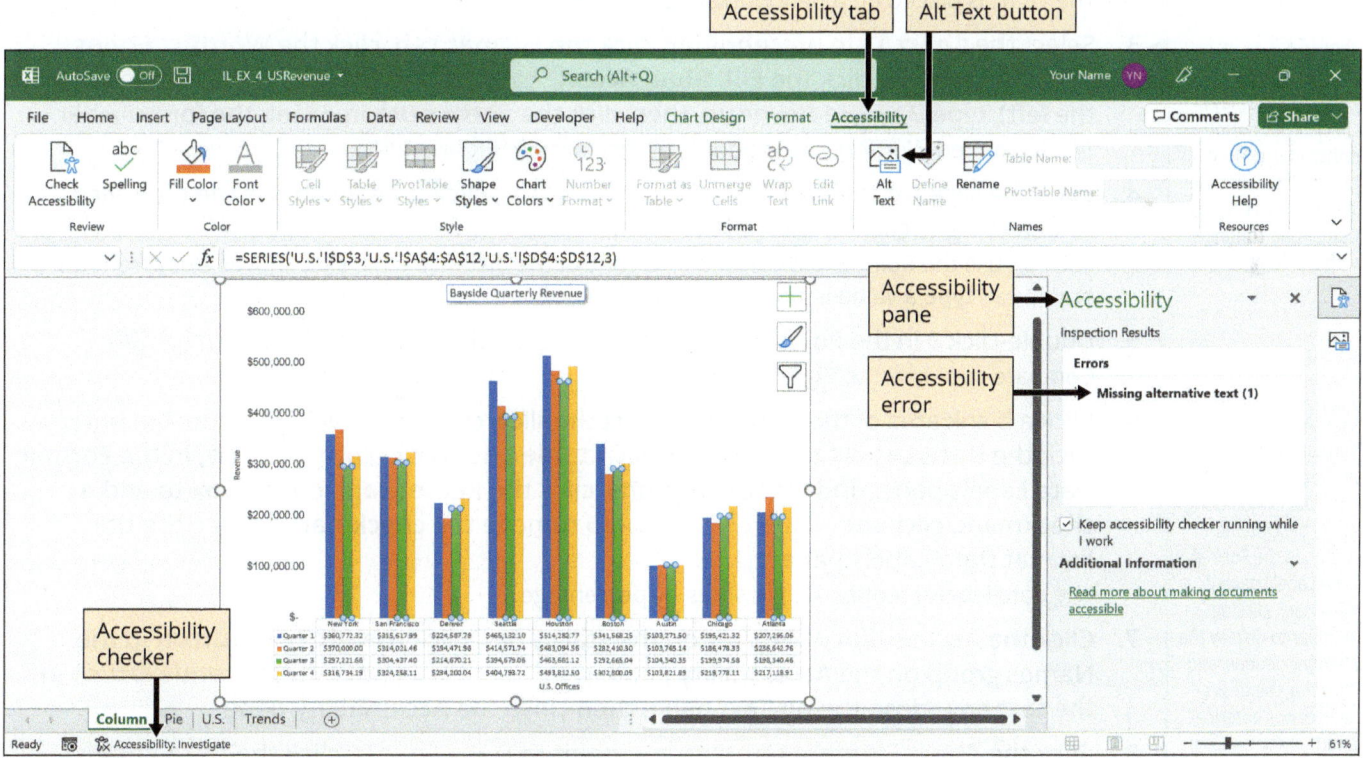

Aligning charts

If you have two or more embedded charts on a worksheet, you can line them up to make them easier to view. First, select the charts by clicking the first chart and holding CTRL, then click the other chart(s). With the charts selected, click the Shape Format tab, click the Align button in the Arrange group, then choose the alignment position for the charts.

Module 4 Working with Charts

Create a Pie Chart

Case At an upcoming meeting, Elena plans to discuss the company's revenue and identify offices that have weak revenue reports. You want to create a pie chart that Elena can use to compare overall revenue performance in the different offices.

Objectives
- Create a pie chart
- Explode a pie chart slice

You can create multiple charts based on the same worksheet data, to illustrate different aspects of the data. For example, while a column chart may reveal top performers month by month, you may want to create a pie chart to compare relative proportions for performances for individual products or regions. Depending on the type of chart you create, you have additional options for calling attention to trends and patterns. With a pie chart, for example, you can emphasize one data point by **exploding**, or moving one slice, as if someone were taking the piece away from the pie.

Steps

1. Click the **U.S. sheet tab** to select it, select the range **A4:A12**, press and hold **CTRL**, select the range **F4:F12**, click the **Insert tab** on the ribbon if necessary, click the **Insert Pie or Doughnut Chart button** in the Charts group, then click the first **2-D Pie** in the chart gallery

2. Click the **chart**, click the **Chart Design tab**, click the **Move Chart button** in the Location group, click the **New sheet option button**, type **Pie** in the New sheet box, then click **OK**
   The chart is placed on a new worksheet named Pie.

Trouble
Your WordArt Styles group may display a Quick Styles button rather than a More button; if so, click the WordArt Quick Styles button and continue with the step.

▶ 3. Select the **Chart Title placeholder**, click the **Format tab**, click the **WordArt Styles More button**, click the **Fill: Blue, Accent color 1; Shadow** fill (first row, second from the left), type **Bayside Revenue**, then click the **Enter button** on the formula bar
   The formatted WordArt title is added, as displayed in **Figure 4-17**.

4. Click the slice for the **San Francisco data point**, click it again so it is the only slice selected, right-click it, then click **Format Data Point**
   You can use the Point Explosion slider to control the distance a pie slice moves away from the pie, or you can type a value in the Point Explosion box.

5. Double-click **0** in the Point Explosion box, type **10**, then click the **Close button**
   Compare your chart to **Figure 4-18**.

Quick Tip
You can change the number format of the data labels by clicking the Label Options button in the Format Data Labels pane if necessary, clicking Number to display the Number options, and choosing the desired category or entering a format code. Also in this pane are options under Label Position to change the position of the data labels to Center, Inside End, and Best Fit.

▶ 6. Click a blank area of the chart to deselect the slice, click the **Chart Elements button**, click the **Data Labels arrow**, click **Outside End**, click **More Options**, in the Format Data Labels pane, under Label Options, click the **Percentage check box** to add a checkmark, click the **Value check box** to remove the checkmark, then close the Format Data Labels pane
   The data labels identify the pie slices by percentage.

7. Click the **Accessibility checker** on the status bar, click the **Alt Text button** in the Names group on the Accessibility pane, type **Percentage of total revenue Office** in the text box, close the Alt Text pane, then close the Accessibility pane

8. Click the **Chart Elements button**, point to **Data Labels**, click the **Data Labels arrow**, click **Data Callout**, click the **Legend check box** to deselect it, click the **Chart Elements button**, click the **Bold button** on the Home tab, then click a blank area of the chart to deselect the callouts
   The data is labeled using percentage callouts in bold formatting, as displayed in **Figure 4-19**.

9. Click the **Insert tab** on the ribbon, click the **Text button**, click the **Header & Footer button** in the Text group, click the **Custom Footer button**, enter your name in the center section, click **OK**, click **OK** again, then save your work

Figure 4-17: Title Formatted using WordArt

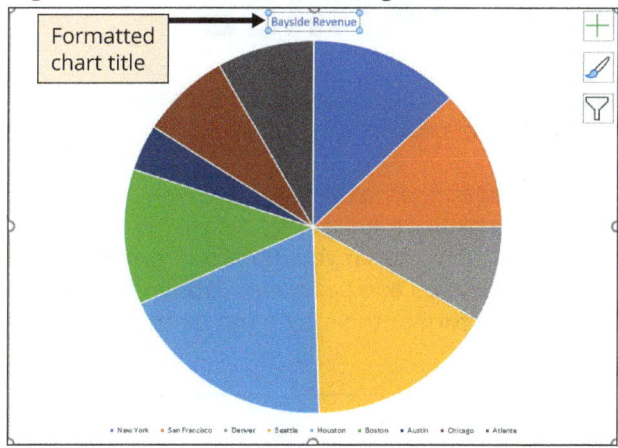

Figure 4-18: Exploded pie slice

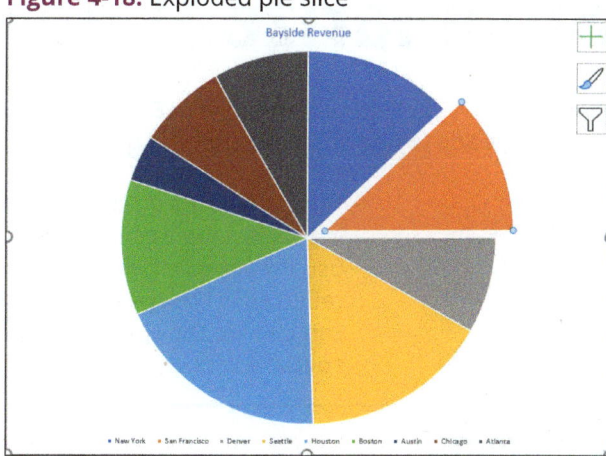

Figure 4-19: Pie chart with percentages

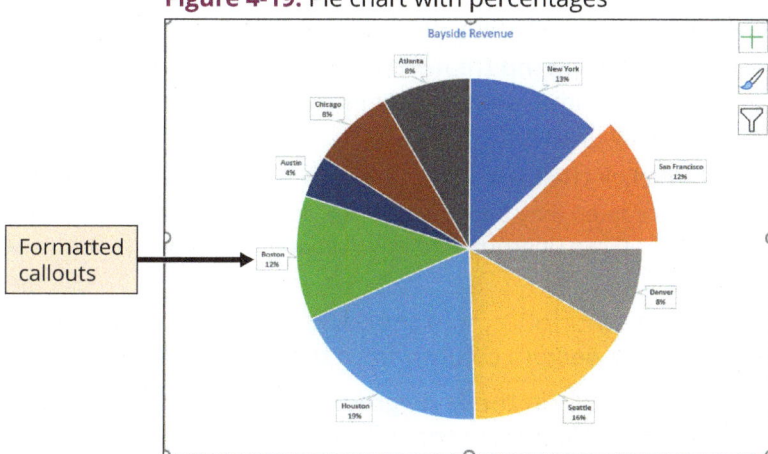

Working with other chart types

Excel includes chart types that are useful for illustrating highly specific types of data. These include Waterfall, Histogram, Funnel, Box & Whisker, Treemap, Scatter, and Sunburst. A **treemap chart** is a hierarchy chart in which each category is placed within a rectangle and subcategories are nested as rectangles within those rectangles. A **sunburst chart** is also a hierarchy chart, but it groups categories within a series of concentric rings, with the upper levels of the hierarchy placed in the innermost rings. To insert one of these chart types, click the Insert tab, click the Insert Hierarchy Chart button in the Charts group, click More Hierarchy Charts, then click the chart type. **Waterfall charts** are used to track the addition and subtraction of values within a sum and **funnel charts** are used to chart the progressive stages of a process. To insert a waterfall or funnel chart, click the Insert tab, click the Insert Waterfall, Funnel, Stock, Surface, or Radar Chart button in the Charts group, then click Waterfall or Funnel. A **histogram chart** displays the distribution of data grouped in bins. These charts look similar to column charts, but each column (or bin) represents a range of values. To insert a histogram chart, click the Insert tab on the ribbon, click the Insert Statistic Chart button in the Charts group, then click the Histogram chart button. You can edit the bins in a histogram chart by double-clicking the x-axis, clicking to expand the Axis Options group on the Format Axis pane, then choosing options under Bins.

A **scatter chart** displays the correlation between two numeric variables. It is a type of **XY scatter chart**, which displays the pattern or relationship between two or more sets of values. Scatter charts look similar to line charts but have two value axes. The data points on a scatter chart display the intersection of the horizontal and vertical axes values. To insert a scatter chart, select the data you want to chart, click the Insert tab, click the Insert Scatter (X,Y) or Bubble Chart button in the Charts group, then choose a scatter chart type.

Module 4 Working with Charts

Summarize Data with Sparklines

Case As a supplement to the charts, Elena wants the U.S. worksheet to illustrate the revenue trends for the year. You decide to add sparklines to tell a quick visual story within the worksheet cells.

Objectives
- Add sparklines to a worksheet
- Format sparklines

You can create a quick overview of your data by adding sparklines to the worksheet cells. A **sparkline** is a small, simple chart located within a cell that serves as a visual indicator of data trends. Sparklines usually appear close to the data they represent. Any changes that you make to a worksheet are reflected in the sparklines that represent the data. After you add sparklines to a worksheet, you can change the sparkline style and color, and you can format their high and low data points in special colors.

Steps

Trouble
You may have to move the Create Sparklines dialog box to select the data range.

1. Click the **U.S. sheet tab**, click cell **G4**, click the **Insert tab** on the ribbon if necessary, click the **Column button** in the Sparklines group, verify that the insertion point is in the Data Range box, select the range **B4:E4** on the worksheet, then click **OK**
   Columns displaying the revenue trend for New York appear in cell G4.

2. With cell G4 selected, drag the **fill handle** ➕ to fill the range **G5:G12**
   The sparkline is copied, and column sparklines reflecting the data for each office are added, as displayed in **Figure 4-20**.

Quick Tip
To insert Win/Loss sparklines, which display upward column symbols for positive values and downward symbols for negative values, click the Win/Loss button in the Type group.

3. Click cell **G4**, then click the **Line button** in the Type group on the Sparkline tab
   When sparklines are copied they become a group, so all the sparklines in this group change to the Line sparkline type. You can ungroup and group sparklines using the Group and Ungroup buttons in the Group group.

4. Click the **Sparkline Color button** in the Style group, then click **Blue, Accent 5, Darker 50%** (last row, second column from the right under Theme Colors)

5. Click the **More button** ▼ in the Style group, then click **Dark Blue, Sparkline Style Accent 1, Darker 50%** (first from the left in the first row)
   The sparkline colors and styles are consistent with the colors on the worksheet.

6. Click the **Marker Color button** in the Style group, point to **High Point**, select **Green Accent 6**, (first row, last column from the left), then click the **Markers check box** in the Show group to add a checkmark
   Data markers indicate each quarter's revenue.

Quick Tip
To clear sparklines, select the sparklines, then click the Clear button in the Group group.

7. Click cell **C4** type **370,000.00**, click the **Enter button** ✓, then compare your screen to **Figure 4-21**
   The sparklines update to reflect the new worksheet data.

8. Click the **Insert tab** on the ribbon, click the **Text button**, click the **Header & Footer button** in the Text group, click the **Go to Footer button** in the Navigation group, enter your name in the center footer section, click **any cell** on the worksheet, click the **Normal button** ▦ on the status bar, then press **CTRL+HOME**

9. Save your changes

Summarize Data with Sparklines   EX 4-17

Figure 4-20: Revenue trend sparklines

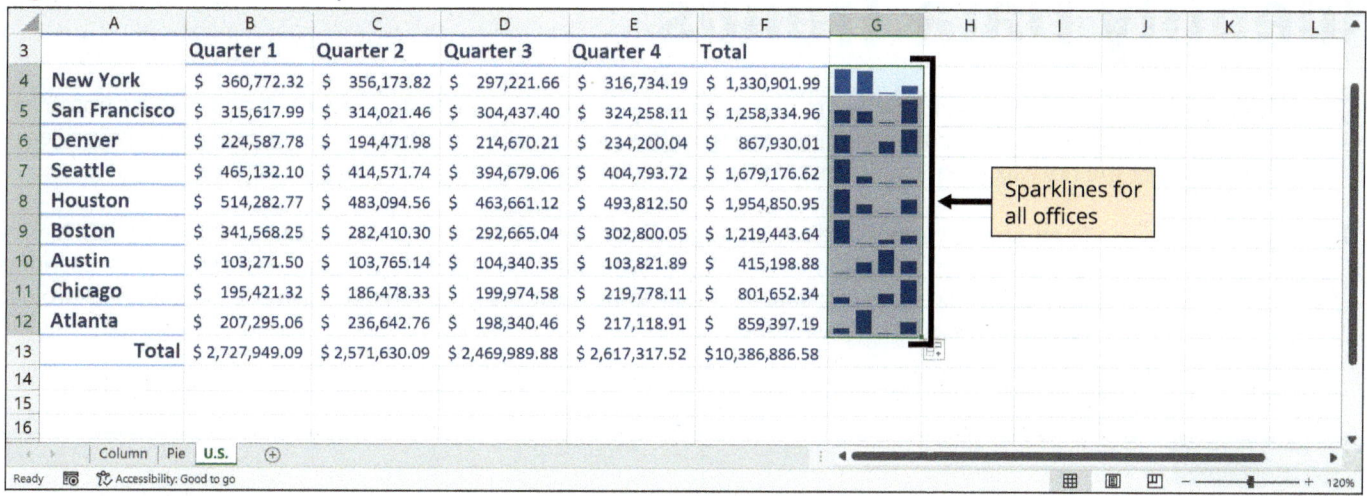

Figure 4-21: Formatted sparklines

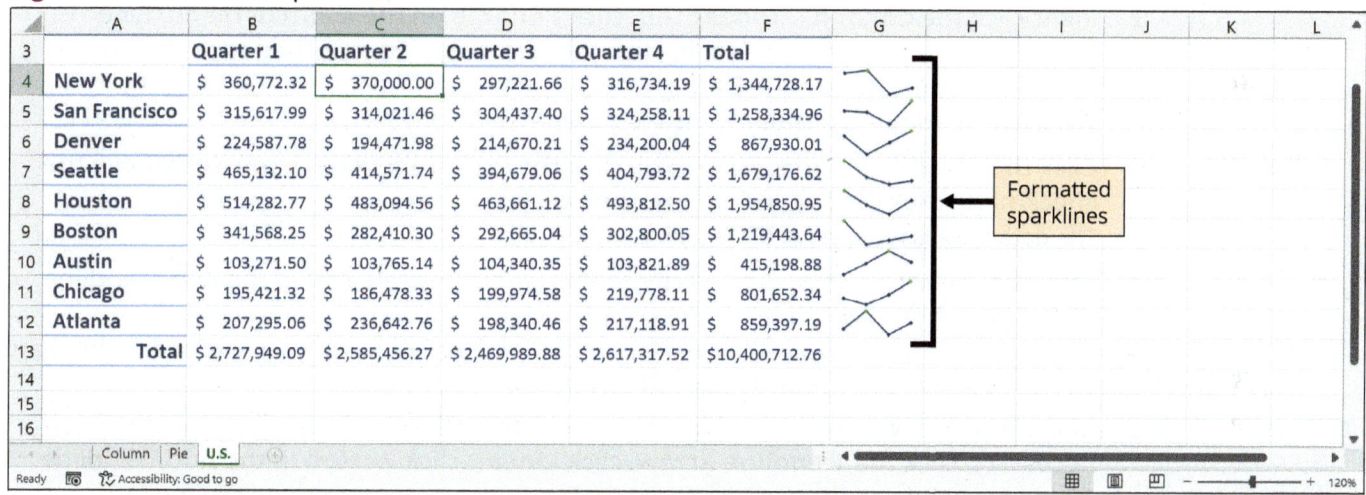

Identify Data Trends

Case As part of her presentation, Elena wants to compare the New York and Boston revenues and discuss possible future trends. You decide to use trendlines to highlight revenue at these offices over the past year and project revenue for the next six months, if their past trends continue.

Objectives
- Compare chart data using trendlines
- Format a trendline
- Forecast future trends using trendlines

To emphasize trends and patterns that occur over a period of time, you can add one or more trendlines to a chart. A **trendline** is a series of data points on a line that displays data values representing the general direction of a data series. In some business situations, you can use trendlines to project future data based on past trends.

Steps

1. Right-click the **Column sheet tab**, click **Move or Copy** on the shortcut menu, click **(move to end)** in the Before sheet box, click the **Create a copy check box** to add a checkmark, then click **OK**
   The new worksheet Column (2) is a copy of the Column sheet.

2. Right-click the **Column (2) sheet tab**, click **Rename** on the shortcut menu, type **Trends**, click the **chart** to select it, click the **Chart Design tab**, then click the **Switch Row/Column button** in the Data group
   The chart now displays quarters along the x-axis.

3. Click the **Chart Elements button**, click the **Data Table check box** to remove the checkmark, click the **Legend arrow**, then click **Bottom**
   The data table is removed and a legend is added.

4. Click the **Trendline checkbox**, verify that **New York** is selected in the Add Trendline dialog box, then click **OK**
   A linear trendline identifying the New York revenue trend in the past year is added to the chart, along with an entry in the legend identifying the line.

Quick Tip
To make sure that a chart element is not selected, simply click away from the element.

5. Make sure the New York trendline is not selected, click the Chart Elements button if necessary, click the **Trendline arrow**, click **Linear**, click **Boston** in the Add Trendline dialog box, click **OK**, then click the **Chart Elements button** to close the menu
   The chart now has two trendlines, making it easy to compare the revenue trends of the New York and Boston offices, as displayed in **Figure 4-22**.

6. Double-click the **New York data series trendline**, in the Format Trendline pane click the **Trendline Options button** if necessary, select **0.0** in the Forward box, type **1**, press **ENTER**, click the **Fill & Line button**, select **1.5** in the **Width box**, type **2.5**, then close the Format Trendline pane
   Trendlines are often used to project future trends. The formatted New York trendline projects an additional quarter of future revenue trends for the office, assuming past trends continue.

7. Double-click the **Boston data series trendline**, click the **Trendline Options button** in the Format Trendline pane if necessary, select **0.0** in the Forward box, type **1**, press **ENTER**, click the **Fill & Line button**, select **1.5** in the **Width box**, type **2.5**, then close the Format Trendline pane
   The formatted Boston trendline also projects an additional quarter of future revenue, if past trends continue.

8. sam↑ Compare your chart to **Figure 4-23**, save your work, preview the Trends sheet, close the workbook, submit the workbook to your instructor, then close Excel

Identify Data Trends   EX 4-19

Figure 4-22: Chart with two trendlines

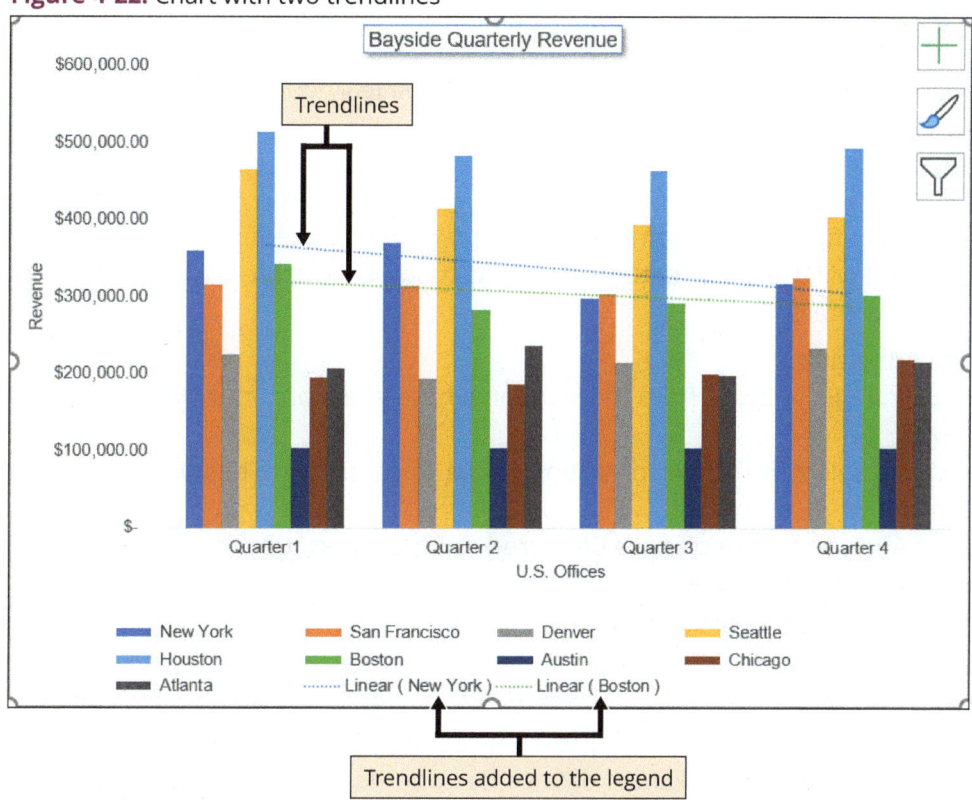

Trendlines added to the legend

Figure 4-23: Revenue chart with trendlines for New York and Boston

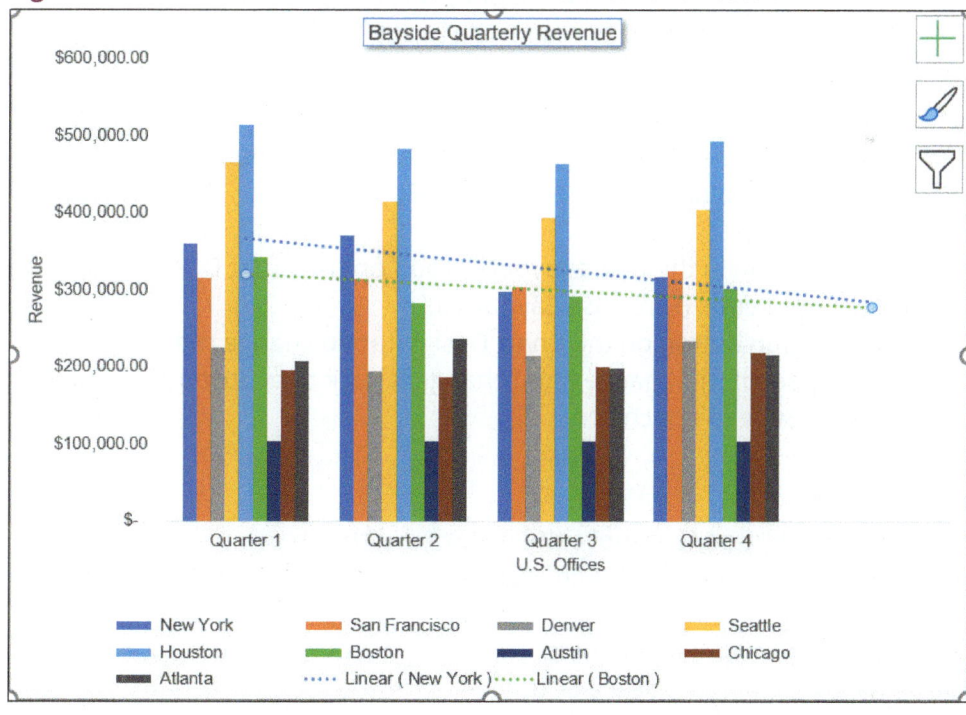

Choosing the right trendline options for your chart

When choosing a trendline, it is important to know which one is best for the information you want to communicate. If the data progression follows a straight line, using a linear trendline helps to emphasize that. If the pattern of a chart's data is linear but the data points don't follow a straight line, you can use a linear forecast trendline to chart a best-fit straight line. When data values increase or decrease in an arc shape, consider using an exponential or power trendline to illustrate this. A two-period moving average smooths out fluctuations in data by averaging the data points.

Practice

In the exercises that follow, you will practice the skills you have learned in this module.

Skills Review

As the manager of TRM, a food service company, you regularly review revenue data from the regional distribution centers. You will use Excel features from this module to create charts displaying the revenue relationships for these centers.

1. **Create a chart with a title.**
   a. Start Excel, open IL_EX_4-2.xlsx from the location where you store your Data Files, then save it as **IL_EX_4_TRM**.
   b. In the worksheet, select the range containing all the sales data and headings. Do not include the totals.
   c. Use the Quick Analysis tool to create a Clustered Column chart. Use the first Clustered Column option, placing the months on the x-axis.
   d. Add the chart title **TRM Revenue** above the chart.
   e. Save your work.

2. **Position a chart.**
   a. Make sure the chart is still selected and close any open panes if necessary.
   b. Move the chart beneath the worksheet data so its upper-left corner is at the upper-left corner of cell A11.
   c. Widen the chart so it extends to the right edge of column H.
   d. Move the chart to a new worksheet, then name the sheet **Column**.
   e. Save your work.

3. **Modify a chart.**
   a. Activate the Q3 & Q4 sheet, then change the value in cell B4 to **80,000.00**. Activate the Column sheet and verify that the revenue value for Maine in July is $80,000.00.
   b. Select the chart if necessary.
   c. Use the Quick Layout button in the Chart Layouts group on the Chart Design tab to move the legend to the right of the charted data. (**Hint**: Use Layout 1.)
   d. Use the Change Chart Type button on the Chart Design tab to change the chart to a Clustered Bar chart, evaluate the impact of this change, then change it back to a Clustered Column chart.
   e. Apply the Style 6 Chart Style to the chart.
   f. Save your work.

4. **Change the chart layout.**
   a. Use the Chart Elements button to remove the gridlines in the chart.
   b. Change the font used in the horizontal and vertical axis labels to Times New Roman with a font size of 11 point.
   c. Change the chart title's font size to 20 point.
   d. Insert **Revenue** as the primary vertical axis title.
   e. Change the font size of the vertical axis title to 16 point.
   f. Add a solid line border to the chart title, using the Orange, Accent 2 color (first row, sixth from left) and a preset shadow of Outer Offset: Bottom Right.
   g. Add a data table to the chart with a legend key, then remove the chart legend.
   h. Save your work.

5. Format a chart.

a. Use the Format tab to change the shape fill of the Vermont data series to Green, Accent 6 (first row of Theme Colors, last column from the left).

b. Change the shape style of the Vermont data series to Colored Fill – Green, Accent 6 (second row, last column from the left), then click the chart area to deselect the Vermont data series.

c. Use the Alt Text pane to add the alternative text **Revenue for July through December**, then close the Alt Text and Accessibility panes.

d. Enter your name in the center footer section, then save your work.

6. Create a pie chart.

a. Switch to the Q3 & Q4 sheet, then select the range A4:A8 and H4:H8. (**Hint**: Holding CTRL allows you to select multiple nonadjacent ranges.)

b. Create a 2-D pie chart, then move the chart beneath the worksheet data so the upper-left corner is at the upper-left corner of cell A11.

c. Resize the chart so its bottom border is at the bottom edge of row 20 and its right border is at the right edge of column E.

d. Add data labels in the outside end position with only category names and percentage options. Do not display the legend.

e. Change the chart title to **Region by Region Comparison** and format the title using the WordArt style Fill: Blue, Accent color 1, Shadow (second style in the first row).

f. Explode the New Hampshire slice from the pie chart at **20%**.

g. Select the chart area then add the alternative text of **Revenue percentage by region** to the chart.

h. Save your work.

7. Summarize data with sparklines.

a. Add a Column sparkline to cell I4 that represents the data in the range B4:G4.

b. Copy the sparkline in cell I4 into the range I5:I8.

c. Apply the Sparkline style Dark Blue, Sparkline Style Accent 1, Darker 25% (second row, first column) to the group.

d. Add high point markers with the color Orange, Accent 2 (first row, sixth from the left).

e. Compare your worksheet to **Figure 4-24**.

f. Add your name to the center footer section of the worksheet, then save the workbook.

Figure 4-24

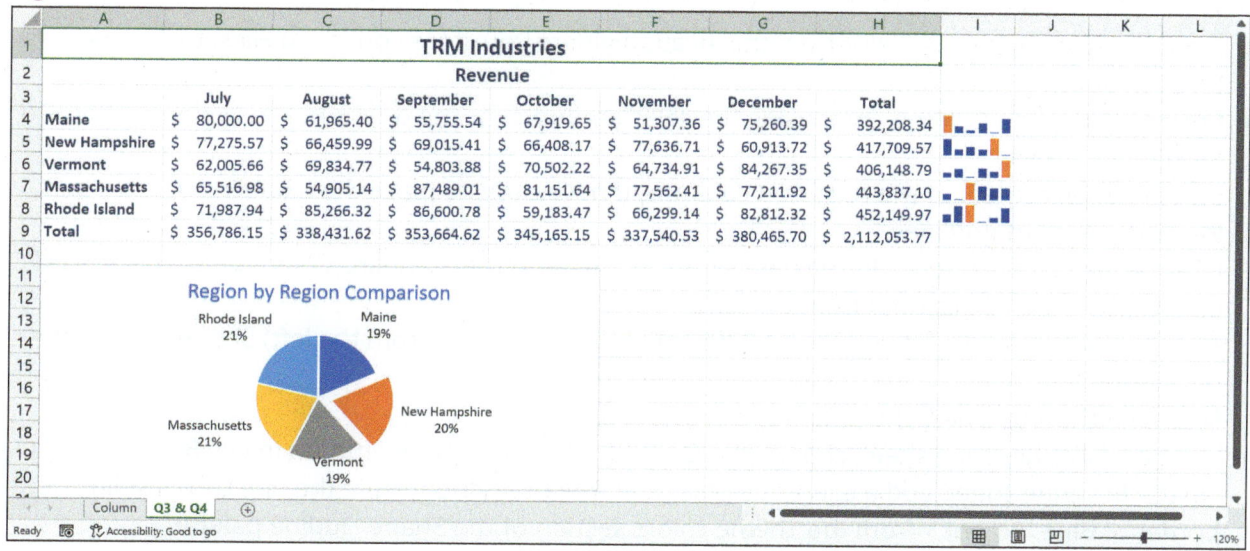

Skills Review (Continued)

8. **Identify data trends.**
   a. Switch to the Column sheet.
   b. Add linear trendlines to the New Hampshire and Massachusetts data series.
   c. Set the forward option to 2.0 periods for both trendlines.
   d. Change the width of both trendlines to 3.
   e. Compare your screen to **Figure 4-25**.
   f. Save the workbook, close the workbook, then submit the workbook to your instructor.
   g. Close Excel.

Figure 4-25

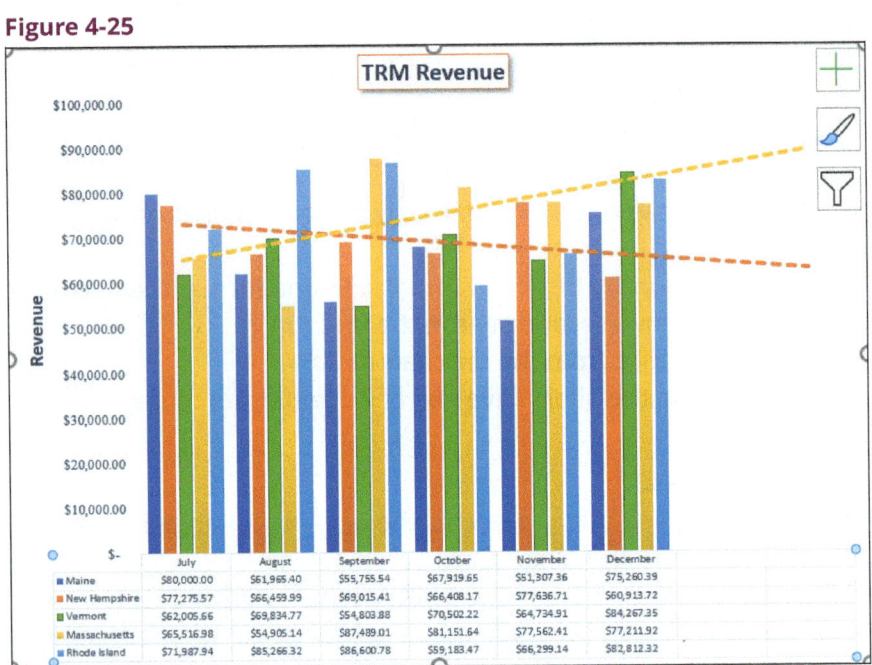

Independent Challenge 1

As an executive assistant for GSI, a global semiconductor engineering firm, you prepare revenue reports for the CEO. You will use charts to illustrate the annual revenue for this year's global sales.

a. Start Excel, open IL_EX_4-3.xlsx from the location where you store your Data Files, then save it as **IL_EX_4_GSI**.
b. Create a Clustered Column chart using the sales amounts for the quarters and regions. (**Hint**: Do not include the totals.)
c. Switch the placement of the rows and columns, if necessary, to place the quarters on the x-axis.
d. Remove the chart gridlines.
e. Change the fill of the South Korea data series to Purple in the Standard Colors section of the Fill Color palette (last row, last column from the left).
f. Add the Subtle effect – Green, Accent 6 (fourth row, last column from the left) Shape Style to the U.S. data series.
g. Move the chart to a new sheet named **Revenue**.
h. On the Global Revenue sheet, change the Quarter 1 Japan revenue amount in cell B7 to **$5,000,000**.
i. On the Revenue sheet, add a chart title of **Global Revenue** and format the title with a solid line border of Blue, Accent 1 from the Theme colors section of the Shape Outline palette.
j. Add a data table, then remove the chart legend.
k. Add trendlines to the Taiwan and U.S. revenue data, with a width of 3 points forecasting one period ahead.
l. Change the chart type to a line chart, then apply the Style 12 chart Style to the chart.

m. Add the alternative text **Global Revenue for all regions** to the chart. Compare your chart to **Figure 4-26**.
n. Enter your name in the center section of the worksheet footer of the Revenue sheet, then save your work.
o. Submit your work to your instructor as directed.
p. Close the workbook, then close Excel.

Figure 4-26

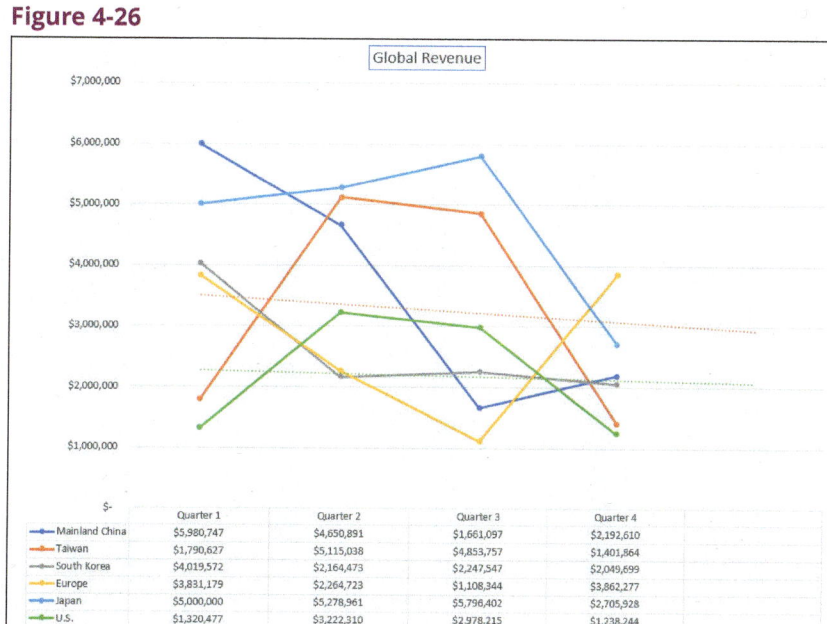

Independent Challenge 2

One of your responsibilities as the director of operations at Quest Adventures is to present occupancy rate data to the executive staff at the end of the year. Your assistant has organized the company's occupancy data by region in a worksheet. You will review the data and create charts to visually represent the occupancy for the year.

a. Start Excel, open IL_EX_4-4.xlsx from the location where you store your Data Files, then save it as **IL_EX_4_Occupancy**.
b. Create a 3-D Clustered Column chart in the worksheet displaying the occupancy data for all four quarters. (**Hint**: The regions, such as Northeast, Mid-Atlantic, and so forth, should appear on the x-axis.)
c. Add a chart title of **Occupancy**, then format the title with the WordArt Quick Style of Fill: Blue, Accent color 1; Shadow (first row, second from left).
d. Move the chart so its upper-left corner is at the upper-left corner of cell H3.
e. On the worksheet, type **Average** in cell F3, then use the Average function to calculate the average Northeast occupancy for the year. Format the average in cell F4 as a percentage with two decimal places.
f. Copy the average formula in cell F4 to the range F5:F8.
g. Add the average data from column F to the chart. (**Hint**: Use the Select Data button on the Chart Design tab to select the new chart data, including the average data.)
h. Change the chart type to Combo Clustered Column - Line chart (first option of combo charts) with the Average data series charted as a line. (**Hint**: After selecting the chart type in the Change Chart Type dialog box, scroll down to make sure all four quarter series are charted as clustered columns and the Average data series is charted as a line. You may need to change the fourth quarter chart type. Do not use the secondary axis options.)
i. Add the alternative text **Occupancy for regions by quarter with average for each region** to the chart.
j. Move the chart to a new sheet named **Occupancy**.
k. Using **Figure 4-27** as a guide, add data labels to the Average data series only. (**Hint**: Select the Average data series on the chart before adding data labels.)

Independent Challenge 2 (Continued)

l. Enter your name in the center footer section of both sheets, then preview the worksheet.
m. Save your work.
n. Submit your work to your instructor as directed, close the workbook, then close Excel.

Figure 4-27

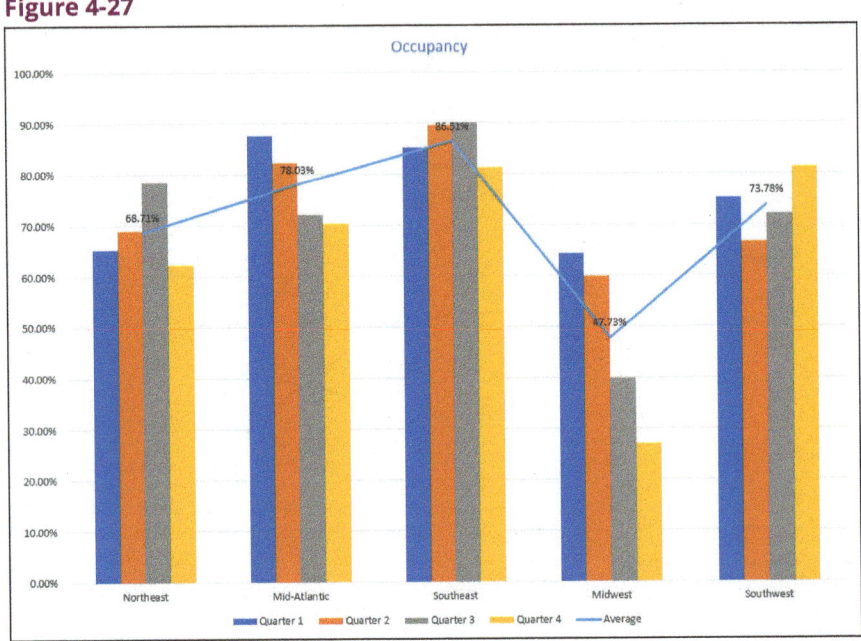

Visual Workshop

Open IL_EX_4-5.xlsx from the location where you store your Data Files, then save it as **IL_EX_4_SUV**. Create, modify, and position the charts to match those in **Figure 4-28**. (**Hint**: Use the CTRL key as needed to select nonadjacent ranges.) You will need to make design changes once you create the chart. (**Hints**: The WordArt used in the pie chart title is Fill: Blue, Accent color 1: Shadow. The Full-size data point in the pie chart is exploded 20%. The sparkline color is Green, Accent 6) The Alternative text for the pie chart is **Annual deliveries for four categories of SUVs**, without a period at the end of the text. Enter your name in the center section of the footer, then save and preview the worksheet. Submit your work to your instructor as directed, then close the workbook and close Excel.

Figure 4-28

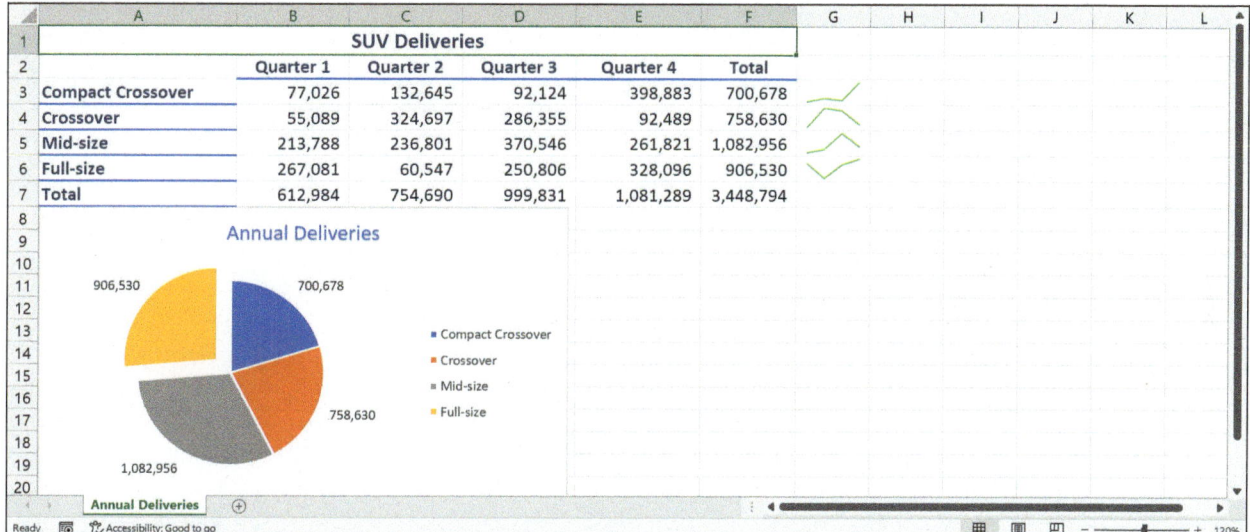

Integration **Module 1**

Integrating Word and Excel

Case
You are working with Ariel Likowski, the Dean of Student Services at Mountain Spring Institute of Technology in Denver, Colorado. Ariel has asked you to explore efficient ways to combine numeric information developed in Excel with text-based documents created in Word. First, you create a report in Word that includes values and a chart created in Excel, and then you embed a paragraph of text that is created in Word into an Excel worksheet.

Module Objectives
After completing this module, you will be able to:
- Identify integration options between Word and Excel
- Copy data from Excel to Word
- Copy a chart from Excel to Word
- Insert linked objects
- Embed a Word file in Excel

Files You Will Need

IL_INT_1-1.xlsx	IL_INT_1-8.docx
IL_INT_1-2.docx	IL_INT_1-9.xlsx
IL_INT_1-3.xlsx	IL_INT_1-10.docx
IL_INT_1-4.docx	IL_INT_1-11.docx
IL_INT_1-5.xlsx	IL_INT_1-12.xlsx
IL_INT_1-6.docx	IL_INT_1-13.xlsx
IL_INT_1-7.xlsx	IL_INT_1-14.docx

Identify Integration Options Between Word and Excel

Case Your work in the Student Services Department at Mountain Spring Institute of Technology often requires you to create documents such as reports and spreadsheets that include data from both Word and Excel. You decide to review some of the ways you integrate data between the two programs.

Objective
- Define copy/paste, link, and embed integration options

Office programs are designed to work together through a process called integration. **Integration** is the combining of objects and data from two or more applications using linking or embedding. When you integrate data from multiple Office programs, you work with both a source file and a destination file. The **source file** is the file in which you create an object that you will place in a destination file. The **destination file** is the file that displays an object from a source file. You can choose from three integration methods: pasting, linking, and embedding.

Details

You can integrate Word and Excel by:

- **Copying and pasting data from the Clipboard**
  You use the Copy and Paste commands to duplicate objects such as text selections, numbers (called values in Excel), and pictures from one program and place them into another program. An **object** is the data to be exchanged between another document or program. After you copy and paste an object, changes that you make to the object in the source file do not appear in the destination file. The report shown in **Figure 1-1** was created in Word and includes two objects that were copied from Excel—the photograph that appears to the right of the document title and the shaded two-column table under the document subtitle.

- **Linking data**
  Sometimes you want to connect the data that is included in two or more files. For example, suppose you copy the contents of a cell containing a formula from an Excel worksheet and paste it into a Word document. When you change the formula values in Excel, you want the corresponding values to change in the Word document. To create a **link** or a connection between data in a source file and a destination file, you select one of the link options that appears when you either click the Paste button arrow or view options in the Paste Special dialog box. You use the term **linked object** to refer to a text selection, value, or picture that is contained in a destination file and linked to a source file. In the report shown in **Figure 1-1**, the value "82%" is a linked object. If this percentage changes in the Excel worksheet, the linked percentage in the Word document also changes.

- **Copying and pasting charts**
  When you copy a chart from Excel and paste it into Word using the Paste command, Word automatically creates a link between the pasted chart and the original chart. In the report shown in **Figure 1-1**, the column chart was copied from Excel and pasted into the Word document. When the chart values are updated in Excel, the same chart values are updated in the chart copied to Word. You can also copy a chart from the source file and then paste it into the destination file as an object that is not linked.

- **Embedding a Word file in Excel**
  You can **embed**, or place an unlinked copy of, the contents of a Word file into an Excel worksheet. You edit the embedded object by double-clicking it and using Word program tools to change text and formatting. This process changes the embedded copy of the Word object in Excel but does not affect the original source document you created in Word. Similarly, any changes to the source Word document are not reflected in the embedded copy in Excel. In the list shown in **Figure 1-2**, the text that describes academic services at Mountain Springs Institute of Technology was inserted in Excel as an embedded Word file.

Identify Integration Options Between Word and Excel   INT 1-3

Figure 1-1: Word report with objects copied from Excel

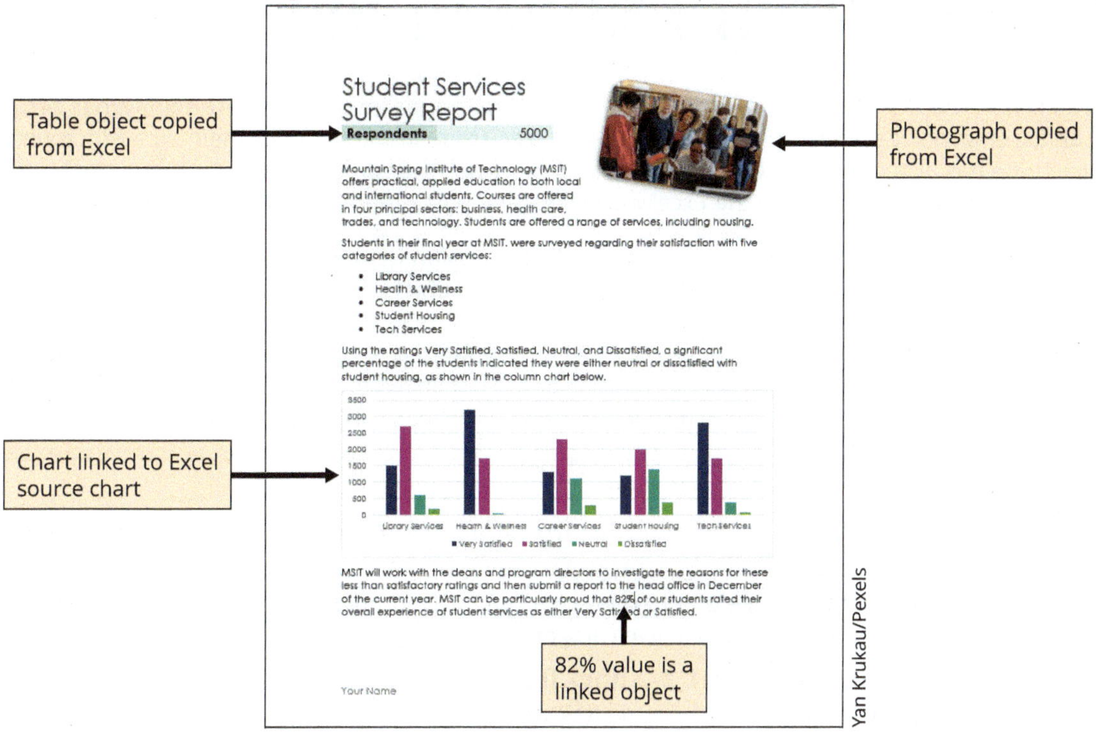

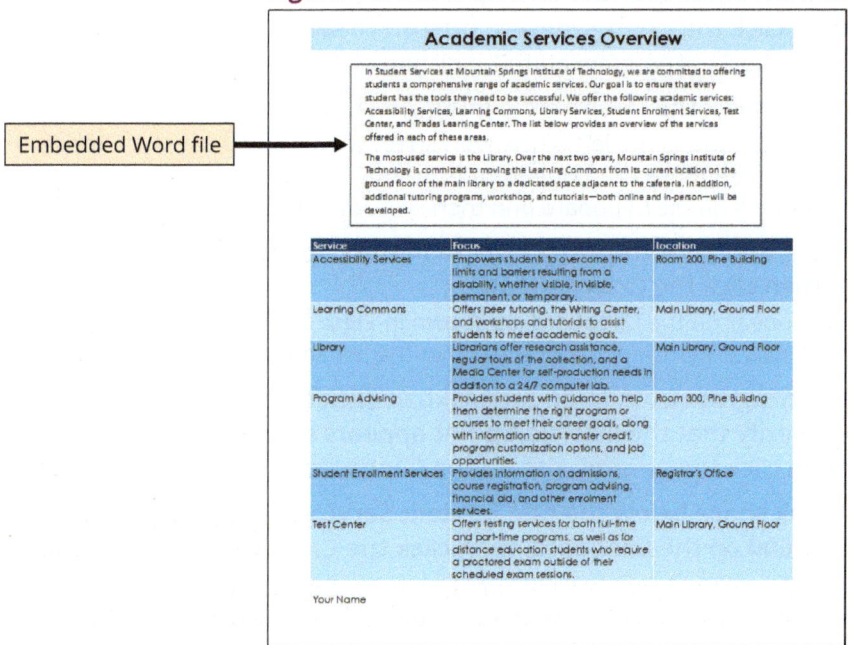

- Table object copied from Excel
- Photograph copied from Excel
- Chart linked to Excel source chart
- 82% value is a linked object

Figure 1-2: List of services with embedded Word file

- Embedded Word file

Understanding object linking and embedding (OLE)

The term **object linking and embedding (OLE)** refers to a technology that lets you share information among the Office programs. You create an object in one program, and then you can choose to either link the object to or embed it in another program. The difference between linking and embedding relates to where the object is stored and how you update the object after you place it in a document. A linked object in a destination file is an image of an object contained in a source file, not a copy of it. Both objects share a single source, which means you make changes to an object only in the source file.

When you embed an object you created in another program, you include a copy in a destination file. To update the object, you double-click it in the destination file and then use the tools of the source program to make changes. You cannot edit the source object using the tools of the destination program.

Module 1 Integrating Word and Excel

Copy Data from Excel to Word

Case Ariel Likowski, the Dean of Student Services at Mountain Springs Institute of Technology, has provided you with an Excel worksheet containing survey data gathered from students about their experience with Student Services. She has also created a report in Word that describes the survey results. To complete the report, she asks you to copy two objects from the Excel worksheet and paste them into the Word report.

Objectives
- Switch between Word and Excel
- Copy objects to the clipboard
- Paste Excel objects into Word

You use the Copy and Paste commands to copy an item from one program to another. The item might be a line of text, a selection of cells, or an object such as a chart or a picture. The procedure is the same as the one you use to copy and paste an object from one location in a document to another location in the same document. By default, an object copied from one program to another retains the original object's formatting and is not linked to the original object. The exception occurs when you copy and paste a chart, which you will learn about in the next lesson.

Steps

1. Start Excel, open **IL_INT_1-1.xlsx** from the location where you store your Data Files, then save it as **IL_INT_1_StudentSurveyResults**
   The values in the range B7:F10 represent the total number of responses in each of the four rating levels for student services in five categories.

2. Start Word, open **IL_INT_1-2.docx** from the location where you store your Data Files, then save it as **IL_INT_1_StudentSurveyReport**
   The Word report contains text that describes the results of the survey.

3. Move the mouse pointer over the **Excel program button** on the taskbar, as shown in **Figure 1-3**, then click the **Excel program button** to switch to Excel
   When you point to the Excel program button, a picture of the worksheet and the filename appear.

Trouble
If items already appear in the Clipboard pane, click Clear All.

4. On the Home tab, click the **Clipboard Dialog Box Launcher**
   The Clipboard pane opens to the left of the worksheet window. You use the Clipboard when you want to copy and paste more than one item from one program to another program. You can "collect" up to 24 items on the Clipboard and then switch to the other program to paste them.

5. Click the photograph, click the **Copy button** in the Clipboard group, select the range **A4:B4**, then click the **Copy button**
   Both items now appear on the Clipboard, as shown in **Figure 1-4**. When you place multiple items on the Clipboard, newer items appear at the top of the list and older items move down.

6. Click the **Word program button** on the taskbar, click the **Clipboard Dialog Box Launcher**, verify that the insertion point appears to the left of the title in the document, then click the photograph on the Clipboard

7. Click in the blank space below the title Student Services Survey Report, click **Respondents 5000** on the Clipboard, then click the **Close button** on the Clipboard pane
   You pasted the object as a table below the document title. When you use the Copy and Paste commands, the default setting is for the copied object to retain the formatting applied to it in the source file.

Trouble
If the alignment guides are not showing, click the Align button in the Arrange group, then click Use Alignment Guides. Don't worry if the text wraps slightly differently in your document.

8. Click the photograph in the Word document, set its height at 1.5" and its width to 2.41", click the **Layout Options button** in the upper-right corner of the photograph, click the **Square option**, close the Layout Options window, then drag the photograph to the right of the first paragraph using the green alignment guides, as shown in **Figure 1-5**

9. Click anywhere in the document to deselect the photograph, then save the document

Copy Data from Excel to Word INT 1-5

Figure 1-3: Word and Excel on the taskbar

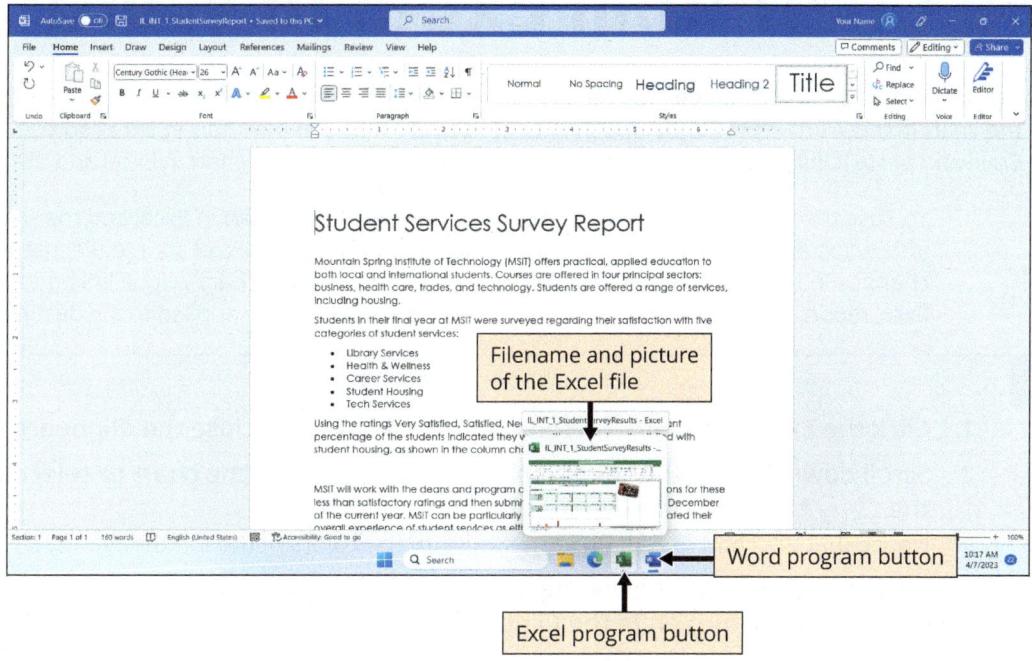

Figure 1-4: Two items collected on the Clipboard

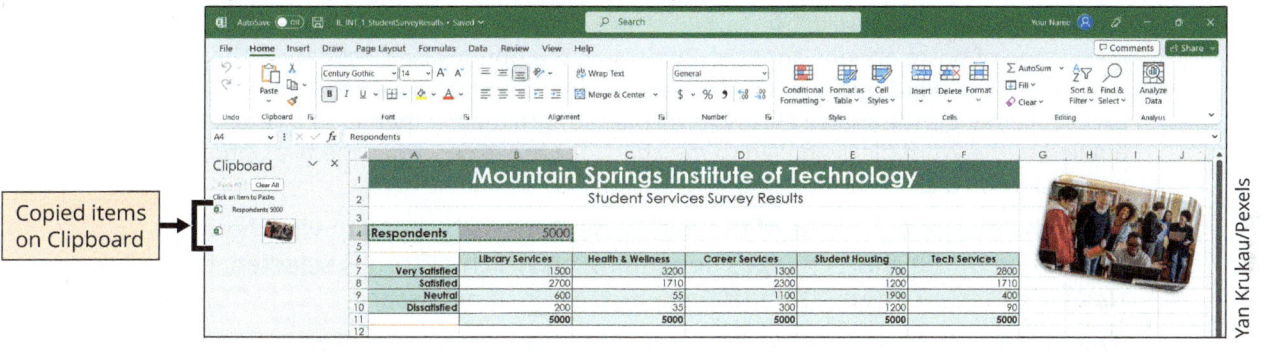

Figure 1-5: Picture positioned in the Word report

Module 1 Integrating Word and Excel

Copy a Chart from Excel to Word

Case You need the Word report to include a column chart representing survey results that are created in Excel. You want the chart in the Word report to be updated if changes are made to the chart in Excel, so you copy the chart from Excel and paste it into Word. By so doing, you create a link between the chart in Excel and the chart in Word.

Objectives
- Copy a chart
- Identify Paste options
- Update a linked chart

You use the Copy and Paste tools to create a link between a chart in Excel and the same chart pasted into a document in Word. When you change the data in the Excel source file, the linked data also changes in the Word destination file. By default, the copied chart will be linked to the chart in the Excel report. However, it will be formatted with the same theme applied to the destination document.

Steps

1. **Click the Excel program button on the taskbar, then close the Clipboard pane**

2. **Scroll down to view the column chart, click an edge of the chart to select it, then click the Copy button in the Clipboard group**
   Notice that the chart in Excel is formatted with the colors of the Ion theme.

3. **Switch to Word, click below the paragraph (that ends with "column chart below."), then click the Paste button in the Clipboard group**
   The chart appears in the Word document formatted with the colors of the Slice theme because this theme was already applied to the Word document. The Paste Options button appears in the lower-right corner of the chart.

4. **Click the Paste Options button (Ctrl) outside the lower-right corner of the pasted chart, as shown in Figure 1-6**
   A selection of paste options appears. By default, the option Use Destination Theme & Link Data is selected. The Word document is the destination file and is formatted with the Slice theme. The Excel document is the source file and is formatted with the Ion theme. As a result, the Slice theme applied to the Word file is applied to the chart. Table 1-1 describes the five options available for pasting a copied chart.

5. **Move the mouse over each of the five Paste Options buttons to view how the formatting of the chart changes depending on which button is selected, then click the Use Destination Theme & Link Data button if necessary**

6. **Switch to Excel, then note the position of the bars for the Student Housing category in the column chart**
   At present, the Dissatisfied column (green) is quite high compared to the Dissatisfied columns for the other categories.

7. **Scroll up, click cell E8, type 2000, press ENTER, click cell E10, type 400, then press ENTER and scroll down to the chart**
   In the chart, the Satisfied column (orange) in the Student Housing category has grown, and the Dissatisfied column (green) has shrunk.

Trouble
If the chart did not update, click the chart, click the Chart Design tab, then click the Refresh Data button in the Data group.

8. **Switch to Word, then verify that the bars for the Student Housing category have changed**
   As shown in Figure 1-7, the bars for the Student Housing category in the column chart change in the linked chart to reflect the changes you made to the chart in Excel.

9. **Save the document, switch to Excel, then save the workbook**

Figure 1-6: Paste Options

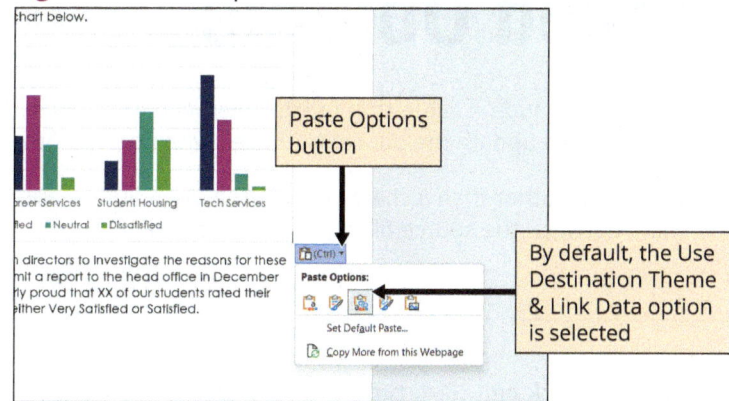

Figure 1-7: Linked chart updated in Word

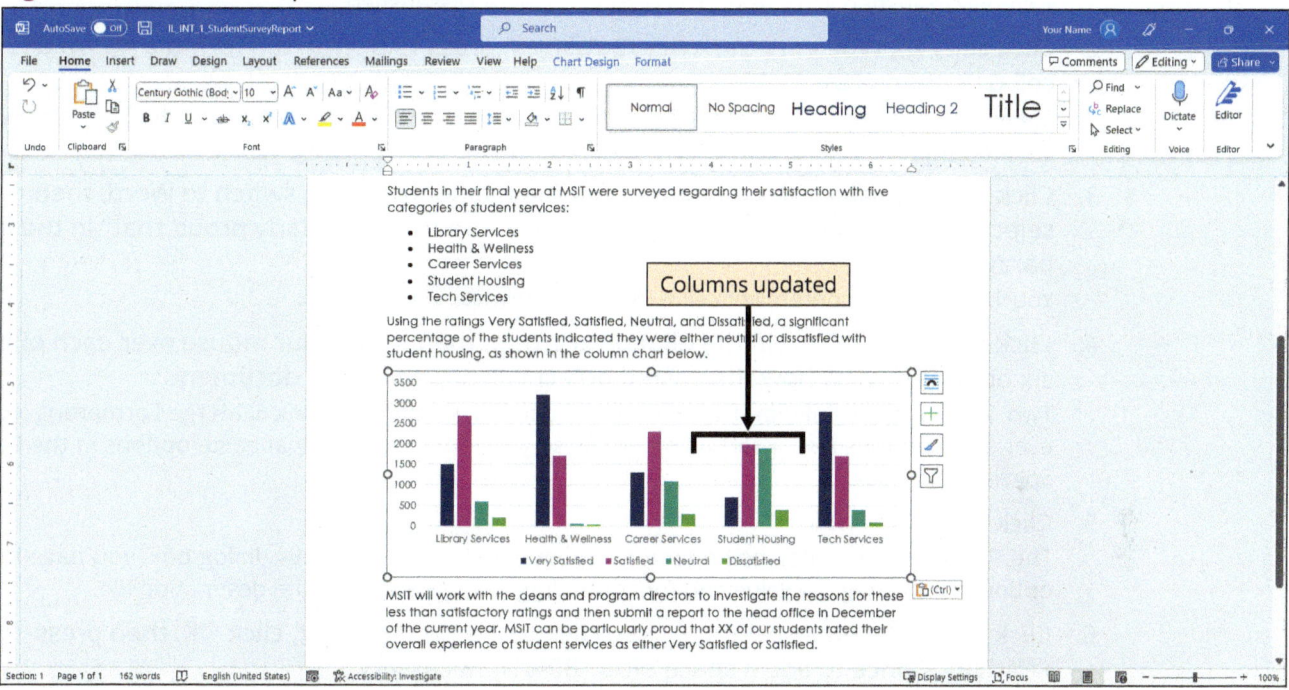

Table 1-1: Paste options for charts

Paste Options button	button name	description
	Use Destination Theme & Embed Workbook	The pasted chart is not linked to the source document, and the pasted chart assumes the formatting of the destination document
	Keep Source Formatting & Embed Workbook	The pasted chart is not linked to the source document, and the pasted chart keeps the same formatting as the source document
	Use Destination Theme & Link Data	This button is selected by default when a chart is pasted into the destination document; the theme of the destination document is applied to the chart, and the chart is linked to the object in the source document
	Keep Source Formatting & Link Data	The pasted chart is linked to the source document, so any changes made to the chart in the source document will be made to the copied chart in the Word document; in addition, the formatting of the source document is retained
	Picture	The chart is pasted as a picture that cannot be modified and uses the same formatting as the chart in the source document

Insert Linked Objects

Case You need the report to include a value that represents average ratings. You decide to link the report to the source file data so you can update the data in both files when new information becomes available.

Objectives
- Use Paste Special to insert a link
- Update a linked object

To link data other than a chart, you use the Copy button and the Paste Special command to create a link between the source file and the destination file.

Steps

1. In Excel, click cell **G14**, type the formula **=AVERAGE(B14:F14)**, press **ENTER**, click cell **G14**, then drag its fill handle to cell **G17** to enter the remaining three percentages
   The value "38%" appears in cell G14. This value indicates that, on average, 38% of the responses were Very Satisfied. Only 4% of the responses were Dissatisfied.

2. Click cell **F18**, type **Very Satisfied/Satisfied**, press **TAB**, type the formula **=G14+G15** in cell G18, then press **ENTER**
   The value "80%" appears in cell G18, indicating that 80% of students rated their experience with student services as Satisfied or Very Satisfied.

3. Click cell **G18**, click the **Copy button** in the Clipboard group, switch to Word, then select **XX** that appears following the phrase "can be particularly proud that" in the last paragraph
   You will paste the contents of cell G18 from Excel over "XX" in Word.

4. Click the **Paste arrow** in the Clipboard group, then move your mouse over each of the six options to view how the pasted object will appear in the document
   Two options allow linking—Link & Keep Source Formatting and Link & Merge Formatting. However, both options also insert a line break, so you look for additional paste options in the Paste Special dialog box.

5. Click **Paste Special**
   The Paste Special dialog box opens, as shown in **Figure 1-8**. In this dialog box, you have more options for pasting the value and for controlling its appearance in the destination file.

6. Click the **Paste link option button**, click **Unformatted Text**, click **OK**, then press **SPACEBAR** once to add a space after "80%" if necessary
   The percentage, 80%, appears in the Word document. You decide to test the link.

7. Switch to Excel, click cell **E7**, type **1200**, press **ENTER**, click cell **E9**, type **1400**, then press **ENTER**
   The Satisfied/Very Satisfied rating in cell G18 is now 82%.

8. Switch to Word, right-click **80%**, then click **Update Link**
   The value 82% appears. The final document is shown in **Figure 1-9**.

Trouble
If your document doesn't fit on one page, adjust the top and bottom margins as needed.

9. **sam↑** Type your name where indicated in the Word footer, save the document, switch to Excel, type your name where indicated in cell A43, save the workbook, submit your files to your instructor, then close the files
   If you print the Excel workbook, make sure you fit it on one page.

Figure 1-8: Paste Special dialog box

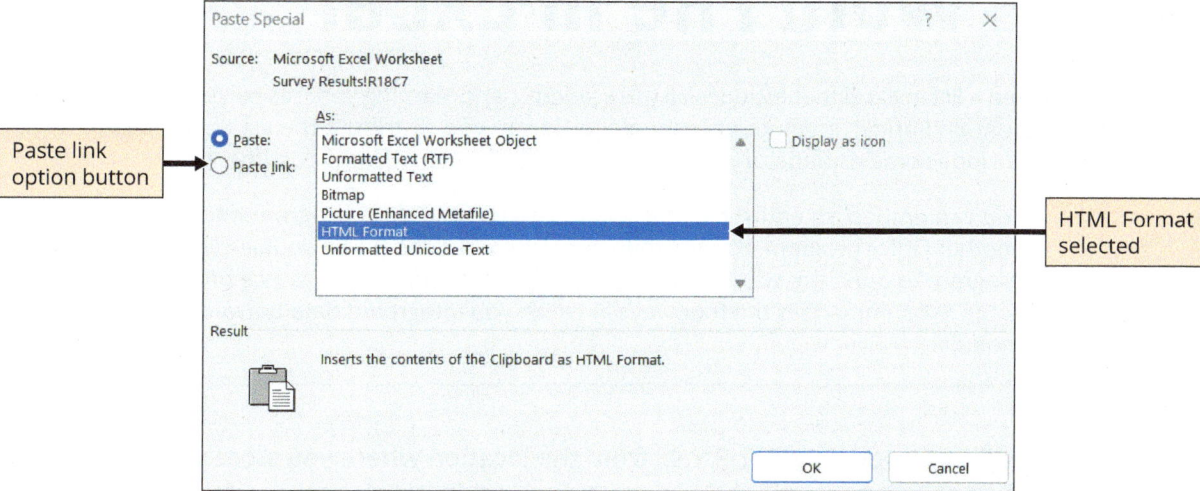

Figure 1-9: Completed report

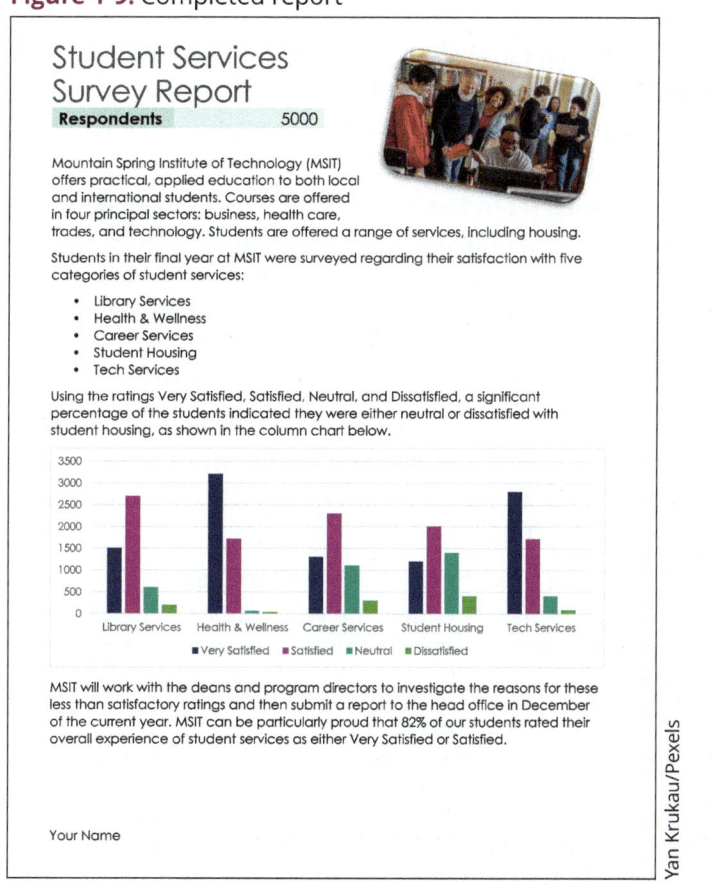

Opening linked files and reestablishing links to charts

When you open a Word file that contains links from an Excel file, a dialog box opens with a message telling you that the document contains links that may refer to other files. The message also asks if you want to update this document with the data from the linked file. Click Yes to update the document with data from the linked file. If you want to change information in both the Excel file and the Word file, you need to open the Excel workbook first, followed by the Word document.

If you make a change to a linked chart in the Excel file, you need to refresh the chart data in Word. To do so, click the chart in Word, click the Chart Design tab, then click the Refresh Data button in the Data group. You also need to manually update any other links by right-clicking the link in Word and then clicking Update Link.

Embed a Word File in Excel

Case You have created a list in Excel that includes all the academic and learning services currently offered by Student Services at Mountain Springs Institute of Technology. Before you distribute the list at an upcoming meeting, you decide to include some explanatory text that you have stored in a Word document.

Objectives
- Insert a Word file as an object
- Edit the Word file in Excel

You can embed an entire file that you create in one Office program into a document created in another Office program. You can then edit the embedded file by double-clicking it in the destination program to open the source program. You use the tools of the source program to make changes. **Table 1-2** summarizes the four ways in which you integrated data between Word and Excel in this module.

Steps

1. In Excel, open **IL_INT_1-3.xlsx** from the location where you store your Data Files, then save it as **IL_INT_1_AcademicServices**; in Word, open **IL_INT_1-4.docx** from the location where you store your Data Files, save it as **IL_INT_1_Overview**, then close the document

2. In Excel, click cell **E3**, click the **Insert tab**, click the **Text button** to display the selection of Text objects, if necessary, then click the **Object button**
   The Object dialog box opens. Here you can choose to either create a new object or insert an object from a file.

3. Click the **Create from File tab**, click **Browse**, navigate to where you stored the **IL_INT_1_Overview** file if necessary, double-click **IL_INT_1_Overview**, then click **OK**
   The text from the Word document appears in a box that starts in cell E3. When you insert an object from another program such as Word, you sometimes need to reposition the current worksheet contents to accommodate the inserted object.

4. Select the range **A4:C10**, move the mouse pointer over any border of the selection to show the pointer, then drag the selection down to cell **A17**

5. Move the mouse pointer over the border of the box containing the Word text to show the pointer, drag the selection to cell **A3**, click a blank cell, then compare your screen to **Figure 1-10**

6. Double-click the box containing the Word text
   Because the object is embedded, the Word ribbon and tabs appear within the Excel window. As a result, you can use the tools from the source program (Word) to edit the text.

   Trouble
   If your embedded Word document opens in a separate window, proceed with the steps, and at the end of Step 8, close the Word window.

7. Click the **Select button** in the Editing group, click **Select All**, click the **Dialog Box Launcher** in the Paragraph group, select the contents of the Left box in the Indentation section, type **.2**, press **TAB**, type **.2** in the Right box, then click **OK**

8. Select **Learning Commons** in paragraph 2, type **Library**, compare the edited object to **Figure 1-11**, then click outside the object to return to Excel
   The embedded object is updated in Excel. The text in the source file is not updated because the source file is not linked to the destination file.

9. Click the **File tab**, click **Print**, click **No Scaling**, click **Fit Sheet on One Page**, then click to return to the workbook
   The embedded Word object and Excel data fit on one page.

10. Type your name where indicated in cell **A25**, save the workbook, submit your files to your instructor, then close the workbook and close Word and Excel

Embed a Word File in Excel INT 1-11

Figure 1-10: Embedded Word file positioned in Excel

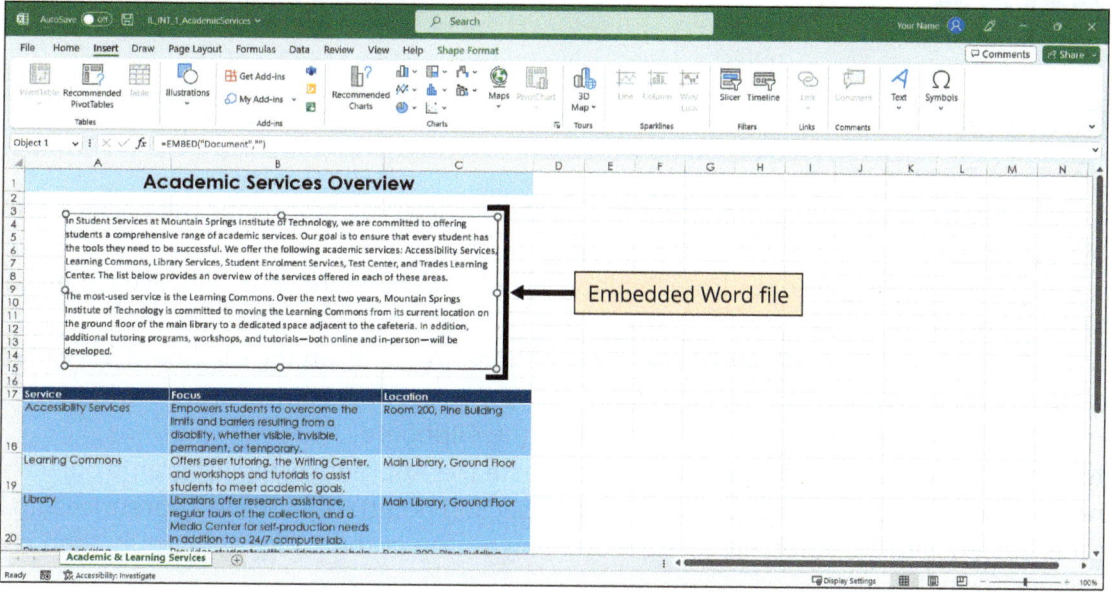

Figure 1-11: Embedded object updated in Excel

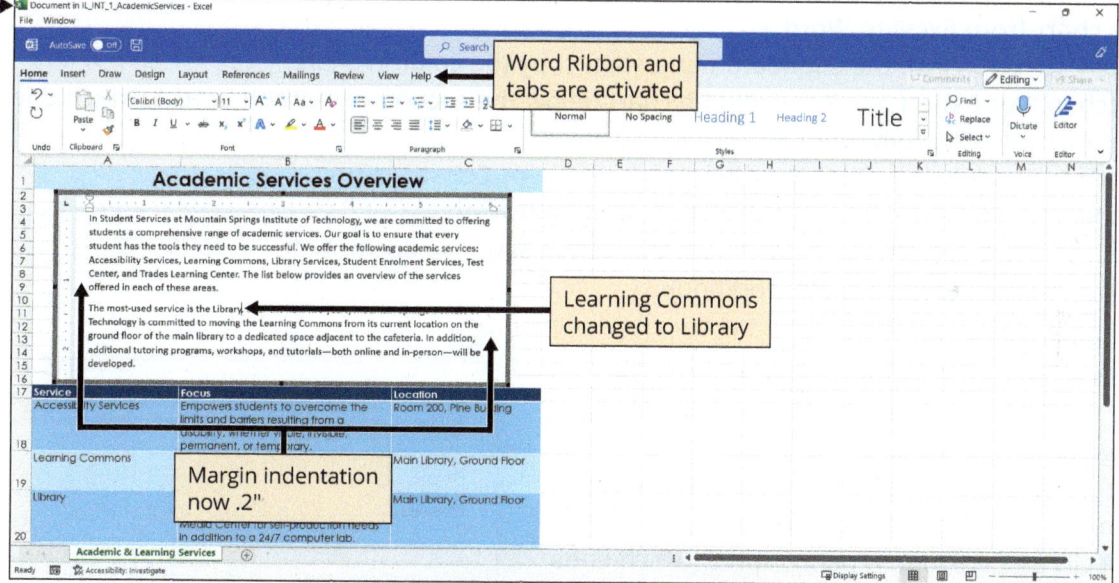

Table 1-2: Module 1 integration tasks

Object	command	source program	destination program	result	connection	page no.
Cells	Copy/Paste	Excel	Word	Object with Excel formatting	Pasted: no link	4
Chart	Copy/Paste	Excel	Word	Object with Word formatting	Linked	6
Cell	Copy/Paste Special/ Paste link	Excel	Word	Formatting varies depending on the formatting option chosen in the Paste Special dialog box	Linked	8
File	Insert/ Object/ Create from File	Word	Excel	Text box containing the Word file: to update, double-click and use Word tools within the Excel destination file	Embedded: no link	10

Practice

Skills Review

1. **Copy data from Excel to Word.**
   a. Start Excel, open the IL_INT_1-5.xlsx from the location where you store your Data Files, then save it as **IL_INT_1_ApprenticeshipData**.
   b. Start Word, open IL_INT_1-6.docx from the location where you store your Data Files, then save it as **IL_INT_1_ApprenticeshipReport**.
   c. Switch to Excel, open the Clipboard pane, then, if there are items on the Clipboard, click Clear All.
   d. Copy the contents of cell A1 to the Clipboard.
   e. Select the range A4:A7, then copy the contents to the Clipboard.
   f. Switch to Word, open the Clipboard pane, then paste the Apprenticeship Programs object at the top of the document (at the current position of the insertion point). **Hint**: If the Apprenticeship Programs object is pasted with a colored fill, click the Shading button in the Paragraph group, then click No Color.
   g. Paste the list of programs on the blank line below the first paragraph.
   h. Close the Clipboard pane, then save the document.

2. **Copy a chart from Excel to Word.**
   a. Switch to Excel, close the Clipboard pane, then copy the column chart.
   b. Switch to Word, then paste the column chart below the second paragraph of text (which ends with "in New York and Pennsylvania").
   c. Switch to Excel, then note the position of the bars for Construction.
   d. Change the value in cell C6 to **15800**, then switch to Word.
   e. Click the chart, refresh the data, if necessary, then save the document.
   f. Switch to Excel, then save the workbook.

3. **Insert linked objects.**
   a. In Excel, enter the formula **=B4-C4** in cell D4.
   b. Use the Fill handle to copy the formula to the range D5:D7.
   c. Select the range A3:D7, copy it, switch to Word, then use the Paste Special command to paste the cells as a link below paragraph 3 (which ends with "...to those in Pennsylvania"), using the Formatted Text (RTF) selection in the Paste Special dialog box.
   d. In Excel, copy cell D4, switch to Word, then use Paste Special to paste the cell over "XX" in the last paragraph as a link using the Unformatted Text option in the Paste Special dialog box. Add a space after the linked object if necessary.
   e. In Excel, change the value in cell B4 to **18000**.
   f. In Word, refresh the chart if necessary.
   g. Update the link in the table so "18000" appears below "New York" and in the last paragraph so that "6710" appears.
   h. Enter your name where indicated in the footer in Word, compare your document to **Figure 1-12**

Figure 1-12

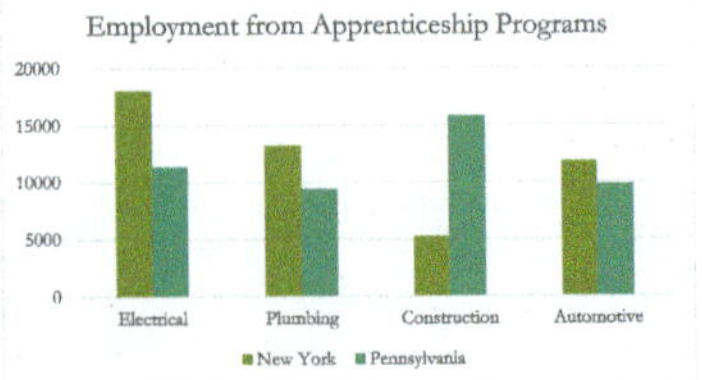

Apprenticeship Programs
The New York Trade Association initiated an Assessment of Apprenticeship Programs to assess and report upon the employment success of students enrolled in apprenticeship programs throughout the state. The following four program areas were assessed:

Electrical
Plumbing
Construction
Automotive

Most of the students enrolled in apprenticeship programs found employment within six months of leaving, except for students who graduated from construction programs. The column chart below compares employment numbers from comparable programs in New York and Pennsylvania.

The following table compares the number of students employed following their apprenticeship in New York to those in Pennsylvania.

Program	New York	Pennsylvania	Difference
Electrical	18000	11290	6710
Plumbing	13200	9300	3900
Construction	5200	15800	-10600
Automotive	11800	9700	2100

The employment of apprentices in New York in all areas except Construction is consistently higher; however, only the employment number for Electrical is significantly higher—by 6710 jobs.

Your Name

and adjust spacing if necessary, save the Word report, submit your file to your instructor, then close the document.

i. In Excel, enter your name in cell A26, save the workbook, submit the file to your instructor, then close the workbook.

4. **Embed a Word file in Excel.**
   a. In Excel, open IL_INT_1-7.xlsx from the location where you store your Data Files, then save it as **IL_INT_1_ApprenticeshipProgramRevenue**.
   b. In Word, open IL_INT_1-8.docx from the location where you store your Data Files, save it as **IL_INT_1_ApprenticeshipPrograms**, then close it.
   c. In Excel, in cell H4, insert the Word file IL_INT_1_ApprenticeshipPrograms.docx as an embedded file.
   d. Select the range A6:E15, then move it to cell A14.
   e. Position the box containing the Word text so its upper-left corner is in cell A4.
   f. Change "XX" to **$740** in the paragraph, then change "ZZ" in paragraph 1 to **80%**.
   g. Click outside the embedded object to return to Excel, adjust the width of the embedded file so its right edge is even with column E if necessary, compare your screen to **Figure 1-13**, enter your name in cell A23, save the workbook, submit the file to your instructor, then close the workbook and close Word and Excel.

Figure 1-13

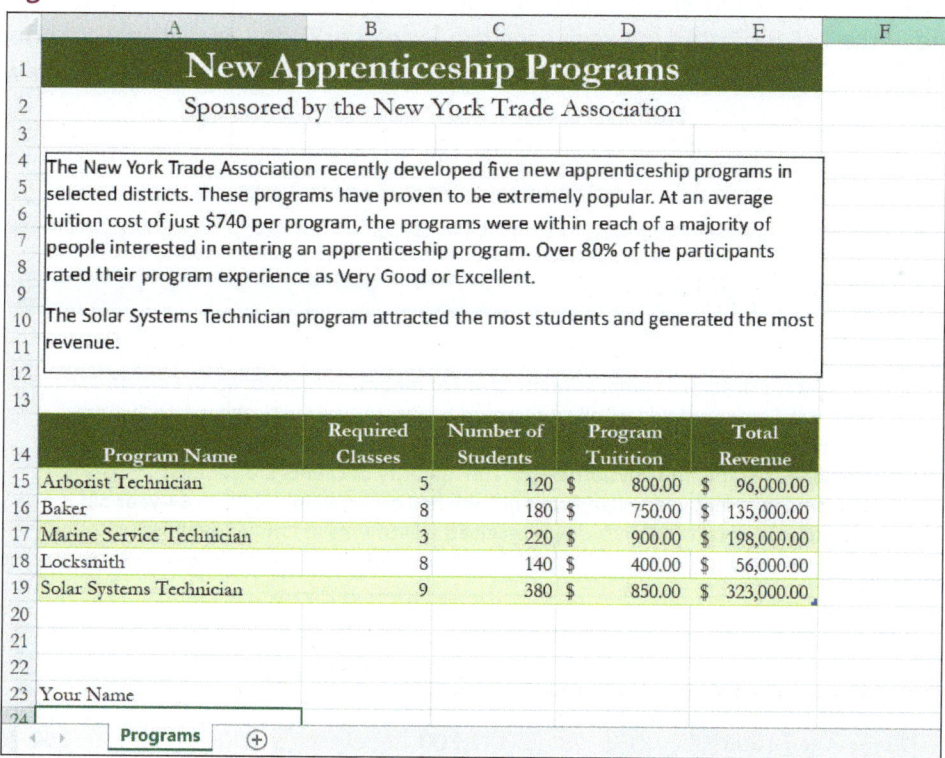

Independent Challenge 1

You assist the office manager at Canyon Wellness Center, a neighborhood facility that provides health and wellness treatments to clients in the community. You've been asked to compile data about the services provided at the Canyon Wellness Center to include in an Excel workbook you'll share at an upcoming meeting of management staff. You want to include text in the workbook that you have stored in a Word document.

a. Start Excel, open IL_INT_1-9.xlsx from the location where you store your Data Files, then save it as **IL_INT_1_CanyonServices**.

b. Start Word, open IL_INT_1-10.docx from the location where you store your Data Files, save it as **IL_INT_1_CanyonClients**, then close it.

c. In a blank area of the Excel worksheet, insert the Canyon Clients file as an embedded object.

d. Adjust the positions of the Excel data and the box containing the Word text so the Word text appears above the Excel data and below the title.

e. In Excel, calculate the total number of treatments provided for Nutrition Services, Massage Therapy, and Physiotherapy in the appropriate cells.

f. In the last row of the table, enter **Total Clients** and right-align it, and then in the next cell, enter a formula to calculate the total number of clients served in all three served categories (Nutrition Services, Massage Therapy, and Physiotherapy).

g. Replace XX in the embedded Word document with the value representing the total number of clients. Indent the text by .2" from the left and right margins.

h. Enter your name in the cell indicated in Excel, save the Excel workbook, view the workbook in Print Preview, and compare it to **Figure 1-14**, submit the file to your instructor, then close the workbook and close Excel.

Figure 1-14

Canyon Wellness Center

The highly skilled and compassionate team of medical professionals at Canyon Wellness Center provide wholly integrated health services with the motto "where wellness is a way of life." Services are offered in three categories: Nutrition, Massage Therapy, and Physiotherapy. The majority of clients are seniors; however, in recent years, significant growth has occurred in the 31 to 64-year old age group. A total of 37,190 clients received treatments at Canyon Wellness Center in the past year.

	Nutrition Services	Massage Therapy	Physiotherapy
Children Aged 0 to 12	300	100	50
Teens Aged 13 to 17	1,100	200	350
Young Adults Aged 18 to 30	2,000	400	890
Adults Aged 31 to 64	4,000	5,200	4,900
Seniors Over 65	5,200	6,300	6,200
Totals	12,600	12,200	12,390
Total Clients	37,190		

Your Name

Independent Challenge 2

As part of your work as an administrator at a Chamber of Commerce in Minnesota, you've been put in charge of organizing a networking event for local business owners. You have already written most of the text required for a proposal that you'll present at an upcoming meeting of Chamber of Commerce staff. Now you need to insert data from Excel that shows the budget items for the event.

a. Start Word, open IL_INT_1-11.docx from the location where you store your Data Files, save it as **IL_INT_1_NetworkingEventProposal**, start Excel, open IL_INT_1-12.xlsx from the location where you store your Data Files, then save it as **IL_INT_1_EventData**.

b. In Excel, open the Clipboard pane, clear all items if necessary, then copy the photograph and cell A1.

c. In Word, open the Clipboard pane, paste the photograph at the top of the Word document, change the text wrapping of the picture to Square, then position the photograph to the right of the first paragraph, keeping within the green guidelines.

d. Click to the left of "Proposal," then paste cell A1.

e. Copy the Networking Event Costs chart from Excel, then paste it into the appropriate area in the Word document.

f. In Excel, change the cost of the Venue Rental to **2,200**; then in Word, refresh the data in the chart if necessary. The Venue Rental slice (red in Word) should be 21%.

g. In cell B7 in Excel, enter a formula to sum the five budget costs, then copy the figure representing the total budget, switch to Word, select "XX" in the paragraph below the chart, view the paste options, then paste the value as a link using the Unformatted Text selection in the Paste Special dialog box. Add or remove a space if necessary.

h. In Excel, change the printing cost for the event to **$300**; then in Word, verify the Printing slice changed to 3% and the link in Word updated to $10,200.00.

i. Type your name in the Word footer, then save the Word document and Excel workbook, submit the files to your instructor, then close them. The completed Word document appears as shown in **Figure 1-15**.

Figure 1-15

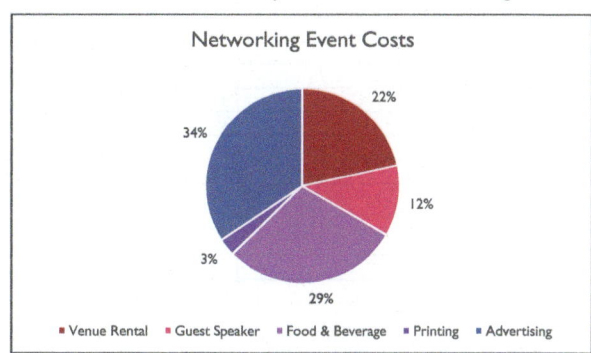

Visual Workshop

Using the Data Files IL_INT_1-13.xlsx and IL_INT_1-14.docx, create the price list shown in **Figure 1-16**. Use formulas to calculate the prices for 50 grams and 100 grams. Save the workbook as **IL_INT_1_RainCoastTeasPriceList**, and save the Word document as **IL_INT_1_RainCoastTeasInformation**. Embed the Word document into the Excel worksheet, position the inserted file and the price list in Excel as shown in **Figure 1-16**, then format the embedded Word object as shown in **Figure 1-16**. (Hint: The indentation on both sides of the text is .2, and the font size is 12 point.) Add your name to the Excel worksheet in the cell indicated, save all files, submit them to your instructor, then close all files.

Figure 1-16

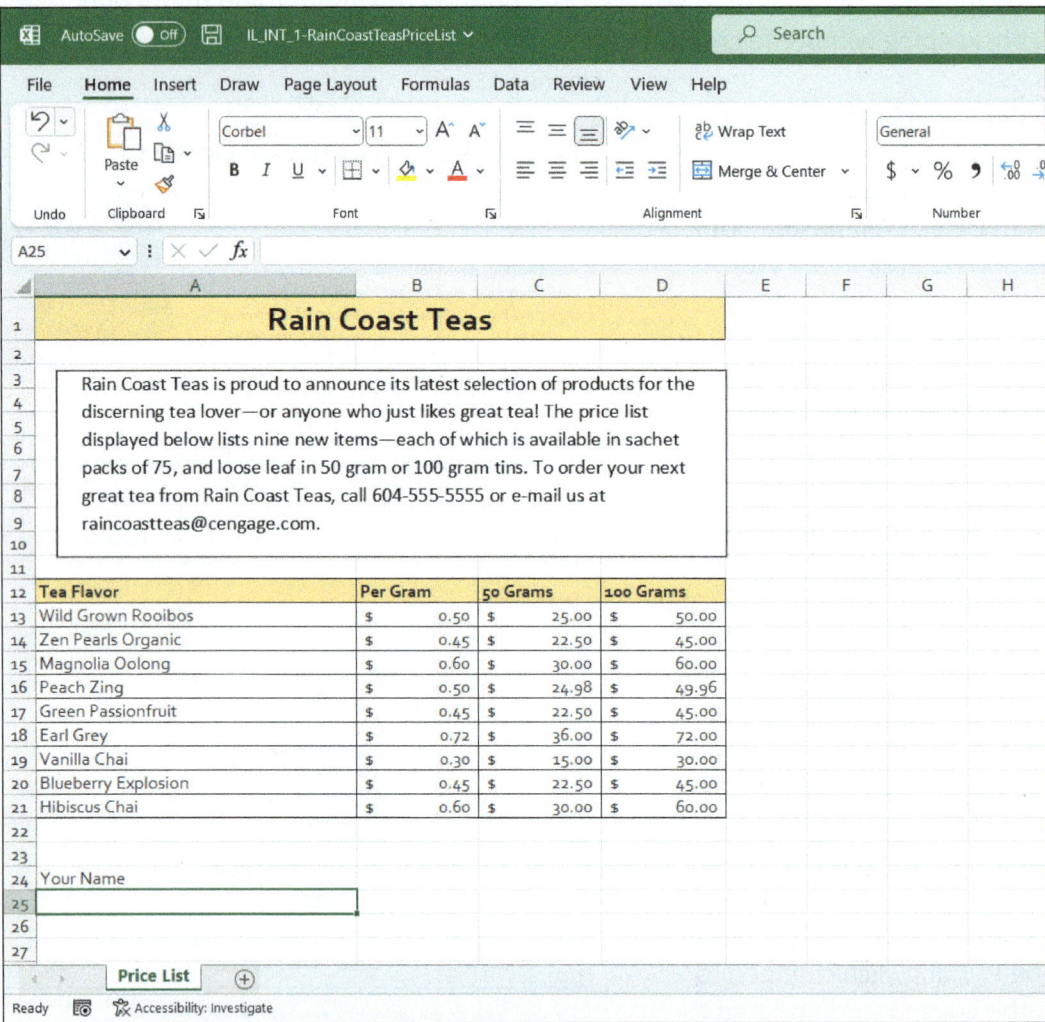

Access Module 1

Getting Started with Access

Case

Sasha Spiros is the special projects director for GIG Placement, a company that helps match employer short-term contract (gig) and full-time employment needs with people who have the required skill set. You will work with Sasha using Microsoft Access 365 to store, maintain, and analyze employment data.

Module Objectives

After completing this module, you will be able to:

- Describe relational databases
- Open and explore a database
- Navigate and enter data
- Edit existing data
- Create a table
- Modify fields
- Create a query
- Create a form
- Create a report
- Save and share a database with OneDrive
- Create a database
- Compact and back up a database

Files You Will Need

IL_AC_1-1.accdb
Support_AC_1_Employees.xlsx
IL_AC_1-2.accdb
Support_AC_1_StatesAndProvs.xlsx
IL_AC_1-3.accdb
IL_AC_1-4.accdb

Describe Relational Databases

Case Sasha has noticed that GIG Placement manages copies of several lists of data in Excel. She asks you to help her review the advantages of managing data in a relational database model that Access uses compared to the single-list spreadsheet approach that Excel uses.

Objectives
- Describe relational database concepts.
- Explain when to use a database.
- Compare a relational database to a spreadsheet.

Microsoft Access 365 is relational database software that runs on the Windows operating system. You use **relational database software** to manage data organized into lists, such as information about customers, products, vendors, employees, projects, or sales. Some companies track lists of information in a spreadsheet program such as Microsoft Excel. Although Excel offers some list management features, Access provides many more tools and advantages for managing data. Access uses a relational database model to manage data, whereas Excel manages data as a single list. **Table 1-1** compares the two programs.

Details

The advantages of using Access for database management include the following:

- **Duplicate data is minimized**
  Figures 1-1 and **1-2** compare how you might store data in a single list in an Excel spreadsheet versus managing the same data using multiple tables in an Access relational database. With Access, you enter company data only once no matter how many jobs the company offers.

- **Information is more accurate, reliable, and consistent because duplicate data is minimized**
  When data is not duplicated, it is more accurate, reliable, and consistent.

- **Data entry is faster and easier using Access forms**
  Data entry forms (screen layouts) make data entry faster, easier, and more accurate than entering data in a spreadsheet.

- **Information can be viewed and sorted in many ways using Access queries, forms, and reports**
  In Access, you can save queries (questions about the data), data entry forms, and reports, allowing users to view the same data in different ways.

- **Information is more secure using Access forms, passwords, and security features**
  Access databases can be encrypted and password protected. Forms can be created to protect and display only specific data.

- **Several users can share and edit information at the same time**
  More than one person can use an Access database at the same time. You do not need to have multiple independent copies of a database that need to be merged later. Having all users work on the same, single set of data at the same time is enormously accurate and reliable.

Describe Relational Databases   AC 1-3

Figure 1-1: Using a spreadsheet to organize data

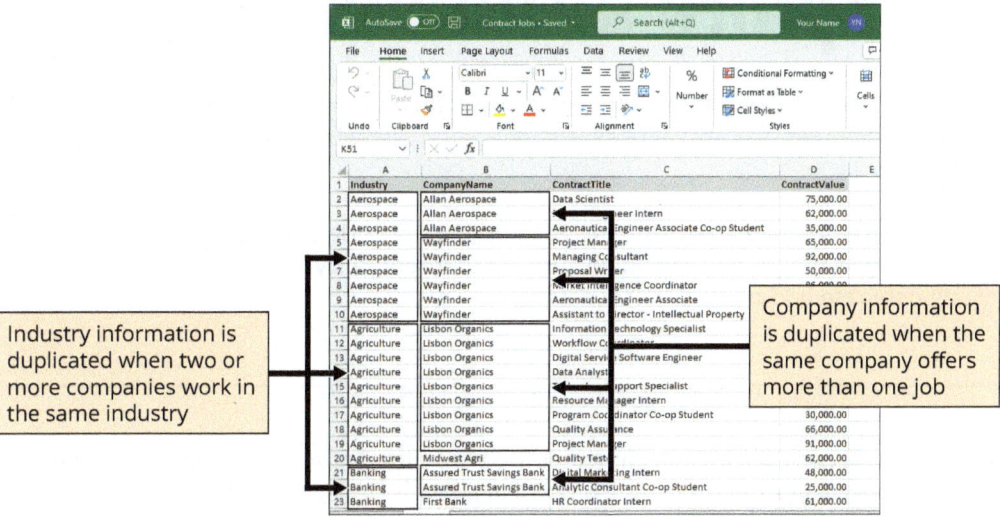

Industry information is duplicated when two or more companies work in the same industry

Company information is duplicated when the same company offers more than one job

Figure 1-2: Using a relational database to organize data

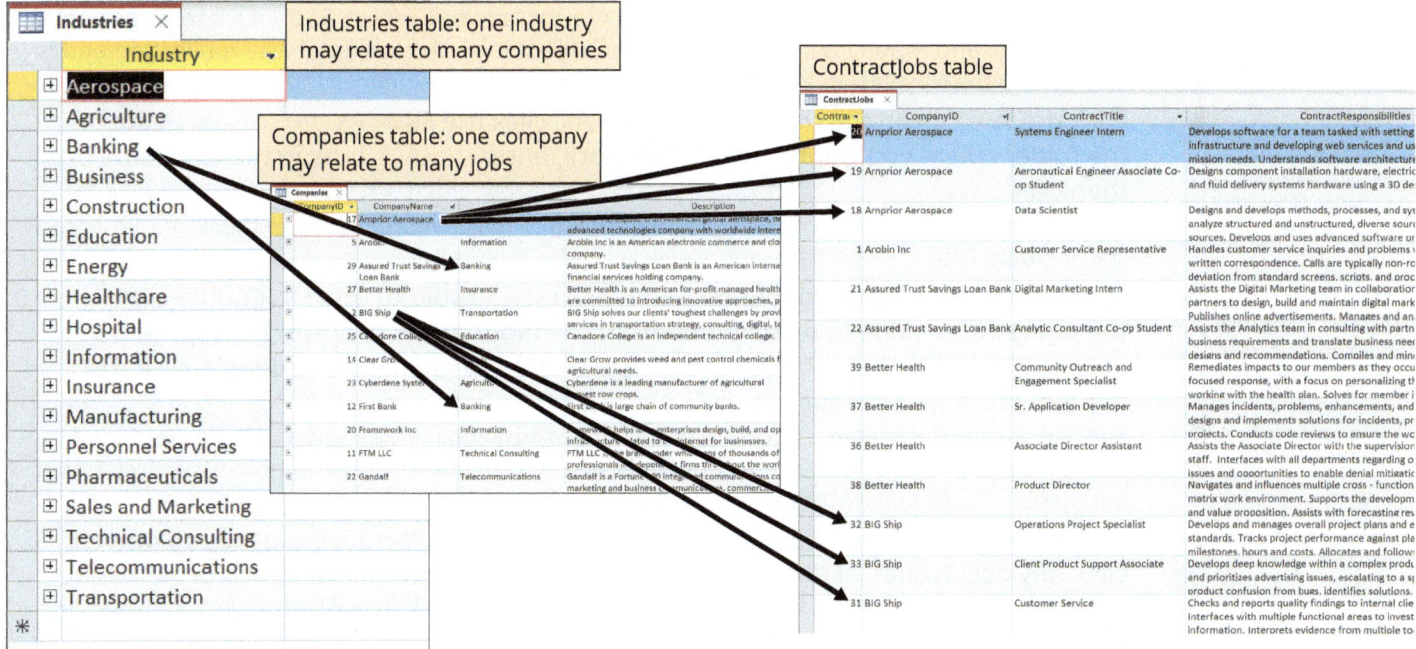

Industries table: one industry may relate to many companies

Companies table: one company may relate to many jobs

ContractJobs table

Table 1-1: Comparing Excel with Access

feature	Excel	Access
Data entry	Provides only one spreadsheet layout	Allows you to create an unlimited number of data entry forms
Storage	Restricted to a single file's limitations	Virtually unlimited when used with Microsoft SQL Server to store data
Data model	Manages single lists of information	Manages data in a relational database with related tables, which tremendously reduces data redundancy and improves data integrity
Reporting	Provides a printout of the spreadsheet	Allows you to create and save an unlimited number of reports that summarize and organize data in different ways
Security	Limited to file security options such as marking the file "read-only" or protecting a range of cells	When used with SQL Server, provides extensive security down to the user and data level
Multiuser capabilities	Limited to one user at a time	Allows multiple users to simultaneously enter and update data

Open and Explore a Database

Case Sasha has developed a research database containing information about previous job opportunities that GIG Placement has managed. She asks you to start Access 365 and review this database so you can help her maintain the data.

Objectives
- Start Access.
- Save a database.
- Identify object characteristics.

The fastest way to open an existing Access database is to double-click its file or shortcut icon. If you start Access on its own, a window appears that requires you to choose between opening an existing database and creating a new database.

Steps

1. **sam↓** Start Access, click **Open** in the left pane, click **Browse**, navigate to the location where you store your Data Files, double-click the **IL_AC_1-1.accdb database** to open it, then click the **Maximize button** ■ if the Access window is not already maximized

   The IL_AC_1-1 database contains four tables of data named Companies, ContractJobs, FullTimeJobs, and Industries. It also includes four queries, six forms, and one report. Each of these items (table, query, form, and report) is a different type of **object** in an Access database application and is displayed in the **Navigation Pane**. The purpose of each object is defined in **Table 1-2**.

   Trouble
   If a yellow Security Warning bar appears below the ribbon, click Enable Content.

2. Click the **File tab** on the ribbon, click **Save As**, click the **Save As button**, navigate to the folder where you want to save your work, enter **IL_AC_1_Jobs** in the File name box, then click **Save**

   If you need to redo the exercises, return to this step to make another copy of the IL_AC_1-1.accdb starting Data File.

   Trouble
   If the Navigation Pane is not open, click the Shutter Bar Open/Close button ‹‹ to open it and view the database objects.

3. In the Navigation Pane, double-click the **Industries table** to open it, double-click the **Companies table** to open it, note that the Industry for Arnprior Aerospace is Construction, double-click the **ContractJobs table** to open it, then double-click the **FullTimeJobs table** to open it

   The Industries, Companies, ContractJobs, and FullTimeJobs tables open in Datasheet View to display the data they store. An Access **table** is the fundamental building block of a relational database because tables store all the data.

4. In the Navigation Pane, double-click the **ContractJobsByIndustry query** to open it, click any occurrence of **Construction** in the Industry column for Arnprior Aerospace, click the **list arrow**, click **Aerospace** in the list, then click any other row, as shown in **Figure 1-3**

   An Access **query** selects a subset of data from one or more tables. Because the Industry field value for Arnprior Aerospace is stored only once in the Arnprior Aerospace record in the Companies table, changing one occurrence of that value in the query changes all records that select that company.

5. Double-click the **CompanyEntry form** in the Navigation Pane to open it, note that Arnprior Aerospace's Industry value is Aerospace, then click the **Next button** in the upper-right corner of the form two times

   An Access **form** is a data entry screen that often includes command buttons to make common tasks such as moving between records easy to perform. Forms are the most common way to enter and edit data. The change to Arnprior Aerospace's record in the form reflects the change you made to Arnprior Aerospace in the ContractJobsByIndustry query.

6. Double-click the **FullTimeJobsByHighestSalary report** in the Navigation Pane to open it

   An Access **report** is a professional printout that can be distributed electronically or on paper. The Aerospace update to Arnprior Aerospace carried through to the report, demonstrating the power and productivity of a relational database.

7. Click the **Close button** ✕ on each object tab except for the Companies table, notice that the Industry for Arnprior Aerospace is now set to Aerospace in the Companies table, then close it

   Changes to data are automatically saved as you work.

Figure 1-3: IL_AC_1_Jobs.accdb database

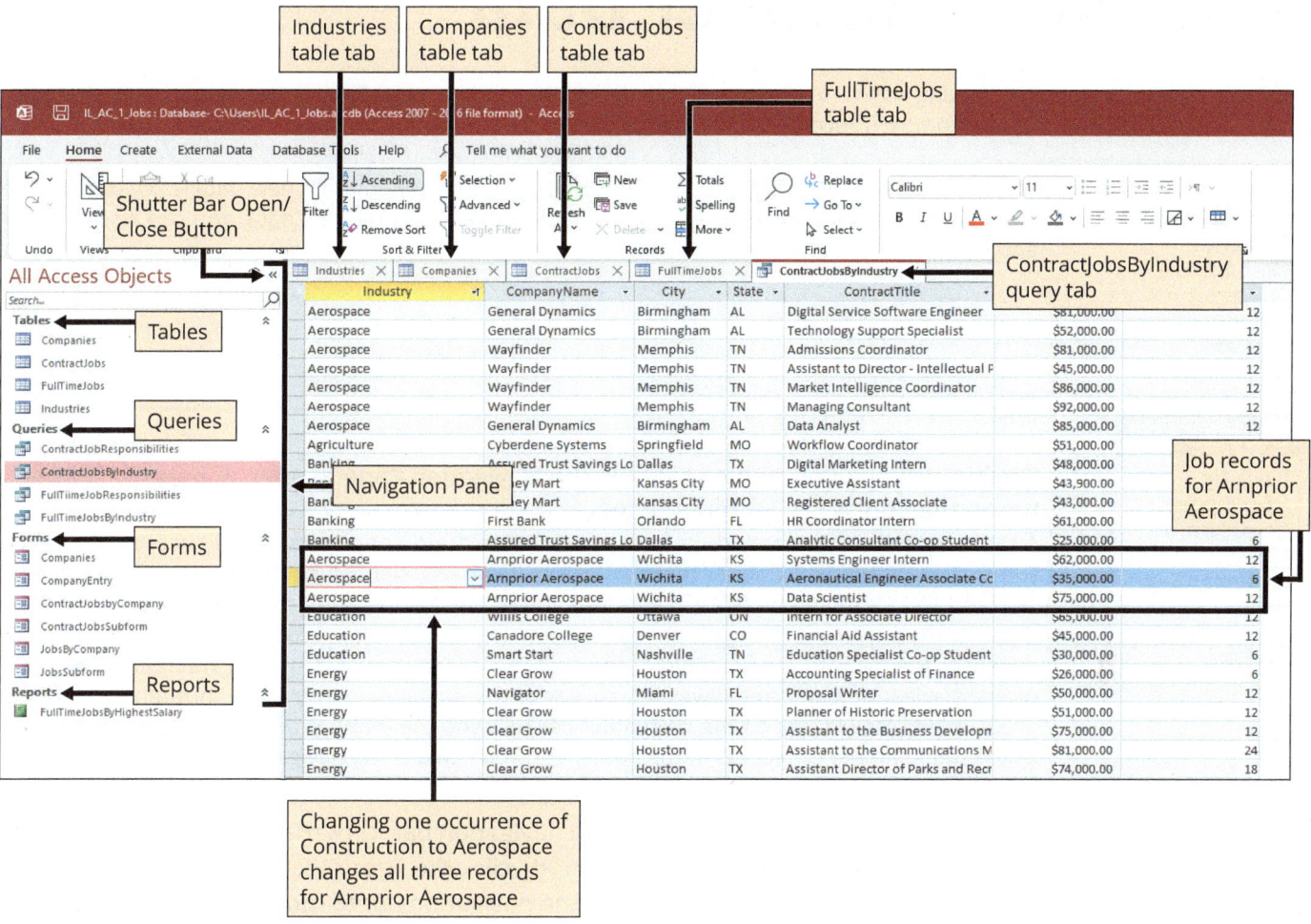

Table 1-2: Access objects and their purpose

object	icon	purpose
Table		Contains all the data in the database in a spreadsheet-like view called **Datasheet View**; tables are linked with a common field to create a relational database
Query		Allows you to select a subset of fields or records from one or more tables; create a query when you have a question about the data
Form		Provides an easy-to-use data entry screen
Report		Provides a professional presentation of data with headers, footers, graphics, and calculations on groups of records

Navigate and Enter Data

Case GIG Placement is working with a new company to help recruit candidates to fill their job openings. Sasha asks you to enter the new company record into the Companies table.

Objectives
- Navigate records in a datasheet.
- Enter records in a datasheet.
- Define essential database terminology.

Your skill in navigating through the database and accurately entering new data is key to your success. While the form object is the primary object used to enter new data, you can also navigate and enter data directly in a table datasheet.

Steps

Quick Tip
Access databases are **multiuser**, which means that more than one person can enter and edit data in the same database at the same time.

▶ 1. **Double-click the Companies table in the Navigation Pane to open it, press TAB three times, then press ENTER three times**

A table datasheet presents data in columns called **fields** and rows called **records**. **Table 1-3** summarizes essential database terminology. As you navigate through the records, note that both TAB and ENTER move the focus to the next field. The **focus** refers to the data you would edit if you started typing. When you navigate to the last field of the record, pressing TAB or ENTER advances the focus to the first field of the next record. You can also use the **navigation buttons** on the navigation bar in the lower-left corner of the datasheet to navigate through the records. The **Current record box** on the navigation bar tells you the number of the current record as well as the total number of records in the datasheet. You can use the navigation bar to practice record navigation.

2. **Click the Next record button ▶ on the navigation bar, click the Previous record button ◀, click the Last record button ▶|, click the First record button |◀, then click the New (blank) record button ▶* on the navigation bar to move to a new record**

You navigate to and enter new records at the end of the datasheet. A complete list of navigation keystrokes is shown in **Table 1-4**.

Quick Tip
Press TAB in the CompanyID AutoNumber field.

▶ 3. **At the end of the datasheet, enter the new record, as shown in Figure 1-4, using Jara Group as the CompanyName, Information as the Industry, Jara provides data science services including modeling and machine learning. as the Description, Chicago as the City, and IL as the State**

The **edit record symbol** 🖉 appears to the left of the record you are currently editing. When you move to a different record, Access automatically saves the data.

Your CompanyID value might differ from the one in **Figure 1-4**. The CompanyID field is an **AutoNumber** field, which means that Access automatically enters the next consecutive number into the field as it creates the record. If you delete a record or are interrupted when entering a record, Access discards the value in the AutoNumber field and does not reuse it. Therefore, AutoNumber values do not represent the number of records in your table. Instead, they only provide a unique value per record.

Changing from Navigation mode to Edit mode

If you navigate to another area of the datasheet by clicking with the mouse pointer instead of pressing TAB or ENTER, you change from Navigation mode to Edit mode. In Edit mode, Access assumes that you are making changes to the current field value, so keystrokes such as CTRL+END, CTRL+HOME, ←, and → move the insertion point within the field. To return to Navigation mode, press TAB or ENTER (which moves the focus to the next field), or press ↑ or ↓ (which moves the focus to a different record).

Figure 1-4: Adding a new record to the Companies table

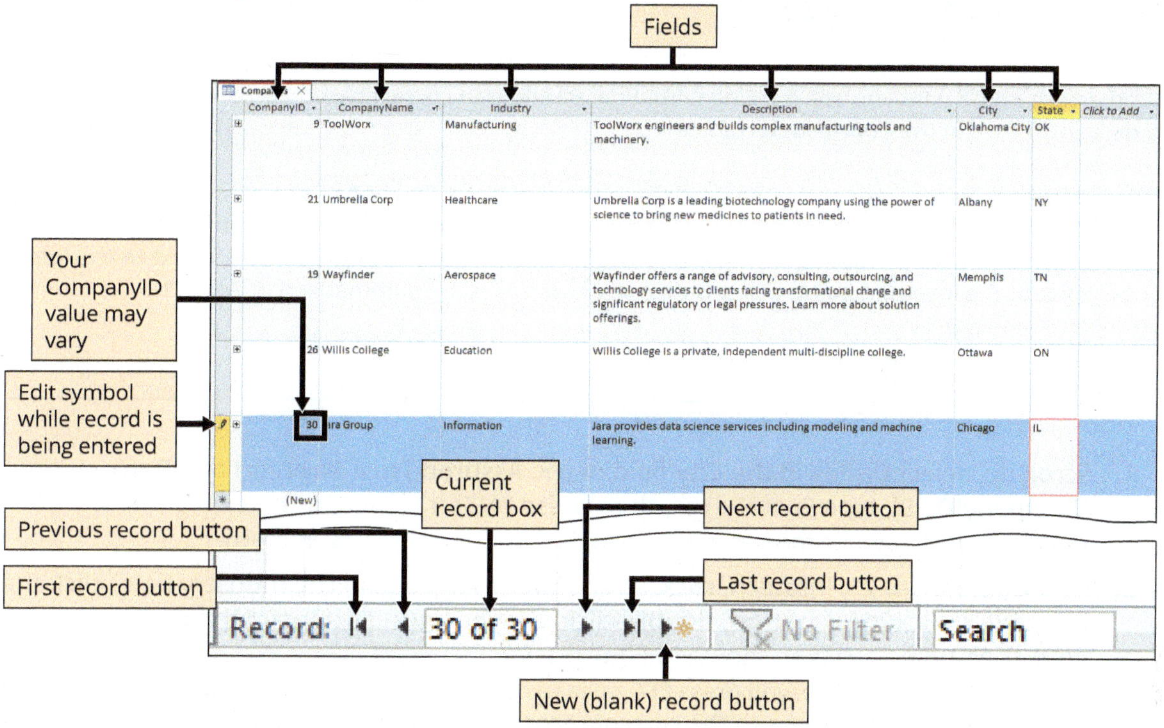

[Screenshot of Companies table datasheet with callouts:]
- Fields (pointing to column headers: CompanyID, CompanyName, Industry, Description, City, State, Click to Add)
- Your CompanyID value may vary
- Edit symbol while record is being entered
- Current record box
- Next record button
- Previous record button
- Last record button
- First record button
- New (blank) record button

Record: 30 of 30 | No Filter | Search

Table 1-3: Essential database terminology

term	description
Field	A specific piece or category of data such as a company name, first name, last name, city, state, or phone number
Record	A group of related fields that describes a person, place, thing, or transaction such as a company or job
Primary key field	A field that contains unique information for each record, such as a CompanyID value for a company
Table	A collection of records for a single subject such as industries, companies, or jobs
Relational database	Multiple tables that are linked together to address a business process such as managing industries, companies, and jobs at GIG Placement
Object	A part of an Access database that helps you view, edit, manage, and analyze the data; Access has six major objects: tables, queries, forms, reports, macros, and modules

Table 1-4: Navigation mode keyboard shortcuts

shortcut key	moves to the
TAB, ENTER, or →	Next field of the current record
SHIFT+TAB or ←	Previous field of the current record
HOME	First field of the current record
END	Last field of the current record
CTRL+HOME or F5	First field of the first record
CTRL+END	Last field of the last record
↑	Current field of the previous record
↓	Current field of the next record

Resizing and moving datasheet columns

You can resize the width of a field in a datasheet by dragging the column separator, the thin line that separates the field names, to the left or right. The pointer changes to ↔ as you make the field wider or narrower. Release the mouse button when you have resized the field. To adjust the column width to accommodate the widest entry in the field (called the best fit), double-click the column separator. To move a column, click the field name to select the entire column, then drag the field name left or right.

Edit Existing Data

Case Sasha found errors in the data you are working with. She asks you to correct two records in the Companies table and delete a record in the ContractJobs table.

Objectives
- Edit data in a datasheet.
- Delete records in a datasheet.
- Preview and print a datasheet.

Database users frequently update data in the database. To change the contents of an existing record, navigate to the field you want to change and type the new information. You can delete unwanted data by clicking the field and using BACKSPACE or DELETE to delete text to the left or right of the insertion point. Other data entry keystrokes are summarized in **Table 1-5**.

Steps

1. Scroll up, select **Dallas** in the City field of the Assured Trust Savings Loan Bank record (CompanyID 29), type **Fort Worth**, then press **ENTER**
   You also need to update the Description and City for CompanyID 28, Infotech.

   Quick Tip
   Click the Undo arrow in the Undo group on the Home tab to display the action you can undo.

2. Find CompanyID 28, Infotech, click **Telecommunications** in the Industry field, click the **list arrow**, click **Information**, double-click **telecommunications** in the Description field, then type **media** as shown in **Figure 1-5**
   While editing a field value, you press ESC once to remove the current field's editing changes, and twice to remove all changes to the current record. When you move to another record, Access saves your edits, so you can no longer use ESC to remove editing changes to the current record. You can, however, click the Undo button in the Undo group to undo the last saved action.

3. Double-click the **ContractJobs table** in the Navigation Pane to open it in Datasheet View, click the **record selector** for the second last record (ContractID 89, Arobin Inc, Care Management Associate), click the **Delete button** in the Records group, then click **Yes**

   Quick Tip
   If your instructor asks you to print the Companies or ContractJobs datasheet, click the Print button, then click OK.

   A message warns that you cannot undo a record deletion. The Undo button in the Undo group is dimmed, indicating that you cannot use it. The ContractJobs table now has 83 records. The last five are shown in **Figure 1-6**.

4. Click the **File tab**, click **Print**, then click **Print Preview** to preview the printout of the ContractJobs table before printing

   Quick Tip
   It's a good idea to close an object if you are not currently working with it.

5. Click the **Close Print Preview button** in the Close Preview group, then right-click each **table tab** and click **Close**

Figure 1-5: Editing records in the Companies table

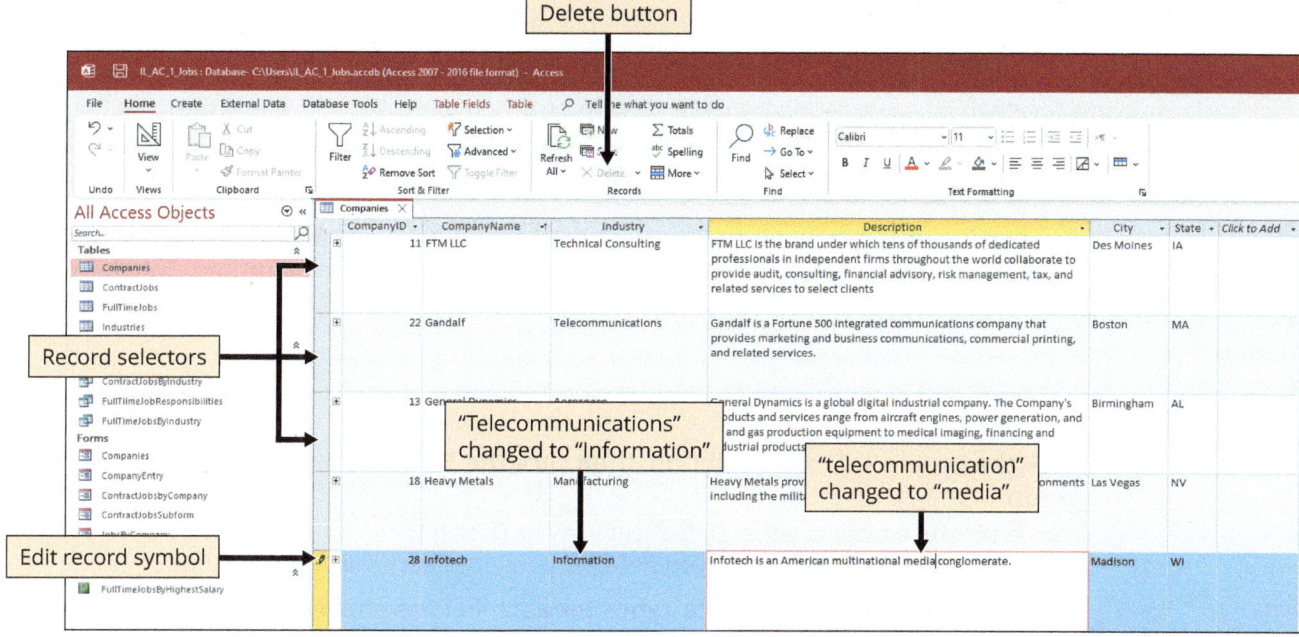

Figure 1-6: Deleting a record in the ContractJobs table

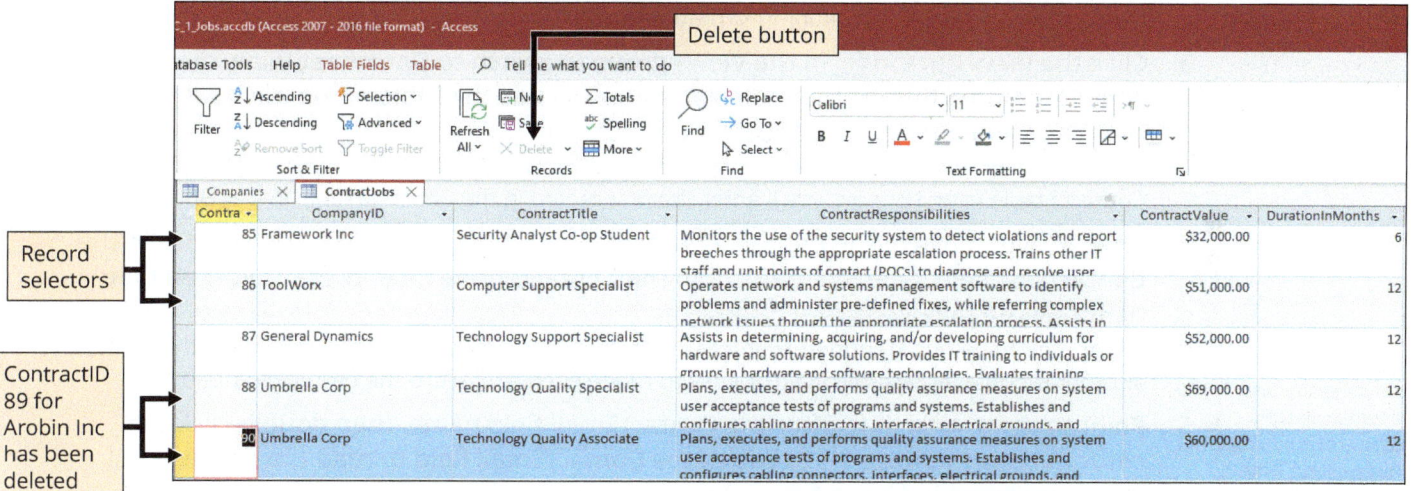

Table 1-5: Edit mode keyboard shortcuts

editing keystroke	action
BACKSPACE	Deletes one character to the left of the insertion point
DELETE	Deletes one character to the right of the insertion point
F2	Switches between Edit and Navigation mode
ESC	Undoes the change to the current field
ESC, ESC	Undoes all changes to the current record
F7	Starts the spell-check feature
CTRL+'	Inserts the value from the same field in the previous record into the current field
CTRL+;	Inserts the current date in a Date field

Create a Table

Case Sasha asks you to create another table to store information about people GIG regularly communicates with at each company. Together you have decided what fields of information to track and to name the table Contacts. Eventually, the Contacts table will be connected to the Companies table so that each record in the Companies table may be related to many records in the Contacts table.

Objectives
- Create a table in Table Design View.
- Set appropriate data types for fields.

Creating a table consists of the following essential tasks: naming the fields in the table, selecting an appropriate data type for each field, naming the table, and determining how the table will participate in the relational database.

Steps

1. **Click the Create tab on the ribbon, then click the Table Design button in the Tables group**
   You can create a table in either Datasheet View or Design View, but **Design View** gives you more control over the characteristics called **field properties** of each field in the table.

    Quick Tip: Fields that contain numbers but are not used in calculations such as phone numbers or postal codes should be set as a Short Text data type.

2. **Enter the Field Names and Data Types for each field as shown in Figure 1-7**
   The Contacts table will contain five fields. ContactID is set with an **AutoNumber** data type so each record is automatically numbered by Access. ContactFirst, ContactLast, and ContactPhone are set with the default **Short Text** data type to store the contact's first name, last name, and primary phone number. ContactEmail is set with a **Hyperlink** data type that helps you send an email to that person. Table 1-6 lists more information on field data types.

3. **Click the View button in the Views group to switch to Datasheet View, click Yes when prompted to save the table, type Contacts as the table name, click OK, then click No when prompted to create a primary key**
   A **primary key field** contains unique data for each record. You'll identify a primary key field for the Contacts table later. For now, you'll enter the first record in the Contacts table in Datasheet View.

4. **Press TAB to move to the ContactFirst field, type Nisha, press TAB, type Gupta in the ContactLast field, type 5553327711 in the ContactPhone field, press TAB, then type ngupta@cengage.com**
   So far, you have not identified Nisha Gupta's company affiliation. After you relate the tables in another module, Access will make it easy to relate each contact to the correct company.

    Trouble: The ContactID field is an AutoNumber field, which automatically increments to provide a unique value. If the number has already incremented beyond 1 for the first record, it doesn't matter.

5. **Point to the divider line after the ContactEmail field name, then double-click the column resize pointer ↔ to widen the ContactEmail field to read the entire email value, as shown in Figure 1-8**

6. **Right-click the Contacts table tab, click Close, then click Yes when prompted to save the table**

Creating a table in Datasheet View

You can also create a table in Datasheet View using the commands on the Fields tab of the ribbon. However, if you use Design View to design your table before entering data, you will avoid common data entry errors because Design View helps you focus on the appropriate data type for each field.

Selecting the best data type for each field before entering any data into that field helps prevent incorrect data and unintended typos. For example, if a field has a Number, Currency, or Date/Time data type, you cannot enter text into that field by mistake.

Figure 1-7: Creating a table in Design View

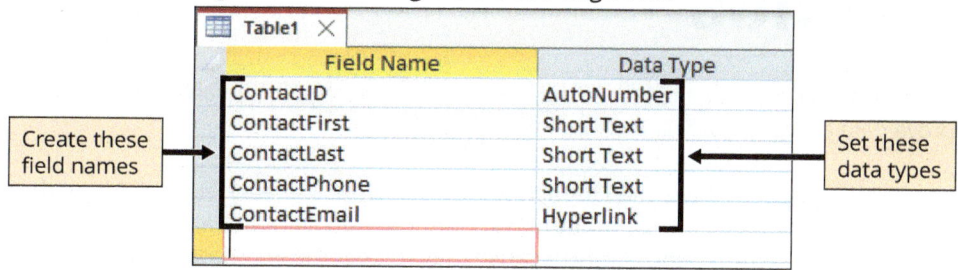

Figure 1-8: Entering a new record in Datasheet View

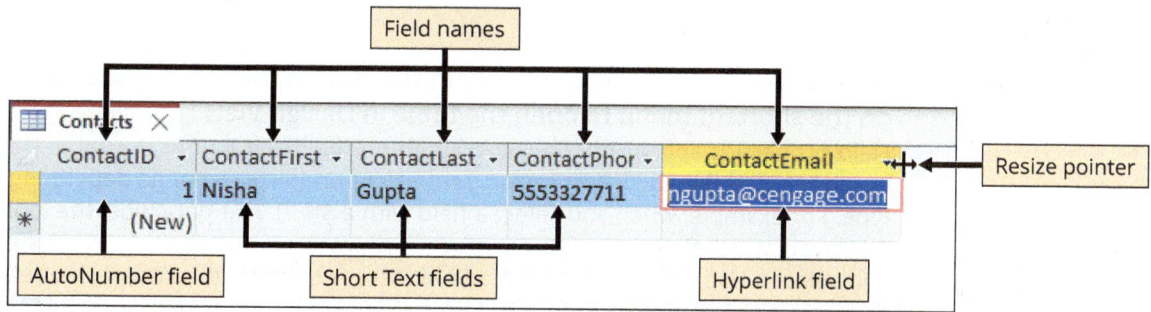

Table 1-6: Data types

data type	description of data
Short Text	Text or numbers not used in calculations such as a name, postal code, or phone number less than 255 characters
Long Text	Lengthy text greater than 255 characters, such as comments or notes
Number	Numeric data that can be used in calculations, such as quantities
Large Number	Provides additional analytical capability and deepens the integration experience when users are importing or linking to BigInt data
Date/Time	Dates and times
Date/Time Extended	Similar to the Date/Time data type, but with a larger date range, greater precision, and compatibility with the SQL Server datetime2 date type
Currency	Monetary values
AutoNumber	Sequential integers controlled by Access
Yes/No	Yes or No or Null (neither Yes nor No)
OLE Object	OLE (Object Linking and Embedding) objects such as an Excel spreadsheet or Word document
Hyperlink	Web and email addresses or links to local files
Attachment	Files such as images, spreadsheets, and documents
Calculated	Result of a calculation based on other fields in the table
Lookup Wizard	The Lookup Wizard is not a data type even though it is on the Data Type list. It helps you set Lookup properties, which display a list of values for the field. After using the Lookup Wizard, the final data type for the field is either Short Text or Number depending on the type of data in the list.

Object views

Each object has more than one view that allows you to complete different tasks. For example, to enter and edit data into the database using a table or query, use Datasheet View. To enter and edit data in a form, use Form View. To verify how a report will appear on a physical sheet of paper, use Print Preview. To display all the available views for an object, click the View arrow in the Views group on the Home tab.

Modify Fields

Case After reviewing the ContractJobs table with Sasha, you decide to change the default value for the DurationInMonths field to improve data entry accuracy and efficiency.

Objectives
- Rename a field.
- Identify field properties.

Field properties are the characteristics that describe each field, such as the Field Name, Data Type, Field Size, Format, Input Mask, Caption, and Default Value. These properties help ensure database accuracy and clarity because they restrict the way data is entered, stored, and displayed. You can modify most field properties in Table Datasheet View and all field properties in Table Design View.

Steps

1. Right-click the **ContractJobs table** in the Navigation Pane, and then click **Design View** on the shortcut menu to open the table in Design View

   Field properties appear on the General tab on the lower half of the Table Design View window, which is called the **Field Properties pane**. Field properties change depending on the field's data type. For example, when you select a field with a Short Text data type, the **Field Size property** is displayed, which determines the number of characters you can enter in the field. However, when you select a Hyperlink or Date/Time field, Access controls the size of the data, so the Field Size property is not displayed. Many field properties are optional, but for those that require an entry, Access provides a default value.

2. Press **DOWN ARROW** to move through each field while viewing the field properties in the lower half of the window

   The **field selector** button to the left of the field indicates which field is currently selected.

3. Click the **DurationInMonths field name**, double-click **0** in the Default Value property box, type **6**, right-click the **ContractJobs tab**, then click **Save** on the shortcut menu

   When a Number field is created, its Default Value setting is 0. GIG contracts are often six months long, so changing the default to 6 will speed up data entry. Table Design View of the ContractJobs table is shown in **Figure 1-9**.

4. Click the **Close button** [x] on the ContractJobs table tab to close the table

Figure 1-9: Modifying field properties

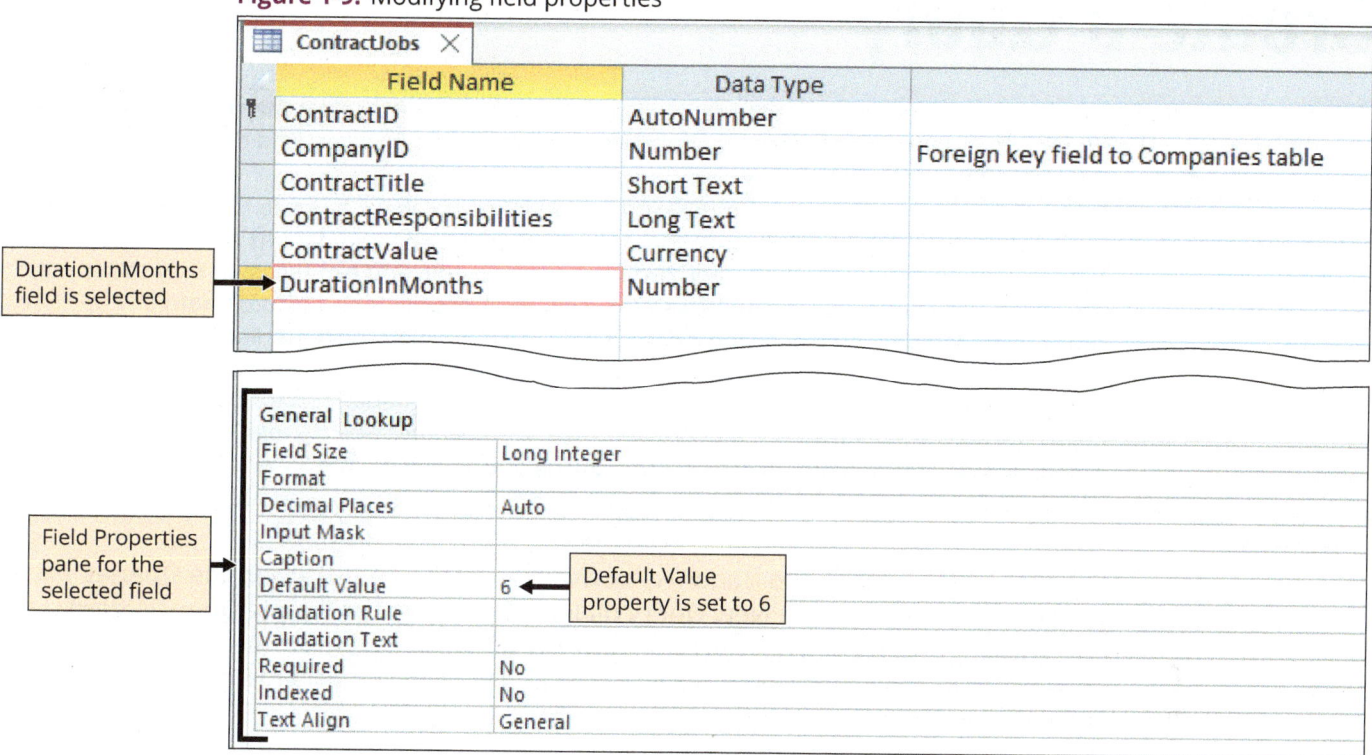

Field properties

Properties are the characteristics that define the field. Two properties are required for every field: Field Name and Data Type. Many other properties, such as Field Size, Format, Caption, and Default Value, are defined in the Field Properties pane in the lower half of a table's Design View. You can also access many common properties on the Fields tab in Table Datasheet View. As you add more property entries, you generally restrict the amount or type of data that can be entered in the field, which increases data entry accuracy. For example, you might change the Field Size property for a State field to 2 to eliminate an incorrect entry such as FLL. Field properties change depending on the data type of the selected field. For example, Date/Time, Currency, and Yes/No fields do not have a Field Size property because Access controls the size of fields with those data types.

Module 1 Getting Started with Access

Create a Query

Case Sasha asks for a listing of contract jobs sorted in ascending order by state that displays the contract value and duration for each job. You will use the Simple Query Wizard to create a query to select and display this data.

Objectives
- Describe the purpose of a query.
- Create a query with the Simple Query Wizard.

A **query** answers a question about the information in the database by selecting a subset of fields and records from one or more tables and presenting the selected data as a single datasheet. A major benefit of working with data through a query is that you can focus on only the specific information you need, rather than navigating through all the fields and records from one or more large tables. You can enter, edit, and navigate data in a query datasheet just like a table datasheet. However, keep in mind that Access data is physically stored only in tables, even though you can select, view, and edit it through other Access objects such as queries and forms. Because a query doesn't physically store the data, a query datasheet is sometimes called a **logical view** of the data. Access provides several tools to create a new query, one of which is the Simple Query Wizard.

Steps

1. **Click the Create tab on the ribbon, click the Query Wizard button in the Queries group, then click OK in the New Query dialog box to start the Simple Query Wizard**
   The **Simple Query Wizard** prompts you for the information it needs to create the query. You can select fields from one or more tables or queries. The fields you want for this query are in the Companies and ContractJobs tables.

   Trouble
   Click the Remove Single Field button **<** if you need to remove a field from the Selected Fields list.

2. **Click the Tables/Queries arrow, click Table: Companies, double-click State in the Available Fields list to move it to the Selected Fields list, click the Tables/Queries arrow, click Table: ContractJobs, double-click ContractTitle, double-click ContractValue, then double-click DurationInMonths as shown in Figure 1-10**
   You've selected four fields for this query from two tables.

   Trouble
   Click Back if you need to move to a previous dialog box in the Simple Query Wizard.

3. **Click Next, click Next to select Detail, select Companies Query in the title text box, type ContractJobsByState as the name of the query, then click Finish**
   The ContractJobsByState datasheet opens, displaying one field from the Companies table (State) and three from the ContractJobs table (ContractTitle, ContractValue, and DurationInMonths). To sort the records by ContractTitle within a State, you can select those two fields then use the Ascending button on the Home tab.

4. **Use the column selector pointer ↓ to drag across the field names of State and ContractTitle to select both columns, click the Home tab on the ribbon, then click the Ascending button in the Sort & Filter group**
   The ContractJobsByState datasheet is sorted in ascending order by the State field, and then in ascending order by the ContractTitle field within each state, as shown in **Figure 1-11**.

5. **Right-click the ContractJobsByState tab, click Close, then click Yes when prompted to save the query**

Simple Query Wizard

The **Simple Query Wizard** is a series of dialog boxes that prompt you for the information needed to create a **Select query**. A Select query selects fields from one or more tables in your database and is by far the most common type of query. The other query wizards—Crosstab, Find Duplicates, and Find Unmatched—are used to create queries that do specialized types of data analysis and are covered in a later module.

Figure 1-10: Using the Simple Query Wizard

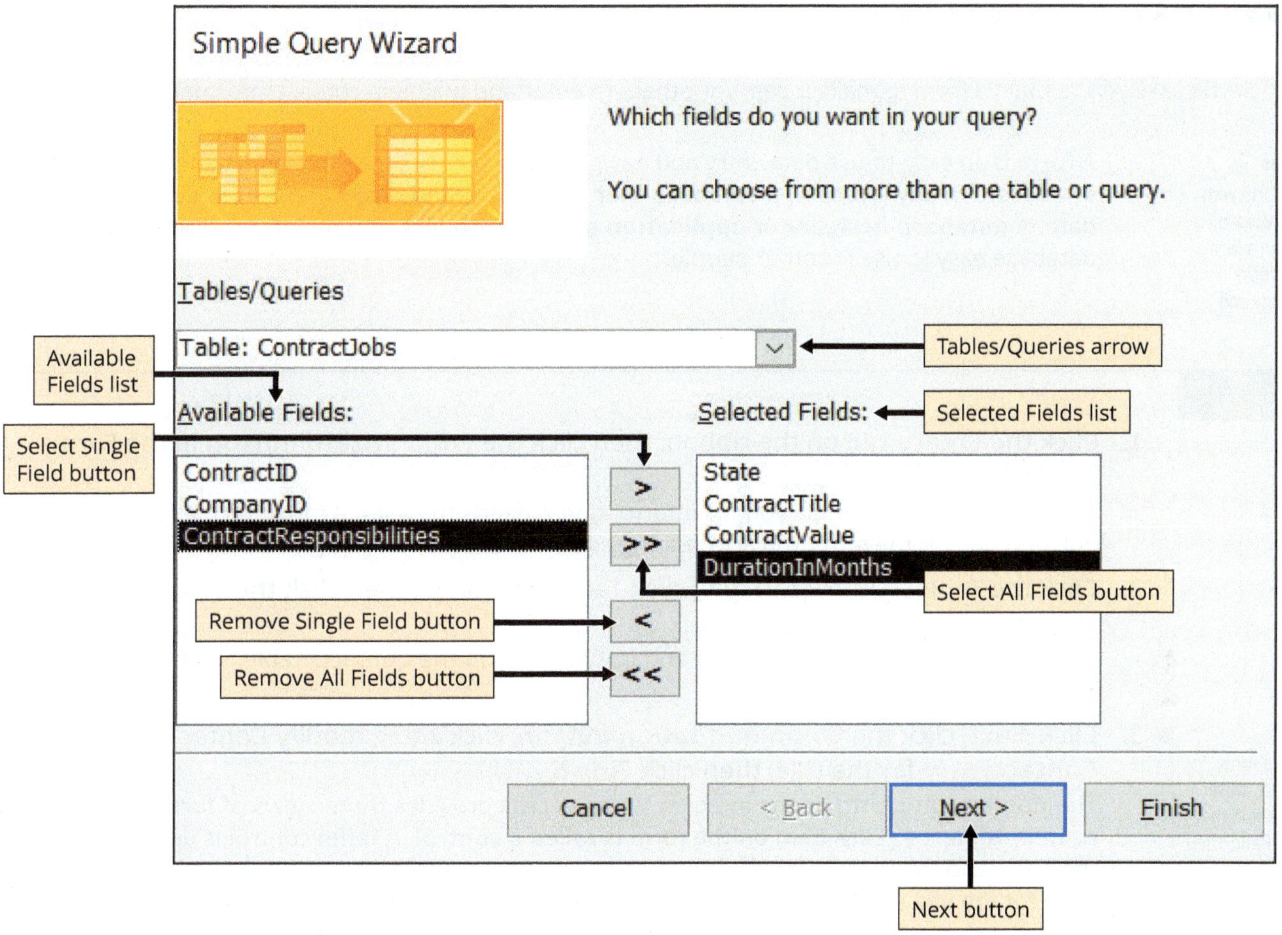

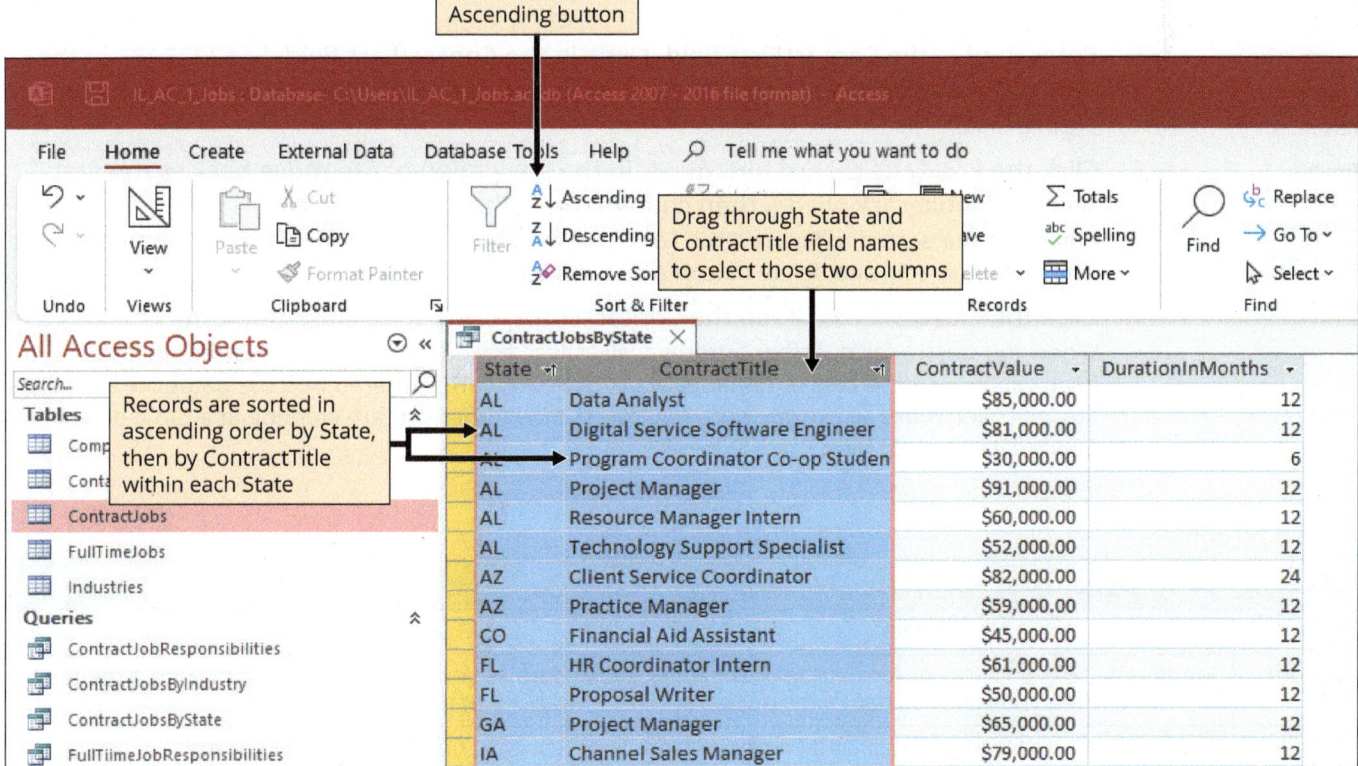

Figure 1-11: Sorting a query datasheet

Create a Form

Case Sasha asks you to build a form to make it easy for others to enter and maintain contact information.

Objectives
- Create a form with the Form Wizard.
- Edit data in a form.
- Describe form terminology and views.

A **form** is an easy-to-use data entry and navigation screen. A form allows you to arrange the fields of a record in any layout so a database user can quickly and easily find, enter, edit, and analyze data. A **database designer** or **application developer** builds and maintains forms to make the database easy to use for other people.

Steps

1. Click the **Create tab** on the ribbon, then click the **Form Wizard button** in the Forms group

   The **Form Wizard** prompts you for information it needs to create a form, such as the fields, layout, and title for the form. You are creating a form to enter and update data in the Contacts table.

2. Click the **Tables/Queries arrow**, click **Table: Contacts**, then click the **Select All Fields button** >>

   You want to create a form to enter and update data in the Contacts table, which contains five fields.

Trouble
To rename a form, or any object, close it, right-click it in the Navigation Pane, then click Rename.

3. Click **Next**, click the **Columnar option button**, click **Next**, modify Contacts to **ContactEntry** for the title, then click **Finish**

   The ContactEntry form opens in **Form View**. Access provides three views of forms, as summarized in **Table 1-7**. Each item on the form is called a **control**. A **label** control is used to describe the data, and the most common control used to display the data is the **text box**. A label is also used for the title of the form, ContactEntry. Text boxes not only display existing data, but they are also used to enter, edit, find, sort, and filter the data.

Quick Tip
Tab through the AutoNumber ContactID field, which automatically increments.

4. Click the **New (blank) record button** in the navigation bar to move to a new, blank record

5. Enter **Raul** in the ContactFirst field, **Ortiz** in the ContactLast field, **5552223333** in the ContactPhone field, and **rortiz@cengage.com** as the ContactEmail value as shown in **Figure 1-12**

Trouble
If you click an email hyperlink in the form, Outlook starts. Close Outlook or click Cancel to stop the process.

6. Click the **Previous record button** in the navigation bar to move back to the first record, double-click **Nisha**, then change the ContactFirst value to **Nishala**

   Compare your screen to **Figure 1-13**. Forms open in Form View are the primary tool for database users to enter, edit, and delete data in an Access database.

7. Click the **Close button** on the ContactEntry form tab to close the form

   When you close a form, Access automatically saves any edits made to the current record. As you have experienced, Access automatically saves new records entered into the database as well as any edits you make to existing data regardless of whether you are working in a table datasheet, query datasheet, or form.

Table 1-7: Form views

view	primary purpose
Form	Find, sort, enter, and edit data
Layout	Modify the size, position, or formatting of controls; shows data as you modify the form, making it the tool of choice when you want to change the appearance and usability of the form while viewing data
Design	Modify the Form Header, Detail, and Footer section, or access the complete range of controls and form properties; Design View does not display data

Figure 1-12: Entering a new record in a form

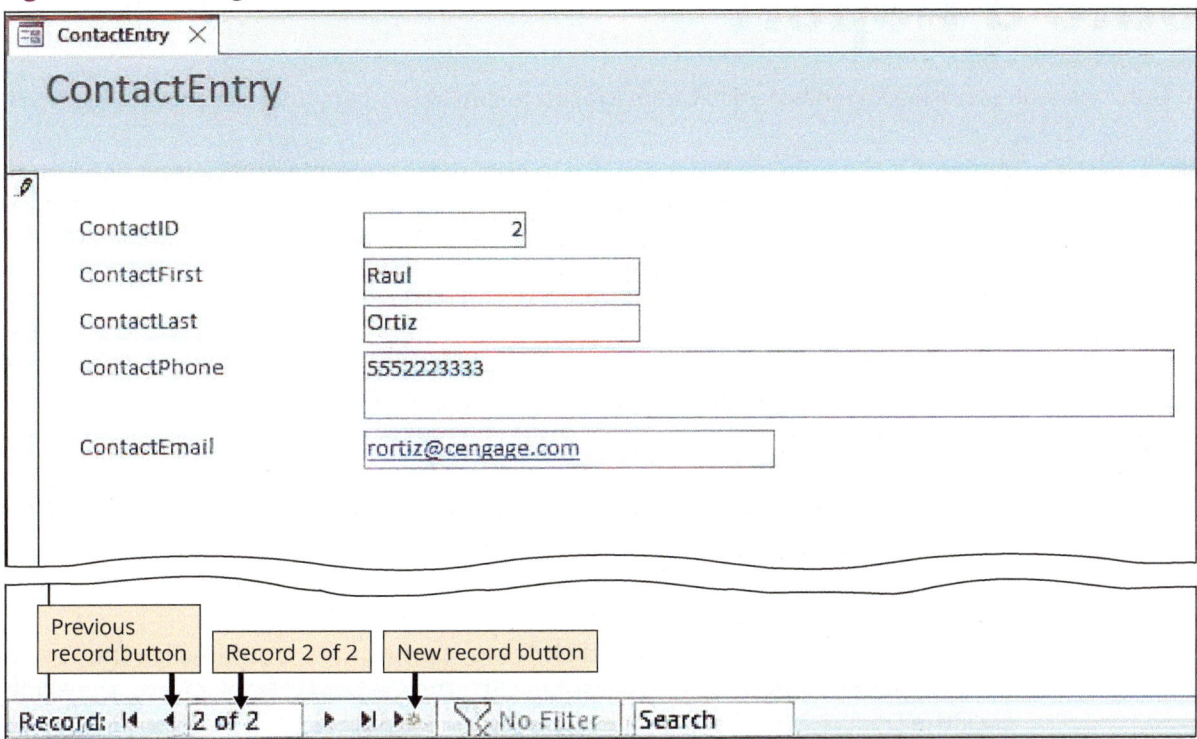

Figure 1-13: Editing an existing record in a form

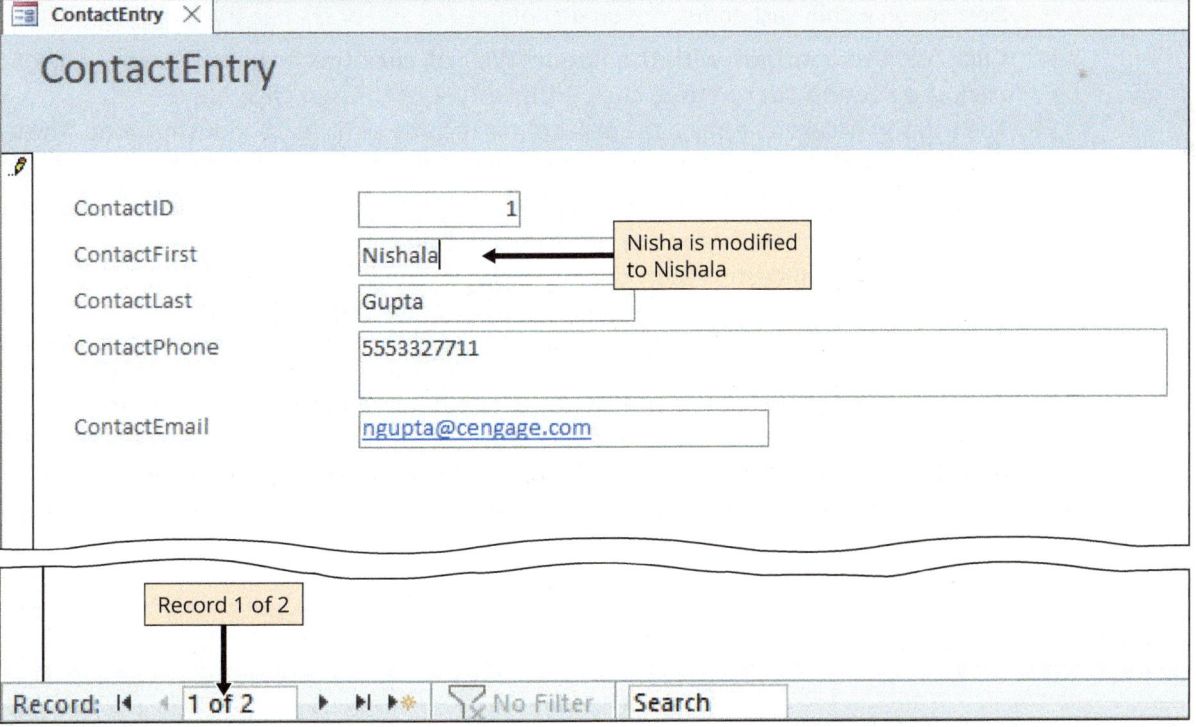

Create a Report

Case Sasha asks you to use the Report Wizard to create a report to display company information within each industry.

Objectives
- Create a report with the Report Wizard.
- Change page orientation.

A **report** is the primary object you use to print database content because it provides the most formatting, layout, and summary options. A report may include various fonts and colors, pictures, lines, headers, and footers. A report can also calculate subtotals, averages, counts, and other statistics for groups of records. You can create reports in Access with the **Report Wizard**, a tool that asks questions to guide you through the initial development of the report. Your responses to the Report Wizard determine the record source, style, and layout of the report. The **record source** is the table or query that defines the fields and records displayed on the report. The Report Wizard also helps you sort, group, and analyze the records.

Steps

1. **Click the Create tab on the ribbon, then click the Report Wizard button in the Reports group**
   The Report Wizard starts, prompting you to select the fields you want on the report. You can select fields from one or more tables or queries.

2. **Click the Tables/Queries arrow, click Table: Companies, double-click the State field, double-click the Industry field, double-click the CompanyName field, then double-click the Description field**
   As you have experienced, the first step of creating a new query, form, or report using the Simple Query Wizard, Form Wizard, or Report Wizard is to select the fields for the new object.

   Quick Tip: Click Back to review previous dialog boxes within a wizard.

3. **Click Next to advance to the report grouping options, as shown in Figure 1-14**
   The Report Wizard suggests grouping the records by Industry and allows you to specify additional grouping levels. Because you are creating a report displaying the State, CompanyName, and Description within each Industry, you do not need to add or change the grouping level.

4. **Click Next to continue with the Report Wizard, click the first sort arrow, click State, click the second sort arrow, click CompanyName, then click Next**
   The two sort orders determine the order of the records within each Industry group. The last questions in the Report Wizard deal with report appearance and the report title.

5. **Click Next to accept the Stepped layout and Portrait orientation, modify Companies to CompaniesByIndustry for the report title, then click Finish**
   The CompaniesByIndustry report opens in **Print Preview**, which displays the report as it appears when printed, as shown in **Figure 1-15**. The records are grouped by Industry, the first one being Aerospace, and then sorted in ascending order by State. If two companies are in the same state and industry, they are further ordered by CompanyName. Reports are **read-only** objects, meaning you can use them to read and display data but not to change (write to) data. As you change data using tables, queries, or forms, reports constantly display those up-to-date edits just like all the other Access objects.

6. **Click the Close button ⓧ on the CompaniesByIndustry report tab to close the report**

Changing page orientation

To change page orientation from **portrait** (8.5" wide by 11" tall) to **landscape** (11" wide by 8.5" tall) and vice versa, click the Portrait button or Landscape button on the Print Preview tab when viewing the report in Print Preview.

Figure 1-14: Setting report grouping fields

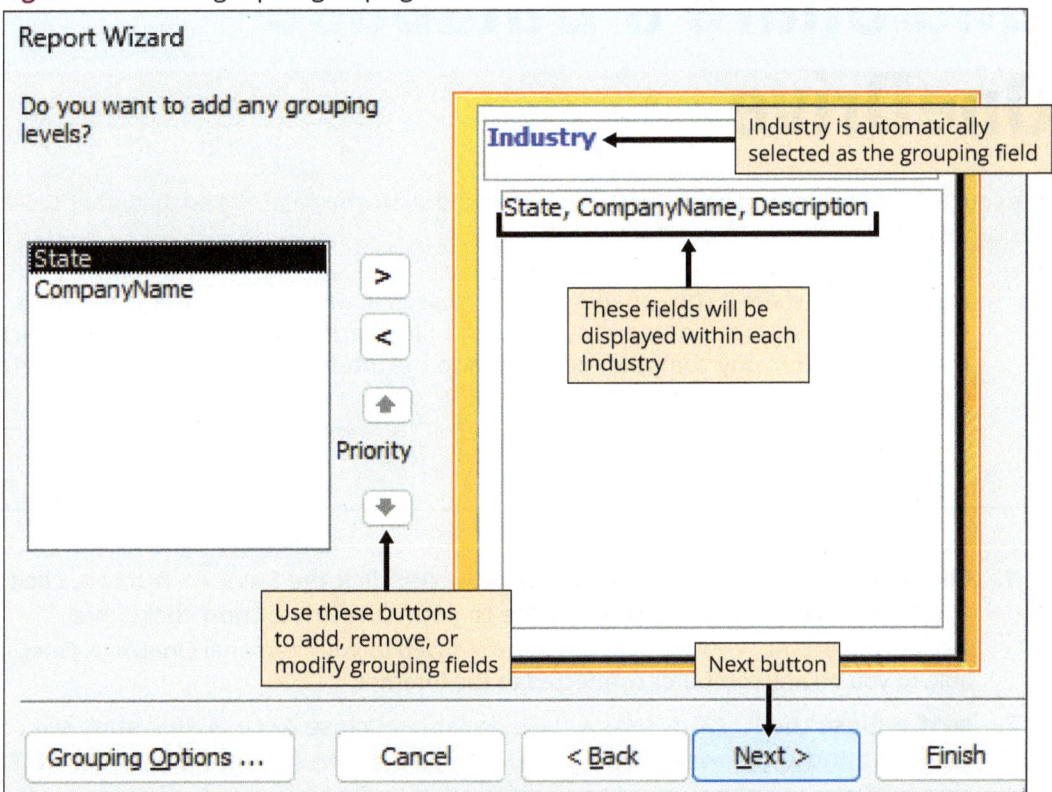

Figure 1-15: Previewing a report

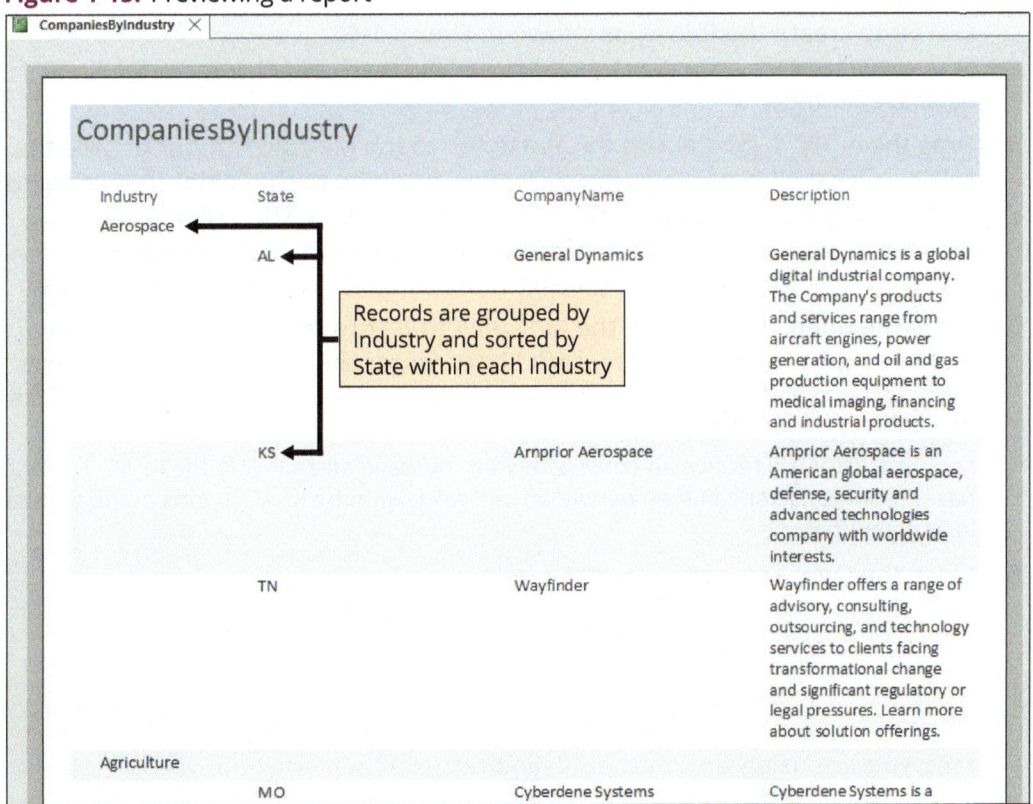

Save and Share a Database with OneDrive

Case Sasha asks you to create a folder on your OneDrive to save and share the database so that other GIG Placement employees can access it.

Objectives
- Create a OneDrive folder.
- Save a file to a OneDrive folder.
- Share a file in a OneDrive folder.

A good way to share a copy of an Access database file with another user is to save it to a shared OneDrive folder, a cloud-based storage and file-sharing service provided by Microsoft that is accessible from any computer connected to the Internet. OneDrive is particularly handy for students who work on many computers.

Steps

Trouble
You must be signed in to your Microsoft account to access your OneDrive. If you do not find OneDrive in Step 1, continue to Step 2 to access it directly and sign in.

1. Click the **File tab** on the ribbon, click **Save As**, click the **Save As button**, click **OneDrive** in the left pane or navigate to your OneDrive, then click **Save**

   A **copy** of the IL_AC_1_Jobs.accdb database is saved to your personal OneDrive. OneDrive is available to you on any computer connected to the Internet.

2. **sam↑** Close the **IL_AC_1_Jobs.accdb database**, close **Access 365**, start **Microsoft Edge** or another browser, type **OneDrive.com** in the Address box, press **ENTER**, then sign in if you are not already connected to your OneDrive.com server space

   The contents of your OneDrive appear. From here, you can upload, delete, move, download, or copy files, similar to how you work with files on your local computer. You want to share the IL_AC_1_Jobs.accdb database with your instructor. You decide to first create a folder for the database. That way, your OneDrive will stay more organized.

3. Click the **New button**, click **Folder**, type **Module1** as the new folder name, then press **ENTER** to create the folder, as shown in **Figure 1-16**

   Now you're ready to open the Module1 folder and then upload or move the IL_AC_1_Jobs.accdb database file into it.

4. Drag the **IL_AC_1_Jobs.accdb database file** to the **Module1 folder** or click the **Module1 folder**, click the **Upload button**, click **Files**, navigate to the folder that contains your IL_AC_1_Jobs.accdb database, click **IL_AC_1_Jobs.accdb**, then click **Open**

   With the IL_AC_1_Jobs.accdb database copied or uploaded to the Module1 folder in OneDrive, you're now ready to invite your instructor to access the IL_AC_1_Jobs.accdb database.

5. If it is not open, double-click the **Module1 folder** to open it, right-click the **IL_AC_1_Jobs.accdb database**, click **Share**, enter the **email address of your instructor**, enter the message **Sharing the IL_AC_1_Jobs.accdb database** as shown in **Figure 1-17**, then click **Send**

   Your instructor will receive an email with your message and a link to the IL_AC_1_Jobs.accdb database. Your instructor can then download and work with the IL_AC_1_Jobs.accdb database on their local computer.

6. Close the OneDrive.com browser window

Cloud computing

Cloud computing means you are using an Internet resource to complete your work. Using **OneDrive**, a free service from Microsoft, you can store files in the "cloud" and retrieve them anytime you are connected to the Internet. Saving your files to OneDrive is one example of cloud computing.

Save and Share a Database with OneDrive   AC 1-21

Figure 1-16: Creating a new folder in OneDrive

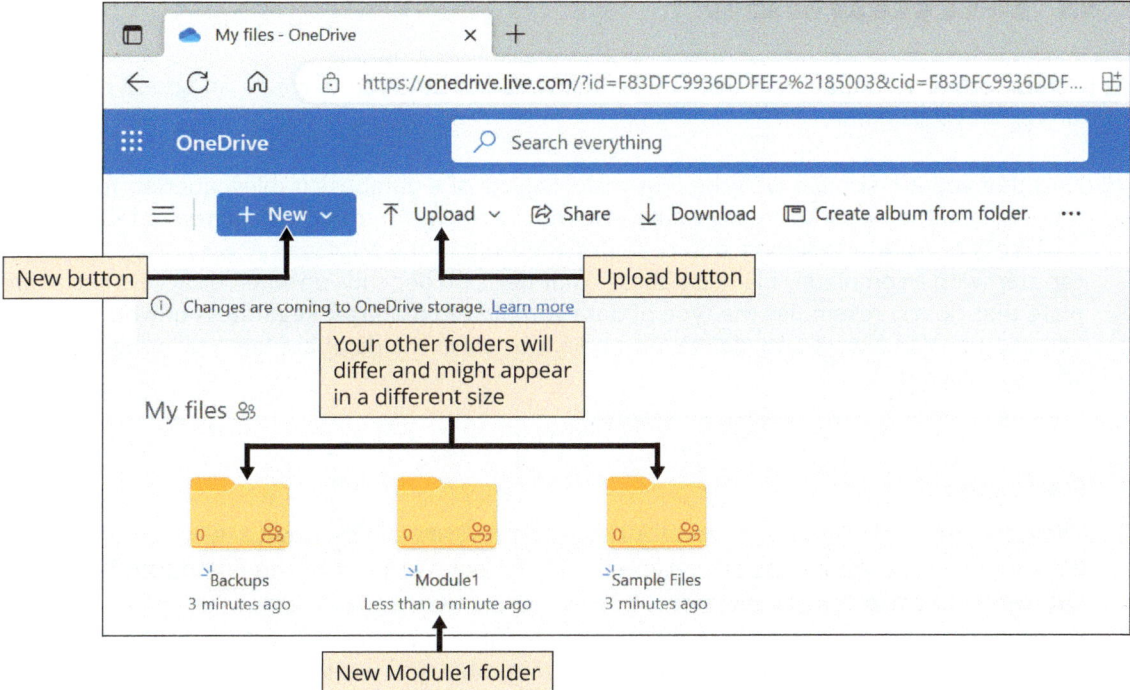

Figure 1-17: Sharing a database with OneDrive

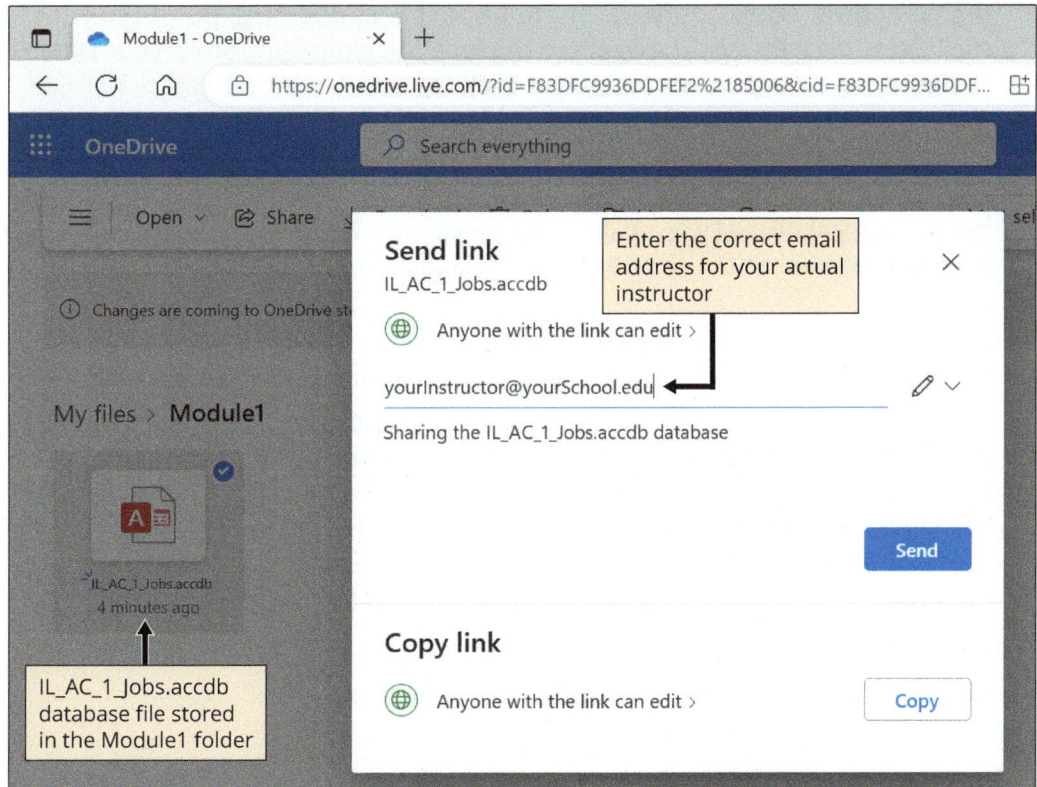

Access is a local application

Unlike Word and Excel, Access is not available in an online version. Access is a **local application** that runs from the hard drive of a local Windows machine. You can share a copy of a database with others using OneDrive, but remember that saving a database to OneDrive creates a copy of the database. For multiple people to work in the same database at the same time, the database must be located in a shared folder on a local file server.

Create a Database

Case Sasha wants to track technical support calls from GIG employees and asks you to create an Access database to store and manage the information.

Objectives
- Create a database.
- Import data from Excel.

Now that you are familiar with the four main objects of a database (tables, queries, forms, and reports), you may want to create a database from scratch. You can create a new database using an Access **template**, a sample database provided within the Microsoft Access program, or you can start with a completely blank database. Your decision depends on whether Access has a template that closely resembles the type of data you plan to manage. Regardless of which method you use, you can always add, delete, or modify objects in the database later, tailoring it to meet your specific needs.

Steps

1. **Start Access**

2. Click the **Blank database icon**, click the **Browse button**, navigate to the location where you store your Data Files, type **IL_AC_1_TechSupport** in the File name box, click **OK**, then click the **Create button**

   Access creates a new database file with a single table currently named Table1. To create the first table needed for this database, the Employees table, you will import the data from an Excel spreadsheet.

3. Right-click the **Table1 tab**, click **Close**, click the **External Data tab** on the ribbon, click the **New Data Source button** in the Import & Link group, point to **From File**, click **Excel**, click **Browse**, navigate to the location where you store your Data Files, click **Support_AC_1_Employees.xlsx**, then click **Open**

   You want to import the data in the file Support_AC_1_Employees.xlsx into a new table.

4. Click **OK** to accept the import option, click the **First Row Contains Column Headings check box**, then click **Next**

   The Import Spreadsheet Wizard allows you to specify information about each field that you are importing as shown in **Figure 1-18**. You can accept the current settings.

5. Click **Next**

   The Import Spreadsheet Wizard prompts you to define a primary key field, which contains unique information for each row. Accept the default option to let Access add the primary key.

6. Click **Next**, type **Employees** as the new table name, click **Finish**, click **Close**, then double-click the **Employees table** in the Navigation Pane to open it

   As shown in **Figure 1-19**, you have imported 58 records, each with nine fields of data from the Support_AC_1_Employees.xlsx spreadsheet into the Employees table in the IL_AC_1_TechSupport.accdb Access database.

7. Click the **Close button** on the Employees table tab to close the table

Create a Database   AC 1-23

Figure 1-18: Using the Import Spreadsheet Wizard

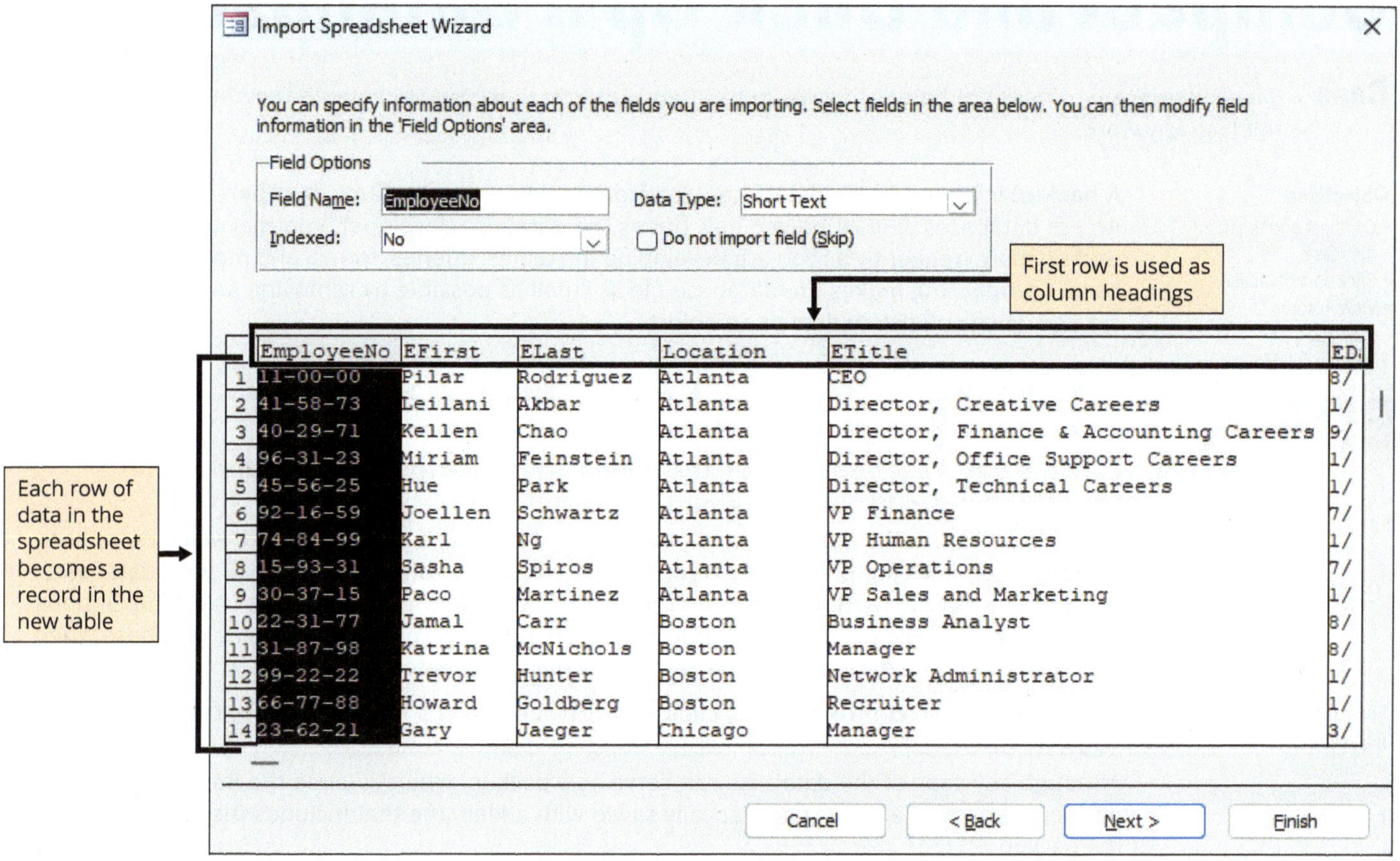

Figure 1-19: Employees table in Datasheet View

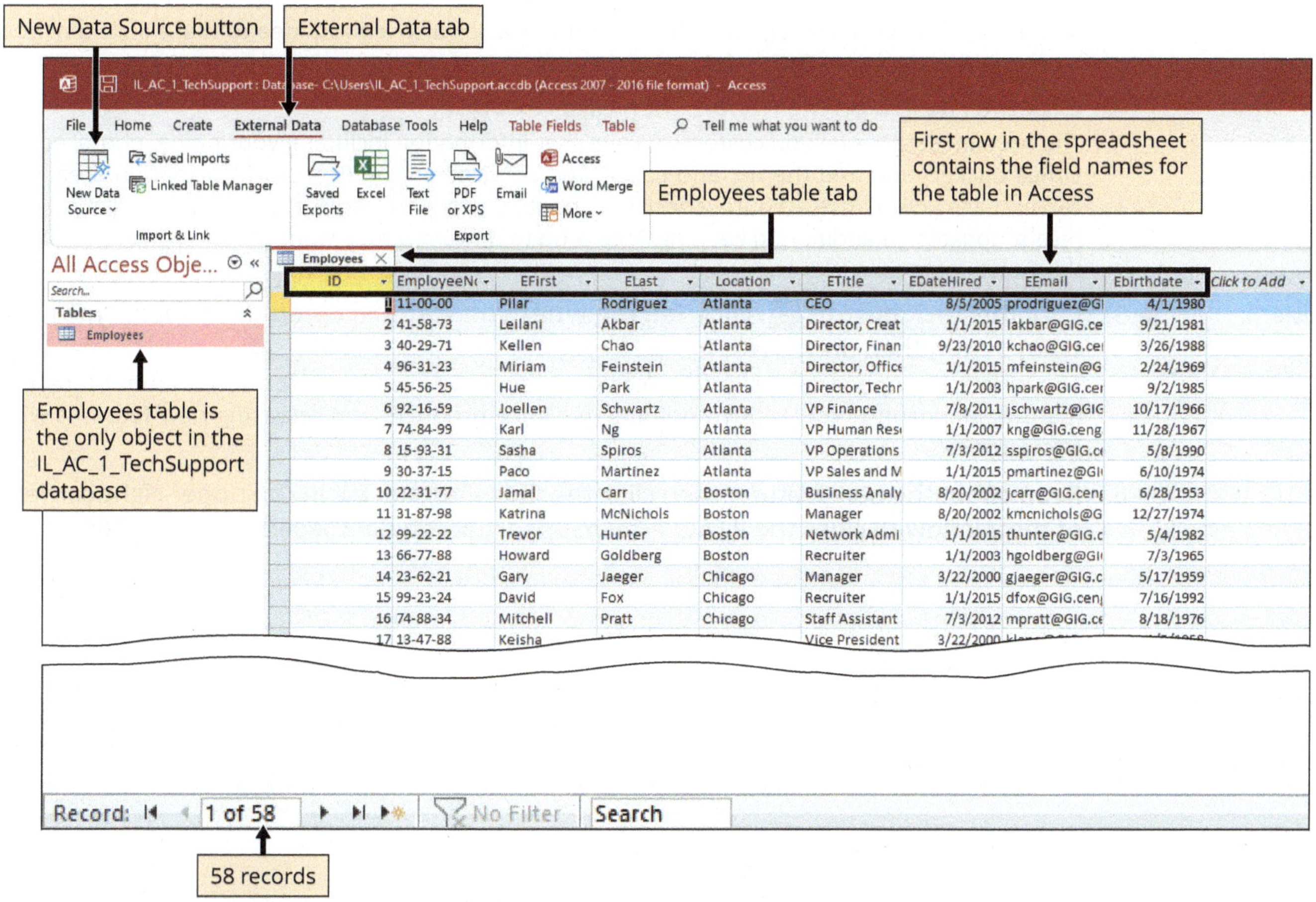

Module 1 Getting Started with Access

Compact and Back Up a Database

Case Sasha wants you to back up the new database frequently as you make significant enhancements so you do not lose any work.

Objectives
- Compact and repair a database.
- Back up a database.
- View Account settings.
- Use the Tell Me box.

A **backup** is a copy of the database. Most companies create backups of important files such as Access databases at least once a day, but as the database developer, you may want to create a backup more frequently as you are developing the tables, queries, forms, and reports in the database. **Compacting** makes the database file as small as possible by removing any unused space created when you delete data or an object.

Steps

1. **Click the Database Tools tab on the ribbon, then click the Compact and Repair Database button in the Tools group**
   When you compact the database, an automatic **repair** feature is also initiated, which helps keep hidden system files up to date. It is a good idea to regularly compact and repair your databases. You can use **Access Options**, default application settings, which you access using the Options command on the File tab, to set an option to automatically compact and repair a database when it is closed. With the database compacted, you're ready to create a backup.

Trouble
If a yellow Security Warning bar appears below the ribbon, click Enable Content.

2. **Click the File tab on the ribbon, click Save As, click Back Up Database, then click the Save As button**
   Although any copy of the database can serve as a backup, when you use the Back Up Database option, the database file is automatically saved with a filename that includes the date you made the backup.

3. **Navigate to the folder where you want to store the backup, then click Save in the Save As dialog box**
   Now that you have a backup copy of your database, it's also a good idea to make sure that you have installed the latest Office updates to keep Access up to date.

4. **Click the File tab on the ribbon, then click Account**
   The Account settings let you customize your user information including your name, photo, email, Office background and theme, and connected services. In the Product Information area, you can manage your Office account, check for updates, and learn more about your application and recent updates. In addition to keeping Access up to date, you may want to read what is new with the latest updates.

Trouble
Click the Learn more link in the What's New in Access window if a browser doesn't open.

5. **Click the Back button ⊙, click Tell me what you want to do on the ribbon, type what's new, then press ENTER**
   The What's New pane opens in the Access window and displays information about a recent feature. Microsoft is constantly updating its Office products and releasing new features with Microsoft 365.

6. Read about the new feature, then click the **Close button** ✕ in the upper-right corner of the window to close the IL_AC_1_TechSupport.accdb database and Access 365

Practice

In the exercises that follow, you will practice the skills you have learned in this module.

Skills Review

As a help desk specialist for a major accounting firm, you provide technical support to the company. Use your knowledge of Access to track support calls and cases from employees.

1. **Describe relational databases.**
   a. In a Word document, enter your name and the current date.
   b. Using a bulleted list, identify five advantages of managing database information in Access versus using a spreadsheet.
   c. Write a sentence to explain how the terms *field*, *record*, *table*, and *relational database* relate to one another.
   d. Save the document with the name **IL_AC_1_Database** then close it and close Word.

2. **Open and explore a database.**
   a. Start Access.
   b. Open the IL_AC_1-2.accdb database from the location where you store your Data Files and save it as **IL_AC_1_SupportDesk**. Click Enable Content if a yellow Security Warning message appears.
   c. Open each of the three tables to study the data they contain. Create and complete the following table in the document you started in the previous step, IL_AC_1_Database.docx.

table name	number of records	number of fields

   d. Open the CaseListing query from the Navigation Pane. Change either occurrence of the last name of "Summers" to **Sung** then move to another record to save your changes. Close the CaseListing query.
   e. Open the EmployeeEntry form from the Navigation Pane. Use the navigation buttons to navigate through the 20 records to observe each employee's cases. When you reach the Hwan Sung record (record 10 of 20), change the extension value to **6230**. Close the EmployeeEntry form.
   f. Open the CallLog report from the Navigation Pane. The records are listed in ascending order by employee last name. Scroll through the report to find the "Sung, Hwan" record. Confirm that the edit to Hwan's last name and the change to his extension value in previous steps are reflected in the report. Close the CallLog report.
   g. In your IL_AC_1_Database.docx document, add another sentence to explain why the edits to Hwan's record in previous steps carried through to the CallLog report. Check the spelling, save your changes, then close the IL_AC_1_Database.docx document.

3. **Navigate and enter data.**
   a. Open the Employees table in Datasheet View, then enter the following record for a new employee:
   EmployeeID: (AutoNumber)
   LastName: Sierra
   FirstName: Anita
   Extension: 6112
   Department: Marketing
   b. For the first record in the table (EmployeeID 3), change the employee name to your name.
   c. Close the Employees table.

Skills Review (Continued)

4. **Edit existing data.**
   a. Open the Cases table in Datasheet View, click the ResolvedDate field for CaseID 1, then enter **4/11/29**. You can use the Calendar Picker to help you enter or update data in a field with a Date/Time data type. You can also type a date using a month/day/year format.
   b. Click the ResolvedDate field for the record with CaseID 5 and enter today's date. You can enter today's date from the keyboard or use the CTRL+; shortcut. (**Hint**: Press and hold the CTRL key while pressing the semicolon ; key.)
   c. Edit the CaseTitle value for CaseID 23 to include the word **automatically** as in "Excel formulas are not automatically updating."
   d. Close the Cases table.

5. **Create a table.**
   a. Create a table in Design View with the following three fields and data types:

field name	data type
StateName	Short Text
StateAbbreviation	Short Text
Capital	Short Text

   b. Save the table with the name **States**. Click No when asked if you want Access to create the primary key field.

6. **Modify fields.**
   a. In Design View of the States table, change the Field Size property for the StateName and Capital fields to **25**, and change Field Size property for the StateAbbreviation field to **2**.
   b. Enter an Input Mask property of **LL;;*** for the StateAbbreviation field. (**Hint**: Do not use the Input Mask Wizard. Enter the property directly into the Input Mask property box.)
   c. Change the Field Name of the StateAbbreviation field to **Abbreviation** instead.
   d. Save the States table, then test the Input Mask by entering the first record into the table for Alabama using the following information:

statename	abbreviation	capital
Alabama	AL	Montgomery

   e. Use the Tell me what you want to do (Search) box to read about the three parts of an Input Mask property and the meaning of the L character.
   f. Close the States table.

7. **Create a query.**
   a. Use the Simple Query Wizard to create a new query with the following fields in the following order: LastName and FirstName from the Employees table, CaseTitle from the Cases table, and CallDateTime from the Calls table.
   b. Select a detail query and title the query **CallList**.
   c. Display the query datasheet and change the last name of Mindi Meyers to **Mora**. Notice that both records that display Mindi's name change to Mora when you move to a new record. Her name was stored only once in the Employees table but selected twice for this query because she has taken two calls.
   d. Save and close the CallList query.

8. **Create a form.**
   a. Use the Form Wizard to create a new form based on all the fields in the Employees table. Use a columnar layout and enter **EmployeeMain** as the title of the form.
   b. Use the record navigation buttons to navigate to the third record to confirm that Mindi Meyers has been changed to Mindi Mora.
   c. Save and close the EmployeeMain form.

9. **Create a report.**
   a. Use the Report Wizard to create a new report based on all the fields of the Employees table.
   b. Group the records by Department and sort them in ascending order by LastName then FirstName.
   c. Use a stepped layout and a landscape orientation.
   d. Title the report **EmployeeMainList** and preview it as shown in **Figure 1-20**.
   e. Use the navigation buttons to locate the Mindi Mora record (in the Research Department) to confirm that the report is also based on the updated data.
   f. Save and close the EmployeeMainList report.

Figure 1-20

Department	LastName	FirstName	EmployeeID	Extension
Accounting				
	Calderon	Nunzi	29	6788
	Hoover	Carlos	12	3557
	Rivas	Jaime	32	3322
	Serrano	Oscar	24	7621
Executive				
	Carson	Victor	16	9862
	Holloway	Martin	19	9682
Human Resources				
	Fuentes	Enrico	9	2002
	Guerra	Chris	33	4411
Marketing				
	Carey	Katelyn	26	7958
	Khan	Mohammed	23	2879
	Short	Peggy	15	1366

10. **Save and share a database with OneDrive.**
    a. Close the IL_AC_1_SupportDesk.accdb database.
    b. Log into your Microsoft OneDrive.com account.
    c. Create a Module1 folder (if you have not already done so).
    d. Upload the IL_AC_1_SupportDesk.accdb database to the Module1 folder.
    e. Through email, share the IL_AC_1_SupportDesk.accdb database with your instructor.

11. **Create a database.**
    a. Start Access and use the Blank desktop database to create a new database named **IL_AC_1_CustomerSurvey** in the folder where you store your Data Files.
    b. Close the Table1 table without saving it.
    c. Build the first table by importing a list of states and provinces from the Excel spreadsheet named **Support_AC_1_StatesAndProvs**.
    d. The first row contains column headings. Accept the default field options but choose StatePostal as the primary key field.

Skills Review (Continued)

   e. Name the new table **StatesAndProvs**, and do not save the import steps.
   f. Open the StatesAndProvs table in Datasheet View to confirm that 64 records were imported, then close the StatesAndProvs table.

12. Compact and back up a database.
    a. Compact and repair the IL_AC_1_CustomerSurvey.accdb database.
    b. Create a backup of the IL_AC_1_CustomerSurvey.accdb database in the folder where you store your Data Files. Be sure to use the Back Up Database option so that the current date is automatically appended to the filename.
    c. View your Account settings, and in a Word document, note your existing Connected Services.
    d. Using the Tell me what you want to do feature, research Connected Services and pick one of the services to explore further. Identify which Connected Service you chose in your Word document, then write at least one sentence explaining why you chose it and one sentence describing the features it offers. Save the document with the name **IL_AC_1_AccessConnectedServices**.
    e. Close the IL_AC_1_CustomerSurvey.accdb database and Access.

Independent Challenge 1

Before working in Access to create a table, you should plan how to set up proper fields for a table. Consider the following 12 subject areas:

- Contacts
- Countries in Europe
- Major League Baseball teams
- College course offerings
- Physical activities
- Ancient wonders of the world
- Restaurant menu
- Electronics
- Vehicles
- Conventions
- Hotel events
- Movie listings

a. For each subject, create a table in a single Word document named **IL_AC_1_SampleTables**. The table should contain four to seven columns and three rows. In the first row, enter appropriate field names that you would expect to find in a table used to manage that subject. Note the guidelines for proper field construction in step c.

b. In the second and third rows of each table, enter two realistic records. The first subject, Contacts, is completed as an example to follow.

Table: Contacts

firstname	lastname	street	zip	phone
Selena	Campos	25 Pacific Street	93023	555-612-3312
Ali	Nadar	1811 Forest Lane	60048	555-612-1179

c. Use the following guidelines as you build each table in Word:
   - Make sure each record represents one item in that table. For the restaurant menu, the following table is a random list of categories of food. These records do not represent one item in a restaurant menu.

beverage	appetizer	meat	vegetable	dessert
Milk	Chicken wings	Steak	Carrots	Chocolate cake
Tea	Onion rings	Salmon	Potato	Cheesecake

A better example of records that describe an item in the restaurant menu would be the following:

category	description	price	calories	spicy
Appetizer	Chicken wings	$10	800	Yes
Beverage	Milk	$2	250	No

- Do not put first and last names in the same field. This prevents you from easily sorting, filtering, or searching on either part of the name later.
- Break street, city, state, zip, and country data into separate fields for the same reasons.
- Do not put values and units of measure such as 5 minutes, 4 pounds, or 6 square miles in the same field. This also prevents you from sorting and calculating with the numeric part of the information.
- Make your field names descriptive such as TimeInMinutes or AreaInSquareMiles so that each record's entries are consistent.
- Remember that this is a conceptual exercise on creating proper fields for a particular subject. Putting all these tables in one Access database would be like putting a letter to your Congressperson, a creative poem, and a cover letter to a future employer all in the same Word file. Use Word for this exercise to focus on the concepts of creating appropriate fields and records for a subject.

d. Save and close the IL_AC_1_SampleTables Word document.

Independent Challenge 2

You are working for a city to coordinate a series of community-wide preparedness activities. You have started a database to track the activities and volunteers who are attending them.

a. Start Access, then open the IL_AC_1-3.accdb database from the location where you store your Data Files. Save it with the name **IL_AC_1_Volunteers** and then enable content if prompted.

b. Open each table's datasheet to study the number of fields and records per table. In the Volunteers table, change the name in the first record (VolunteerID 1) to your name.

c. In a Word document named **IL_AC_1_VolunteerTables**, re-create the following table and fill in the blanks:

table name	number of records	number of fields

d. Close all open tables, then use the Simple Query Wizard to create a query using the following fields in the following order: FirstName and LastName from the Volunteers table, and ActivityName, ActvityDate, and ActivityHours from the Activities table. Show detail records, name the query **VolunteerActivity**, then open it in Datasheet View.

e. In the ActivityName field, change any occurrence of Shelter Fundamentals to **Outdoor Shelter Basics**, then click any other record to save the change, as shown in **Figure 1-21**. Save and close the VolunteerActivity query.

Independent Challenge 2 (Continued)

Figure 1-21

FirstNa	LastName	ActivityName	ActivityDate	ActivityHour
Rhea	Alemani	Outdoor Shelter Basics	7/31/2029	8
Micah	Ati	Managing Volunteers	8/27/2029	8
Young	Bogard	Outdoor Shelter Basics	7/31/2029	8
Andrea	Collins	First Aid	8/1/2029	8
Gabriel	Hammer	Outdoor Shelter Basics	7/31/2029	8
Evan	Bouchart	Forklift Training	8/14/2029	6
Ann	Bovier	Outdoor Shelter Basics	7/31/2029	8
Gabriel	Hammer	Warehouse Logistics	8/19/2029	4
Forrest	Browning	Forklift Training	8/14/2029	6
Polly	Bullock	Cardiopulmonary resuscitation CPR	8/28/2029	4
Kendra	Cheng	Community Preparedness	8/7/2029	16
Denice	Dabong	Water Safety	8/4/2029	6
Angela	Cabriella	Water Safety	8/4/2029	6
Gina	Daniels	Livestock in Disasters	8/22/2029	0
Quentin	Giardino	Personal Safety and Security	8/15/2029	6
Heidi	Kalvert	Grief Counseling	8/6/2029	8
Helen	Hubert	Automated External Defibrillator AED	8/5/2029	4
Jeremiah	Hopper	Hurricane Preparedness	8/26/2029	6
Loraine	Goode	Outdoor Shelter Basics	7/31/2029	8
Karla	Larson	Animals in Disasters	8/8/2029	4
Katrina	Margolis	Incident Management	8/11/2029	4
Harvey	McCord	Food Service	8/13/2029	6
Sally	Olingback	Community Preparedness	8/7/2029	16
Mallory	Olson	Basic Life Support BLS	8/25/2029	4
Joshua	Palmacher	Automated External Defibrillator AED	8/5/2029	4
Quentin	Giardino	Chemical Attacks	8/18/2029	4

f. Use the Form Wizard to create a new form based on all the fields in the Activities table. Use a columnar layout, title the form **ActivityEntry**, and view it in Form View. The Outdoor Shelter Basics record should be the first record in the form. Save and close the ActivityEntry form.

g. Use the Report Wizard to create a new report based on the following fields in the following order: ActivityName from the Activities table and LastName from the Volunteers table. View the data by ActivityName then sort the records in ascending order by LastName. Use a stepped layout and a portrait orientation. Title the report **ActivityAssignment** and preview the report.

h. Close the IL_AC_1_Volunteers.accdb database, then exit Access.

Visual Workshop

Open the IL_AC_1-4.accdb database from the location where you store your Data Files, save it as **IL_AC_1_CollegeCourses**, then enable content if prompted. Use the Simple Query Wizard to create the query shown in **Figure 1-22** that contains the ClassNo, Description, and Credits fields from the Classes table, and the SectionNo, MeetingDay, and Time fields from the Sections table. Name the query **ClassDescriptions**.

Figure 1-22

ClassNo	Description	Credits	SectionNo	MeetingDay	Time
ACCT109	Accounting Concepts	3	52	M	10:00 AM
ACCT111	Small Business Accounting	3	51	T	8:00 AM
ACCT121	Accounting I	3	48	W	10:00 AM
ACCT121	Accounting I	3	49	H	12:00 PM
ACCT121	Accounting I	3	50	M	1:00 PM
ACCT122	Accounting II	3	47	T	11:00 AM
ACCT135	Accounting Apps	3	44	W	9:00 AM
ACCT135	Accounting Apps	3	45	W	8:00 AM
ACCT135	Accounting Apps	3	46	M	9:00 AM
ACCT145	Accounting for Nonprofits	3	43	H	8:00 AM
ACCT155	Cost Accounting	3	42	T	9:00 AM
ACCT165	Managerial Accounting	3	41	W	1:00 PM
ACCT201	Financial Forensics	3	40	H	9:00 AM
BUS120	Managerial Attitudes	3	39	M	2:00 PM
BUS121	Introduction to Business	3	38	T	2:00 PM
BUS123	Personal Finance	3	36	W	10:00 AM
BUS123	Personal Finance	3	37	H	1:00 PM
BUS140	Management Principles	3	34	T	9:00 AM
BUS140	Management Principles	3	35	M	8:00 AM
CIS134	Programming Fundamentals	4	6	M	3:00 PM
CIS134	Programming Fundamentals	4	7	T	6:00 PM
CIS134	Programming Fundamentals	4	8	M	8:00 AM
CIS134	Programming Fundamentals	4	9	T	8:00 AM
CIS162	Database Programming	4	5	W	8:00 AM
CIS162	Database Programming	4	55	M	9:00 AM
CIS162	Database Programming	4	56	T	9:00 AM
CIS162	Database Programming	4	57	W	9:00 AM
CIS162	Database Programming	4	58	W	6:00 PM
CIS208	Mobile Application Development	4	4	H	2:00 PM
CIS260	Database Management	4	3	W	1:00 PM
CIS260	Database Management	4	59	T	6:00 PM
ECON132	Survey of Economics	3	31	M	1:00 PM
ECON132	Survey of Economics	3	32	T	8:00 AM
ECON132	Survey of Economics	3	33	M	11:00 AM
ECON230	Economics I	3	29	W	1:00 PM
ECON230	Economics I	3	30	H	9:00 AM
ECON231	Economics II	3	27	W	9:00 AM
ECON231	Economics II	3	28	T	10:00 AM
ENGR121	Engineering Orientation	2	53	M	2:00 PM

Access Module 2

Building Tables and Relationships

Case
At GIG Placement, you are working with Sasha Spiros, special projects director, to continue developing the Access database that tracks contract and full-time job placement data. You will work with Sasha to make the database more effective by improving tables and linking them together to create a relational database.

Module Objectives
After completing this module, you will be able to:

- Import data from Excel
- Modify fields in Datasheet View
- Modify Number and Currency fields
- Modify Short Text fields
- Modify Date/Time fields
- Create primary key fields
- Design related tables
- Create one-to-many relationships
- Use subdatasheets

Files You Will Need

IL_AC_2-1.accdb
Support_AC_2_States.xlsx
Support_AC_2_Provs.xlsx
IL_AC_2-2.accdb
Support_AC_2_Departments.xlsx
Support_AC_2_Staff.xlsx
IL_AC_2-3.accdb

IL_AC_2-4.accdb
IL_AC_2-5.accdb
Support_AC_2_NewCourses.xlsx
Support_AC_2_Classes.xlsx
Support_AC_2_Enrollments.xlsx
Support_AC_2_Sections.xlsx
Support_AC_2_Students.xlsx

Import Data from Excel

Case Sasha gives you two Excel spreadsheets that list information for USA states and Canadian provinces and asks you to import the data into a new table in the Jobs database. This new table will make it easier to enter and reference state and province information.

Objectives
- Import data from Excel.
- Describe other file formats that work with Access.

Importing enables you to quickly copy data from an external file into an Access database. You can import data from many sources, such as another Access database; Excel spreadsheet; SharePoint site; Outlook email; or text files in an HTML, XML, or delimited text file format. In a **delimited text file**, data is separated by a common character, the **delimiter**, such as a comma, tab, or dash. A **CSV (comma-separated values) file** is a common example of a delimited text file. An **XML file** contains data surrounded by **Extensible Markup Language (XML)** tags that identify field names and data. The most common file format for importing data into an Access database is **Microsoft Excel**, the spreadsheet program in the Microsoft Office suite.

Steps

Quick Tip
Updates to linked data made in the original data source are reflected in the Access database, but linked data cannot be changed in Access.

1. **sam↓** Start Access, open the IL_AC_2-1.accdb database from the location where you store your Data Files, save it as **IL_AC_2_Jobs**, enable content if prompted, click the **External Data tab**, click the **New Data Source button** in the Import & Link group, point to **From File**, click **Excel**, click the **Browse button**, navigate to the location where you store your Data Files, then double-click **Support_AC_2_States.xlsx**

   The **Get External Data - Excel Spreadsheet** dialog box opens, as shown in **Figure 2-1**. You can **import** the records to a new table, **append** the records to an existing table, or **link** to the data source. Both importing and appending create a copy of the data in the database. **Linking** means that the data is not copied into Access; it is only stored in the original data source. **Table 2-1** lists file formats that can share data with Access.

2. Click **OK**

   The **Import Spreadsheet Wizard** helps you import data from Excel into Access and presents a sample of the data to be imported, as shown in **Figure 2-2**.

Quick Tip
You can save the choices you made while importing if you need to repeat the steps regularly.

3. Click the **First Row Contains Column Headings check box**, click **Next**, click **Next** to accept the default field options, click the **Choose my own primary key** option button, click the **StateName arrow**, click **StateAbbrev** to choose it as the primary key field, click **Next**, type **States** as the new table name, click **Finish**, then click **Close**

   The **primary key field** stores unique data for each record. The two-character state abbreviation is unique for each state and will be used later to connect to other tables. You also want to import more data that represents the 13 provinces in Canada.

4. Click the **New Data Source button**, point to **From File**, click **Excel**, click the **Browse button**, navigate to the location where you store your Data Files, then double-click **Support_AC_2_Provs.xlsx**

Trouble
If a "Subscript out of range" error message appears, close the database, reopen it, then repeat Steps 4 and 5.

5. Click the **Append option button** in the Get External Data – Excel Spreadsheet dialog box, click the **Companies arrow**, click **States**, click **OK**, click **Next**, click **Finish**, then click **Close**

   To append data to an existing table, the column names of the Excel spreadsheet must match the field names in the Access table.

6. Double-click the **States table** to view the imported data, note 64 in the record selector box at the bottom of the datasheet, then close the States table

   A better name for the table would be StatesAndProvinces.

Trouble
An object must be closed before you can rename it.

7. Right-click the **States table** in the Navigation Pane, click **Rename**, type **StatesAndProvinces** as the new name, then press **ENTER**

Figure 2-1: Get External Data – Excel Spreadsheet dialog box

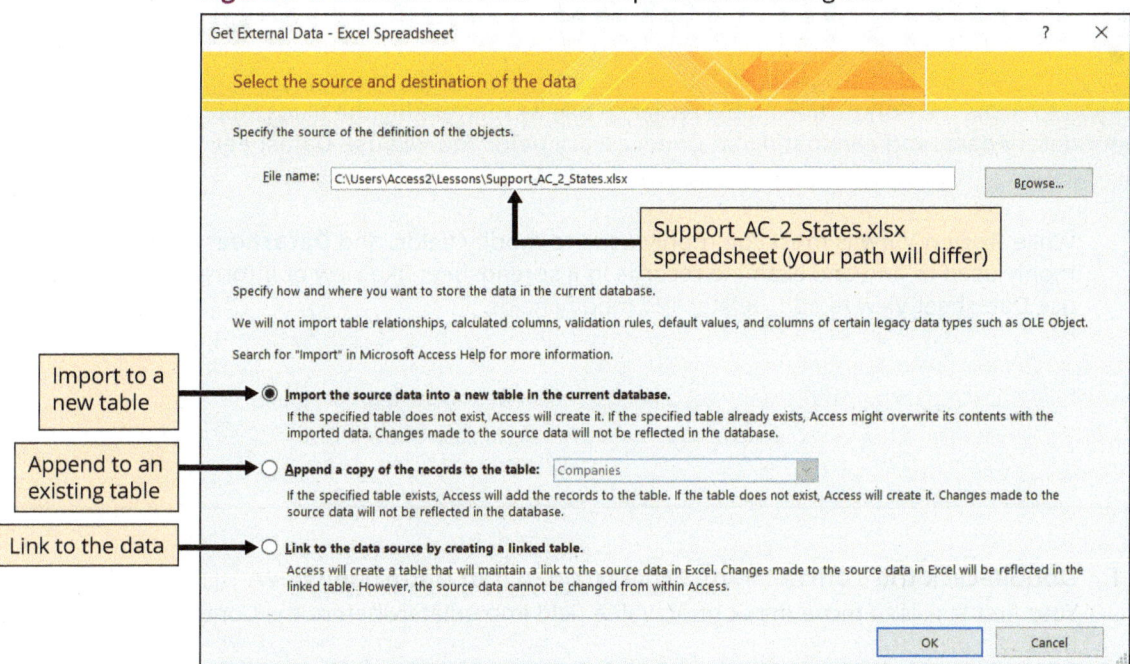

Figure 2-2: Import Spreadsheet Wizard

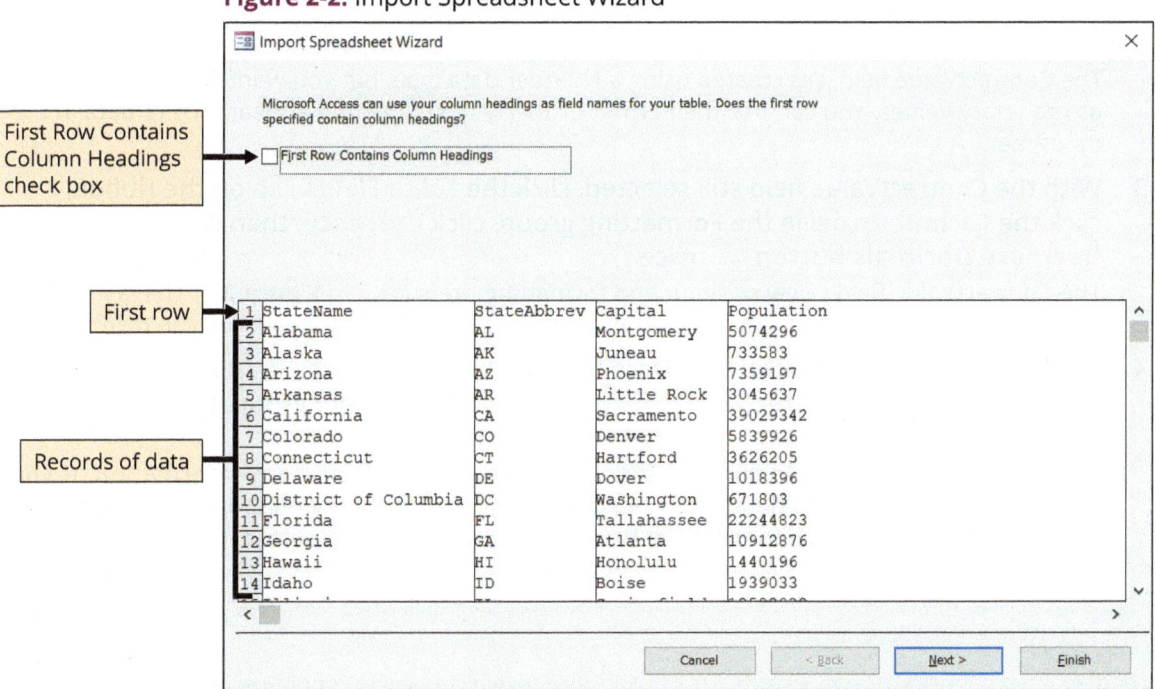

Table 2-1: File formats that Access can link to, import, and export

file format	import	link	export	file format	import	link	export
Access	✓	✓	✓	Azure database	✓		
Excel	✓	✓	✓	dBASE	✓	✓	✓
Word			✓	Dataverse	✓	✓	✓
SharePoint site	✓	✓	✓	HTML document	✓	✓	✓
Email file attachments			✓	PDF or XPS file			✓
Outlook folder	✓	✓		Text file (delimited or fixed width)	✓	✓	✓
ODBC database (such as SQL Server)	✓	✓	✓	XML file	✓		✓

Modify Fields in Datasheet View

Case Sasha asks you to make the ContractJobs table easier to use by rearranging the fields, applying the Currency format to monetary data, and eliminating an unnecessary field. You will use Datasheet View to make the changes.

Objectives
- Move a field in Datasheet View.
- Delete a field in Datasheet View.
- Decrease a field's decimal places.
- Modify the Format property.

While **Design View** is most commonly used to modify fields, and **Datasheet View** is most commonly used to find and examine records in a spreadsheet-like view of information, you can also use Datasheet View to add, delete, and modify fields.

Steps

1. **Double-click the ContractJobs table to open it in Datasheet View**
   Your first task is to move the ContractValue field immediately before the ContractResponsibilities field.

   Quick Tip
   A vertical black line indicates the new position for the field.

2. **Click the ContractValue field name to select the entire column, then use the move pointer to drag the ContractValue field between the ContractTitle and ContractResponsibilities fields**
   The ContractValue field was created using a Number data type, but you want to display the data as monetary values. You can use the Format property to change the appearance of data in the datasheet.

3. **With the ContractValue field still selected, click the Table Fields tab on the ribbon, click the Format arrow in the Formatting group, click Currency, then click the Decrease Decimals button twice**
   The ContractValue field's new position and formatting are shown in **Figure 2-3**. The last field in the table, StartDate, was planned for the ContractJobs table but never used. You can delete it.

4. **Scroll to the right to view the StartDate field, click the StartDate field name to select the entire column, click the Delete button in the Add & Delete group, then click Yes when prompted**
   Because the StartDate field contained no data, you are not losing any information. If you delete a field that contains data, all the values in that field for every record would be deleted. Deleting a field is an action that cannot be reversed with the Undo button.

Figure 2-3: ContractValue field in the ContractJobs table has been moved and formatted

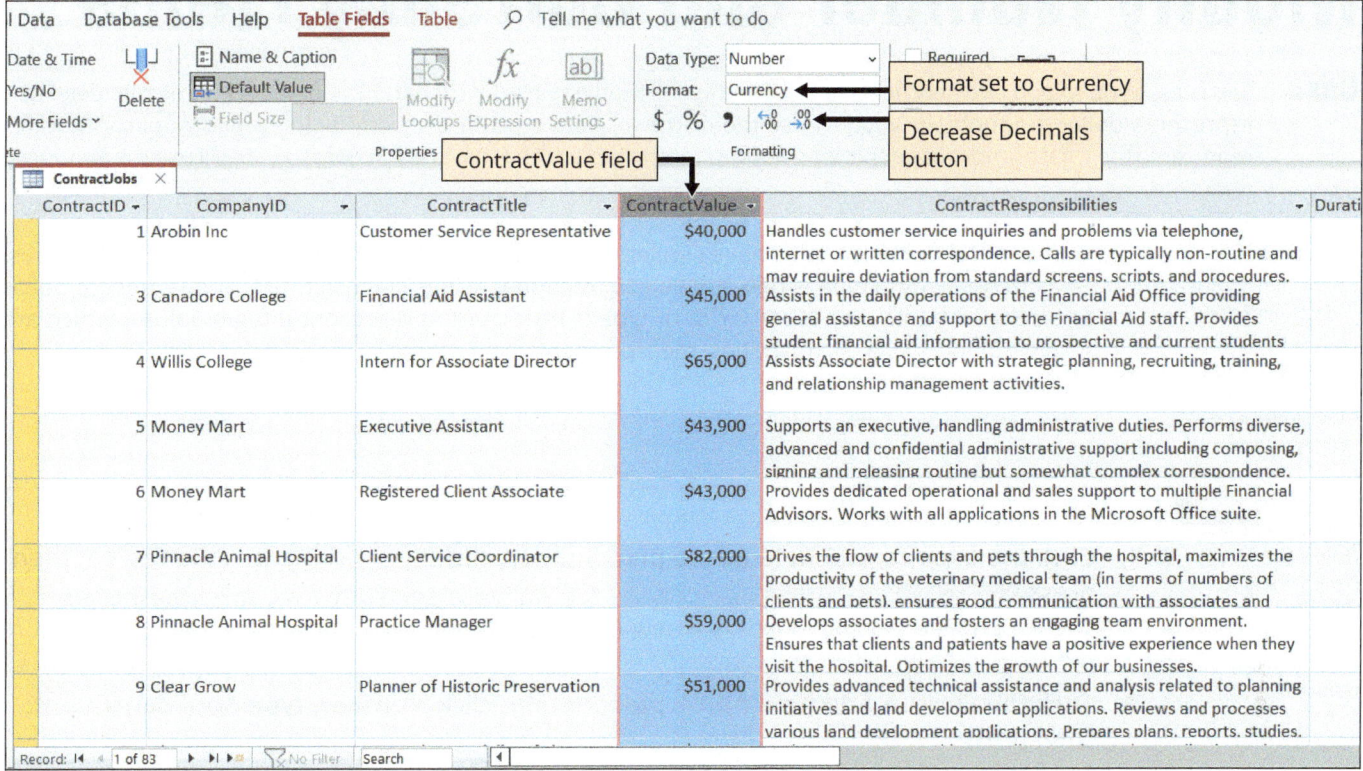

Currency versus Number data type

In general, if a number represents a **fractional** value (such as dollars and cents, not a whole number), choose Currency for its data type. Fractional values should have a Currency data type because a computer works with numbers using a binary system (1s and 0s), which cannot accurately store decimal fractions such as 0.1 or 0.01. The system can lead to rounding errors that all programming languages must address. In Access, the Currency data type includes a special code to avoid these errors. If you are working with **integer** (a whole number, not a fraction) data, however, the Number data type provides faster performance. Whether you choose the Currency or Number data type, you can format the data to look the way you want.

Modify Number and Currency Fields

Case Sasha asks you to add two new fields to the ContractJobs table to track new data. The first field named FindersFee represents dollar amounts, so you will use the Currency data type. The second field named ApplicantCount represents the total number of people who applied for the job, which is never a fraction, so you will use the Number data type.

Objectives
- Add a Currency field.
- Add a Number field.
- Modify the Field Size property for a Number field.
- Modify the Decimal Places property.

Number and Currency fields have similar properties because they both contain numeric values. The **Currency** data type is best applied to fractional values such as those that represent dollar and cent amounts. The **Number** data type is best used to represent integer values, which are whole numbers such as quantities, measurements, and scores.

Steps

Quick Tip
Scroll to the right side of the datasheet to find the Click to Add field name placeholder.

1. Click the **Click to Add field name placeholder**, click **Currency**, type **FindersFee**, then press **ENTER**

   The FindersFee field is added as a new Currency field in the ContractJobs table. It will store monetary data in dollars and cents.

2. Click the **Click to Add field name placeholder**, click **Number**, type **ApplicantCount**, then press **ENTER**

   The ApplicantCount field is added as a new Number field in the ContractJobs table. Test your new fields with sample data.

3. Click the **FindersFee field** for the first record, type **225.25**, press **TAB**, type **50**, then click the second record to display the data you've entered, as shown in **Figure 2-4**

   Access automatically formatted the value in the FindersFee field as $225.25. You can set some field properties in both Datasheet View and Design View.

4. Click the **FindersFee field**, click the **Table Fields tab** on the ribbon if not already selected, click the **Default Value button** in the Properties group, replace the 0 with **250.25**, click **OK** in the Expression Builder dialog box, click the **ApplicantCount field**, then click the **Increase Decimals button** in the Formatting group

   The **Default Value property** automatically enters the default value, 250.25 in this case, for all new records. The **Decimal Places property** displays the value with the specified number of digits to the right of the decimal point. Because the ApplicantCount field will store only whole numbers, displaying the decimal place does not make good sense. You will switch to Table Design View to change the Decimal Places property value for the ApplicantCount field back to 0.

5. Right-click the **ContractJobs table tab**, click **Design View**, select the **ApplicantCount field**, click the **Decimal Places property box**, change the value to **0**, then press **ENTER**

   Because **Table Design View** gives you access to *all* field properties, it is generally the preferred way of changing field properties.

   The **Field Size property** determines the size or length of the maximum value for that field. Choosing the smallest Field Size for your Number fields helps improve database performance. **Table 2-2** lists Number Field Size property options. The Integer field size is large enough to hold any potential entry in the ApplicantCount field.

Quick Tip
Double-click a property name to toggle through the choices.

6. With the ApplicantCount field still selected, click the **Field Size property**, click the **Field Size arrow**, then click **Integer**

   Compare your Table Design View to **Figure 2-5**.

7. Save the **ContractJobs table** then close it

Modify Number and Currency Fields AC 2-7

Figure 2-4: Adding a Currency field and a Number field

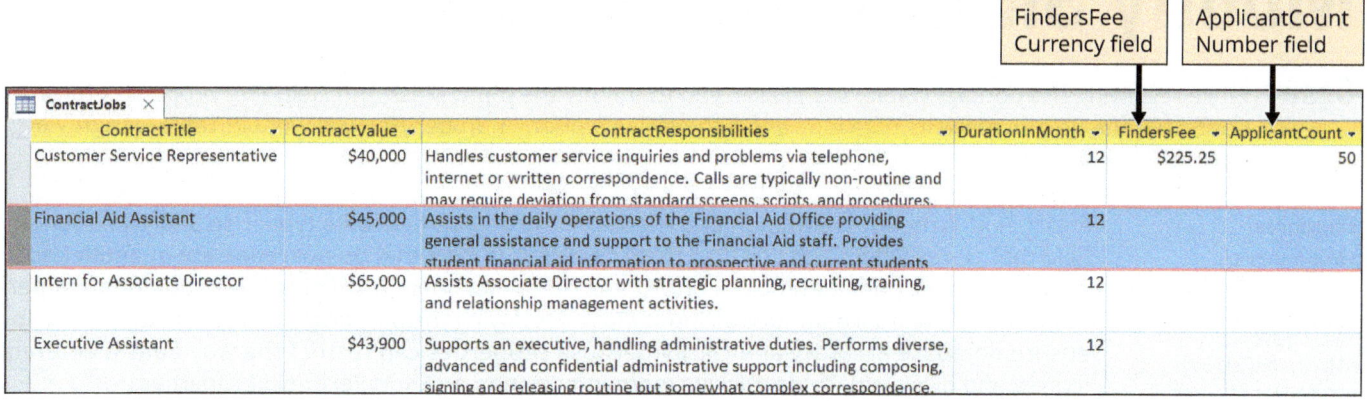

Figure 2-5: Modifying Number field properties in Table Design View

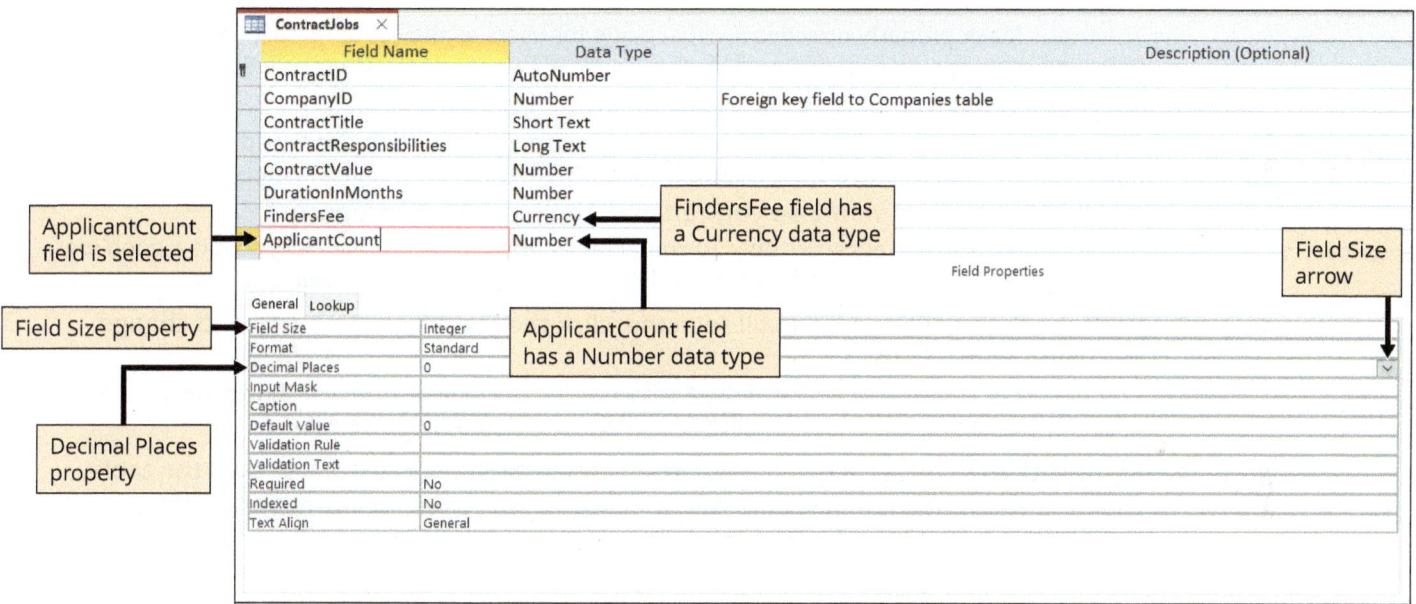

Table 2-2: Number Field Size property options

property	description
Byte	Stores numbers from 0 to 255 (no fractions)
Integer	Stores numbers from −32,768 to 32,767 (no fractions)
Long Integer	Stores numbers from −2,147,483,648 to 2,147,483,647 (no fractions)
Single	Stores numbers (including fractions with six digits to the right of the decimal point) times 10 to the −38th to +38th power
Double	Stores numbers (including fractions with more than 10 digits to the right of the decimal point) in the range of 10 to the −324th to +324th power

Modify Short Text Fields

Case While reviewing the Contacts table, Sasha asks you to modify the Input Mask and Field Size properties for the ContactPhone field to make its data look and behave like a phone number. You will work in Table Design View to make the changes.

Objectives
- Modify the Input Mask property.
- Enter data using an input mask.
- Modify the Field Size property.

Short Text is the most common and therefore the default field data type. Use Short Text for any field that stores letters and any field that contains numbers that do not represent quantities such as postal codes, phone numbers, or product numbers. Short Text fields have additional properties unique to textual data such as Input Mask. Modifying the properties of a Short Text field helps ensure database accuracy and clarity because properties can restrict the way data is entered, stored, and displayed. **Table 2-3** lists more information on Short Text field properties.

Steps

1. **Right-click the Contacts table in the Navigation Pane, then click Design View on the shortcut menu**
   The **Input Mask** property provides a visual guide for users as they enter data. The ContactPhone field is a good candidate for an Input Mask because phone numbers are consistently entered with 10 numeric characters for each record.

   Trouble
   The Build button [...] is located on the right side of the Input Mask property box.

2. **Click ContactPhone, click the Input Mask property box, click the Build button [...], click the Phone Number input mask, click Next, click Next, click Finish, then click the ContactPhone field name so you can read the Input Mask property**
   This Input Mask lets users enter only 10 characters in the ContactPhone field, so it is a good idea to change the Field Size property from the default value of 255 to 10 as well.

3. **With the ContactPhone field still selected, click the Field Size property and change the value from 255 to 10**
   Compare your Table Design View of the Contacts table to **Figure 2-6**, which shows the Input Mask property created for the ContactPhone field and the updated Field Size value of 10.

4. **Right-click the Contacts table tab, click Datasheet View, click Yes to save the table, click Yes when warned that data might be lost, press TAB three times to move to the ContactPhone field for the first record, type 5558675309, press ENTER, then resize the first four fields to their best fit**
   No data was lost because no existing value in the ContactPhone field is greater than 10 characters. The Input Mask property creates an easy-to-use visual guide to help you enter accurate and consistent data in the ContactPhone field.
   Compare your Contacts table to **Figure 2-7**.

5. **Right-click the Contacts table tab, click Close, then click Yes to save your changes**

Figure 2-6: Modifying the Input Mask property

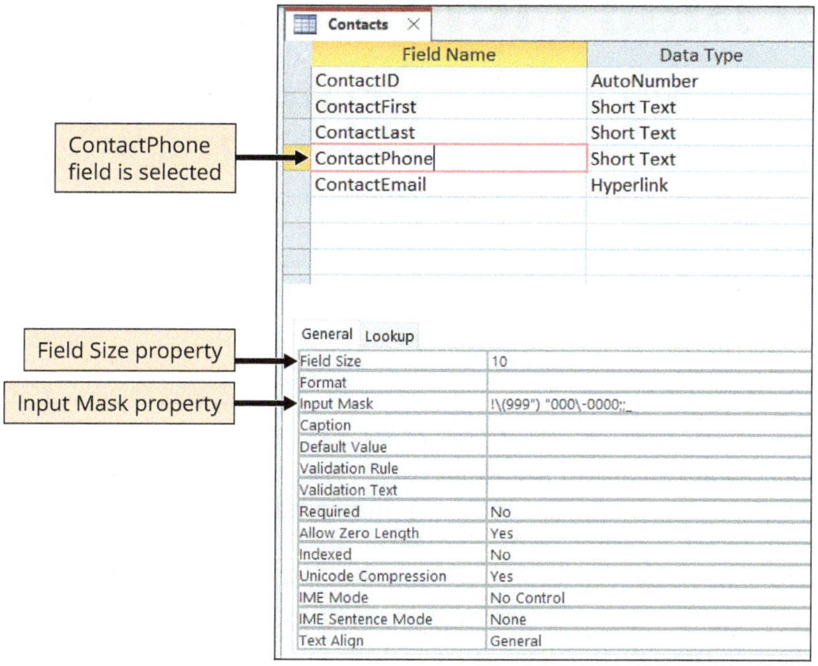

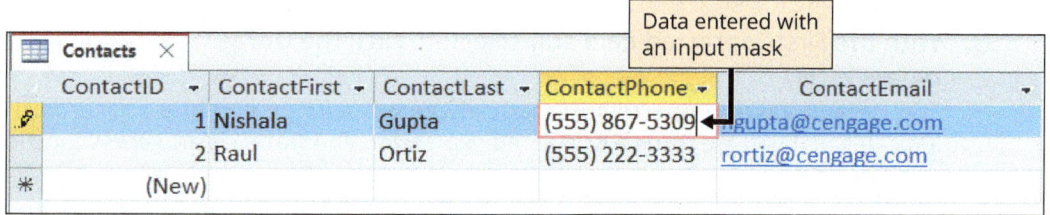

Figure 2-7: Entering data with an input mask

Table 2-3: Common Short Text field properties

property	description	sample field	sample property entry
Field Size	Controls how many characters can be entered into the field	State	2
Format	Controls how information will be displayed and printed	State	> (displays all characters in uppercase)
Input Mask	Provides a pattern for data to be entered	Phone	!(999) 000-0000;1;_
Caption	Describes the field in the first row of a datasheet, form, or report; if the Caption property is not entered, the field name is used to label the field	EmpNo	Employee Number
Default Value	Displays a value that is automatically entered in the field for new records	City	Des Moines
Required	Determines if an entry is required for this field	LastName	Yes

Working with the Input Mask property

The Input Mask property provides a pattern for entering data. The pattern uses three parts, each separated by a ; (semicolon). The first part provides a pattern for what type of data can be entered. For example, 9 represents an optional number, 0 a required number, ? an optional letter, and L a required letter. The second part determines whether all displayed characters (such as dashes in a phone number) are stored in the field. For the second part of the input mask, a 0 entry stores all characters, such as 555-1199, and a 1 entry stores only the entered data, 5551199. The third part of the input mask determines which character Access uses to guide the user through the mask. Common choices are the asterisk (*), underscore (_), or pound sign (#).

Module 2 Building Tables and Relationships

Modify Date/Time Fields

Case Sasha asks you to add a new field to the Contacts table to contain the date of first contact. You will create a new field named FirstContacted and set its properties to handle this request.

Objectives
- Modify the Format property.
- Modify the Default Value property.
- Modify the Required property.

Fields with a **Date/Time** data type store dates, times, or both. Many properties of Date/Time fields work the same way as they do for Short Text or Number fields. One difference, however, is the **Format property**, which helps you format dates in various ways such as January 25, 2029; 25-Jan-29; or 01/25/2029.

Steps

1. Right-click the **Contacts table** in the Navigation Pane, click **Design View** on the shortcut menu, click the **Field Name cell** just below ContactEmail, type **FirstContacted**, press **TAB**, click the **Data Type arrow**, then click **Date/Time**
   With the field name and data type set, you can use field properties to further describe the field.

2. With the FirstContacted field still selected, click the **Format property box**, click the **Format list arrow**, then click **Medium Date**
   The Format property changes the way the data is displayed *after it is entered*. All dates in Access are *entered* in a month/day/year pattern.

3. With the FirstContacted field still selected, click the **Default Value property box**, then type **=Date()**
   The Default Value property automatically enters a value in all new records. The equal sign indicates that you are using a calculated expression and **Date()** is an Access function that returns the current date.
   The updated Table Design View for the Contacts table is shown in **Figure 2-8**.

Trouble
The current date will obviously be the date you perform these steps.

▶ 4. Right-click the **Contacts table tab**, click **Save**, right-click the **Contacts table tab** again, then click **Datasheet View**
   The current date is already entered in the FirstContacted field for the new record. To change the value, you can type dates using a month/day/year pattern or pick a date from a pop-up calendar using the **Date Picker**.

5. Press **TAB** five times to move to the FirstContacted field, click the **Date Picker icon** 📅, click a date of your choice on the pop-up calendar, click the **FirstContacted field** for the second record, click the **Date Picker icon** 📅, then click a date of your choice on the calendar for the second record
   With valid dates in the FirstContacted field of both records, you can set the Required property to Yes for the FirstContacted field.

6. Click the **FirstContacted field name**, click the **Table Fields tab** on the ribbon, then click the **Required check box** as shown in **Figure 2-9**
   The **Required** property will create an error message if the user attempts to enter a record in the database without a date in the FirstContacted field.

7. Close the Contacts table

Figure 2-8: Creating a Date/Time field

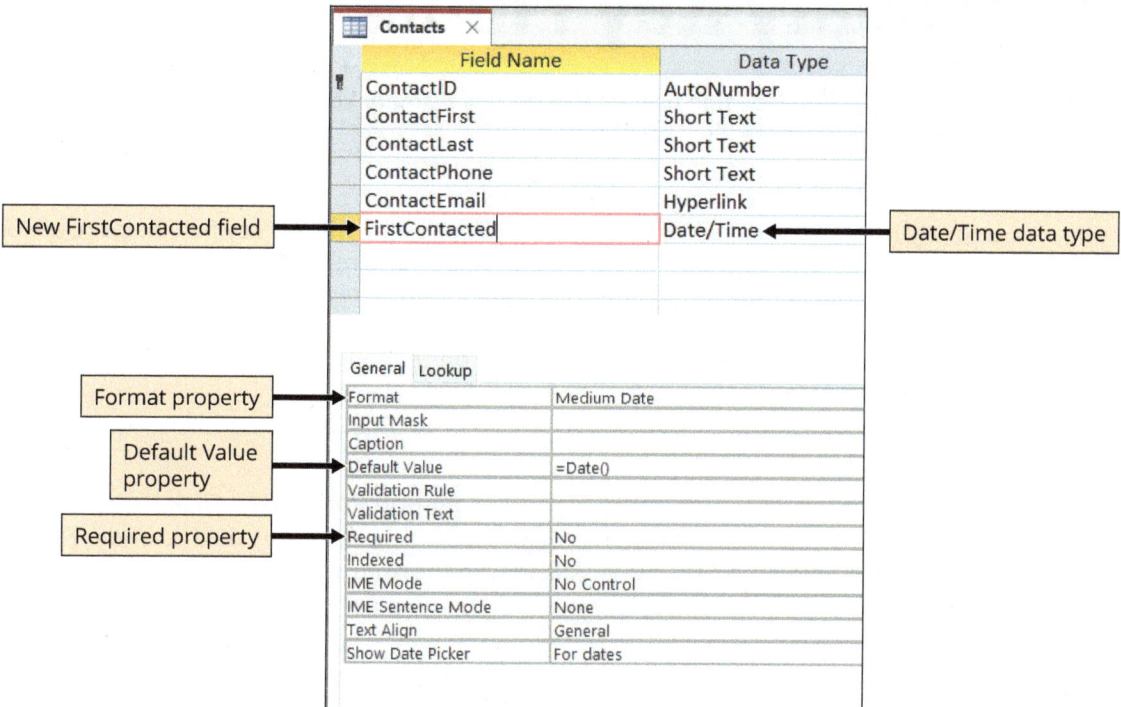

Figure 2-9: Working with dates

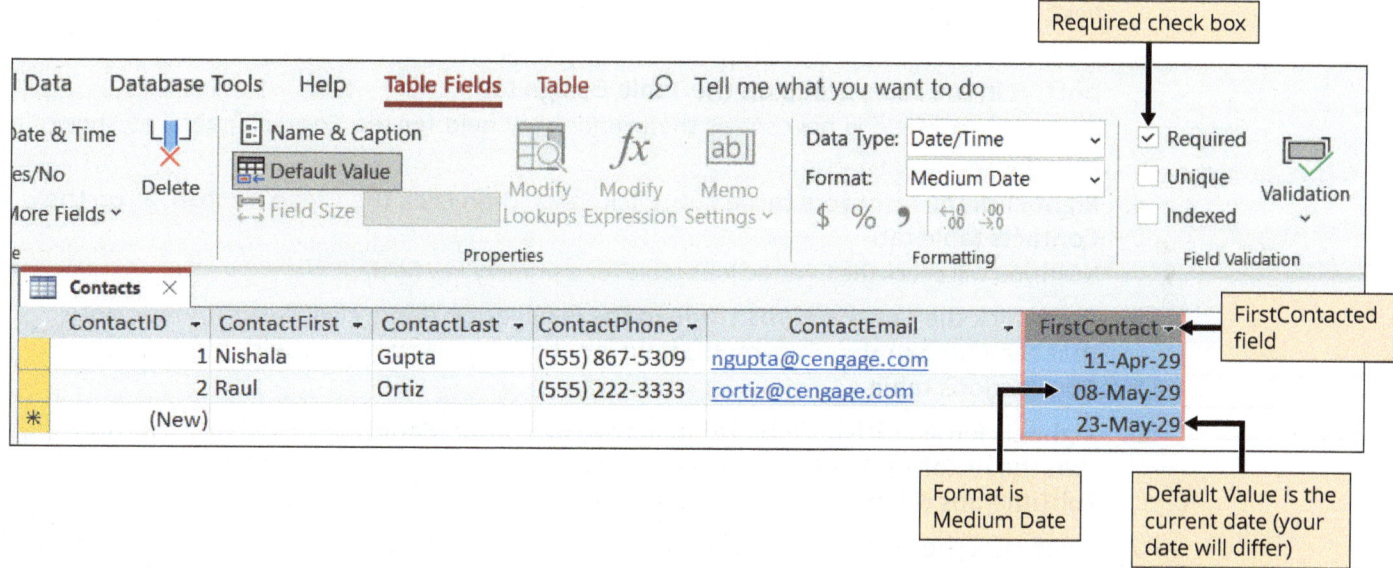

Entering dates

If you type the date for a Date/Time field instead of choosing a date from the pop-up calendar, Access assumes that years entered with two digits from 30 to 99 refer to the years 1930 through 1999, and 00 to 29 refers to the years 2000 through 2029. To enter a year before 1930 or after 2029, you must type all four digits of the year.

Using Action Tags

Action Tags are buttons that automatically appear in certain conditions. They provide a short menu of options to help you work with the task at hand. For example, in Table Design View, Access provides the **Property Update Options** Action Tag to help you quickly apply property changes to other objects of the database that use the field. The **Error Indicator** Action Tag helps identify potential errors.

Create Primary Key Fields

Case Sasha asks you to confirm that each table has an appropriate primary key field so that you can create table relationships to improve the database.

Objective
- Create a primary key field.

The **primary key field** of a table serves two important purposes. First, it contains data that uniquely identifies each record in that table. Second, the primary key field helps relate one table to another in a **one-to-many relationship**, where one record from one table may be related to many records in the second table. For example, one record in the Companies table may be related to many records in the ContractJobs table. (One company may have many contract job openings.) The primary key field is always on the "one" side of a one-to-many relationship between two tables.

Steps

1. Right-click the **Companies table** in the Navigation Pane, then click **Design View**
   The CompanyID AutoNumber field has been set as the primary key field as evidenced by the **key symbol** to the left of the field name. A field with the AutoNumber data type is a good candidate for the primary key field in a table because it automatically contains a unique number for each record.

2. Click the **Close button** ☒ on the Companies table tab, right-click the **Contacts table** in the Navigation Pane, then click **Design View**
   The Contacts table does not have a primary key field. The best choice would be the ContactID field.

3. Click the **ContactID field** if it is not already selected, then click the **Primary Key button** in the Tools group on the Table Design tab
   The ContactID field is now set as the primary key field for the Contacts table, as shown in **Figure 2-10**.

4. Right-click the **Contacts table tab**, click **Save**, then click the **Close button** ☒ on the Contacts table tab
   Next, you will check the ContractJobs table for a primary key field.

5. Right-click the **ContractJobs table** in the Navigation Pane, click **Design View**, note that the AutoNumber ContractID field is set as the primary key field, then close the ContractJobs table

6. Right-click the **FullTimeJobs table** in the Navigation Pane, click **Design View**, note that the AutoNumber JobID field is set as the primary key field, then close the FullTimeJobs table

7. Right-click the **Industries table** in the Navigation Pane, click **Design View**, note that the Short Text Industry field is set as the primary key field, then close the Industries table tab

8. Right-click the **StatesAndProvinces table** in the Navigation Pane, click **Design View**, note that the Short Text StateAbbrev field is set as the primary key field as shown in **Figure 2-11**, then close the StatesAndProvinces table
   Often, the primary key field is the first field in the table, but that is not a requirement. If you do not make any design changes to an object, you are not prompted to save it when you close it.

Figure 2-10: Setting the primary key field in Design View of the Contacts table

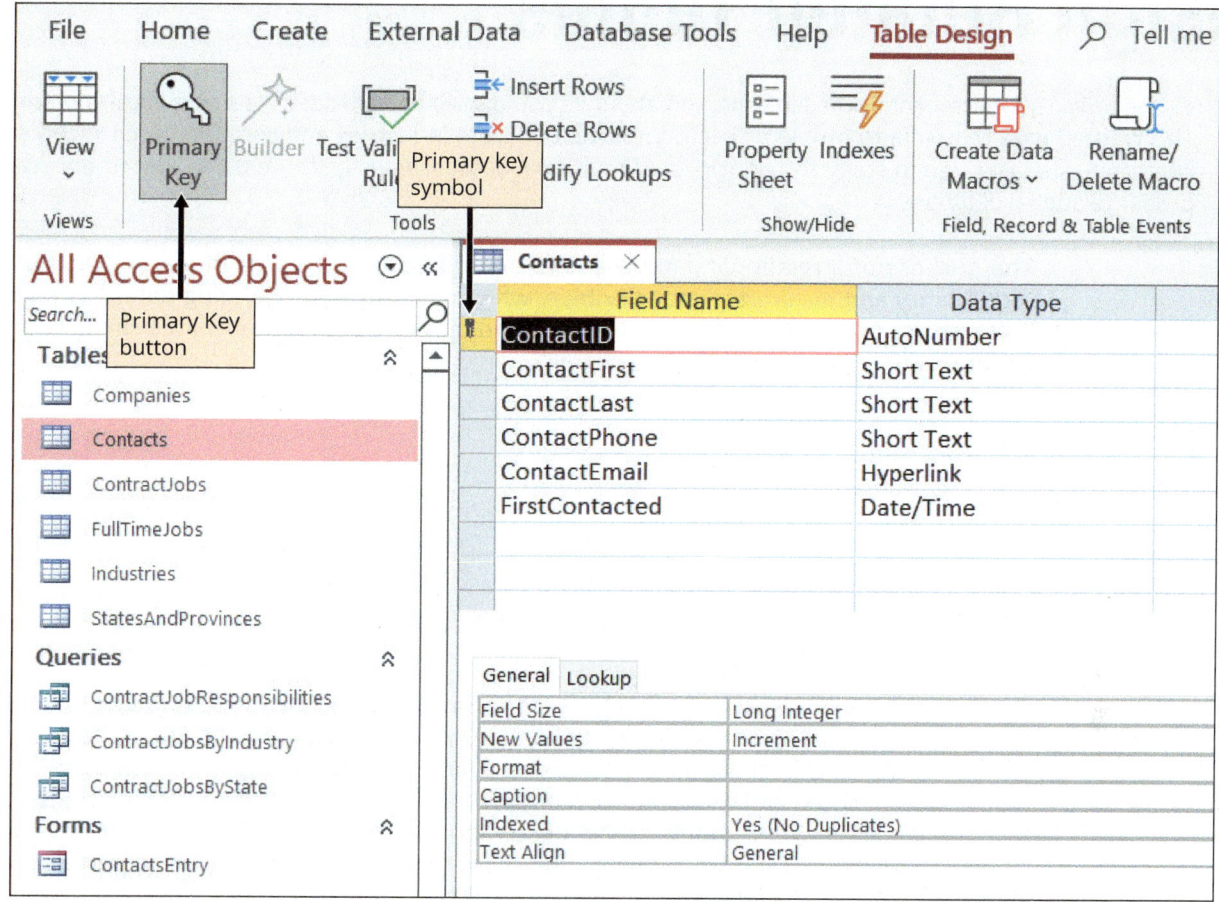

Figure 2-11: Design View of the StatesAndProvinces table

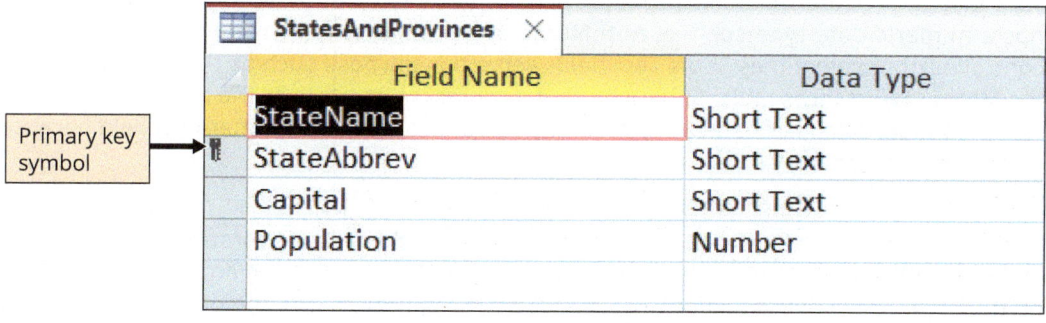

Design Related Tables

Case At one time, GIG Placement tracked information about its companies and jobs using a single Excel spreadsheet. This created data redundancy problems because of the duplicate industries and companies for each job and contact. Sasha asks you to study the principles of relational database design to help GIG Placement create a proper relational database.

Objectives
- Identify the terminology used when creating a relational database.
- Identify the steps to create a relational database.
- Analyze one-to-many relationships.

The purpose of a relational database is to organize and store data in a way that minimizes redundancy and maximizes your flexibility when querying and analyzing data. To accomplish these goals, a relational database uses multiple related tables rather than a single large table of data.

Details

To design a relational database, complete the following steps:

- **Design each table to contain fields that describe only one subject**

  Each table in the GIG Placement database stores records that describe only one of the following subjects: Companies, Contacts, ContractJobs, FullTimeJobs, Industries, and StatesAndProvinces. If you stored the data for these subjects in a single large table, the company information would be repeated for each job and each contact. Many problems are created when data is duplicated such as extra data entry work; additional data entry inconsistencies and errors; larger physical data storage requirements; and limitations on the ability to search for, analyze, and report on the data. A properly designed relational database minimizes these problems.

- **Identify a primary key field for each table**

  The primary key field contains unique information for each record. You have already made sure that each of the six tables has a proper primary key field. Generally, the primary key field has a numeric data type such as AutoNumber (automatically increments) or Number (user controlled), but sometimes Short Text fields serve this purpose such as the StateAbbrev field in the StatesAndProvinces table. Although using a contact's last name as the primary key field might work in a small database, names are generally a poor choice for the primary key field because two records may legitimately have the same name.

- **Build foreign key fields and one-to-many relationships**

  To tie the information from one table to another, one field must be common to each table. This linking field is the primary key field on the "one" side of the relationship and the **foreign key field** on the "many" side of the relationship. You are not required to give the primary and foreign key fields the same name, although doing so may clarify which fields are used to relate two tables.

  The current relational database design for the Jobs database is shown in **Figure 2-12**. It is only partially completed. Currently, one record in the Industries table is related to many records in the Companies table using the common Industry field. One record in the Companies table is related to many records in the ContractJobs and FullTimeJobs tables using the common CompanyID field. The StatesAndProvinces as well as the Contacts tables are not currently participating in the relational database, but you will correct that in the next lesson. **Table 2-4** summarizes important relational database terminology.

Table 2-4: Terminology used when creating a relational database

term	definition
Field	A column of information in a table. A field should not contain more than one piece of data. For example, always separate first and last names into two fields so you can sort, filter, and find either name. Do not enter numbers and units of measurement such as *10 minutes* or *5 hours* into a single field. Doing so prevents you from easily sorting and calculating the numeric part of the information.

term	definition
Record	A group of related fields that describes a person, place, thing, or transaction such as a company or a job; a row
Table	A collection of records for a single subject such as Industries or Companies
Primary key field	A field that contains unique data for each record. Often an AutoNumber or Number field, a primary key field may also have a Short Text data type and may be used on the parent table ("one" table) side of a one-to-many relationship.
Foreign key field	A field in the child table ("many" table) that connects each record to the appropriate record in the parent table ("one" table)
Parent table	The table on the "one" side of a "one-to-many" relationship
Parent record	A record in the parent table
Child table	The table on the "many" side of a "one-to-many" relationship
Child record	A record in the child table
One-to-many relationship	A link between two tables that relates one record in the parent table to many records in the child table. For example, one record in the Industries table can be related to many records in the Companies table.
One-to-one relationship	A link between two tables that relates one record in the parent table to one record in the child table. One-to-one relationships are rare because this relationship can be simplified by moving all the fields into a single table.
Many-to-many relationship	If two tables have a many-to-many relationship, one record in one table may be related to many records in the other table and vice versa. You cannot directly create a many-to-many relationship between two tables in Access. To connect two tables with this relationship, you must establish a third table called a **junction table** and create two one-to-many relationships from the original two tables using the junction table as the child table for both relationships. For example, at a school, the Students and Classes tables have a many-to-many relationship because one student can be in many classes and one class can have many students. To connect the Students and Classes tables, create a third table, such as Enrollments, as the junction table. One student can be enrolled in many classes. One class can have many enrollments.
Junction table	The table between two tables that have a many-to-many relationship; the junction table is a child table to the other two tables.
Referential integrity	A set of rules that helps prevent orphan records in a child ("many") table. With referential integrity enforced, you cannot enter a value in a foreign key field of the child ("many") table that does not have a match in the linking field of the parent ("one") table. Referential integrity also prevents you from deleting a record in the parent ("one") table if the foreign key field of the child ("many") table has a matching entry.
Orphan record	A record in a child ("many") table that has no match in the parent ("one") table. Orphan records cannot be created in a child table if referential integrity is enforced.
Scrubbing or data cleansing	Removing and fixing orphan records in a relational database

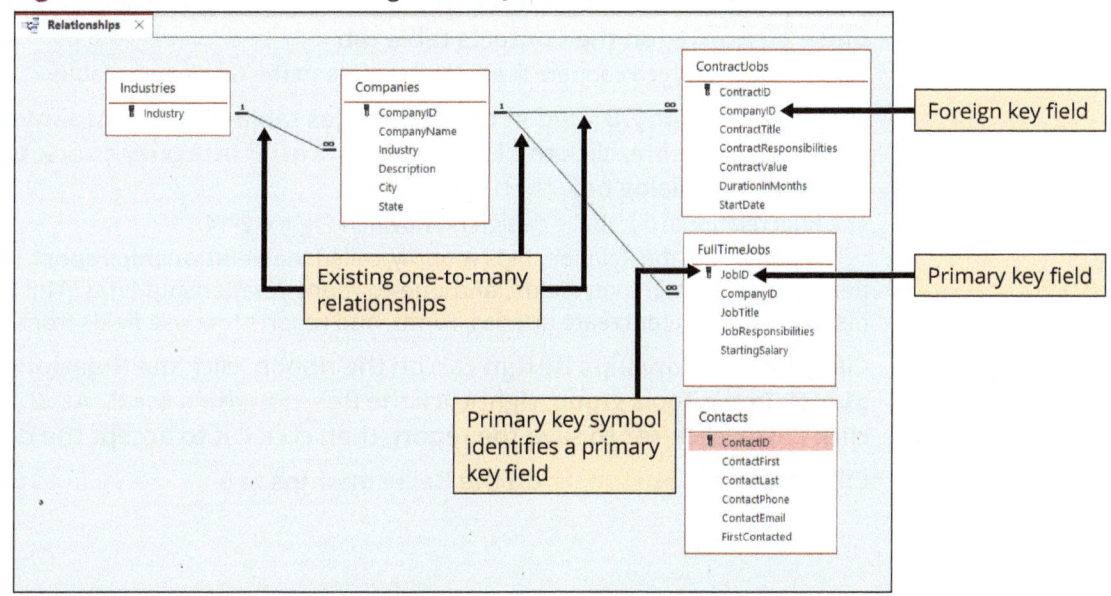

Figure 2-12: Initial relational design for the Jobs database

Create One-to-Many Relationships

Case Sasha asks you to complete the relational database by connecting the StatesAndProvinces and Companies tables in a one-to-many relationship. You can then combine data from both tables in queries, forms, and reports.

Objectives
- Create a foreign key field.
- Create one-to-many relationships.
- Set referential integrity.
- Create a Relationship report.

You must connect the tables in your database in proper one-to-many relationships to enjoy the benefits of a relational database. You use a common field in each table to create a one-to-many relationship between the tables. The common field is always the primary key field in the parent ("one") table and is called the foreign key field in the child ("many") table. **Table 2–5** describes a few common one-to-many relationships.

Steps

1. Click the **Database Tools tab** on the ribbon, click the **Relationships button**, then drag the **StatesAndProvinces table** from the Navigation Pane to the Relationships window

   Each table in the database is represented by a small **field list** window that displays the table's field names. A **key symbol** identifies the primary key field in each table. To relate the two tables in a one-to-many relationship, you connect them using a common field, which is always the primary key field on the parent ("one") side of the relationship.

   Quick Tip: Drag a field list by its title bar to move the field list.

2. Drag the **StateAbbrev field** in the **StatesAndProvinces table** to the **State field** in the **Companies table**

   The Edit Relationships dialog box opens, as shown in **Figure 2-13**, which provides information about the tables and fields that will participate in the relationship and includes the option to enforce referential integrity.

   Trouble: If you need to delete a relationship, right-click a relationship line, then click Delete.

3. Click the **Enforce Referential Integrity check box**, then click **Create**

   A **one-to-many join line** appears between the StatesAndProvinces table and the Companies table. The parent ("one") side, as indicated by the "1" symbol on the line, identifies the primary key field used in the relationship. The child ("many") side, as indicated by the **infinity symbol**, identifies the foreign key field used in the relationship.

   The Contacts table does not have a corresponding foreign key field, which you need to create a one-to-many relationship.

4. Right-click the **Contacts table field list**, click **Table Design**, click the **blank Field Name cell** just below the **FirstContacted field**, type **CompanyID**, click the **Data Type arrow**, click **Number**, right-click the **Contacts table tab**, click **Save**, then click the **Close button** ✕ on the Contacts table tab

   Now you are ready to connect the Contacts table to the Companies table.

5. Drag the **CompanyID field** in the Companies table to the **CompanyID field** in the **Contacts table**, click the **Enforce Referential Integrity check box** in the Edit Relationships dialog box, then click **Create**

   The final relational database design is shown in **Figure 2-14**.

   A printout of the Relationships window, called the **Relationship report**, includes table names, field names, primary key fields, and one-to-many relationship lines. This printout is a helpful resource as you later create queries, forms, and reports that use fields from multiple tables.

6. Click the **Relationships Design tab** on the ribbon, click the **Relationship Report button** in the Tools group, right-click the **Relationships for IL_AC_2_Jobs report tab**, click **Close**, click **Yes** to save the report, then click **OK** to accept the default report name

7. Click the **Close button** ✕ on the **Relationships tab**

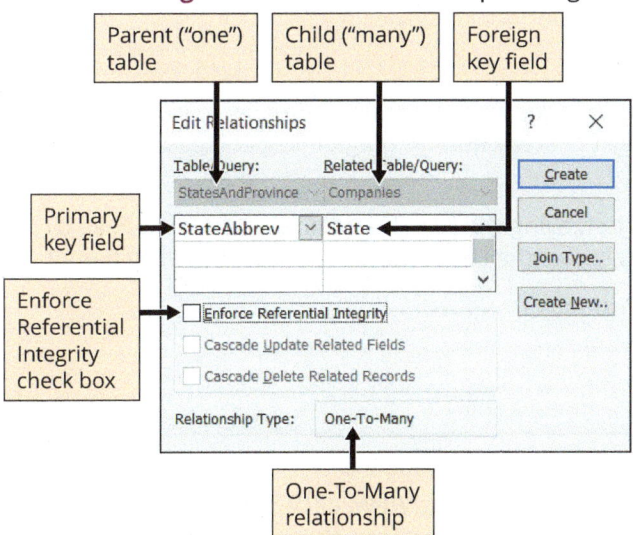

Figure 2-13: Edit Relationships dialog box

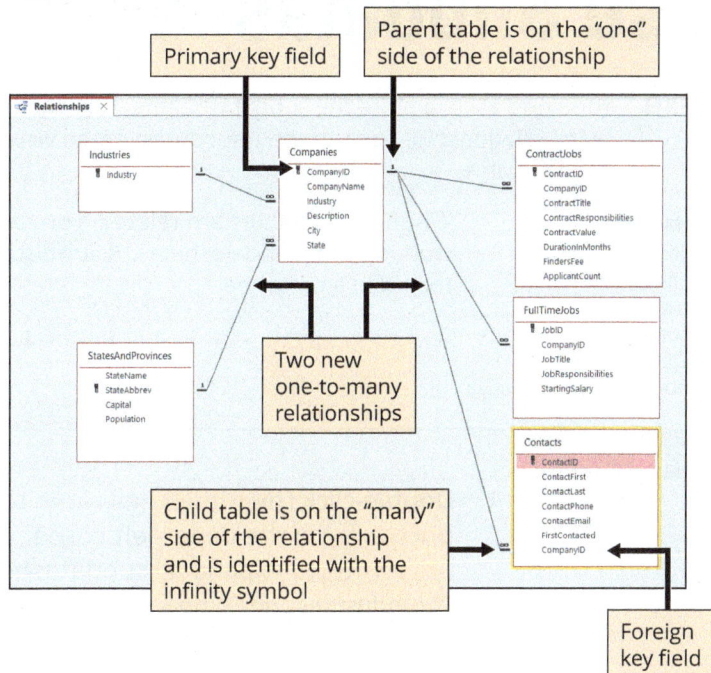

Figure 2-14: Final Relationships window

Table 2-5: Common one-to-many relationships

table on "one" side	table on "many" side	linking field	description
Products	Sales	ProductID	A ProductID field must have a unique entry in a Products table, but it is listed many times in a Sales table
Students	Enrollments	StudentID	A StudentID field must have a unique entry in a Students table, but it is listed many times in an Enrollments table as the student enrolls in multiple classes
Employees	Promotions	EmployeeID	An EmployeeID field must have a unique entry in an Employees table, but it is listed many times in a Promotions table as the employee is promoted to new job positions over time

Specifying the data type of the foreign key field

The foreign key field in the child table must have the same data type (Short Text or Number) as the primary key it is related to in the parent table. An exception to this rule is when the primary key field in the parent table has an AutoNumber data type. In this case, the linking foreign key field in the child table must have a Number data type. A Number field used as a foreign key field must also have a Long Integer Field Size property to match the Field Size property of the AutoNumber primary key field.

Cascade options

Cascade Update Related Fields means that if a value in the primary key field (the field on the "one" side of a one-to-many relationship) is modified, all values in the foreign key field (the field on the child ("many") side of a one-to-many relationship) are automatically updated as well. **Cascade Delete Related Records** means that if a record on the parent ("one") side of a one-to-many relationship is deleted, all related records in the child ("many") table are also deleted. Because both of these options automatically change or delete data in the child ("many") table behind the scenes, they should be used with caution.

Use Subdatasheets

Case You and Sasha explore the subdatasheet feature that Access provides when two tables are related in a one-to-many relationship. You can use a subdatasheet to view and edit related data without opening and navigating to another table.

Objectives
- Expand and collapse subdatasheets.
- Use data in a subdatasheet.
- Customize the status bar.

When all the tables are related, you can start enjoying the benefits of a relational database by working with subdatasheets. A **subdatasheet** shows the child records connected to each parent record in a datasheet.

Steps

1. **Double-click the Industries table to open it in Datasheet View, click the Select All button in the upper-left corner of the Industries datasheet, then click any Expand button + to expand all subdatasheets at the same time, as shown in Figure 2-15**
   The Industries and Companies tables are linked in a one-to-many relationship, so the subdatasheet for each industry record displays related child records from the Companies table. The records in the subdatasheet also have Expand buttons.

2. **Click the Expand button + to the left of the Arnprior Aerospace record (the second record in the Aerospace subdatasheet)**
   The Companies table participates as the parent table in three one-to-many relationships, so you are presented with the Insert Subdatasheet dialog box, asking which child table you want to select.

3. **Click ContractJobs in the Insert Subdatasheet dialog box**
   The CompanyID field is automatically added to the Link Child Fields and Link Master Fields boxes, as shown in Figure 2-16, because it is the field that connects the Companies and ContractJobs tables.

4. **Click OK in the Insert Subdatasheet dialog box**
   Three records in the ContractJobs table are linked to the Arnprior Aerospace record in the Companies table and are now displayed in the Arnprior Aerospace subdatasheet. You can use subdatasheets to enter and edit data.

5. **Enter 250.25 as the FindersFee field value for each of the three contract job records in the Arnprior Aerospace subdatasheet, click the Select All button in the upper-left corner of the Industries datasheet, click the Collapse button − to the left of the Aerospace record, click the Close button × on the Industries table tab, then click No when asked to save changes to the Companies table**

6. **Double-click the ContractJobs table to open it in Datasheet View, scroll down to the records for the Arnprior Aerospace company (ContractIDs 18 through 20), then scroll to the right to view the 250.25 entries you made to the FindersFee field in a subdatasheet**
   When working with data in Datasheet View, subdatasheets make it easy to view child records.
   As you are working with Access, you may notice messages and indicators that appear in the status bar at the bottom of the Access window. Table 2-6 lists information on status bar indicators. To turn these indicators on and off, right-click the status bar then select the indicator you want to change. Most of the indicator messages appear in the right corner of the status bar.

7. **sam'↑ Click the Close button × on the ContractJobs table tab, click the Database Tools tab, click the Compact and Repair Database button, then close Access**

Use Subdatasheets   AC 2-19

Figure 2-15: Expanding subdatasheets for the Industries table

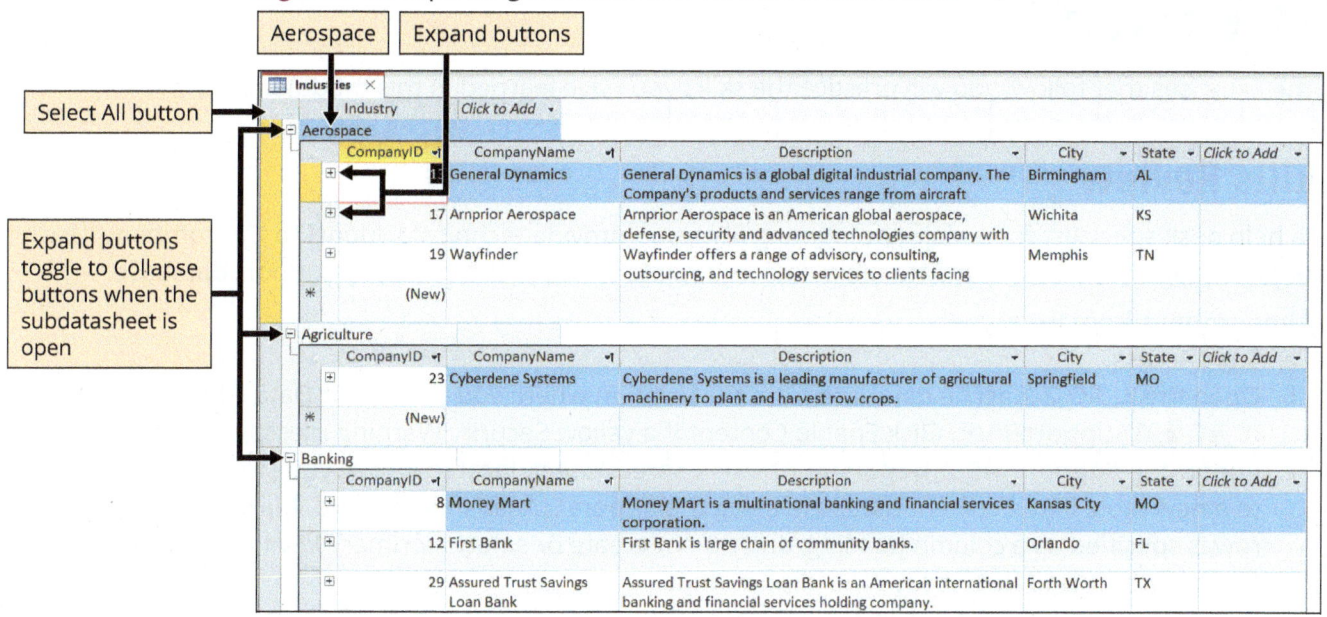

Figure 2-16: Insert Subdatasheet dialog box

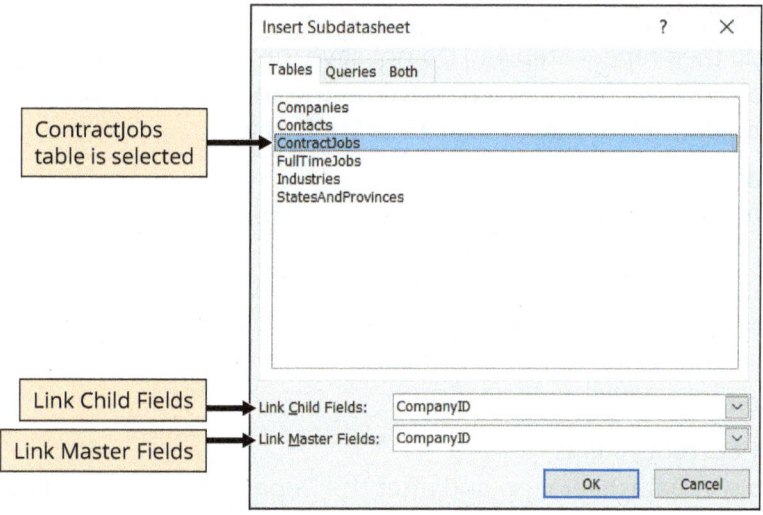

Table 2-6: Status bar indicators

status bar indicator	text displayed in the status bar
Caps Lock	Caps Lock when the Caps Lock is toggled on
Kana Mode	Kana, short for Katakana, a Japanese writing system; you must have a special installation of Access to enter these characters
Num Lock	Num Lock when the Num Lock is toggled on
Scroll Lock	Scroll Lock when the Scroll Lock is toggled on
Overtype	Overtype when Overtype mode (rather than Insert mode) is toggled on
Filtered	Filtered when using the filter features
Move Mode	Move Mode when using customized insertion point and key behaviors
Extended Selection	Extended Selection when using extend mode, a feature that allows you to select text more easily without using a mouse

Practice

In the exercises that follow, you will practice the skills you have learned in this module.

Skills Review

As a help desk specialist for a major accounting firm, you provide technical support to the company. Use your knowledge of Access to update table data and relate tables in the company support database.

1. **Import data from Excel.**
    a. Start Access.
    b. Open the IL_AC_2-2.accdb database from the location where you store your Data Files and save it as **IL_AC_2_ITSupportDesk**. Click Enable Content if a yellow Security Warning message appears.
    c. Import the **Support_AC_2_Departments.xlsx** spreadsheet, located where you store your Data Files, to a new table in the current database using the Import Spreadsheet Wizard. Make sure that the first row is specified as a column heading, and do not create or select a primary key field. Name the table **Departments** and do not save the import steps.
    d. Open the Departments table in Table Datasheet View to confirm that the import worked properly. The Departments table should have eight records. Close the Departments table.
    e. Append the records from the **Support_AC_2_Staff.xlsx** spreadsheet, located where you store your Data Files, to the existing Staff table. (**Hint**: If a "Subscript out of range" error appears, close the database, reopen it, then repeat Step 1e.) Do not save the import steps.
    f. Open the Staff table in Table Datasheet View to confirm that the append process worked properly. The Staff table should have 26 records. Close the Staff table.

2. **Modify fields in Datasheet View.**
    a. Open the SupportCalls table in Datasheet View and delete the last field, **CallPriority**, which currently has no data.
    b. Move the CallMinutes field between the CallDateTime and CallNotes fields.
    c. Decrease decimals on the CallMinutes field to **0** and make sure the Format property is set to **Standard**.
    d. Save and close the SupportCalls table.

3. **Modify Number and Currency fields.**
    a. Open the Staff table in Datasheet View and after the Department field, add a new field named **Salary** with a Currency data type.
    b. After the Salary field, add another field named **Dependents** with a Number data type.
    c. Enter **66000** for the Salary field and **4** for the Dependents field for the first employee (Robbie Reyes, EmployeeID 3).
    d. Decrease the decimals for the Salary field to **0.**
    e. Make the Default Value for the Dependents field **1**.
    f. Save and close the Staff table.

4. **Modify Short Text fields.**
    a. Open the Staff table in Design View and after the Dependents field, add a new field named **EmergencyPhone** with a Short Text data type.
    b. Save the Staff table, then use the Input Mask Wizard to add a Phone Number input mask. Use the asterisk (*****) as the Placeholder character and accept the other default settings.

c. Change the Field Size property of the EmergencyPhone field to **10**.
d. Change the Field Size property of the Department field to **15**.
e. Save the Staff table and click **Yes** when prompted about losing data. No data will be lost because no existing entries exceed the new Field Size property limits you set.
f. Display the Staff table in Datasheet View, tab to the EmergencyPhone field for the second record (Tony Roth EmployeeID 6), then type **5553338888** to enter the phone number using the Input Mask property.
g. Close the Staff table.

5. **Modify Date/Time fields.**
   a. Open the SupportCases table in Design View and change the Format property for both the OpenedDate and the ResolvedDate fields to **Short Date**.
   b. Change the Default Value for the OpenedDate field to **=Date()** to provide today's date.
   c. Change the Required Value for the OpenedDate field to **Yes**.
   d. Save the table, click Yes when prompted to test the data, then close the SupportCases table.

6. **Create primary key fields.**
   a. Open the Departments table in Design View and set the Department field as the primary key field. Save and close the Departments table.
   b. Open each of the other tables, Staff, SupportCalls, and SupportCases, in Design View to view and confirm that they have a primary key field. In each case, the first field is designated as the primary key field and has an AutoNumber data type. A field with an AutoNumber data type will automatically increment to the next number as new records are entered into that table. Close the tables.

7. **Design related tables.**
   a. Open the Relationships window to study the existing relationships between the tables.
   b. Drag the edges of the field lists so that all fields are clearly visible and drag the field list title bars as needed to clearly position the tables so that the SupportCalls table is to the right of the SupportCases table and the SupportCases table is to the right of the Staff table.
   c. Be ready to discuss these issues in class or in an online discussion thread.
      - Why is it important to relate tables in the first place?
      - What are the relationships in this database?
      - What role does the primary key field in each table play in the relationships identified in Step 7a?
      - What is the foreign key field in each of the relationships?
      - What parent ("one") tables exist in this database?
      - What child ("many") tables exist in this database?
      - What do the "1" and infinity symbols tell you about the relationship?
   d. Save the Relationships window.

8. **Create one-to-many relationships.**
   a. Add the Departments table to the Relationships window. Position it to the left of the Staff table.
   b. Create a one-to-many relationship between the Departments table and the Staff table using the common Department field.
   c. Enforce referential integrity on the relationship.
   d. Save the Relationships window, as shown in **Figure 2-17**, then close it.

Skills Review (Continued)

Figure 2-17

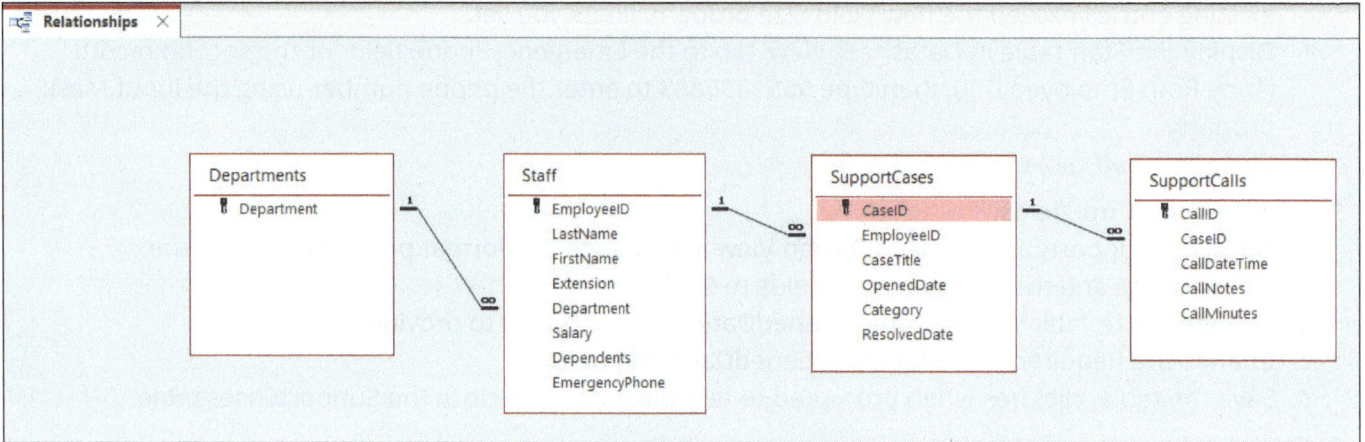

9. **Use subdatasheets.**
   a. Open the Departments table in Datasheet View. Expand the Accounting Department's subdatasheet to display the staff who work in that department.
   b. Change the Extension value of EmployeeID 29 (Sean Calderon) from 6788 to **6789** in the subdatasheet.
   c. Use the subdatasheet to add a new employee with your first and last names and **7777** as the Extension field value.
   d. Expand the subdatasheet for EmployeeID 29 (Sean Calderon) to display the cases linked to that employee.
   e. Expand the subdatasheet for CaseID 18 (Google doesn't look right) to display the calls linked to that case.
   f. Collapse all subdatasheets and close the Departments table.
   g. Compact and repair the database and close Access.

Independent Challenge 1

As the manager of Homefront, a company that provides personal support workers (PSWs) to patients, you have created a database to manage the schedules that connect each healthcare provider with the PSWs that the provider needs to efficiently handle patient visits. In this exercise, you create the primary keys and relationships required to create a relational database.

   a. Start Access. Open the **IL_AC_2-3.accdb** database from the location where you store your Data Files and save it as **IL_AC_2_Homefront**. Click Enable Content if a yellow Security Warning message appears.
   b. Open the Relationships window. Drag the ScheduleItems table from the Navigation Pane to the Relationships window, positioning it in the middle of the four other tables. (**Hint**: You can also add tables to the Relationships window by clicking the Add Tables button in the Relationships group on the Relationships Design tab.)
   c. With all five tables in the Relationships window, notice that each table has a primary key field except for the ScheduleItems table. Open the ScheduleItems table in Design View, set the TransactionNo field as the primary key field, then save and close the table to return to the Relationships window.

d. To connect the tables, you decide how "one" record in a parent table relates to "many" records in a child table. In this case, the ScheduleItems table is the child table to each of the four other tables. Therefore, build four one-to-many relationships with referential integrity as follows:
   - Drag the ScheduleNo field from the ScheduleDate table to the ScheduleNo field of the ScheduleItems table.
   - Drag the LocationNo field from the Locations table to the LocationNo field of the ScheduleItems table.
   - Drag the DoctorNo field from the Providers table to the DoctorNo field of the ScheduleItems table.
   - Drag the PSWNo field from the PSWs table to the PSWNo field of the ScheduleItems table.
e. Be sure to enforce referential integrity on each relationship. Doing so will add the "1" and "infinity" symbols to the relationship line. If they are missing, double-click the relationship line to open the Edit Relationships dialog box, where you can check the Enforce Referential Integrity check box.
f. Create a Relationship report, as shown in **Figure 2-18**.
g. Save and close the report with the default name of **Relationships for IL_AC_2_Homefront**, then save and close the Relationships window.
h. Compact and repair the database then close Access.

Figure 2-18

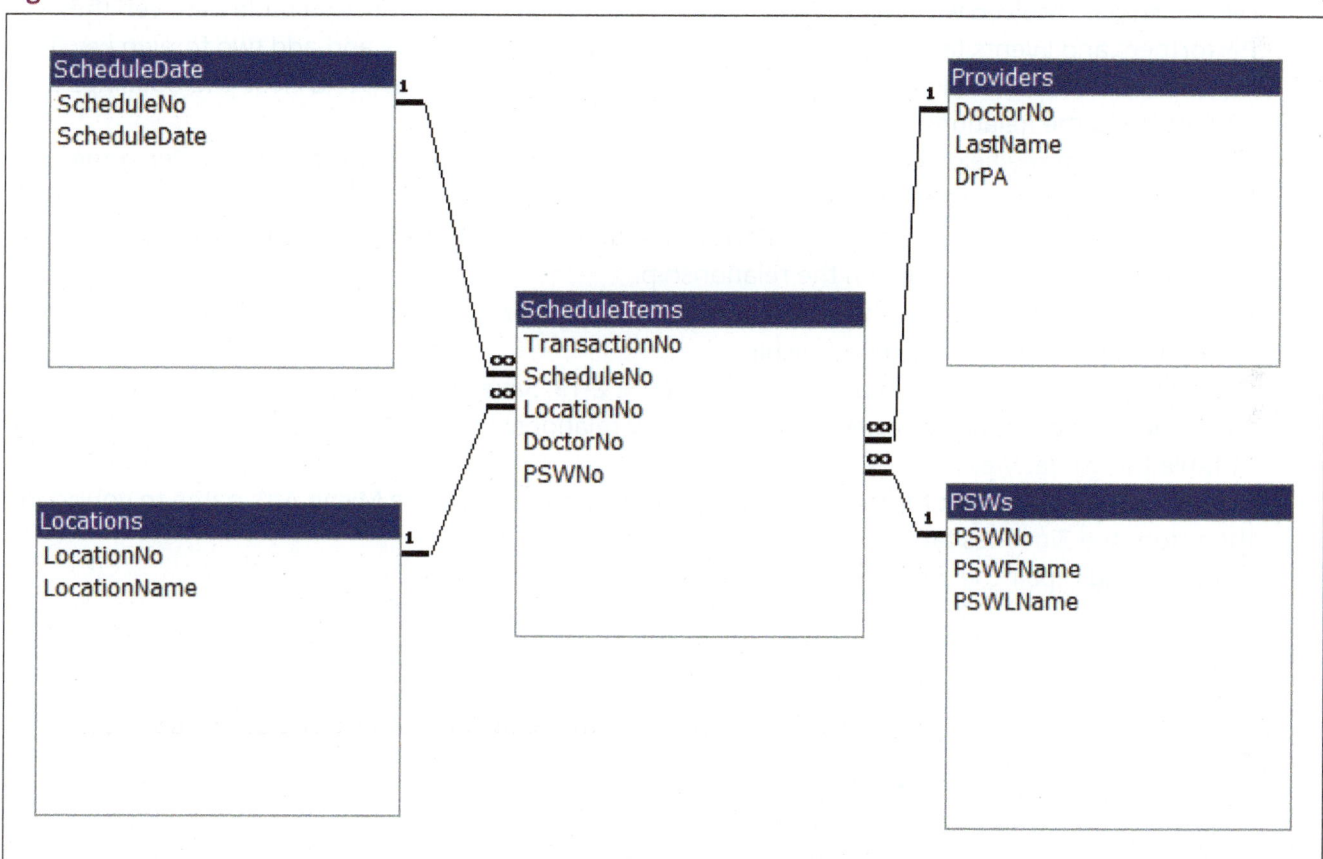

Independent Challenge 2

You are working for a city to coordinate a series of community entertainment events. You have started a database to track the events and performers who are booked for each event.

a. Start Access. Open the **IL_AC_2-4.accdb** database from the location where you store your Data Files and save it as **IL_AC_2_Performers**. Click Enable Content if a yellow Security Warning message appears.

b. To best manage this relational database, start at the table level and review the table relationships. Open the Relationships window and drag the tables from the Navigation Pane to the Relationships window in this order: Zipcodes, Performers, Bookings, and Events. (**Hint**: You can also add tables to the Relationships window by clicking the Add Tables button in the Relationships group on the Relationships Design tab.)

c. Some relationships are more obvious than others. For example, one record in the Zipcodes table may be related to many records in the Performers table. To establish this relationship, drag the Zip field from the Zipcodes table to the Zipcode field in the Performers table and enforce referential integrity on the relationship.

d. The Performers, Bookings, and Events tables are more difficult to analyze because one performer may be related to many bookings and one booking may have many performers. This many-to-many relationship is resolved with the Bookings table, which serves as the junction table between the Performers and Events tables. Open the Bookings table in Design view and add two foreign key fields named **PerformerID** and **EventID**, each with a Number data type. Save and close the Bookings table and return to the Relationships window.

e. With the foreign key fields in the Bookings table established, you are ready to link the Performers, Bookings, and Events tables by building these two relationships:
   - Drag the PerformerID field from the Performers table to the PerformerID field in the Bookings table. Enforce referential integrity on the relationship.
   - Drag the EventID field from the Event table to the EventID field in the Bookings table. Enforce referential integrity on the relationship.

f. Compare your final Relationships window to **Figure 2-19**. Save and close the Relationships window.

g. Open the Zipcodes table to review its one-to-many relationship with the Performers table by working in Table Datasheet View.

h. Expand the subdatasheet for the 64145 Springfield KS record, change Micah Ati's name to your name, then close the Zipcodes table.

i. Compact and repair the database and close Access.

Figure 2-19

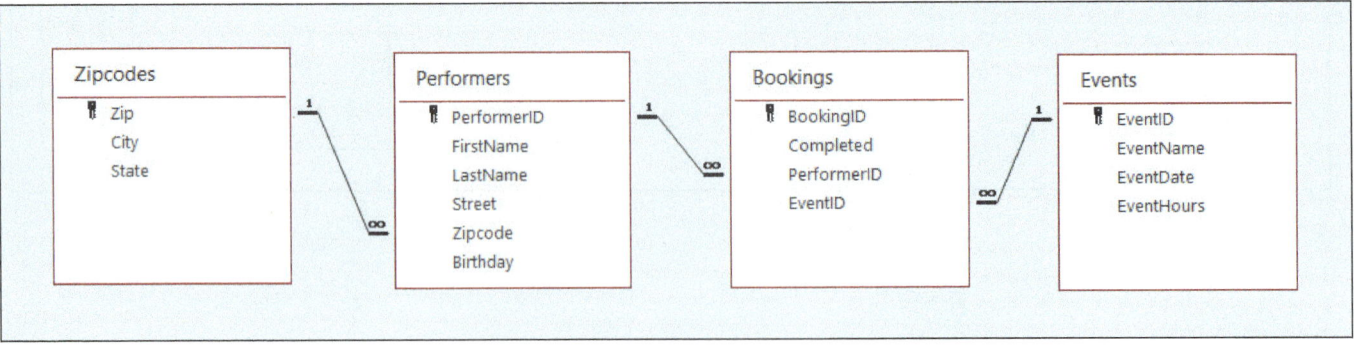

Visual Workshop

Open the **IL_AC_2-5.accdb** database from the location where you store your Data Files and save it as **IL_AC_2_CyberCourses**, then enable content if prompted. Import the **Support_AC_2_NewCourses.xlsx** Excel spreadsheet and append the records to the Courses table. Do not save the import steps.

Import the following spreadsheets as new tables with the following names. For each import, use the first row as the column headings and other default options of the Import Spreadsheet Wizard. Do not save the import steps.

- Import **Support_AC_2_Classes.xlsx** as **Classes** and set ClassNo as the primary key field.
- Import **Support_AC_2_Enrollments.xlsx** as **Enrollments** and set EnrollmentID as the primary key field.
- Import **Support_AC_2_Sections.xlsx** as **Sections** and set SectionNo as the primary key field.
- Import **Support_AC_2_Students.xlsx** as **Students** and set StudentID as the primary key field.

In the Relationships window, relate the tables in one-to-many relationships using **Figure 2-20** as a guide. Enforce referential integrity on each relationship. Save and close the Relationships window.

Figure 2-20

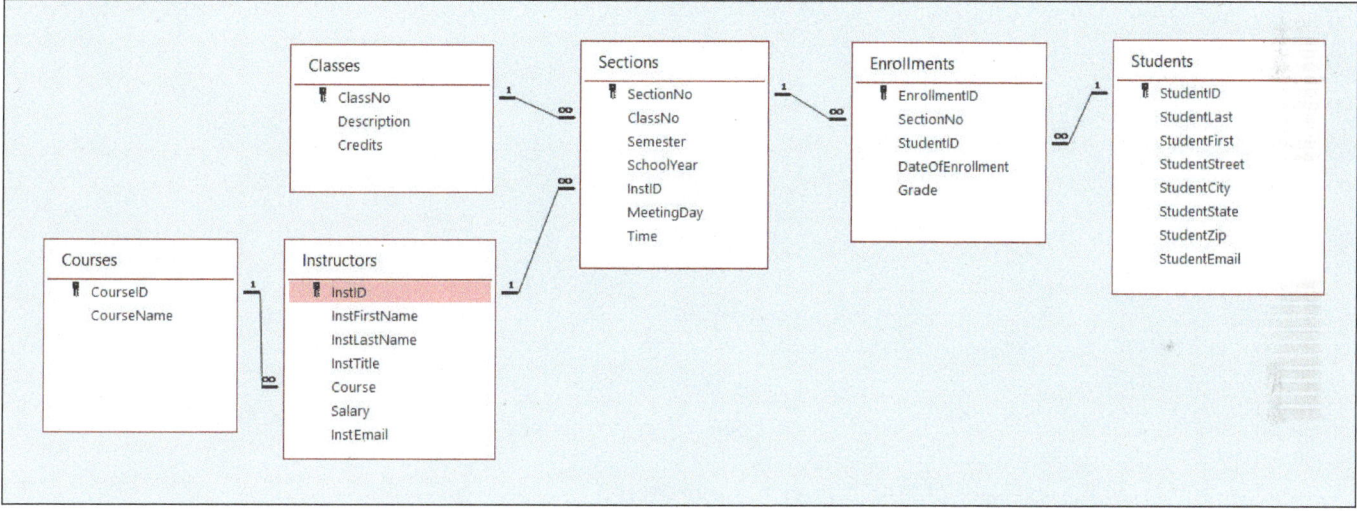

Access Module 3

Creating Queries

Case

Now that you've updated the tables in the database for GIG Placement and linked them in one-to-many relationships to create a relational database, you're ready to mine the data for information. You'll develop queries to provide Sasha Spiros, special projects director, with fast and accurate answers.

Module Objectives

After completing this module, you will be able to:

- Use Query Datasheet View
- Use Query Design View
- Use SQL View
- Sort data
- Find and replace data
- Filter data
- Enter and save criteria
- Apply AND criteria
- Apply OR criteria
- Create calculated fields
- Format a datasheet

Files You Will Need

IL_AC_3-1.accdb
IL_AC_3-2.accdb
IL_AC_3-3.accdb
IL_AC_3-4.accdb
IL_AC_3-5.accdb

Use Query Datasheet View

Case In the Jobs database, some contract job data is incomplete and some is out of date, so Sasha asks you to change the contract job data currently organized in a query. You'll work in Query Datasheet View to make the updates.

Objectives
- Edit and delete records.
- Hide and unhide columns.
- Freeze and unfreeze columns.

A **query** answers a question about the information in a database by allowing you to select a subset of fields and records from one or more tables and present them in a single datasheet. You can enter, edit, and navigate data in **Query Datasheet View**, which displays each field as a column and each record as a row just like Table Datasheet View. All data is stored only in tables, so any edits, additions, or deletions you make in Query Datasheet View are automatically reflected elsewhere in the database.

Steps

1. **sam↓** Start Access, open the **IL_AC_3-1.accdb database** from the location where you store your Data Files, save it as **IL_AC_3_Jobs**, enable content if prompted, then double-click the **ContractJobsByIndustry query** to open it in Datasheet View

    Each time you open a query, it shows a current view of the data. The datasheet displays one record for every job. One company may be connected to many jobs.

    The records for General Dynamics in Birmingham do not have a value in the State field. Although data is stored in tables, you can edit data in Query Datasheet View.

2. Click the **State field cell** for any General Dynamics record, type **AL**, then click any other record

    All records for General Dynamics in this query update to show AL (Alabama) in the State field because General Dynamics is related to six records in the ContractJobs table.

3. Click the **record selector** to the left of the sixteenth record (CompanyID 8 and ContractTitle of Executive Assistant), click the **Delete button** in the Records group, then click **Yes**

    You can delete records from a query datasheet the same way you delete them from a table datasheet. The navigation bar now indicates that you have 82 records in the datasheet as shown in **Figure 3-1**.

    In large datasheets, you may want to freeze certain fields so that they remain displayed at all times.

Quick Tip
To unfreeze a field, right-click any field name, then click Unfreeze All Fields on the shortcut menu.

4. Right-click the **CompanyName field name** to select the entire column, click **Freeze Fields** on the shortcut menu, press **TAB** as needed to move to the **ApplicantCount field** for the first record, then type **15**

    The CompanyName field is now positioned as the first field in the datasheet and doesn't scroll off the screen as you press TAB. In large datasheets, you may also want to hide fields.

Quick Tip
To unhide a field, right-click any field name, click Unhide Fields on the shortcut menu, click the check box beside the field that you want to unhide, then click Close.

5. Press **TAB** as needed to move to the **Description field**, right-click the **Description field name** to select the entire column, as shown in **Figure 3-2**, then click **Hide Fields** on the shortcut menu

    Hiding a field in a query datasheet doesn't remove it from the query; it merely hides it on the datasheet.

6. Right-click the **ContractJobsByIndustry tab**, click **Save**, then click the **Close button** ✕ on the ContractJobsByIndustry tab

    Saving your changes to this query saves the changes you made to freeze the CompanyName field and hide the Description field. Edits to data are automatically saved as you work.

Figure 3-1: Editing data in Query Datasheet View

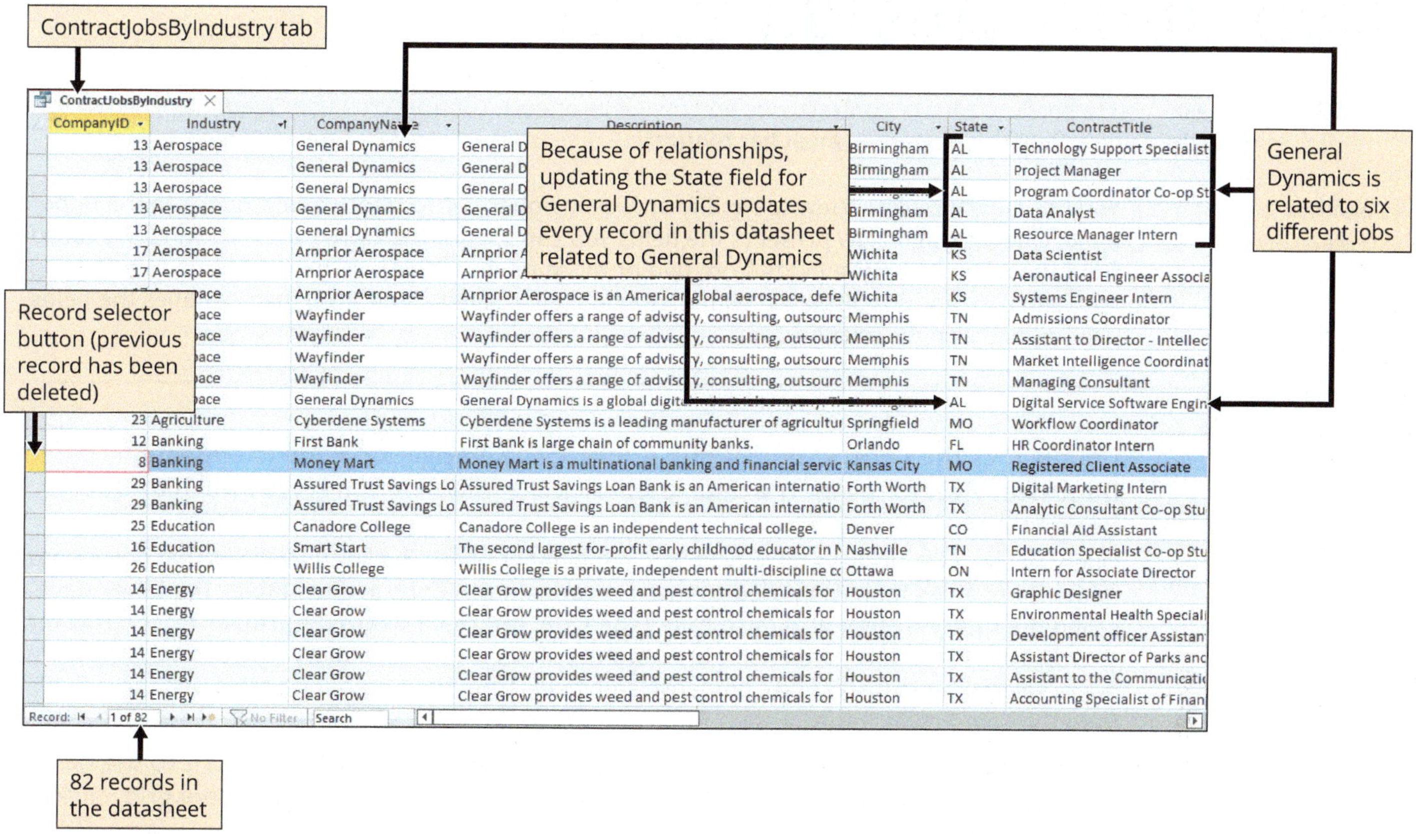

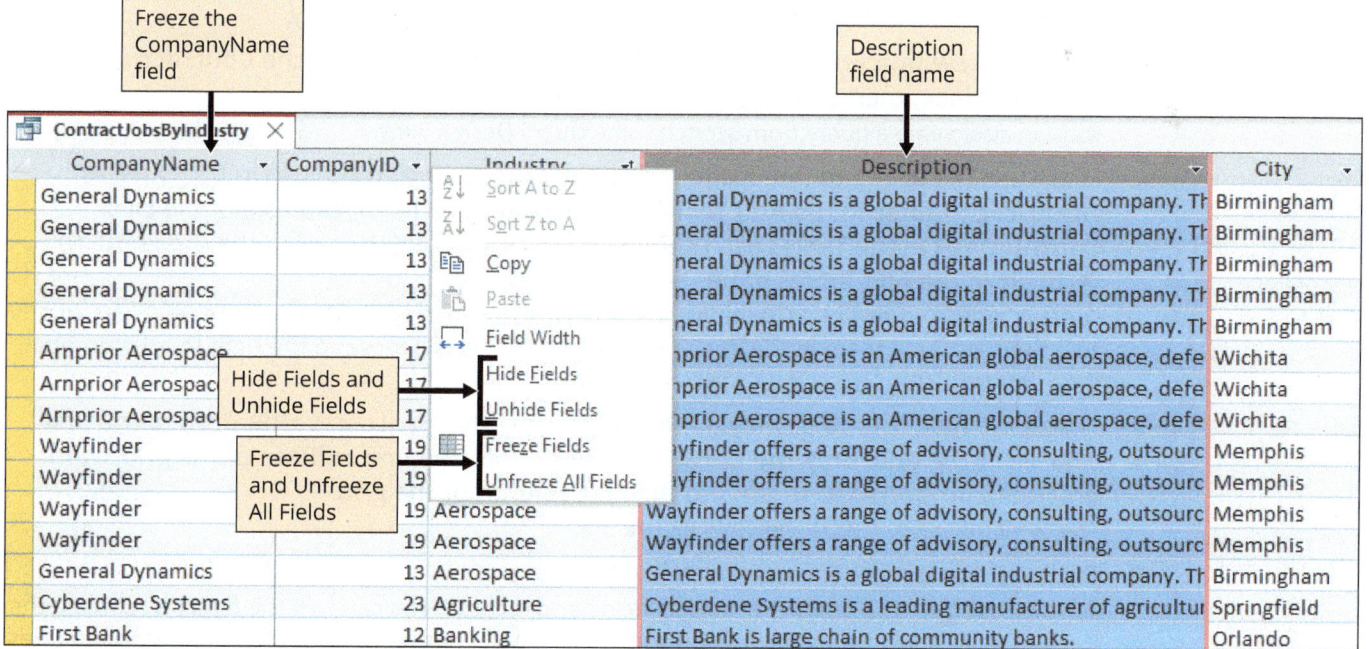

Figure 3-2: Freezing and hiding columns in Query Datasheet View

Use Query Design View

Case Sasha asks you to produce a list of contract jobs and the value of each contract. You use Query Design View to modify the ContractJobsValue query to meet her request.

Objectives
- Create a query in Query Design View.
- Add, remove, and move fields in Query Design View.

You use **Query Design View** to modify an existing query or to create a new query. In the upper pane, Query Design View presents the fields you can use for that query in small windows called **field lists**. If you use the fields from two or more related tables in the query, the relationship between two tables is displayed with a **join line** (also called a **link line**) that identifies the fields used to establish the relationship.

Steps

Quick Tip
You can toggle the Table row on and off in the query grid by clicking the Table Names button on the ribbon.

1. **Double-click the ContractJobsValue query in the Navigation Pane to open it in Datasheet View to review the data, then click the View button to switch to Query Design View**

   Query Design View displays table field lists in the upper pane. The link line shows that one record in the Companies table is related to many records in the ContractJobs table. The lower pane, called the **query design grid** (also called the **QBE**, **query by example grid**, or **query grid** for short), displays the field names, sort orders, and criteria used in the query. The ContractJobsValue query selects the Industry and CompanyName fields from the Companies table and three fields from the ContractJobs table.

Quick Tip
You can also click a field name in the first row of the grid, click the arrow, then select a new field from the list.

2. **Double-click the ContractValue field in the ContractJobs field list to add it to the next available column of the query grid, click the CompanyID field in the query grid, click the Delete Columns button in the Query Setup group, click the CompanyName field selector, then use the arrow pointer to drag the CompanyName field to the first column of the grid**

   The resulting query grid is shown in **Figure 3-3**. Removing a field from the query grid does not delete the field from its table. It simply removes the field from this query.

3. **Click the View button to switch to Datasheet View, right-click the ContractJobsValue tab, click Close, then click Yes to save changes**

   You can also create a query from scratch using Query Design View.

Trouble
If the Add Tables pane is not open, click the Add Tables button in the Query Setup group.

4. **Click the Create tab on the ribbon, click the Query Design button in the Queries group, click Tables in the Add Tables pane to display a list of tables, double-click ContractJobs in the Tables list, double-click Companies, then click the Close button to close the Add Tables pane**

   For this query, you want to include three fields. You can drag fields from the field lists to any column to position them in the query. Any existing fields will move to the right to accommodate the new field.

Quick Tip
You can also add a new column to the grid by clicking the Insert Columns button in the Query Setup group.

5. **Resize the field lists to display all the fields, drag the ContractValue field to the first column of the grid, drag the ContractTitle field to the first column of the grid, then drag the CompanyName field to the first column of the grid**

   The resulting query grid is shown in **Figure 3-4**.

6. **Click the Datasheet View button to run the query**

   For a **select query**, a query that selects fields and records, you can **run** the query by clicking the Datasheet View button or the Run button. In an **action query**, clicking the Run button modifies all the selected records. Because the Datasheet View button never changes data no matter what type of query you are building, it is a safe way to run a select query or view selected fields and records for an action query. You learn about action queries that change data in later modules.

7. **Right-click the Query1 tab, click Save, type CompanyContracts as the new query name, then click OK**

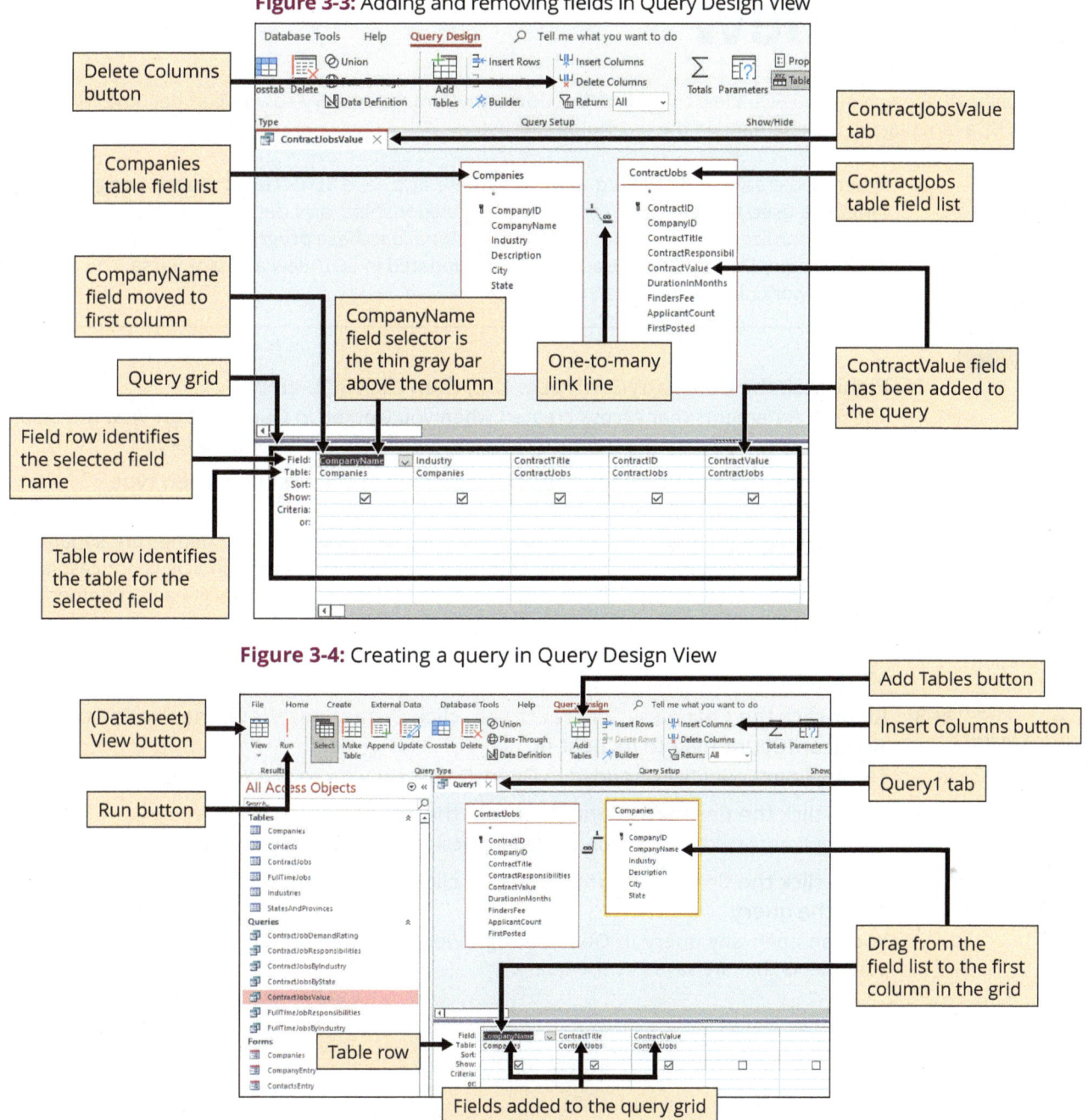

Figure 3-3: Adding and removing fields in Query Design View

Figure 3-4: Creating a query in Query Design View

Adding or deleting a table in Query Design View

You might want to add a table's field list to the upper pane of Query Design View to select fields from that table for the query. To add a new table to Query Design View, drag it from the Navigation Pane to the upper pane, or click the Add Tables button in the Query Setup group on the Query Design tab. To delete an unneeded table from Query Design View, click its title bar, then press DELETE.

Linking tables in Query Design View

If tables are joined in the Relationships window, they are automatically joined in Query Design View. If tables are not joined in the Relationships window, you can join them in Query Design View by dragging the linking field from one field list to another. However, you cannot enforce referential integrity on a relationship created in Query Design View. Also, a relationship created in Query Design View is established for that query only. Creating one-to-many relationships for the database in the Relationships window provides many productivity and application performance benefits over relating tables within individual queries.

Use SQL View

Case Sasha suggests you use SQL View to update the CompanyContracts query so you can become familiar with SQL, a language in high demand in the technology industry.

Objectives
- Modify a query in SQL View.
- Describe common SQL keywords.

When you create and save a query, you create and save **Structured Query Language (SQL)**, a language used to create and modify tables, relationships, and data in a relational database. SQL is a standardized language that all major relational database programs use. Whatever actions you take in Query Design View are automatically updated in SQL View and vice versa. You can use **SQL View** to work directly with the SQL code.

Steps

1. Right-click the **CompanyContracts tab**, then click **SQL View**
   The SQL statements that Access created when you worked in Query Design View are displayed. You can enter SQL statements directly into this window to modify your query.

2. Click to the right of ContractJobs.ContractValue in the first line, then type
   , ContractJobs.ApplicantCount
   The resulting SQL code is shown in **Figure 3-5**. In SQL, table and field names are separated by a period (.) and multiple fields are separated by a comma (,). Although SQL is not case-sensitive, it is customary to write the SQL keywords in all capital letters and to start each statement with an SQL keyword to make the code easier to read.
   A select query starts with the SQL keyword **SELECT**. **Table 3-1** lists some of the most common SQL keywords.

Trouble
If you receive an error message, make sure you use a comma (,) to separate the new field name and spell the table and field name correctly.

3. Right-click the **CompanyContracts tab**, click **Datasheet View**, then resize the ApplicantCount field to its best fit
   The ApplicantCount field is added to Query Datasheet View as shown in **Figure 3-6**.

4. Right-click the **CompanyContracts tab**, then click **Design View**
   The Applicants field is also added to Query Design View as shown in **Figure 3-7**.

5. Right-click the **CompanyContracts tab**, click **Close**, then click **Yes** when prompted to save the query
   You can open any query in Query Design View and then switch to SQL View to see the SQL statements that are saved by the query.

Figure 3-5: Adding the ApplicantCount field in SQL View

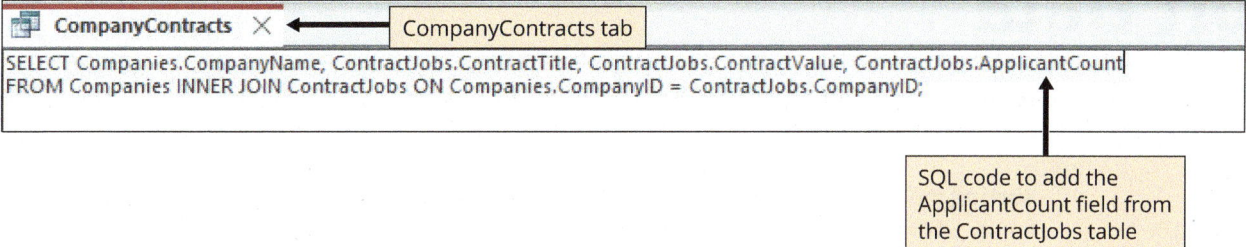

Figure 3-6: Viewing the ApplicantCount field in Query Datasheet View

CompanyName	ContractTitle	ContractValue	ApplicantCount
RSW Health	Project Manager	$65,000.00	31
BIG Ship	Customer Service	$65,000.00	4
BIG Ship	Operations Project Specialist	$69,000.00	25
BIG Ship	Client Product Support Associate	$72,000.00	31
KPMG	Microsoft PowerPoint specialist	$49,000.00	22
Talent Tree	Program Manager	$72,000.00	16

Figure 3-7: Viewing the ApplicantCount field in Query Design View

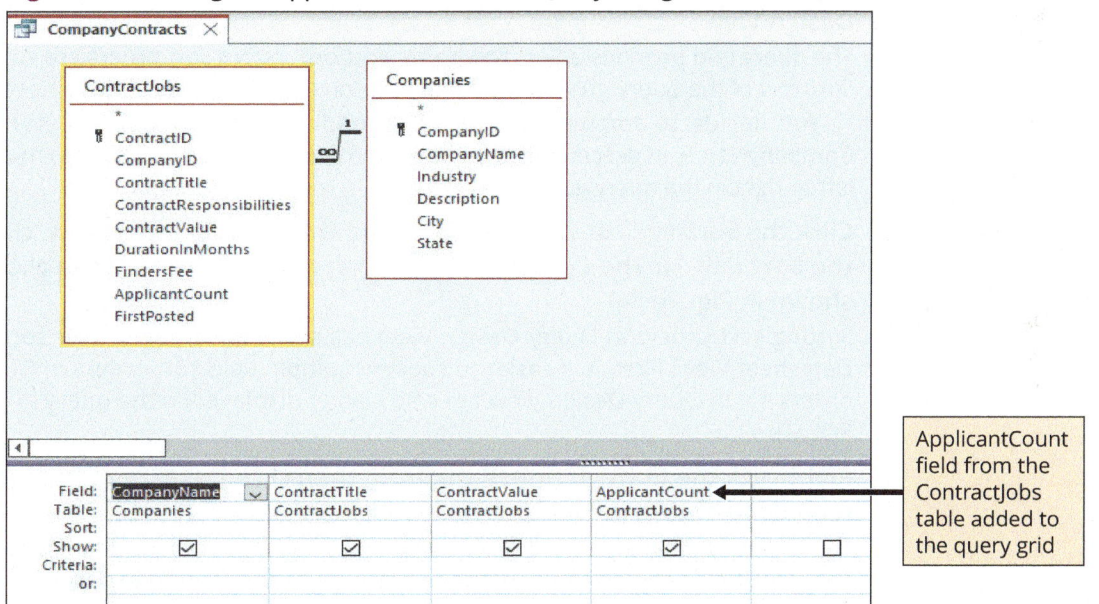

Table 3-1: Common SQL keywords

keyword	identifies...
SELECT	which fields you want to include in a select query
FROM	what tables contain the fields you have selected
WHERE	criteria used to limit the number of records selected
ORDER BY ... ASC (DESC)	sort order for the records; ASC means ascending, DESC means descending
INNER JOIN ... ON	which records will be selected when choosing fields from more than one table (there must be a match in both tables)
INSERT	the data and fields used when adding a new record
UPDATE ... SET	the data and fields used when updating specific records
DELETE	records to delete

Sort Data

Case Sasha asks you to sort the ContractJobsValue query to more clearly show the records with a high contract value.

Objectives
- Sort records in Query Datasheet View.
- Sort records in Query Design View.

Sorting means to order records in ascending or descending order based on values in one or more fields. Sorting helps you organize records to quickly find and analyze data. **Table 3-2** describes the Sort buttons on the Home tab. In Datasheet View, you can also click the arrow beside a field name to access sort options. Query Design View helps you add and save sort orders and is especially useful when you want to sort on multiple fields.

Steps

Quick Tip
Double-click the column resize pointer ↔ to widen a field to display the widest entry.

1. **Double-click the ContractJobsValue query** in the Navigation Pane to open it in Datasheet View, click the **ContractValue field**, click the **Descending button** in the Sort & Filter group, then use the column resize pointer ↔ to widen the ContractID and ContractValue fields as shown in **Figure 3-8**

   The ContractJobsValue query now lists the records from highest ContractValue to lowest, and the ContractValue field displays a descending sort indicator by the field name. However, sort orders applied to Datasheet View are not automatically added to Design View.

2. **Right-click the ContractJobsValue tab**, then click **Design View** to switch to Query Design View

   The query grid provides a **Sort row** to set sort orders. No sort orders are currently specified in the Sort row of the query grid even though you sorted the records in Datasheet View.

   You decide to sort the records in ascending order by CompanyName, and within each CompanyName, in descending order by ContractValue. Access evaluates multiple sort orders from left to right in the query grid.

3. **Click the Sort cell for the CompanyName field**, click the **arrow**, click **Ascending**, click the **Sort cell for the ContractValue field**, click the **arrow**, then click **Descending** as shown in **Figure 3-9**

   Setting sort orders in Query Design View has some advantages over sorting records in Query Datasheet View. First, it is easier to specify multiple field sort orders in Query Design View. Sort orders set in Query Design View are also clearly displayed in the query grid and are reflected in SQL View.

4. **Right-click the ContractJobsValue tab**, then click **Datasheet View** to view the sorted records as shown in **Figure 3-10**

   The first, or primary, sort order is ascending by CompanyName. When two or more records have the same CompanyName value, the records are further sorted in descending order based on the ContractValue field.

5. **Right-click the ContractJobsValue tab**, click **Close**, then click **Yes** when prompted to save changes

   Sort orders set in Query Design View are always saved with the query.

Figure 3-8: Sorting in Query Datasheet View

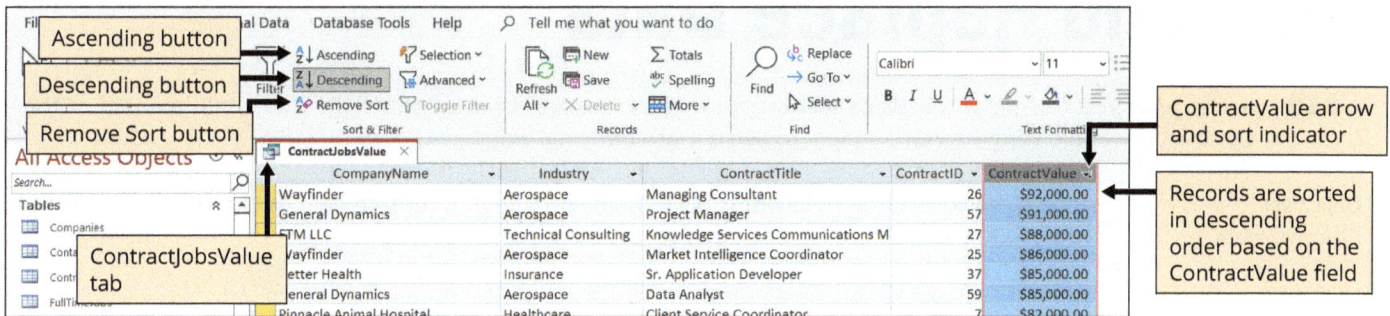

Figure 3-9: Sorting by multiple fields in Query Design View

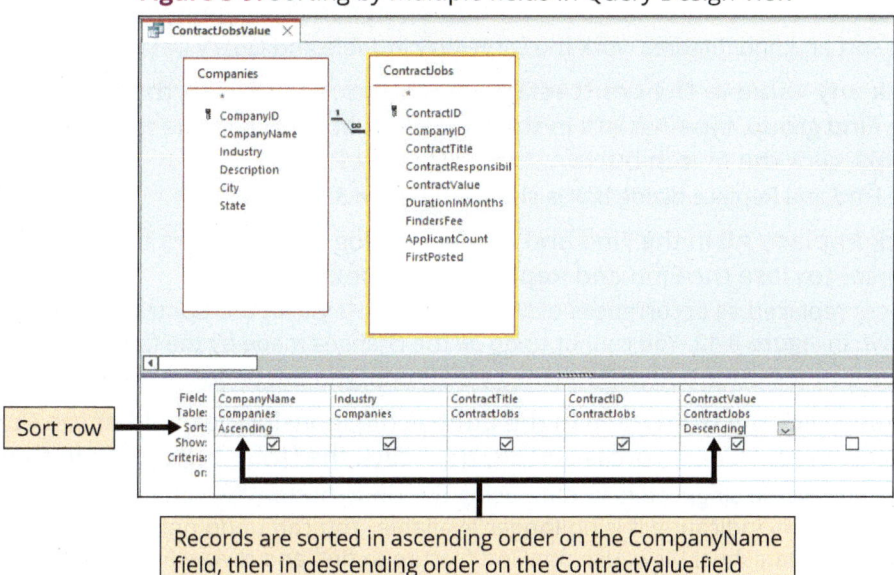

Figure 3-10: Final ContractJobsValue datasheet

CompanyName	Industry	ContractTitle	ContractID	ContractValue
Arnprior Aerospace	Aerospace	Data Scientist	18	$75,000.00
Arnprior Aerospace	Aerospace	Systems Engineer Intern	20	$62,000.00
Arnprior Aerospace	Aerospace	Aeronautical Engineer Associate Co-op	19	$35,000.00
Arobin Inc	Information	Customer Service Representative	1	$40,000.00
Assured Trust Savings Loan	Banking	Digital Marketing Intern	21	$48,000.00
Assured Trust Savings Loan	Banking	Analytic Consultant Co-op Student	22	$25,000.00
Better Health	Insurance	Sr. Application Developer	37	$85,000.00
Better Health	Insurance	Product Director	38	$78,000.00
Better Health	Insurance	Community Outreach and Engagement	39	$77,000.00
Better Health	Insurance	Associate Director Assistant	36	$60,000.00

Table 3-2: Datasheet View Sort buttons

name	button	purpose
Ascending	⬆	Sorts records based on the selected field in ascending order (0 to 9, A to Z)
Descending	⬇	Sorts records based on the selected field in descending order (Z to A, 9 to 0)
Remove Sort		Removes the current sort order

Find and Replace Data

Case Sasha asks you to find and replace all occurrences of "assists" in the ContractResponsibilities field of the ContractJobs table with the word "helps" to use a more informal word.

Objectives
- Find and replace data.
- Undo edits.

Access provides some excellent tools to help you find and replace data in Query Datasheet View. **Table 3-3** describes the Find buttons on the Home tab.

Steps

1. Double-click the **ContractJobs table** to open it in Datasheet View
   The sort and find features work the same way in Table and Query Datasheet View.

2. Click **any value in the ContractResponsibilities field**, click the **Replace button** in the Find group, type **Assists** in the Find What box, click in the **Replace With box**, type **Helps**, click the **Match button**, then click **Any Part of Field**
   The Find and Replace dialog box is shown in **Figure 3-11**.

3. Click **Replace All** in the Find and Replace dialog box, click **Yes** to continue, then click **Cancel** to close the Find and Replace dialog box
   Access replaced all occurrences of "Assists" with "Helps" in the ContractResponsibilities field, as shown in **Figure 3-12**. You cannot undo *all* the changes made by the find and replace feature, but if you click the Undo button in the Undo group, you can undo the last replacement.

4. Double-click the word **daily** in the ContractResponsibilities field of the ContractID 3 record, press **DELETE**, press **ENTER**, then click the **Undo button** in the Undo group
   You can reverse single edits to data using the Undo button. After you click it once, the Undo button is dim, indicating it is no longer available. You can undo only the most recent edit when working in Datasheet View. Use the Find feature to find and review field values.

5. Click **any value in the ContractResponsibilities field**, click the **Find button** in the Find group, type **targets** in the Find What box, click **Find Next**, click **Find Next** one more time to find the two occurrences of "targets," then click **Cancel** to close the Find and Replace dialog box
   If you wanted to search the entire datasheet versus the current field, you could use the Look In option in the Find and Replace dialog box, which allows you to check values in every field in the entire datasheet.

6. Click the **Close button** on the ContractJobs tab, then click **Yes** if prompted to save changes
   All updates to data made in Query Datasheet View are automatically updated in all objects.

Figure 3-11: Find and Replace dialog box

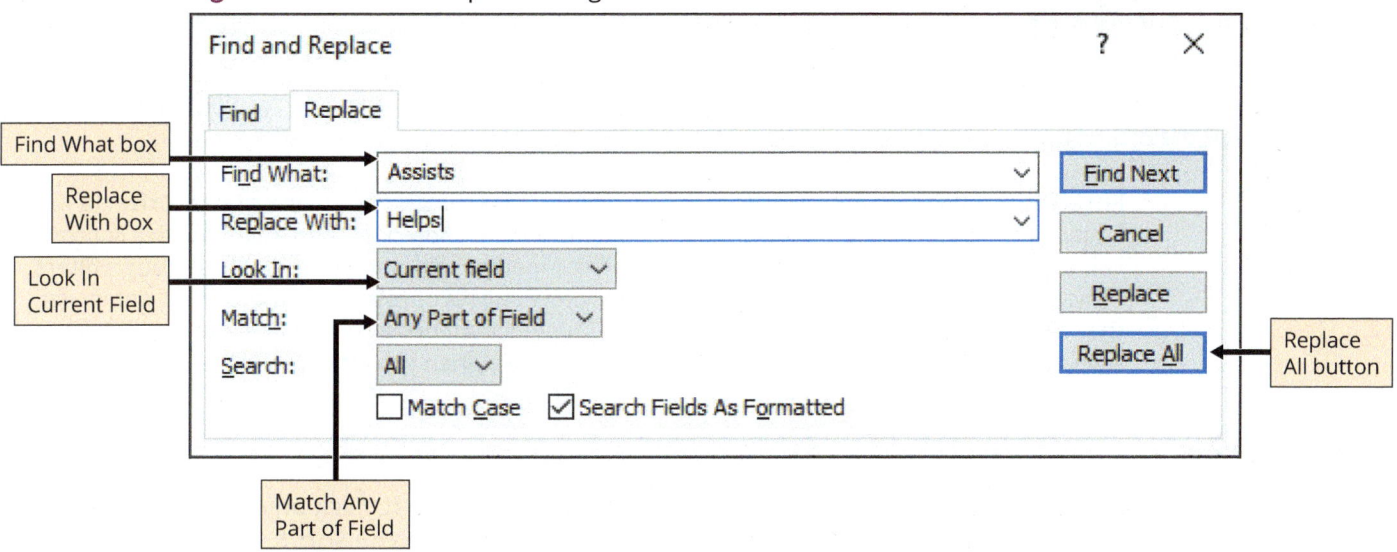

Figure 3-12: ContractJobs table in Datasheet View

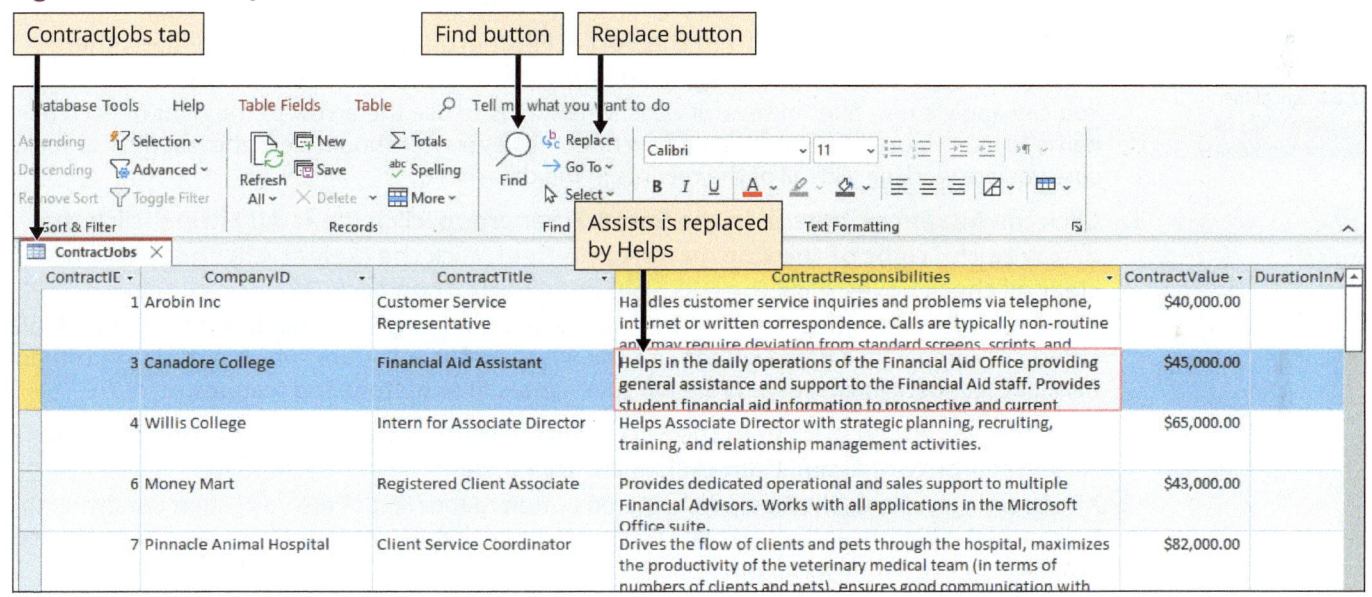

Table 3-3: Find buttons

Find		Opens the Find and Replace dialog box to find data
Replace		Opens the Find and Replace dialog box to find and replace data
Go To		Helps you navigate to the first, previous, next, last, or new record
Select		Helps you select a single record or all records in a datasheet

… Module 3 Creating Queries

Filter Data

Case Sasha asks several questions about the jobs listed in the ContractJobsByIndustry query. You will use filters to answer these questions.

Objectives
- Apply and clear filters.
- Use Filter by Selection and Filter by Form.

Filtering a datasheet *temporarily* displays records that match the given criteria. **Criteria** are limiting conditions you set. For example, you might want to show only contract jobs with a contract value greater than a certain amount or those companies in a particular state. Although filters provide a quick and easy way to display a temporary subset of records in the current datasheet, they are not as powerful or flexible as queries. The most important difference is that a query is a saved object in the database, whereas a filter is removed when you close the datasheet. **Table 3-4** compares filters and queries.

Steps

Quick Tip
Filters work the same way in Table and Query Datasheet Views.

1. Double-click the **ContractJobsByIndustry query** to open it, click any occurrence of **Energy** in the Industry field, click the **Selection button** in the Sort & Filter group, then click **Equals "Energy"**

   Nine records from two companies are selected, as shown in **Figure 3-13**. A filter icon appears to the right of the Industry field name. Filtering by the selected field value, called **Filter By Selection**, is a fast and easy way to filter records for an exact match.

Quick Tip
The Filtered button to the right of the navigation buttons also toggles the filter.

2. Click the **Toggle Filter button** in the Sort & Filter group to toggle off the filter, then click the **Toggle Filter button** again to apply the last filter to the datasheet

   You can apply a new filter in several ways. One way is to use the arrow to the right of each field name to filter data. Before applying a new filter, however, you should clear the last filter to make sure you are working with all of the records in the datasheet.

3. Click the **Advanced button** in the Sort & Filter group, click **Clear All Filters**, click the **arrow to the right of the CompanyName field**, click the **(Select All) check box** to clear all check boxes, click the **BIG Ship check box**, then click **OK**

   Three records match the criteria of *BIG Ship* for the CompanyName field. To filter for multiple criteria or comparative data, you can use the **Filter By Form** feature, which provides maximum flexibility for specifying criteria. **Table 3-5** summarizes filter buttons and features.

4. Click the **Advanced button** in the Sort & Filter group, click **Clear All Filters**, click the **Advanced button** again, then click **Filter By Form**

   After clearing all filters, the Filtered/Unfiltered button to the right of the navigation buttons at the bottom of the datasheet displays "No Filter" to indicate that all previous filters have been cleared. The Filter by Form window opens.

Quick Tip
You can clear the Filter by Form grid by clicking the Advanced button, then clicking Clear Grid.

5. Click the **ContractValue cell**, type **>=50000**, click the **ApplicantCount cell**, then type **<=10** as shown in **Figure 3-14**

   If more than one criterion is entered, a record must satisfy the requirements for each criterion to be selected.

6. Click the **Toggle Filter button** in the Sort & Filter group, then resize fields as necessary to display their entire field names

   The datasheet selects 14 records that match both of the filter criteria, as shown in **Figure 3-15**. Filter icons appear next to the ContractValue and ApplicantCount field names.

7. Click the **Close button** ✕ on the ContractJobsByIndustry tab, then click **Yes** if prompted

   Filters are *temporary* views of the data. Filters are *not* saved with a table or query datasheet after you close the datasheet even if you save the datasheet. If you want to save criteria, create a query.

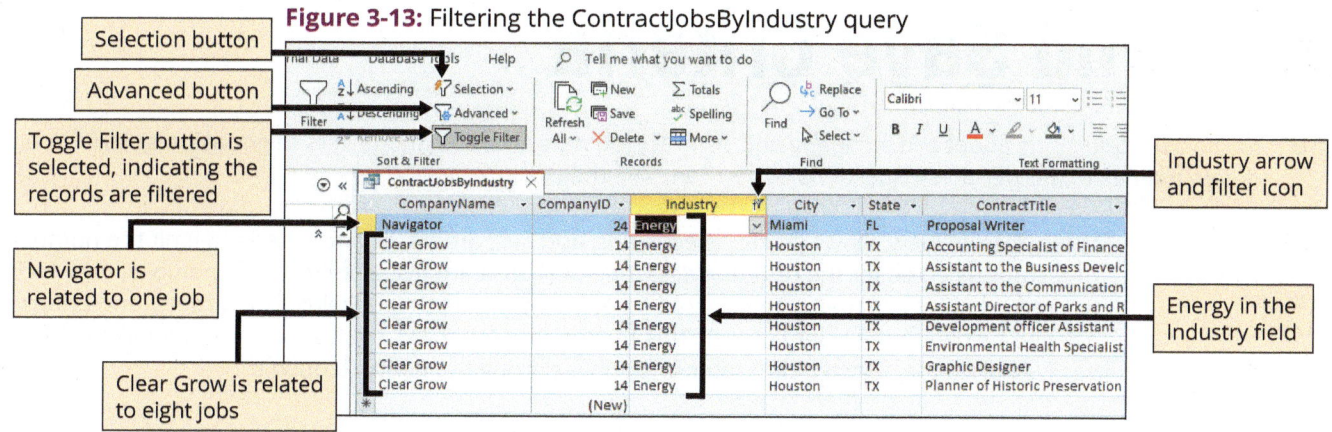

Figure 3-13: Filtering the ContractJobsByIndustry query

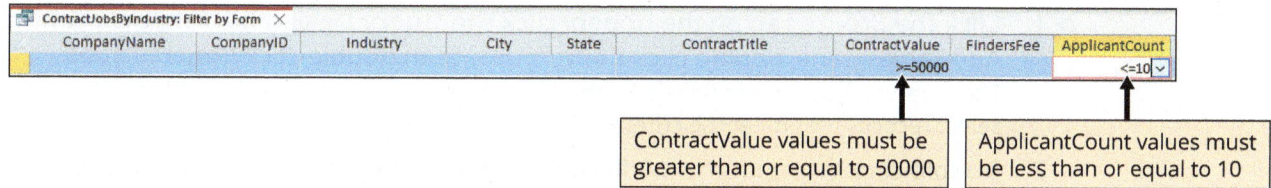

Figure 3-14: Filter by Form

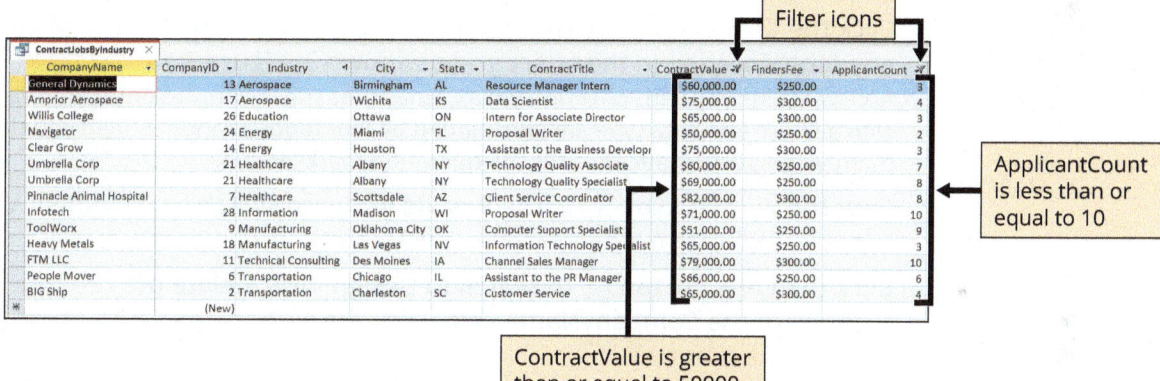

Figure 3-15: Filtering by form with two fields

Table 3-4: Filters vs. queries

characteristic	filters	queries
Are saved as an object in the database		●
Can be used to select a subset of records in a datasheet	●	●
Can be used to select a subset of fields in a datasheet		●
Resulting datasheet used to enter and edit data	●	●
Resulting datasheet used to sort, filter, and find records	●	●
Commonly used as the source of data for a form or report		●
Can calculate sums, averages, counts, and other types of summary statistics across records		●
Can be used to create calculated fields		●

Table 3-5: Filter buttons

name	button	purpose
Filter		Provides a list of values in the selected field that can be used to customize a filter
Selection		Filters records that equal, do not equal, or are otherwise compared with the current value
Advanced		Provides advanced filter features such as Filter By Form, Save As Query, and Clear All Filters
Toggle Filter		Applies or removes the current filter

Enter and Save Criteria

Case Sasha asks questions about the company and contract job data that she and others might ask regularly. You create queries to answer these questions so you can save the criteria.

Objectives
- Add a criterion to a Short Text field.
- Add a criterion to a Number field.
- Add a criterion to a Date/Time field.

Query Design View allows you to select fields, add sort orders, or add criteria to limit the number of records selected for the resulting datasheet. **Criteria** are tests, or limiting conditions, for which the record must be true to be selected for the query datasheet. Fields, sort orders, and criteria are all saved with the query object. This means that once you create and save a query, you can easily analyze the selected data later by double-clicking the query to open it.

Steps

Quick Tip
Drag the bottom edge of a field list to resize it to display all fields.

1. **Click the Create tab on the ribbon, click the Query Design button, click Tables in the Add Tables pane, double-click Companies, then double-click ContractJobs**
   This query will select one field from the Companies table and three from the ContractJobs table to select records that meet the criteria you specify.

2. **Double-click CompanyName in the Companies field list, then in the ContractJobs field list, double-click ContractTitle, FindersFee, and FirstPosted**
   Criteria are limiting conditions you set in the query design grid.

Quick Tip
Query criteria are not case-sensitive, but using proper uppercase and lowercase text makes criteria easier to read.

3. **Click the Criteria cell for the CompanyName field, type People Mover, then click any other location in the query grid as shown in Figure 3-16**
   Access assists you with **criteria syntax**, rules that specify how to enter criteria. Criteria for fields with a Short Text data type are surrounded by "quotation marks" though you do not need to type them. Access automatically adds the quotation marks for you.

4. **Click the View button in the Results group to switch to Datasheet View**
   Eight records match the criterion of People Mover in the CompanyName field.

5. **Click the View button to switch to Design View, delete the "People Mover" criterion in the CompanyName field, click the FindersFee Criteria cell, type 300, then click the View button**
   Criteria in Number, Currency, and Yes/No fields are not surrounded by any characters. Twenty-nine records are selected where the FindersFee field equals 300.

6. **Click the View button, delete the 300 criterion in the FindersFee field, click the FirstPosted Criteria cell, type 1/4/2029, then click any other location in the query grid as shown in Figure 3-17**
   Criteria for fields with a Date/Time data type are surrounded by #pound signs# though you do not need to type them. The pound sign symbol (#) is also known as the number sign, hashtag, and octothorpe.

7. **Click the View button**
   Seven records are selected where the FirstPosted field equals 1/4/2029.

8. **Right-click the Query1 tab, click Save, type FirstPostedJan4, click OK, then click the Close button on the FirstPostedJan4 tab**
   The query is saved with the new name, FirstPostedJan4, as a new query object in the database. Criteria entered in Query Design View are saved with the query.

Enter and Save Criteria   AC 3-15

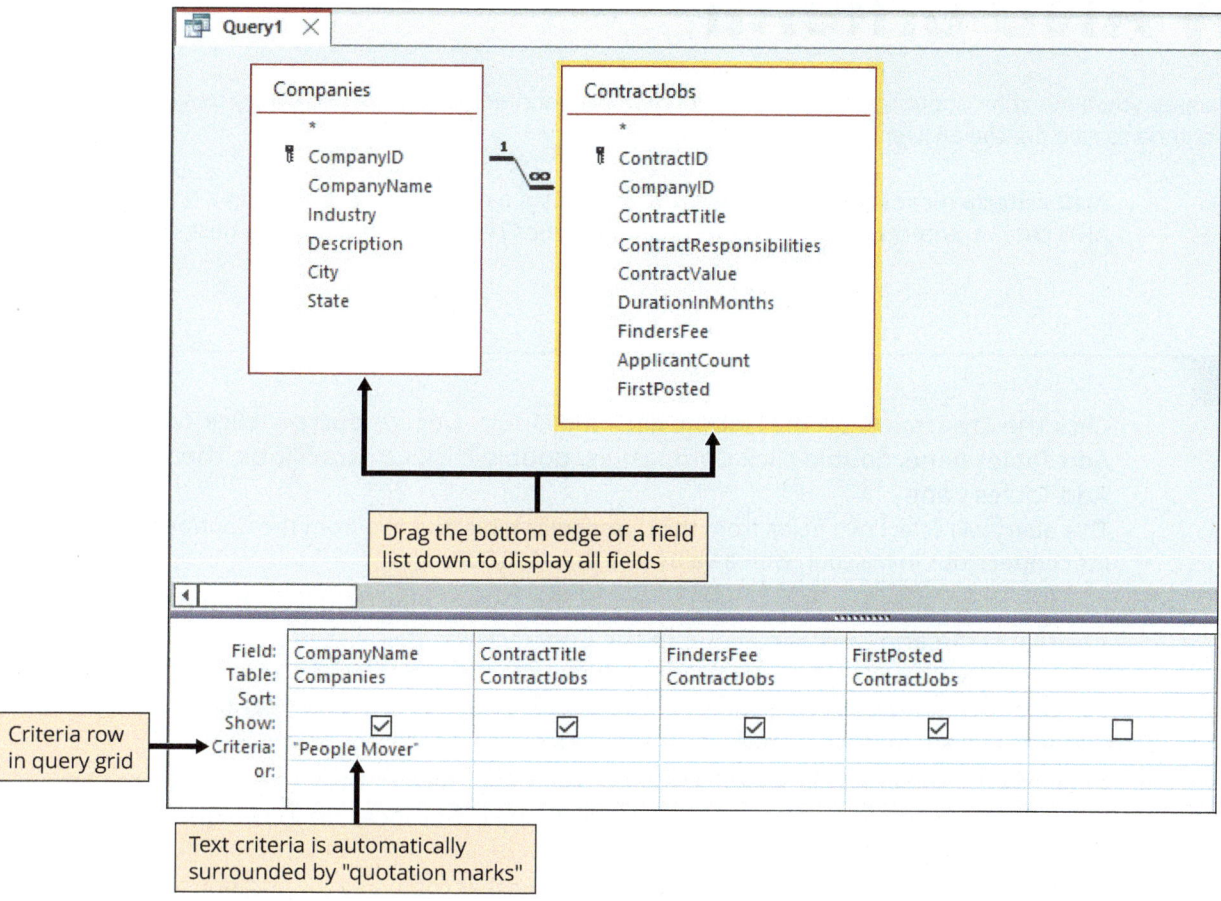

Figure 3-16: Entering text criteria

Figure 3-17: Entering date criteria

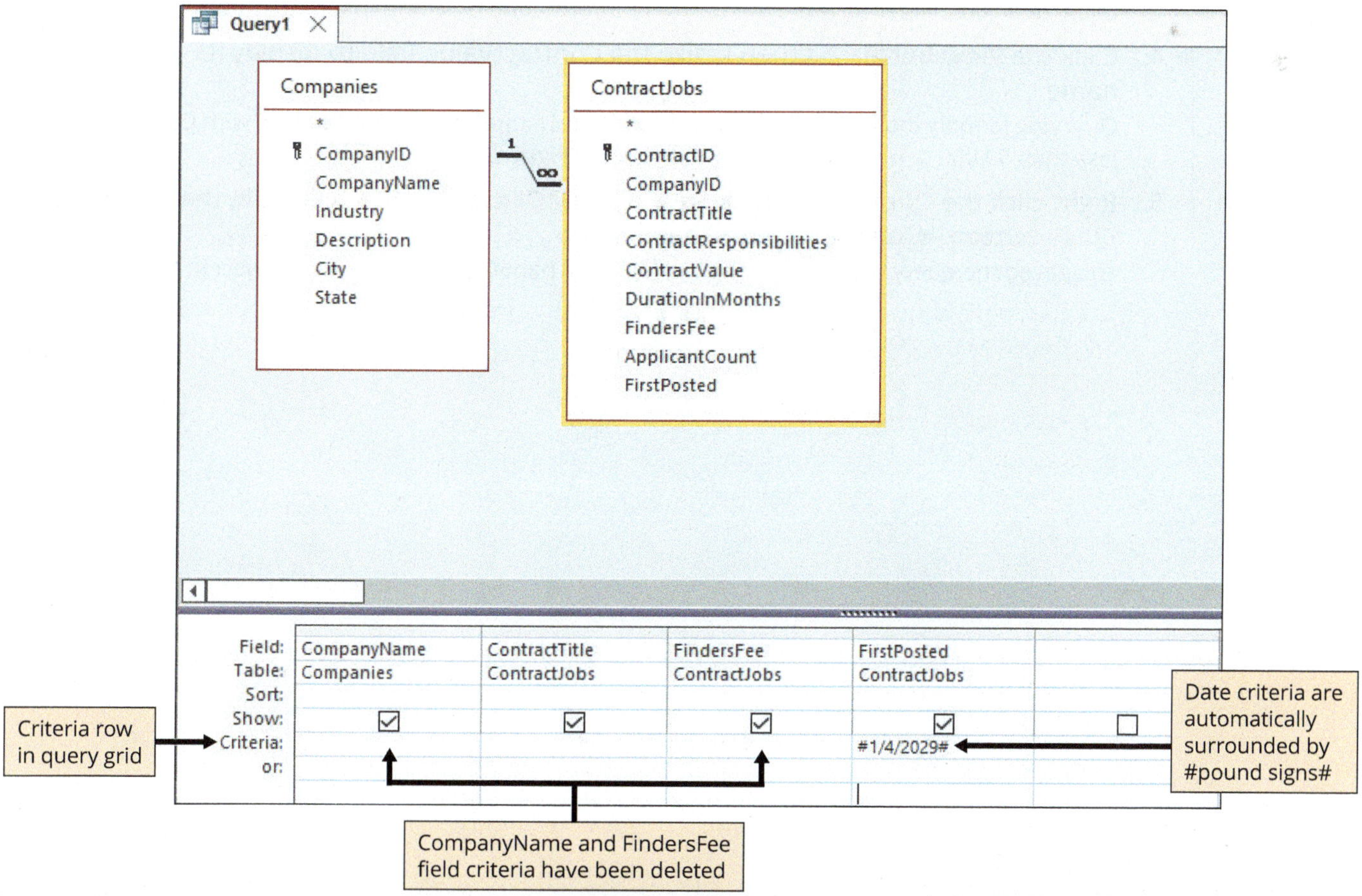

Module 3 Creating Queries

Apply AND Criteria

Case Sasha asks you a question about the data that meets multiple conditions. You will use Query Design View with AND criteria to give her the answer.

Objectives
- Enter AND criteria in a query.
- Use comparison operators.

AND criteria means that *all* criteria must be true for a record to be selected in a query. To create AND criteria, enter two or more criteria on the *same* Criteria row of the query design grid.

Steps

1. **Click the Create tab on the ribbon, click the Query Design button, click Tables in the Add Tables pane, double-click Companies, double-click ContractJobs, then close the Add Tables pane**
   This query will select two fields from the Companies table and two from the ContractJobs table to list contract jobs in Missouri with a value less than $50,000.

   Quick Tip
   Drag or double-click the bottom edge of a field list to resize it to display all fields.

2. **Double-click CompanyName and State in the Companies field list, then double-click ContractTitle and ContractValue in the ContractJobs field list**
   You enter AND criteria, where each criterion must be true to select a record, on the *same* row. For every new criterion on the same row, you potentially *reduce* the number of selected records because a record must be true for *each* criterion.

3. **Click the Criteria cell for the State field, type MO, click in the Criteria cell for the ContractValue field, type <50000, then click any other location in the query grid as shown in Figure 3-18**
   The less than symbol (<) is a **comparison operator** that compares the criterion to the values in the ContractValue field. In this case, it selects all records with a ContractValue less than 50,000. If you do not enter a comparison operator, Access assumes an equal sign (=) and selects records equal to 50,000. Refer to **Table 3-6** for more information on comparison operators.

   Trouble
   If your datasheet doesn't match **Figure 3-19**, return to Query Design View and compare your criteria with that of **Figure 3-18**.

4. **Click the View button then resize the ContractValue field to display its entire field name**
   Querying for only those jobs in the state of Missouri (state abbreviation of MO) with ContractValues less than 50,000 selects two records as shown in **Figure 3-19**.

5. **Right-click the Query1 tab, click Save, type MOLessThan50K, click OK, then click the Close button on the MOLessThan50K tab**
   You saved the query with the new name, MOLessThan50K, as a new query object in the database.

Apply AND Criteria   AC 3-17

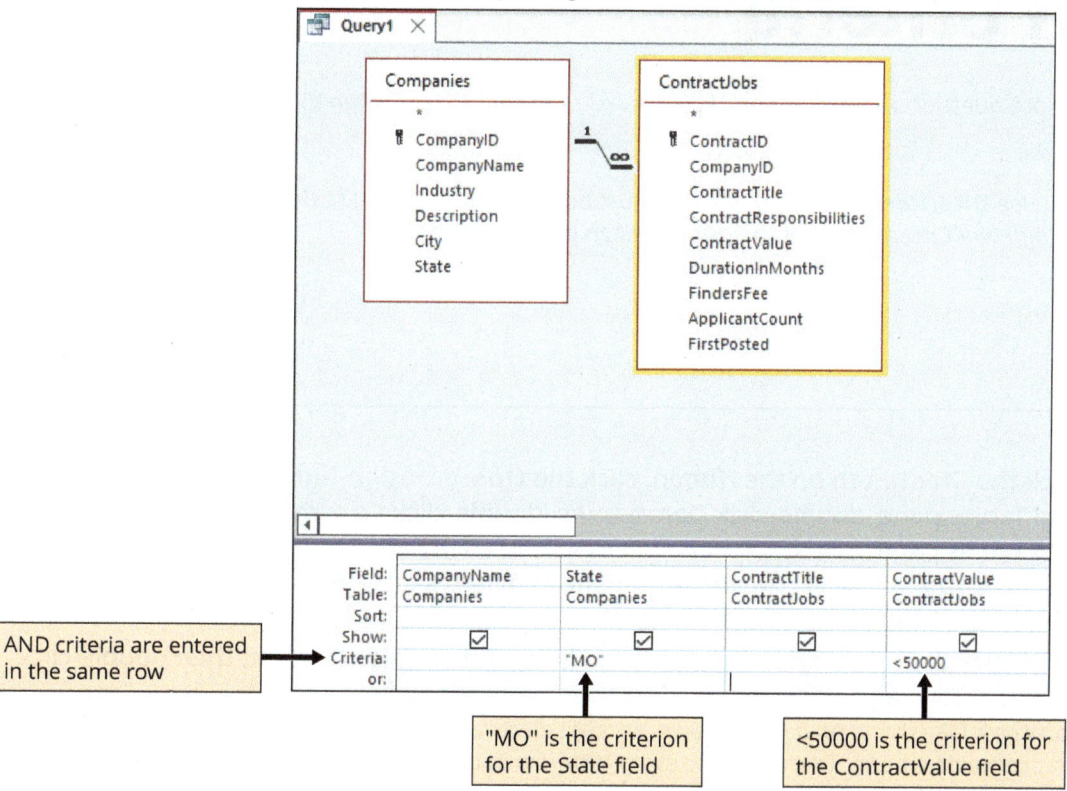

Figure 3-18: Query Design View with AND criteria

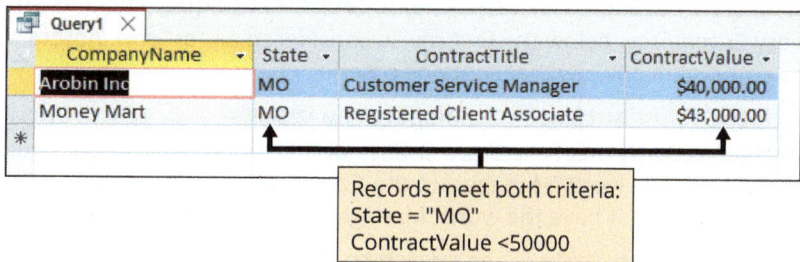

Figure 3-19: Results of query with AND criteria

Table 3-6: Comparison operators

operator	description	expression	meaning
>	Greater than	>500	Numbers greater than 500
>=	Greater than or equal to	>=500	Numbers greater than or equal to 500
<	Less than	<"Elder"	Names from A to Elder, but not Elder
<=	Less than or equal to	<="Liang"	Names from A through Liang, inclusive
<>	Not equal to	<>"Vazquez"	Any name except for Vazquez
=	Equal to	="Kapoor" =500	Equal to Kapoor Equal to 500 Note that the equal sign is assumed when no other comparison operator is used.

Searching for blank fields

Is Null and Is Not Null are two other types of common criteria. The **Is Null** criterion finds all records where no entry has been made in the field. **Is Not Null** finds all records where the field contains any entry, even if the entry is 0. Primary key fields cannot have a null entry.

Module 3 Creating Queries

Apply OR Criteria

Case Sasha asks you more questions about the contract jobs. You will use Query Design View with OR criteria to give her the answers.

Objectives
- Enter OR criteria in a query.
- Enter criteria with a wildcard.
- Enter both AND and OR criteria in a query.

You use **OR criteria** when *any one row* must be true for the record to be selected. Enter OR criteria on *different* Criteria rows of the query design grid.

Steps

1. Click the **Create tab** on the ribbon, click the **Query Design button**, click **Tables** in the Add Tables pane, double-click **Companies**, double-click **ContractJobs**, then close the Add Tables pane

   For this query, you select two fields from the Companies table and two from the ContractJobs table to list managers in Missouri or Texas.

2. Double-click **CompanyName** and **State** in the Companies field list, then double-click **ContractTitle** and **ContractValue** in the ContractJobs field list

   You enter OR criteria on *different* rows. Access selects a record if it matches the criteria for *any row* that contains criteria. Therefore, for every new row of criteria, you potentially *increase* the number of records that are selected.

Quick Tip
The query grid provides eight criteria rows by default, but you can add more by clicking the Insert Rows button in the Query Setup group on the Query Design tab.

▶ 3. Click the **Criteria cell for the State field**, type **MO**, click the **or Criteria cell for the State field**, type **TX**, then click any other location in the query grid as shown in **Figure 3-20**

   Every Criteria row below the first row is considered an "or" row. Access selects records that match the criterion in *any* row that contains criteria.

4. Click the **View button** to display the results

   Fourteen records meet the State criteria of MO or TX. In addition, you want to select only those records with the word "Manager" in the ContractTitle field. You use asterisk characters (*) to help select records that have the word "Manager" in any position in the ContractTitle field value.

5. Click the **View button** to switch to Design View, click the **Criteria cell for the ContractTitle field**, type ***Manager***, then click the **View button** to display the results

   Twelve records are displayed. The first record meets the State criteria of MO with the word "Manager" in the ContractTitle field criteria. The other records meet the State criteria of TX but aren't limited by the word "Manager" in the ContractTitle criteria.

6. Click the **View button** to switch to Design View, click **the second Criteria cell for the ContractTitle field**, type ***Manager***, then click any other location in the query grid as shown in **Figure 3-21**

   Access adds the **Like** keyword to criteria that contain the asterisk (*) wildcard character.

Quick Tip
Resize fields to display the entire field names and values by dragging or double-clicking the border to the right of the field name.

▶ 7. Click the **View button** to display the results

   Three records meet the State criteria of MO or the State criteria of TX with the word "Manager" in the ContractTitle field, as shown in **Figure 3-22**.

8. Right-click the **Query1 tab**, click **Save**, type **MOTXManager**, click **OK**, then click the **Close button** on the MOTXManager tab

   You can also use **AND OR** SQL keywords in your criteria. A simpler approach is to remember these rules: Criteria on a *single row must all be true* for a record to be selected. Criteria on *different rows are separate tests* that the record may satisfy to be selected.

Figure 3-20: Query Design View with OR criteria

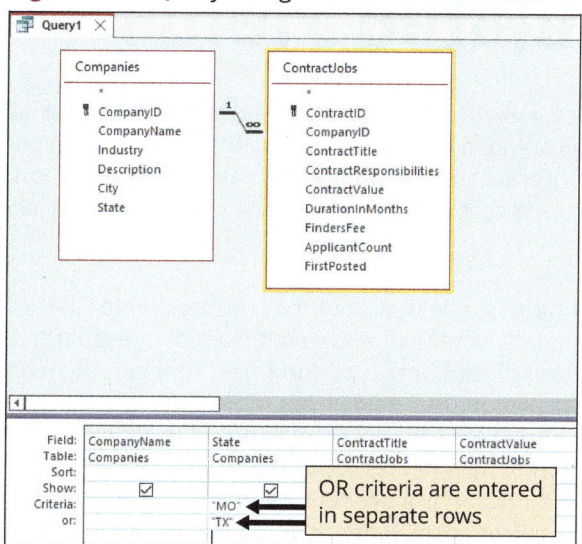

Figure 3-21: Query Design View with AND and OR criteria

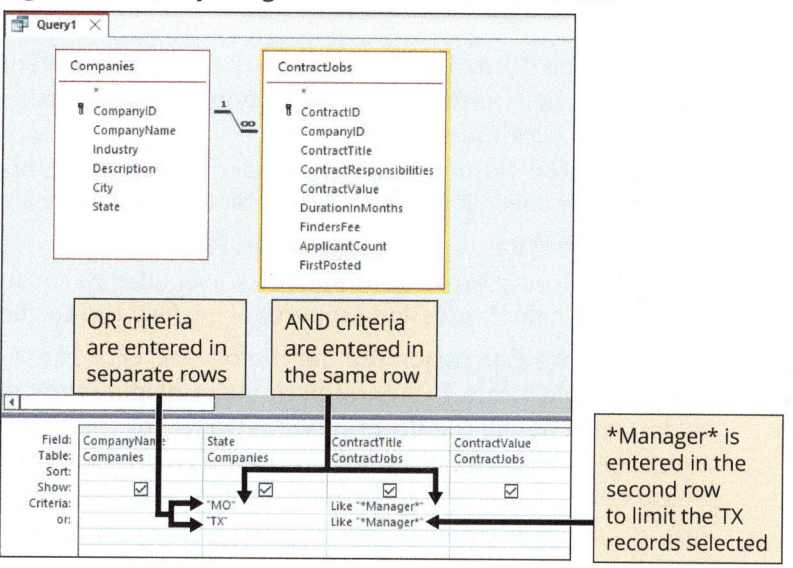

Figure 3-22: Results of query with AND and OR criteria

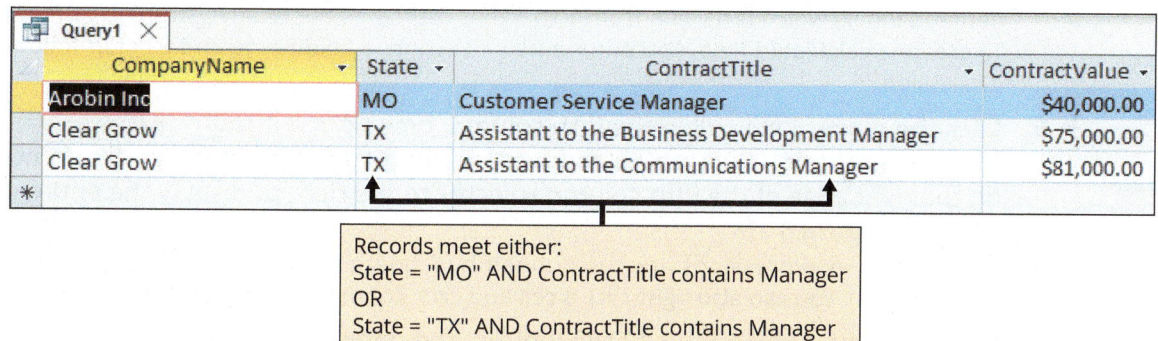

Using wildcard characters

To search for a pattern, you can use a wildcard character to represent any character in the condition entry. Use a question mark (?) to search for any single character and an asterisk (*) to search for any number of characters. Access uses the **Like** keyword when your criterion contains wildcard characters. For example, the criterion Like "12/*/29" finds all dates in December of 2029, and the criterion Like "G*" finds all values that start with the letter G.

Create Calculated Fields

Case Sasha asks you to calculate a contract job placement commission for each contract position that GIG Placement helps fill. You will create a calculated field in the ContractJobs table to satisfy this request. Sasha also asks you to create an internal contract job rating calculation based on the job's contract value and an industry demand index. Because that data is stored in two tables, you will create a calculated field in a query for this answer.

Objectives
- Create a field with a Calculated data type.
- Create calculated fields in queries.
- Define functions and expressions.

A **calculated field** is a field of data that can be created based on the values of other fields. By calculating the data instead of entering it from the keyboard, the data is always accurate. Access provides the **Calculated** data type for a field that can be defined using other fields in the *same* table. If the calculation uses fields from more than one table, it must be calculated in a query. To create a calculated field, you enter an expression that describes the calculation. An **expression** is a combination of field names, **operators** (such as +, –, /, and *), and functions that result in a single value. A **function** is a predefined formula that returns a value such as a subtotal, count, average, or the current date. Refer to **Table 3-7** for more information on arithmetic operators and **Table 3-8** for more information on Access functions.

Steps

1. Right-click the **ContractJobs table** in the Navigation Pane, click **Design View**, click the **Field Name cell below FirstPosted**, type **Commission**, press **TAB**, click the **Data Type arrow**, then click **Calculated**

   The **Expression Builder** dialog box opens to help you build an expression by providing information about built-in functions, constants (such as True and False), and operators.

2. Type **[ContractValue]*0.1** as shown in **Figure 3-23**

   Field names used in expressions must be surrounded by square brackets. [ContractValue]*0.1 is now entered in the **Expression property** of the field and can be modified in Table Design View.

Quick Tip
To modify the expression of a calculated field in Datasheet View, right-click it, then click Modify Expression.

▶ 3. Click **OK** in the Expression Builder dialog box, click the **View button** 🔳, click **Yes** to save the table, press **TAB** enough times to display the ContractValue and Commission fields, then change the ContractValue value for the first record to **47000**

   The Commission value for the first record correctly updates to 4700 as shown in **Figure 3-24**. The second calculation involves data from multiple tables, so you will use a query.

4. Click the **Close button** ✕ on the ContractJobs tab, right-click the **ContractJobDemandRating query** in the Navigation Pane, then click **Design View**

   The Contract Job Index calculation is defined as the contract value divided by 1,000 times the job demand index, which is a value from 1 to 5 that estimates the relative strength of that industry. To create a calculated field, you enter a new descriptive field name and a colon followed by an expression.

Quick Tip
You can also use expressions as query criteria.

▶ 5. Click the **blank Field cell** in the fifth column, type **ContractJobIndex: [ContractValue]/1000*[JobDemandIndex]**, then drag the column resize pointer ↔ on the right edge of the fifth column selector to the right to display the entire entry as shown in **Figure 3-25**

   Field names in expressions are surrounded by [square brackets] not {curly braces} and not (parentheses). You can also right-click a cell and click Zoom to enter a long expression.

6. Click the **View button** 🔳, edit the JobDemandIndex value for any record with the Industry value of Personnel Services from 3 to **4**, then click any other record

   The ContractJobIndex value for all jobs in the Personnel Services industry is recalculated when you change the JobDemandIndex value used in the expression for that calculated field.

7. Click the **Save button** 💾 on the Quick Access toolbar, then click the **Close button** ✕ on the ContractJobDemandRating tab

   Some database experts encourage you to create all calculations using queries because the Calculated field data type doesn't convert well to other relational database systems.

Create Calculated Fields

Figure 3-23: Creating a calculated field in Table Design View

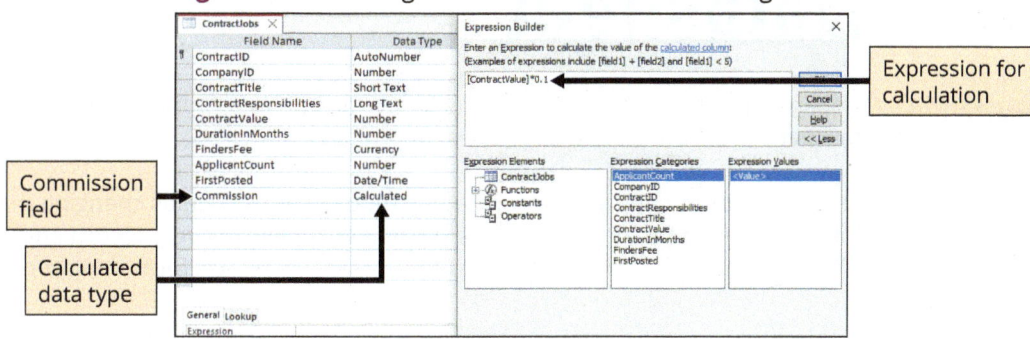

Figure 3-24: Calculated field in Table Datasheet View

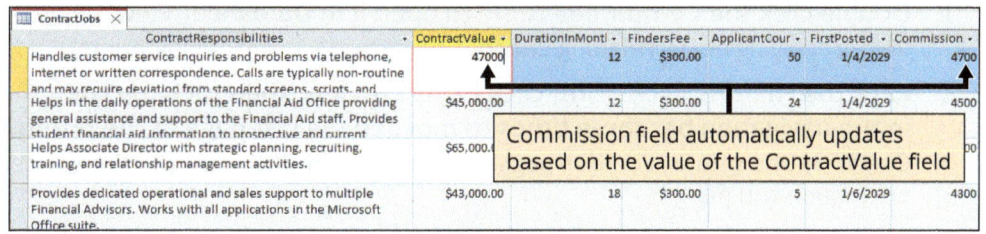

Figure 3-25: Creating a calculated field in Query Design View

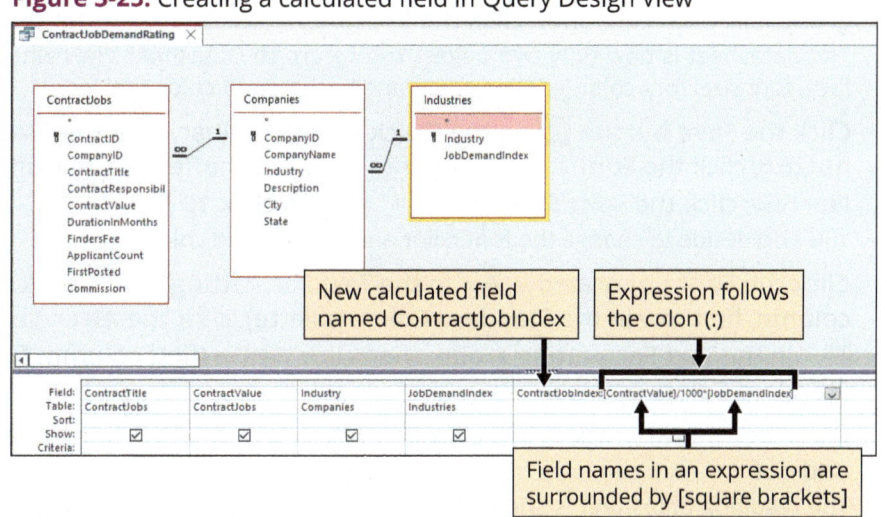

Table 3-7: Arithmetic operators

operator	description
+	Addition
−	Subtraction
*	Multiplication
/	Division
^	Exponentiation

Table 3-8: Common functions

function	sample expression and description
DATE	DATE()-[BirthDate] Calculates the number of days between today and the date in the BirthDate field; Access expressions are not case sensitive, so DATE()-[BirthDate] is equivalent to date()-[birthdate] and DATE()-[BIRTHDATE]; therefore, use capitalization in expressions in any way that makes the expression easier to read
PMT	PMT([Rate],[Term],[Loan]) Calculates the monthly payment on a loan where the Rate field contains the monthly interest rate, the Term field contains the number of monthly payments, and the Loan field contains the total amount financed
LEFT	LEFT([LastName],2) Returns the first two characters of the entry in the LastName field
RIGHT	RIGHT([PartNo],3) Returns the last three characters of the entry in the PartNo field
LEN	LEN([Description]) Returns the number of characters in the Description field

Format a Datasheet

Case Sasha asks you to prepare a printout of the companies list to include in a monthly report. You format the Companies table datasheet to improve its appearance when printed.

Objectives
- Change page orientation.
- Change margins.
- Format a datasheet.

In a datasheet, you can apply basic formatting modifications such as changing the font size, font face, colors, and gridlines. Formatting in a datasheet applies to every record and works the same way in Table and Query Datasheet Views. **Table 3-9** lists common formatting commands.

Steps

1. Double-click the **Companies table** to open it in Datasheet View
   Before applying new formatting enhancements, preview the default printout.

2. Click the **File tab**, click **Print**, click **Print Preview**, then click the **Next Page button** in the navigation bar three times to move to the last page of the printout
   Currently, the printout is four pages, but you can reduce that number by changing the page orientation and margin.

3. Click the **Landscape button** in the Page Layout group on the Print Preview tab to switch the report to landscape orientation, click the **Margins button** in the Page Size group, click **Narrow**, then click the **Previous Page button** to display the first page
   The datasheet is now only two pages. You return to Datasheet View where you can make font face, font size, font color, gridline color, and background color choices.

4. Click the **Save button** on the Quick Access toolbar, click the **Close Print Preview button**, click the **Font arrow** Calibri (Detail) in the Text Formatting group, click **Arial Narrow**, click the **Font Size arrow** 11, then click **10**
   You also decide to change the font color and background color.

5. Click the **Font Color arrow** in the Text Formatting group, click **Dark Blue** (fourth column, first row in the Standard Colors palette), click the **Alternate Row Color arrow** in the Text Formatting group, then click **White** (first column, first row in the Standard Colors palette)

6. Click the **File tab**, click **Print**, click **Print Preview**, then click the **preview** to zoom in and out
   The resulting datasheet is shown in **Figure 3-26**. The preview contains two pages in landscape orientation.

7. **sam↑** Right-click the **Companies tab**, click **Close**, click **Yes** when prompted to save changes, then click the **Close button** on the title bar to close the database and Access

Format a Datasheet   AC 3-23

Figure 3-26: Formatted Companies datasheet

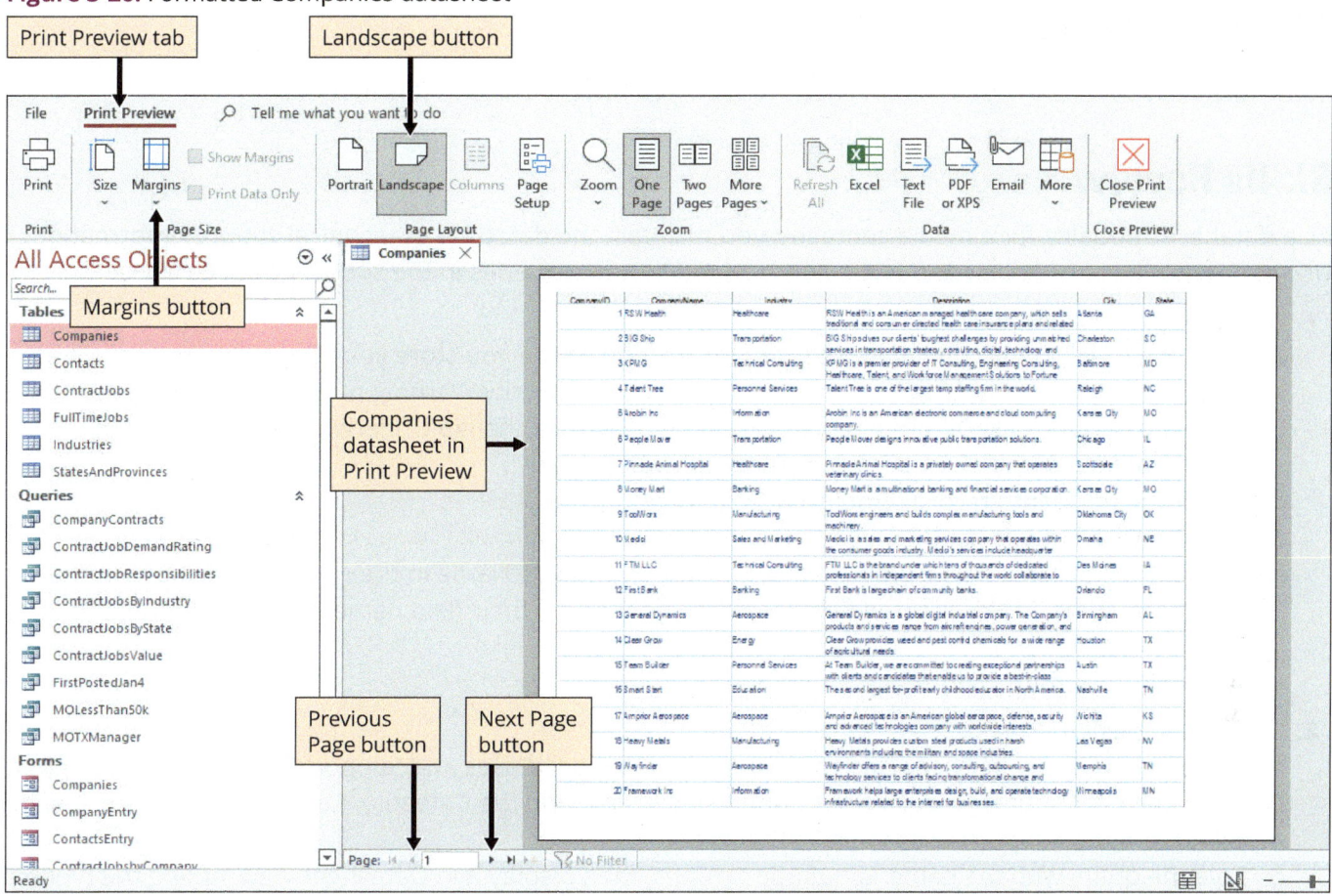

Table 3-9: Useful formatting commands

button	button name	description
Calibri (Detail)	Font	Changes the font face of the data
11	Font Size	Changes the font size of the data
B	Bold	Toggles bold on or off
I	Italic	Toggles italic on or off
U	Underline	Toggles underline on or off
A	Font Color	Changes the font color of the data
	Background Color	Changes the background color
	Align Left	Left-aligns the data
	Center	Centers the data
	Align Right	Right-aligns the data
	Alternate Row Color	Changes the background color of alternate records
	Gridlines	Changes the gridlines

Practice

In the exercises that follow, you will practice the skills you have learned in this module.

Skills Review

As a database specialist for a media company, you maintain the database of technical support information. Use your knowledge of Access and SQL to update and improve queries in the support desk database.

1. **Use Query Datasheet View.**
   a. Open the IL_AC_3-2.accdb database from the location where you store your Data Files and save it as **IL_AC_3_SupportDesk**. Click Enable Content if a yellow Security Warning message appears.
   b. Open the SupportCaseDetails query in Datasheet View and change Underwood to **Underhill** in the LastName field of the eleventh record for EmployeeID 14.
   c. Delete the thirteenth record (EmployeeID 16, Victor Carson).
   d. Hide the Dependents field.
   e. Freeze the first three fields: EmployeeID, LastName, and FirstName in their current positions in the datasheet. (Hint: Select all three fields by dragging through their field names before selecting the Freeze Fields option.)
   f. Save and close the SupportCaseDetails query.

2. **Use Query Design View.**
   a. Create a new query in Query Design View. Add the SupportCases and SupportCalls tables.
   b. Select the CallMinutes field from the SupportCalls table and the Category, CaseTitle, and EmployeeID fields from the SupportCases table, in that order.
   c. Save the query with the name **LongSupportCalls**, then display it in Datasheet View, noting the types of calls taking more than 30 minutes to resolve and the employees associated with those calls.

3. **Use SQL View.**
   a. Open the LongSupportCalls query in SQL View.
   b. Add the CallID field from the SupportCalls table and the CaseID field from the SupportCases table to the query after the EmployeeID field.
   c. Save the query then view it in Datasheet View to make sure you enter the SQL statement correctly. Save and close the LongSupportCalls query.

4. **Sort data.**
   a. Open the TotalCallMinutes query in Datasheet View, sort the records in ascending order by the TotalTime field, then save and close the query.
   b. Open the SupportCaseDetails query in Design View, then add an ascending sort order to the LastName and FirstName fields. Add a descending sort order to the CallMinutes field.
   c. Save the SupportCaseDetails query, then view it in Datasheet View.
   d. Be prepared to discuss this question in class or on a discussion thread: Were all three sort fields used to determine the order of the records? If so, where?
   e. Close the SupportCaseDetails query.

5. **Find and replace data.**
   a. In Datasheet View of the SupportCases table, search for all occurrences of **Local Network** in the Category field and replace it with **LAN** using the Whole Field match.
   b. Press CTRL+Z to undo your last replacement, but not all replacements.
   c. Edit the Category entry to **LAN** in the record containing Local Network in the Category field.
   d. Save and close the SupportCases table datasheet.

Skills Review

6. **Filter data.**
   a. Open the SupportCaseDetails query in Datasheet View and filter for all records where the Department is **Human Resources** and the CallMinutes is **greater than or equal to 30**. Your datasheet should show three records that meet these criteria.
   b. You can apply a filter in several ways, including using the filter buttons in the Sort & Filter group on the Home tab, the Filter by Form feature, and the options listed in the sort and filter menu when you click the arrow to the right of the field name in the datasheet. In class or a discussion group, be prepared to explain which technique you chose to apply the filter.
   c. Save and close the SupportCaseDetails query. Reopen it to see that all records are shown. In class or a discussion group, be prepared to explain why the filter criteria were not reapplied to the query.

7. **Enter and save criteria.**
   a. Create a query in Query Design View with the SupportCases and Staff tables.
   b. Add the following fields, in this order: CaseID and Category from the SupportCases table and LastName and FirstName from the Staff table.
   c. Add criteria to select only those records with **LAN** in the Category field.
   d. Save the query with the name **LANSupportCases**, display it in Datasheet View to make sure you have selected the correct records, and then close the LANSupportCases query.

8. **Apply AND criteria.**
   a. Right-click the LANSupportCases query, copy it, and then paste it using **LANResearchSupportCases** as the query name.
   b. Open the LANResearchSupportCases query in Design View, add the Department field from the Staff table to the last column in the query grid, then add criteria to select all records with **LAN** in the Category field and **Research** in the Department field.
   c. Display the results in Datasheet View, resizing fields to display the entire field name and values as shown in **Figure 3-27**, then save and close the query.

   Figure 3-27

CaseID	Category	LastName	FirstName	Department
14	LAN	Montoya	Olivia	Research
19	LAN	Montoya	Olivia	Research
(New)				

9. **Apply OR criteria.**
   a. Copy the LANResearchSupportCases, then paste it using **LANResearchExecutiveSupportCases** as the query name.
   b. Open the LANResearchExecutiveSupportCases query in Design View, then add criteria to select the records in the **Research** or **Executive** Department with **LAN** as the Category field value.
   c. Display the results in Datasheet View as shown in **Figure 3-28**, then save and close the query.

   Figure 3-28

CaseID	Category	LastName	FirstName	Department
11	LAN	Holloway	Martin	Executive
14	LAN	Montoya	Olivia	Research
19	LAN	Montoya	Olivia	Research
(New)				

Skills Review (Continued)

10. **Create calculated fields.**
    a. Open the Staff table in Design View then add field named **Monthly** with a Currency format and Calculated data type.
    b. Use the expression **[Salary]/12** to calculate the values for the new Monthly field.
    c. Save the Staff table and display it in Datasheet View.
    d. Change the salary for Carlos Hoover (Employee ID 12) from $44,000 to **54000** then click anywhere else in the datasheet to observe the automatic update to the Monthly field.
    e. Add a new record to the end of the Staff table using your name in the LastName and FirstName fields and no other data.
    f. Save and close the Staff table.
    g. Create a query in Query Design View with the Staff, SupportCases, and SupportCalls tables.
    h. Add the LastName field from the Staff table, the CaseTitle field from the SupportCases table, and the CallMinutes field from the SupportCalls table, in that order.
    i. Add a calculated field to the fourth column of the query grid with the following field name and expression: **TotalTime: [CallMinutes]+10** to estimate the total time required per call, assuming a five-minute gap before and after each call.
    j. Add another calculated field to the fifth column of the query grid using **Cost: ([Staff].[Monthly]*[TotalTime])/(30*8*60)** as the field name and expression to calculate the approximate dollar costs of the calls assuming 30 days in a month, eight hours in a day, and an hour being 60 minutes long.
    k. Save the query with the name **TotalCallMinutesCost** and display it in Datasheet View. Change the CallMinutes value for the first record (Cabrera, "User got the blue screen of death") from 2 minutes to **8** minutes, then click anywhere else in the datasheet. Increase the column width as necessary to display the values. The TotalTime field value should update to 18 and the Cost field value should increase accordingly.
    l. Save and close the TotalCallMinutesCost query.
    m. In class or a discussion group, be prepared to discuss the TotalTime calculated field in the TotalCallMinutesCost query. What are the advantages and disadvantages of creating this field in a query instead of in the Calls table?

11. **Format a datasheet.**
    a. In the SupportCases table datasheet, apply the Garamond font and **12**-point font size.
    b. Change the alternate row color to Green, Accent 6, Lighter 80% (tenth column, second row in the Theme Colors palette), and the gridlines to None.
    c. Display the SupportCases datasheet in Print Preview, then switch the orientation to Landscape and the margins to Narrow. The datasheet should now fit on a single sheet of paper.
    d. Save the SupportCases datasheet, and then close it.
    e. Close Access.

Independent Challenge 1

As the manager of Homefront, a personal support worker resource company, you have created a database to manage the schedules that connect each healthcare provider with the personal support workers (PSWs) that the provider needs to efficiently handle patient visits. In this exercise, you create a query to answer a special scheduling question at the company.

   a. Start Access. Open the IL_AC_3-3.accdb database from the location where you store your Data Files and save it as **IL_AC_3_Homefront**. Click Enable Content if a yellow Security Warning message appears.

b. Create a new query in Query Design View with the Locations, ScheduleItems, ScheduleDate, and PSWs tables.
c. Add the following fields to the query in this order: LocationName from the Locations table, ScheduleDate from the ScheduleDate table, and PSWLName and PSWFName from the PSWs table.
d. Sort the records in ascending order first by ScheduleDate then by PSWLName.
e. Save the query with the name **EastWest**.
f. Add criteria to select only the records that have a LocationName of **East** or **West**, a PSWLName value of **Kennedy** or **Kowalewski**, and a ScheduleDate **on or after 10/1/2029**, then display the query in Query Datasheet View, as shown in **Figure 3-29**.
g. Save and close the EastWest query, then close the database and exit Access.

Figure 3-29

LocationName	ScheduleDate	PSWLName	PSWFName
East	10/12/2029	Kennedy	Jill
East	10/14/2029	Kennedy	Jill
East	10/15/2029	Kennedy	Jill
West	10/15/2029	Kowalewski	Karin
West	10/17/2029	Kowalewski	Karin
East	10/18/2029	Kennedy	Jill
East	10/21/2029	Kennedy	Jill
East	10/22/2029	Kennedy	Jill
East	10/23/2029	Kennedy	Jill
East	10/24/2029	Kennedy	Jill
East	10/28/2029	Kennedy	Jill
East	10/29/2029	Kennedy	Jill
East	10/30/2029	Kennedy	Jill
East	10/31/2029	Kennedy	Jill
East	11/4/2029	Kennedy	Jill
East	11/5/2029	Kennedy	Jill
East	11/6/2029	Kennedy	Jill
East	11/7/2029	Kennedy	Jill
East	11/8/2029	Kennedy	Jill
East	11/11/2029	Kennedy	Jill
East	11/12/2029	Kennedy	Jill
East	11/14/2029	Kennedy	Jill
East	11/18/2029	Kennedy	Jill
East	11/21/2029	Kennedy	Jill
East	11/25/2029	Kennedy	Jill
East	11/26/2029	Kennedy	Jill
East	12/6/2029	Kennedy	Jill
East	12/9/2029	Kennedy	Jill
East	12/10/2029	Kennedy	Jill
East	12/12/2029	Kennedy	Jill
East	12/13/2029	Kennedy	Jill
East	12/16/2029	Kennedy	Jill

Independent Challenge 2

You are working for a city to coordinate a series of community entertainment events. You have started a database to track the events and performers who are booked for each event. In this exercise, you create a query to answer a special event question from city planners.

a. Start Access. Open the IL_AC_3-4.accdb database from the location where you store your Data Files and save it as **IL_AC_3_Performers**. Click Enable Content if a yellow Security Warning message appears.
b. Create a new query in Query Design View with the Performers, Bookings, and Events tables.
c. Add the following fields to the query in this order: FirstName and LastName from the Performers table, Completed from the Bookings table, EventName and EventHours from the Events table.
d. Sort the records in ascending order on LastName.
e. Add criteria to select only those records with **Fest** anywhere in the EventName field and an EventHours value **greater than or equal to 8**.
f. Add a calculated field with the following name and expression to estimate the value of the performers' time within that activity: **Labor: [EventHours]*15**.
g. Save the query with the name **LaborCalculation**, display it in Datasheet View, resize the fields to display complete names and values, then change the record for Angela Cabriella to have your first and last names, as shown in **Figure 3-30**.
h. Close the database and exit Access.

Figure 3-30

FirstName	LastName	Completed	EventName	EventHours	Labor
Forrest	Browning	☑	Heavy Fest	8	120
Patch	Bullock	☑	Heavy Fest	8	120
StudentFirstname	StudentLastname	☑	Heavy Fest	8	120

Visual Workshop

Open the IL_AC_3-5.accdb database from the location where you store your Data Files and save it as **IL_AC_3_CyberCourses**, then enable content if prompted. Create a query in Query Design View based on the Classes, Instructors, Sections, Enrollments, and Students tables with the following fields as shown in **Figure 3-31**: StudentLast and StudentFirst from the Students table, Description and Credits from the Classes table, Grade from the Enrollments table, and InstLastName from the Instructors table. Add criteria to select only those records where the Grade field value is **A** or **B** and the Credits field value equals **3**. Display the query in Datasheet View, widen the columns to display all of the data, then save the query with the name **3CreditsAB**. Close the 3CreditsAB query then exit Access.

Figure 3-31

StudentLast	StudentFirst	Description	Credits	Grade	InstLastName
Lincoln	Douglas	Cybersecurity Cost Accounting	3	A	Foxhoven
Chow	Ling	Cybersecurity Cost Accounting	3	B	Foxhoven
Cadbury	Louise	Cybersecurity for Managers	3	B	Foxhoven
Bush	Brad	Cybersecurity Fraud Examination	3	A	Foxhoven
Mitchell	Irma	Cybersecurity Fraud Examination	3	B	Foxhoven
Davis	Timothy	Cybersecurity Fraud Examination	3	A	Foxhoven
Kalam	Archie	Cybersecurity Fraud Examination	3	B	Foxhoven
Bush	Brad	Managing Cybersecurity	3	A	Garland
Mitchell	Irma	Managing Cybersecurity	3	B	Garland
Kalam	Archie	Managing Cybersecurity	3	B	Garland
Norton	Mary Jane	Managing Cybersecurity	3	B	Garland
Bach	Kristen	Principles of Cybersecurity	3	A	Garland
York	Erin	Principles of Cybersecurity	3	B	Garland
York	Erin	Survey of Cybersecurity Economics	3	B	Daniels
Jobs	Arno	Survey of Cybersecurity Economics	3	A	Ringgold
York	Erin	Cybersecurity I	3	B	Nordgren
Ali	Toni	Global Cybersecurity	3	B	Patrick
Owen	Leo	Global Cybersecurity	3	B	Patrick
John	Dominique	Home Cybersecurity	3	B	Patrick
Rafi	Erica	Retail Cybersecurity	3	B	Edwards
Ali	Toni	Retail Cybersecurity	3	B	Edwards
Simmons	Michael	Retail Cybersecurity	3	B	Edwards
Gayle	John	Retail Cybersecurity	3	A	Edwards
Cotton	Hobart	Retail Cybersecurity	3	B	Edwards
York	Erin	Retail Cybersecurity	3	B	Edwards
Adams	Jean	Retail Cybersecurity	3	B	Edwards
Owen	Leo	Advertising Cybersecurity	3	B	Stanton

Record: 1 of 27

Access **Module 4**

Working with Forms and Reports

Case
Sasha Spiros, special projects director at GIG Placement, asks you to create forms to make job and company information easier to access, enter, and update. She also wants you to create some reports that provide a professional presentation and analysis of selected data.

Module Objectives
After completing this module, you will be able to:

- Use Form View
- Use Form Layout View
- Use Form Design View
- Use Report Layout View
- Use Report Design View
- Add conditional formatting
- Use the Format Painter and themes

Files You Will Need

IL_AC_4-1.accdb
IL_AC_4-2.accdb
IL_AC_4-3.accdb
IL_AC_4-4.accdb
IL_AC_4-5.accdb

Use Form View

Case Sasha asks you to find and enter company data in the database. You will use a form to complete the work.

Objectives
- Navigate records in a form.
- Enter records in a form.

A form allows you to arrange the fields of a record in any layout so a database **user** can quickly and easily find, enter, edit, and analyze data. You can use several tools to create forms, as shown in **Table 4-1**. Each form has three views, and each view has a primary purpose, as described in **Table 4-2**, although you can complete some tasks in multiple views. **Form View** provides an easy-to-use data entry and navigation screen.

Steps

1. **sam↓** Start Access, open the **IL_AC_4-1.accdb database** from the location where you store your Data Files, save it as **IL_AC_4_Jobs**, enable content if prompted, then double-click the **CompanyEntry form** to open it in Form View

   The CompanyEntry form organizes all the fields of the Companies table to clearly display the data from one record at a time. Forms contain **controls** such as labels to describe information, text boxes and combo boxes to help you enter information, and command buttons to help you work with the form. Forms also provide **navigation buttons** in the lower-left corner, which help you navigate through the data.

2. Click the **Next record button** ▶ in the navigation bar three times to navigate to the fourth record

   The **Current Record box** identifies the record you are currently viewing and the total number of records. The navigation buttons also provide a way to move to the first or last record in the form quickly.

3. Click the **Last record button** ▶| in the navigation bar

   To move to a prior record, you use the Previous record and First record buttons.

4. Click the **Previous record button** ◀ in the navigation bar, then click the **First record button** |◀ to return to the first record

   In addition, you can type a number in the Current Record box to quickly move to that record.

5. Click the **Current Record box**, type **21**, press **ENTER**, then change the Industry field value to **Aerospace**

   Changes are saved as you move from record to record. You always enter new records at the end of the form.

6. Click the **New (blank) record button** ▶*, then enter a new company record, as shown in **Figure 4-1** and described as follows

Company ID:	TAB (AutoNumber field that automatically increments)
Company Name:	**Got Your Six Cybersecurity**
Industry:	**Information**
Description:	**Cybersecurity design, implementation, and training**
City:	**Ottawa**
State:	**ON**

7. Right-click the **CompanyEntry tab**, then click **Close**

   When you close a form, Access automatically saves data in the current record.

Figure 4-1: Adding a new record to the CompanyEntry form in Form View

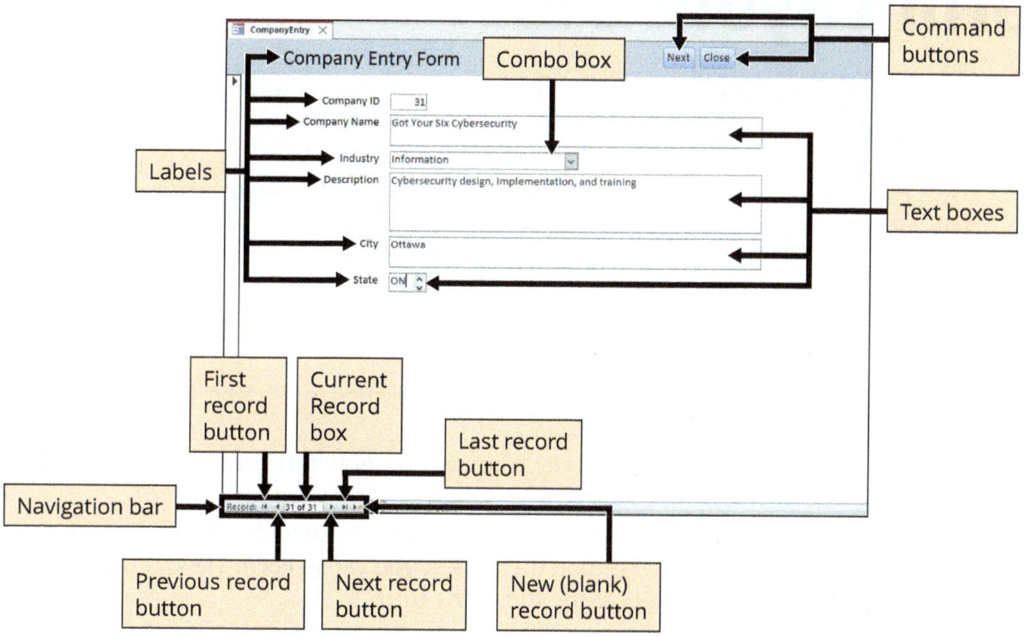

Table 4-1: Form creation tools

tool	icon	creates a form
Form		with one click based on the selected table or query
Form Design		from scratch in Form Design View
Blank Form		from scratch in Form Layout View
Form Wizard		by answering a series of questions provided by the Form Wizard dialog boxes
Navigation		to navigate or move between different areas of the database
More Forms		for Multiple Items, Datasheet, Split Form, or Modal Dialog arrangements
Split Form		with two panes, the upper showing one record at a time and the lower displaying a datasheet of many records

Table 4-2: Form views

view	primary purpose
Form	To find, sort, enter, and edit data
Layout	To modify the size, position, or formatting of controls; shows data as you modify the form, making it the tool of choice when you want to change the appearance and usability of the form while viewing data
Design	To modify the Form Header, Detail, and Footer section, to work with form rulers and gridlines, or to access the complete range of controls and form properties; Design View does not display data

Use Form Layout View

Case Sasha asks you to change some design elements in the ContractJobsEntry form to make it more attractive and easier to use. You make these changes in Form Layout View.

Objectives
- Format controls in Form Layout View.
- Edit labels in Form Layout View.

You can use Form Layout View and Form Design View to create and modify a form. The most significant benefit of **Form Layout View** is that it lets you make design changes to the form while browsing the data. This helps you productively resize and format the controls on the form. Although the data appears in Form Layout View, you cannot enter or edit it in this view. **Table 4-3** lists several of the most popular formatting commands on the Format tab of the ribbon that help you work effectively in Layout View.

Steps

1. Right-click the **ContractJobsEntry form** in the Navigation Pane, then click **Layout View**

   Layout View opens and looks similar to Form View. In Layout View, you can move through the records, but you cannot enter or edit the data as you can in Form View. You decide to enhance the Contract Jobs Entry Form label at the top of the form.

   Quick Tip
   You can also apply formatting commands in Form Design View.

2. Click the **Contract Jobs Entry Form label** in the Form Header section, click the **Format tab** on the ribbon, click the **Bold button** [B], click the **Font Color arrow** [A▼], click **Green, Accent 6** (tenth column, first row in the Theme Colors palette), click the **Font Size arrow** [11 ▼], then click **22**

   You often use Layout View to make minor design changes, such as editing labels and changing formatting characteristics.

3. Click the **Contract Responsibilities label** to select it, click the **Contract Responsibilities label** again to position the insertion point in the label, edit the text to be **Responsibilities** (delete the word Contract), then press **ENTER**

   Your users do not need the Next button because they use the buttons in the navigation bar, so you can delete the Next command button.

4. Click the **Next command button**, then press **DELETE**

   You can change the style, shape, and outline of the Close button.

   Quick Tip
   You can undo multiple formatting actions by clicking the Undo button [↶] on the Home tab.

5. Click the **Close command button**, click the **Quick Styles button**, click the **Colored Fill – Green, Accent 6 style** (seventh column, second row in the Quick Styles gallery), click the **Shape Outline button**, then click **Transparent** near the bottom of the menu

   You decide to center the data in the Contract ID text box to make it easier to read.

   Trouble
   Be sure to modify the text box instead of the Contract ID label on the left.

6. Click **1** in the box to the right of the Contract ID label, then click the **Center button** [≡] in the Font group

   Compare your ContractJobsEntry form to **Figure 4-2**. The form title label is more pronounced, the Close button is styled, and the Contract ID data is easier to read.

Figure 4-2: Modifying controls in Form Layout View

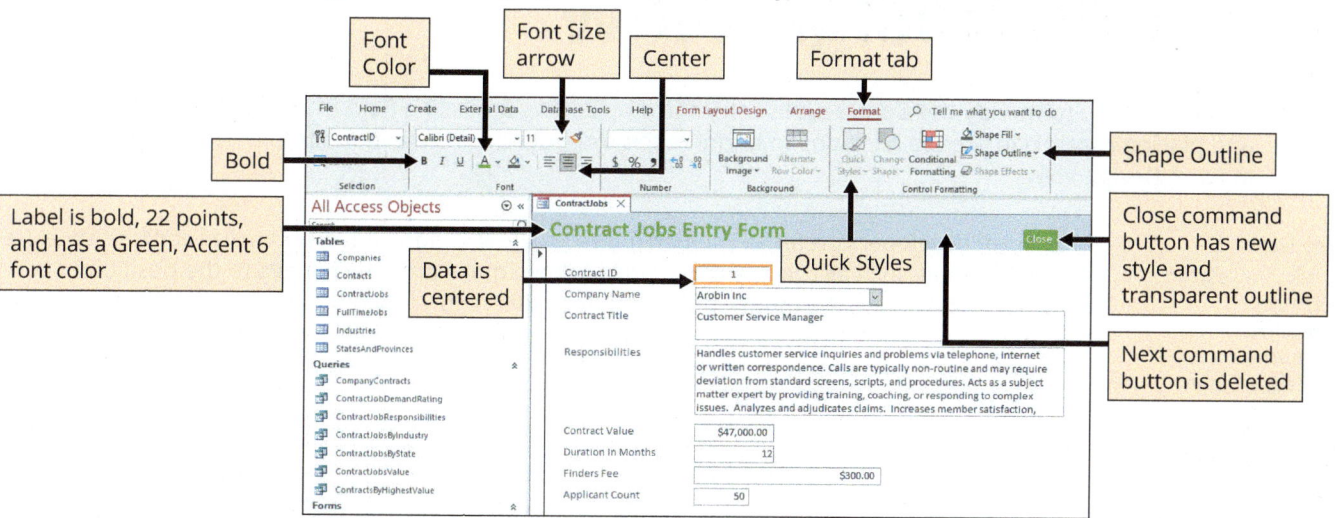

Table 4-3: Useful formatting commands

button	button name	description
B	Bold	Toggles bold on or off for the selected control(s)
I	Italic	Toggles italic on or off for the selected control(s)
U	Underline	Toggles underline on or off for the selected control(s)
A	Font Color	Changes the text color of the selected control(s)
	Background Color or Shape Fill	Changes the background color of the selected control(s)
	Align Left	Left-aligns the selected control(s) within its own border
	Center	Centers the selected control(s) within its own border
	Align Right	Right-aligns the selected control(s) within its own border
	Alternate Row Color	Changes the background color of alternate records in the selected section
	Shape Outline	Changes the border color, thickness, or style of the selected control(s)
	Shape Effects	Changes the special visual effect of the selected control(s)
	Quick Styles	Changes the color, outline, and effects with one selection

Use Form Design View

Case Sasha asks you to modify the ContractJobsEntry form by adding a missing field from the ContractJobs table and placing controls in precise positions to improve the form design. You respond to her request by working in Form Design View.

Objectives
- Format controls in Design View.
- Move controls in Design View.
- Add Fields in Design View.

Most form developers prefer to use **Form Design View** to add, move, and resize controls because it provides tools such as rulers and gridlines to help make precise changes to the position of controls. **Table 4-4** shows the mouse pointer shapes that help you work effectively in Form or Report Design View to select, resize, and move controls.

Steps

Quick Tip
You can also open the Field List and add a field to a form in Form Layout View.

1. **Right-click the ContractJobs tab, click Design View, click the Form Design tab on the ribbon, then click the Add Existing Fields button in the Tools group to open the Field List**
   The **Field List** opens, listing the fields available for this form. You can drag the title bar of the Field List to move it or double-click the title bar to dock the Field List to the right.

Quick Tip
If you make a mistake, click the Undo button and try again.

2. **Drag the top of the Form Footer bar down about 0.5", then use the move pointer to drag the FirstPosted field to the form below the Applicant Count text box, as shown in Figure 4-3**
   When you add the FirstPosted field to the form, you add two controls: a label and a text box. The **label** on the left describes the data. By default, the label displays the field name, though you can modify the text. The **text box** on the right displays the data from the field. It *must* contain the actual field name to stay connected (also called **bound**) to the data.

3. **Click the FirstPosted label, click the FirstPosted label a second time to place the insertion point in the text, modify the text to be First Posted, press ENTER, click the Format tab on the ribbon, click the Font Color arrow, then click Automatic**
   Automatic is the default color for text, which is Black in this case. You also want to align and format the new controls.

Trouble
Labels are on the left, and text boxes are on the right.

4. **With the First Posted label selected, press and hold CTRL, click the Applicant Count label to select both labels at the same time, click the Arrange tab on the ribbon, click the Align button, then click Left**
   You left-aligned the First Posted label with the Applicant Count label above it, which is different from left-aligning the text within the label. Now left-align the Applicant Count and First Posted text boxes and the text they contain.

5. **Click the ApplicantCount text box, press and hold CTRL, click the FirstPosted text box, click the Align button, click Left, click the Format tab on the ribbon, then click the Align Left button**
   You added, moved, and aligned the new controls for the FirstPosted field on the form. As a final touch, you want to add a label to the Form Footer section with the text "GIG Placement" to include the company name on the form.

Quick Tip
You can also add and edit labels in Form Layout View.

6. **Drag the bottom of the Form Footer bar down about 0.5", click the Form Design tab on the ribbon, click the Label button, click at about the 1" mark in the Form Footer section, type GIG Placement, then press ENTER**
   You are ready to review the final ContractJobsEntry form in Form View.

7. **Right-click the ContractJobsEntry tab, click Save, right-click the ContractJobsEntry tab again, then click Form View as shown in Figure 4-4**
   In general, you use Form Layout View for formatting changes and Form Design View to add and position new controls. However, the two views share many features.

8. **Close the ContractJobsEntry form**

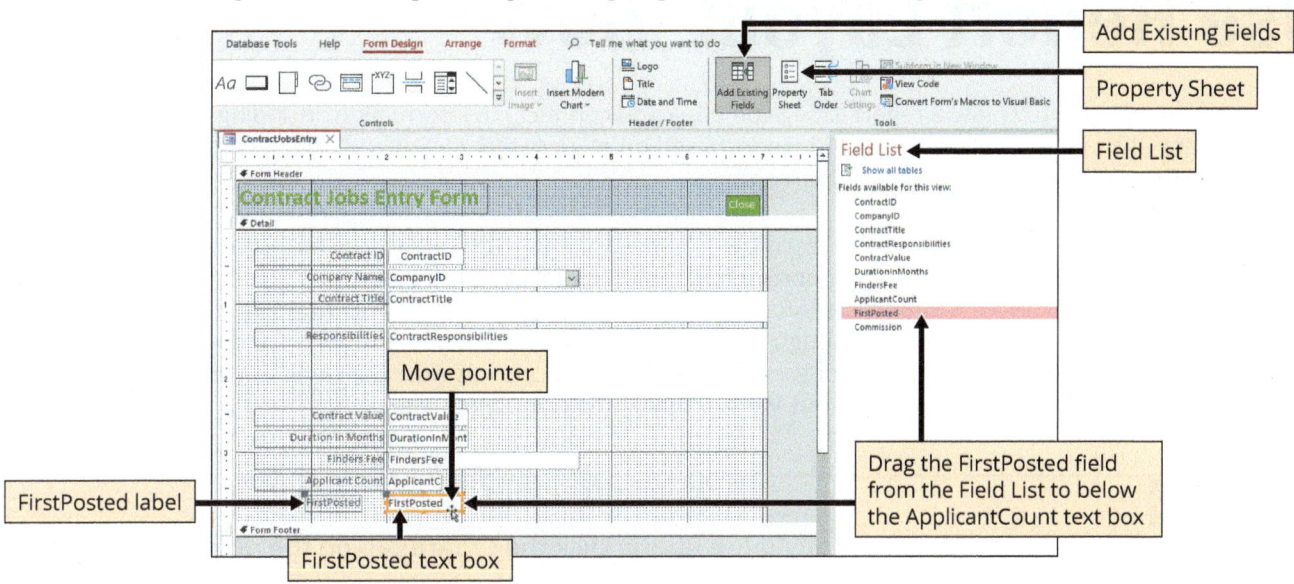

Figure 4-3: Adding, moving, and aligning controls in Form Design View

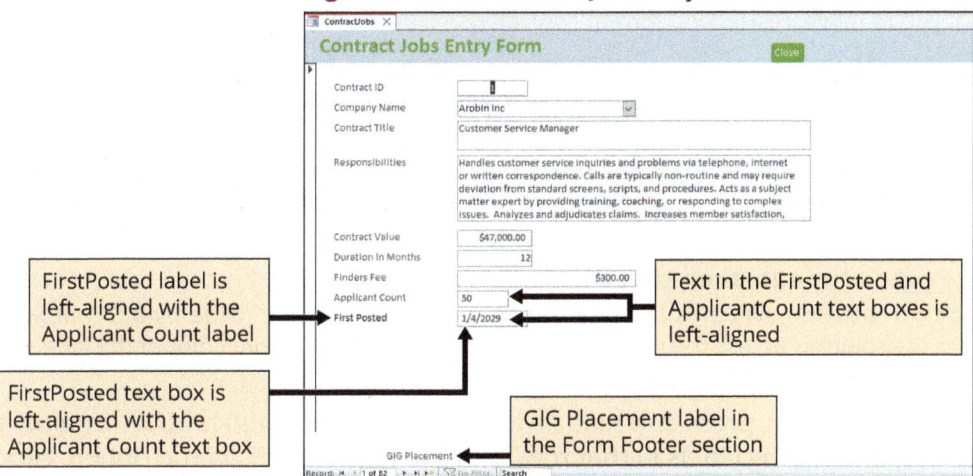

Figure 4-4: Final ContractJobsEntry form in Form View

Table 4-4: Mouse pointer shapes in Form or Report Design View

shape	when does this shape appear?	action
▷	When you point to any unselected control on the form (the default mouse pointer)	Single-clicking with this mouse pointer selects a control
✥	When you point to the upper-left corner or edge of a selected control in Form Design View or the middle of the control in Form Layout View	Dragging with this mouse pointer moves the selected control(s)
↕ ↔ ⤡ ⤢	When you point to any sizing handle (except the larger one in the upper-left corner in Form Design View)	Dragging with one of these mouse pointers resizes the control

Bound versus unbound controls

Controls are either bound or unbound. **Bound controls** display values from a field such as text boxes and combo boxes. The most common bound control is the text box. **Unbound controls** describe data or enhance the appearance of the form. Labels are the most common type of unbound control, but other types include lines, images, tabs, and command buttons. Another way to distinguish bound from unbound controls is to observe the form as you move from record to record. Because bound controls display data, their contents change as you move through the records, displaying data from the field of the current record. Unbound controls such as labels, lines, and command buttons do not change as you move through the records in a form.

Use Report Layout View

Case Sasha asks you to create a report listing company and contract job information, including contract values, for financial analysis. You can create the report based on a query that includes all the necessary fields and then use Report Layout View to modify the report.

Objectives
- Create a report with the Report tool.
- Move, resize, and format controls in Report Layout View.
- Change page orientation.

Reports allow you to organize, group, sort, and subtotal records for professional presentations of data. You create reports using multiple tools and multiple views just as you do forms. Refer to **Table 4-5** for more information on report creation tools and **Table 4-6** for more information on report views. Although you use forms for data entry and reports for data distribution, many tasks such as formatting, moving, and resizing controls work the same way in the two objects. For example, **Report Layout View** is similar to Form Layout View.

Steps

Trouble
If the Field List opens, close it.

1. Click the **ContractJobsValue query**, click the **Create tab** on the ribbon, then click the **Report button**
   A report based on the ContractJobsValue query opens in Report Layout View, which displays data and allows you to move, resize, and format controls.

2. Click any value in the **Industry column**, then use the two-headed arrow pointer ↔ to narrow the column to about half its size, as shown in **Figure 4-5**
   A benefit of resizing controls in Report Layout View rather than Report Design View is that you can keep track of how the data fits as you resize the control. The report is still too wide to fit on a standard piece of paper in **portrait orientation** (8.5" wide by 11" tall), as indicated by the dashed line on the right.

3. Click the **Page Setup tab**, then click the **Landscape button**
   Landscape orientation switches the orientation of the paper to 11" wide by 8.5" tall, which allows for more columns across the page. You also want to change the font color of the labels that serve as column headings so they are more noticeable.

4. Click the **Industry label**, press and hold **SHIFT**, then click the **ApplicantCount label** to select all column heading labels in that row, click the **Format tab** on the ribbon, click the **Font Color arrow** [A ▾], then click **Automatic**
   Your last change is to move the ContractValue column to the far right.

5. Click the **ContractValue label**, press and hold **SHIFT**, click **any value** in the ContractValue column, then use the move pointer to drag the column to the right of the ApplicantCount column
   The final ContractJobsValue report is shown in **Figure 4-6**.

6. Right-click the **ContractJobsValue tab**, click **Save**, click **OK** to accept the default name, right-click the **ContractJobsValue tab**, then click **Print Preview** to preview the report as it would fit on a piece of paper

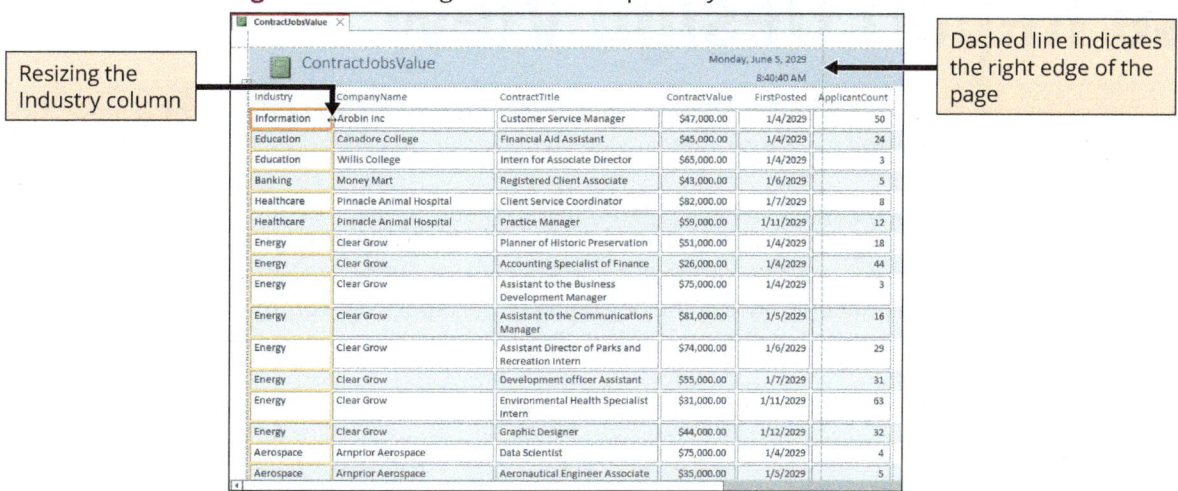

Figure 4-5: Resizing a column in Report Layout View

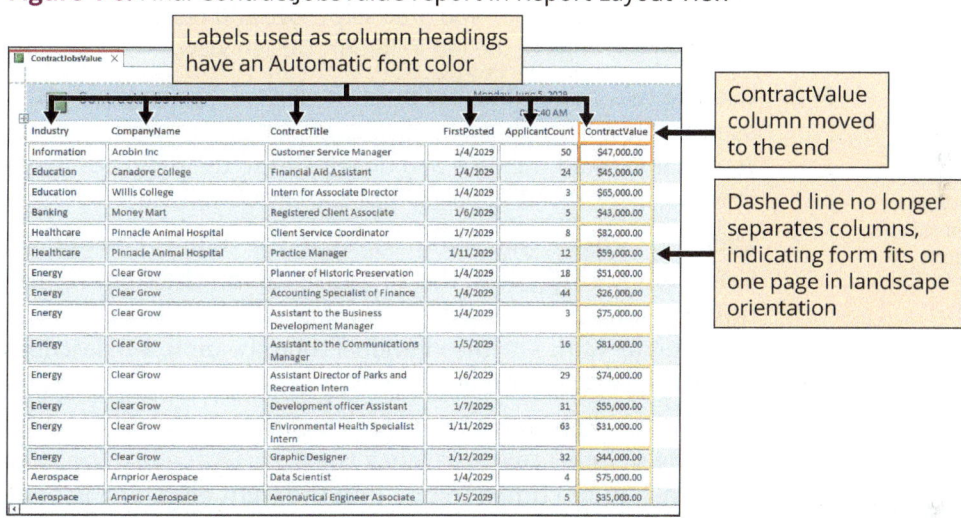

Figure 4-6: Final ContractJobsValue report in Report Layout View

Table 4-5: Report creation tools

tool	icon	creates a report
Report		with one click based on the selected table or query
Report Design		from scratch in Report Design View
Blank Report		from scratch in Report Layout View
Report Wizard		by answering a series of questions provided by the Report Wizard dialog boxes
Labels		by answering a series of questions provided by the Label Wizard dialog boxes

Table 4-6: Report views

view	primary purpose
Report View	To quickly review the report without page breaks
Print Preview	To review each page of an entire report as it will appear if printed
Layout View	To modify the size, position, or formatting of controls; shows live data as you modify the report, making it the tool of choice when you want to change the appearance and positioning of controls on a report while also reviewing live data
Design View	To work with report sections or to access the complete range of controls and report properties; Design View does not display data

Use Report Design View

Case Sasha asks you to modify the ContractJobsValue report to fine-tune the design by removing clutter and improving readability. You use Report Design View to make the changes.

Objectives
- Modify controls in Report Design View.
- Group and ungroup controls in Report Design View.
- Change report width.

Report Design View gives you maximum control over all report modifications by providing extra design tools such as rulers and section bars. Report **sections** determine where and how often controls in that section print in the final report. For example, controls in the Report Header section print only once at the beginning of the report, but controls in the Detail section print once for every record the report displays. **Table 4-7** describes report sections.

Steps

1. **Right-click the ContractJobsValue tab, then click Design View**
   Five report **section bars** are displayed that identify the report sections. The **horizontal ruler** is also shown, which helps you precisely move and resize controls. To narrow the entire report, you drag the right edge to the left in Report Design View.

Quick Tip
If a report is too wide to fit on a piece of paper, a green error indicator appears in the upper-left corner of the report.

2. **Use the two-headed arrow pointer ↔ to drag the right edge of the report as far left as possible**
   You want to move the date and time boxes to the right, but they are part of a control layout. To move or resize an individual control in a layout, you must first remove the layout.

3. **Click the ContractJobsValue label in the Report Header section, click the Control Selection icon ⊕, click the Arrange tab on the ribbon, then click the Remove Layout button**
   Now you can work with the individual controls. **Table 4-8** describes control layout buttons on the Arrange tab that are useful in report formatting.

Quick Tip
Though you can move controls in Report or Form Design View by dragging them, the arrow keys let you precisely position controls.

4. **Click the background of the report, click the =Date() text box, press and hold CTRL, click the =Time() text box, click the Size/Space button, click Group, then press RIGHT ARROW enough times to position the right edge of the controls at the 9" mark on the horizontal ruler**
   Compare your screen to **Figure 4-7**. You also want to make some formatting changes to the title of the report.

5. **Click the ContractJobsValue label in the Report Header, click the Format tab on the ribbon, click the Font Color arrow A ▾, click Automatic, click the Font Size arrow 11 ▾, click 22, click the ContractJobsValue label again to place the insertion point in the text, then add spaces so that the label reads Contract Jobs Value**
   Your final modification will be to change the background color of the ContractValue data.

Quick Tip
You edit labels and format controls the same way in Form Design View and Form Layout View.

6. **Click the ContractValue text box in the Detail section, click the Background Color arrow ▾, then click the Green 3 box (seventh column, fourth row in the Standard Colors palette)**
   Compare your final Report Design View to **Figure 4-8**. To review your modifications, display the report in Print Preview.

7. **Right-click the ContractJobsValue tab, click Save, right-click the ContractJobsValue tab, click Print Preview, click the Next Page button ▶ to navigate the pages of the report, right-click the ContractJobsValue tab, then click Close**
   When you preview each page of a report, you can confirm it contains no blank pages and examine how the report sections print on each page.

Use Report Design View AC 4-11

Figure 4-7: Working in Report Design View

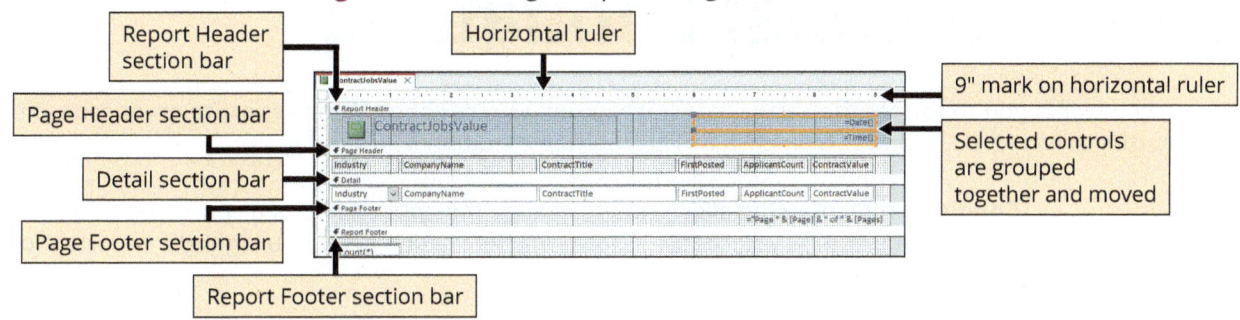

Figure 4-8: Final ContractJobsValue report in Report Design View

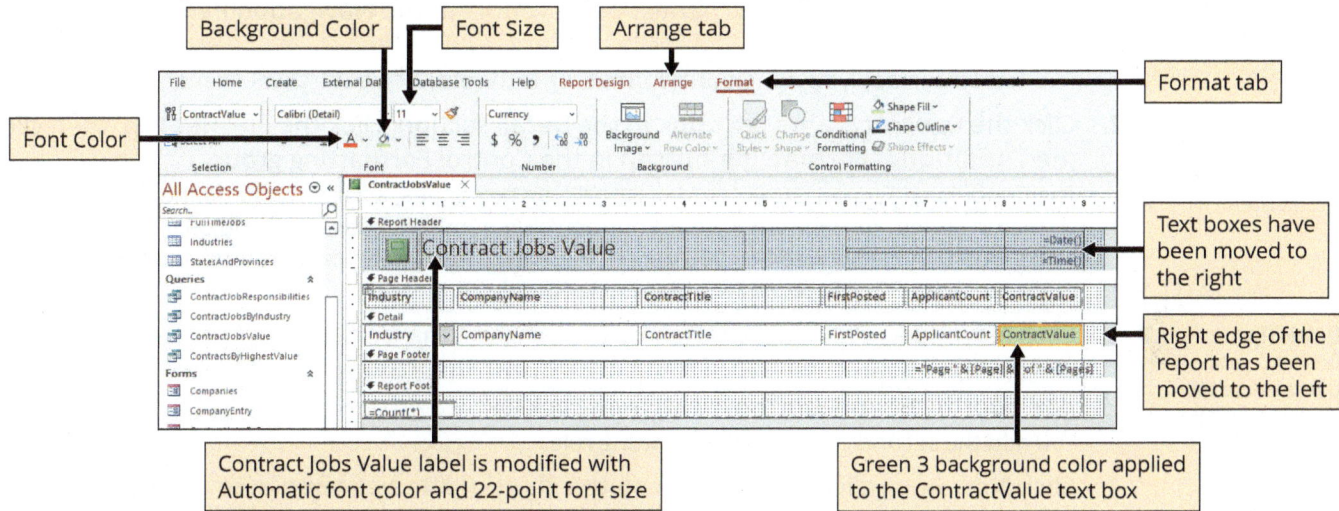

Table 4-7: Report sections

section	where does this section print?
Report Header	At the top of the first page
Page Header	At the top of every page (but below the Report Header on the first page)
Detail	Once for every record
Page Footer	At the bottom of every page
Report Footer	At the end of the report

Table 4-8: Control layout buttons

button		description	button		description
Gridlines		Applies gridlines in different colors, widths, and borders to the cells of the control layout	Select Layout		Selects the entire layout
			Select Column		Selects a single column of a layout
Stacked		Applies a vertical layout with labels on the left and text boxes on the right	Select Row		Selects a single row of a layout
Tabular		Applies a horizontal layout similar to a spreadsheet	Merge		Merges cells in a layout
			Split Vertically		Splits cells into two rows
Remove Layout		Removes a layout	Split Horizontally		Splits cells into two columns
Insert Above		Inserts a row above the layout	Move Up		Moves cells into the section above the current section
Insert Below		Inserts a row below the layout			
Insert Left		Inserts a column to the left of the layout	Move Down		Moves cells into the section below the current section
Insert Right		Inserts a column to the right of the layout			

Add Conditional Formatting

Case Sasha wants you to format the salary data in the ContractsByHighestValue report to emphasize different starting salary levels. You will accomplish this by applying conditional formatting.

Objective
- Apply conditional formats.

Conditional formatting allows you to change the appearance of a control on a form or report based on the criteria you specify. Conditional formatting helps you highlight important or exceptional data on a form or report.

Steps

1. Right-click the **ContractsByHighestValue report** in the Navigation Pane, then click **Design View**

   The first step in applying conditional formatting is to select the control you want to format.

Trouble
Be sure to select the ContractValue text box (not the label).

2. Click the **ContractValue text box** in the Detail section, click the **Format tab**, then click the **Conditional Formatting button** in the Control Formatting group

   The Conditional Formatting Rules Manager dialog box opens, asking you to define the conditional formatting rules. You want to format ContractValue numbers between 0 and 59,999 with a yellow background, those between 60,000 and 79,999 with a light green background, and those equal to or greater than 80,000 with a light blue background.

Quick Tip
Between . . . and criteria include both values in the range.

3. Click **New Rule**, click the **text box to the right of the between arrow**, type **0**, click the **and box**, type **59999**, click the **Background color arrow**, click the **Yellow box** (fourth column, bottom row), then click **OK**

   You add the second conditional formatting rule.

4. Click **New Rule**, click the **text box to the right of the between arrow**, type **60000**, click the **and box**, type **79999**, click the **Background color arrow**, click the **Light Green box** (fifth column, bottom row), then click **OK**

   You add the third conditional formatting rule.

5. Click **New Rule**, click the **between arrow**, click **greater than or equal to**, click the **value box**, type **80000**, click the **Background color arrow**, click the **Light Blue box** (seventh column, bottom row), then click **OK**

   Compare your Conditional Formatting Rules Manager dialog box with three rules to **Figure 4-9**.

Quick Tip
Conditional formatting works the same way in Form and Report Layout and Design Views.

6. Click **OK** in the Conditional Formatting Rules Manager dialog box, right-click the **ContractsByHighestValue tab**, then click **Print Preview**

   Conditional formatting rules applied a yellow, light green, or light blue background color to the ContractValue text box for each record, as shown in **Figure 4-10**.

7. Right-click the **ContractsByHighestValue tab**, click **Save**, then click the **Close button** ☒ on the ContractsByHighestValue tab

Figure 4-9: Conditional Formatting Rules Manager dialog box

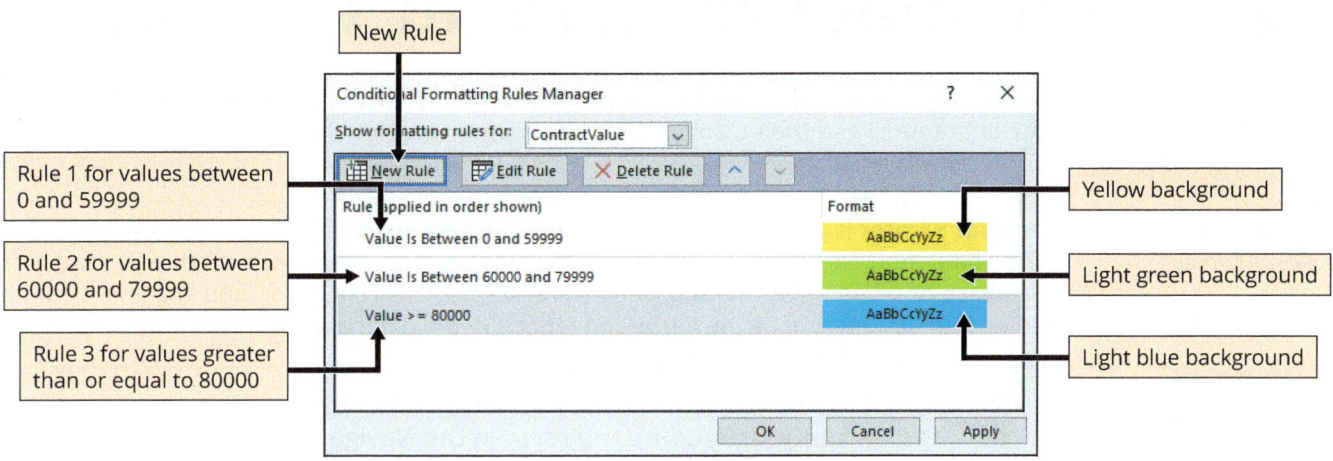

Figure 4-10: Conditional formatting applied to the ContractsByHighestValue report

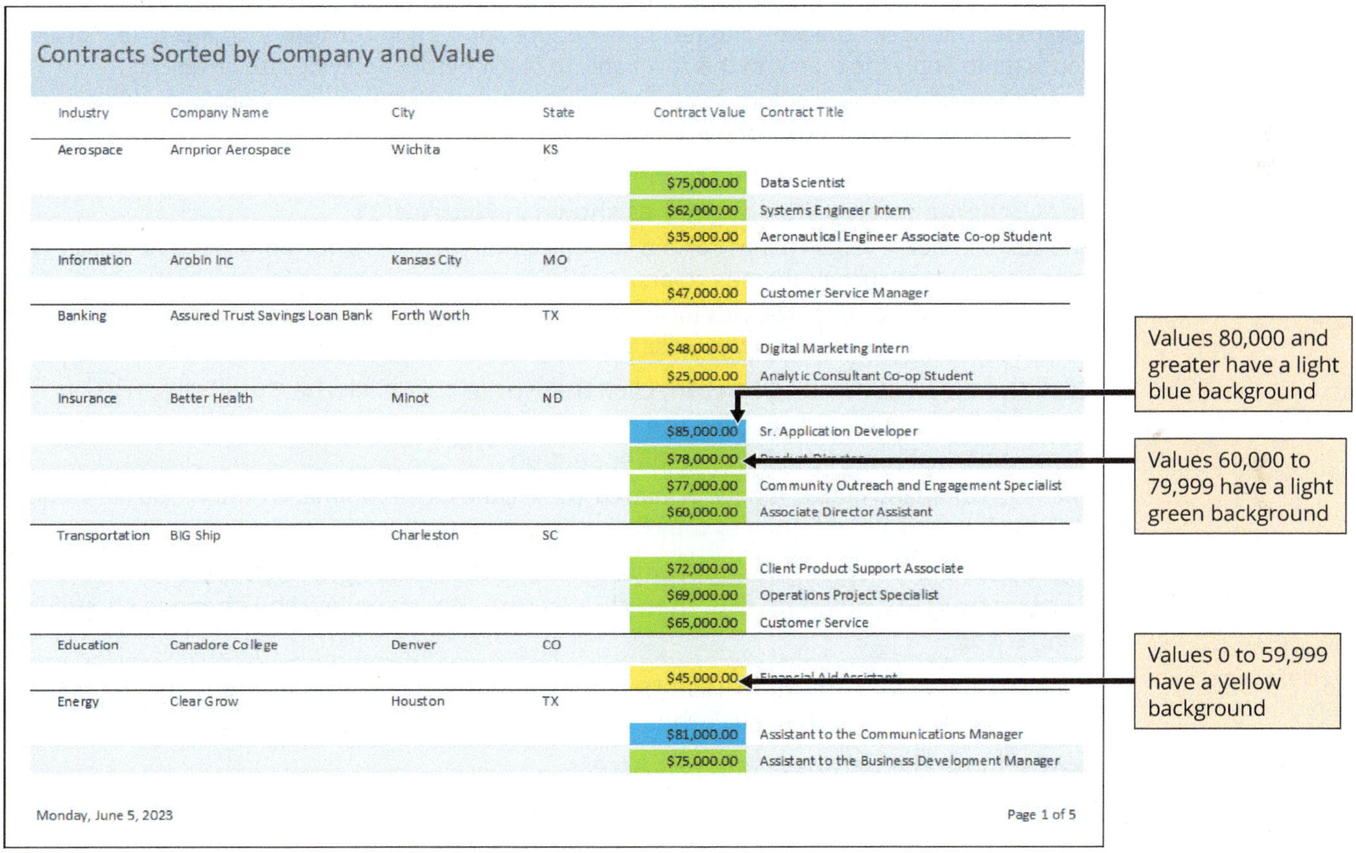

Use the Format Painter and Themes

Case Sasha wants to improve the appearance of the ContractJobsByCompany form. You can do so by applying a built-in theme to the entire form and then using the Format Painter to quickly copy and paste formatting characteristics from one label to another.

Objectives
- Format with Format Painter.
- Apply a theme.

The **Format Painter** is a tool you use to copy formatting properties from one control to another in Form and Report Design or Layout Views. **Themes** are predefined formats that you apply to the database to set all the formatting enhancements, such as font, color, and alignment, for an individual form or report or all the forms and reports in the database.

Steps

1. Right-click the **ContractJobsByCompany form** in the Navigation Pane, click **Design View**, click the **Themes button**, point to several themes and wait until each of their names appear, right-click the **Gallery theme**, then click **Apply Theme to This Object Only**

   If you click (rather than right-click) a theme, it is applied to all the forms and reports in the database. This keeps the look and feel of the entire application consistent. In this case, however, you want to apply the theme to this form only to test it before applying it to all objects.

   A theme applies new colors, fonts, alignment, and other formatting options. You can also choose to change only the colors or only the fonts.

   Quick Tip
   You can apply themes, theme fonts, or theme colors in Form and Report Layout and Design views.

2. Click the **Fonts button** in the Themes group, right-click **Garamond**, then click **Apply Font Scheme to This Object Only** as shown in **Figure 4-11**

   The current theme fonts change for the current form. The Colors button works in a similar way, changing only the current theme's colors.

   The Print command button was formatted previously and does not look the same as the Close button. To copy formats quickly, you use the Format Painter.

3. Click the **Close command button**, click the **Home tab**, click the **Bold button** [B] in the Text Formatting group, click the **Format Painter button**, then click the **Print command button** in the Form Header section

   The Print command button is now formatted just like the Close command button. You can double-click the Format Painter button to copy formatting to more than one control.

   Quick Tip
   The Format Painter works the same way in Form and Report Layout and Design Views.

4. Right-click the **ContractJobsByCompany tab**, click **Save**, right-click the **ContractJobsByCompany tab**, then click **Form View** to review the changes shown in **Figure 4-12**

5. Click the **Close command button** to close the ContractJobsByCompany form, click the **Database Tools tab**, then click the **Compact and Repair Database button**

6. **sam↑** Close the database and exit Access

Use the Format Painter and Themes   AC 4-15

Figure 4-11: Applying themes

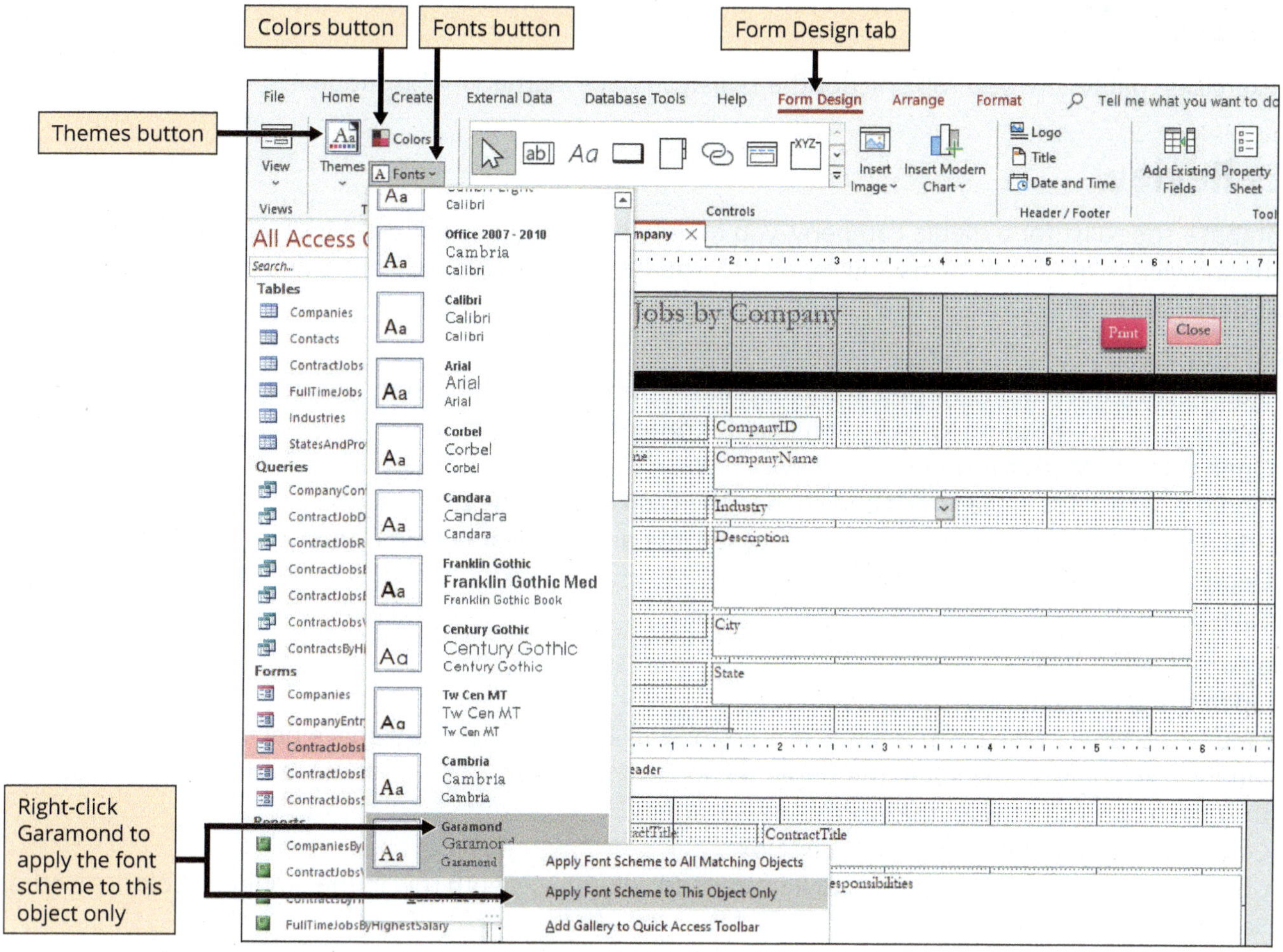

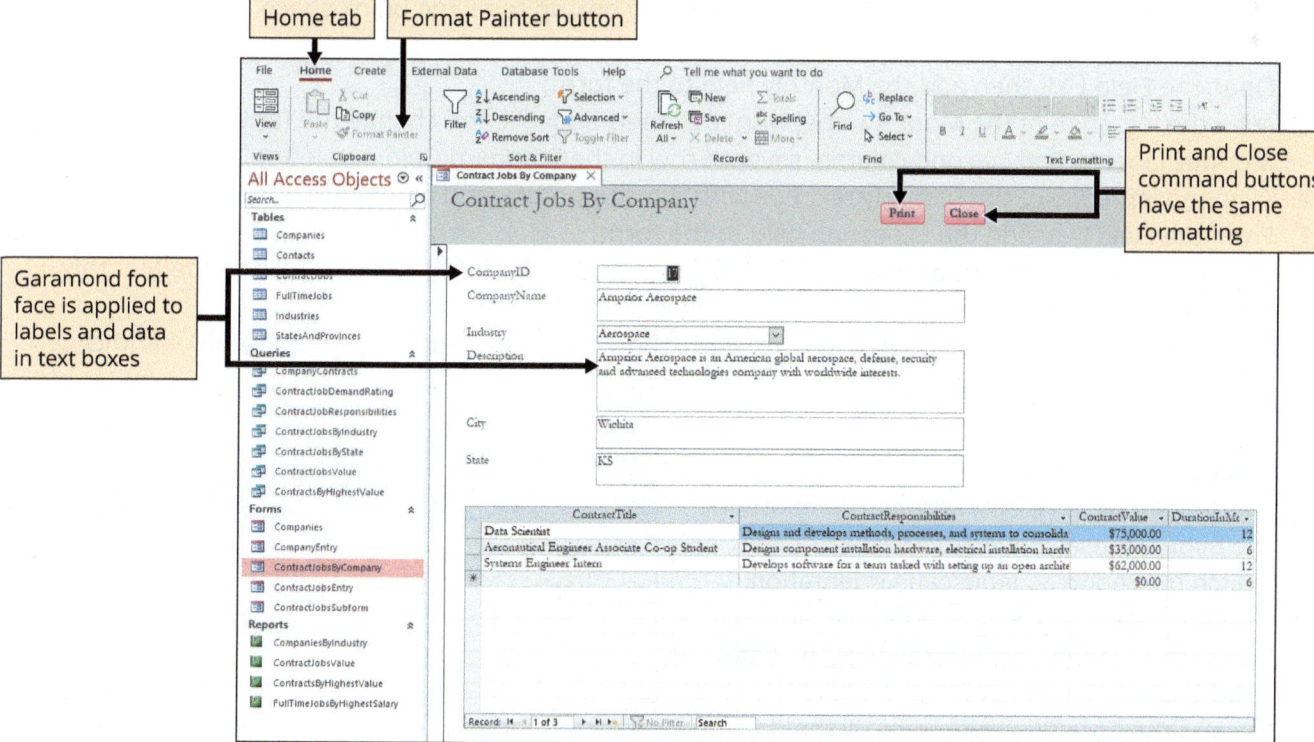

Figure 4-12: Final ContractJobsByCompany form

Practice

In the exercises that follow, you will practice the skills you have learned in this module.

Skills Review

As a database specialist for a media company, you maintain the database of technical support information. Use your knowledge of Access forms and reports to update and improve data entry and reporting for the support desk database.

1. **Use Form View.**
   a. Start Access, open the IL_AC_4-2.accdb database from the location where you store your Data Files, save it as **IL_AC_4_SupportDesk**, then enable content if prompted.
   b. Open the StaffMaster form in Form View.
   c. Find the record for Kayla James and change the LastName value to **Munson**.
   d. Add a new record with your name in the LastName and FirstName fields, and **Research** in the Department field.
   e. Save the StaffMaster form.

2. **Use Form Layout View.**
   a. Open the StaffMaster form in Layout View.
   b. Modify the label in the Form Header section to **Staff Master** so it has a space between the words.
   c. Modify the labels on the left in the Detail section to **Employee ID**, **Last Name**, and **First Name** so they have spaces between the words.
   d. Center the data in the EmployeeID text box.
   e. Change the font color for all labels to Red (second column, seventh row in the Standard Colors palette).
   f. Save the StaffMaster form.

3. **Use Form Design View.**
   a. Open the StaffMaster form in Design View.
   b. Move the Department label and Department combo box up to fill the blank space after the FirstName controls.
   c. Open the Field List, then add the Monthly field to the form.
   d. Align the left edge of the Monthly label with the labels above it and change the font color for the Monthly label to Red (second column, seventh row in the Standard Colors palette).
   e. Align the left edge of the Monthly text box with the combo box and text boxes above it.
   f. From the Field List, add the Extension field to the form.
   g. Make the same alignment and font color changes to the Extension field as you did to the Monthly label and text box.
   h. Save the StaffMaster form, open it in Form View, then navigate to record 6 (EmployeeID 14, Michael Underhill) as shown in **Figure 4-13**.
   i. Close the StaffMaster form.

4. **Use Report Layout View.**
   a. Use the Report tool to create a new report on the SupportCases table.
   b. Switch the report to landscape orientation.
   c. In Layout View of the new report, reduce the size of the Category column so that the data just fits.
   d. Expand the CaseTitle column so all the data fits without text wrapping except for the longest

Figure 4-13

Staff Master	
Employee ID	14
Last Name	Underhill
First Name	Michael
Department	Marketing
Monthly	$4,333.33
Extension	3924

case title, which starts with "I keep seeing." That data can still wrap to another line so that the report fits on one landscape page.
   e. Move the label and text box of the OpenedDate column to be the third column in the report.
   f. Modify the font color of the SupportCases label in the Report Header section to Green (sixth column, last row in the Standard Colors palette) and the font size to **20**.
   g. Delete the date and time controls in the Report Header section.
   h. Modify the font color of the labels that identify every column heading to also be Green, with a font size of **12**.
   i. Save the report with the name **SupportCaseInfo**.
5. **Use Report Design View.**
   a. Switch the SupportCaseInfo report to Report Design View.
   b. Narrow the report as much as possible horizontally.
   c. Select all the controls then remove the control layout in the Page Header, Detail, and Report Footer sections.
   d. Resize the =Count(*) text box in the Report Footer to be tall enough to display the entire expression. (**Hint**: This expression was created by the Report tool when the report was initially created to calculate the total number of records in the report.)
   e. Move and align the =Count(*) text box in the Report Footer section so that its top edge is touching the Report Footer section bar and its left edge is aligned with the left edge of the text box in the Page Footer section that contains the page number expression.
   f. Delete any extra space in the Report Footer section by dragging the bottom of the report up as far as possible.
   g. Select all the labels in the Page Header section and group them together so that they will move as a group should you want to reposition them later.
   h. Select all the text boxes in the Detail section and change their font to Consolas size **10**. Reduce the height of the text boxes so that their names just fit in the text box with no extra space.
   i. Save the SupportCaseInfo report.
6. **Add conditional formatting.**
   a. With the SupportCaseInfo report still open in Report Design View, add a conditional formatting rule to the Category text box. If the field value is equal to **LAN**, change the font color to Red (second column, last row of the Standard Colors palette).
   b. Add a second conditional formatting rule to the Category text box. If the field value is equal to **Printer**, change the font color to Green (sixth column, last row of the Standard Colors palette).
   c. Save the SupportCaseInfo report, switch to Print Preview to make sure the conditional formats are applied correctly, then return to Report Design View.
7. **Use the Format Painter and themes.**
   a. In Report Design View, use the Format Painter to copy the format from the page expression text box in the Page Footer section to the =Count(*) control in the Report Footer section.
   b. Apply the Garamond-TrebuchetMS theme font to the SupportCaseInfo report object only.
   c. Apply the Violet theme color to the SupportCaseInfo report object only.
   d. Save the SupportCaseInfo report and switch to Print Preview, as shown in **Figure 4-14**.

Figure 4-14

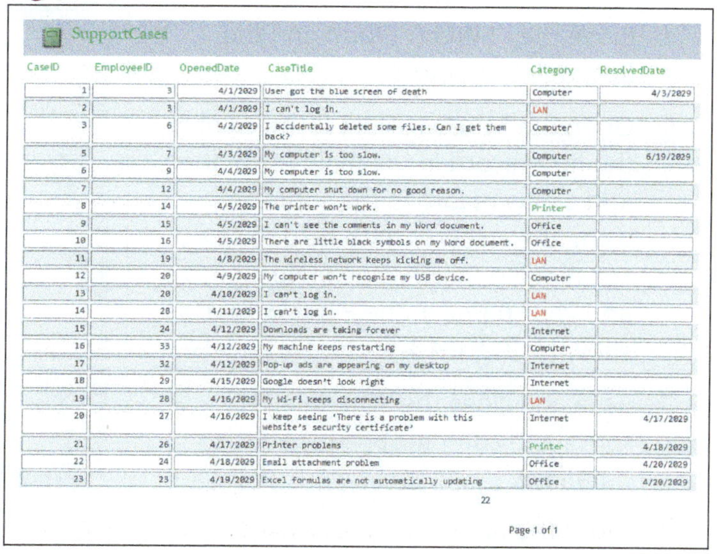

Skills Review (Continued)

e. Close the SupportCaseInfo report, then compact and repair the database.

f. Close the database and exit Access.

Independent Challenge 1

As the manager of Homefront, a personal support worker resource company, you have created a database to manage the schedules that connect each healthcare provider with personal support workers (PSWs) to efficiently handle patient visits. In this exercise, you modify a form to help users find, enter, and edit data.

a. Start Access. Open the IL_AC_4-3.accdb database from the location where you store your Data Files and save it as **IL_AC_4_Homefront**. Click Enable Content if a yellow Security Warning message appears.

b. Open the ScheduleDate form in Form Layout View.

c. Change the font face for all controls in the Detail section, including those in the subform, to Arial Narrow and a **10**-point font size. (**Hint**: This form contains a subform, the ScheduleItemsSubform. You can change the font face and font size for the controls directly in Form Layout View of the ScheduleDate form, or you can close the ScheduleDate form and apply the formats to the ScheduleItemsSubform in Form Layout View.) After making the changes, save any open forms.

d. Open the ScheduleDate form in Design View. Modify the Work Schedule label in the Form Header section to read **Doctor and PSW Schedule**. Change the font size to **17** and resize the label as needed to display the text clearly.

e. The Detail section has five command buttons with the following captions: Day, Doctor, PSW, by Location, and by PSW. Format the Day command button with the Light 1 Outline, Colored Fill – Orange, Accent 6 quick style (seventh column, third row in the Quick Styles gallery).

f. Use the Format Painter to copy the formatting from the Day command button to the Doctor, PSW, by Location, and by PSW command buttons.

g. Save the ScheduleDate form and switch to Form View.

h. Click the PSW command button, then click the New (blank) record button to position your insertion point at a new record at the end of the form. Enter your name as a new record.

i. Close the PSWEntry form and the ScheduleDate form.

j. Open the ScheduleDate form, display the first record in the main form, then add a new record in the subform using the arrow in each field to select LocationNo **South**, DoctorNo **Northy**, and your name in the PSWNo field, as shown in **Figure 4-15**.

k. Save and close the ScheduleDate form, and compact and repair the database.

l. Close the database, then exit Access.

Figure 4-15

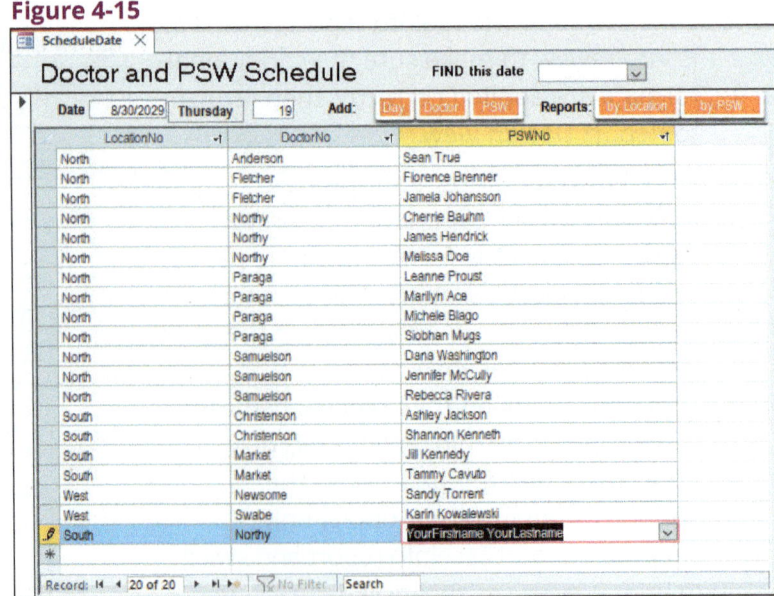

Independent Challenge 2

You are working for a city to coordinate a series of community entertainment events. You have created a database to track the events and performers who are performing at each event. In this exercise, you create and modify a report to summarize data.

a. Start Access, open the IL_AC_4-4.accdb database from the location where you store your Data Files, save it as **IL_AC_4_Performers**, then enable content if prompted.

b. Use the Report tool to create a new report on the Events table.

c. In Report Layout View, resize the EventID column to be about one inch wide, if necessary. Make sure the column remains wide enough to display the column heading label on one line.

d. Resize the EventName column so the entire Event Name fits on one line in the field with no text wrapping.

e. Switch to Report Design View and remove the control layout from the controls in the Report Header section.

f. Delete the report image to the left of the Events label in the Report Header section. Delete the =Time() text box in the Report Header section.

g. Group the remaining two controls in the Report Header section, then move the group to the left edge of the report.

h. Delete the =Count(*) text box and any other controls in the Report Footer section.

i. Move the text box that contains the page number expression to the left edge of the report.

j. Drag the right edge of the report as far to the left as possible to narrow the report.

k. Apply the Garamond font theme to this report only.

l. Save the report with the name **EventList**, then display it in Print Preview, as shown in **Figure 4-16**.

m. Save and close the EventList report, then compact and repair the database.

n. Close the database and exit Access.

Figure 4-16

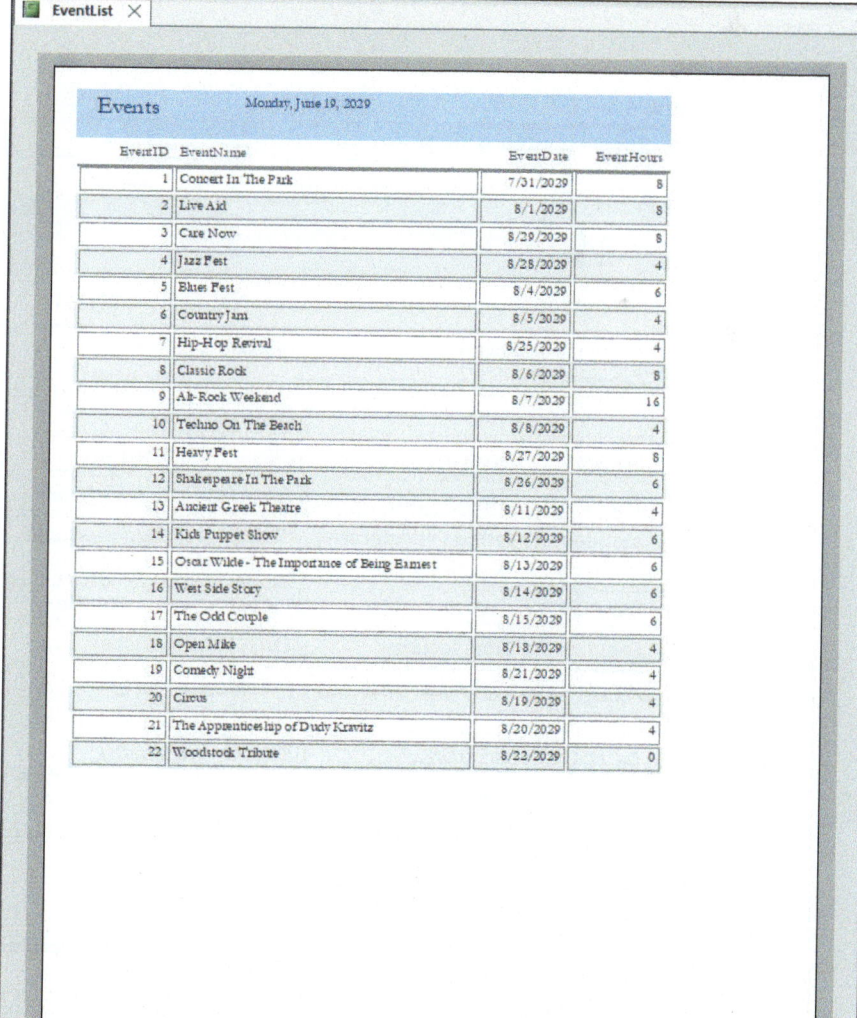

Visual Workshop

Start Access, open the IL_AC_4-5.accdb database from the location where you store your Data Files, save it as **IL_AC_4_CyberCourses**, then enable content if prompted.

In Query Design View, create a query with the following fields from the following tables:

- Description from the Classes table
- ClassNo from the Sections table
- Grade from the Enrollments table
- StudentFirst and StudentLast from the Students table

Save the query with the name **StudentMarks**, display it in Datasheet View, change any occurrence of Yehudah Cooper to your name, then close the StudentMarks query.

Use the Report tool to create a report on the StudentMarks query.

Use Report Layout View to narrow the ClassNo, Grade, StudentFirst, and StudentLast columns. Move the Grade column to be the last. Modify the report title to be **Student Marks Listing**.

Use Report Design View to delete all the controls in the Page Footer and Report Footer sections. Delete the text boxes in the Report Header section that calculate the current date and the current time. Narrow the width of the report to 8.5" or less. Save the report with the name **StudentMarksListing** and preview it in Print Preview, as shown in **Figure 4-17**. Compact and repair the database, then close the database and exit Access.

Figure 4-17

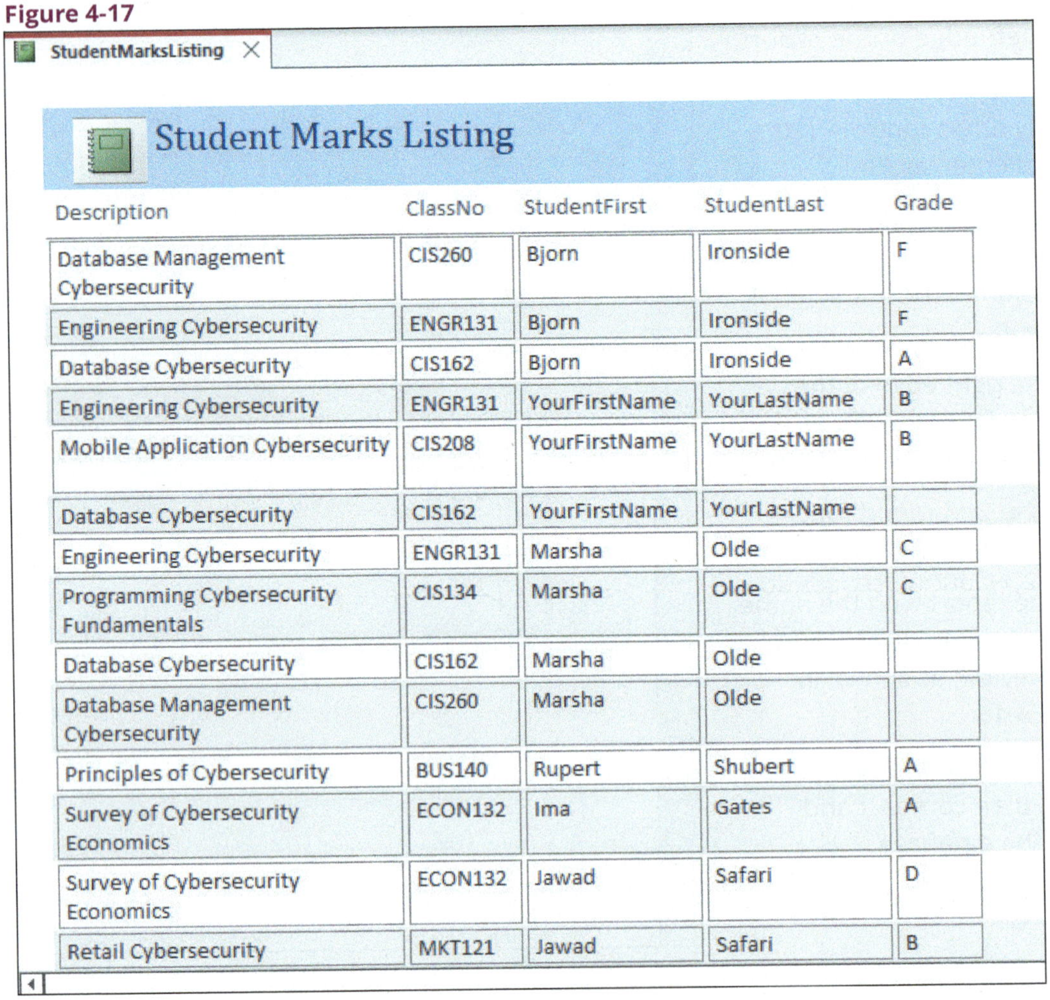

Student Marks Listing

Description	ClassNo	StudentFirst	StudentLast	Grade
Database Management Cybersecurity	CIS260	Bjorn	Ironside	F
Engineering Cybersecurity	ENGR131	Bjorn	Ironside	F
Database Cybersecurity	CIS162	Bjorn	Ironside	A
Engineering Cybersecurity	ENGR131	YourFirstName	YourLastName	B
Mobile Application Cybersecurity	CIS208	YourFirstName	YourLastName	B
Database Cybersecurity	CIS162	YourFirstName	YourLastName	
Engineering Cybersecurity	ENGR131	Marsha	Olde	C
Programming Cybersecurity Fundamentals	CIS134	Marsha	Olde	C
Database Cybersecurity	CIS162	Marsha	Olde	
Database Management Cybersecurity	CIS260	Marsha	Olde	
Principles of Cybersecurity	BUS140	Rupert	Shubert	A
Survey of Cybersecurity Economics	ECON132	Ima	Gates	A
Survey of Cybersecurity Economics	ECON132	Jawad	Safari	D
Retail Cybersecurity	MKT121	Jawad	Safari	B

Integration Module 2

Integrating Word, Excel, and Access

Case

Ariel Likowski, the Dean of Student Services at Mountain Springs Institute of Technology in Denver, CO, asks you to use Word, Excel, and Access in Office to organize and process data related to a state-wide funding program.

Module Objectives

After completing this module, you will be able to:

- Identify Integration Options among Word, Excel, and Access
- Import an Excel worksheet into Access
- Copy a Word table to Access
- Link an Access table to Excel and Word
- Copy an Access table to Word

Files You Will Need

IL_INT_2-1.xlsx
Support_INT_2_ProgramInformation.docx
IL_INT_2-2.docx
IL_INT_2-3.xlsx
Support_INT_2_FinancialServices.docx
IL_INT_2-4.docx

Support_INT_2_ProductPriceList.docx
IL_INT_2-5.xlsx
Support_INT_2_BentallAccountants.docx
IL_INT_2-6.xlsx
IL_INT_2-7.xlsx

Module 2 Integrating Word, Excel, and Access

Identify Integration Options Among Word, Excel, and Access

Case Ariel Likowski asks you to create a report in Word to describe the funding received from the state-wide Training Grant Program. The information you need for this report is contained in Excel, Access, and Word files. Before you create the report, you decide to review some of the ways information can be shared among Word, Excel, and Access.

Objective
- Define import, copy/paste, and link integration options

You can increase efficiency by integrating the information you create in Word, Excel, and Access so it works together. For example, you can enter data into an Access database, make calculations using that data in Excel, and then create a report in Word that incorporates the Excel data and the Access table. You can also import data from an Excel spreadsheet into Access and copy a table created in Word into an Access table.

Details

You can integrate Word, Excel, and Access by:

- **Importing an Excel worksheet into Access**
  You can enter data directly into an Access database table, or you can import data from other sources such as an Excel workbook, another Access database, or even a text file. You use the Get External Data command in Access to import data from an outside source. **Figure 2-1** shows how data entered in an Excel file appears when imported into a new table in an Access database. During the import process, you can change the field names and the data types of selected fields.

- **Copying a Word table into Access**
  You can also create a table in Word that contains data you want to include in an Access database. To save time, you can copy the table from Word and paste it into a new or existing Access table. By doing so, you save typing time and minimize errors.

- **Linking an Access table to Excel and Word**
  You link an Access table to Excel and then to Word when you want the data in all three applications to always remain current. To link Access data to Excel, you first use the Copy command in Access to copy an Access table and then you use the Paste Special command to paste the copied Access table into Excel as a link. You can then make calculations using Excel tools that are not available in Access. Any changes you make to the data in Access are also reflected in the linked Excel copy. However, you cannot change the structure of the linked Access table in Excel. For example, you cannot delete any of the columns or rows that contain copied data. The data used in the Excel calculations is linked to the source file in Access. When the data in Access is changed, the results of the formulas in Excel also change.

  Once you have made calculations based on the data in Excel, you can then copy the data from Excel and paste it as a link into Word. When you change the data in Access, the data in both the Excel and the Word files also changes. **Figure 2-2** shows a Word document that contains two tables. The top table is linked to both Excel and Access. The table was copied from Access and pasted as a link into Excel, additional calculations were made in Excel, and then the table was copied to the Word report and pasted as a link.

- **Copying an Access table to Word**
  You can use the Copy and Paste Special commands to copy a table from Access and then paste it into a Word document. You can then format the table attractively. In **Figure 2-2**, the bottom table was copied from Access, pasted into Word, and then reformatted.

Identify Integration Options Among Word, Excel, and Access   INT 2-3

Figure 2-1: Excel data imported to an Access table

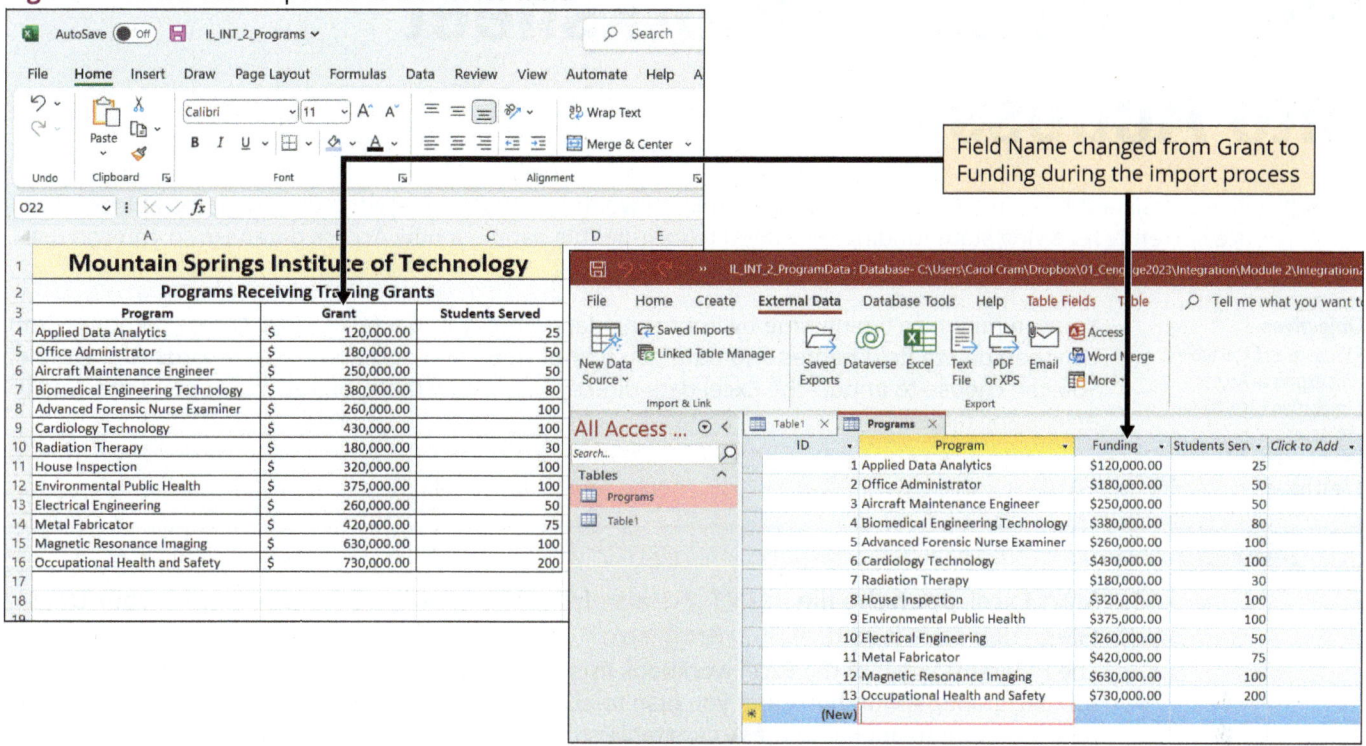

Figure 2-2: Word report with links to Excel and Access

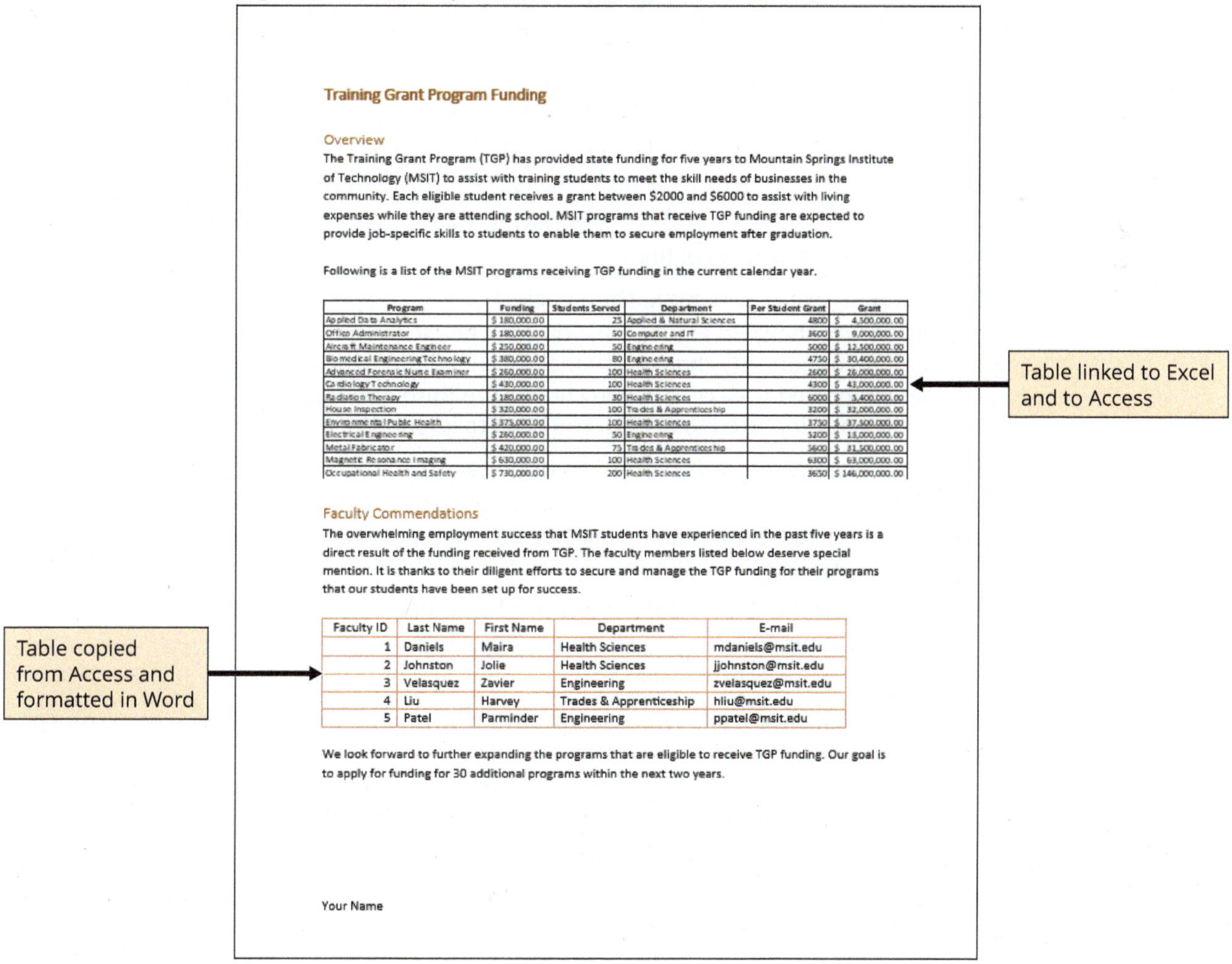

Import an Excel Worksheet into Access

Case Ariel's assistant has already compiled data in an Excel workbook that is related to the programs at MSIT that are currently receiving state funding. You need to include this data in a new Access database so you can use Access functions to analyze it.

Objectives
- Prepare an Excel table for export to Access
- Import an Excel table to Access
- Rename imported field names

You can minimize typing time by importing data directly into a table in an Access database. You can then delete field names and data you do not need and add additional records to the table. You can choose to import the Excel data directly into a new table, or you can append the data to an existing table.

Steps

1. Start Excel, open the file **IL_INT_2-1.xlsx** from the location where you store your Data Files, then save it as **IL_INT_2_Programs**
   The Programs sheet of the Excel workbook lists the programs at MSIT that are currently receiving training grants. A workbook that you plan to export from Excel into Access must contain only the data you want to appear in the Access table so you remove titles, subtitles, charts, and any other extraneous data.

2. Move the mouse pointer to the left of row 1, click and drag to select **rows 1** and **2**, click the **right mouse button**, click **Delete**, then save and close the workbook

3. Start Access, click **Blank database**, replace the current filename with **IL_INT_2_ProgramData** in the File name box, click the **Browse button**, navigate to the location where you store your Data Files, click **OK**, then click **Create**

4. Click the **External Data tab**, click **New Data Source** in the Import & Link group, point to **From File**, click **Excel**, click **Browse**, then navigate to the location where you stored the IL_INT_2_Programs.xlsx file

5. Click **IL_INT_2_Programs.xlsx**, then click **Open**
   In the dialog box shown in **Figure 2-3**, you can choose from three options. When you select the first or second option, any change you make to the data in the Excel source file will not be made to the data imported to Access. If you choose the third option, the imported Excel source file is linked to the data imported to Access. You want to import the data.

6. Click **OK** to accept the default option and start the Import Spreadsheet Wizard, then verify the **First Row Contains Column Headings check box** is selected
   The column headings in the Excel spreadsheet become field names in the Access table. A preview of the Access table appears, with the column names shown in gray header boxes.

Quick Tip
In this dialog box, you can also change the data types of imported data using the Data Type arrow.

7. Click **Next**, click the **Grant** column in the Table Preview to select the entire Grant column, then type **Funding** as shown in **Figure 2-4**
   The field name changes in the Field Name text box and the table preview.

8. Click **Next**, click **Next** to let Access add the primary key, verify that **Programs** appears as the table name, click **Finish**, then click **Close**
   Access creates a new table called Programs. You can work with this table in the same way you work with any table you create in Access.

9. Double-click **Programs** in the list of tables, double-click between the **Program** column and the Funding column to show all the text, click below "Occupational Health and Safety", then compare the table to **Figure 2-5**
   The imported Excel data now appears in a new Access table. You chose to import the data without links, so any changes you make to the Excel source data will not be reflected in the Access table.

Import an Excel Worksheet into Access   INT 2-5

Figure 2-3: Selecting a data source in the Get External Data dialog box

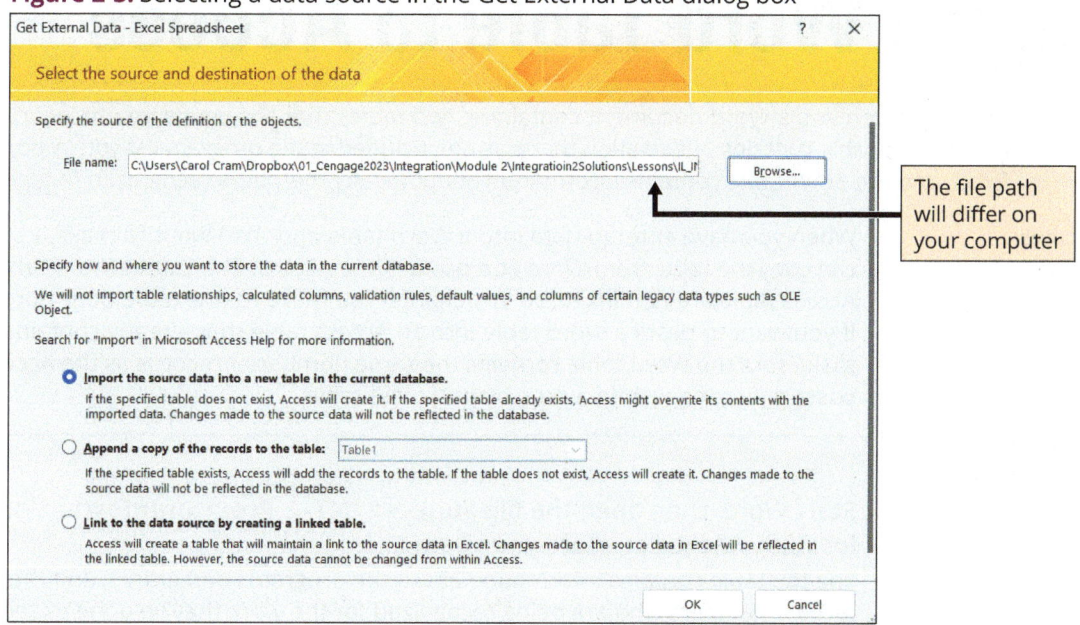

Figure 2-4: Changing a field name in an imported table

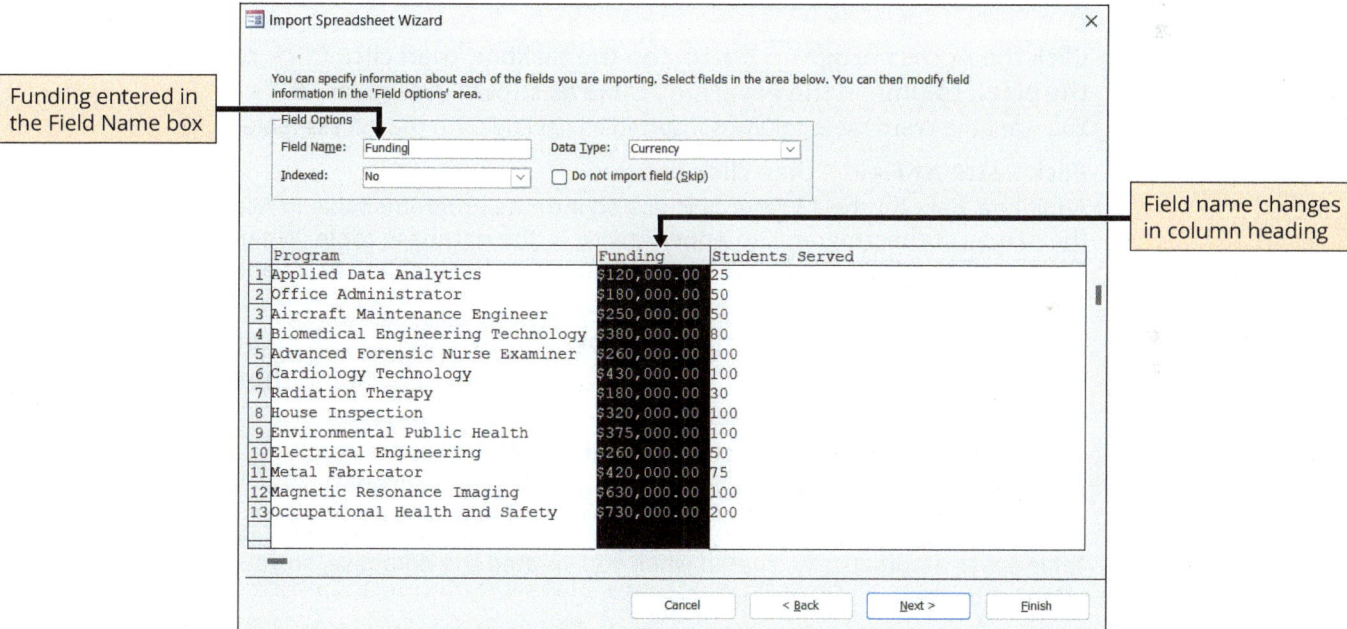

Figure 2-5: Excel data imported to an Access table

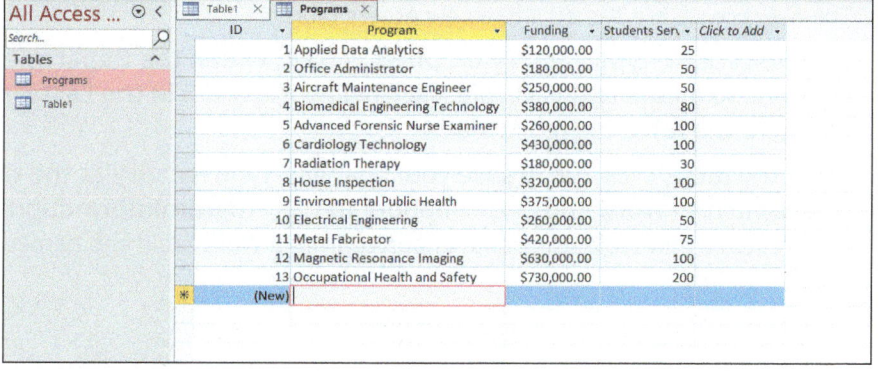

Copy a Word Table to Access

Case Ariel has given you a Word document containing two tables that she wants you to incorporate into the Word report. One table contains information that was not included in the program list you imported into Access from Excel, and the other table contains information about faculty members recognized for special commendation.

Objectives
- Copy a Word table to an existing Access table
- Copy a Word table to a new Access table

When you have entered data into a Word table and then want to make it part of a database, you can copy the table from Word and paste it into Access. The source Word table and the destination Access table are not linked, so any change you make to one table does not affect the other table. If you want to paste a Word table into an Access table that already contains records, you need to make sure the Word table contains the same number of records as the Access table. You can also paste a Word table into a new, blank Access table.

Steps

1. Start Word, then open the file **Support_INT_2_ProgramInformation.docx** from the location where you store your Data Files

   The top table contains information about the programs and grants, and the bottom table lists the faculty members who are being recognized for the work they've done to secure state funding.

2. Click **Program** in the top table, click the **table select button** ⊞, then click the **Copy button** in the Clipboard group

   You copied the selected table to the Clipboard.

   Quick Tip
   If you want to import additional records to an existing database, make sure the imported Excel data contains the same number of fields (columns) as the database.

3. Click the **Access program button** on the taskbar, then click **Click to Add** at the top of the blank column in the **Programs** table as shown in **Figure 2-6**

   You want the Word table columns inserted as new fields in the Access table.

4. Click **Paste as Fields**, then click **Yes**

   Additional data for the 13 records is pasted into the Programs table in Access. You do not need the names of the programs to appear twice in the database table. When you copy data from another source and paste it into an Access table, you can delete fields and records in the same way you normally do in Access.

5. Click anywhere in the table, right-click **Program1**, click **Delete Field**, click **Yes**, widen the Department field so all the records are visible, then click in the blank field below Occupational Health and Safety

   The Programs table appears as shown in **Figure 2-7**.

6. Close the **Programs** table, then click **Yes** to save it

   You can copy a table directly from Word into a new blank table in Access. A blank table called Table 1 was automatically created when you created the database, so you can place the copied information there.

7. Switch to Word, scroll down, and select the table containing the list of faculty members, click the **Copy button** in the Clipboard group, switch to Access, click the **Home tab**, click **Click to Add** in Table 1, click **Paste as Fields**, then click **Yes**

   The five records are pasted into a new Access table.

8. Double-click **ID**, type **Faculty ID**, press **ENTER**, widen the Department and E-mail columns so all the text is visible, click below **Record 5** in the Last Name field, then compare the table to **Figure 2-8**

9. Close the table, click **Yes** to save your changes, type **Faculty** as the table name, click **OK**, then switch to Word and close Support_INT_2_ProgramInformation.docx

   You created a new table using data imported from a Word table and named it Faculty.

Figure 2-6: Selecting the location for copied data

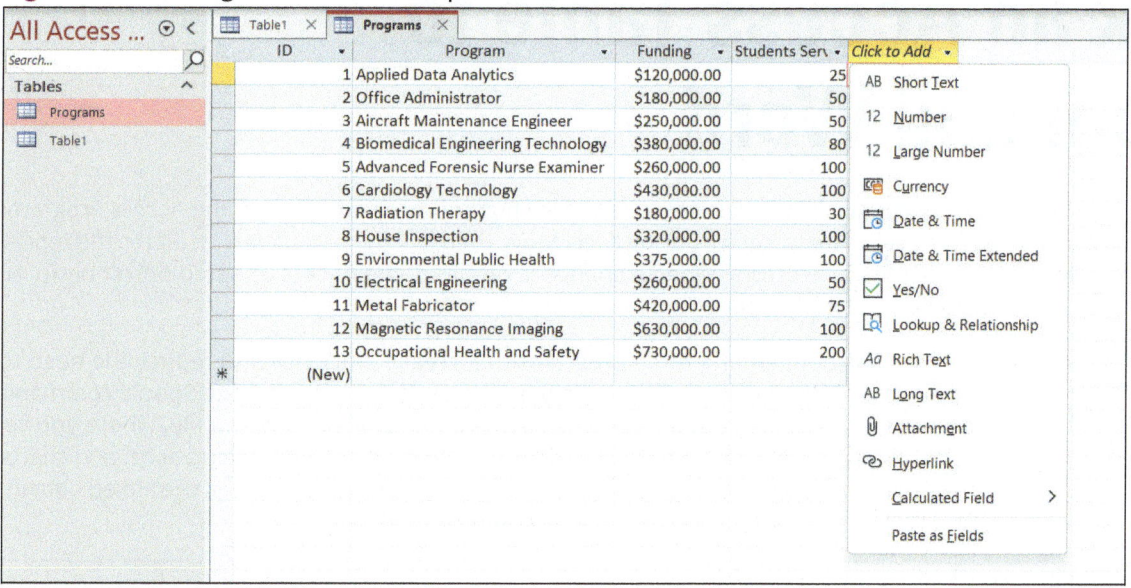

Figure 2-7: Table containing data copied from Word

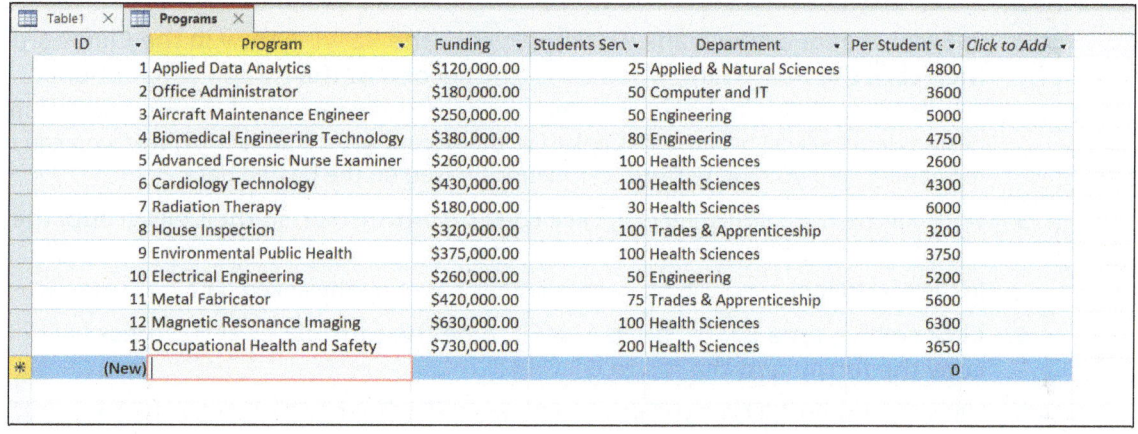

Figure 2-8: Renaming the ID field

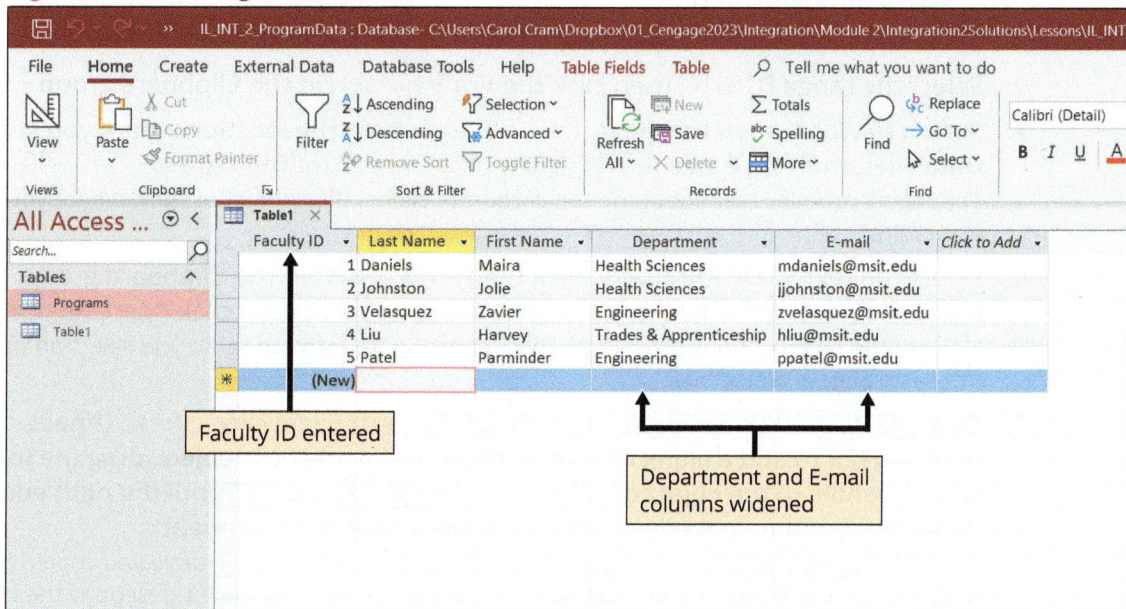

Faculty ID entered

Department and E-mail columns widened

Link an Access Table to Excel and Word

Case You want your report to include the full amount of each grant received. You link the Access Programs table to an Excel worksheet, calculate the grants using Excel tools, then link the calculation results to the report in Word. You link the files to minimize errors. When a change is required, the data is updated once only in Access and then is automatically updated in the linked Excel and Word files.

Objectives
- Use Copy and Paste Special to create links
- Update linked data

You can link data among three programs to increase efficiency and reduce the need to enter the same data more than once. To do this, you can use the Copy and Paste Special commands to create a link between an Access database object and an Excel destination file, where you can perform calculations and create charts. You can then copy the Excel data, calculations, and charts to a Word document. When you change the data in the source Access database, the linked data in both Excel and Word are updated to reflect the new information.

Steps

Quick Tip
Click cell A1 if necessary to select it before pasting. If you do not see the Paste Link button, return to Access and copy the table again.

1. In Access, click the **Programs table** in the list of tables if necessary, then click the **Copy button** in the Clipboard group

2. In Excel, create a new blank workbook, click the **Paste arrow** in the Clipboard group, then click the **Paste Link button** (the second of the three Paste options)
   The Programs table appears in Excel. You cannot delete any of the rows or columns in the pasted data in Excel because it is linked to the Access source table. However, you can modify cell formatting, and you can perform calculations based on the pasted data.

3. With all the data still selected, click the **Format button** in the Cells group, then click **AutoFit Column Width**
   In the copied table, you can make calculations based on the linked data.

4. Click cell **G1**, type **Grant**, press **ENTER**, type the formula **=C2*D2**, press **ENTER**, then copy the formula to the range **G3:G14**

5. With the range G2:G14 still selected, press and hold **CTRL**, select the range **C2:C14**, release **CTRL**, click the **Accounting Number Format button** $ in the Number group, click cell **A15**, increase column widths if needed, then save the workbook as **IL_INT_2_GrantRevenue**
   The values in columns C and G are formatted in the Accounting format as shown in **Figure 2-9**.

6. Select the range **B1:G14**, then click the **Copy button** in the Clipboard group

7. Switch to Word, open the file **IL_INT_2-2.docx** from the location where you store your Data Files, then save it as **IL_INT_2_TrainingGrantFundingReport**
   The report contains text about the top corporate clients. Placeholders show where you will paste two tables.

8. Select the text **PROGRAM LIST**, click the **Paste arrow** in the Clipboard group, move the mouse over the paste icons to view paste options, then click **Paste Special**
   None of the Paste options provide you with appropriate formatting, so you select an option from the Paste Special dialog box.

9. Click the **Paste link option button**, click **Microsoft Excel Worksheet Object**, click **OK**, press **ENTER** to add a blank line, click the pasted worksheet object, drag the top-left corner handle of the object down and to the right about 2.5" until the right edge is about 1" from the right edge of the page, then save the document
   The table appears as shown in **Figure 2-10**. This table is linked to the table you copied from Excel, which, in turn, is linked to the table you copied from Access. **Table 2-1** describes the differences between the three Paste options you have used in these lessons.

Link an Access Table to Excel and Word

Figure 2-9: Copied data formatted in Excel

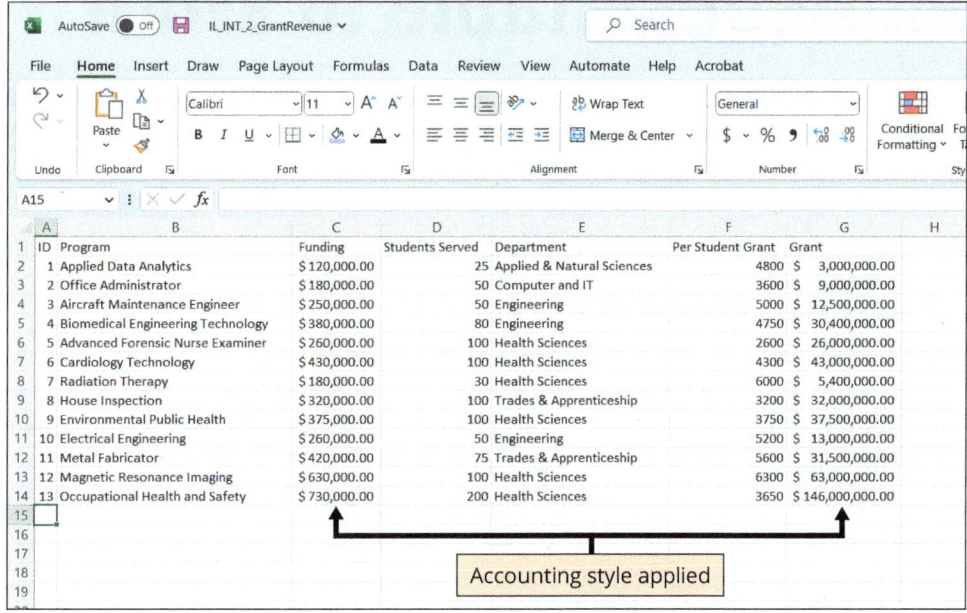

Figure 2-10: Excel data pasted and linked in Word

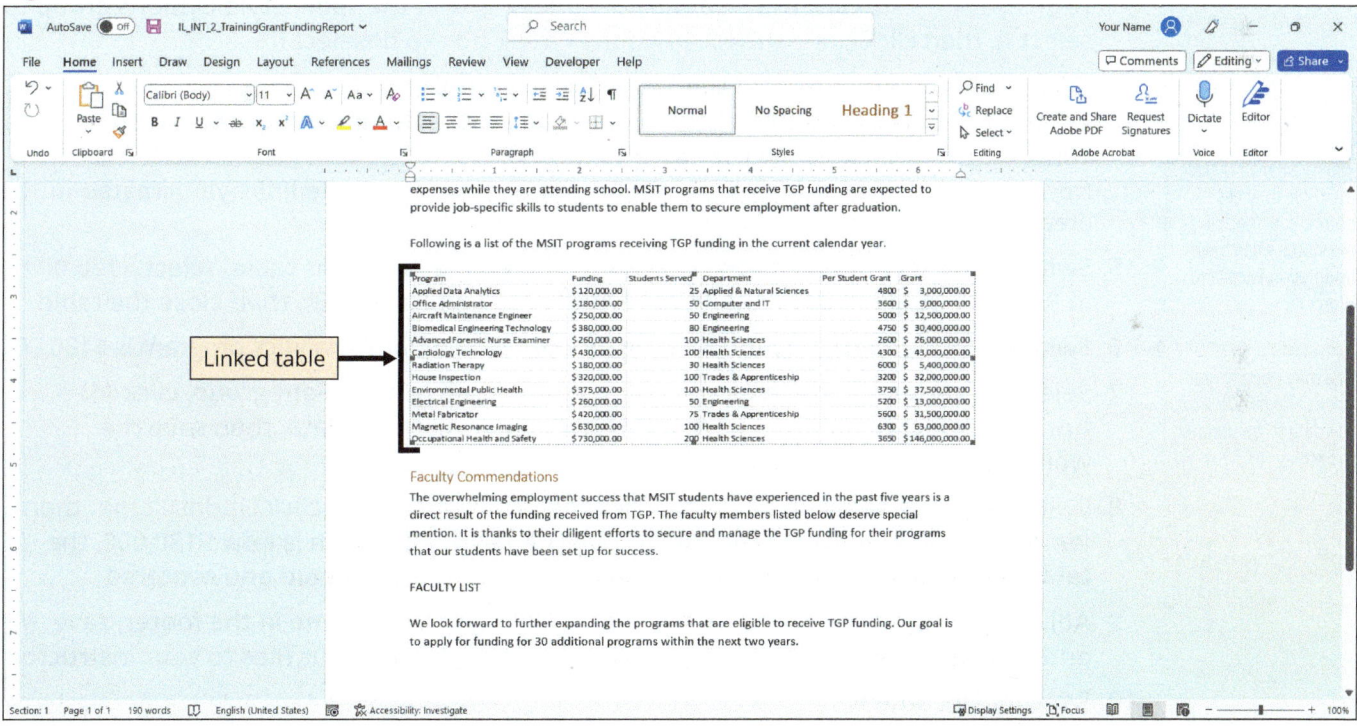

Table 2-1: Paste options

command	location	use to
Paste	Paste button in Word and Excel	Paste an object without creating a link; the exception is a chart—when you copy a chart from Excel and paste it into Word, the chart is, by default, linked to the source file in Excel
Paste Special	Paste button list shows Paste Special selection in Word and Excel	Paste an object when you want to create a link or you want to select from a variety of formatting options for the pasted object, whether linked or not
Paste Link	Paste button list shows Paste Link button in Excel	Paste an object such as a copied table from Access into Excel as a link

Copy an Access Table to Word

Case The Word report needs to contain a list of the five faculty members being recognized for special commendation. You copy the Faculty table from Access and paste it into Word, then test the links you created in the previous lesson.

Objective
- Copy an Access table to Word

If you don't need to use Excel to make calculations based on Access data, you can copy an Access table and paste it directly into Word where you can use Word tools to modify the formatting of the pasted table so the table communicates the data clearly. **Table 2-2** summarizes the integration tasks you performed in this module.

Steps

1. Switch to Access, click **Faculty** in the list of tables to select it, click the **Copy button** in the Clipboard group, then switch to Word

2. Select the text **FACULTY LIST** below paragraph 2, click the **Paste arrow** in the Clipboard group, click **Paste Special**, click **Formatted Text (RTF)**, then click **OK**

   The Faculty table is pasted as formatted text in Word and is not linked to the Access database. You can format the table using Word table tools.

3. Click the **pasted table**, click the **table select button** to select the table, click the **Table Design tab**, click the **Header Row check box** in the Table Style Options group to select it, then click the **Banded Columns check box** to deselect it

4. Click the **More button** in the Table Styles group, click **Grid Table 6 Colorful - Accent 2**, double-click between any two columns to autofit the table contents, then click below the table to deselect it

   Now that you have formatted the table, you decide to test the links you created in the previous lesson.

   Quick Tip
   You must always close the table in Access before you check if linked data has been updated in Excel and Word.

5. Switch to Access, double-click **Programs** to open the Programs table, select **$120,000** in Record 1 (Applied Data Analytics), type **180000**, press **ENTER**, then close the table

   Trouble
   You may need to wait about two minutes for the data to be updated in Excel.

6. Switch to Excel, then verify the funding for the Applied Data Analytics program is $180,000

7. Select the range **A1:G14**, click the **Borders arrow** in the Font group, click **All Borders**, select the range **A1:G1**, apply bold and center the data, then save the workbook

8. Switch to Word, scroll up and right-click the **Programs table**, click **Update Link**, then verify that the funding for the Applied Data Analytics program is now $180,000, the table is formatted with border lines, and the text in row 1 is bold and centered

9. Adjust spacing as needed to match **Figure 2-11**, type your name in the footer, save and close all files and exit all open programs, then submit your files to your instructor

10. Save the document

Opening linked files and enabling content

When you open files created in different applications, you need to create them on the same computer logged in as the same user. Open them in the order in which they were created. For example, if you want to change the Word report and need to maintain links, open the Access database first, followed by the Excel workbook. When you open a linked Excel file, click Enable Content if prompted, click Update in response to the message, then, if prompted, click Yes. The exact order of these steps varies depending on how often you have opened the files. In Word, click Yes in response to the message. If all the files were created on the same computer by the same user, the links will all update.

When you email your files to another user, such as your instructor, the links will not work. However, the new user may view the files. After opening the workbook in Excel, they click No, close the workbook without saving it, then reopen the workbook and click Don't Update. In Word, they click No to update links.

Copy an Access Table to Word INT 2-11

Figure 2-11: Completed Word report

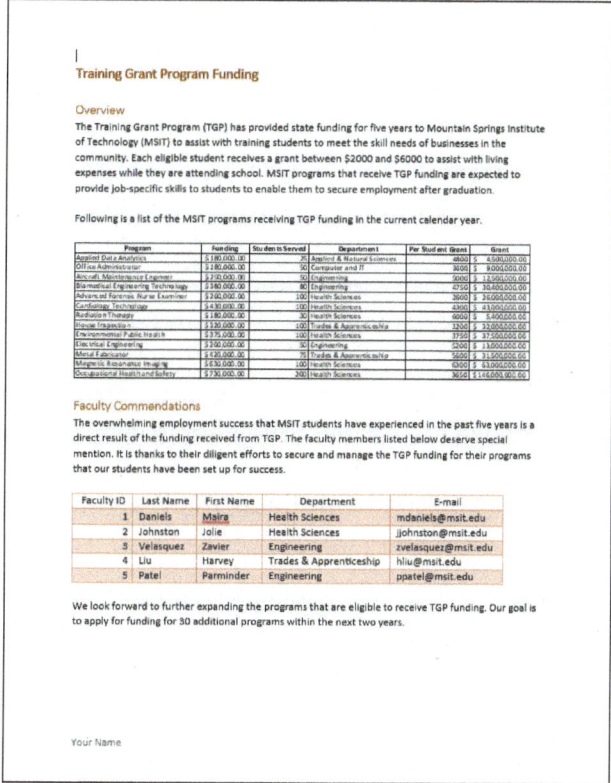

Table 2-2: Module 2 integration tasks

object	commands	source program(s)	destination program	result	connection	page no.
Excel file	External Data/Excel	Excel	Access	Excel spreadsheet is imported into a new table in Access; the spreadsheet must contain only the rows and columns required for the Access table	None	4
Word table	Copy/Paste	Word	Access	Word table is pasted in a new or existing table in Access; if an existing table, the Word table should contain the same number of records as the Access table	None	6
Access table	Copy/Paste Special/Paste Link	Access	Excel	Access table is pasted into Excel as a link; the linked data can be formatted in Excel and included in formulas but cannot be modified or deleted	Linked	8
Linked Access table in Excel	Copy/Paste Link in Excel Copy/Paste Special/Paste Link in Word	Access and Excel	Word	Access table is linked to Excel and then to Word; changes made in Access appear in Excel and Word	Linked	8
Access table	Copy/Paste Special	Access	Word	Access table is pasted in Word and can be formatted using Word tools	None	10

Practice

Skills Review

1. **Import an Excel worksheet into Access.**
   a. Start Excel, open the file IL_INT_2-3.xlsx from the location where you store your Data Files, then save it as **IL_INT_2_KPLWorkshopList**.
   b. Delete rows 1 and 2, then save and close the workbook.
   c. Start Access, then create a new blank database called **IL_INT_2_KPLWorkshops** in the location where you store your Data Files.
   d. In Access, import the file **IL_INT_2_KPLWorkshopList.xlsx** file from Excel as external data. In the Import Spreadsheet Wizard, change the name of the People field to **Attendees**, then name the new table **Financial Workshops**.
   e. Close the wizard, open the Financial Workshops table, then widen columns as necessary.

2. **Copy a Word table to Access.**
   a. Start Word, open the file Support_INT_2_FinancialServices.docx from the location where you store your Data Files.
   b. Select the top table (which contains the list of workshops), copy it, then switch to Access.
   c. Paste the table in the Financial Workshops table, delete the duplicate column, widen columns as needed, then save and close the table.
   d. In Word, select the table containing the list of financial management services, copy the table, then paste it as a new table in Access.
   e. Change the ID field to **Services ID**, widen columns as necessary to display data, then close the table and name it **Services**.
   f. In Word, close the FinancialServices file.

3. **Link an Access table to Excel and Word.**
   a. In Access, copy the Financial Workshops table.
   b. Create a new Excel workbook, paste the Financial Workshops table as a link in cell A1, save the workbook as **IL_INT_2_KPLWorkshopData**, then adjust column widths where necessary.
   c. Enter **Total Revenue** in cell G1, adjust the column width, then in cell G2, enter a formula to multiply the Per Person Rate by the Attendees.
   d. Copy the formula to the range G3:G16, then format the values in columns C and G in the Accounting Number format.
   e. Copy the range B1:G16, switch to Word, open the file IL_INT_2-4.docx from the location where you store your Data Files, then save it as **IL_INT_2_KPLServices**.
   f. In the Word document, select the text WORKSHOP LIST, paste the copied data as a linked Microsoft Excel Worksheet Object, add a blank line above or below the table if necessary, reduce the width of the table so its right edge is approximately .5" from the right margin, then save the document.

4. **Copy an Access table to Word.**
   a. In Access, copy the Services table, switch to Word, then select the SERVICES LIST placeholder.
   b. Paste the copied table as a Formatted Text (RTF) object, add a blank line above the table, then format the table with the List Table 2 - Accent 5 table design with the Header Row check box selected and the Banded Columns check box deselected. Adjust column widths so none of the lines wrap.
   c. In Access, open the Financial Workshops table, change the number of attendees at the Business Mastery workshop (Record 5) to **200**, then close the table.
   d. In Excel, verify the total revenue value for the Business Mastery workshop is $30,000.00. You may need to wait a few minutes.
   e. Select the range A1:G16, add border lines to all cells, select the range A1:G1, then apply bold and centering.

f. In Word, update the link to the table that lists the workshops, then verify the Business Mastery total changes to $30,000.00 and the header row changes to the new format.
g. Compare the completed report to **Figure 2-12**, make any necessary spacing adjustments, type your name where indicated in the footer, save and close all open files and programs, then submit your files to your instructor.

Figure 2-12

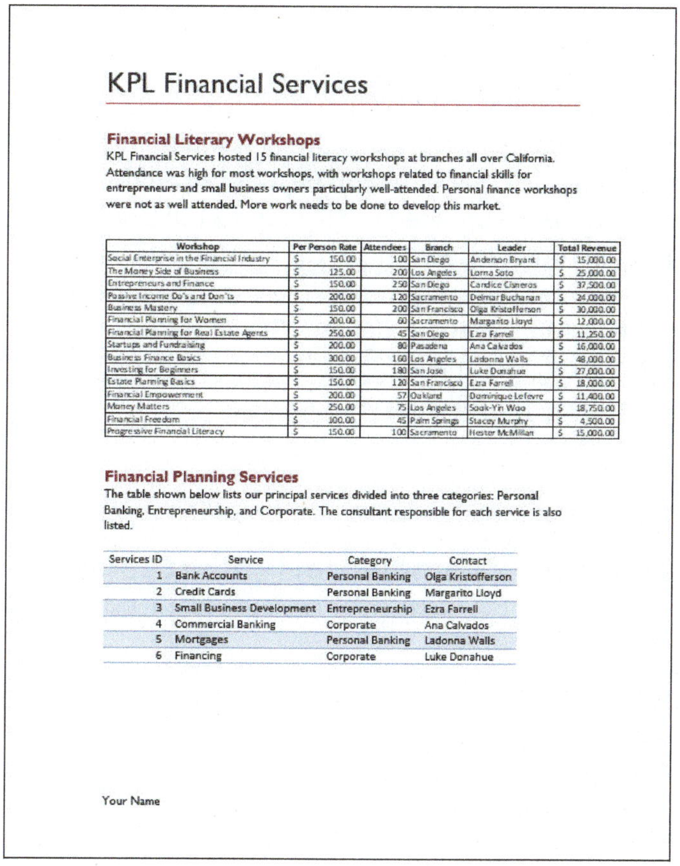

KPL Financial Services

Financial Literary Workshops

KPL Financial Services hosted 15 financial literacy workshops at branches all over California. Attendance was high for most workshops, with workshops related to financial skills for entrepreneurs and small business owners particularly well-attended. Personal finance workshops were not as well attended. More work needs to be done to develop this market.

Workshop	Per Person Rate	Attendees	Branch	Leader	Total Revenue
Social Enterprise in the Financial Industry	$ 150.00	100	San Diego	Anderson Bryant	$ 15,000.00
The Money Side of Business	$ 125.00	200	Los Angeles	Lorna Soto	$ 25,000.00
Entrepreneurs and Finance	$ 150.00	250	San Diego	Candice Cisneros	$ 37,500.00
Passive Income Do's and Don'ts	$ 200.00	120	Sacramento	Delmar Buchanan	$ 24,000.00
Business Mastery	$ 150.00	200	San Francisco	Olga Kristofferson	$ 30,000.00
Financial Planning for Women	$ 200.00	60	Sacramento	Margarito Lloyd	$ 12,000.00
Financial Planning for Real Estate Agents	$ 250.00	45	San Diego	Ezra Farrell	$ 11,250.00
Startups and Fundraising	$ 200.00	80	Pasadena	Ana Calvados	$ 16,000.00
Business Finance Basics	$ 300.00	160	Los Angeles	Ladonna Walls	$ 48,000.00
Investing for Beginners	$ 150.00	180	San Jose	Luke Donahue	$ 27,000.00
Estate Planning Basics	$ 150.00	120	San Francisco	Ezra Farrell	$ 18,000.00
Financial Empowerment	$ 200.00	57	Oakland	Dominique Lefevre	$ 11,400.00
Money Matters	$ 250.00	75	Los Angeles	Sook-Yin Woo	$ 18,750.00
Financial Freedom	$ 100.00	45	Palm Springs	Stacey Murphy	$ 4,500.00
Progressive Financial Literacy	$ 150.00	100	Sacramento	Hester McMillan	$ 15,000.00

Financial Planning Services

The table shown below lists our principal services divided into three categories: Personal Banking, Entrepreneurship, and Corporate. The consultant responsible for each service is also listed.

Services ID	Service	Category	Contact
1	Bank Accounts	Personal Banking	Olga Kristofferson
2	Credit Cards	Personal Banking	Margarito Lloyd
3	Small Business Development	Entrepreneurship	Ezra Farrell
4	Commercial Banking	Corporate	Ana Calvados
5	Mortgages	Personal Banking	Ladonna Walls
6	Financing	Corporate	Luke Donahue

Your Name

Independent Challenge 1

You work for Aloha Cleaning, a start-up company in Hawai'i that sells eco-friendly commercial cleaning products. The company has partnered with a cleaning company to provide cleaning products. You need to develop a system for keeping track of the products purchased by partner companies. You have a price list saved in a Word document. You transfer the price list into an Access database, then add some new records. You then perform calculations on the data in Excel and verify that when you update data in the Access database, the data in Excel also changes.

a. Start Word, open the file Support_INT_2_ProductPriceList.docx from the location where you store your Data Files.
b. Copy the table, create a new database in Access called **IL_INT_2_AlohaProducts** in the location where you store your Data Files, then paste the copied table into a new table named **Products**.
c. Add two new records to the Products table with the following information:

Product	Category	Price per Gallon
Disinfectant	Ultra	$45.00
Glass Cleaner	Scent Free	$40.00

Independent Challenge 1 (Continued)

d. Adjust column widths so all text is visible, close and save the table, copy it, and paste it as a link into a new Excel workbook, then add a new column in Excel called **Gallons Sold**.
e. Enter **20** as the number of gallons sold for the first four products and **50** as the number of gallons sold for the last eight products.
f. Add a new column called **Revenue**, calculate the total revenue for each product, then save the workbook as **IL_INT_2_AlohaProductSales**.
g. Format the Price per Gallon and Revenue values with the Accounting Number format, then adjust column widths as necessary so all the text is visible.
h. Note the current revenue amount for the first two products ($700 and $800).
i. In the Access Products table, change the price of the first Multi-Purpose Cleaner to $45.00 and the price of the second Multi-Purpose Cleaner to $50.00, then close the table.
j. In Excel, verify the values have been updated to $900 and $1,000. You may need to wait a few minutes.
k. Bold and center the labels in row 1, insert a new row 1, enter **Aloha Cleaning Commercial Product Sales**, merge and center it across the range A1:F1, increase the font size to 16 point, apply bold formatting, then apply the Green, Accent 6, Lighter 80% fill color.
l. Type your name in cell A16, compare the completed workbook to **Figure 2-13**, save and close all open files and programs, then submit your files to your instructor.

Figure 2-13

	A	B	C	D	E	F
1		Aloha Cleaning Commercial Product Sales				
2	ID	Product	Category	Price per Gallon	Gallons Sold	Revenue
3	1	Multi-Purpose Cleaner	Ultra	$ 45.00	20	$ 900.00
4	2	Multi-Purpose Cleaner	Scent Free	$ 50.00	20	$1,000.00
5	3	Bathroom Cleaner	Ultra	$ 45.00	20	$ 900.00
6	4	Bathroom Cleaner	Scent Free	$ 35.00	20	$ 700.00
7	5	Multi-Purpose Cleaner	Neutral	$ 32.00	50	$1,600.00
8	6	Heavy Duty Cleaner	Scent Free	$ 35.00	50	$1,750.00
9	7	Laundry Wash	Ultra	$ 52.00	50	$2,600.00
10	8	Laundry Wash	Scent Free	$ 33.00	50	$1,650.00
11	9	Carpet & Upholstery Cleaner	Hypoallergenic	$ 35.00	50	$1,750.00
12	10	Air Purifier	Ultra	$ 27.00	50	$1,350.00
13	11	Disinfectant	Ultra	$ 45.00	50	$2,250.00
14	12	Glass Cleaner	Scent Free	$ 40.00	50	$2,000.00
15						
16	Your Name					
17						
18						

Independent Challenge 2

Bentall Accounting in Albany, NY, provides accounting services to small business owners. You have been asked to build a database that the owner can use to keep track of contracts. The owner would also like you to create a report that analyzes sales trends.

a. Start Excel, open the file **IL_INT_2-5.xlsx** from the location where you store your Data Files, then save it as **IL_INT_2_Bentall Contracts**.
b. Delete any rows and objects that cannot be imported into Access, then save and close the workbook.
c. Create a database in Access called **IL_INT_2_BentallServices**, and save it in the location where you store your Data Files.

d. Import the Excel file **IL_INT_2_BentalContracts.xlsx** into the Access database, change the Description field name to **Service**, and accept **Contracts** as the table name.

e. Start Word, open the file Support_INT_2_BentallAccountants.docx from the location where you store your Data Files, copy the table, close the document, then paste the table into the Contracts table in Access.

f. Delete the Client Name1 column from the pasted information, widen columns as needed, then save and close the table.

g. Copy the Contracts table, paste it as a linked file into cell A1 of a new Excel workbook, then adjust the column widths.

h. Calculate the total revenue from each contract total based on an hourly rate of $90. (**Hint**: Add two new columns—one called "Rate" with "90" entered for each record and one called "Total" with the formula entered for each record.)

i. Format the values in columns G and H with the Accounting Number format, then save the Excel workbook as **IL_INT_2_BentallContractRevenue**.

j. In Word, open a new document and enter the text (but not the table) shown in the completed document in **Figure 2-14**, then save it as **IL_INT_2_BentallCurrentContracts**. Format the title in 22 point, bold and the subtitle in 14 point, bold.

k. Copy the range B1:H11 from Excel, paste it as a link using the Microsoft Excel Worksheet Object option in the Paste Special dialog box below the text paragraph in the IL_INT_2_BentallCurrentContracts document, resize the object so it matches the width of the text (**Hint**: Drag the top-left corner sizing handle down), then save the document.

l. In the Contracts table in Access, change the number of hours for Loretta Garza (Record 2) to **50**, close the table, then verify the revenue from Loretta Garza has changed to $4,500 in the Excel file. Remember, you may need to wait a few minutes for the values to update.

m. Format the range A1:H11 with border lines around all cells, and bold and center column titles.

n. Update the worksheet object in the Word file.

o. Add your name below the worksheet object, compare the completed document to **Figure 2-14**, save all files and close all programs, then submit your files to your instructor.

Figure 2-14

Bentall Accounting

Current Contracts

Bentall Accounting provides a wide range of accounting services to small business owners in the Albany, NY, area. The table below lists the clients currently working with Bentall Accounting.

Client Name	Service	Hours	Consultant	Location	Rate	Total
Chelsea Crawford	Bookkeeping	22	Gene Gonzalez	Head Office	$ 90.00	$ 1,980.00
Loretta Garza	Payroll	50	Barbara Woodward	Client's Office	$ 90.00	$ 4,500.00
Sherman Hays	Inventory Management	35	Velma Tan	Client's Home	$ 90.00	$ 3,150.00
Emmanuel Silva	Month End Close	12	Gene Gonzalez	Head Office	$ 90.00	$ 1,080.00
Tamika Carr	Budgeting	60	Norris Nunez	Client's Home	$ 90.00	$ 5,400.00
Daniel Chung	Strategic Consultation	45	Barbara Woodward	Client's Office	$ 90.00	$ 4,050.00
Irma Delacruz	Bookkeeping	15	Gene Gonzalez	Head Office	$ 90.00	$ 1,350.00
Tyler Kostiuk	Financial Modeling	25	Quinn Salazar	Head Office	$ 90.00	$ 2,250.00
Maryanne Lane	Benefits Administration	60	Quinn Salazar	Head Office	$ 90.00	$ 5,400.00
Jasjit Singh	Insurance Administration	75	Velma Tan	Client's Home	$ 90.00	$ 6,750.00

Your Name

Visual Workshop

Create the Word document shown in **Figure 2-15** by combining elements from Excel and Access. In Excel, open IL_INT_2-6, xlsx, save it as **IL_INT_2_PineCrestData**, remove any rows that cannot be exported to Access, then create a new database called **IL_INT_2_PineCrestExploration** in the location where you store your Data Files and import the Excel file, changing the Days field name to **Duration** and saving the table with the name provided. Copy the Site Visits table, then paste it as linked data in a new Excel workbook. Save the workbook as **IL_INT_2_PineCrestExpenses**. Refer to Figure 2-15: add two new columns, enter a daily rate of $500 for all managers, and calculate the total expenses for each manager. Adjust column widths and format the table as shown in Figure 2-15, then save the workbook. In Word, open IL_INT_2-7.docx, save it as **IL_INT_2_PineCrestReport**, then paste the data from IL_INT-2_PineCrestExpenses as a linked Microsoft Excel Worksheet Object in the appropriate place. In the Access source table, change the number of days that Deanna Reyes was away to 5 and the number of days that Armand Jordan was away to 10, then close the table. Verify that links have been updated in the Excel and Word files. Include your name in cell A14 in the Excel file and the footer in Word, save and close all open files and programs, then submit your files to your instructor.

Figure 2-15

Pine Crest Exploration
1300 County Road, Knoxville, TN 37917, Phone: 865-555-0147
www.pinecrestexploriong.biz

First Quarter Site Visits

In the first quarter of the current year, Pine Crest Exploration site managers visited 11 established energy providers worldwide to investigate opportunities for alternative energy developments. Of these visits, the ones to Iceland to investigate geothermal energy and Chile to investigate solar energy yielded the most valuable data.

Site Manager Expenses

The table below presents data related to each site manager's expenses. The shortest and therefore least expensive visits were to locations in North America. International locations required managers to stay longer, thereby incurring higher expenses.

ID	First Name	Last Name	Energy Type	Destination	Duration	Daily Rate	Total
1	Deanna	Reyes	Solar	Arizona	5	$ 500.00	$ 2,500.00
2	Grace	Kim	Tidal	South Korea	12	$ 500.00	$ 6,000.00
3	Michael	Olson	Biomass	Denmark	8	$ 500.00	$ 4,000.00
4	Camille	Carey	Tidal	Maine	3	$ 500.00	$ 1,500.00
5	Hazel	Masson	Wind	New Mexico	5	$ 500.00	$ 2,500.00
6	Sanford	Nicholson	Geothermal	Montana	5	$ 500.00	$ 2,500.00
7	Frances	Cordova	Hydropower	British Columbia	8	$ 500.00	$ 4,000.00
8	Armand	Jordan	Tidal	Nova Scotia	10	$ 500.00	$ 5,000.00
9	Eula	Clayton	Geothermal	Iceland	10	$ 500.00	$ 5,000.00
10	Barrett	Wong	Solar	Chile	12	$ 500.00	$ 6,000.00
11	Silva	Miguel	Wind	Portugal	8	$ 500.00	$ 4,000.00

PowerPoint Module 1

Creating a Presentation in PowerPoint

Case
XcR Global is a fast-growing digital project management company based in Orlando, Florida. You work for Tanya Scheving, who has asked you to help create a presentation that describes the company's teams, workflow, and product development process. You use PowerPoint to create the presentation.

Module Objectives

After completing this module, you will be able to:

- Define presentation software
- Plan an effective presentation
- Examine the PowerPoint window
- Add text to a slide
- Add a new slide
- Format text
- Apply a design theme
- Compare presentation views
- Insert and resize a picture
- Check spelling
- Print a PowerPoint presentation

Files You Will Need

Support_PPT_1_Team.jpg
IL_PPT_1-1.pptx
Support_PPT_1_Hackers.jpg

IL_PPT_1-2.pptx
IL_PPT_1-3.pptx
Support_PPT_1_Office.jpg

Define Presentation Software

Case You need to start working on the company presentation. Because you are only somewhat familiar with PowerPoint, you get to work exploring its capabilities.

Objective
- Describe presentation software

Presentation software (also called presentation graphics software) is a computer program you use to organize and present information to others. Presentations are typically in the form of a **slide show**, a series of electronic pages containing text and graphics. Whether you are explaining a new product or moderating a meeting, presentation software can help you effectively communicate your ideas. You can use PowerPoint to create informational slides that you print or display on a monitor, share in real time on the web, or save as a video for others to watch.

Details

You can easily complete the following tasks using PowerPoint:

- **Enter and edit text easily**
  Text editing and formatting commands in PowerPoint are organized by the task you are performing at the time, so you can enter, edit, and format text information simply and efficiently to produce the best results in the least amount of time.

- **Change the appearance of information**
  PowerPoint has many effects that can transform the way text, graphics, and slides appear. By exploring some of these capabilities, you discover how easy it is to change the appearance of your presentation.

- **Organize and arrange information**
  Once you start using PowerPoint, you won't have to spend much time making sure your information is correct and in the right order. With PowerPoint, you can quickly and easily rearrange and modify text, graphics, and slides in your presentation.

- **Include information from other sources**
  Often, when you create presentations, you use information from a variety of sources. With PowerPoint, you can import text, photographs, videos, numerical data, and other information from files created in programs such as Adobe Photoshop, Microsoft Word, Microsoft Excel, and Microsoft Access. You can also import information from other PowerPoint presentations as well as graphic images from a variety of sources such as the Internet, storage devices, computers, a camera, or other graphics programs. Always be sure you have permission to use any work that you did not create yourself.

- **Present information in a variety of ways**
  With PowerPoint, you can present information using a variety of methods. For example, you can print handout pages or an outline of your presentation for audience members. You can display your presentation as an on-screen slide show using your computer, or if you are presenting to a large group, you can use a video projector and a large screen. If you want to reach an even wider audience, you can broadcast the presentation or upload it as a video to the Internet so people anywhere in the world can use a web browser to view your presentation. **Figure 1-1** shows how a presentation looks printed as handouts. **Figure 1-2** shows how the same presentation might look saved as a video.

- **Collaborate with others on a presentation**
  PowerPoint makes it easy to collaborate or share a presentation with colleagues and coworkers using the Internet. You can use your email program to send a presentation as an attachment to a colleague for feedback. If you have several people that need to work together on a presentation, you can save the presentation to a shared workspace such as a network drive or OneDrive so authorized users in your group with an Internet connection can access the presentation.

Figure 1-1: PowerPoint handout

Fauxels/Pexels

Figure 1-2: Presentation saved as a video

Using PowerPoint on a touchscreen

You can use PowerPoint on a Windows computer with a touch-enabled monitor or any other compatible touchscreen, such as a tablet. Using your fingers, you can use typical touch gestures to create, modify, and navigate presentations. To enable touch mode capabilities in PowerPoint, you need to add the Touch Mode button to the Quick Access Toolbar. Click the Customize Quick Access Toolbar button , click Touch/Mouse Mode, click the Touch/Mouse Mode button on the Quick Access Toolbar, then click Touch. In Touch mode, additional space is added around all of the buttons and icons in the ribbon and the status bar to make them easier to touch. Common gestures that you can use in PowerPoint include double-tapping text to edit it and tapping a slide then dragging it to rearrange it in the presentation.

Module 1 Creating a Presentation in PowerPoint

Plan an Effective Presentation

Case Because your presentation needs to be as effective as possible, you review the planning guidelines below.

Objective
- Determine presentation content and design

Before you create a presentation, you need to have a general idea of the information you want to communicate. PowerPoint is a powerful and flexible program that gives you the ability to start a presentation simply by entering the text of your message. If you have a specific design in mind that you want to use, you can start the presentation by working on the design. In most cases, you'll probably enter the text of your presentation into PowerPoint first and then tailor the design to the message and audience. When preparing your presentation, you need to keep in mind not only whom you are giving it to, but also how you are presenting it. For example, if you are going to record your presentation and then share it on the Internet, you need to have a shared online location where others can open the presentation. **Figure 1-3** illustrates a storyboard for a well-planned presentation.

Details

In planning a presentation, it is important to:

- **Determine and outline the message you want to communicate**
  The more time you take developing the message and outline of your presentation, the better your presentation will be in the end. A presentation with a clear message that reads like a story and is illustrated with appropriate graphic elements, such as 3-D pictures, animation, and video will have the greatest impact on your audience. Start the presentation by providing a general description of the company teams and users. Refer to **Figure 1-3**.

- **Identify your audience and where and how you are giving the presentation**
  Audience and the delivery method are major factors in the type of presentation you create. For example, a presentation you develop for a staff meeting that is held in a conference room would not necessarily need to be as sophisticated or detailed as a presentation that you develop for a large audience to be presented over the Internet. Room lighting, natural light, screen position, and room layout can affect how the audience responds to your presentation. With PowerPoint, you can broadcast your presentation over the Internet to several people who view the presentation on their computers in real time or you can record your presentation and post it to a shared location for others to view. Your presentation will be broadcast over the Internet.

- **Determine the type of output**
  Output choices for a presentation include an on-screen slide show, a recorded video, an animated recording, or an online broadcast. Consider time demands and computer equipment availability as you decide which output types to produce. Because your presentation will be broadcast over the Internet, the default output settings work just fine.

- **Determine the design**
  Visual appeal, graphics, and presentation design work together to communicate your message. You can choose one of the professionally designed themes that come with PowerPoint, modify one of these themes, or create one of your own. You decide to choose one of PowerPoint's design themes for your presentation.

Figure 1-3: Storyboard of the presentation

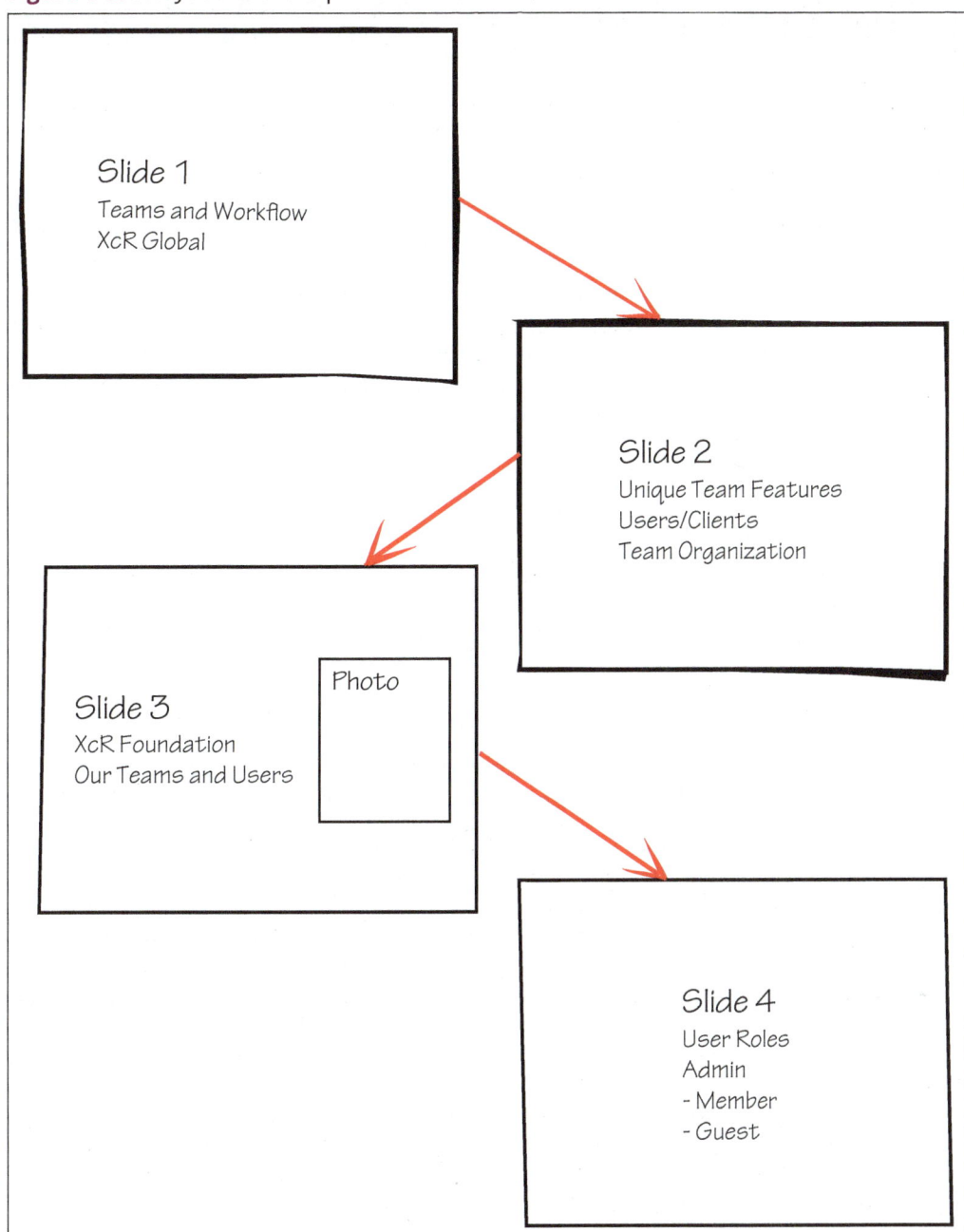

Understanding copyright

Intellectual property is any unique idea or creation of the human mind. Copyright law is a type of intellectual property law that protects works of authorship, including books, webpages, computer games, music, artwork, and photographs. Copyright protects the expression of an idea, but not the underlying facts or concepts. In other words, the general subject matter is not protected, but how you express it is, such as when several people photograph the same sunset. Copyright attaches to any original work of authorship as soon as it is created; you do not have to register it with the Copyright Office or display the copyright symbol, ©. Fair use is an exception to copyright and permits the public to use copyrighted material for certain purposes without obtaining prior consent from the owner. Determining whether fair use applies to a work depends on its purpose, the nature of the work, how much of the work you want to copy, and the effect on the work's value. Unauthorized use of protected work (such as downloading a photo or a song from the web) is known as copyright infringement and can lead to legal action.

Examine the PowerPoint Window

Case You want to create your presentation as efficiently as possible, so you review the elements of the PowerPoint window.

Objectives
- Explain PowerPoint window elements
- Open PowerPoint
- Create a blank presentation

When you first start PowerPoint, you can choose what kind of presentation you want to use to start—a blank one, or one with a preformatted design. You can also open and work on an existing presentation. PowerPoint has different **views** that allow you to see your presentation in different ways. By default, the PowerPoint window opens in **Normal view**, which is the primary view that you use to write, edit, and design your presentation. Normal view is divided into sections called **panes**: the pane on the left, called the **slide thumbnail pane** (or just the thumbnail pane), displays the slides of your presentation as small images, called **slide thumbnails**. The large pane is the Slide pane where you do most of your work on the slide.

Steps

1. **sam↓** Start **PowerPoint**
   PowerPoint starts and the PowerPoint start screen opens, as shown in **Figure 1-4**.
2. **Click the Blank Presentation slide thumbnail**
   The PowerPoint window opens in Normal view, as shown in **Figure 1-5**.

Details

Using **Figure 1-5** as a guide, examine the elements of the PowerPoint window, then find and compare the elements described below:

- The **ribbon** is a wide band spanning the top of the PowerPoint window that organizes all of PowerPoint's primary commands. Each set of primary commands is identified by a **tab**; for example, the Home tab is selected by default, as shown in **Figure 1-5**. Commands are further arranged into **groups** on the ribbon based on their function. So, for example, text formatting commands such as Bold, Underline, and Italic are located on the Home tab, in the Font group.
- The thumbnail pane is on the left side of the window. You can navigate through the slides in your presentation by clicking the slide thumbnails. You can also add, delete, or rearrange slides using this pane.
- The **Slide pane** displays the current slide in your presentation.
- The **Design Ideas pane** on the right side of the Slide pane appears automatically (unless it is turned off) which provides you with several presentation design suggestions. You may choose one of these suggestions or close the pane.
- The **View buttons** on the status bar allow you to switch quickly between PowerPoint views.
- The **Notes button** on the status bar opens the Notes pane and is used to enter text that references a slide's content. You can print these notes and refer to them when you make a presentation or use them as audience handouts. The Notes pane is not visible in Slide Show view.
- The **status bar**, located at the bottom of the PowerPoint window, shows messages about what you are doing and seeing in PowerPoint, including which slide you are viewing and the total number of slides. In addition, the status bar displays the Zoom slider controls, the Fit slide to current window button, and other functionality information.
- The **Zoom slider** on the lower-right corner of the status bar is used to zoom the slide in and out.

Figure 1-4: PowerPoint start screen

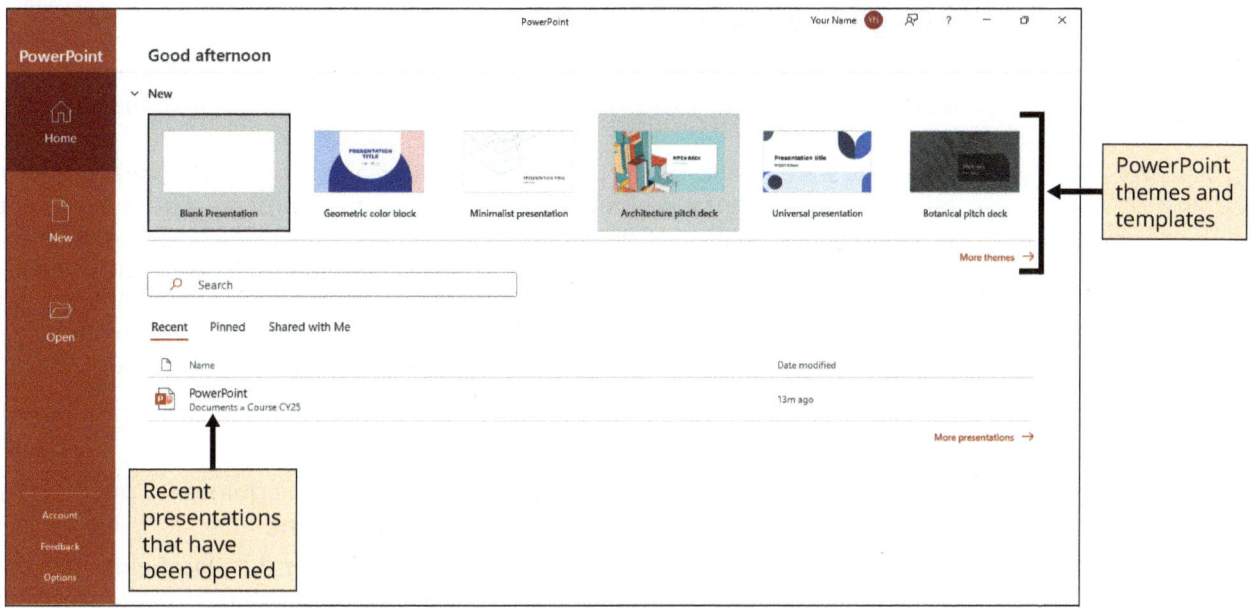

Figure 1-5: PowerPoint window in Normal view

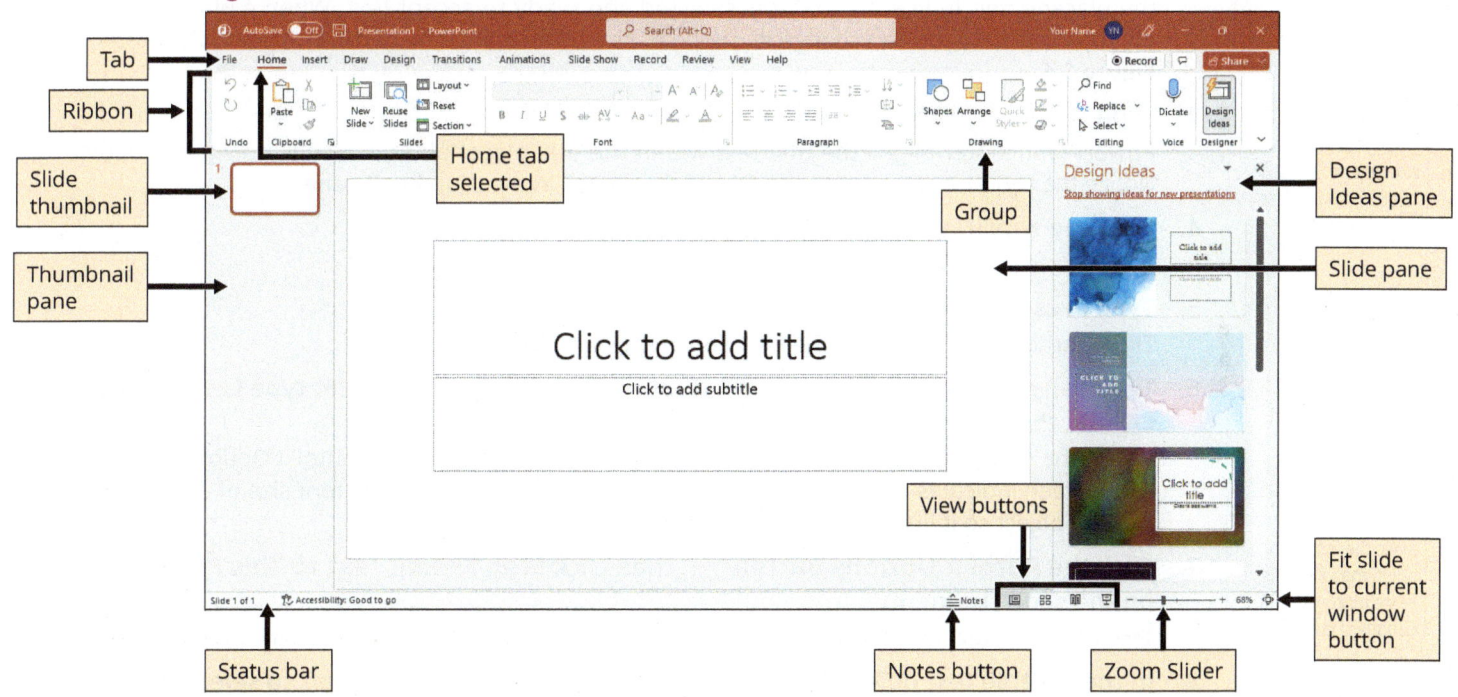

Creating a presentation using a template

PowerPoint offers you a variety of ways to create a presentation, including starting with a blank presentation, a theme, a template, or an existing presentation. A **template** is a type of presentation that contains design information on the slide master and often includes text and design suggestions for information you might want to include in the presentation. You have access to sample templates in PowerPoint and online at the Microsoft.com website. To create a presentation using a template, click the File tab on the ribbon, click New, locate the template, then click Create.

Module 1 Creating a Presentation in PowerPoint

Add Text to a Slide

Case Because text is an important part of your presentation, you begin by entering text on the title slide.

Objectives
- Create text on a slide
- Change slide text

When you start a blank PowerPoint presentation, an empty title slide appears in Normal view. The title slide has two **text placeholders**—boxes with dotted borders—where you enter text. The top text placeholder on the title slide is the **title placeholder**, labeled "Click to add title." The bottom text placeholder on the title slide is the **subtitle placeholder**, labeled "Click to add subtitle." To enter text in a placeholder, click the placeholder and then type your text. After you enter text in a placeholder, the placeholder becomes a text object. An **object** is any item on a slide that can be modified. Objects are the building blocks that make up a presentation slide.

Steps

1. Click the Design Ideas Close button ✖, then move the pointer over the title placeholder labeled **Click to add title** in the Slide pane

    The pointer changes to I when you move the pointer over the placeholder. In PowerPoint, the pointer often changes shape, depending on the task you are trying to accomplish.

2. Click the **title placeholder** in the Slide pane

    The **insertion point**, a blinking vertical line, indicates where your text appears when you type in the placeholder. A **selection box** with a dashed line border and **sizing handles** appears around the placeholder, indicating that it is selected and ready to accept text. When a placeholder or object is selected, you can change its shape or size by dragging one of the sizing handles. Refer to **Figure 1-6**.

Trouble
If you press a wrong letter, press BACKSPACE to erase the character.

▶ 3. Type **Teams and Workflow**

    PowerPoint center-aligns the title text within the title placeholder, which is now a text object. Notice the text also appears on the Slide 1 thumbnail in the thumbnail pane.

4. Click the **subtitle placeholder** in the Slide pane

    The subtitle placeholder is ready to accept text.

5. Type **Presented by**, then press **ENTER**

    The insertion point moves to the next line in the text object.

Quick Tip
To copy text, select the text, click the Home tab, click the Copy button in the Clipboard group, place the insertion point, then click the Paste button in the Clipboard group.

▶ 6. Type **Tanya Scheving**, press **ENTER**, type **XcR Global**, press **ENTER**, type **Leader**, press **ENTER**, then type **Technical Division**

    Notice the AutoFit Options button appears near the text object. The AutoFit Options button on your screen indicates that PowerPoint has automatically decreased the font size of all the text in the text object so it fits inside the text object.

7. Click the **AutoFit Options button**, then click **Stop Fitting Text to This Placeholder** on the shortcut menu

    The text in the text object changes back to its original size and no longer fits inside the text object.

8. In the subtitle text object, position I to the right of **Leader**, drag left to select the whole word, press **BACKSPACE**, then click outside the text object in a blank area of the slide

    The Leader line of text is deleted and the AutoFit Options menu closes, as shown in **Figure 1-7**. Clicking a blank area of the slide deselects all selected objects on the slide.

9. Click the **File tab** on the ribbon to open Backstage view, click **Save As**, click Browse, then save the presentation as **IL_PPT_1_XCR** in the location where you store your Data Files

    In the Save As screen, you have the option of saving your presentation to your computer or OneDrive. Notice that PowerPoint automatically entered the title of the presentation as the file name in the Save As dialog box.

Figure 1-6: Title placeholder selected

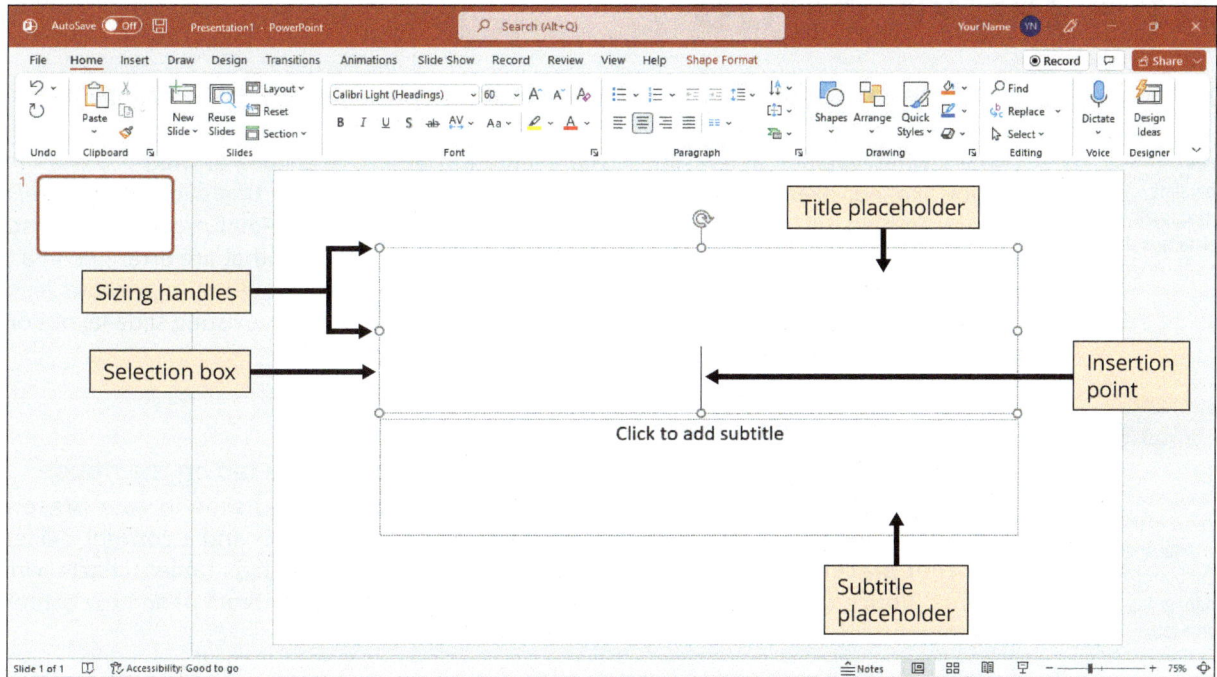

Figure 1-7: Text on title slide

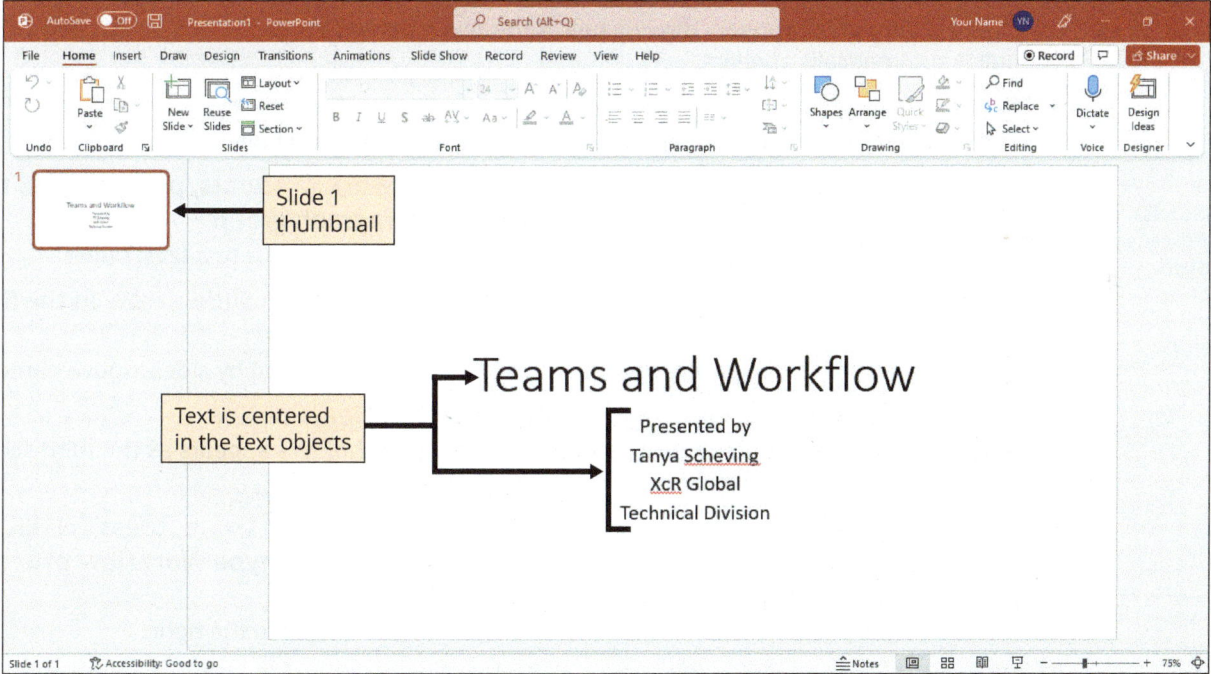

Aligning paragraph text

PowerPoint offers six ways to align paragraph text within a text object: Top, Middle, Bottom, Top Centered, Middle Centered, and Bottom Centered. To change paragraph text alignment, click the Home tab on the ribbon, select the text you want to change, then click the Align Text button in the Paragraph group to open the Align Text menu. To see all the alignment options, click More Options in the Align Text menu, then click the Vertical alignment arrow.

Add a New Slide

Case Teamwork is an important part of working at XcR, so you create a slide that describes XcR company teams.

Objectives
- Add a new slide
- Change text levels
- Modify slide layout

Usually, when you add a new slide to a presentation, you have an idea of what you want the slide to look like. For example, you may want to add a slide that has a title over bulleted text and a picture. To help you add a slide like this quickly and easily, PowerPoint provides many standard slide layouts. A **slide layout** contains text and object placeholders that are arranged in a specific way on the slide. You have already worked with the Title Slide layout in the previous lesson. If a standard slide layout does not meet your needs, you can modify an existing slide layout or create a new, custom slide layout.

Steps

Quick Tip
To delete a slide, select the slide in the thumbnail pane, then click the Cut button in the Clipboard group on the Home tab.

▶ 1. **Click the New Slide button in the Slides group on the Home tab on the ribbon**
A new blank slide (now the current slide) appears as the second slide in your presentation, as shown in **Figure 1-8**. The new slide contains a title placeholder and a content placeholder. A **content placeholder** can be used to insert text or objects such as tables, charts, videos, or pictures. Notice the status bar indicates Slide 2 of 2 and the thumbnail pane now contains two slide thumbnails.

2. **Type Unique Team Features, then click the bottom content placeholder**
The text you typed appears in the title placeholder, and the insertion point is now at the top of the bottom content placeholder.

3. **Type Collection of Users, then press ENTER**
The insertion point appears directly below the text when you press ENTER, and a new first-level bullet automatically appears.

4. **Press TAB**
The new first-level bullet is indented and becomes a second-level bullet.

Quick Tip
You can also press SHIFT+TAB to decrease the indent level.

▶ 5. **Type Users can be associated directly with XcR work products, press ENTER, then click the Decrease List Level button in the Paragraph group**
The Decrease List Level button changes the second-level bullet into a first-level bullet.

6. **Type Organize and view work by Team, then click the New Slide arrow in the Slides group**
The Office Theme layout gallery opens. Each slide layout is identified by a descriptive name.

7. **Click the Two Content slide layout, then type The Heart of XcR**
A new slide with a title placeholder and two content placeholders appears as the third slide. The text you typed is the title text for the slide.

8. **Click the left content placeholder, type Our Teams plus our Users, press ENTER, click the Increase List Level button in the Paragraph group, type Workflow process, press ENTER, then type Innovative work products**
The Increase List Level button moves the insertion point one level to the right.

9. **Click a blank area of the slide, then click the Save button on the Title bar**
The Save button saves all of the changes to the file. Compare your screen with **Figure 1-9**.

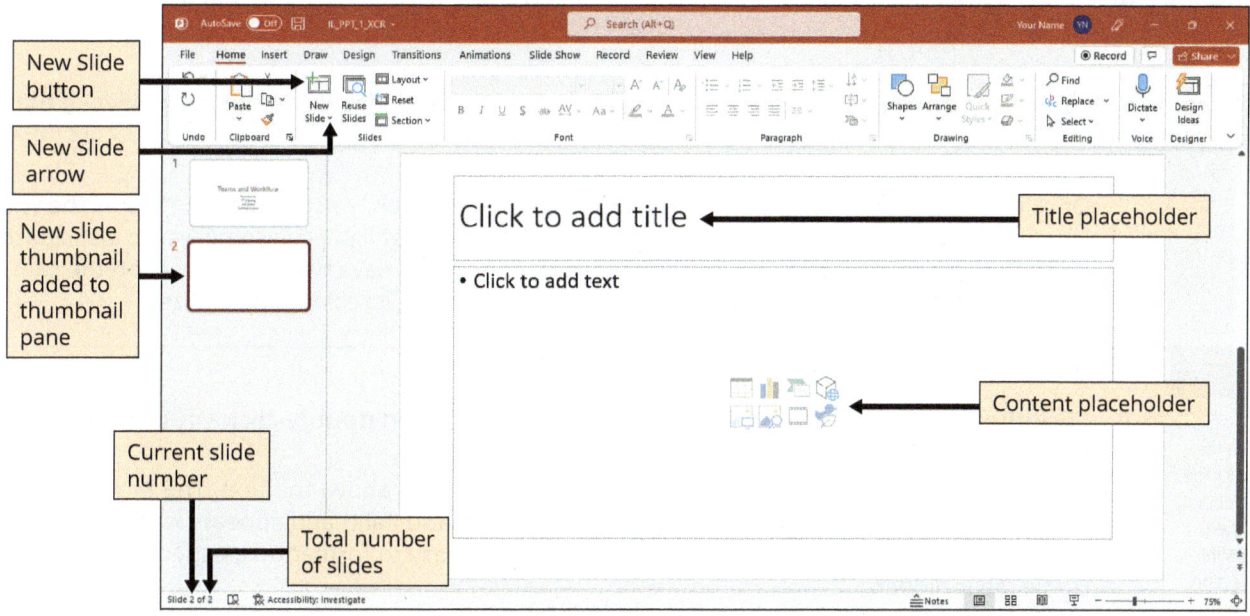

Figure 1-8: New blank slide in Normal view

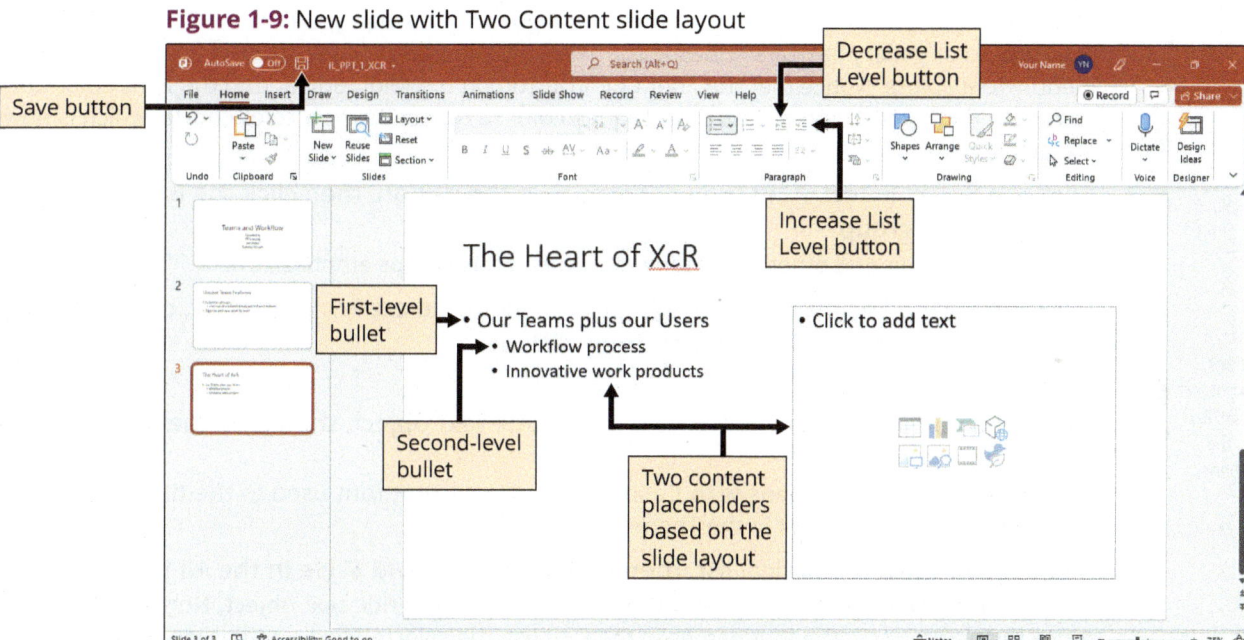

Figure 1-9: New slide with Two Content slide layout

Viewing your presentation in grayscale or black and white

Viewing your presentation in grayscale (using shades of gray) or pure black and white is useful when you are printing a presentation on a black-and-white printer and you want to make sure your presentation prints correctly. To see how your color presentation looks in grayscale or black and white, click the View tab, then click either the Grayscale or Black and White button in the Color/Grayscale group.

Depending on which button you select, the Grayscale or the Black and White tab appears, and the ribbon displays different settings that you can customize. If you don't like the way an individual object looks in black and white or grayscale, you can change its color. Click the object while still in Grayscale or Black and White view, then choose an option in the Change Selected Object group on the ribbon.

Format Text

Case To emphasize the importance of teamwork at XcR, you decide to format selected text on two slides of the presentation.

Objective
- Modify text characteristics

Once you have entered and edited the text in your presentation, you can modify the way the text looks to emphasize your message. Important text should be highlighted in some way to distinguish it from other text or objects on the slide. For example, if you have two text objects on the same slide, you could draw attention to one text object by changing its color, font, or size.

Steps

Quick Tip
To show or hide the Mini toolbar, click the File tab on the ribbon, click Options, then click the Show Mini Toolbar on selection check box.

1. **Click the Slide 2 thumbnail in the thumbnail pane, then double-click Unique in the title text object**
   The word "Unique" is selected, and a Mini toolbar appears above the text. The **Mini toolbar** contains basic text-formatting commands, such as bold and italic, and appears when you select text using the mouse. This toolbar makes it quick and easy to format text, especially when the Home tab is hidden.

2. **Move over the Mini toolbar, click the Font Color arrow, then click the Dark Red color box in the Standard Colors row**
   The text changes color to dark red, as shown in **Figure 1-10**. When you click the Font Color arrow, the Font Color gallery appears showing the Theme Colors and Standard Colors. ScreenTips help identify font colors. Notice that the Font Color button on the Mini toolbar and the Font Color button in the Font group on the Home tab change color to reflect the new color choice, which is now the active color.

Quick Tip
To select an unselected text object, press SHIFT, click the text object, then release SHIFT.

3. **Click the Bold button in the Font group on the ribbon, then click the Italic button in the Font group**
   Changing the color and other formatting attributes of text helps emphasize it.

Quick Tip
For more text formatting options, right-click a text object, then click Format Text Effects to open the Format Shape pane.

4. **Click the Slide 1 thumbnail in the thumbnail pane, select Presented by, click the Font Size arrow in the Mini toolbar, then click 28**
   The text increases in size to 28.

5. **Select the text Teams and Workflow in the title text object, then click the Font arrow in the Font group**
   A list of available fonts opens with Calibri Light, the current font used in the title text object, selected at the top of the list in the Theme Fonts section.

6. **Scroll down the alphabetical list, then click Bookman Old Style in the All Fonts section**
   The Bookman Old Style font replaces the original font in the title text object. Notice that as you move the pointer over the font names in the font list, the selected text on the slide displays a Live Preview of the available fonts.

7. **Click the Underline button in the Font group, then click the Increase Font Size button in the Font group**
   All of the text now displays an underline and increases in size to 66.

8. **Click a blank area of the slide outside the text object to deselect it, then save your work**
   Clicking a blank area of the slide deselects all objects that are selected. Compare your screen to **Figure 1-11**.

Figure 1-10: Selected word with Mini toolbar open

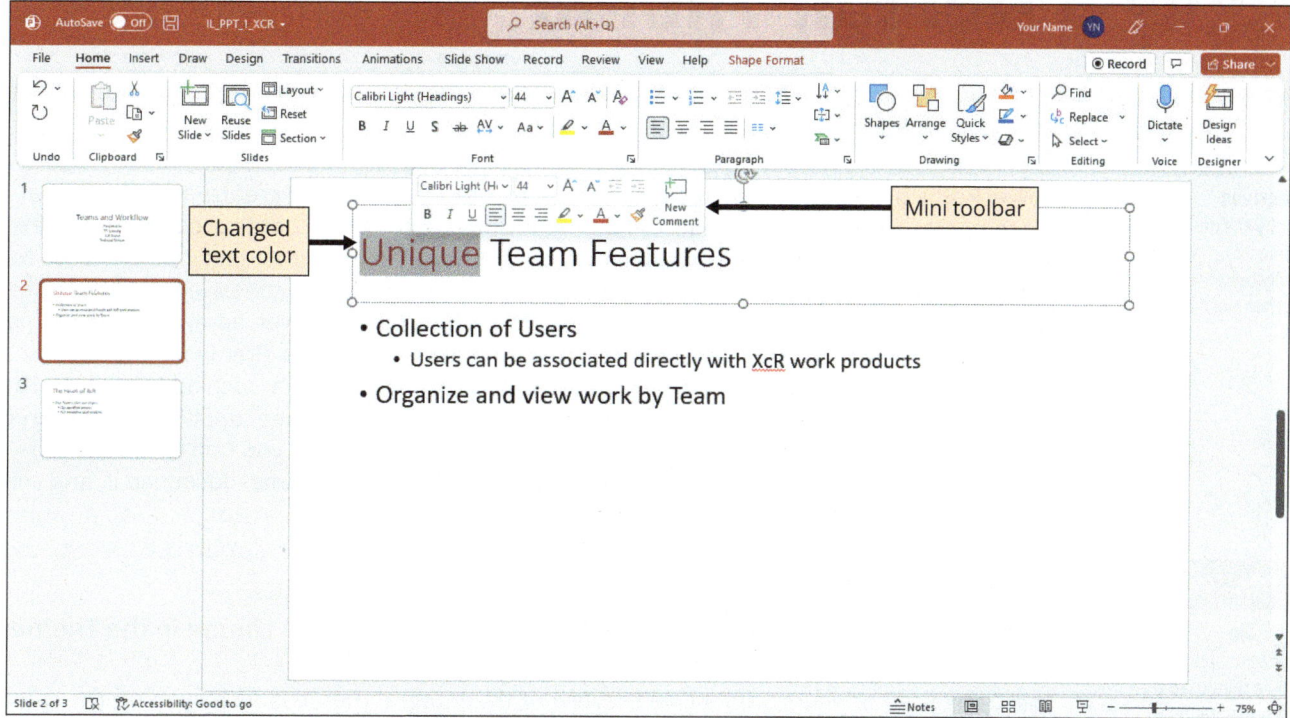

Figure 1-11: Formatted text

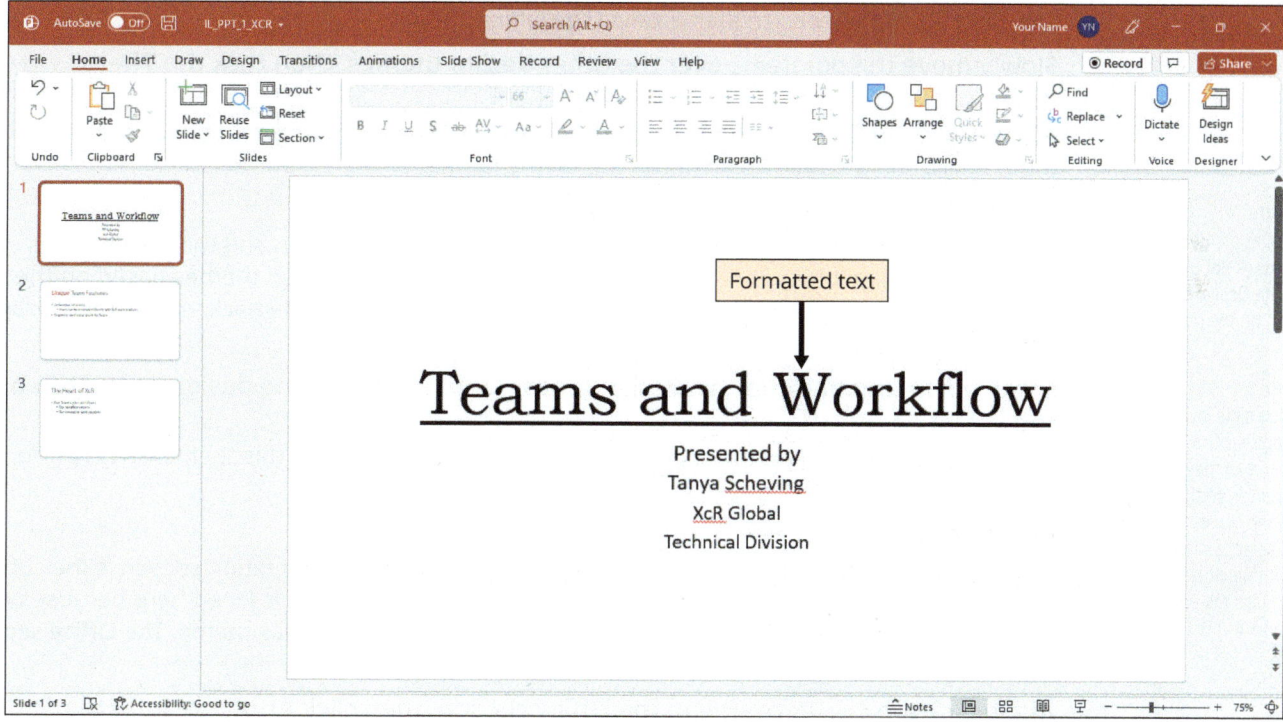

Adding bullets to paragraphs

In PowerPoint, paragraph text is often preceded by either a number or some kind of bullet. Common bullets include graphic images such as arrows, dots, or blocks. To add or change bullets, select the text or text object, click the Bullets arrow in the Paragraph group on the ribbon, then select a bullet.

Module 1 Creating a Presentation in PowerPoint

Apply a Design Theme

Case It is important that your presentation be visually appealing, so you decide to change the default design theme in the presentation to a new one.

Objectives
- Modify the design theme
- Navigate between slides in Normal view

PowerPoint provides many design themes to help you quickly create a professional and contemporary-looking presentation. A **theme** includes a set of 12 coordinated colors for text, fill, line, and shadow, called **theme colors**; a set of fonts for titles and other text, called **theme fonts**; and a set of effects for lines and fills, called **theme effects** to create a cohesive look. In most cases, you would apply one theme to an entire presentation; you can, however, apply multiple themes to the same presentation. You can use a design theme as is, or you can alter individual elements of the theme as needed. Unless you need to use a specific design theme, such as a company theme or product design theme, it is faster and easier to use one of the themes supplied with PowerPoint. If you design a custom theme, you can save it to use in the future. If you don't have a theme that you need, go to https://templates.office.com, search the template name, download it, and store it in your template storage location.

Steps

Quick Tip
One way to apply multiple themes to the same presentation is to click the Slide Sorter button on the status bar, select a slide or a group of slides, then click the theme.

1. **Click the Design tab on the ribbon, then point to the Integral theme in the Themes group, as shown in Figure 1-12**
   The Design tab appears, and a Live Preview of the Integral theme is displayed on the selected slide. A **Live Preview** allows you to see how your changes affect the slide before actually making the change. The Live Preview lasts about 1 minute, and then your slide reverts to its original state. The first (far-left) theme thumbnail identifies the current theme applied to the presentation, in this case, the default design theme called the Office Theme.

2. **Slowly move the pointer over the other design themes, then click the Themes group down scroll arrow**
   A Live Preview of the theme appears on the slide each time you pass your pointer over the theme thumbnails, and a ScreenTip identifies the theme names.

Trouble
If the Design Ideas pane does not open, click the Design Ideas button on the ribbon.

3. **Move over the design themes, then click the Atlas theme**
   The Atlas design theme is applied to all the slides in the presentation and the Design Ideas pane opens. The Design Ideas pane provides additional customized design themes based on the current design theme applied to your presentation. Notice the new slide background color, graphic elements, fonts, and text color.

Trouble
The top slide layout that appears on your screen may be different from the one in **Figure 1-13**. If so, select a slide layout that closely resembles the one in **Figure 1-13**.

4. **Scroll down and back up the Design Ideas pane, then click the design at the top of the list**
   The presentation displays the suggested design theme. You decide this theme isn't right for the presentation.

5. **Click the More button in the Themes group**
   The Themes gallery opens. At the top of the gallery in the This Presentation section is the current theme applied to the presentation. Notice that just the Atlas theme is listed here because when you changed the theme, you replaced the default theme with the Atlas theme. The Office section identifies all of the standard themes that come with PowerPoint.

6. **Right-click the Berlin theme in the Office section, then click Apply to Selected Slides**
   The Berlin theme is applied only to Slide 1. You like the Berlin theme better and decide to apply it to all slides.

7. **Right-click the Berlin theme in the Themes group, then click Apply to All Slides**
   The Berlin theme is applied to all three slides. You decide to preview the next slide in the presentation to see how it looks.

8. **Click the Next Slide button at the bottom of the vertical scroll bar, click the Close button in the Design Ideas pane, then save your changes**
   Compare your screen to **Figure 1-13**.

Apply a Design Theme   PPT 1-15

Figure 1-12: Slide showing a different design theme

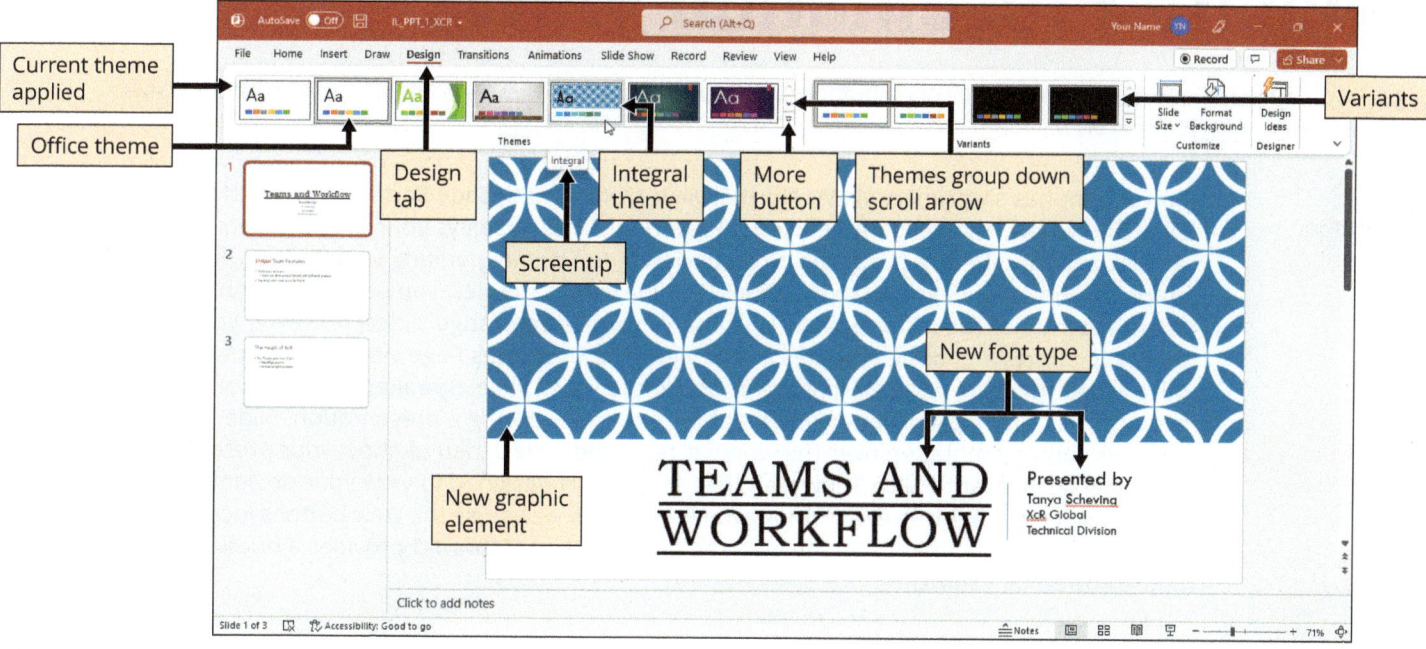

Figure 1-13: Presentation with Berlin theme applied

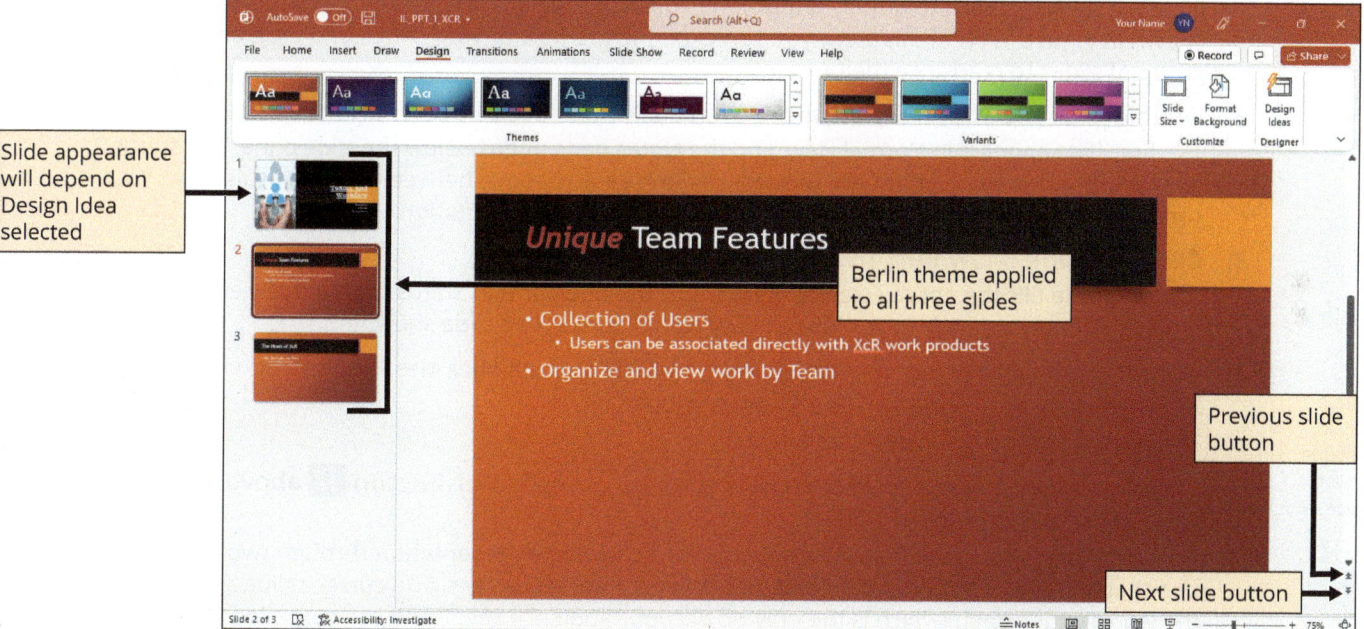

Changing theme colors

You are not limited to using the standard theme colors PowerPoint provides; you can also modify theme colors or create your own custom theme. For example, you might want to incorporate your school's or company's colors on the slide background of the presentation. To change existing theme colors, click the Design tab on the ribbon, click the More button in the Variants group, point to Colors then select a color theme. You can also create a new color theme from scratch by clicking the More button in the Variants group, pointing to Colors, then clicking Customize Colors. The Create New Theme Colors dialog box opens where you can select the theme colors you want and then save the color theme with a new name.

Compare Presentation Views

Case As you plan how you will share your presentation with colleagues, you examine some of the PowerPoint views, starting with Normal view.

Objective
- Select PowerPoint views

PowerPoint has six primary views: Normal view, Outline view, Slide Sorter view, Notes Page view, Slide Show view, and Reading view. Each PowerPoint view displays your presentation differently and is used for different purposes. Normal view is the primary editing view where you add text, graphics, and other elements to the slides. Outline view is the view you use to focus on the text of your presentation. Slide Sorter view is primarily used to rearrange slides; however, you can also add slide effects and design themes in this view. You use Notes Page view to type speaker notes (also called notes) to yourself that are important for each slide. **Speaker notes** usually relate to slide content and is information you want to remember during a presentation. Slide Show view displays your presentation over the whole screen and is designed to show your presentation to an audience. Similar to Slide Show view, Reading view is designed to view your presentation on a computer screen. To move easily among the PowerPoint views, use the View buttons located on the status bar or the commands on the View tab on the ribbon. **Table 1-1** provides a brief description of the PowerPoint views.

Steps

1. Click the **View tab** on the ribbon, then click the **Slide Sorter button** in the Presentation Views group

   Slide Sorter view opens to display a thumbnail of each slide in the presentation in the window, as shown in **Figure 1-14**. In this view, you can examine the flow of your slides and drag any slide or group of slides to rearrange their order.

2. Double-click the **Slide 1 thumbnail**, then click the **Notes button** on the status bar

   The first slide appears in Normal view, and the Notes pane opens below the slide pane. The status bar controls at the bottom of the window make it easy to move between slides in this view. You can type notes to yourself in the Notes pane to guide your presentation.

3. Click the **Slide Show button** on the status bar

   The first slide fills the entire screen now without the title bar and status bar. In this view, you can practice running through your slides as they would appear in a slide show.

Quick Tip
You can also press ENTER, SPACEBAR, Page Up, Page Down, or the arrow keys to advance the slide show.

4. Click the **left mouse button** to advance to Slide 2, then click the **More slide show options button** on the Slide Show toolbar

   The slide show options menu opens.

5. Click **Show Presenter View**, then click the **Pause the timer button** above the slide, as shown in **Figure 1-15**

   Presenter view is a view that you can use when showing a presentation through two monitors; one that you see as the presenter and one that your audience sees. The current slide appears on the left of your screen (which is the only object your audience sees), and the next slide in the presentation appears on the right side of the screen. Speaker notes, if you entered any In the Notes pane, appear in the lower-right corner. The timer you paused identifies how long the slide has been viewed by the audience.

Quick Tip
You can start a slide show from Slide 1 by clicking the From Beginning button in the Start Slide Show group on the Slide Show tab.

6. Click, click **Hide Presenter View**, then click the **left mouse button** to advance through the slide show until you see a black slide, then press **SPACEBAR**

   At the end of a slide show, you return to Normal view and the last slide of the slide show, in this case, Slide 3.

7. Click the **Home tab** on the ribbon

Compare Presentation Views   PPT 1-17

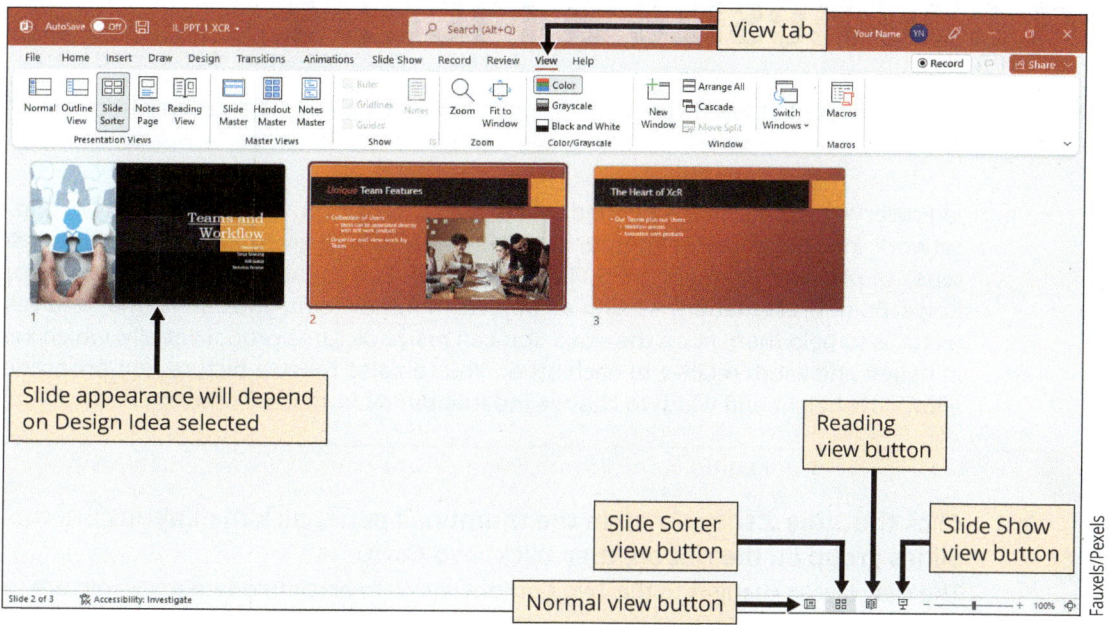

Figure 1-14: Slide Sorter view

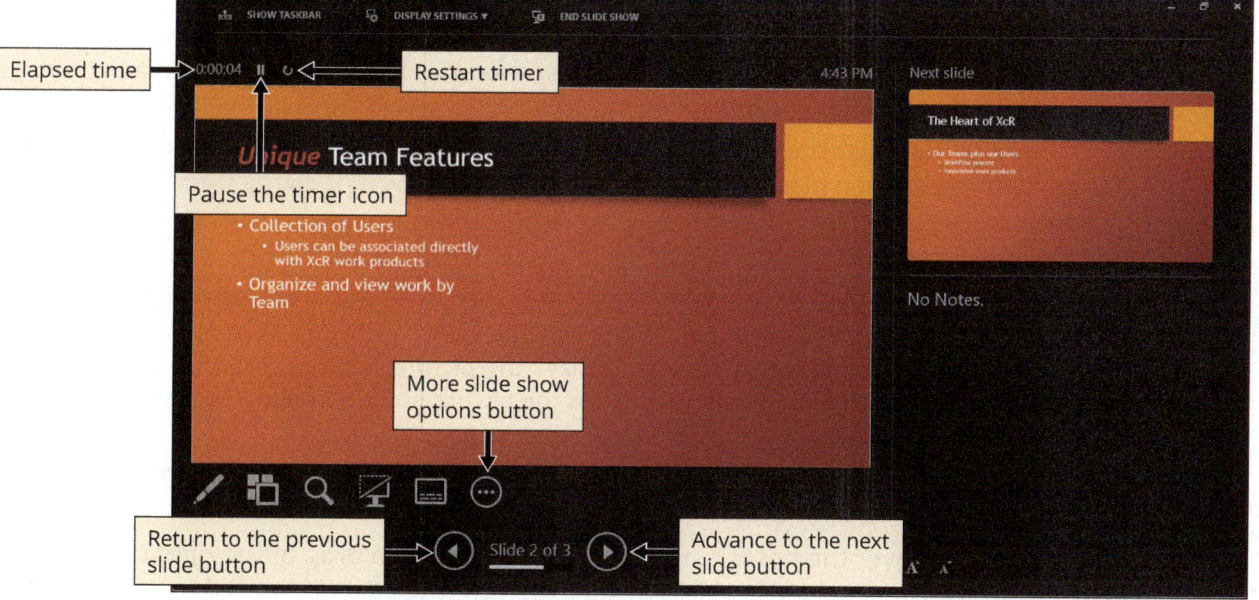

Figure 1-15: Slide 2 in Presenter view

Table 1-1: PowerPoint views

view name	button	button name	displays
Normal	🔲	Normal	The Slide pane and the thumbnail pane at the same time
Outline View	(no View button on status bar)		An outline of the presentation and the Slide pane at the same time
Slide Sorter	🔡	Slide Sorter	Thumbnails of all slides
Slide Show	🖥	Slide Show	Your presentation on the whole computer screen
Reading View	📖	Reading View	Your presentation in a large window on your computer screen
Notes Page	(no View button on status bar)		A reduced image of the current slide above a large text box

Insert and Resize a Picture

Case To help illustrate the concept of teamwork at XcR, Tanya has given you a stock picture to insert and resize in your presentation.

Objectives
- Insert a picture
- Resize and move a picture

In PowerPoint, a **picture** is defined as a digital photograph, a piece of line art or clip art, or other artwork that is created in another program. PowerPoint gives you the ability to insert different types of pictures, including JPEG File Interchange Format and BMP Windows Bitmap files into a PowerPoint presentation. As with all objects in PowerPoint, you can format and resize inserted pictures to help them fit on the slide. You can resize pictures proportionally, which keeps changes in height and width relative to each other. You can also resize a picture non-proportionally, which allows the height and width to change independently from each other.

Steps

Quick Tip
You can also insert a picture by clicking the Pictures button in the Images group on the Insert tab.

1. Click the **Slide 2 thumbnail** in the thumbnail pane, click the **Layout button** in the Slides group on the ribbon, then click **Two Content**

   The slide layout changes to the Two Content layout to accommodate a new picture.

2. Click the **Pictures icon** in the content placeholder on the slide, navigate to the location where you store your Data Files, select the picture file **Support_PPT_1_Team .jpg**, then click **Insert**

   The Insert Picture dialog box opens displaying the pictures available in the default Pictures folder. The newly inserted picture fills the content placeholder on the slide, and the Picture Format tab opens on the ribbon. The Design Ideas pane also opens offering you design suggestions for the slide.

Quick Tip
To select all the objects on a slide, click the Home tab on the ribbon, click the Select arrow in the Editing group, then click Select All.

3. Scroll through the suggestions in the Design Ideas pane, click the **Close button** in the Design Ideas pane, then place the pointer over the **middle-right sizing handle** on the picture

   The pointer changes to ⇔.

4. Drag the **sizing handle** to the right as shown in **Figure 1-16**, then release the mouse button

   Dragging any of the middle sizing handles resizes the picture non-proportionally, whereas dragging one of the corner sizing handles resizes the picture proportionally. The picture would look better if it was resized proportionally.

Quick Tip
You can also resize a picture proportionally by entering specific height or width values in the Height or Width text boxes in the Size group on the Picture Format tab.

5. Click the **Home tab** on the ribbon, then click the **Undo button** in the Undo group

   The picture reverts to its original size.

6. Place the pointer over the **bottom-right sizing handle**, then drag to the right until the right side of the picture edge is about a half inch from the edge of the slide

   The picture is now resized proportionally. To see a portion of a slide close up, you can zoom in.

7. Drag the **Zoom slider** on the status bar to the right until the picture fills the slide pane

   The selected picture fills the pane.

8. Click the **Fit slide to current window button** on the status bar, click a blank area of the slide, then save your work

   The zoom setting returns to its previous position and the slide fits in the Slide pane. Compare your screen to **Figure 1-17**.

9. Replace Tanya's name with your name on slide 1, save your work, click the **File tab** on the ribbon, then click **Close**

   The presentation file closes.

Figure 1-16: Picture sized non-proportionally

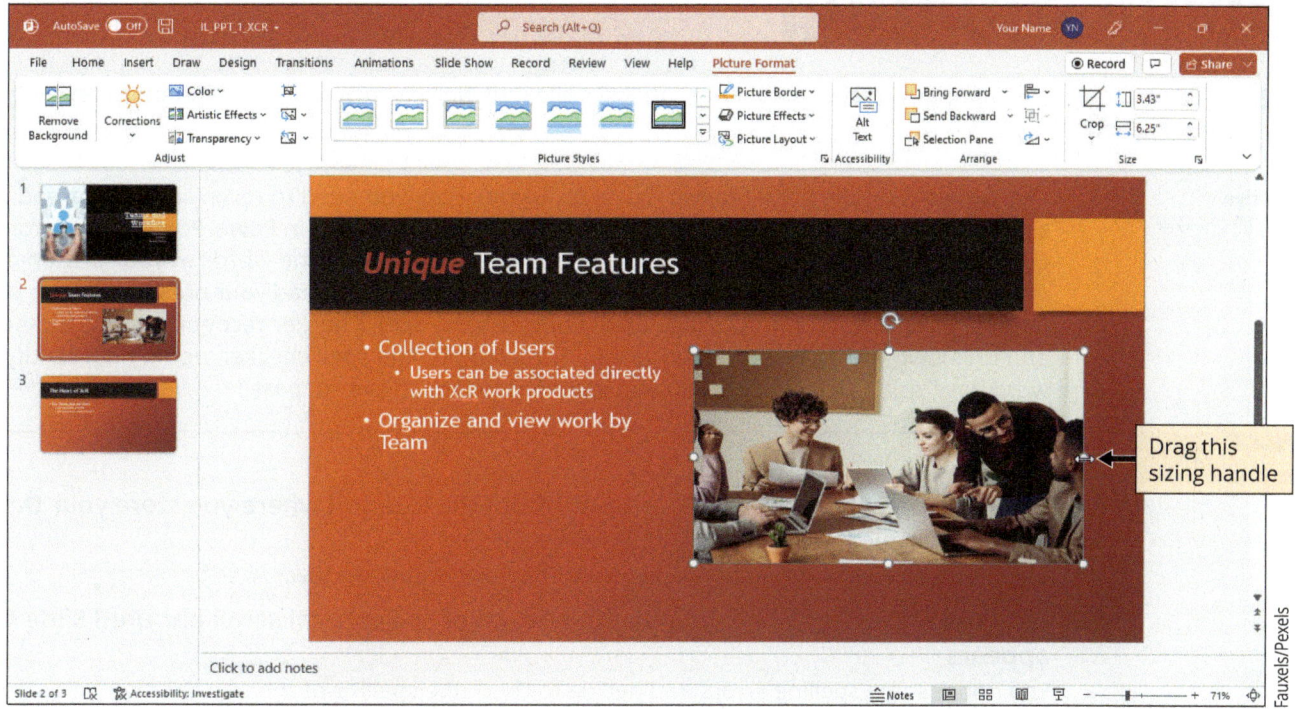

Figure 1-17: Picture sized proportionally

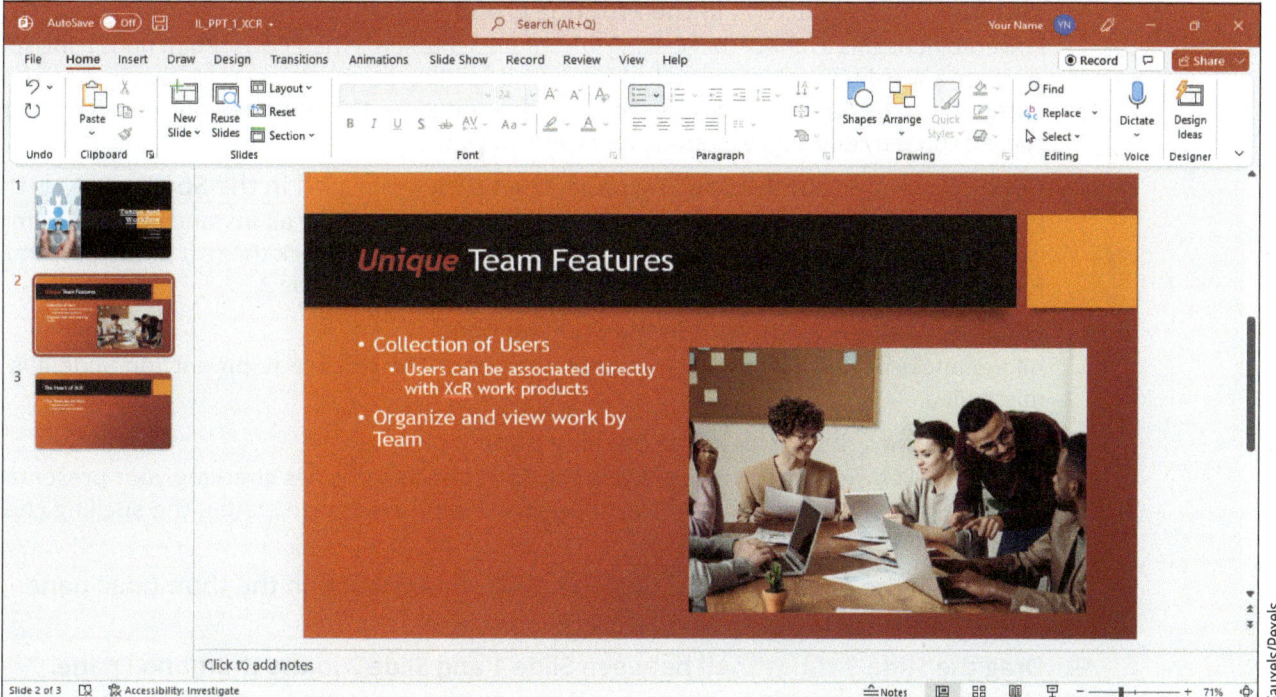

Rehearse with the Speaker coach

Speaker coach is a presentation delivery trainer in PowerPoint that evaluates your speaking technique as you speak during a slide show. When Speaker coach is on and you speak into your microphone, it evaluates multiple aspects of your speaking technique, such as your pace (or words per minute), your use of repetitive language and filler words, your voice pitch, and your language originality. When you are finished rehearsing, a report opens with advice and recommendations. To open the Speaker coach, click the Slide Show tab on the ribbon, then click the Rehearse with Coach button in the Rehearse group.

Module 1 Creating a Presentation in PowerPoint

Check Spelling

Case To help meet the company goal of excellence, an XcR colleague has given you a presentation to review and spell check.

Objective
Use Spell Checker

As your work on the presentation file nears completion, you need to review and proofread your slides thoroughly for errors. You can use the Spell Checker feature in PowerPoint to check for and correct spelling errors. This feature compares the spelling of all the words in your presentation against the words contained in the dictionary. You still must proofread your presentation for punctuation, grammar, and word usage errors because the Spell Checker recognizes only misspelled and unknown words, not misused words. For example, the spell checker would not identify the word "last" as an error, even if you had intended to type the word "past."

Steps

1. Open the presentation **IL_PPT_1-1.pptx** from the location where you store your Data Files, then save it as **IL_PPT_1_MyReview**
   A presentation with a new name appears in the PowerPoint window.

2. Click the **Next Slide button** at the bottom of the vertical scroll bar until Slide 4 appears
   You notice some spelling errors and decide to check the spelling of the presentation.

3. Click the **Previous Slide button** at the bottom of the vertical scroll bar until Slide 1 appears, then click the **Review tab** on the ribbon

4. Click the **Spelling button** in the Proofing group
   PowerPoint begins to check the spelling in your presentation. When PowerPoint finds a misspelled word or a word that is not in its dictionary, the Spelling pane opens, as shown in **Figure 1-18**. In this case, the Spell Checker identifies a name on Slide 1, but it does not recognize that it's spelled correctly and suggests some replacement words.

5. Click **Ignore Once** in the Spelling pane, then click **Ignore All** in the Spelling pane
   PowerPoint ignores this one instance of the name then ignores all instances of the company name XcR in the presentation. The Spell Checker continues to check the rest of the presentation for errors. PowerPoint finds the misspelled word "language" on Slide 3.

6. Click the **Change All button** in the Spelling pane
   All instances of this misspelled word are corrected. The word "equipment" on Slide 4 is also misspelled.

7. Click the **Change button** in the Spelling pane
   The misspelled word is corrected. When the Spell Checker finishes checking your presentation, the Spelling pane closes, and an alert box opens with a message stating the spelling check is complete.

8. Click **OK** in the Alert box, then click the **Slide 3 thumbnail** in the thumbnail pane
   The alert box closes.

9. Drag the **Slide 3 thumbnail** between Slide 1 and Slide 2 in the thumbnail pane.
   Slide 3 moves and becomes the second slide in the presentation. Compare your screen to **Figure 1-19**.

Figure 1-18: Window with Spelling pane open

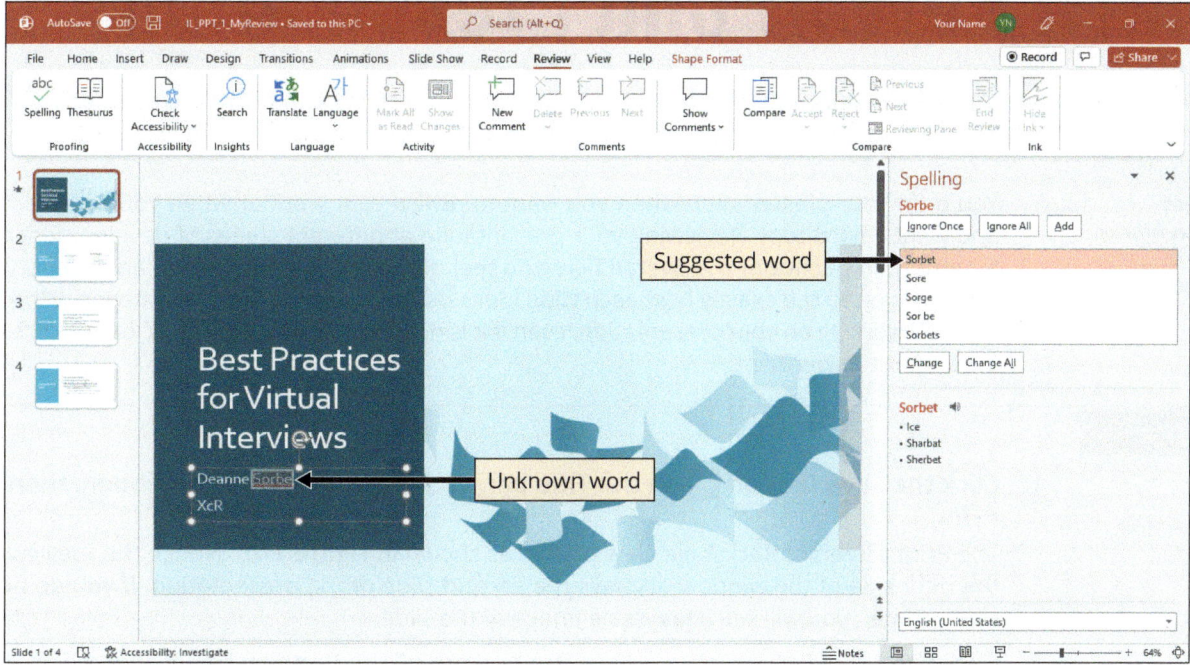

Figure 1-19: Moved slide

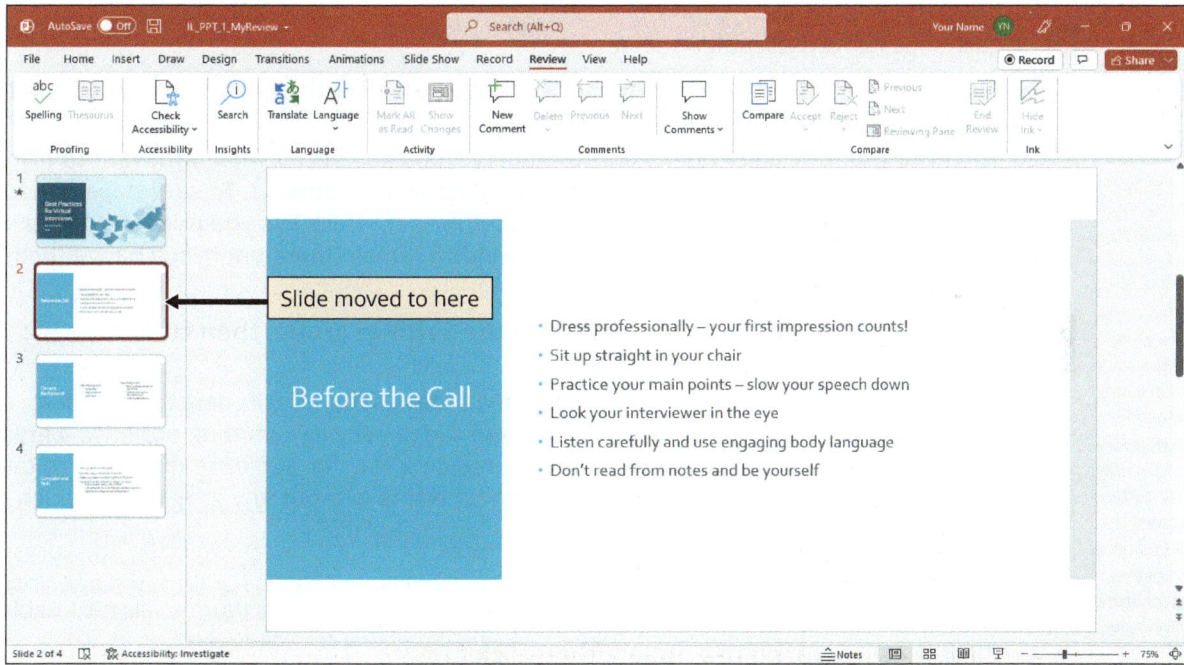

Checking spelling as you type

By default, PowerPoint checks your spelling as you type. If you type a word that is not in the dictionary, a wavy red line appears under it. To correct an error, right-click the misspelled word, then review the suggestions, which appear in the shortcut menu. You can select a suggestion, add the word you typed to your custom dictionary, or ignore it. To turn off automatic spell checking, click the File tab, then click Options to open the PowerPoint Options dialog box. Click Proofing in the left column, then click the Check spelling as you type check box to deselect it. To temporarily hide the wavy red lines, click the Hide spelling and grammar errors check box to select it. Contextual spelling in PowerPoint also identifies common grammatically misused words; for example, if you type the word "their" and the correct word is "there," PowerPoint will identify the mistake and place a wavy red line under the word. To turn contextual spelling on or off, click Proofing in the PowerPoint Options dialog box, then click the Mark grammar errors as you type check box.

Print a PowerPoint Presentation

Case To save paper, you preview your presentation, then you print the slides and notes pages so you can review them later. Before leaving for the day, you close the file and exit PowerPoint.

Objectives
- Print a presentation
- Select print settings
- Modify color settings

You print your presentation when you want to review your work or when you have completed it and want a hard copy. Reviewing your presentation at different stages of development gives you a better perspective of the overall flow and feel of the presentation. You can also preview your presentation to see exactly how each slide looks before you print the presentation. When you are finished working on your presentation, even if it is not yet complete, you can close the presentation file and exit PowerPoint.

Steps

1. Click the **Save button** on the Title bar, click the **File tab** on the ribbon, then click **Print**

   The Print screen of Backstage view opens, as shown in **Figure 1-20**. Notice the Preview pane on the right side of the window displays the second slide of the presentation. If you do not have a color printer, you will see a grayscale image of the slide.

   Quick Tip
   To quickly print the presentation with the current Print options, display the Quick Access toolbar in the Title bar, then add the Quick Print button to the toolbar.

2. Click the **Next Page button** at the bottom of the Preview pane, then click again

   The slides of the presentation appear in the Preview pane.

3. Click the **Print button**

   Each slide in the presentation prints.

4. Click the **File tab** on the ribbon, click **Print**, then click the **Full Page Slides button** in the Settings group

   The Print Layout gallery opens. In this gallery, you can specify what you want to print (slides, handouts, notes pages, or outline), as well as other print options. To save paper when you are reviewing your slides, you can print in handout format, which lets you print up to nine slides per page. The options you choose in the Print window remain there until you change them or close the presentation.

   Quick Tip
   To print slides appropriate in size for overhead transparencies, click the Design tab, click the Slide Size button in the Customize group, click Custom Slide Size, click the Slides sized for arrow, then click Overhead.

5. Click **3 Slides**, click the **Color button** in the Settings group, then click **Pure Black and White**

   PowerPoint removes the color and displays the slides as thumbnails next to blank lines, as shown in **Figure 1-21**. Using the Handouts with three slides per page printing option is a great way to print your presentation when you want to provide a way for audience members to take notes. Printing using the pure black-and-white option prints without any gray tones, which can save printer ink.

6. Click the **Print button**

   The presentation prints three slides of the presentation per page as thumbnails next to blank lines.

7. Click the **File tab** on the ribbon, then click **Close**

   If you have made changes to your presentation, a Microsoft PowerPoint alert box opens asking you if you want to save the changes you have made to your presentation file.

8. Click **Save**, if necessary, to close the alert box

   Your presentation closes.

9. **sam↑** Click the **Close button** on the Title bar

   The PowerPoint program closes, and you return to the Windows desktop.

Figure 1-20: Print window

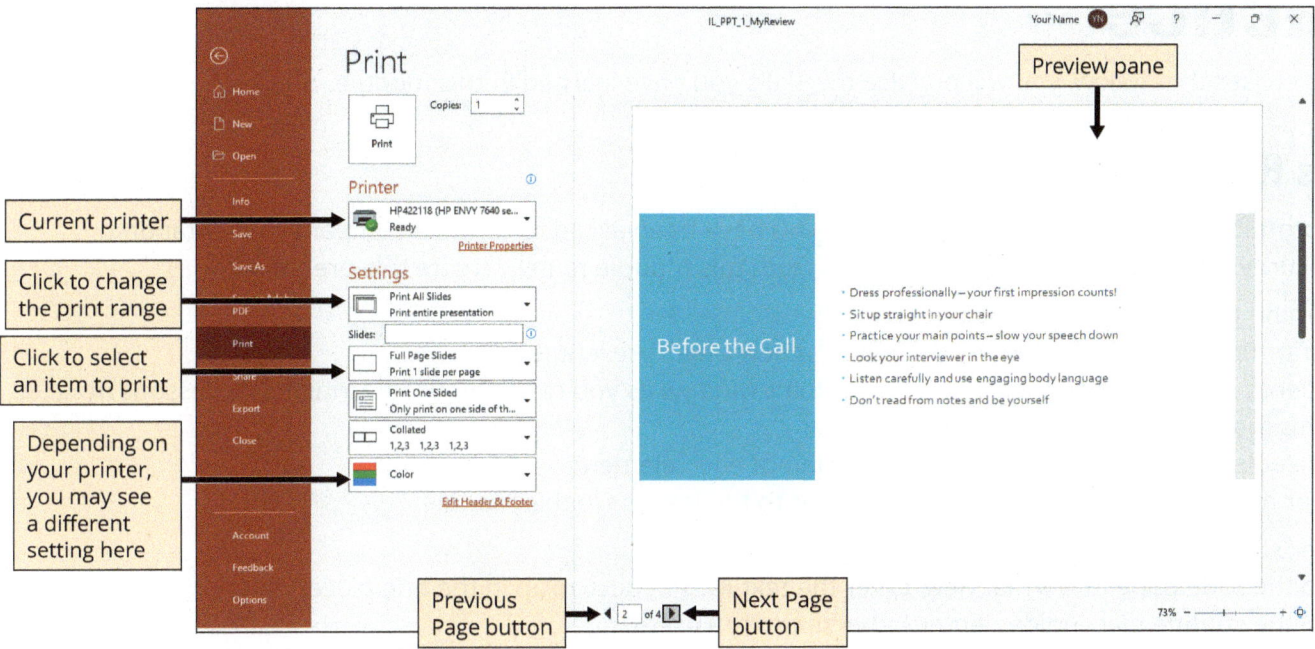

Figure 1-21: Print window with changed settings

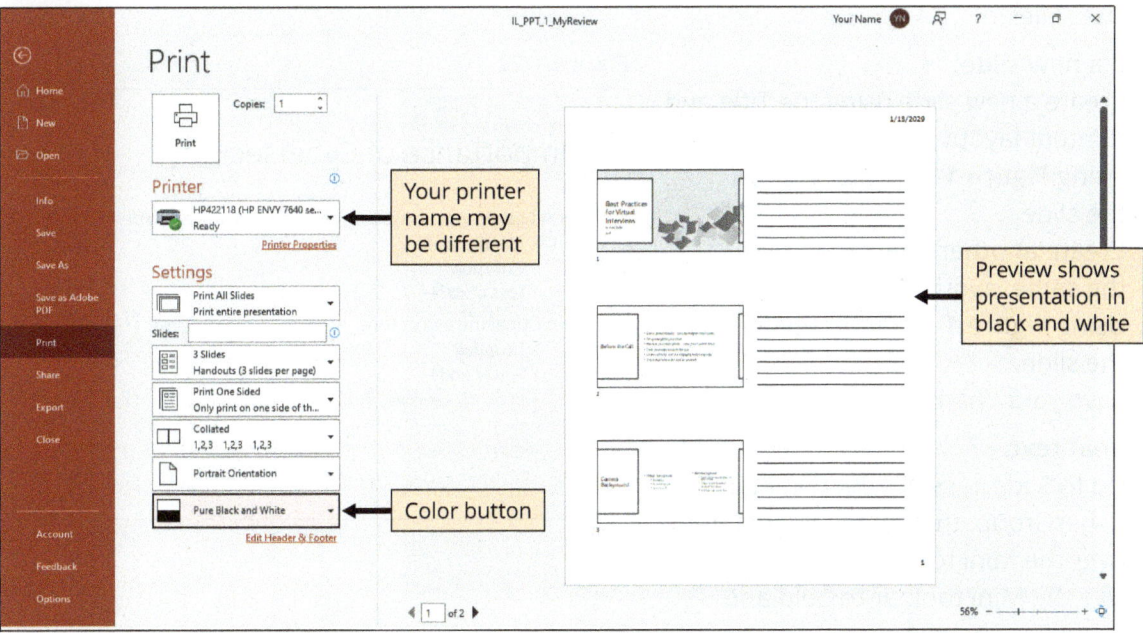

Office for the Web Apps

Some Office programs, PowerPoint for example, include the capability to incorporate feedback—called online collaboration—across the Internet or a company network. Using **cloud computing** (work done in a virtual environment), you can take advantage of web programs called Microsoft 365, which are simplified versions of the programs found in the Microsoft Office suite. Because these programs are online, they take up no computer disk space and are accessed using Microsoft OneDrive, a free service from Microsoft. Using Microsoft OneDrive, you and your colleagues can create and store documents in the "cloud" and make the documents available to whomever you grant access. To use Microsoft OneDrive, you need to create a free Microsoft account, which you obtain at the Microsoft website.

Practice

In the exercises that follow, you will practice the skills you have learned in this module.

Skills Review

As the production assistant for LB Cybergroup, you have been asked to create a company presentation on cybersecurity. You will use PowerPoint features from this module to help create this presentation.

1. **Examine the PowerPoint window.**
   a. Start PowerPoint, if necessary then open a new blank presentation.
   b. Identify as many elements of the PowerPoint window as you can without referring to the lessons in this module.
   c. Be able to describe the purpose or function of each element.
   d. For any elements you cannot identify, refer to the lessons in this module.

2. **Enter slide text.**
   a. In the Slide pane in Normal view, enter the text **KLB CyberGroup** in the title placeholder.
   b. In the subtitle placeholder, enter **Cybersecurity Threats**.
   c. On the next line of the placeholder, enter your name.
   d. Deselect the text object.
   e. Save the presentation using the file name **IL_PPT_1_Security** to the location where you store your Data Files.

3. **Add a new slide.**
   a. Create a new slide using the Title and Content layout.
   b. Using **Figure 1-22**, enter text on the slide.
   c. Create another new slide using the same layout.
   d. Using **Figure 1-23**, enter text on the slide.
   e. Save your changes.

4. **Format text.**
   a. Go to Slide 1, select the text KLB CyberGroup, then move the pointer over the Mini toolbar.
   b. Use the Mini toolbar to bold and underline the text.
   c. Select the text Cybersecurity Threats, use the Mini toolbar to italicize it, then increase its font size to 72 points.
   d. Go to Slide 2, select the word "benefit", use the Font Color arrow to change its color to Purple under Standard Colors.
   e. Go to Slide 3, select the word "extort" below "Ransomware", use the Font Size arrow to change its size to 32.
   f. Use the Font button to change the font to Arial Black, then save your changes.

Figure 1-22

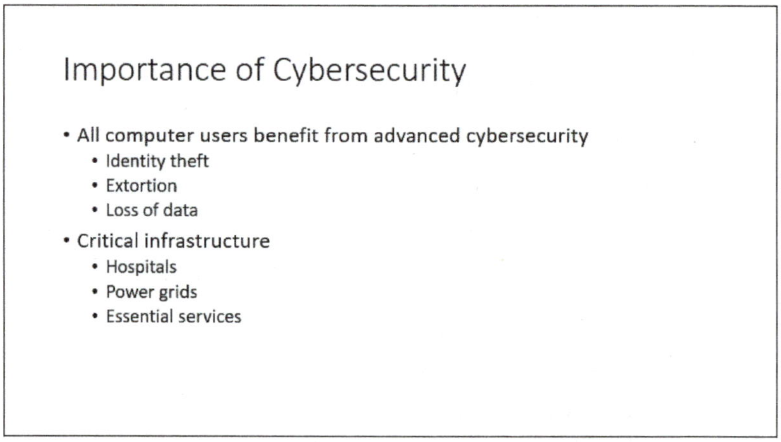

Importance of Cybersecurity

- All computer users benefit from advanced cybersecurity
  - Identity theft
  - Extortion
  - Loss of data
- Critical infrastructure
  - Hospitals
  - Power grids
  - Essential services

Figure 1-23

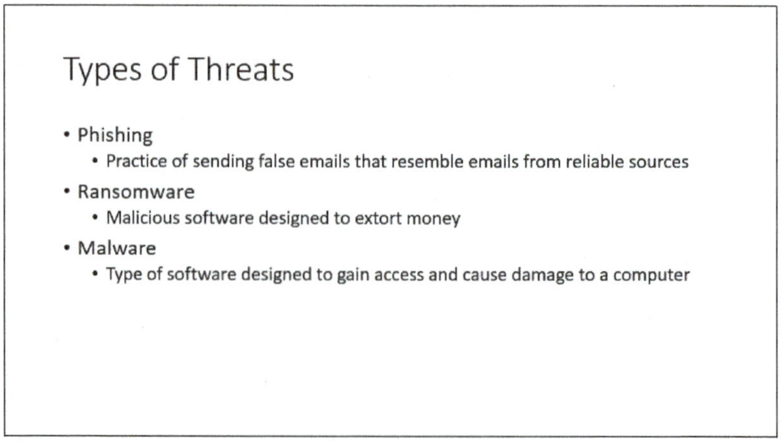

Types of Threats

- Phishing
  - Practice of sending false emails that resemble emails from reliable sources
- Ransomware
  - Malicious software designed to extort money
- Malware
  - Type of software designed to gain access and cause damage to a computer

5. **Apply a design theme.**
   a. Select the Design tab.
   b. Using the Themes group More button, point to all of the themes, noting the effect of each one.
   c. Locate the Wisp theme, then apply it to the selected slide.
   d. Go to Slide 1, click the Themes group More button, locate the Circuit theme, then apply it to Slide 1.
   e. Apply the Circuit theme to all of the slides in the presentation.
   f. Select the first design in the Design Ideas pane, then close the Design Ideas pane.
   g. Use the Next Slide button to move to Slide 2, then save your changes.

6. **Compare presentation views.**
   a. Go to the View tab, then click the Slide Sorter button in the Presentation Views group.
   b. Click the Normal button in the Presentation Views group, then click the Notes button on the status bar again to hide the Notes pane.
   c. Click the Notes button on the status bar, then click the Next Slide button.
   d. Click the Slide Show button on the status bar.
   e. Click the More slide show options button, click Show Presenter View, then click the Pause button.
   f. Click the More slide show options button, then click Hide Presenter View.
   g. Advance the slides until a black screen appears, then click to end the presentation.
   h. Save your changes.

7. **Insert and resize a picture.**
   a. Select Slide 2 in the thumbnail pane, then go to the Home tab.
   b. Use the Layout button to change the slide layout to Two Content, then insert the picture **Support_PPT_1_Hackers.jpg** from the location where you store your Data Files.
   c. Close the Design Ideas pane, then drag the picture's left-middle sizing handle to the left.
   d. Use the Undo button to undo the resizing, then drag the bottom-left corner sizing handle down to the left about a half inch to increase the picture size.
   e. Drag the Zoom slider on the status bar to the right until 100% appears next to the Zoom slider.
   f. Click the Fit slide to current window button on the status bar, save your changes, then close the presentation.

8. **Check spelling.**
   a. Open the presentation IL_PPT_1-2.pptx from the location where you store your Data Files, add your name to the title slide, then save it as **IL_PPT_ 1_ClockWorks**.
   b. Use the Next Slide button at the bottom of the vertical scroll bar to view Slide 2.
   c. Use the Previous Slide button at the bottom of the vertical scroll bar to return to Slide 1, then go to the Review tab.
   d. Use the Spelling button in the Proofing group to begin spell checking. The word "ClockWorks" on Slide 1 appears in the Spelling tab.
   e. Click Ignore All, make sure the word "Employee" on Slide 2 is selected in the Spelling pane, then click the Change All button. The word "management" is also misspelled. Depending on the language settings in your Office installation, your spellcheck dictionary may not flag "employe" as incorrectly spelled. You can just continue with the spell check.
   f. Click the Change button in the Spelling pane.
   g. Click OK in the alert box, then save your changes.

9. **Print a PowerPoint presentation.**
   a. Print all the slides as handouts, 3 Slides, in color, if you have a color printer.
   b. Close the file, saving your changes.
   c. Exit PowerPoint.

Independent Challenge 1

You work in the School of Nursing for the State University in Houston, Texas. You have been asked to put together a presentation on the University's summer internship program. The presentation will be used to recruit students from the Nursing program to fill internships offered in hospitals and other medical facilities throughout the state.

a. Start PowerPoint, then open a new blank presentation.
b. In the title placeholder on Slide 1, type **State University**.
c. In the subtitle placeholder, type **School of Nursing Summer Program**, press ENTER, then type your name.
d. Underline the text School of Nursing Summer Program, then italicize your name.
e. Save your presentation with the file name **IL_PPT_1_StateU** to the location where you store your Data Files.
f. Use **Figure 1-24** and **Figure 1-25** to add two more slides to your presentation then select Slide 1.
g. Apply the Organic design theme to the presentation, click the second design theme from the top in the Design Ideas pane, then close the Design Ideas pane.
h. On Slide 3, format the color, font type, and font size of the words "Shift work" to Green, 24 pt, Arial.
i. Use the buttons on the View tab to switch between PowerPoint's views, then open and close Presenter View.
j. Print the presentation using handouts, 3 Slides, in pure black and white.
k. Save and close the file, then exit PowerPoint.

Figure 1-24

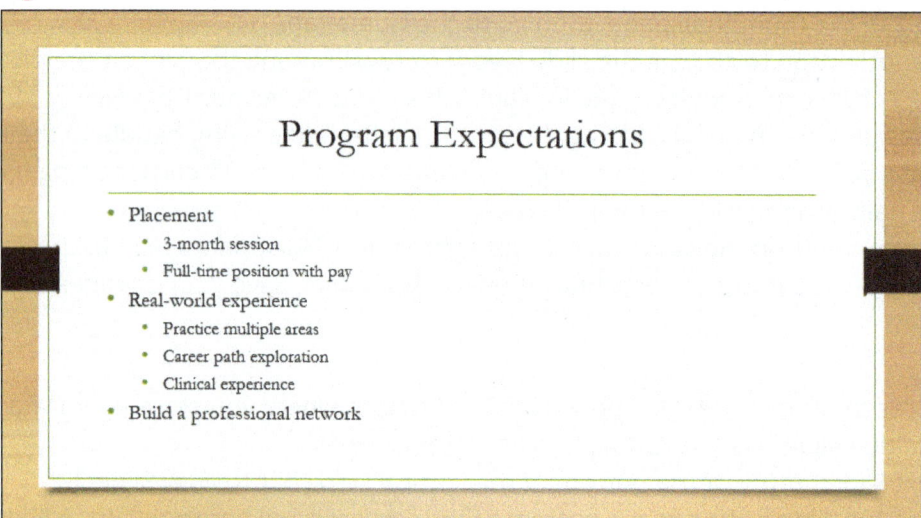

Figure 1-25

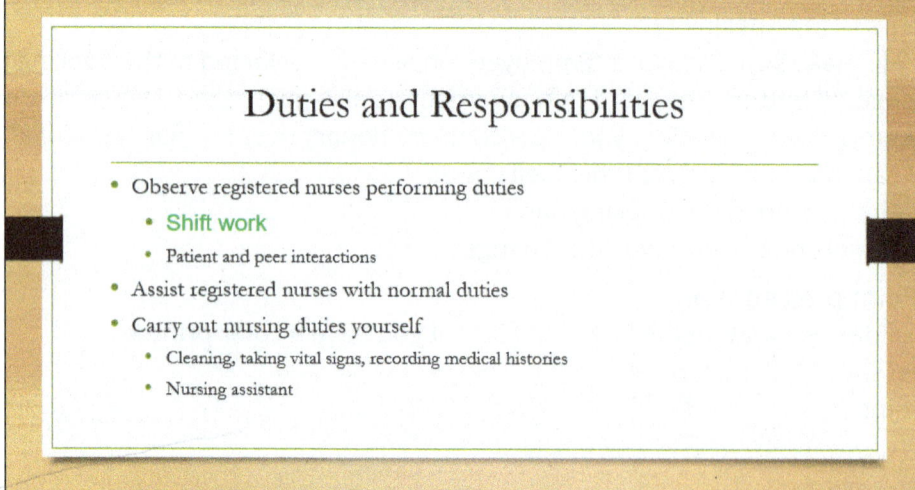

Independent Challenge 2

You work for World Systems, a business that offers high-speed broadband Internet service and network server management to its customers. One of your jobs is to present company products and services to potential corporate clients. You have already started working on the presentation and now you add and resize a picture, add a design theme, and run a spell check.

   a. Start PowerPoint, open the presentation IL_PPT_1-3.pptx from the location where you store your Data Files, and save it as **IL_PPT_1_World**.
   b. Apply the Celestial design theme to all the slides, apply a design theme from the Design Ideas pane similar to one shown in **Figure 1-26**, then close the Design Ideas pane.
   c. Spell-check the presentation. There is a misspelled word on Slide 3.
   d. Drag Slide 3 above Slide 2 in the thumbnail pane.
   e. On Slide 3, change the slide layout to Two Content, then Insert the picture **Support_PPT_1_Office.jpg** from the location where you store your Data Files into the right content placeholder.
   f. Resize the picture using a middle sizing handle, then undo the action by clicking the Undo button.
   g. Enlarge the picture using the lower-right corner sizing handle, click the second design in the Design Ideas pane, or one similar to the one shown in **Figure 1-27**, then close the Design Ideas pane.
   h. View the presentation using all the views on the status bar. Run through the slide show at least once.
   i. Open and close Presenter view.
   j. Add your name and today's date to Slide 1, then close the presentation and exit PowerPoint.

Figure 1-26

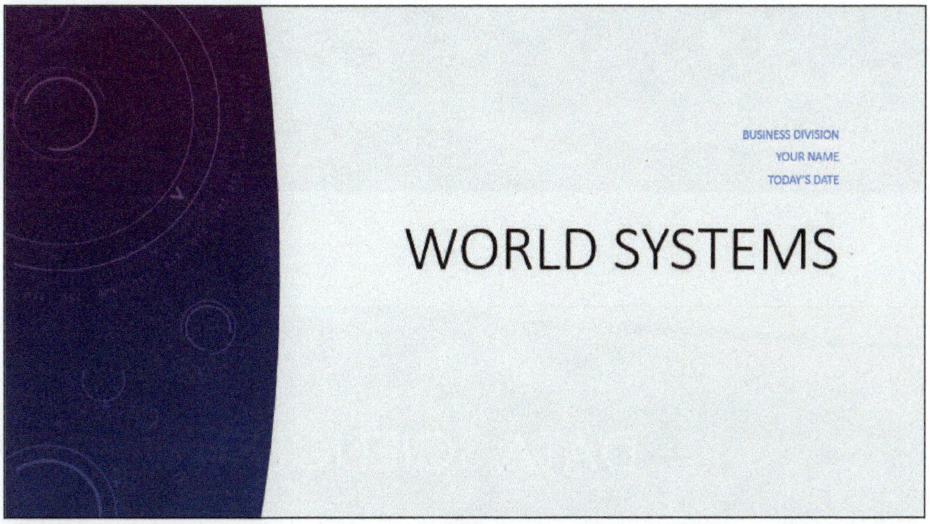

Figure 1-27

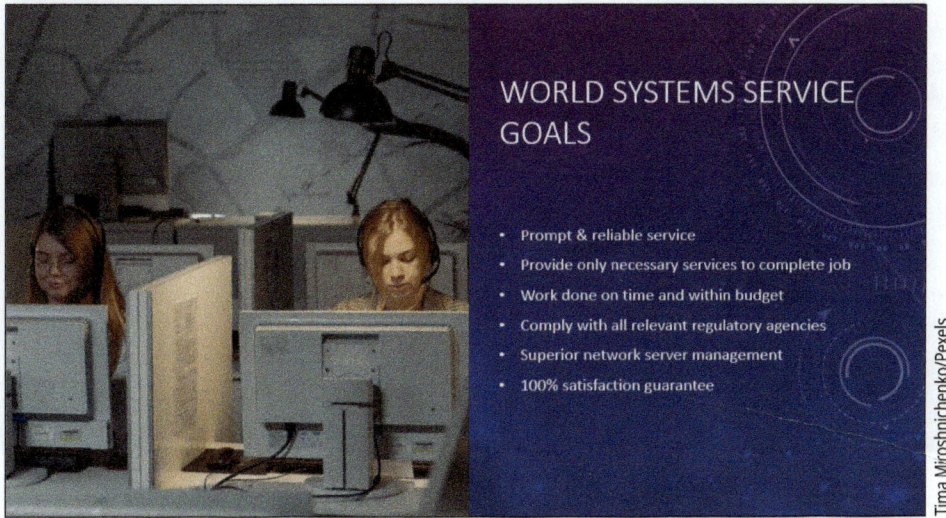

Tima Miroshnichenko/Pexels

Visual Workshop

Create the presentation shown in **Figure 1-28** and **Figure 1-29**. Make sure you include your name on the title slide. Insert the picture Support_PPT_1_Hackers.jpg on Slide 2 as shown in **Figure 1-29**, then spell check the presentation and fix any issues. Save the presentation as **IL_PPT_1_Morgan** to the location where you store your Data Files. Print the slides.

Figure 1-28

Figure 1-29

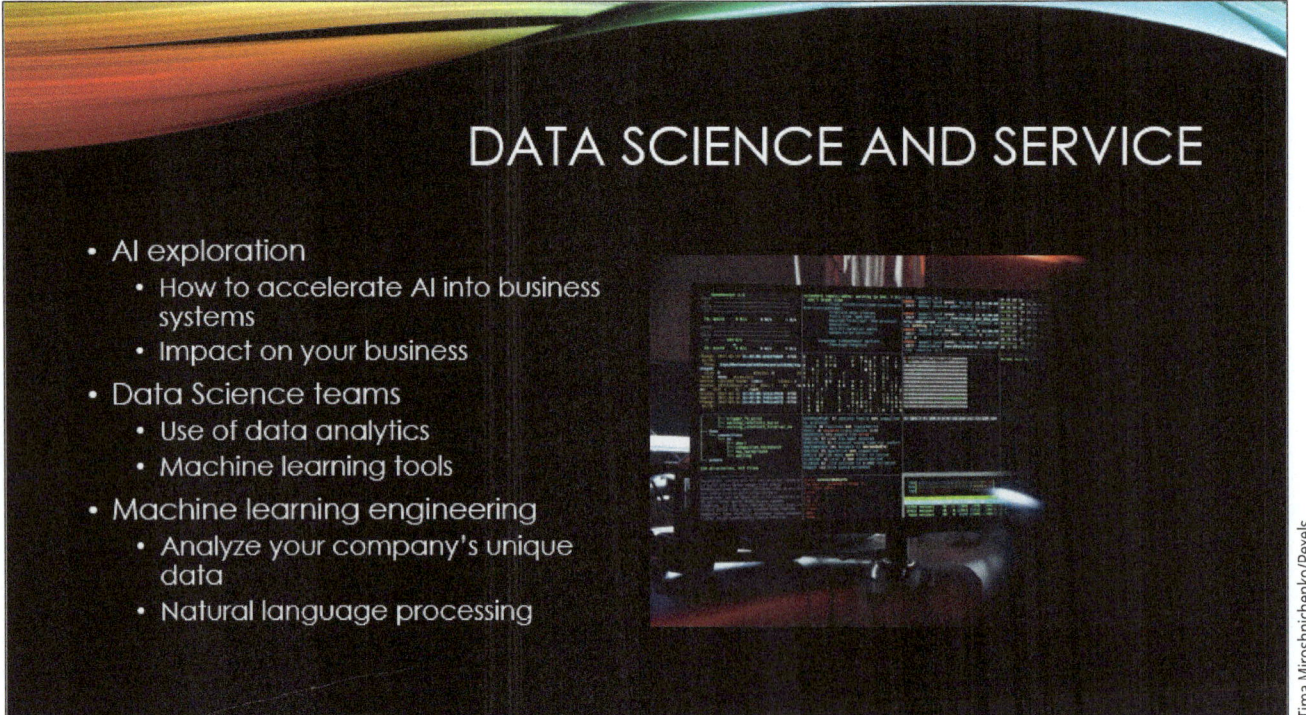

PowerPoint **Module 2**

Modifying a Presentation

Case

You continue working on your company team and workflow presentation. In this module, you'll create a SmartArt graphic, draw and work with shapes, add slide footer information, and set slide transitions and timings in the presentation.

Module Objectives

After completing this module, you will be able to:

- Convert text to SmartArt
- Insert and style shapes
- Rotate and modify shapes
- Rearrange and modify shapes
- Edit and duplicate shapes
- Align and group objects
- Add slide footers
- Set slide transitions and timings

Files You Will Need

IL_PPT_2-1.pptx
IL_PPT_2-2.pptx
IL_PPT_2-3.pptx
IL_PPT_2-4.pptx
IL_PPT_2-5.pptx

Convert Text to SmartArt

Case You want the presentation to appear visually dynamic, so you convert the text on Slide 4 to a SmartArt graphic.

Objectives
- Create a SmartArt graphic
- Modify the SmartArt design
- Change the SmartArt layout

Sometimes when you are working with text, it just doesn't capture your attention. The ability to convert text to a SmartArt graphic provides a creative way to convey a message to your audience using text and graphics. A **SmartArt** graphic is a professional-quality diagram using circles, squares, or arrows that graphically illustrates text. For example, you can show steps in a process or timeline, show proportional relationships, or show how parts relate to a whole. You can create a SmartArt graphic from scratch or create one by converting existing text you have entered on a slide.

Steps

1. **sam↓** Start PowerPoint, open the presentation **IL_PPT_2-1.pptx** from the location where you store your Data Files, then save it as **IL_PPT_2_XCR**

   A presentation with the new filename appears in the PowerPoint window.

2. Click the **Slide 5 thumbnail** in the thumbnail pane, click **Owner** in the text object, then click the **Convert to SmartArt Graphic button** in the Paragraph group

   A gallery of SmartArt graphic layouts opens. As with many features in PowerPoint, you can preview how your text will look before applying the SmartArt graphic layout by using PowerPoint's Live Preview feature. You can review each SmartArt graphic layout and see how it changes the appearance of the text.

3. Move over several **SmartArt graphic layouts** in the gallery

   Notice how the text becomes part of the graphic and changes each time you move the pointer over a different graphic layout. SmartArt graphic names appear in ScreenTips.

   Quick Tip: Text objects in the SmartArt graphic can be moved and edited like any other text object in PowerPoint.

4. Click the **Continuous Block Process layout** in the SmartArt graphics gallery

   A SmartArt graphic appears on the slide in place of the text object, and the SmartArt Design tab opens on the ribbon, as shown in **Figure 2-1**. A SmartArt graphic consists of two parts: the SmartArt graphic and a Text pane where you type and edit text.

   Quick Tip: To open the Text pane, click the Text pane control on the SmartArt graphic.

5. Click the **Text pane control** on the SmartArt graphic to close the Text pane, click the **More button** in the Layouts group, click **More Layouts** to open the Choose a SmartArt Graphic dialog box, click **Matrix**, click the **Grid Matrix layout icon**, then click **OK**

   The text pane closes and the SmartArt graphic changes to the new graphic layout. You can change how the SmartArt graphic looks by applying a SmartArt Style. A **SmartArt Style** is a preset combination of simple and 3-D formatting options that follows the presentation theme.

6. Move slowly over the styles in the SmartArt Styles group, then click the **More button** in the SmartArt Styles group

   A Live Preview of each style is displayed on the SmartArt graphic. The SmartArt styles are organized into sections; the top group offers suggestions for the best match for the document, and the bottom group shows you all the possible 3-D styles that are available.

   Quick Tip: To convert a SmartArt graphic to a standard text object, click the Convert button in the Reset group, then click Convert to Text.

7. Move over the styles in the gallery, click **Powder** in the 3-D section, click in a blank area of the slide outside the SmartArt graphic, then save your work

   Notice how the Powder style adds a shadow and a beveled edge to achieve a 3-D effect. Compare your screen to **Figure 2-2**.

Figure 2-1: Text converted to a Continuous Block Process layout SmartArt graphic

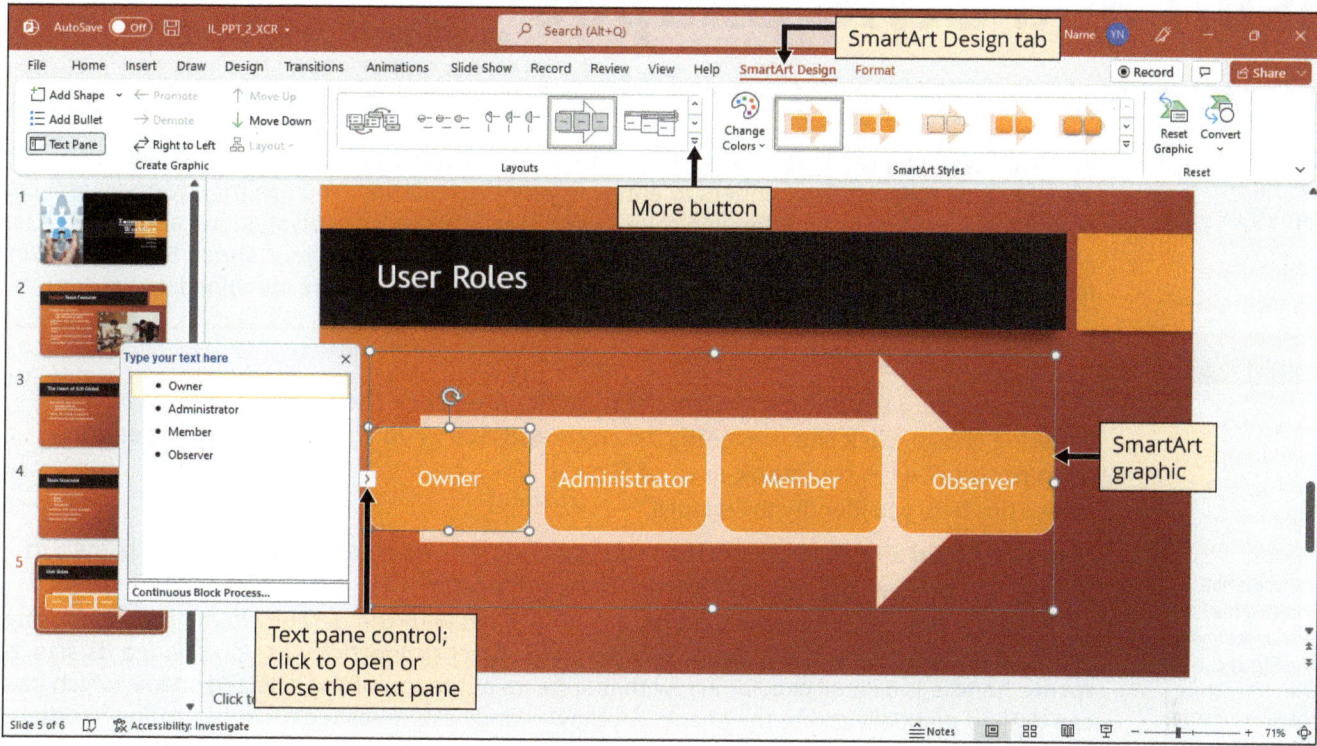

Figure 2-2: Final Grid Matrix with Powder 3-D effect SmartArt graphic

Fauxels/Pexels

Entering and printing notes

You can add notes to your slides when you want to remember certain facts during a presentation or when there is additional information you want to print for your audience. Notes do not appear on the slides when you run a slide show. Use the Notes pane in Normal view or Notes Page view to enter notes for your slides. To open or close the Notes pane, click the Notes button on the status bar. To enter text notes on a slide, click in the Notes pane, then type the note. If you want to insert graphics as notes, you must use Notes Page view. To open Notes Page view, click the View tab on the ribbon, then click the Notes Page button in the Presentation Views group. You can print your notes by clicking the File tab on the ribbon to open Backstage view. Click Print, click Full Page Slides in the Settings group (this button retains the last setting for what was printed previously so it might differ) to open the gallery, and then click Notes Pages. Once you verify your print settings, click the Print button. If you don't enter any notes in the Notes pane and print the notes pages, the slides print as large thumbnails with blank space below the thumbnails to handwrite notes.

Insert and Style Shapes

Case You decide to draw some shapes on Slide 4 of your presentation that complement the slide content.

Objectives
- Create a shape
- Modify a shape's style

In PowerPoint, you can insert many different types of shapes, including lines, geometric figures, arrows, stars, callouts, and banners to enhance your presentation. You can modify many aspects of a shape, including its fill color, line color, and line style, as well as add shadows and 3-D effects. A quick way to alter the appearance of a shape is to apply a Quick Style. A **Quick Style** is a set of formatting options that determines how fonts, fill color, and effects are combined.

Steps

1. **Click the Slide 4 thumbnail in the thumbnail pane, click the Shapes button in the Drawing group, click the Isosceles Triangle button △ in the Basic Shapes section, then position ✛ in the blank area of Slide 4**
   ScreenTips help you identify the shapes.

Trouble
If your shape is not approximately the same size as the one shown in **Figure 2-3**, drag one of the corner sizing handles to resize the object.

2. **Press and hold SHIFT, drag ✛ down and to the right to create the shape, as shown in Figure 2-3, release the mouse button, then release SHIFT**
   An isosceles triangle shape appears on the slide, filled with the default theme color. Pressing SHIFT while you create the object maintains the object proportions as you change its size. A **rotate handle** is a small circular arrow that appears at the top of the selected shape, which you can drag to manually rotate the shape. A yellow-orange circle—called an **adjustment handle**—appears in the top portion of the shape that you drag to change the shape's proportions. Some shapes have an adjustment handle that can be moved to change the most prominent feature of an object, in this case, the shape of the triangle.

3. **Drag the adjustment handle to the right, over the right sizing handle**
   The tip of the triangle moves and changes the shape to a right triangle.

4. **Click the Shape Fill arrow in the Shape Styles group**
   The color palette that appears shows the ten theme colors associated with the current design theme. These colors are used to color the slide background, text, and graphic elements, such as lines and shapes. Theme colors vary depending on the theme applied to your presentation. Below the Theme Colors in the palette are ten Standard Colors, which remain the same regardless of which theme is applied. Additional options are listed in the lower part of the palette.

5. **Click Aqua, Accent 4**
   A blue fill color is applied to the shape.

6. **Click the Shape Outline arrow in the Shape Styles group, click White, Text 1, click the Shape Outline arrow again, point to Dashes, then click the Dash outline style**
   The shape outline changes to a white dash. You also have the option of using a Quick Style to format a shape.

7. **Click the More button ▼ in the Shape Styles group, move ⇗ over the styles in the gallery to review the effects on the shape, then click Intense Effect—Lavender, Accent 5**
   A lavender Quick Style with coordinated gradient fill, line, and shadow color is applied to the shape.

Quick Tip
To change the transparency of a shape or text object filled with a color, right-click the object, click Format Shape, click Fill in the Format Shape pane, then move the Transparency slider.

8. **Click the Shape Effects button in the Shape Styles group, point to Bevel, move ⇗ over the effect options to review the effect on the shape, then click Convex**
   A bevel appears around the shape, as shown in **Figure 2-4**.

9. **Click a blank area of the slide, then save your work**
   Clicking a blank area of the slide deselects all selected objects.

Figure 2-3: Triangle shape added to slide

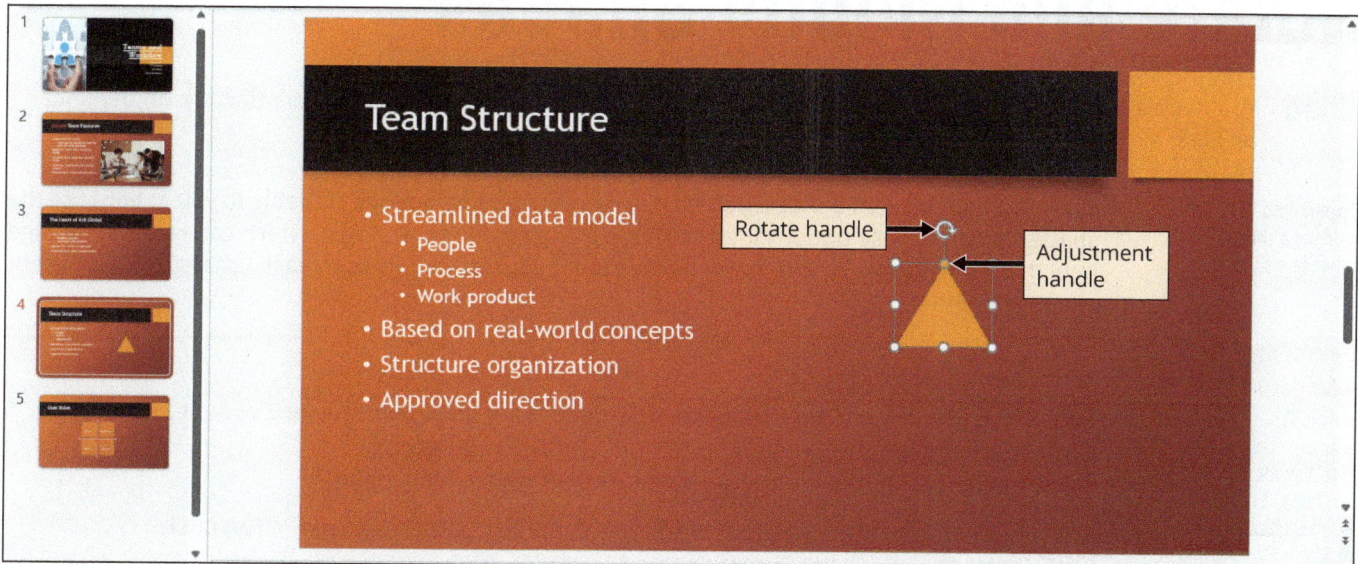

Fauxels/Pexels

Figure 2-4: Styled triangle shape

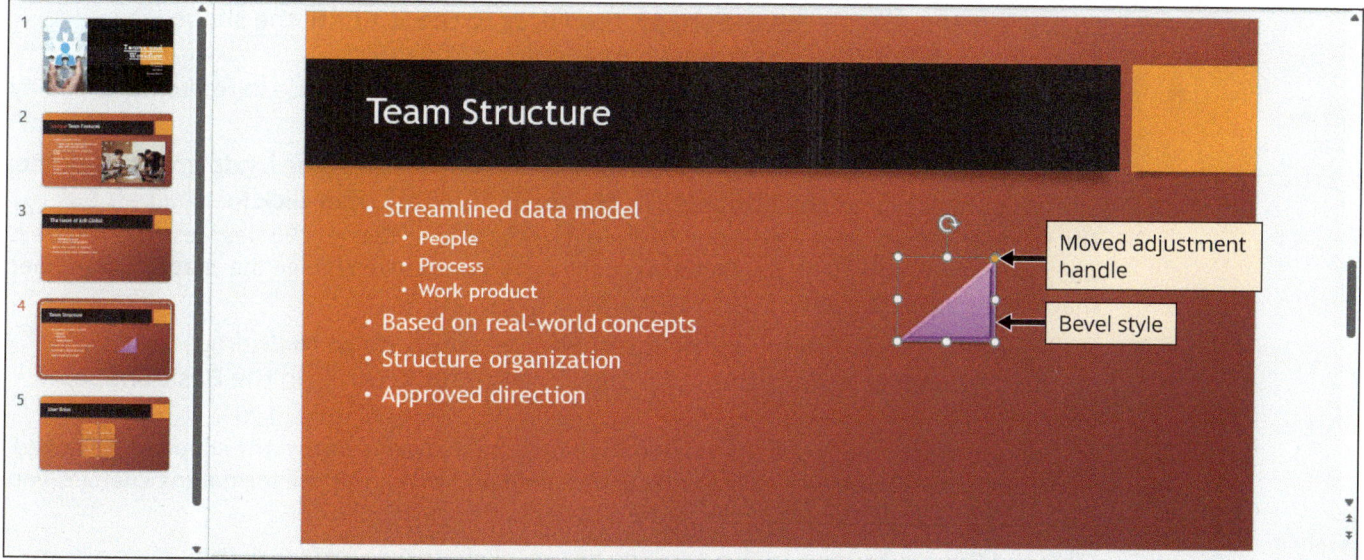

Fauxels/Pexels

Using the Eyedropper to match colors

As you develop your presentation and work with different shapes and pictures, sometimes from other sources, there may be a certain color that is not in the theme colors of the presentation that you want to capture and apply to objects in your presentation. To capture a color on a specific slide, select any object on the slide, click any button with a color feature, such as the Shape Fill arrow or the Shape Outline arrow in the Shape Styles group on the Shape Format tab, then click Eyedropper. Move the ✏ over the color you want to capture and pause. As you point to a color, a Live Preview of the color appears and the RGB (Red Green Blue) values, called coordinates, appear in a ScreenTip. When you have pointed to the color you want to capture, click to apply that color to the selected object. The new color now appears in any color gallery under Recent Colors. If you decide not to capture a new color, press ESC to close the Eyedropper without making any change.

Module 2 Modifying a Presentation

Rotate and Modify Shapes

Case You decide that the shape you created can be more visually appealing, so you continue to work on the shape on Slide 4.

Objectives
- Format a shape
- Change a shape

Once you have created a shape, you have several formatting options available to you to enhance the shape. Some of these options include flipping and rotating the shape, which can radically change how the shape looks. Or, if a shape doesn't meet your needs, you can easily change to a different shape altogether.

Steps

Quick Tip
To apply a picture fill to a shape, select the shape, click the Shape Fill button in the Shape Styles group on the Shape Format tab, click Picture, then locate and insert a picture.

1. Select the **triangle shape** on Slide 4, if necessary click the **Shape Format tab** on the ribbon, then click the **Rotate button** in the Arrange group
   The Rotate menu appears with two rotate options and two flip options.

2. Move over all of the options to review the effect on the shape, then click **Flip Vertical**
   Notice that the triangle top is now pointing down with the rotate handle on the bottom right, indicating that the shape has flipped vertically, as shown in **Figure 2-5**.

3. Click the **rotate handle** on the shape, then drag to the left until the shape is approximately 45 degrees from where it started
   The top of the shape is now pointing toward the text object. You decide to rotate the shape by a specific amount.

4. Click the **Home tab** on the ribbon, click the **Undo button** in the Undo group, click the **Shape Format tab** on the ribbon, click the **Rotate button**, then click **Rotate Left 90°**
   The top of the shape is now pointing to the right side of the slide. It is 90 degrees from where it was just pointing and the rotate handle is to the right. It is easy to change the shape to any other shape in the shapes gallery.

5. Click the **Edit Shape button** in the Insert Shapes group, point to **Change Shape** to open the shapes gallery, then click the **Pentagon button** in the Basic Shapes section
   The triangle shape changes to a pentagon shape. Notice that even though the shape has changed, it is still rotated 90 degrees from its original position and maintains the formatting changes you have already applied. You decide to rotate it back to its original position.

6. Click the **Rotate button** in the Arrange group, click **Rotate Left 90°**, then click a blank area of the slide
   The shape is rotated back to its original position, as shown in **Figure 2-6**.

7. Click the **Slide 4 thumbnail** in the thumbnail pane, then save your work

Figure 2-5: Flipped triangle shape

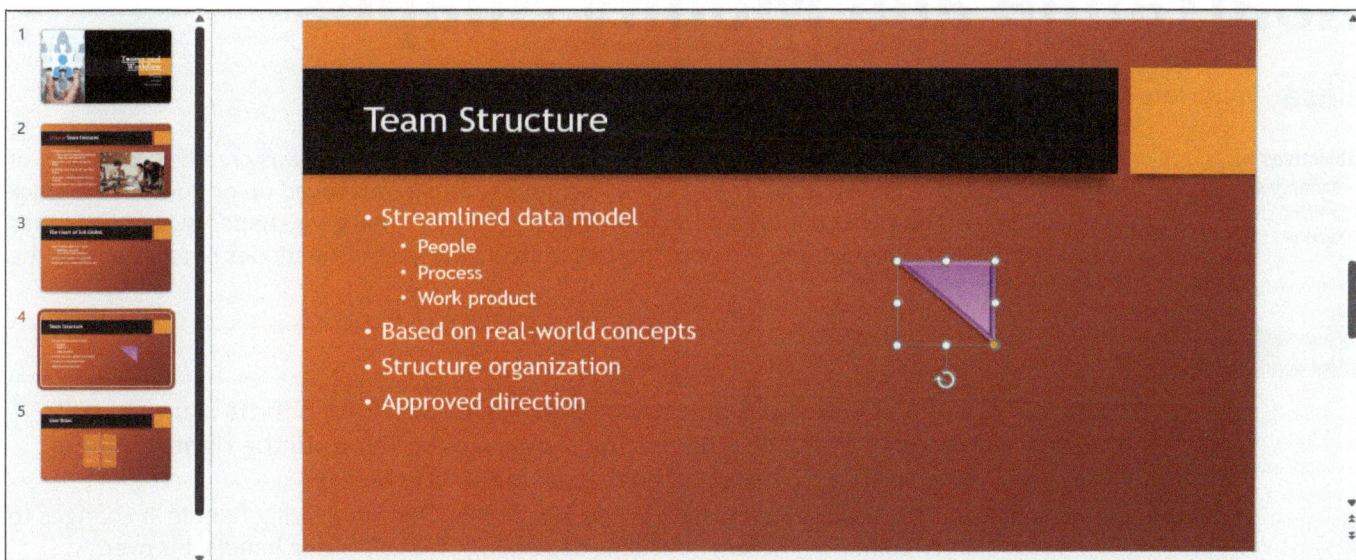

Fauxels/Pexels

Figure 2-6: Pentagon shape

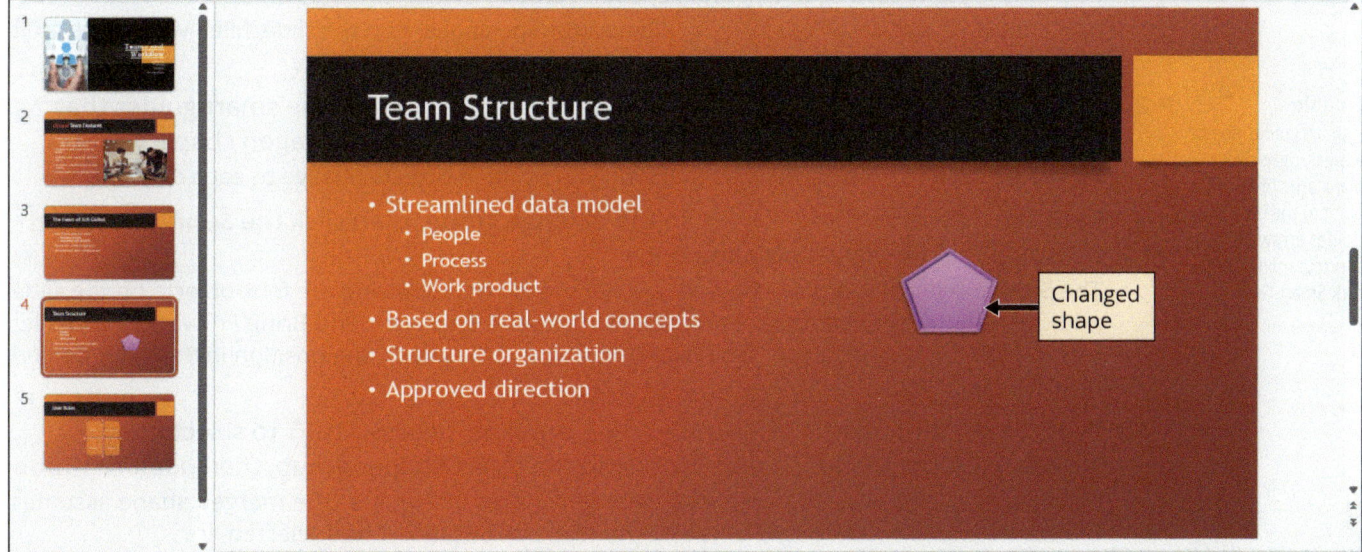

Fauxels/Pexels

Inking a slide

In Normal view, you can add freehand pen and highlighter marks, also known as **inking**, to the slides of your presentation to emphasize information. To begin inking, go to the slide you want to mark up, click the Draw tab on the ribbon, then click one of the drawing tools in the Drawing Tools group. If you are using a touchscreen, you can use your finger or a stylus to mark up a slide. To customize the thickness or color of your pen, click the down arrow on the selected pen. You can also click the Highlighter button in the Drawing Tools group to insert highlighter strokes on your slide. To erase inking on the slide, click the Eraser tool in the Drawing Tools group, then click the ink or mark you want to erase. To exit inking mode, click the Draw button in the Input Mode group.

Rearrange and Modify Shapes

Case You create a diamond shape on Slide 4, then merge it with the pentagon shape.

Objectives
- Rearrange shapes
- Combine shapes together

Every object on a slide is placed, or stacked, on the slide in the order it was created, like a deck of cards placed one on top of another. Each object on a slide can be moved up or down in the stack depending on how you want the objects to look on the slide. **Merging** shapes, which combines multiple shapes, provides you the potential to create unique geometric shapes not available in the shapes gallery.

Steps

1. Click **Streamlined** in the text object, position ⟲ over the **right-middle sizing handle** until it becomes ⟺, then drag the **sizing handle** to the left until the right border of the text object is next to the word "concepts" in the text object
   The width of the text object decreases. When you position ⟲ over a sizing handle, it changes to ⟺. This pointer points in different directions depending on which sizing handle it is over.

2. Click a blank area of the slide, click the **Shapes button** in the Drawing group, click the **Diamond button** ◇ in the Basic Shapes section, press and hold SHIFT, drag down and to the right to create the shape, then release SHIFT
   Compare your screen to **Figure 2-7**. A diamond shape appears on the slide, filled with the default theme accent color. You can move shapes by dragging them on the slide.

Trouble
If smart guides do not appear, right-click a blank area of the slide, point to the Grid and Guides arrow on the shortcut menu, then click Smart Guides.

▶ 3. Drag the **diamond shape** over the pentagon shape, then use the smart guides that appear to position the diamond shape in the center of the pentagon shape
   Smart guides are dashed red lines that help you position objects relative to each other.

4. Click the **Selection Pane button** in the Arrange group, then click the **Send Backward button** ⌄ in the Selection pane once
   The Selection pane opens on the right side of the window showing the four objects on the slide and the order they are stacked on the slide. The Send Backward and Bring Forward buttons let you change the stacking order. The diamond shape moves back one position in the stack behind the pentagon shape.

5. Press **SHIFT**, click the **pentagon shape** on the slide, release **SHIFT** to select both shapes, click the **Merge Shapes button** in the Insert Shapes group, then point to **Union**
   The two shapes appear to merge, or combine, to form one shape. The merged shape assumes the theme and formatting style of the diamond shape because it was selected first.

Quick Tip
To move an object to the top of the stack, click the Bring Forward arrow in the Arrange group, then click Bring to Front. To move an object to the bottom of the stack, click the Send Backward arrow, then click Send to Back.

▶ 6. Move ⟲ over the other **merge shapes options** to review the effect on the shape, click a blank area of the slide, click the **diamond shape**, then click the **Bring Forward button** ⌃ in the Selection pane once
   Each merge option produces a different result. The diamond shape moves back to the top of the stack. Now, you want to see what happens when you select the pentagon shape first before you merge the two shapes together.

7. Click the **pentagon shape**, press **SHIFT**, click the **diamond shape**, release **SHIFT**, click the **Shape Format tab** on the ribbon, click the **Merge Shapes button** in the Insert Shapes group, then point to **Union**
   The merged shape adopts the theme and formatting style of the pentagon shape.

8. Point to each of the **merge shapes options**, then click **Union**
   The two shapes merge into one shape. This merge option combines the area of all shapes from the first shape you selected, so in this case, the area of the diamond shape is combined with the pentagon shape. The merged shape is identified as a sequentially numbered Freeform in the Selection pane. Refer to **Figure 2-8**.

9. Click the **Selection Pane button** in the Arrange group, click a blank area of the slide, then save your work

Rearrange and Modify Shapes   PPT 2-9

Figure 2-7: Diamond shape added to slide

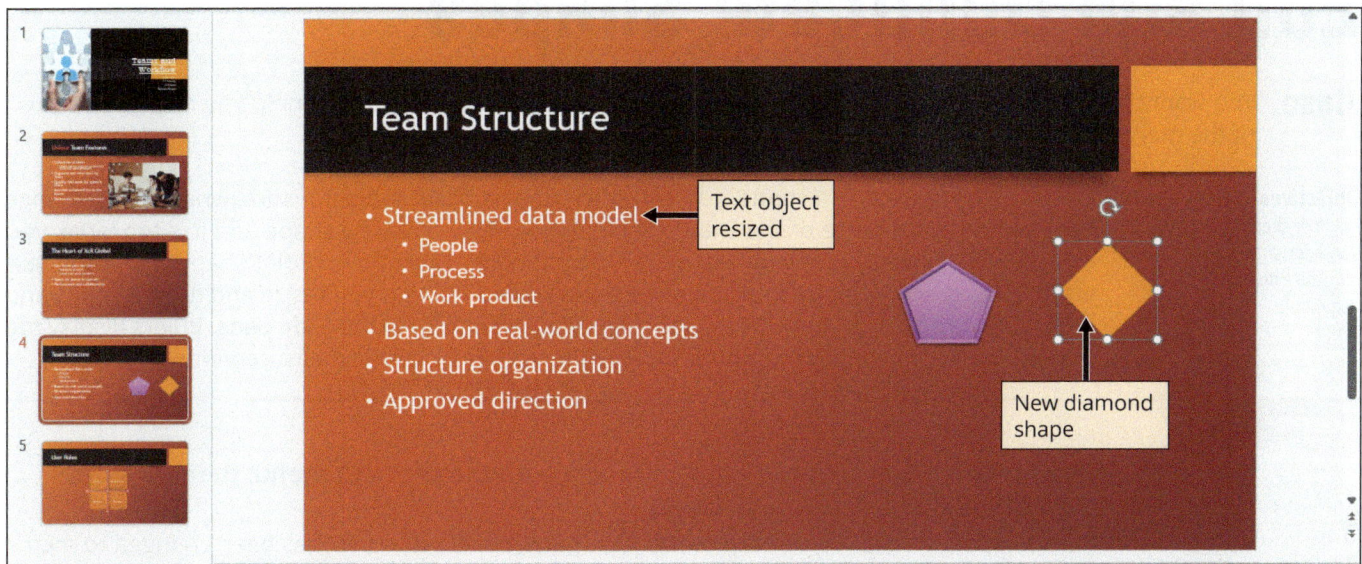

Fauxels/Pexels

Figure 2-8: New merged shape

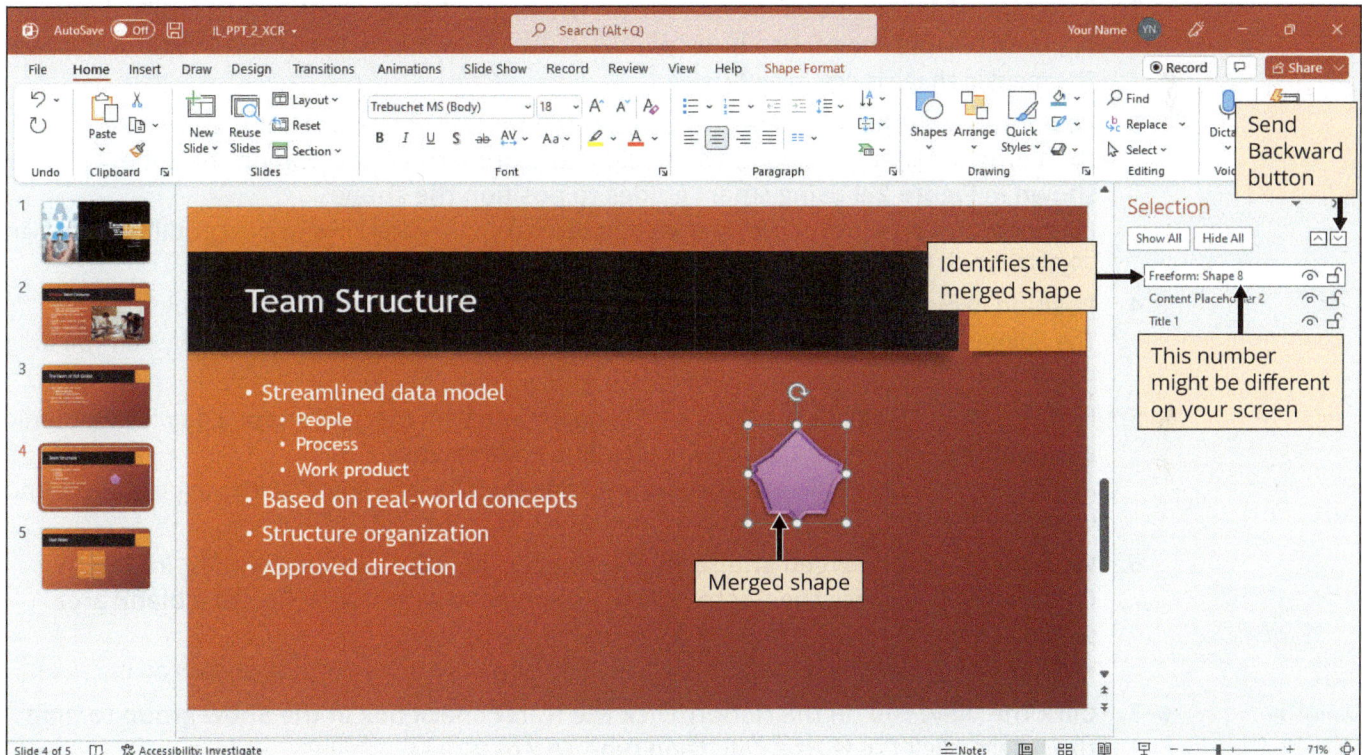

Fauxels/Pexels

Changing the size and position of shapes

Usually, when you resize a shape you can simply drag one of the corner sizing handles on the outside of the shape, but sometimes you may need to resize a shape more precisely. When you select a shape, the Shape Format tab appears on the ribbon, offering you many different formatting options, including some sizing controls located in the Size group. The Width and Height controls in the Size group allow you to change the height and width of a shape. You can also right-click an object and click Format Shape to open the Format Shape pane, which allows you to change many features of a shape, including its rotation, scale, and position on the slide.

Edit and Duplicate Shapes

Case You want three identical shapes on Slide 4. You first display the ruler on the slide to help you change the size of the merged shape you have already created, then you make copies of it.

Objectives
- Modify shape size and design
- Produce duplicate shapes

Once you have created a shape, you can still refine its basic characteristics, which helps change the size and appearance of the shape. For example, if you create a shape and it is too large, you can reduce its size by dragging any of its sizing handles. Most PowerPoint shapes can have text attached to them. All shapes can be moved and copied. To help you resize and move shapes and other objects precisely, PowerPoint has rulers you can display in the Slide pane. Rulers display the measurement system your computer uses, either inches or metric measurements.

Steps

1. **Right-click a blank area of Slide 4, click Ruler on the shortcut menu, then click the edge of the merged shape to select it**
   Rulers appear on the left and top of the Slide pane. Unless the ruler has been changed to metric measurements, it is divided into inches with ½" and ⅛" marks. Notice the current location of the pointer is identified on both rulers by a small dotted red line.

2. **Drag the middle-right sizing handle on the merged shape to the right approximately ½", then release the mouse button**
   The merged shape is now slightly wider.

3. **Position pointer over the left edge of the selected merged shape so that it changes to move pointer, then drag the merged shape to the 0.00 horizontal ruler position on the slide, as shown in Figure 2-9 using smart guides to position the shape**
   PowerPoint uses a series of evenly spaced horizontal and vertical lines—called **gridlines**—to align objects, which force objects to "snap" to the grid.

4. **Position pointer over the bottom part of the merged shape, then press and hold CTRL**
   The pointer changes to copy pointer, indicating that PowerPoint makes a copy of the shape when you drag the mouse.

5. **Holding CTRL, drag the merged shape down until the merged shape copy is in a blank area of the slide, release the mouse button, then release CTRL**
   A duplicate copy of the merged shape appears on the slide and smart guides appear above and below the shape as you drag the new shape, which helps you align shapes.

6. **With the second merged shape still selected, click the Copy button in the Clipboard group, click the Paste button, then move the new shape to a blank area of the slide**
   You have duplicated the merged shape twice and now have three identical shapes on the slide.

Quick Tip
Press and hold ALT to temporarily turn the snap-to-grid feature off while dragging objects on the slide or dragging a sizing handle to make precise adjustments.

7. **Click the View tab on the ribbon, click the Ruler check box in the Show group to hide the rulers, click the Home tab, then type Teams**
   The ruler closes, and the text you type appears in the selected merged shape and becomes a part of the shape. Now if you move or rotate the shape, the text moves with it. Compare your screen with Figure 2-10.

8. **Click the middle merged shape, type Workflows, click the top merged shape, type Projects, click in a blank area of the slide, then save your work**
   All three merged shapes include text.

Figure 2-9: Merged shape moved on slide

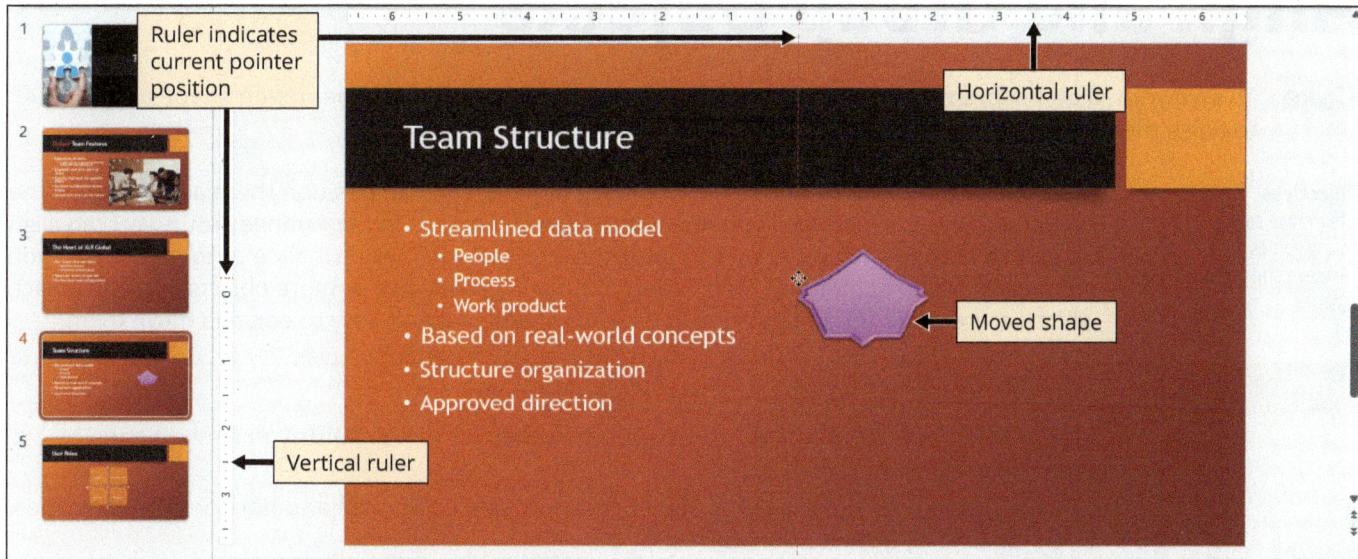

Fauxels/Pexels

Figure 2-10: Duplicated shapes

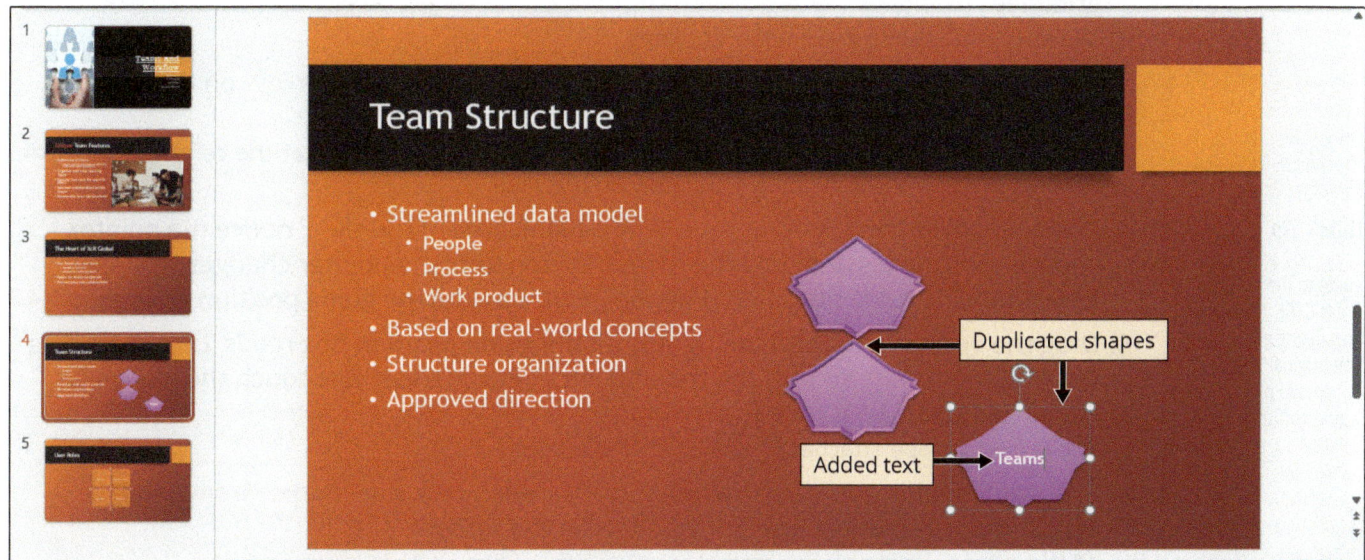

Fauxels/Pexels

Editing points of a shape

If you want to customize the form (or outline) of any shape in the shapes gallery, you can modify its edit points. To display a shape's edit points, select the shape you want to modify, click the Shape Format tab on the ribbon, click the Edit Shape button in the Insert Shapes group, then click Edit Points. Black edit points appear on the shape. To change the form of a shape, drag a black edit point. When you click a black edit point, white square edit points appear on either side of the black edit point, which allow you to change the curvature of a line between two black edit points. When you are finished with your custom shape, you can save it as a picture and reuse it in other presentations or other files. To save the shape as a picture, right-click the shape, then click Save as Picture.

Module 2 Modifying a Presentation

Align and Group Objects

Case To give your slide a more orderly look, you decide to position and group the pentagon shapes on Slide 4 to finish the slide.

Objectives
- Rearrange shapes using guides
- Arrange and group shapes

After you are finished creating and modifying objects, you can position them accurately on the slide to achieve the look you want. Using the Align commands in the Arrange group, you can align objects relative to each other by snapping them to the gridlines on a slide or to guides that you manually position on the slide. The Group command groups two or more objects into one object, which secures their relative position to each other and makes it easy to edit and move them.

Steps

1. Right-click a blank area of the slide, point to the **Grid and Guides arrow** on the shortcut menu, then click **Gridlines**
   Gridlines appear on the slide as a series of evenly spaced vertical and horizontal dotted lines. Gridlines can help you position objects on the slide.

2. Drag the **Projects shape** until it snaps into place on a set of gridlines near its current position, click the **View tab**, then click the **Gridlines check box** to remove the gridlines
   The shape snaps into place using gridlines.

3. Right-click a blank area of the slide, point to **Grid and Guides arrow** on the shortcut menu, then click **Guides**
   The guides appear as dotted lines on the slide and usually intersect at the center of the slide. Guides help you position objects precisely on the slide.

Quick Tip
To quickly add a new guide to the slide, press CTRL, then drag an existing guide. The original guide remains in place. Drag a guide off the slide to delete it.

4. Position over the **horizontal guide** in a blank area of the slide, notice the pointer change to ✢, press and hold the mouse button until the pointer changes to a measurement guide box, then drag the **guide** up until the guide position box reads **1.42**

5. Drag the **vertical guide** to the right until the guide position box reads **2.00**, then drag the **Projects shape** so that the top and left edges of the shape touch the guides, as shown in **Figure 2-11**
   The Projects shape attaches or "snaps" to the guides.

6. Press and hold SHIFT, click the **Workflows shape**, click the **Teams shape**, release SHIFT, then click the **Shape Format tab** on the ribbon
   All three shapes are now selected.

7. Click the **Align button** in the Arrange group, then click **Align Right**
   The two lower frame shapes move to the right and align with the top frame shape along their right edges.

Trouble
Make sure there is some space between the shapes before you distribute them vertically.

8. Click the **Align button**, click **Distribute Vertically**, click the **Group button** in the Arrange group, then click **Group**
   The shapes are now distributed evenly among themselves and are grouped together to form one object without losing their individual attributes. Notice that the sizing handles and rotate handle now appear on the outer edge of the grouped object as shown in **Figure 2-12**, not around each individual object.

9. Drag the **horizontal guide** to the middle of the slide until its guide position box reads **0.00**, then drag the **vertical guide** to the middle of the slide until its guide position box reads **0.00**

10. Click the **View tab** on the ribbon, click the **Guides check box** in the Show group, click a blank area of the slide, then save your work
    The guides are no longer displayed on the slide.

Figure 2-11: Repositioned shape

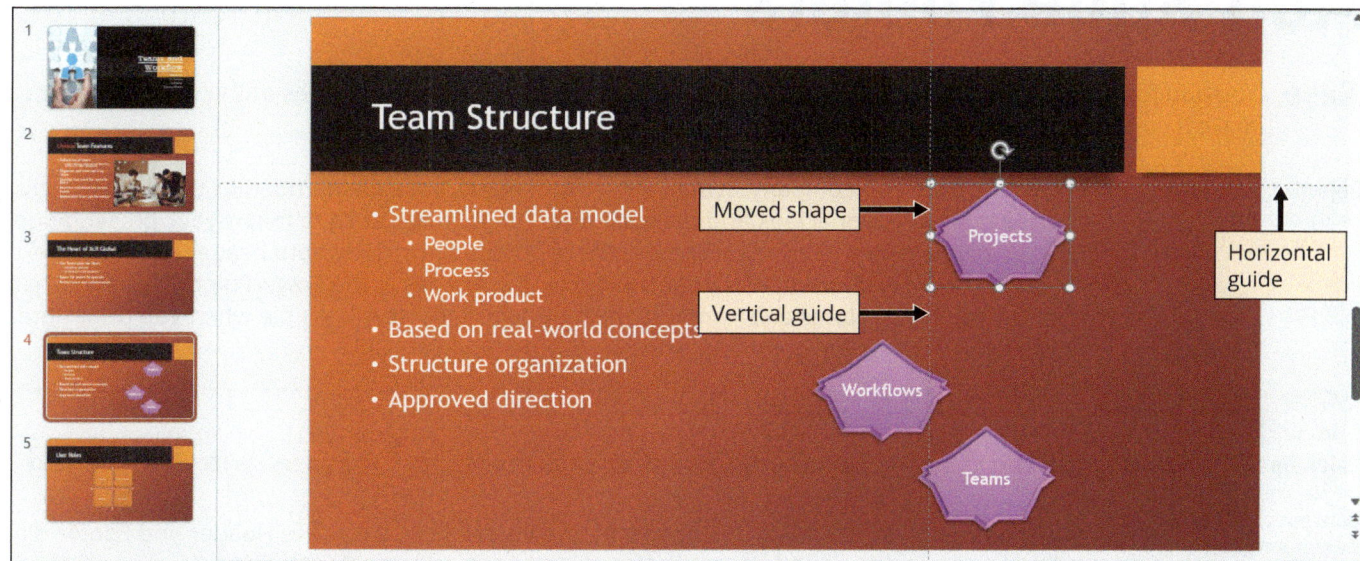

Figure 2-12: Grouped shapes

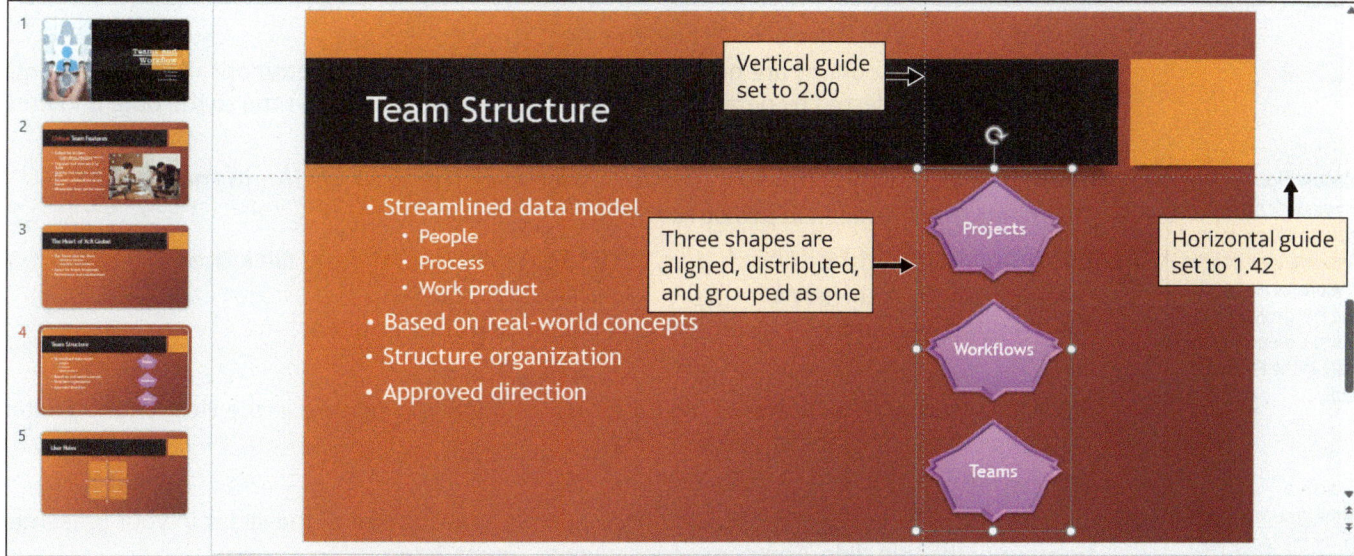

Distributing objects

There are two ways to distribute objects in PowerPoint: relative to each other and relative to the slide edge. If you choose to distribute objects relative to each other, PowerPoint evenly divides the empty space between all the selected objects. When distributing objects in relation to the slide, PowerPoint evenly splits the empty space from slide edge to slide edge between the selected objects. To distribute objects relative to each other, click the Align button in the Arrange group on the Shape Format tab, then click Align Selected Objects, if it is not already selected. To distribute objects relative to the slide, click the Align button in the Arrange group on the Shape Format tab, then click Align to Slide.

Add Slide Footers

Case You add footer text that includes the date, slide number, and your name to the slides of the presentation to make it easier for the audience to follow.

Objective
- Add footer text to slides

Footer text, such as a company, school, or product name, the slide number, or the date, can give your slides a professional look and make it easier for your audience to follow your presentation. Slides do not have headers. However, notes or handouts can include both header and footer text. You can review footer information that you apply to the slides in the PowerPoint views and when you print the slides. Notes and handouts header and footer text is visible when you print notes pages, handouts, and the outline.

Steps

Quick Tip
The placement of the footer text objects on the slide is dependent on the presentation theme.

1. **Click the Insert tab on the ribbon, then click the Header & Footer button in the Text group**
   The Header and Footer dialog box opens, as shown in **Figure 2-13**. The Header and Footer dialog box has two tabs: a Slide tab and a Notes and Handouts tab. The Slide tab is selected. There are three types of footer text: Date and time, Slide number, and Footer. The bold rectangles in the Preview box identify the default position of the three types of footer text placeholders on the slides.

2. **Click the Date and time check box to select it**
   The date and time options are now available to select. The Update automatically date and time option button is selected by default. This option updates the date and time to the date and time set by your computer every time you open or print the file.

Quick Tip
If you want a specific date to appear every time you view or print the presentation, click the Fixed date option button, then type the date in the Fixed text box.

3. **Click the Update automatically arrow, then click the fifth option in the list**
   The month is abbreviated in this option.

4. **Click the Slide number check box, click the Footer check box, click the Footer text box, then type your name**
   The Preview box now shows all three footer placeholders are selected.

5. **Click the Don't show on title slide check box**
   Selecting this check box prevents the footer information you entered in the Header and Footer dialog box from appearing on the title slide.

Trouble
If the grouped shapes cover the footer text, drag them out of the way.

6. **Click Apply to All**
   The dialog box closes, and the footer information is applied to all of the slides in your presentation except the title slide. Compare your screen to **Figure 2-14**.

7. **Click the Slide 1 thumbnail in the thumbnail pane, then click the Header & Footer button in the Text group**
   The Header and Footer dialog box opens again.

Trouble
If you click Apply to All in Step 9, click the Undo button on the Quick Access Toolbar and repeat Steps 7, 8, and 9.

8. **Click the Don't show on title slide check box to deselect it, click the Footer check box, then select the text in the Footer text box**

9. **Type Teams Are Our Success, click Apply, then save your work**
   The text in the Footer text box appears on the title slide. Clicking Apply applies this footer information to just the current slide.

Module 2 Modifying a Presentation

Figure 2-13: Header and Footer dialog box

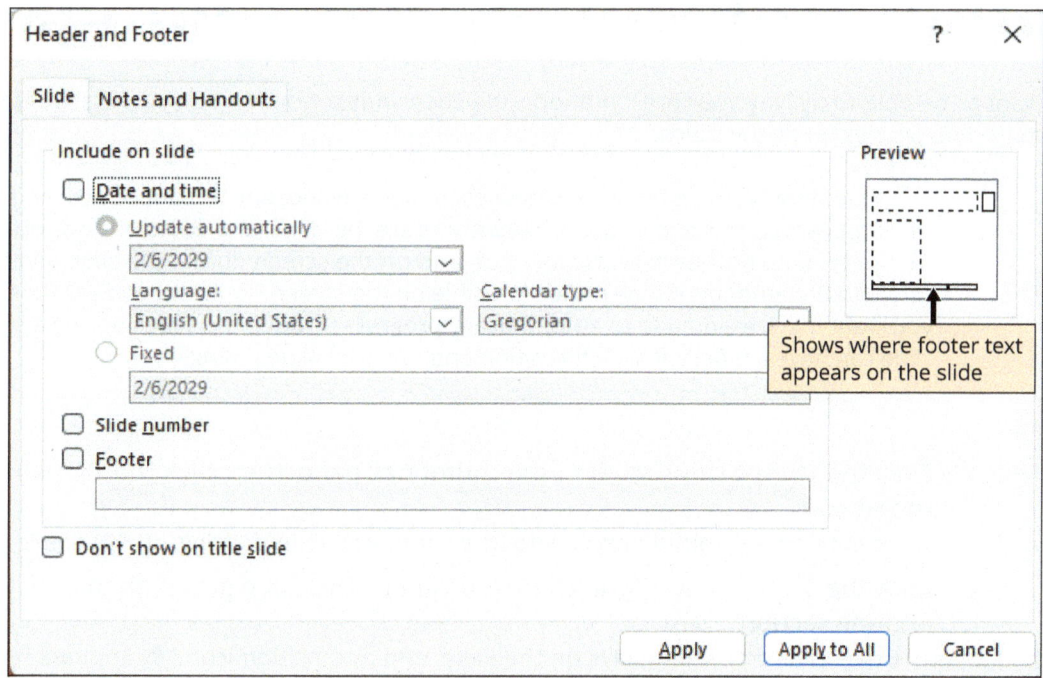

Figure 2-14: Footer information added to presentation

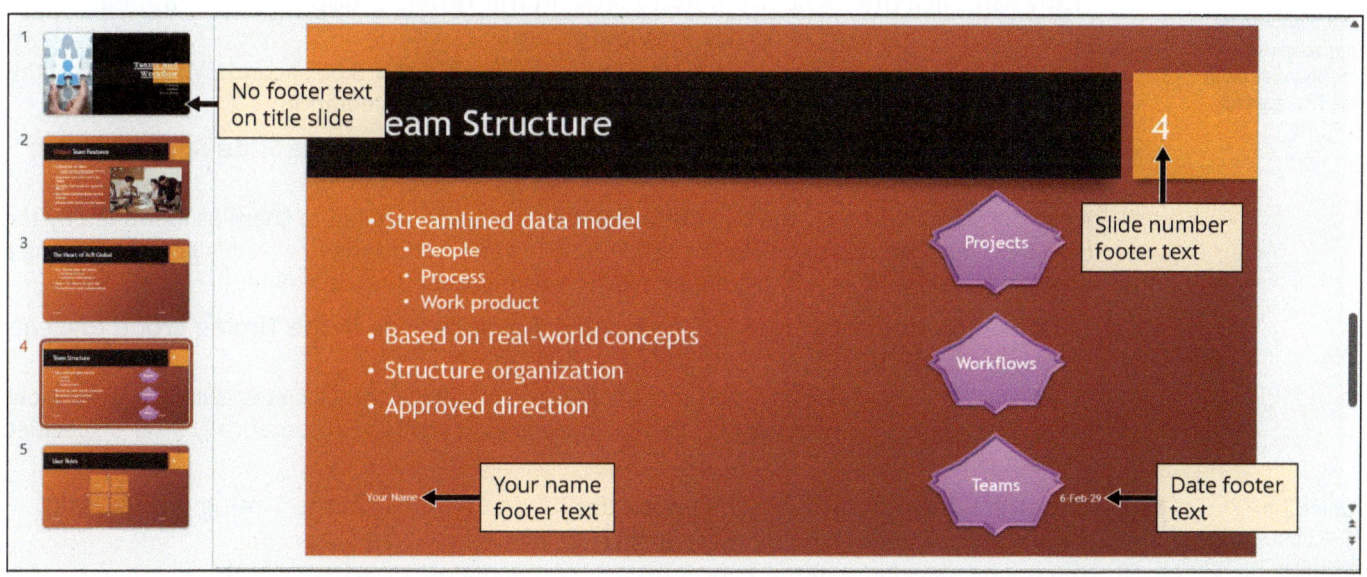

Fauxels/Pexels

Creating superscript and subscript text

Superscript or subscript text is a number, figure, symbol, or letter that appears smaller than other text and is positioned above or below the normal line of text. A common superscript in the English language is the sign indicator next to a number, such as 1st or 2nd. Other examples of superscripts are the trademark symbol™ and the copyright symbol©. To create superscript text in PowerPoint, select the text, number, or symbol, then press CTRL SHIFT + at the same time. Probably the most familiar uses of subscript text are the numerals in chemical compounds and formulas, for example, H_2O and CO_2. To create subscript text, select the text, number, or symbol, then press CTRL = at the same time. To change superscript or subscript text back to normal text, select the text, then press CTRL SPACEBAR.

Module 2 Modifying a Presentation

Set Slide Transitions and Timings

Case You want to be able to display your presentation slide show independently, so you set slide transitions and 7-second slide timings for all the slides.

Objectives
- Apply and modify a transition
- Modify slide timings

In a slide show, you can determine how each slide advances in and out of view and how long each slide appears on the screen. **Slide transitions** are the visual and audio effects you apply to a slide that determine how each slide moves on and off the screen during the slide show. **Slide timing** refers to the amount of time a slide is visible on the screen. Typically, you set slide timings only if you want the presentation to automatically progress through the slides during a slide show. Each slide can have a different slide transition and different slide timing.

Steps

1. Click the **Slide 4 thumbnail** in the thumbnail pane, then click the **Transitions tab** on the ribbon

   Transitions are organized by type into three groups: Subtle, Exciting, and Dynamic Content.

2. Click the **More button** in the Transition to This Slide group, then click **Glitter** in the Exciting section

   The new slide transition plays on the slide, and a transition icon appears next to the slide thumbnail in the thumbnail pane as shown in **Figure 2-15**. You can change the direction and speed of the slide transition.

   Quick Tip
   You can add a sound that plays with the transition using the Sound arrow in the Timing group.

3. Click the **Effect Options button** in the Transition to This Slide group, click **Hexagons from Top**, click the **Duration down arrow** in the Timing group until **3.00** appears, then click the **Preview button** in the Preview group

   The Glitter slide transition now plays from the top of the slide for 3.00 seconds. You can apply this transition with the custom settings to all of the slides in the presentation.

4. Click the **Apply To All button** in the Timing group, then click the **Slide Sorter button** on the status bar

   All of the slides now have the customized Glitter transition applied to them as identified by the transition icon located below each slide. You can also determine how slides progress during a slide show—either manually by mouse click or automatically by slide timing.

5. Click the **On Mouse Click check box** under Advance Slide in the Timing group to clear the checkmark

   When this option is selected, you have to click to manually advance slides during a slide show. Now, with this option disabled, you can set the slides to advance automatically after a specified amount of time.

   Quick Tip
   Click the transition icon under any slide in Slide Sorter view to see its transition play.

6. Click the Slide 4 thumbnail, then click the **After up arrow** in the Timing group until **00:07.00** appears in the text box, then click the **Apply To All button**

   The timing between slides is 7 seconds as indicated by the time under each slide thumbnail in **Figure 2-16**. When you run the slide show, each slide will remain on the screen for 7 seconds. You can override a slide's timing and speed up the slide show by pressing ENTER or using any of the other manual advance slide commands.

7. Click the **Slide Show button** on the status bar

   The slide show advances automatically. A new slide appears every 7 seconds using the Glitter transition.

8. **sam** When you see the black slide, press **SPACEBAR**, double-click the **Slide 1** thumbnail, save your changes, submit your presentation to your instructor, then exit PowerPoint

   The slide show ends, and you return to Slide Sorter view with Slide 5 selected.

Set Slide Transitions and Timings — PPT 2-17

Figure 2-15: Applied slide transition

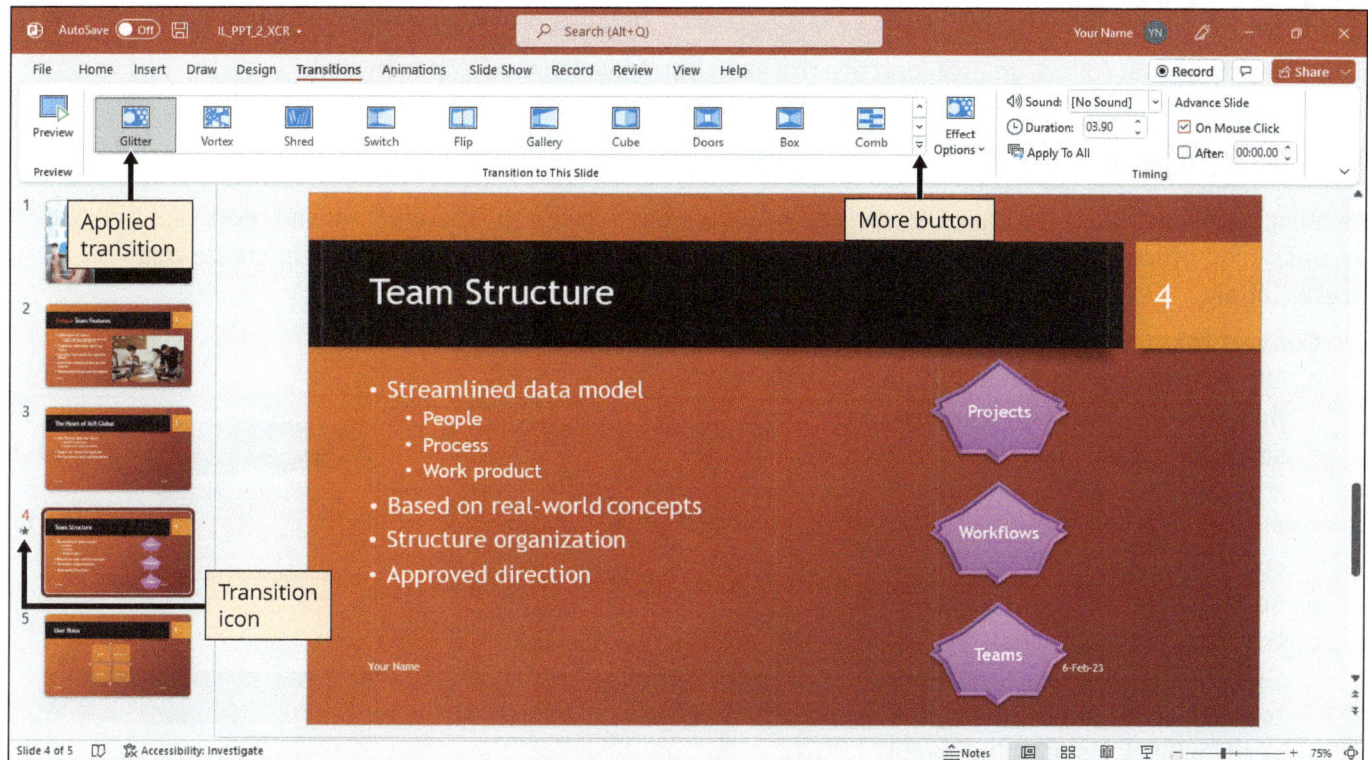

Fauxels/Pexels

Figure 2-16: Slide Sorter view showing applied transition and timing

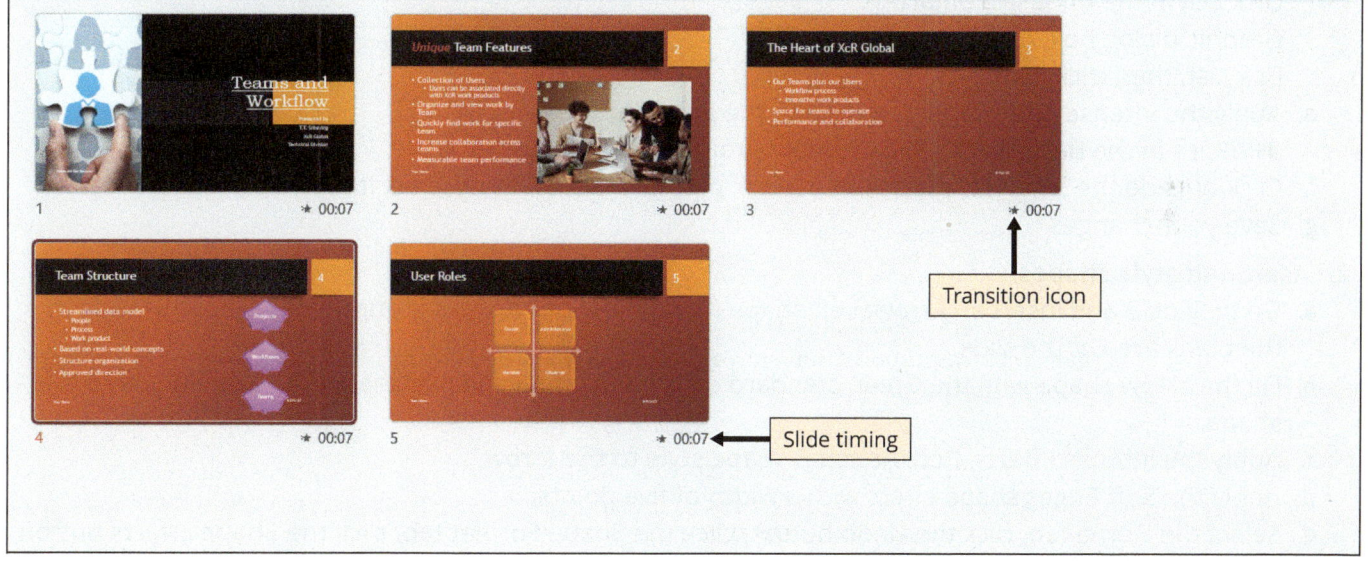

Fauxels/Pexels

Inserting hyperlinks in a webpage

While creating a presentation there may be information on the Internet you want to reference or view during a slide show. Instead of re-creating the information in PowerPoint, you can insert a hyperlink on a slide that when clicked during a slide show will open the webpage directly from the Internet. To insert a hyperlink, select an object on the slide, such as a picture or text object, then click the Insert tab on the ribbon. Click the Link button in the Links group to open the Insert Hyperlink dialog box. Click the Existing File or Web Page button in the link to section, locate the webpage you want to link, enter it in the Address bar in the dialog box, then click OK. Now during a slide show, click the object with the hyperlink and you will view the linked webpage.

Practice

In the exercises that follow, you will practice the skills you have learned in this module.

Skills Review

As an accounts assistant for Blair Enterprises, you have been asked to create a financial report for an upcoming office meeting. You will use PowerPoint features from this module to help create this presentation.

1. **Convert text to SmartArt.**
   a. Open the presentation IL_PPT_2-2.pptx from the location where you store your Data Files, then save it as **IL_PPT_2_Blair**. Refer to **Figure 2-17** for an example of a completed presentation.
   b. Select the text object on Slide 2.
   c. Use the Convert to SmartArt Graphic button to convert the text to a SmartArt graphic, using the Vertical Block List graphic layout.
   d. Click the More button in the Layouts group, click More Layouts, click List in the Choose a SmartArt Graphic dialog box, click Vertical Box List, then click OK.
   e. Apply the Intense Effect SmartArt style to the graphic. (**Hint**: It's in the Best Match for Document group.)
   f. Click outside the SmartArt graphic in a blank part of the slide to deselect it.
   g. Save your changes.

Figure 2-17

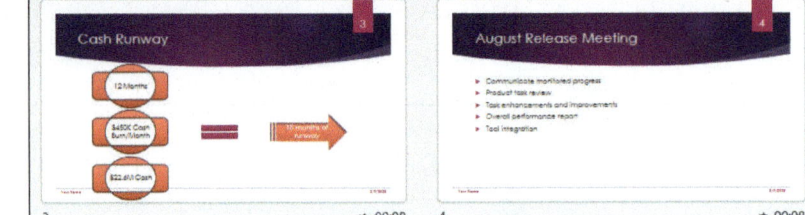

2. **Insert and style shapes.**
   a. Go to Slide 3 and insert an Arrow: Left shape (from the Block Arrows group) that is about 3" wide in the blank area of the slide.
   b. Fill the arrow shape with the Green standard color, then apply the Sketched Freehand outline to the shape.
   c. Apply the Intense Effect—Red, Accent 3 shape style to the arrow.
   d. Apply the Soft Edges shape effect with a width of five points.
   e. Select the Home tab, click the Undo button, click the Shape Format tab, click the Shape Effects button, then point to Shadow.
   f. Click Inside: Top Right, then save your changes.
   g. Drag the left adjustment handle to the right slightly to reduce the size of the arrow tip.

3. **Rotate and modify shapes.**
   a. With the arrow shape still selected, use the Rotate button in the Arrange group to flip the arrow horizontally.
   b. Use the object's Rotate handle so that the arrow points to the top of the slide, then undo the action.
   c. Use the Rotate button to flip the arrow horizontally.
   d. Use the Edit Shape command in the Insert Shapes group to change the shape to the Arrow: Striped Right shape in the Block Arrows group, then save your work.

4. **Rearrange and merge shapes.**
   a. Select the orange circle shape on Slide 3.
   b. Drag the circle shape on the top of the rectangle shape, then center it on the rectangle using the smart guides, as shown in **Figure 2-18**.
   c. Send the circle shape back one level.
   d. Select both the rectangle and the circle shape, then click the Merge Shapes button in the Insert Shapes group.
   e. Point to each of the merge shapes options, click a blank area of the slide twice, then select the rectangle shape.
   f. Send the rectangle shape back one level, then deselect it.
   g. Select both the circle and the rectangle, merge them using the Combine option, then save your work.

Figure 2-18

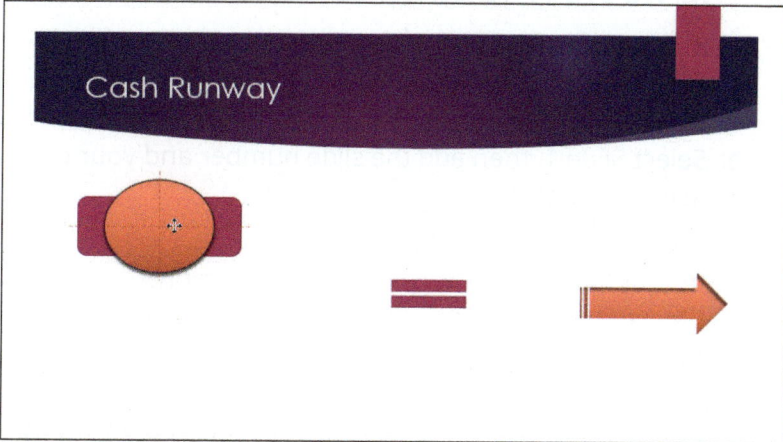

5. **Edit and duplicate shapes.**
   a. Show the rulers, select the equal sign shape on the slide, align the shape on the 0 of the horizontal ruler and 1 on the vertical ruler, hide the rulers, then select the merged rectangle shape.
   b. Using CTRL make a copy of the rectangle shape below the original.
   c. Copy the rectangle shape, then paste it.
   d. Move the newest rectangle shape below the previous rectangle, then type **$22.6M Cash**. (You'll adjust the rectangles' position in the next section.)
   e. Select the top rectangle shape, type **12 Months**, select the middle rectangle shape, type **$450K Cash**, press ENTER, then type **Burn/Month**.
   f. Click the arrow shape, then type **18 Months of runway**.
   g. Deselect the shape, show the gridlines in the Slide pane, then save your changes.

6. **Align and group objects.**
   a. Drag the top rectangle shape until its right edge snaps to the fifth vertical gridline from the left side of the slide (right under the title graphic).
   b. Use SHIFT to select all three rectangles, then align their right sides and distribute them vertically.
   c. Hide the gridlines, display the guides, then move the vertical guide to the right until 3.08 appears in the ScreenTip.
   d. Move the arrow shape until it is centered over the vertical guide, move the vertical guide back to 0.00, then hide the guides.
   e. Drag the equal sign and the arrow so they align horizontally with the middle rectangle.
   f. Adjust the object positions, if necessary, then select all five shapes.
   g. Group the selected objects. Refer to **Figure 2-19**.

Figure 2-19

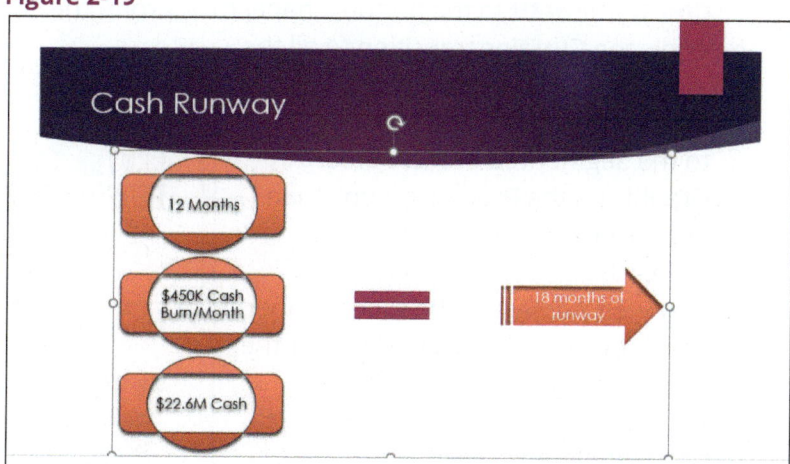

Skills Review (Continued)

7. **Add slide footers.**
   a. Add a footer to all the slides except the title slide showing the date and time, using a fixed date format, add the slide number, then add your name in the Footer text box.
   b. Select Slide 1, then add the slide number and your class name to the title slide footer only.
   c. Save your changes.

8. **Set slide transitions and timings.**
   a. In Slide Sorter view, with the Slide 1 thumbnail selected, apply the Clock transition.
   b. Change the effect option to Counterclockwise, change the transition duration to 3.00, then apply to all the slides.
   c. Change the slide timing so the slides advance automatically after 8 seconds.
   d. Switch to Normal view, view the slide show, then save your work.
   e. Submit your presentation to your instructor, close the presentation, then exit PowerPoint.

Independent Challenge 1

You are the director of the Center for the Performing Arts (CPA) in Council Bluffs, Iowa, and one of your many duties is to raise funds to help cover operating costs. One of the primary ways you do this is by speaking to businesses, community clubs, and other organizations throughout the region. Every year you speak to many organizations, where you give a short presentation detailing CPA's plans for the upcoming season. You need to continue working on the presentation you started earlier.

a. Start PowerPoint, open the presentation IL_PPT_2-3.pptx from the location where you store your Data Files, and save it as **IL_PPT_2_CPA**.
b. On Slide 3, display the guides in the Slide pane, move the horizontal guide down to 2.50, then move the vertical guide right to 2.00.
c. Drag the frame shape so its bottom and left edges snap to align with the guides.
d. Move the adjustment handle on the frame shape to the right slightly to change the width of the shape's frame, then save your work.
e. Change the frame shape fill color to Orange, Accent 1 Lighter 40%, then change the shape outline weight to solid 3-point.
f. Duplicate the shape twice, align the shapes along their left edges on the vertical guide, distribute the shapes vertically, move both guides back to 0.00, then hide the guides.
g. Type **Season Tickets** in the top shape, type **Priority Seating Selection** in the middle shape, then type **Charity Benefit** in the bottom shape, then group the shapes together.
h. Apply the Curtains transition to all the slides with an 8.00 duration time.
i. Change the bulleted text on Slide 4 to the Segmented Process SmartArt Graphic (in the Process group), then apply the Intense Effect SmartArt style.
j. Add your name and the slide number as a footer on all the slides except the title slide, then save your changes. Refer to **Figure 2-20** for an example of a completed presentation.
k. Submit your presentation to your instructor, close your presentation, then exit PowerPoint.

Figure 2-20

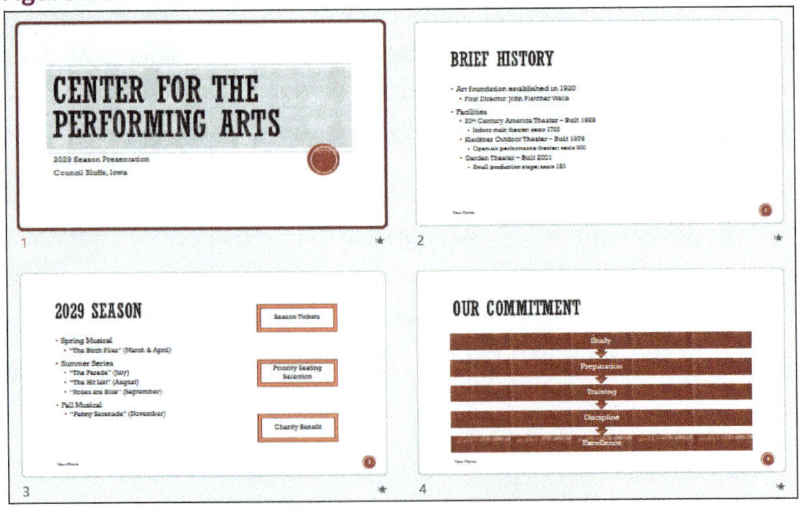

Independent Challenge 2

You are one of the marketing assistants at TimeSHARE Corp., an employee tracking and management software company. You have been asked by your manager to develop a presentation outlining the details of the company TimeSHARE app for an upcoming online meeting. You continue working on the presentation you have already started.

a. Start PowerPoint, open the presentation IL_PPT_2-4.pptx from the location where you store your Data Files, and save it as **IL_PPT_2_Timeshare**.

b. Go to Slide 3, show the rulers in the Slide pane, then drag the middle-right sizing handle on the shape to the right until the pointer reaches the 5" mark in the horizontal ruler.

c. Draw a 1.5" proportional "Flowchart: Stored data" shape from the Flowchart section of shapes, then hide rulers in the Slide pane. (**Hint**: Use the Shift key to create the proportional shape. To draw a specific size shape, position your pointer to align with the 0 of a ruler and drag until your pointer reaches the size you want on the ruler.)

d. Using the Shape Format tab, flip the shape horizontally, then drag the shape's rotate handle until the rotate handle is on the left side of the shape.

e. Select both shapes, then apply Subtle Effect—Aqua, Accent 3 shape style.

f. Apply the Preset 4 shape effect, then merge the two shapes together using the Union option, as shown in **Figure 2-21**.

g. Show gridlines in the Slide pane, drag the merged shape until the shape's left and bottom edges are touching gridlines, then hide the gridlines.

h. Apply the Vortex transition to all the slides with a duration of 5.00, then change the effect option to From Bottom.

i. Set an automatic slide timing to all slides of 5.00, add the slide number and your name as a footer on all the slides, then save your changes. Refer to **Figure 2-22** for an example of a completed presentation.

j. Run the slide show, submit your presentation to your instructor, close your presentation, then exit PowerPoint.

Figure 2-21

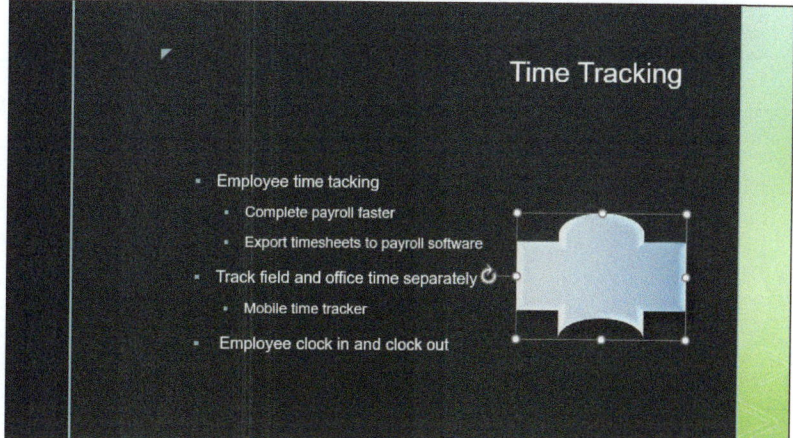

Figure 2-22

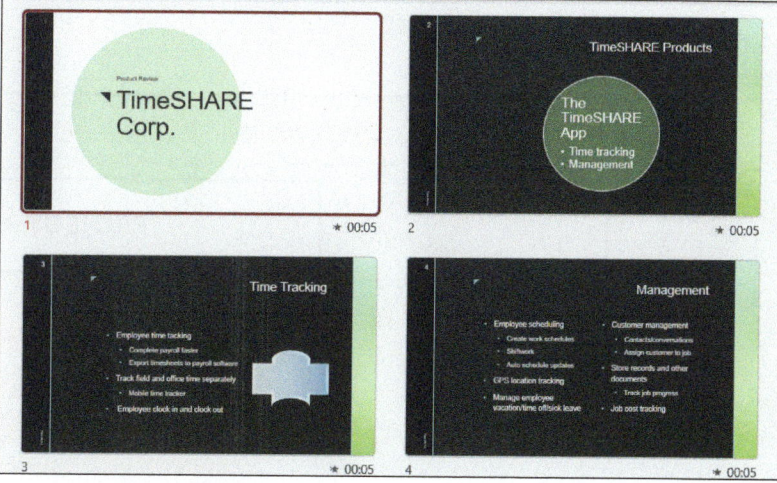

Visual Workshop

Open the presentation IL_PPT_2-5.pptx from the location where you store your Data Files and save it as **IL_PPT_2_JorDee**. Create the presentation shown in **Figure 2-23** and **Figure 2-24**. Create and duplicate the merged shape, which is made with a Plus Sign shape and a Diamond shape. The Plus Sign shape is a 2" proportional shape and the Diamond shape is a 1½" proportional shape. Apply the Subtle Effect—Gold, Accent 1 style to the shapes. Set the horizontal guide to 2 and the vertical guide to 5, as shown in **Figure 2-23** to place the shapes, then move the guides back to 0. The SmartArt graphic in **Figure 2-24** is created with the Vertical Curved List layout and has the Polished style applied to it. Review your slides in Slide Show view, then add the slide number and your name as a footer to all the slides but the title slide. Add today's date as the date on the title slide only, then save your changes. Submit your presentation to your instructor, close the presentation, then exit PowerPoint.

Figure 2-23

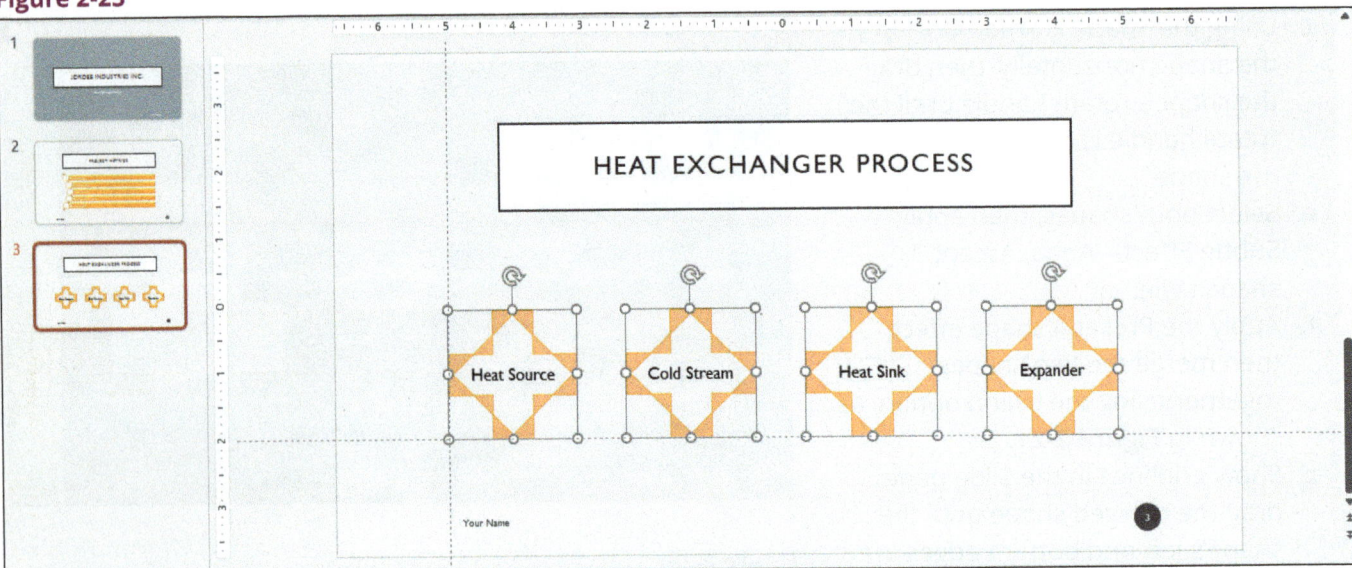

Figure 2-24

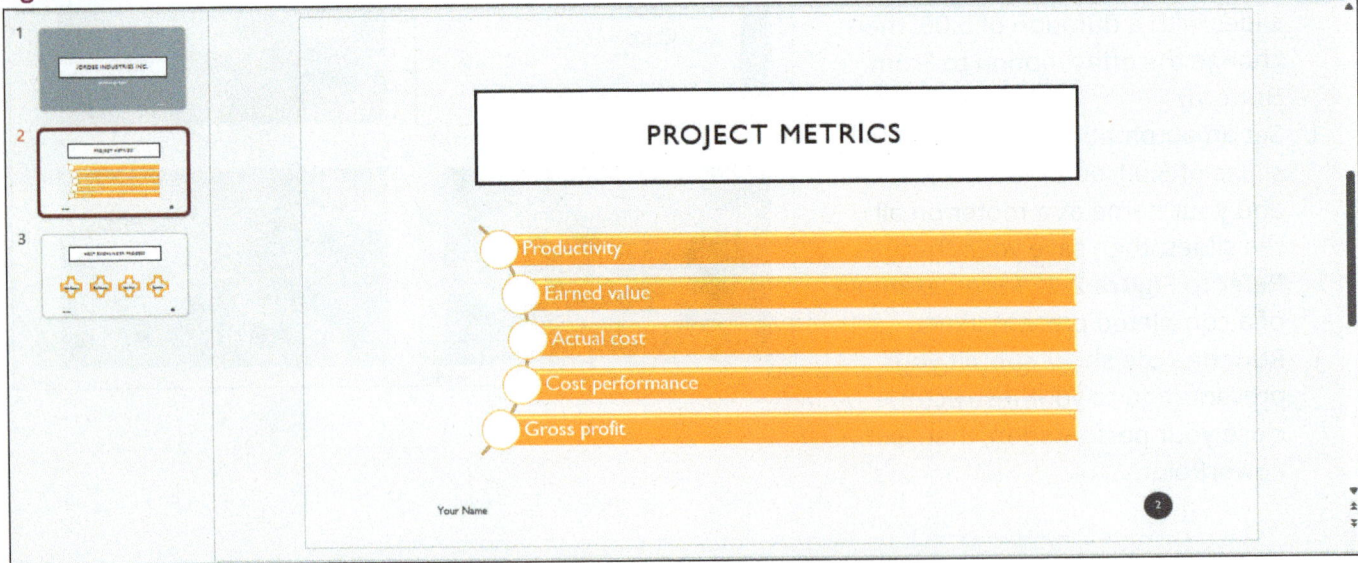

PowerPoint Module 3

Inserting Objects into a Presentation

Case
In this module, you continue working on the XcR presentation by inserting and formatting a text box and then cropping and styling a picture. You also add visual elements to the presentation, including a chart, slides from another presentation, and a table. You format these objects using the powerful object-editing features in PowerPoint.

Module Objectives
After completing this module, you will be able to:

- Insert a text box
- Revise and crop a picture
- Insert a chart
- Enter and edit chart data
- Insert slides from other presentations
- Insert a table
- Insert and format WordArt
- Animate objects
- Insert and edit digital video

Files You Will Need

IL_PPT_3-1.pptx
Support_PPT_3_Team.jpg
Support_PPT_3_Workflow.pptx
Support_PPT_3_Group.mp4
IL_PPT_3-2.pptx
Support_PPT_3_Fire.jpg

Support_PPT_3_Emergency.pptx
Support_PPT_3_Patient.mp4
IL_PPT_3-3.pptx
Support_PPT_3_Strategy.pptx
Support_PPT_3_Advisor.jpg
IL_PPT_3-4.pptx

Insert a Text Box

Case You want to emphasize information about XcR user roles, so you create a text box next to the SmartArt graphic on Slide 5, then edit and format the text.

Objectives
- Insert a text box
- Format text in a text box
- Change and move a text box

In most cases, you enter slide text in a title or content placeholder that is arranged on the slide based on a slide layout. But sometimes you need additional text on a slide where the traditional placeholder does not place text. You can add two types of text boxes: a text **label**, used for a small phrase where the text doesn't automatically wrap inside the text box boundaries, and a **word-processing box**, used for a sentence or paragraph where the text wraps inside a text box. You can format and edit either type of text box just like any other text object.

Steps

1. **sam↓** Start PowerPoint, open the presentation **IL_PPT_3-1.pptx** from the location where you store your Data Files, then save it as **IL_PPT_3_XCR**

2. Click the **Slide 5 thumbnail** on the Thumbnails pane, click the **Insert tab** on the ribbon, then click the **Text Box button** in the Text group
   The pointer changes to ↓ when you move the pointer over the slide.

   Quick Tip
   To create a text label, click the Text Box button, position the pointer on the slide, click once, then enter your text.

3. Move ↓ to the blank area to the right of the SmartArt object on the slide, then drag the pointer + down and toward the right about 3" to create a text box
   When you begin dragging, an outline of the text box appears, indicating the size of the text box you are drawing. After you release the mouse button, a blinking insertion point appears inside the text box, in this case a word-processing box, indicating that you can enter text.

4. Type **Current user roles defined in XcR workflow teams**
   Notice the text box increases in size as your text wraps to additional lines inside the text box. Your screen should appear similar to **Figure 3-1**. After entering the text, you decide to edit the sentence.

5. Drag I over the word **workflow** to select it, position ↘ on top of the selected word, then press and hold the **left mouse button**
   The pointer changes to ↘.

6. Drag the selected word just to the left of the word "user", release the mouse button, then click to the right of the text box
   A grey insertion line appears as you drag, indicating where PowerPoint places the text when you release the mouse button. The word "workflow" moves after the word "Current". Notice there is no space between the words "workflow" and "user" and the spelling error is identified by a wavy red underline.

7. Right-click the **red underlined words** in the text box, then click **"workflow user"** on the shortcut menu
   A space is added between the two words in the text box.

8. Move I to the edge of the text box until the pointer changes to ↔, click the **text box border** (it changes to a solid line), then click the **Shape Format tab** on the ribbon

   Quick Tip
   Click the Shape Effects arrow in the Shape Styles group, then click one of the preset effects to change the style of a text object.

9. Click the **Shape Fill arrow** in the Shape Styles group, click the **Green, Accent 3 color**, click the **Shape Outline arrow** in the Shape Styles group, point to **Weight,** then click **3 pt**
   The text object is now filled with a green color and has a thicker outline.

10. Position ↔ over the text box edge, drag the **text box** to the Smart Guide on the slide as shown in **Figure 3-2**, then save your changes

Figure 3-1: New text object

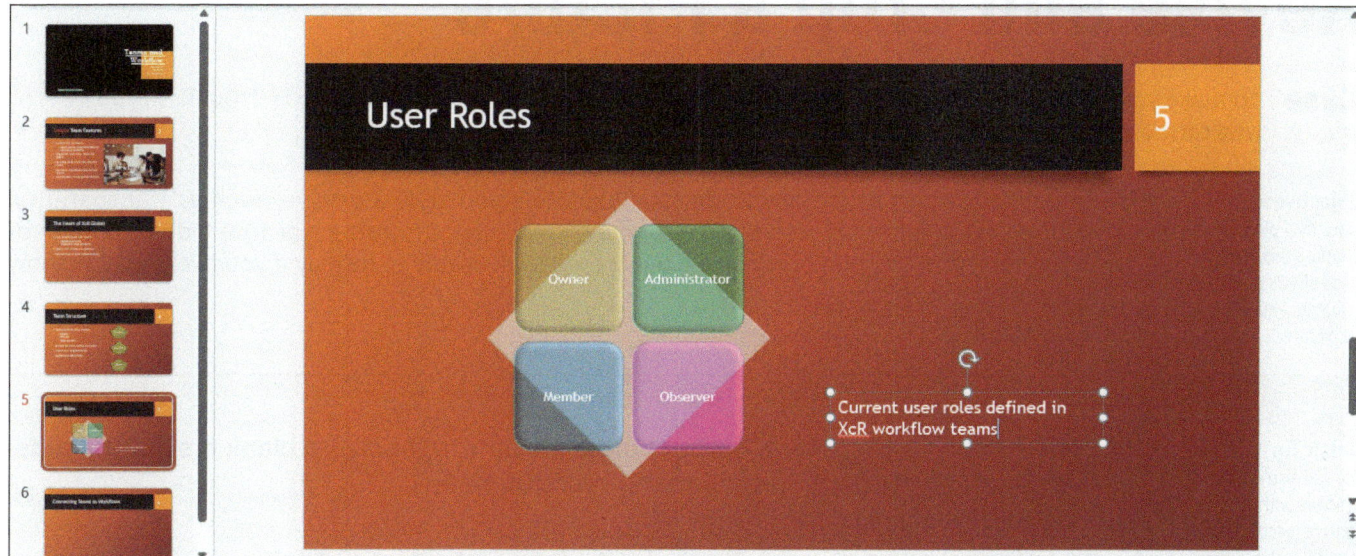

Fauxels/Pexels

Figure 3-2: Formatted text object

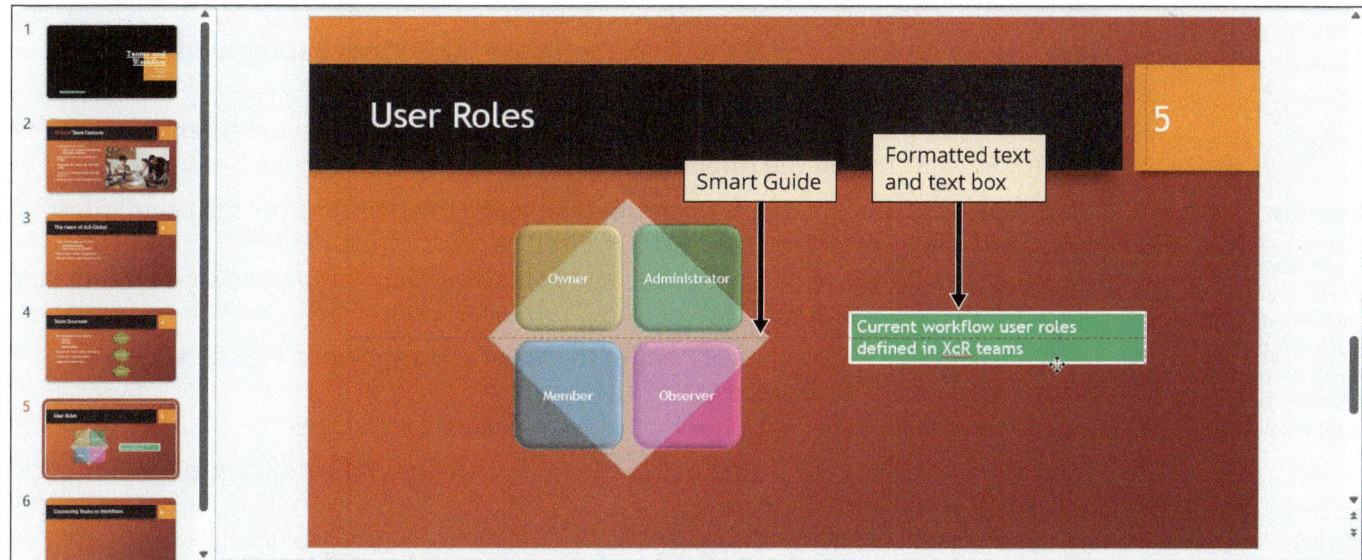

Fauxels/Pexels

Changing text box defaults

You can change the default formatting characteristics of text boxes you create using the Text Box button on the Insert tab. To change the formatting defaults for text boxes, select an existing formatted text box, or create a new one and format it using any of the PowerPoint formatting commands. When you are ready to change the text box defaults of a text box that is not selected, press SHIFT, right-click the formatted text box, release SHIFT, then click Set as Default Text Box on the shortcut menu. Now, any text boxes you create will display the formatting characteristics of this formatted text box.

Revise and Crop a Picture

Case To make your presentation more visually appealing, you crop and style a picture on Slide 2, but first, you insert and format a picture on the Slide Master.

Objectives
- Modify a picture
- Apply a picture style
- Add effects to a picture
- Change and move a picture

PowerPoint provides many editing tools that help you style a picture, such as transparency, sharpening or softening edges, color tone, and cropping. **Cropping** a picture hides a portion of the picture. The cropped portion of a picture is still available to display if you ever want to show that part of the picture again.

Steps

Quick Tip
You can also insert a picture without a content placeholder by clicking the Pictures button in the Images group on the Insert tab.

1. Click the **Slide 1 thumbnail** in the thumbnail pane, right-click a blank area of the slide, then click **Format Background** on the shortcut menu
   The Format Background pane opens.

2. Click the **Picture or texture fill option button** in the Format Background pane, click **Insert**, click **From a File** in the Insert Pictures dialog box, navigate to the location where you store your Data Files, select the picture file **Support_PPT_3_Team.jpg**, then click **Insert**
   The picture fills the slide.

3. Drag the **Transparency Slider** to **40%**, then close the Format Background pane
   The slide background picture on Slide 1 is more transparent.

4. Click the **Slide 2 thumbnail** in the thumbnail pane, click the **picture**, then click the **Picture Format tab** on the ribbon

Quick Tip
Click the Crop arrow to take advantage of other crop options, including cropping to a shape from the Shapes gallery and cropping to a common photo size or aspect ratio.

5. Click the **Crop button** in the Size group, then place the pointer over the **middle-left cropping handle** on the picture
   The pointer changes to ⊣. When the Crop button is active, cropping handles appear next to the sizing handles on the selected object.

6. Drag the **middle cropping handle** right to the location shown in **Figure 3-3**, release the mouse button, then press **ESC**
   The picture would look better on the slide if it had a different color tone.

7. If necessary, reselect the picture, click the **Color button** in the Adjust group, then click **Grayscale** in the Recolor section
   The options in the Recolor section give you a variety of choices to recolor your picture.

Quick Tip
If you have multiple pictures on a slide, you can align them using guides or Smart Guides.

8. Click the **More button** in the Picture Styles group, then click **Soft Edge Rectangle (1st row)**
   The picture now has a blurred edge all around it. Notice the picture has a rotate handle that you can move.

9. Drag the **picture** upward to align with the top of the text object, click a blank area on the slide, then save your changes
   Compare your screen to **Figure 3-4**.

Figure 3-3: Using the cropping pointer to crop a picture

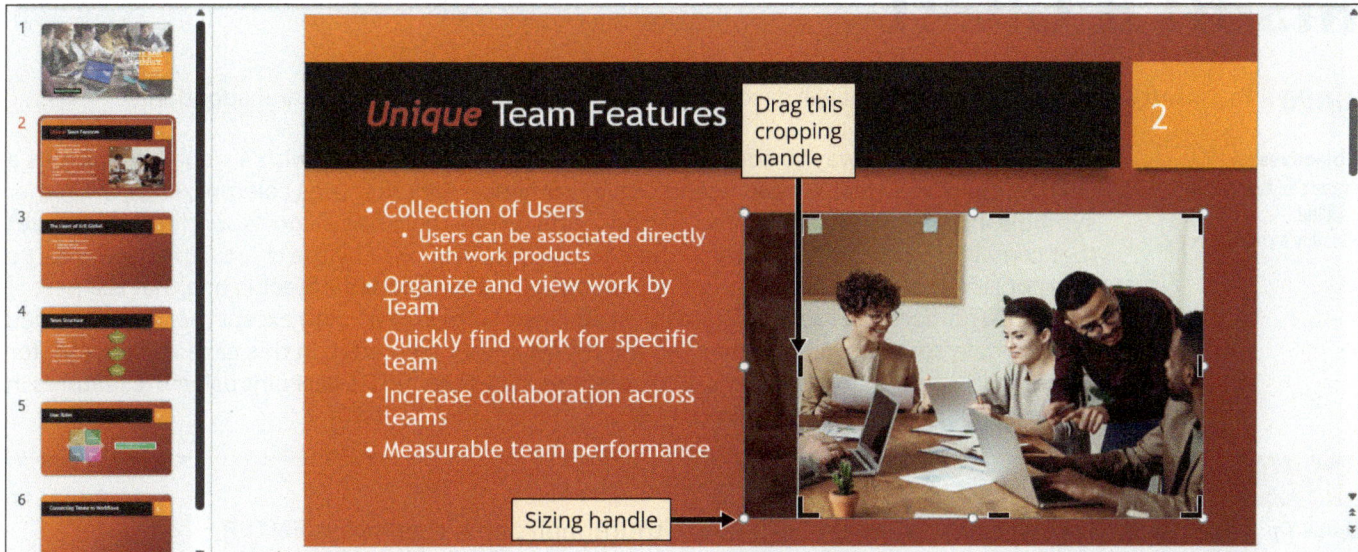

Fauxels/Pexels

Figure 3-4: Cropped and styled picture

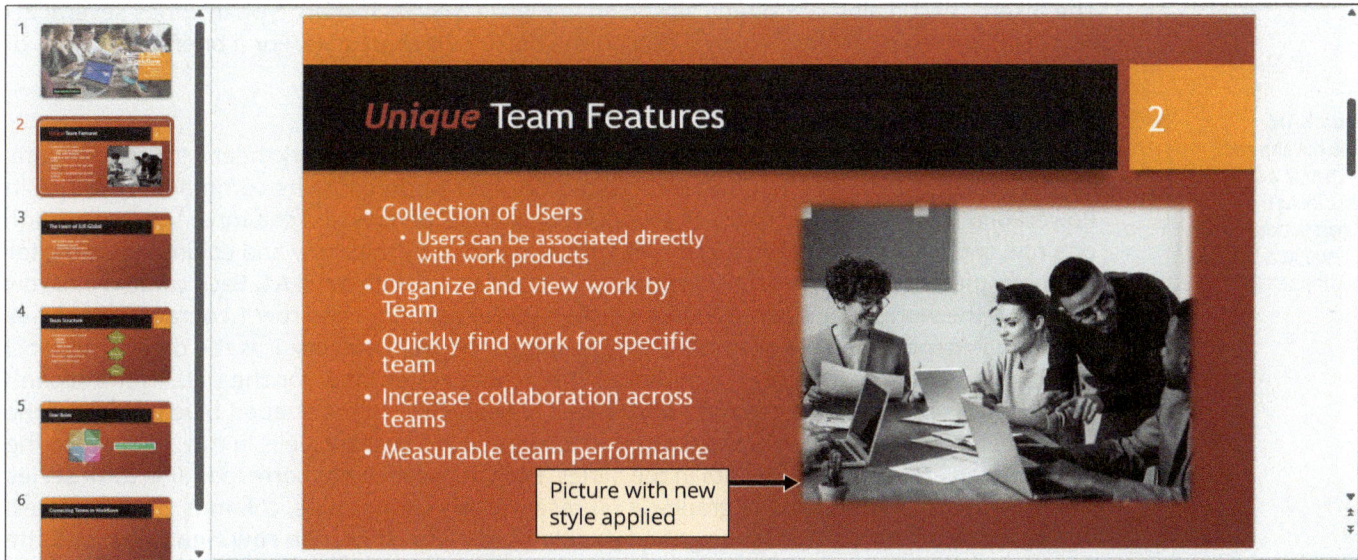

Fauxels/Pexels

Inserting a screen recording

Using the Screen Recording button in the Record group on the Record tab, you can record your computer screen with audio and insert the recording in a slide. For example, if you want to make a recording of an Internet video, locate and display the video on your computer screen. In PowerPoint on the slide where you want to insert the recording, click the Screen Recording button. On the toolbar, click the Select Area button, drag a selection box around the video, click the Audio button, if necessary, then click the Record button on the toolbar. Click the video play button. When finished recording, click Windows Logo+SHIFT+Q to stop recording. PowerPoint opens and the recording appears on your slide. Click the Play button to review your recording.

Module 3 Inserting Objects into a Presentation

Insert a Chart

Case You insert a chart on a new slide that will describe the latest data on user activations and adoptions.

Objectives
- Insert a new chart on a slide
- Modify a chart layout

Frequently, the best way to communicate numerical information is with a visual aid such as a chart. A **chart** is a graphical representation of numerical data that uses columns, lines, and other symbols. PowerPoint uses Excel to create charts. Every chart has a corresponding **worksheet** that contains the rows and columns of numerical data displayed by the chart. When you insert a chart object into PowerPoint, you are embedding it. An **embedded object** is one that is a part of your presentation (just like any other object you insert into PowerPoint) except that an embedded object's data source can be opened by the program that created it, in this case using Excel, for editing purposes. Changes you make to an embedded object in PowerPoint using the features in PowerPoint do not affect the data source.

Steps

Quick Tip
Right-click a slide in the thumbnail pane, then click Duplicate Slide to create an exact copy of the slide.

1. **Click the Slide 6 thumbnail in the thumbnail pane, then press ENTER**
   Pressing ENTER adds a new slide to your presentation with the slide layout of the selected slide, in this case, the Title and Content slide layout.

2. **Click the Title placeholder, type User Activations and Adoptions, then click the Insert Chart icon in the Content placeholder**
   The Insert Chart dialog box opens as shown in **Figure 3-5**. Each chart type includes several 2D and 3D styles. The Clustered Column chart is the default 2D chart style. For a brief explanation of common chart types, refer to **Table 3-1**.

Quick Tip
You can also add a chart to a slide by clicking the Chart button in the Illustrations group on the Insert tab.

3. **Click OK**
   The PowerPoint window displays a clustered column chart below a worksheet with sample data, as shown in **Figure 3-6**. The Chart Design tab on the ribbon contains commands you use in PowerPoint to work with the chart. The worksheet consists of rows and columns. The intersection of a row and a column is called a **cell**. Cells are referred to by their row and column location; for example, the cell at the intersection of column A and row 1 is called cell A1. Each column and row of data in the worksheet is called a **data series**. Cells in column A and row 1 contain **data series labels** that identify the data or values in the column and row. "Category 1" is the data series label for the data in the second row, and "Series 1" is a data series label for the data in the second column. Cells below and to the right of the data series labels, in the shaded blue portion of the worksheet, contain the data values that are represented in the chart. Cells in row 1 appear in the chart **legend** and describe the data in the series. Each data series has corresponding **data series markers** in the chart, which are graphical representations such as bars, columns, or pie wedges. The boxes with the numbers along the left side of the worksheet are **row headings**, and the boxes with the letters along the top of the worksheet are **column headings**.

4. **Move the pointer over the worksheet, then click cell B3**
   The pointer changes to ⊕. Cell B3, containing the value 2.5, is the selected cell, which means it is now the **active cell**. The active cell has a thick green border around it.

5. **Click the Close button ✕ on the worksheet title bar, then click the Quick Layout button in the Chart Layouts group**
   The worksheet window closes, and the Quick Layout gallery opens.

6. **Move over the layouts in the gallery, then click Layout 9**
   This new layout moves the legend to the right side of the chart and increases the size of the data series markers.

7. **Click in a blank area of the slide to deselect the chart, then save your changes**
   The Chart Design tab is no longer active.

Figure 3-5: Insert Chart dialog box

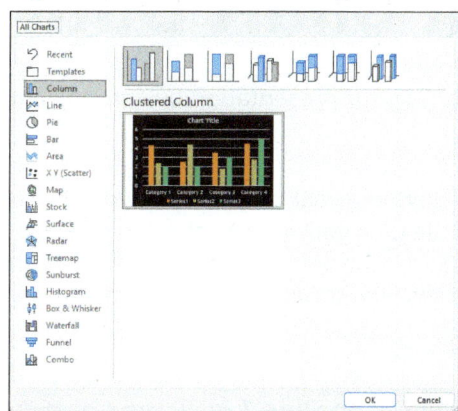

Figure 3-6: Worksheet open showing chart data

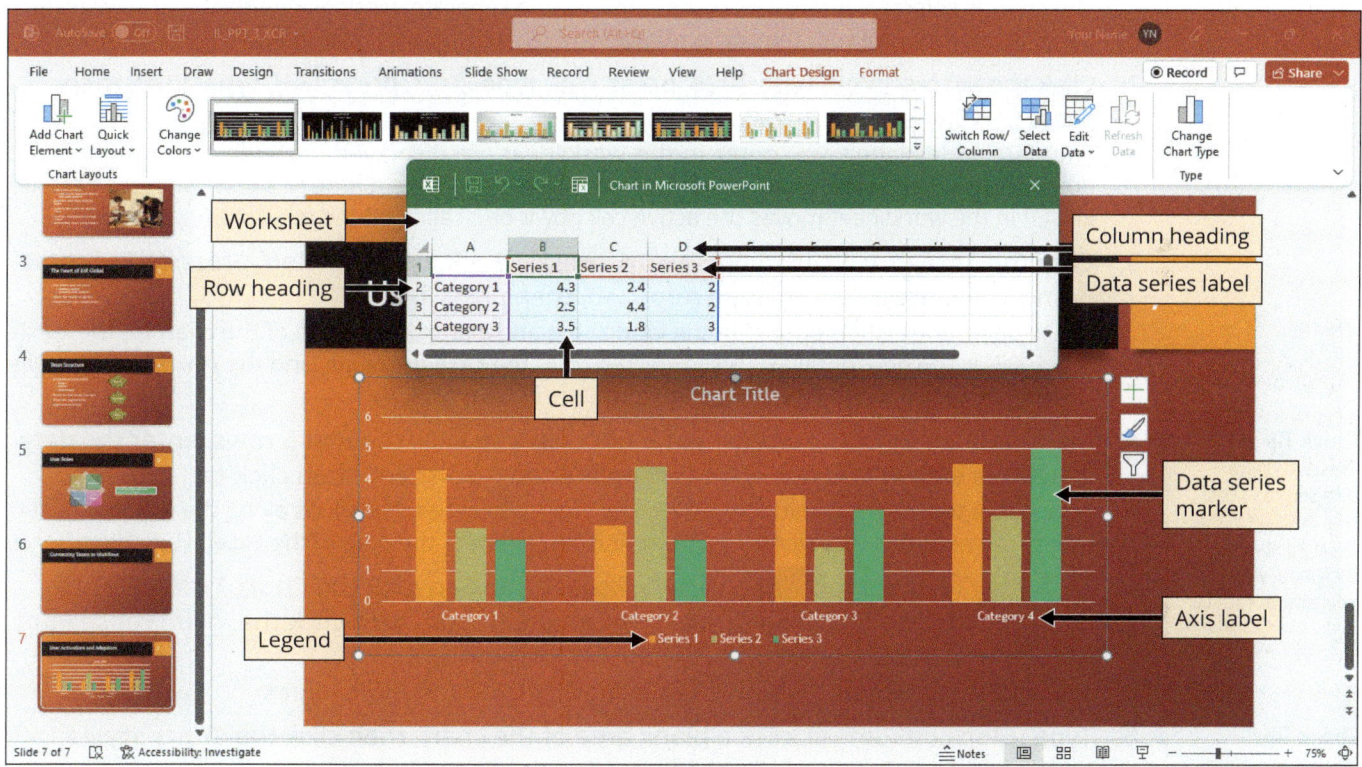

Fauxels/Pexels

Table 3-1: Common chart types

chart type	icon	use to
Column		Track values over time or across categories
Line		Track values over time
Pie		Compare individual values to the whole
Bar		Compare values in categories or over time
Area		Show contribution of each data series to the total over time
X Y (Scatter)		Compare pairs of values
Stock		Show stock market information or scientific data
Surface		Show value trends across two dimensions
Radar		Show changes in values in relation to a center point
Combo		Use multiple types of data markers to compare values

Enter and Edit Chart Data

Case In this lesson you continue to build your presentation by entering and formatting internal company data on user activations and adoptions.

Objectives
- Change chart data values and labels
- Format a chart

After you insert a chart into your presentation, you need to replace the sample data with the correct data. If you have the data you want to chart in an Excel worksheet, you can import it from Excel; otherwise, you can type the data into the worksheet on the slide. As you enter data and make other changes in the worksheet, the chart on the slide automatically reflects the new changes.

Steps

1. Click the **chart object** on Slide 7, click the **Chart Design tab** on the ribbon, then click the **Edit Data button** in the Data group
   The chart is selected and the worksheet opens in a separate window. The data in the worksheet needs to be replaced with the correct data.

2. Click the **Series 1 cell**, type **2026**, press **TAB**, type **2027**, press **TAB**, type **2028**, then press **ENTER**
   The data series labels you enter in the worksheet are displayed in the legend on the chart. Pressing TAB moves the active cell from left to right one cell at a time in a row, whereas pressing ENTER in the worksheet moves the active cell down one cell at a time in a column.

3. Click the **Category 1 cell**, type **Signup**, press **ENTER**, type **Verified**, press **ENTER**, type **Completed**, press **ENTER**, type **Adopted**, then press **TAB**
   These data series labels appear in the worksheet and along the bottom of the chart on the *x*-axis. The *x*-axis is the horizontal axis also referred to as the **category axis**, and the *y*-axis is the vertical axis also referred to as the **value axis**.

▶ 4. Increase the size of the worksheet if necessary to view the first 5 rows, enter the data exactly as shown in **Figure 3-7** to complete the worksheet, then click **cell E5**
   Notice that the height of each column in the chart, as well as the values along the *y*-axis, adjust to reflect the numbers you typed. You have finished entering the data in the Excel worksheet.

5. Click the **Close button** ✕ on the worksheet title bar, click the **Chart Title text box object** in the chart, click the **Home tab** on the ribbon, then click the A˄ **Increase Font Size button** in the Font group
   The worksheet window closes. The text in the Chart Title text box is larger.

▶ 6. Type **Adoption Funnel**, click a blank area of the chart, then click the **Chart Styles button** ✎ to the right of the chart to open the Chart Styles gallery
   The Chart Styles gallery opens on the left side of the chart with Style selected.

7. Scroll down the gallery, click **Style 6**, click **Color** at the top of the Chart Styles gallery, then click the **Colorful Palette 3** in the Colorful section
   The new chart style and color give the column data markers a professional appearance as shown in **Figure 3-8**.

8. Click a blank area on the slide, then click the **Slide 1 thumbnail** in the thumbnail pane
   The Chart Styles gallery closes and Slide 1 appears in the Slide pane.

9. Type **Your Name** at the bottom of the subtitle object, then save the presentation

Quick Tip
To view a chart's data source values, click the chart in the PowerPoint window, then move your pointer over each bar in the chart.

Quick Tip
You can also change the chart style by clicking a style option in the Chart Styles group on the Chart Design tab.

Figure 3-7: Worksheet data for the chart

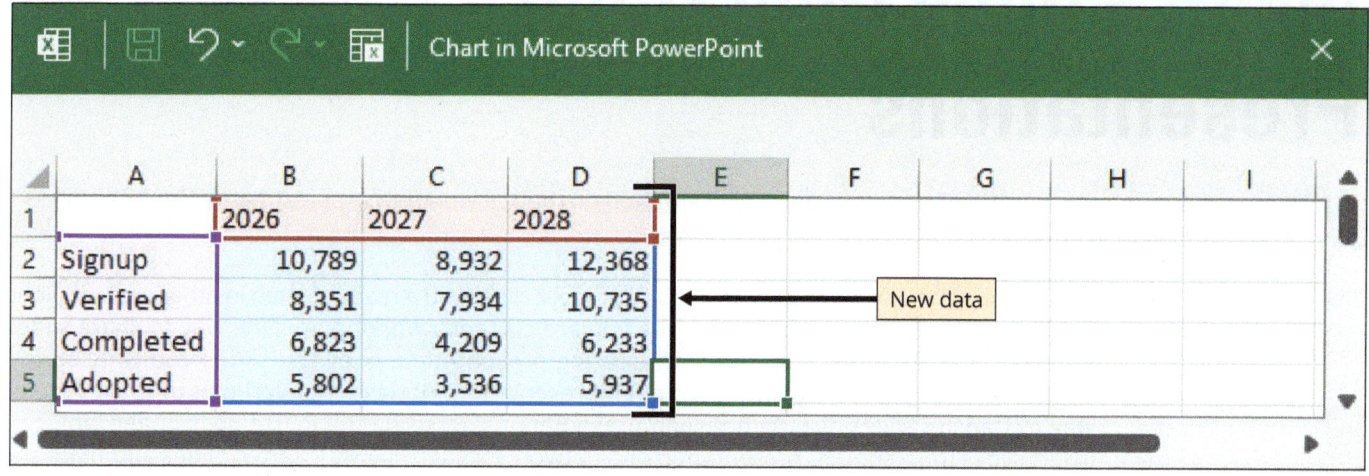

Figure 3-8: Formatted chart

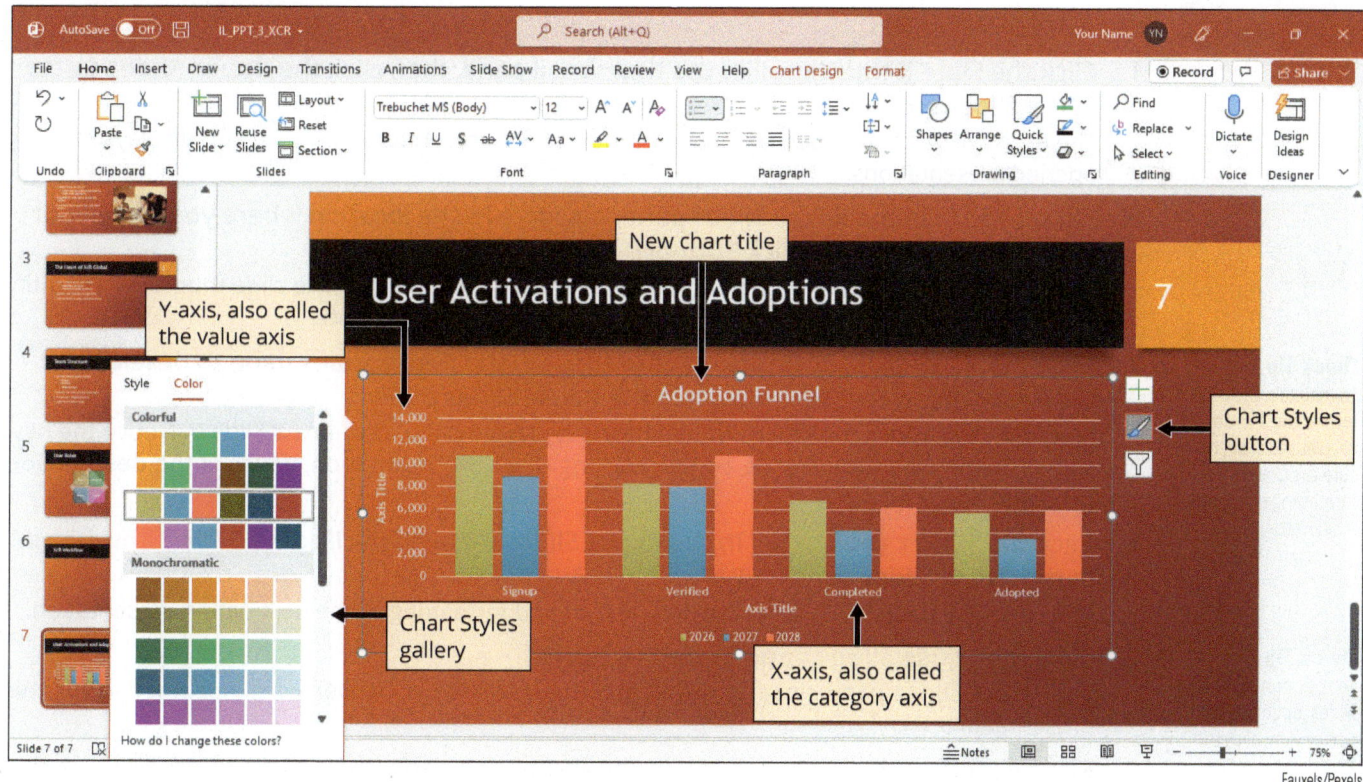

Fauxels/Pexels

Adding a hyperlink to a chart

You can add a hyperlink to any object in PowerPoint, including a chart. Select that chart, click the Insert tab on the ribbon, then click the Link button in the Links group. If you are linking to another file, click the Existing File or Web Page button, locate the file you want to link to the chart, then click OK. Or, if you want to link to another slide in the presentation, click the Place in This Document button, click the slide in the list, then click OK. Now, during a slide show, you can click the chart to open the linked object. To remove the link, click the chart, click the Link button in the Links group, then click Remove Link.

Insert Slides from Other Presentations

Case You have been given slides from a colleague's presentation on the XcR workflow process that you need to insert into your presentation.

Objectives
- Insert slides from another presentation
- Rearrange slides in Slide Sorter view

To save time and energy, you can insert one or more slides you already created in other presentations into an existing presentation or the one you are currently working on. One way to share slides between presentations is to open an existing presentation, copy the slides you want to the Clipboard, then paste them into your open presentation. However, PowerPoint offers a simpler way to transfer slides directly between presentations. By using the Reuse Slides pane, you can insert slides from another presentation or a network location. Newly inserted slides automatically take on the theme of the open presentation, unless you decide to use slide formatting from the original source presentation.

Steps

1. Click the **Slide 5 thumbnail** in the thumbnail pane, then click the **Reuse Slides button** in the Slides group
   The Reuse Slides pane opens on the right side of the presentation window and displays recently opened presentations.

2. Click **Browse** in the Reuse Slides pane, navigate to the location where you store your Data Files, then double-click **Support_PPT_3_Workflow.pptx**
   Slide thumbnails are displayed in the pane as shown in **Figure 3-9**. The slide thumbnails identify the slides in the **source presentation**, Support_PPT_3_Workflow.pptx.

   Quick Tip: To maintain the formatting and design of a reused slide, make sure the Use source formatting check box is selected.

3. Click the **Use source formatting check box** in the Reuse Slides pane to deselect it, then click the **Slide 1 thumbnail** in the Reuse Slides pane
   The new slide appears in the thumbnail pane and Slide pane as the new Slide 6. Notice the new slide assumes the design style and formatting of your presentation, which is the **destination presentation**.

4. Click the **Slide 2 thumbnail** in the Reuse Slides pane, then click the **Slide 3 thumbnail** in the Reuse Slides pane
   The new Slides 7 and 8 assume the design style and formatting of the destination presentation.

   Quick Tip: To copy noncontiguous slides, open Slide Sorter view, click the first slide thumbnail, press and hold CTRL, click each additional slide thumbnail, release CTRL, then click the Copy button.

5. Click the **Reuse Slides pane Close button**
   The Reuse Slides pane closes. You realize the last slide you inserted is not needed for this presentation.

6. Right-click the **Slide 8 thumbnail** in the thumbnail pane, then click **Delete Slide** in the shortcut menu
   Slide 8 is deleted.

7. Click the **Slide Sorter button** in the status bar, then drag **Slide 7** to the right of Slide 5

8. Click the **Normal button** in the status bar, then save the presentation
   Slide 7 becomes Slide 6. Compare your screen to **Figure 3-10**.

Figure 3-9: Presentation window with Reuse Slides pane open

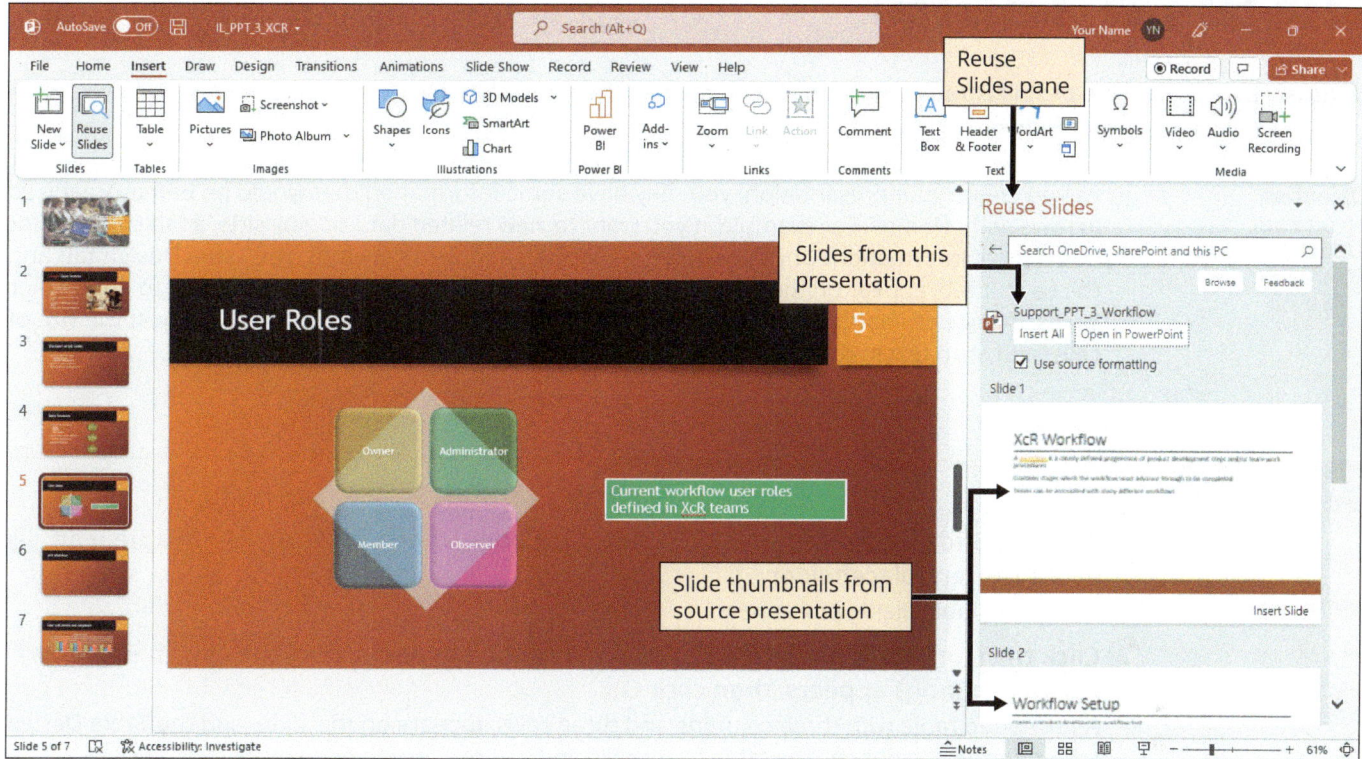

Fauxels/Pexels

Figure 3-10: New slides added to presentation

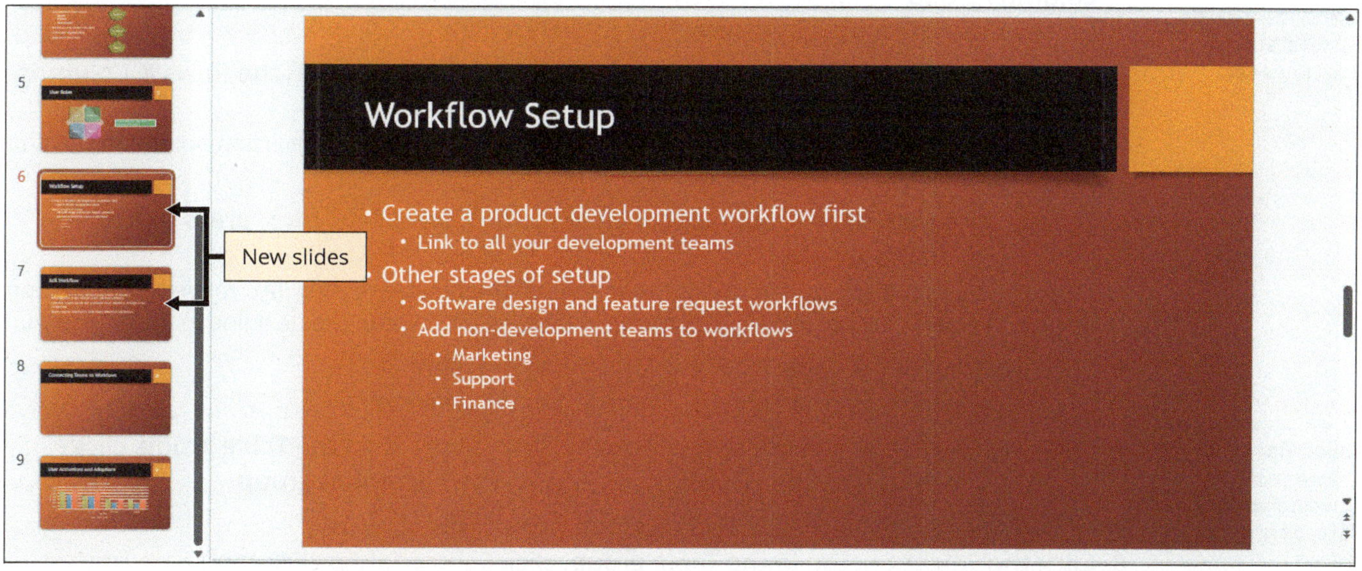

Working with multiple windows

Another way to work with information in multiple presentations is to arrange the presentation windows on your monitor so you view each window side by side. Open each presentation, click the View tab on the ribbon in any presentation window, then click the Arrange All button in the Window group. Each presentation you have open is placed next to each other so you can easily drag, or transfer, information between the presentations. If you are working with more than two open presentations, you can overlap the presentation windows on top of one another. Open all the presentations you want, then click the Cascade button in the Window group. Now you can easily jump from one presentation to another by clicking the presentation title bar or any part of the presentation window.

Insert a Table

Case Because a table best illustrates the connection between the four XcR teams and their specific workflows, you create a table on Slide 8.

Objectives
- Insert a table
- Add text to a table
- Change table size and layout

As you create your presentation, you may have some information that would be better organized in rows and columns. For example, if you want to view related data side by side, a table is ideal for this type of information. Once you have created a table, two new tabs, the Table Design tab and the Layout tab, appear on the ribbon. You can use the commands on the table tabs to apply color styles, change cell borders, add cell effects, add rows and columns to your table, adjust the size of cells, and align text in the cells.

Steps

1. Click the **Slide 8 thumbnail** in the thumbnail pane, then click the **Insert Table icon** in the content placeholder
   The Insert Table dialog box appears.

2. Click the **Number of columns down arrow** until **3** appears, click the **Number of rows up arrow** until **3** appears, then click **OK**
   A formatted table with three columns and three rows appears on the slide, and the Table Design tab opens on the ribbon. The table has 9 cells and you realize you need more cells.

   Quick Tip: Press TAB when the insertion point is in the last cell of a table to insert a new row.

3. Click the **Layout tab** on the ribbon, then click the **Insert Below button** in the Rows & Columns group
   A new row is added to the table below the current row.

4. Click the **top-left cell** in the table, click the **Insert Left button** in the Rows & Columns group, then click the **top-left cell** again
   The table has a new column to the left of the current column and the insertion point is in the first cell of the table ready to accept text.

5. Type **Product**, press **TAB**, type **Website**, press **TAB**, type **Analytics**, press **TAB**, type **Finance**, then press **TAB**
   The text you typed appears in the top four cells of the table. Pressing TAB moves the insertion point to the next cell; pressing ENTER moves the insertion point to the next line in the same cell.

6. Enter the rest of the table information shown in **Figure 3-11**
   The table would be more attractive if it were formatted differently.

   Quick Tip: Change the height or width of any table cell by dragging its borders.

7. Click the **top-left cell** in the table, click the **Select button** in the Table group, click **Select Row**, then click the **Center button** in the Alignment group
   The text in the top row is centered horizontally in each cell.

8. Click the **Select button** in the Table group, click **Select Table**, click the **Table Design tab** on the ribbon, click the **More button** in the Table Styles group, scroll to the **bottom** of the gallery, then click **Dark Style 1 - Accent 3**
   The table color changes to reflect the table style you applied.

9. Click the **Effects button** in the Table Styles group, point to **Cell Bevel**, then click **Soft Round** (2nd row)
   The 3D effect makes the cells of the table stand out.

   Quick Tip: To change the cell color behind the text, click the Shading arrow in the Table Styles group, then choose a color.

10. Drag the table to the center of the blank area of the slide, click a blank area of the slide, then save the presentation
    Compare your screen with **Figure 3-12**.

Figure 3-11: Inserted table with data

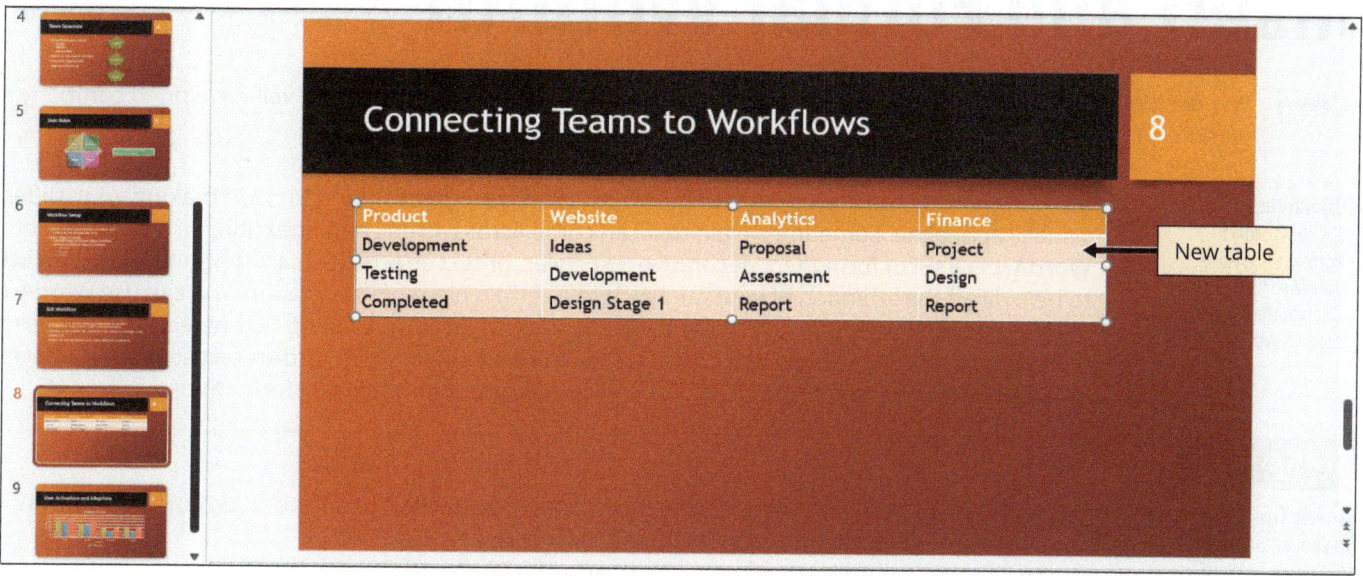

Figure 3-12: Formatted table

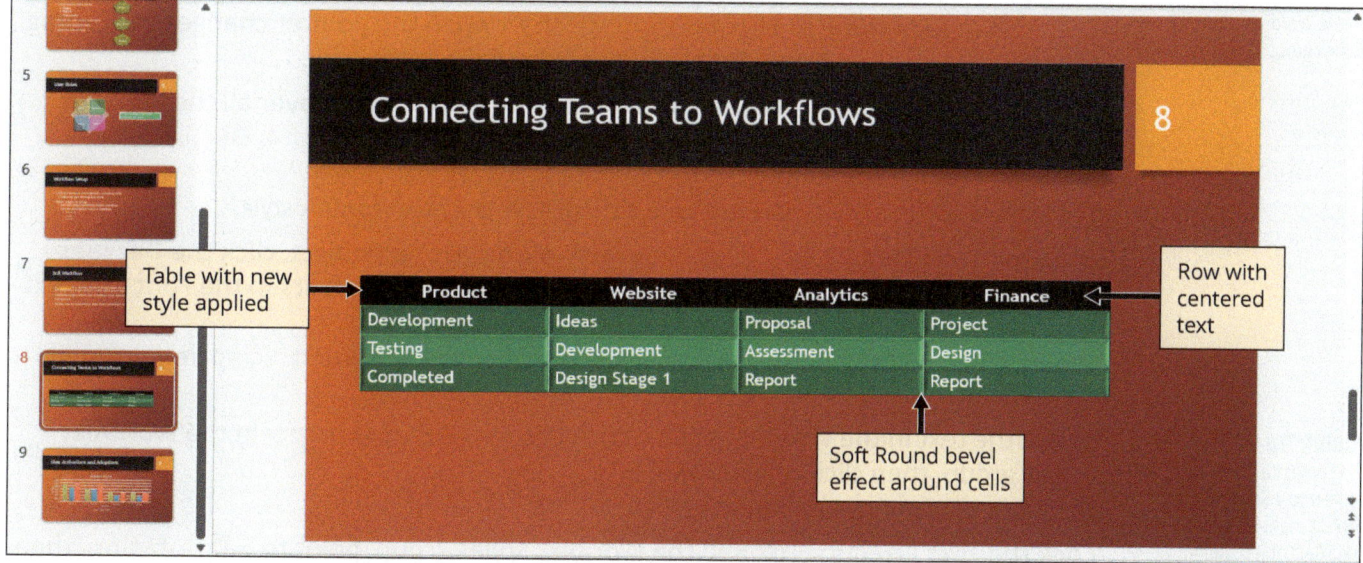

Setting permissions

In PowerPoint, you can set specific access permissions for people who review or edit your work so you have better control over your content. For example, you may want to give a user permission to edit or change your presentation but not allow them to print it. You can also restrict a user by permitting them to view the presentation without the ability to edit or print the presentation, or you can give the user full access or control of the presentation. To use this feature, you first access the information rights management services company. Then, to set user access permissions, click the File tab on the ribbon, click Info, click the Protect Presentation button, point to Restrict Access, then click an appropriate option.

Insert and Format WordArt

Case You decide to create a new WordArt text object on Slide 6 to show the importance of well-developed company workflows.

Objectives
- Create WordArt
- Format and resize WordArt
- Change the text fill color in WordArt

As you work to create an interesting presentation, your goal should include making your slides visually appealing. Sometimes plain text can come across as dull and unexciting in a presentation. **WordArt** is a set of formatted, decorative text styles, or text effects, you can apply to any text object to help direct the attention of your audience to a certain piece of information. You can use WordArt in two different ways: you can apply a WordArt text style to an existing text object that converts the text into WordArt, or you can create a new WordArt object. The WordArt text styles and effects include text shadows, reflections, glows, bevels, 3D rotations, and transformations.

Steps

Quick Tip
To convert any text or text object to WordArt, select the text or text object, click the Shape Format tab on the ribbon, then click a WordArt style option in the WordArt Styles group.

1. **Click the Slide 6 thumbnail** in the thumbnail pane, click the **Insert tab** on the ribbon, then click the **WordArt button** in the Text group
   The WordArt gallery appears displaying 20 WordArt text styles.

2. Click **Fill: Aqua, Accent color 4; Soft Bevel** (first row)
   A text object appears in the middle of the slide displaying sample text with the WordArt style you just selected. The Shape Format tab appears on the ribbon.

3. Click the edge of the **WordArt text object**, then when the pointer changes to ✥, drag the text object to the blank area at the bottom right of the slide

4. Click the **More button** ▼ in the WordArt Styles group, move ▷ over all the WordArt styles in the gallery, then click **Gradient Fill: Aqua, Accent color 4; Outline: Aqua, Accent color 4** (second row)
   The sample text in the WordArt text object changes to the new WordArt style.

5. Drag to select the text **Your text here** in the WordArt text object, click the **Decrease Font Size button** A˅ **twice** in the Mini toolbar so that **44** appears in the Font Size text box, then type **Better Workflows Better Outcomes**
   The text, "Better Workflows Better Outcomes" is on the slide as WordArt. Compare your screen to **Figure 3-13**.

Quick Tip
To convert a WordArt object to a SmartArt object, right-click the WordArt object, point to Convert to SmartArt on the shortcut menu, then click a SmartArt layout.

6. Select the text in the WordArt object, click the **Text Outline arrow** in the WordArt Styles group, then click **White, Text 1**
   The WordArt outline is now white.

7. Click the **Text Effects button** in the WordArt Styles group, point to **3-D Rotation**, then click **Perspective: Left** in the Perspective section (first row)
   The off-axis effect is applied to the text object. You are unsure of this effect and apply an additional effect.

8. Click the **Text Effects button**, point to **Reflection**, then click **Tight Reflection: Touching** in the Reflection Variations section (first row)
   The effect is applied to the text object along with the perspective effect.

9. Press **SHIFT**, drag the **lower-left sizing handle** down ¼ inch, release **SHIFT**, click a blank area of the slide, then save your work
   The text object is proportionally larger. Compare your screen to **Figure 3-14**.

Figure 3-13: WordArt inserted on slide

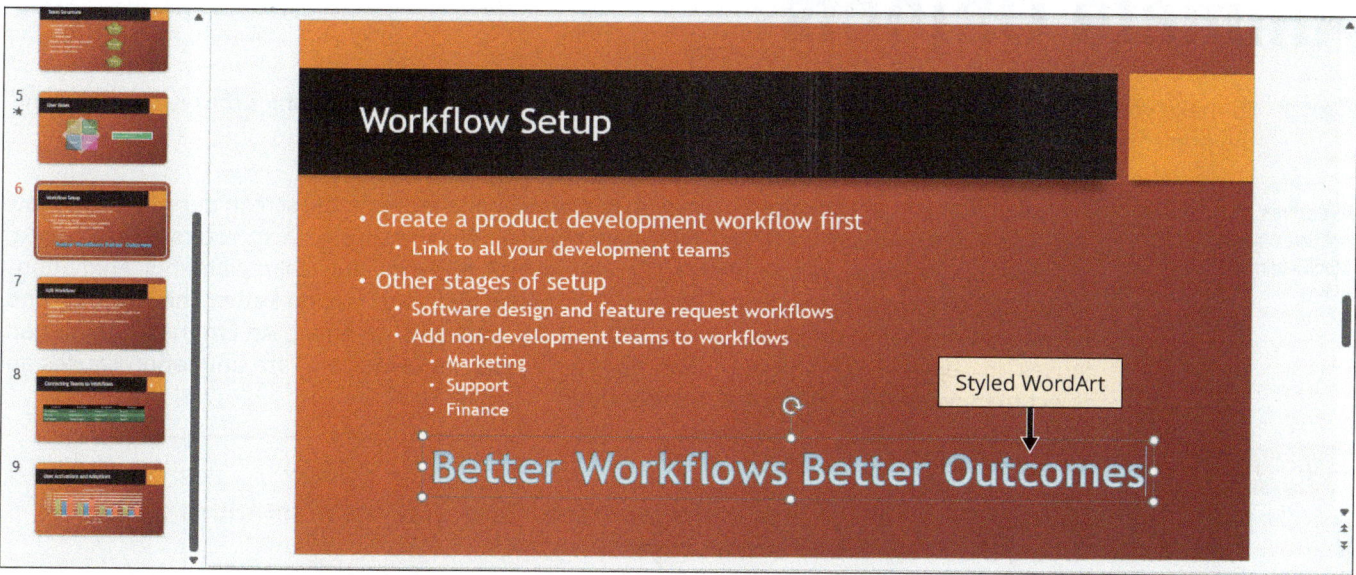

Figure 3-14: Formatted WordArt object

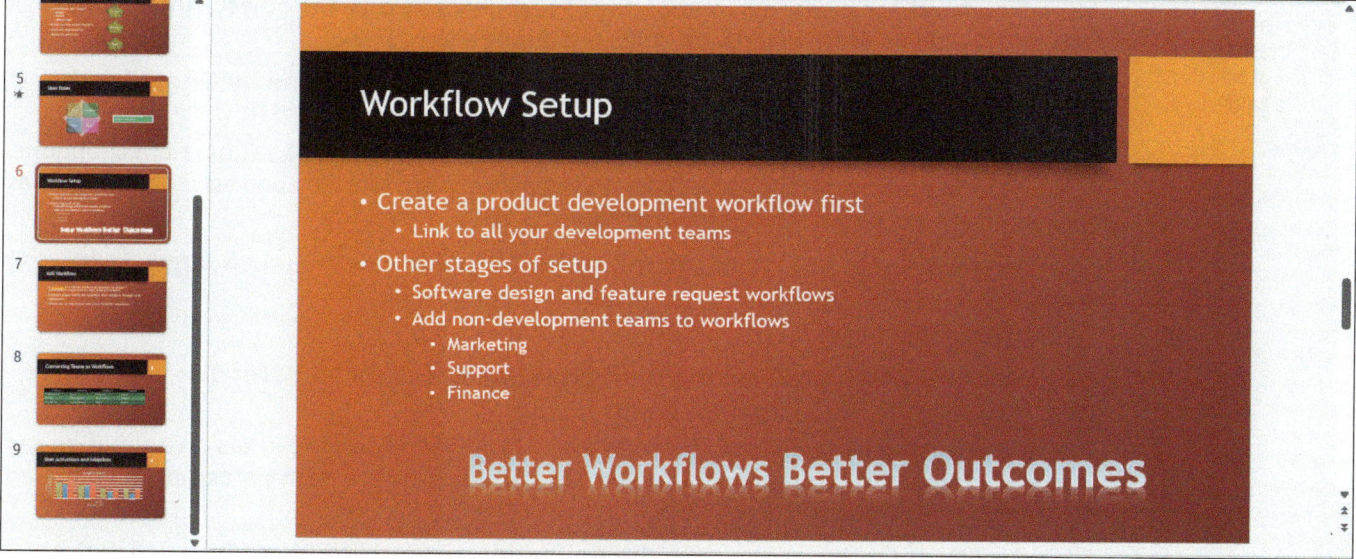

Coauthoring a presentation

By using collaboration software, such as SharePoint Online or saving a presentation to a OneDrive location, you can work with others on a presentation over the Internet at the same time. To set up a presentation to be coauthored with you as the original author, click the File tab, click Share, click Share with People, click Save To Cloud, then click your OneDrive location. Choose a shared location or server to store a primary copy of your presentation, then click the Save button. Open the presentation and begin working, and if someone else is working on the presentation, you will see their thumbnail picture in the upper-right corner of the Ribbon. All changes made to the presentation are recorded, including who is working on the presentation and where in the presentation they are working. When you save the presentation, PowerPoint notifies you about changes made by the coauthors. To use this feature, all authors must have PowerPoint 2010 or later installed on their computers.

Animate Objects

Case To make your presentation more interesting to watch, you animate the text and graphics on several slides in the presentation.

Objectives
- Animate objects
- Modify animation effects

Animations let you control how objects and text appear and move on the screen during a slide show and allow you to manage the flow of information and emphasize specific facts. You can animate text, pictures, sounds, hyperlinks, SmartArt diagrams, charts, and individual chart elements. Animations are organized into four categories: Entrance, Emphasis, Exit, and Motion Paths. The Entrance and Exit animations cause an object to enter or exit the slide with an effect. An Emphasis animation causes an object visible on the slide to have an effect, and a Motion Path animation causes an object to move on a specified path on the slide.

Steps

1. **Click the Slide 5 thumbnail in the thumbnail pane, click the Animations tab on the ribbon, then click the SmartArt object**
   Text as well as other objects, such as a shape or picture, can be animated during a slide show.

2. **Click the More button in the Animation group, then click Float In in the Entrance section**
   A small numeral 1, called an animation tag, appears next to the object. **Animation tags** identify the order in which objects are animated during a slide show.

   Quick Tip: There are additional animation options for each animation category located at the bottom of the animations gallery.

3. **Click the Effect Options button in the Animation group, click One by One, click the Effect Options button, then click Float Down**
   Effect options are different for every animation, and some animations don't have effect options. All 5 objects in the SmartArt animate separately in a downward direction and each object now has an animation tag. Compare your screen to **Figure 3-15**.

4. **Click the Slide Show button on the status bar, click your mouse 5 times, then press ESC**
   The SmartArt object animates.

5. **Click the Slide 3 thumbnail in the thumbnail pane, click the bulleted list text object, then click Wipe in the Animation group**
   The text object is animated with the Wipe animation. Each line of text has an animation tag with each paragraph displaying a different number. Accordingly, each paragraph is animated separately.

6. **Click the Effect Options button in the Animation group, click All at Once, click the Duration up arrow in the Timing group until 02.00 appears, then click the Preview button in the Preview group**
   Notice the animation tags for each line of text in the text object now have the same numeral (1), indicating that each line of text animates at the same time.

7. **Click Heart in the title text object, click in the Animation group, scroll down, then click Loops in the Motion Paths section**
   A motion path object appears on the slide and identifies the path of the animation. If needed, you can resize or change the direction of the motion path. Notice the numeral 2 animation tag next to the title text object indicating that it is animated *after* the bulleted list text object. Refer to **Figure 3-16**.

   Quick Tip: If you want to individually animate the parts of a grouped object, then you must ungroup the objects before you animate them.

8. **Click the Move Earlier button in the Timing group, click the Slide Show tab on the ribbon, then click the From Beginning button in the Start Slide Show group**
   Slide 1 appears in Slide Show view.

9. **Press SPACE to advance the slides and animations, when you reach the black slide, press ENTER, then save your changes**

Figure 3-15: Animation applied to SmartArt object

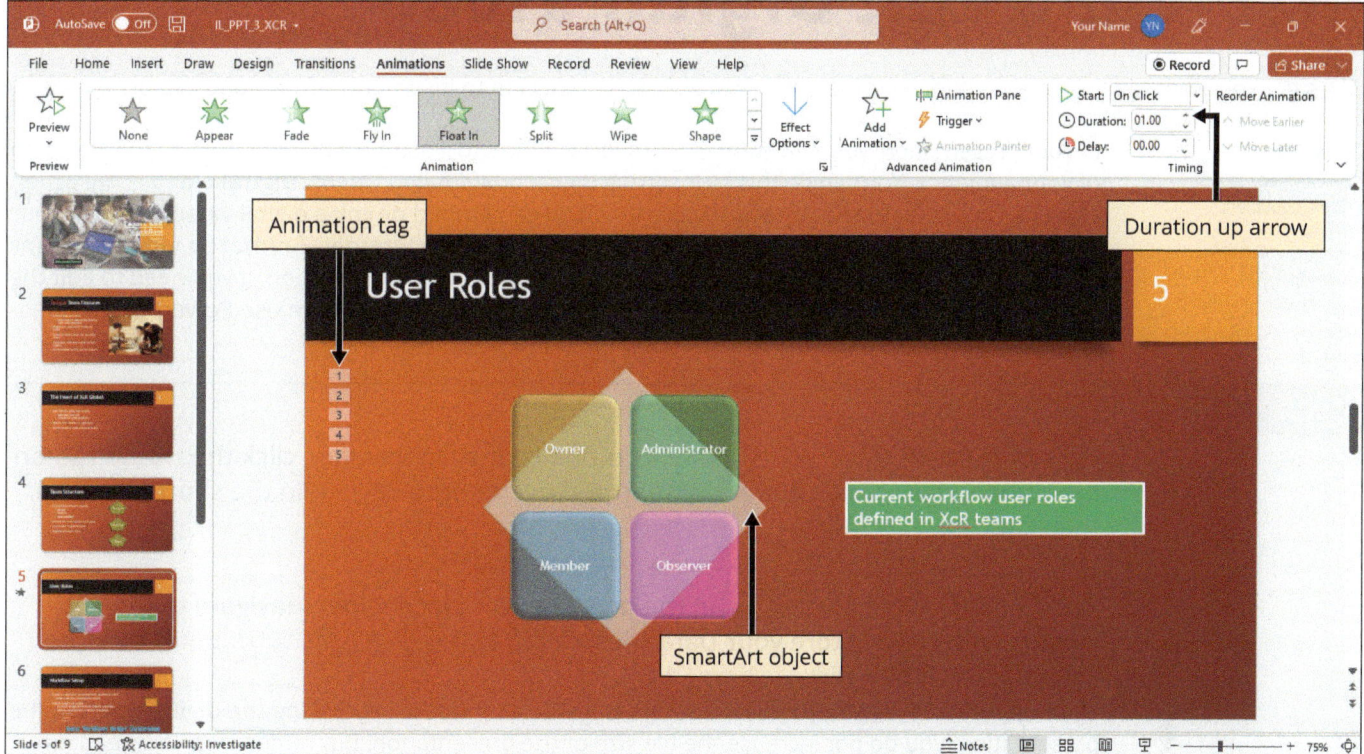

Figure 3-16: Motion path applied to title text object

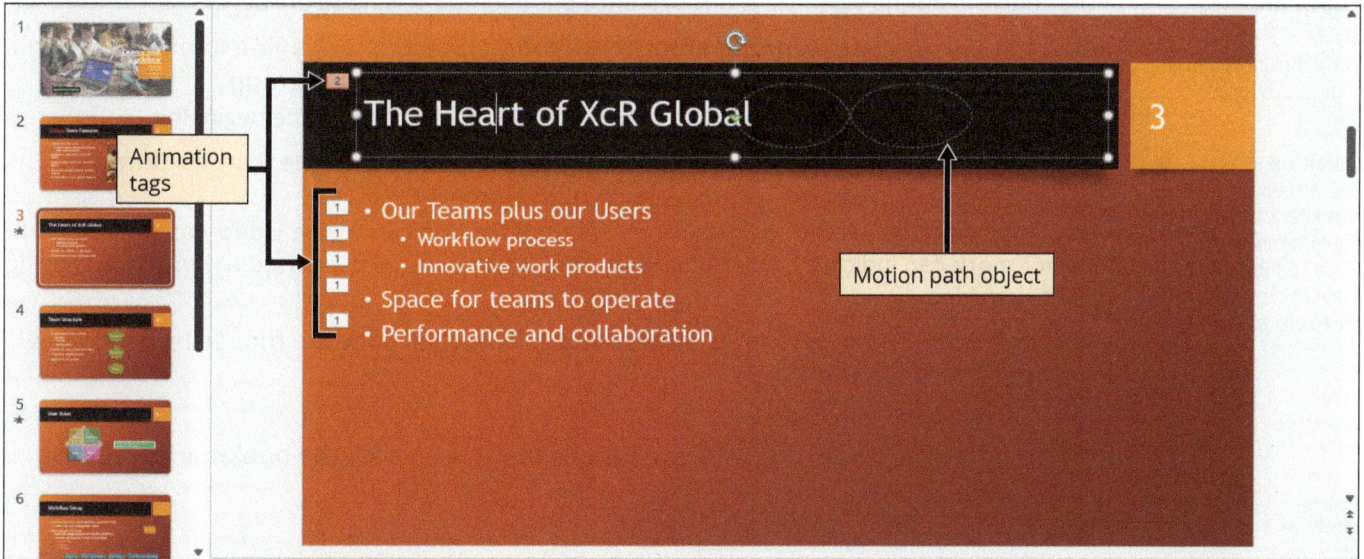

Attaching a sound to an animation

Text or objects that have animation applied can be customized further by attaching a sound for extra emphasis. First, select the animated object, then on the Animations tab, click the Animation Pane button in the Advanced Animation group. In the Animation Pane, click the animation you want to apply the sound to, click the Animation's list arrow, then click Effect Options to open the animation effect's dialog box. In the Enhancements section, click the Sound list arrow, then choose a sound. Click OK when you are finished. Now, when you run the slide show, the sound you applied will play with the animation.

Module 3 Inserting Objects into a Presentation

Insert and Edit Digital Video

Case You want to illustrate the concept of teamwork at XcR, so you decide to insert and edit a video clip on Slide 3.

Objectives
- Link a video
- Add a bookmark

In your presentation, you may want to use special effects to illustrate a point or capture the attention of your audience. You can do this by inserting digital or animated videos. **Digital video** is live action captured in digital format by a video camera. You can embed or link a digital video file from your hard drive or link a digital video file from a webpage on the Internet. **Animated video** contains multiple images that stream together or move to give the illusion of motion. If you need to edit the length of a video or add effects or background color to a video, you can use PowerPoint's video-editing tools to accomplish those and other basic editing tasks.

Steps

1. Click the **Slide 3 thumbnail** in the thumbnail pane if necessary, click the **Home tab** on the ribbon, right-click a blank area of the slide, point to **Layout** in the shortcut menu, then click **Two Content**

   The slide layout changes and has two content placeholders.

2. Click the **Insert Video icon** in the new Content placeholder, navigate to the location where you store your Data Files, click **Support_PPT_3_Group.mp4**, click the **Insert arrow**, then click **Link to File**

   The Support_PPT_3_Group.mp4 video clip is linked to the slide. By linking the digital video to the presentation, you do not increase the file size of the presentation, but remember, you need direct access to the location where the video file is stored in order to play it.

   Quick Tip: For videos with sound, adjust the volume of the video using the Mute/Unmute control on the video control timeline.

3. Click the **Play/Pause button** in the video control bar

   The short 30-second video plays through once but does not rewind to the beginning.

4. Click the **Playback tab** on the ribbon, click the **Rewind after Playing check box** in the Video Options group, then click the **Play button** in the Preview group

   The video plays through once, and this time the video rewinds back to the beginning.

   Quick Tip: You can also add fade effects to the beginning and end of a video using the Fade Duration commands in the Editing group.

5. Click the **video control timeline** at about **00:16.00**, then click the **Add Bookmark button** in the Bookmarks group as shown in **Figure 3-17**

   A yellow circle appears in the video control timeline, indicating the video has a bookmark. A **bookmark** can indicate a point of interest in a video; it can also be used to jump to a specific point in a video.

6. Click the **Slide Show button** on the status bar, then click the mouse twice to view the animations on the slide

   The text object animations play.

7. Move over the video, the pointer changes to , then click the bookmark as shown in **Figure 3-18**

   The video moves to the bookmarked frame.

8. Click the **Play/Pause button** on the video

   The video plays from the bookmarked frame to the end of the video and then rewinds to the beginning.

   Quick Tip: Click the Reset Design button in the Adjust group to remove all formatting changes you made to the video.

9. Press **ESC**, click the **Video Format tab** on the ribbon, click the **More button** in the Video Styles group, then click **Snip Diagonal Corner, Gradient** in the Moderate section

   A snipped corner with a shaded gradient effect is added to the video.

10. **sam↑** Click a blank area of the slide, save your work, submit your presentation to your instructor, then exit PowerPoint

Figure 3-17: Video clip inserted on the slide

Fauxels/Pexels; Mikhail Nilov/Pexels

Figure 3-18: Video in Slide Show view with selected bookmark

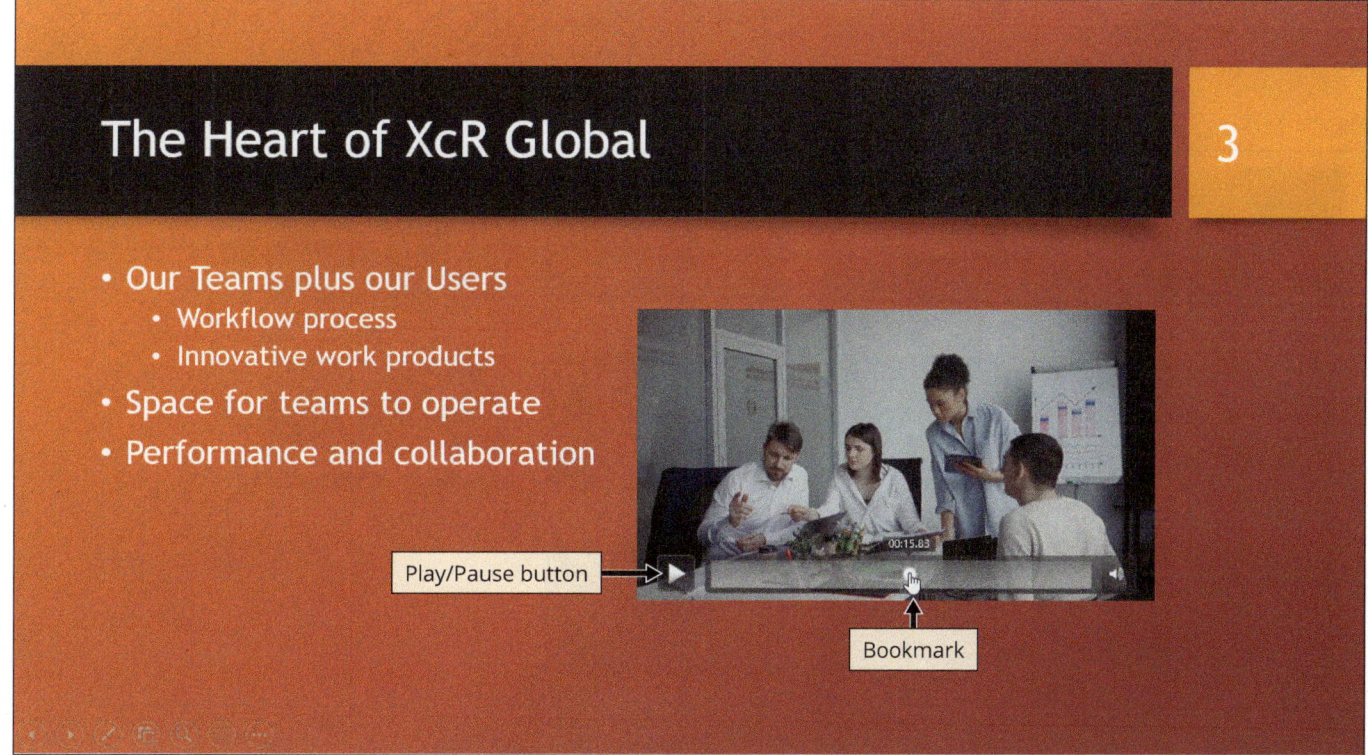

Mikhail Nilov/Pexels

Saving a presentation as a video

You can save your PowerPoint presentation as a full-fidelity video, which incorporates all slide timings, transitions, animations, and narrations. The video can be distributed using a thumb drive, the Internet, or email. Depending on how you want to display your video, you have four resolution settings from which to choose: Ultra HD (4K), Full HD (1080p), HD (720p), and Standard (480p). The largest two settings, Ultra HD (3840 × 2160) and Full HD (1920 × 1080), are used for viewing on a computer monitor, projector, or other high-definition displays. The next setting, HD (1280 × 720), is used for uploading to the web or copying to a standard DVD. The smallest setting, Standard (852 × 480), is used on portable media players. To save your presentation as a video, click the File tab, click Export, click Create a Video, choose your settings, then click the Create Video button.

Practice

In the exercises that follow, you will practice the skills you have learned in this module.

Skills Review

You work for Jefferson County EMS Services, and you have been asked to create a presentation on scene hazards and vehicle extrication for an upcoming meeting. You will use PowerPoint features from this module to help create this presentation.

1. **Insert a text box.**
   a. Open IL_PPT_3-2.pptx from the location where you store your Data Files, then save it as **IL_PPT_3_Jefferson**. You will work to create the completed presentation as shown in **Figure 3-19**.
   b. On Slide 3, insert a text box below the text objects, then type **Size-up is performed by arriving officer first to the scene**
   c. Move the word "first" after the word "by", then add space between words, as necessary.
   d. Select the text object, then click the More button in the Shape Styles group on the Shape Format tab.
   e. Apply the style Intense Effect – Green, Accent 4, then resize the text box to fit the text, if necessary.
   f. Using Smart Guides, drag the text object so it is centered on the slide in the blank space below the two text boxes.

Figure 3-19

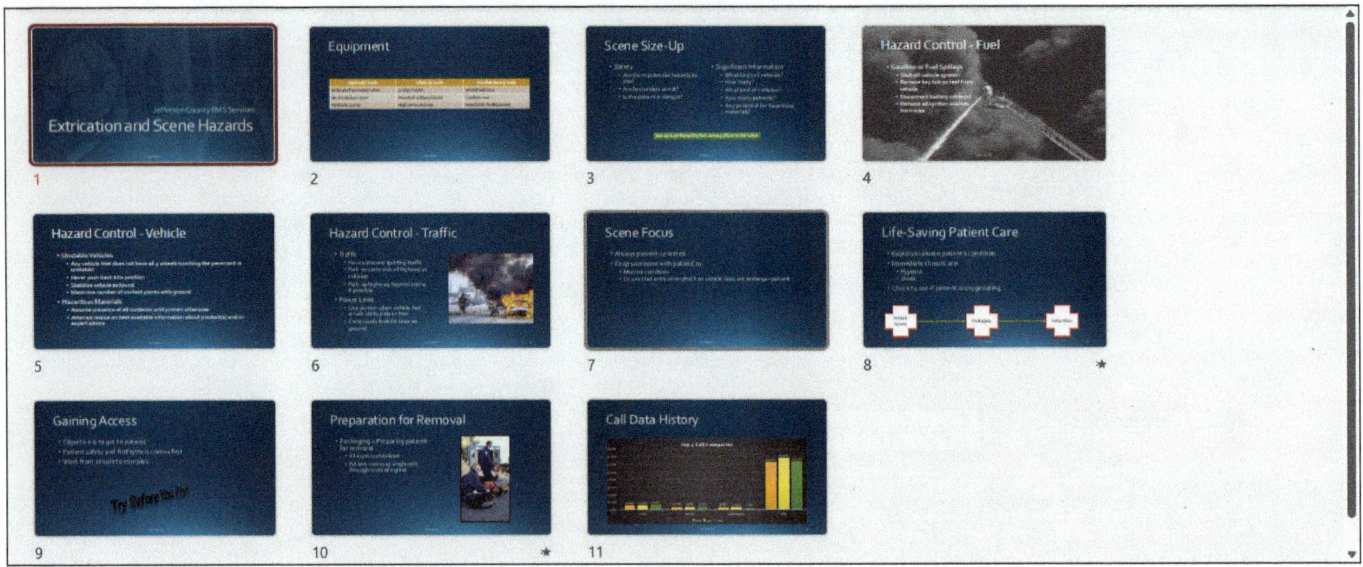

Onur Uslu/Pexels; StyRodnae Productions/PexelsEves Exantus/Pexels

2. **Revise and crop a picture.**
   a. Select Slide 6 in the thumbnail pane, then crop the right side of the picture up to the burning car.
   b. Drag the picture to the center of the blank area of the slide.
   c. Change the picture color tone to Temperature: 4700 K, then using the Corrections button change the sharpness of the picture to Soften: 50%.
   d. Change the picture style to Center Shadow Rectangle.
   e. Select Slide 4 in the thumbnail pane, then open the Format Background pane.
   f. Click the Insert button in the pane, click From a File, then insert the picture Support_PPT_3_Fire.jpg from the location where you store your Data Files.
   g. Change the picture transparency to 30%, close the Format Background pane, then save your changes.

3. **Insert a chart.**
   a. Create a new slide after Slide 7 with a Title and Content layout and title it **Call Data History**.
   b. Insert a Clustered Column chart, close the worksheet, then apply the Layout 3 quick layout to the chart.
   c. Drag the chart to the center of the slide using the vertical Smart Guide.

4. **Enter and edit chart data.**
   a. Show the worksheet, enter the data shown in **Table 3-2** into the worksheet, then close the worksheet.
   b. Type **Top 4 Call Categories** in the chart title text object then increase the font size of the chart title to 24 using the Increase Font Size button.
   c. Click the Chart Styles button next to the chart, then change the chart style to Style 8.
   d. Click Color in the Charts Styles gallery, then change the color to Colorful Palette 4 in the Colorful section.
   e. Close the Charts Styles gallery, click a blank area of the slide, then save your changes.

Table 3-2

	2026	2027	2028
Fires	5.82%	6.19%	7.02%
Vehicle	4.20%	3.96%	4.64%
False Alarms	3.89%	3.19%	2.75%
EMS	63.2%	67.9%	64.4%

5. **Insert slides from other presentations.**
   a. Go to Slide 7, then open the Reuse Slides pane.
   b. Open Support_PPT_3_Emergency.pptx from the location where you store your Data Files, then deselect the Use source formatting option in the Reuse Slides pane.
   c. Insert the second slide thumbnail, insert the third slide thumbnail, then insert the first slide thumbnail.
   d. Close the Reuse Slides pane, then open the Slide Sorter view.
   e. Move Slide 10 between Slide 6 and Slide 7, switch to Normal view, then save your work.

6. **Insert a table.**
   a. Go to Slide 2, then insert a table with two columns and three rows.
   b. On the Layout tab, add one more row and one more column to the table, then enter the information shown in **Table 3-3**.
   c. On the Table Design tab, change the table style to Medium Style 2 – Accent 6.
   d. On the Layout tab, select the top row, then center the text.
   e. Select the whole table, open the Table Design tab, click the Effects button, point to Cell Bevel, then apply the Angle effect.
   f. Using Smart Guides, move the table to the center of the blank area of the slide, then save your changes.

Table 3-3

Hydraulic Tools	Lift/Crib Tools	Forcible Entry Tools
Dedicated spreader/cutter	2-step chocks	Windshield saw
Short/medium rams	Assorted cribbing blocks	Cordless saws
Hydraulic pump	High-pressure bags	Hand tools (halligan/axe)

7. **Insert and format WordArt.**
   a. Go to Slide 9, then insert a WordArt text object using the style Fill White, Text color 1; Shadow.
   b. Type **Try Before You Pry!**, apply the text effect Half Reflection: Touching to the text object, then move the text object to the middle of the blank area of the slide.
   c. Apply the 3-D Rotation text effect Perspective: Contrasting Right (third row in the Perspective section).
   d. Change the text fill color to Gold, Accent 6, Lighter 40%, then change the text outline to Black, Background 1.
   e. Increase the size of the WordArt object proportionally, re-center the object on the slide, then view the slide in Slide Show view.
   f. Switch back to Normal view, then save your changes.

Skills Review (Continued)

8. **Animate objects.**
   a. Go to Slide 8, display the Animations tab, then select the two orange arrow lines on the slide. (**Hint**: Use SHIFT to select the shapes.)
   b. Apply the Wipe animation effect to the objects, then apply the From Left effect option.
   c. Change the animation duration to 01.00, then preview the animations.
   d. Apply the Fade animation to the bulleted text object, then apply the All at Once effect option.
   e. Move the text object animation to be earlier (**Hint**: Use the Move Earlier button in the Timing group), select the Extrication object, then apply the Pulse animation.
   f. Apply the Loops motion path animation to the title object, then open Slide Show view.
   g. Use SPACEBAR to go through the animations on Slide 8, press ESC when you reach Slide 9, then save your work.

9. **Insert and edit digital video.**
   a. Go to Slide 10, change the slide layout to Two Content, then use the Insert Video icon to link the file Support_PPT_3_Patient.mp4 from the location where you store your Data Files, click the Insert arrow, then click Link to File.
   b. Use the Playback tab to set the video to rewind after playing, then add a bookmark at about the 00:05.00 point on the video control timeline.
   c. On the Video Format tab, apply the video style Simple Frame, Black, preview the video clip in Slide Show view, then add your name and the slide number as a footer to all slides.
   d. Save your work, submit your presentation to your instructor, close your presentation, then exit PowerPoint.

Independent Challenge 1

You are an associate at Chamberlin & Foster Inc., a large financial investment and management company, located in Las Vegas, NV. One of your responsibilities is to create general presentations for use on the company website. As part of this presentation, you insert a chart, insert a video, add a WordArt object, and insert slides from another presentation. You finish the presentation by adding slide transitions and animations to the slides.

   a. Open IL_PPT_3-3.pptx from the location where you store your Data Files, then save it as **IL_PPT_3_Chamberlin**. You will work to create the completed presentation as shown in **Figure 3-20**.

Figure 3-20

Kindel Media/Pexels

b. Apply the Ion Boardroom Design Theme, select the thumbnail in the Design Ideas pane that most closely resembles Slide 1 in **Figure 3-20**, then close the pane.
c. Insert a clustered column chart on Slide 2, then enter the data in **Table 3-4** into the worksheet.

Table 3-4

	Bonds	Stocks	Mutual Funds
1-Year	1.7	4.9	4.3
3-Year	2.8	5.3	7.9
5-Year	4.3	7.6	5.4
10-Year	3.5	6.2	6.7

d. Close the worksheet, format the chart using Style 4, change the color to Colorful Palette 2, then using Smart Guides move the chart to the center of the blank area of the slide.
e. Type **Annualized Return** in the chart title text object, then decrease its font size to 18 point.
f. Open the Reuse Slides pane, open Support_PPT_3_Strategy.pptx from the location where you store your Data Files, deselect the Use source formatting check box, then insert Slides 2, 3, and 4.
g. Close the Reuse Slides pane, open Slide Sorter view, move Slide 3 between Slide 5 and Slide 6, then display Slide 3 in Normal view.
h. Insert a WordArt object using the Fill: Orange, Accent color 4; Soft Bevel style, type **The biggest risk is not taking one**, then change the font size to 48.
i. Click the Text Effects button, point to Transform, apply the Chevron: Down text effect from the Warp section, then move the WordArt object to the center of the blank area at the bottom of the slide.
j. Go to Slide 6, change the slide layout to Two Content, then insert the picture Support_PPT_3_Advisor.jpg from the location where you store your Data Files.
k. Crop the left side of the picture up to the woman's arm, apply the Bevel Rectangle picture style (3rd row) to the picture, then change the color tone to Temperature: 8800 K.
l. Change the sharpness of the picture to Sharpen: 50%, then go to Slide 2.
m. Apply the animation Float In to the chart, apply the By Element in Series effect option, then set the duration to 01.50.
n. Apply the animation Wipe to the slide title, then reorder the slide title animation to run first in the animation sequence.
o. Add your name and slide number as the footer on all of the slides, view the presentation in Slide Show view, then save your work.
p. Submit the presentation to your instructor, close the presentation, then exit PowerPoint.

Independent Challenge 2

TimeSHARE Corp. is an employee tracking and management software company. You continue working on the presentation you have already started for an upcoming meeting.

a. Start PowerPoint, open IL_PPT_3-4.pptx from the location where you store your Data Files, then save it as **IL_PPT_3_Meeting**. You will work to create the completed presentation as shown in **Figure 3-21**.
b. Add your name and the slide number as the footer on all the slides.

Independent Challenge 2 (Continued)

Figure 3-21

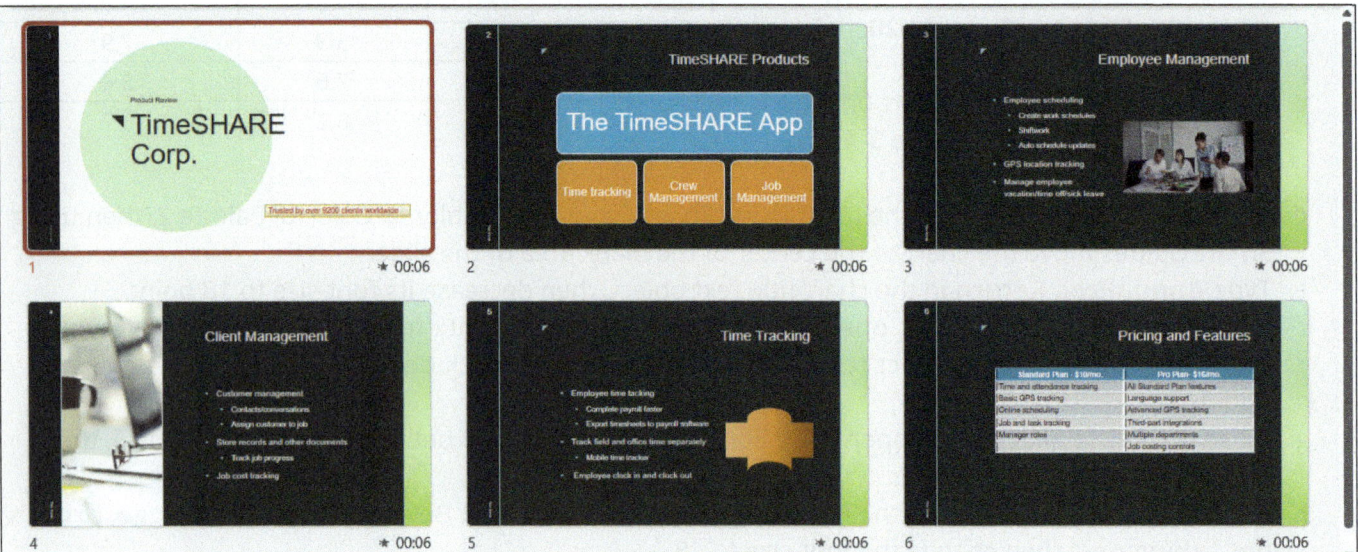

Mikhail Nilov/Pexels

c. Go to Slide 3, change the slide layout to Two Content, click the Insert Video icon in the content placeholder, then link the video Support_PPT_3_Group.mp4 from the location where you store your Data Files. (**Hint**: Be sure to use the Link to File option in this step.)

d. Insert a bookmark at about 00:05.00, rewind the video after playing, then apply the Center Shadow Rectangle video style.

e. Go to Slide 1, insert a text box in a blank area of the slide, type **Trusted by over 9200 clients worldwide**, then change the text color to dark red.

f. Apply the shape style Subtle Effect - Tan, Accent 4 to the text object, then apply the Offset: Bottom shadow shape effect.

g. Go to Slide 5, create a new slide, type **Pricing and Features** in the title placeholder, create a table, then enter the data in **Table 3-5**.

h. Apply the table style Medium Style 1 - Accent 3, apply the Cutout bevel effect, then center the text in the top row of the table.

i. On Slide 2 apply the Random Bars animation to the SmartArt object, change the effect option direction to Vertical and the sequence to One by One, then change the duration to 01.25.

j. Add a Cube transition to all slides with a From Bottom effect, then add a duration time of 02.00.

k. Add a 06.00 slide timing to all the slides, save your work, then view the final presentation from Slide 1 in Slide Show view.

l. Submit the presentation to your instructor, close the file, then exit PowerPoint.

Table 3-5

Standard Plan - $10/mo.	Pro Plan - $16/mo.
Time and attendance tracking	All Standard plan features
Basic GPS tracking	Language support
Online scheduling	Advanced GPS tracking
Job and task tracking	Third-party integrations
Manager roles	Multiple departments
	Job costing controls

Visual Workshop

Create a one-slide presentation (use a Blank slide layout) that looks like **Figure 3-22**. To complete this presentation, insert the picture file Support_PPT_3_Team.jpg from the location where you store your Data Files to the slide background, then change the picture transparency to 40%. The text box font size is 60-point with a Semitransparent – Gold, Accent 4, No Outline shape style applied to it. Add your name as footer text to the slide, change the footer text color to Black, Text 1, save the presentation as **IL_PPT_3_College** to the location where you store your Data Files, submit your presentation to your instructor, close the file, then exit PowerPoint.

Figure 3-22

Fauxels/Pexels

Integration **Module 3**

Integrating Word, Excel, Access, and PowerPoint

Case

Ariel Likowski, the Dean of Student Services at Mountain Springs Institute of Technology in Denver, CO, creates presentations for faculty and students that often include objects from Word, Excel, and Access. She asks you to explore how to use linking and embedding in Office and then how to insert linked objects from Word, Excel, and Access into a PowerPoint presentation.

Module Objectives

After completing this module, you will be able to:

- Identify integration options among Word, Excel, Access, and PowerPoint
- Import a Word outline into PowerPoint
- Embed an Excel worksheet in PowerPoint
- Link Access and Excel objects to PowerPoint
- Update and break links

Files You Will Need

IL_INT_3-1.docx
IL_INT_3-2.accdb
IL_INT_3-3.docx
IL_INT_3-4.accdb
IL_INT_3-5.docx
IL_INT_3-6.accdb
IL_INT_3-7.docx
IL_INT_3-8.accdb
IL_INT_3-9.accdb

Identify Integration Options among Word, Excel, Access, and PowerPoint

Case Before you create the presentation, you review some of the ways you can integrate information among Word, Excel, Access, and PowerPoint.

Objective
- Define import, embed, and link integration options

You can integrate information into a PowerPoint presentation using the linking and embedding techniques you learned with Word, Excel, and Access. As with those programs, you embed data created in other programs in PowerPoint when you want to be able to edit the data from within the destination file. You use linking when you want the linked data in the destination file to be updated when you change the data in the source file. In addition, you can import a Word outline into PowerPoint to automatically create slides without having to reenter information. The PowerPoint presentation in **Figure 3-1** includes information created in Word, Excel, and Access.

Details

You can integrate Word, Excel, Access, and PowerPoint by:

- **Importing a Word outline into PowerPoint**
  In the course of your work, you may create Word documents that contain information that you also want to use in a PowerPoint presentation. Instead of retyping the information in PowerPoint, you can save time by importing it directly from Word into PowerPoint. **Figure 3-1** displays how a Word outline appears before and after it is imported into a PowerPoint presentation. Each Level 1 heading in the outline becomes a slide, and the Level 2 headings become bullets on the slides. Before you import a Word outline, you need to make sure all the headings and subheadings are formatted with heading styles. When you import an outline from Word to PowerPoint, you cannot create a link between the two files.

- **Embedding objects**
  Recall that when you embed an object, you do not create a link to the source file. However, you can use the source program tools to edit the embedded object within the destination file. An embedded object becomes a part of the PowerPoint file, which means that the file size of the PowerPoint presentation increases relative to the file size of the embedded object; a large embedded object, such as a graphic, will increase the size of the PowerPoint presentation considerably. To embed an object in a PowerPoint presentation, you use the Object command in the Text group on the Insert tab. In **Figure 3-1**, the table on Slide 3 is an embedded Excel worksheet object.

  To edit an embedded object, you double-click it. The source program starts, and the Ribbon and tabs of the source program appear inside the PowerPoint window.

- **Linking objects**
  When you link an object to a PowerPoint slide, a picture of the object is placed on the slide instead of the actual object. This representation of the object is connected, or linked, to the original file. The object is still stored in the source file in the source program, unlike an embedded object, which is stored directly on the PowerPoint slide. Any change you make to a linked object's source file is reflected in the linked object. The pie chart included on Slide 4 of the presentation in **Figure 3-1** is linked to values entered in an Excel worksheet, which is, in turn, linked to data entered in an Access database. The differences between embedding and linking are summarized in **Table 3-1**.

  You can open the source file and make changes to the linked object as long as all files remain on your computer. When you move files among machines or transmit files to other people, the links will not be maintained. However, recipients can open and view the linked files. After opening the workbook in Excel, they need to click No, close the workbook without saving it, then reopen the workbook and click Don't Update. In Word, they click No to update links.

Figure 3-1: PowerPoint presentation with integrated objects

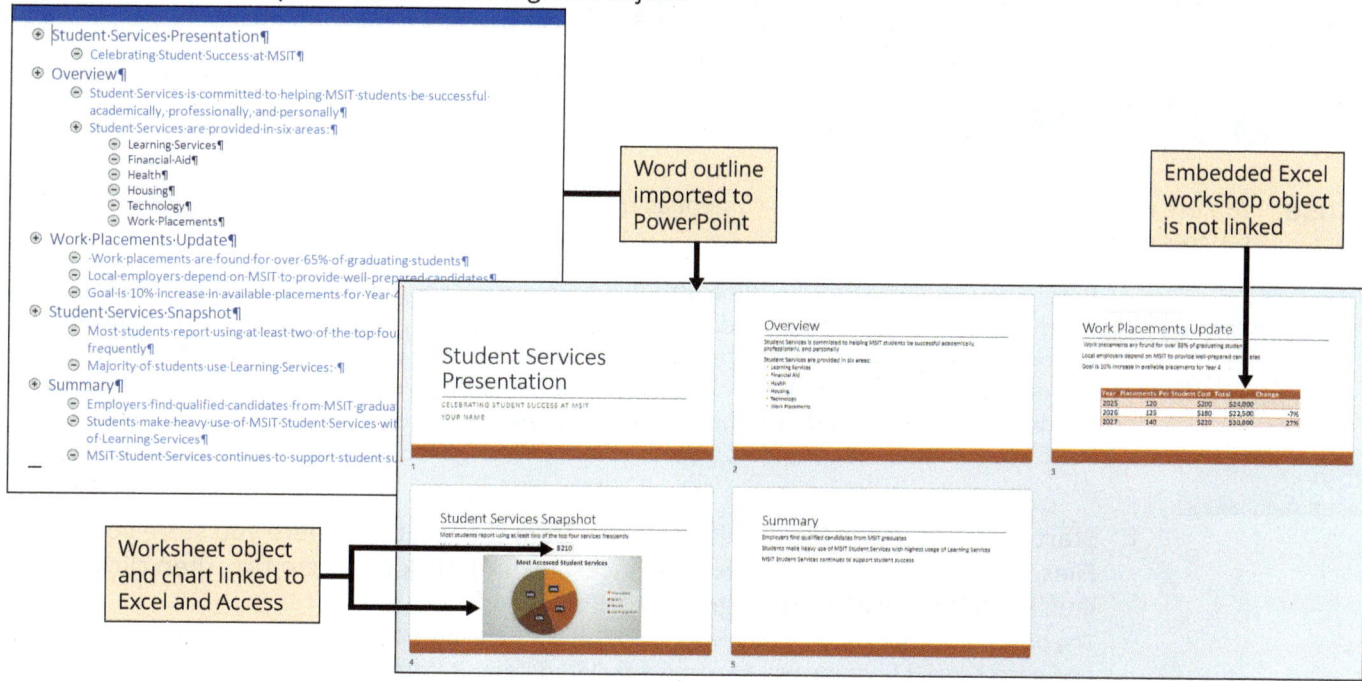

Table 3-1: Embedding vs. linking

	embed	link
User	You are the only user of an object and you want the object to be a part of your presentation	The object's source file is shared on a network or other users have access to the file and can change it
Availability	You want to open the object in its source program, even when the source file is not available	You can open the source file
Timeliness	Information does not change over time	You always want the object to include the latest information
Updating	You want to update the object manually while working in PowerPoint	You want the object to update automatically
File size	File size is not an issue	You want to keep the presentation's file size small

Import a Word Outline into PowerPoint

Case You use information included in a Word document as the basis of a PowerPoint presentation about student services at MSIT.

Objectives
- Prepare a Word outline for PowerPoint
- Import a Word outline into PowerPoint

Before you import a Word outline into PowerPoint, you should ensure that each Word outline heading is formatted with a heading style such as Heading 1, Heading 2, and so on. PowerPoint imports all text formatted with the Heading 1 style as a slide title and all text formatted with the Heading 2 style as a Level 1 item in a bulleted list. Any block of text that is not formatted with a heading style is not included in the PowerPoint presentation.

Steps

1. Start Word, open the file **IL_INT_3-1.docx** from the location where you store your Data Files, save it as **IL_INT_3_StudentServicesOutline**, click the **View tab**, then click the **Outline button** in the Views group

   The document appears in Outline view. Each Level 1 heading will become a slide title in PowerPoint, and each Level 2 heading will become a bulleted item. Before you import a Word outline into a PowerPoint presentation, you check that all the headings and subheadings are positioned at the correct levels.

   Quick Tip: You can also use TAB and SHIFT+TAB to demote and promote headings in Outline view.

2. Click **Celebrating Student Success at MSIT** (the second line), then click the **Demote button** → in the Outline Tools group once

   The text moves to the right by one tab stop and changes to a Level 2 heading. In PowerPoint, this text will appear as a bulleted item under the slide title "Student Services Presentation."

3. Click **Overview** (the third line), click the **Promote button** ← in the Outline Tools group, click **Learning Services** in the list of student services, press **TAB** to demote it to level 3, then compare your Word outline to **Figure 3-2**

4. Save and close the document

5. Start PowerPoint, create a blank presentation, close the Designer pane if it is open, then save the presentation as **IL_INT_3_StudentServicesPresentation** in the location where you store your Data Files

6. Click the **New Slide arrow** in the Slides group, click **Slides from Outline**, navigate to the location where you stored IL_INT_3_StudentServicesOutline.docx, then double-click **IL_INT_3_StudentServicesOutline.docx**

   The Thumbnail pane and the status bar indicate the presentation now contains six slides. Slide 1 is blank, and Slides 2 through 6 represent the Level 1 headings in the Word outline.

7. Click **Slide 1** in the Thumbnail pane, press **DELETE**, click the **Layout button** in the Slides group, click **Title Slide**, click the **View tab**, click the **Outline View button** in the Presentation Views group, click after **Celebrating Student Success at MSIT** on Slide 1, press **ENTER**, then type your name

   You change the slide layout for the first slide so the title and subtitle of the presentation and your name appear in the middle of the slide.

   Quick Tip: When you import slides into PowerPoint, you need to reset the layout of the slides to conform to the PowerPoint slide design you have applied.

8. Click the **Design tab**, click the **More button** ▼ in the Themes group, then click the **Retrospect theme**

9. Click the **View tab**, click the **Guides check box** in the Show group to show placement guides, if necessary click the **Slide Sorter button** in the Presentation Views group, press **CTRL+A** to select all the slides, click the **Home tab**, click the **Reset button** in the Slides group, click away from the slides to deselect them, then save the presentation

   The formatted presentation appears in Slide Sorter view (refer to **Figure 3-3**).

Import a Word Outline into PowerPoint   INT 3-5

Figure 3-2: Edited outline in Word Outline view

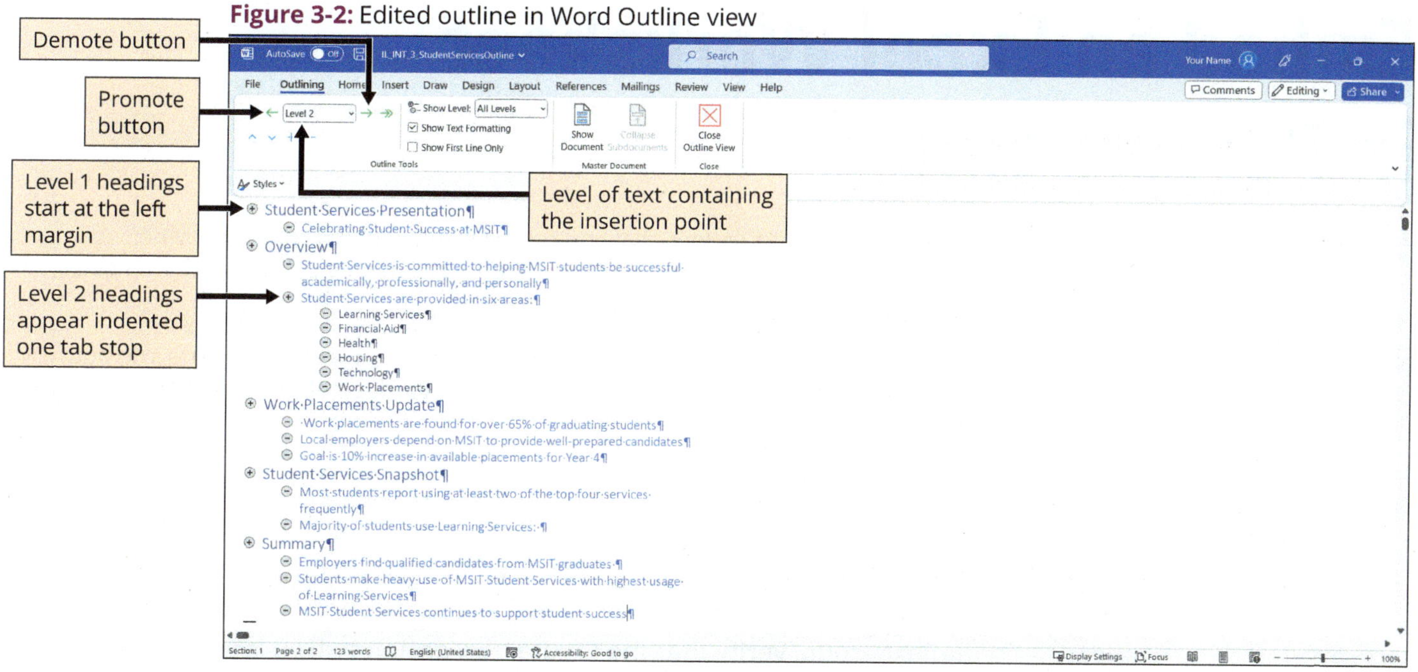

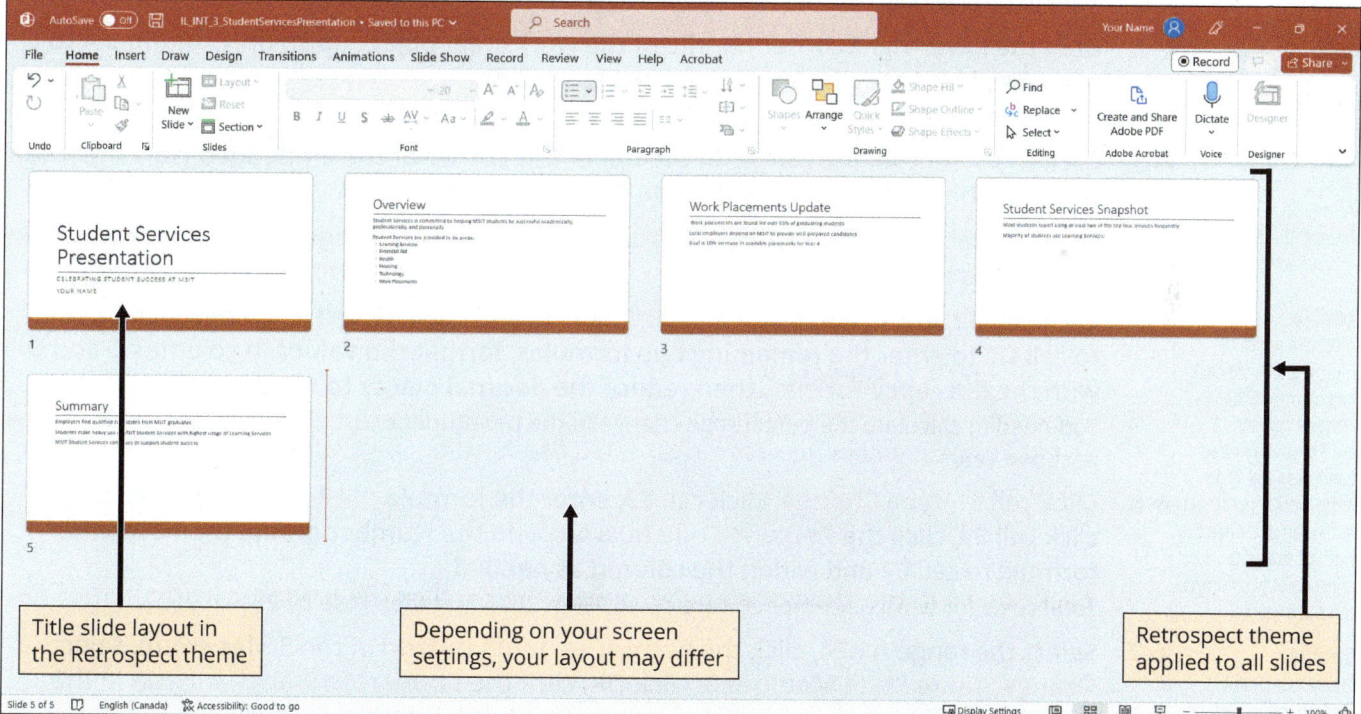

Figure 3-3: Formatted presentation in Slide Sorter view

Embed an Excel Worksheet in PowerPoint

Case You want Slide 3 to include a worksheet with calculations that you can edit from within PowerPoint when you obtain new data. You create an Excel worksheet on the slide to indicate the number of work placements arranged for MSIT students and the per-student cost and then edit it using Excel tools.

Objectives
- Embed a Worksheet object in PowerPoint
- Edit an embedded worksheet

You can use the Object command to embed Excel objects such as worksheets and charts into both Word and PowerPoint documents. When you double-click the embedded object, you can then use the tools of the source program to edit the object.

Steps

Trouble
You move the mouse over the bottom-right corner of the embedded worksheet until the resize pointer appears, then drag up and to the left until only columns A to E and rows 1 to 4 are displayed.

1. Click the **View tab**, click the **Normal button** in the Presentation Views group, click **Slide 3** in the Thumbnail pane to move to Slide 3, click the **Insert tab**, click the **Object button** in the Text group, verify that the Create new option button is selected, scroll to and click **Microsoft Excel Worksheet**, then click **OK**

   An Excel worksheet is placed on the PowerPoint slide, and the Excel Ribbon and tabs are active. The PowerPoint title bar and menu bar, above the Excel tools, indicate that Excel is operating within PowerPoint. When you embed a worksheet object in a PowerPoint slide, you generally want to display only the cells that contain data.

Trouble
If necessary, press the arrow keys, use the scroll bars, or press CTRL+HOME to move to the top of the embedded worksheet.

2. Drag the lower-right corner handle of the worksheet object up so only columns A to E and rows 1 to 4 are displayed (refer to **Figure 3-4**)

   You want the data you need to enter into the worksheet object to be easy to read.

3. Click the **Select All button** in the upper-left corner of the embedded worksheet to select all the worksheet cells, change the font size to **24 point**, then click cell **A1**

4. Enter the labels and values in the range **A1:D4** as shown in **Figure 3-5**, widening columns as needed

Trouble
To set the width of column E, double-click the column divider between columns E and F (you may need to increase the width of the workshop object first), then decrease the width of the workshop object so only columns A to E are visible.

5. Click cell **D2**, enter the formula **=B2*C2**, press **ENTER**, click cell **D2**, drag its fill handle to cell **D4** to enter the remaining two formulas, format the values in columns C and D with the **Currency format**, then reduce the decimal places to **0**

   You need to calculate the percentage change in the per-student cost of work placements over the past two years.

6. Click cell **E1**, type **Change**, click cell **E3**, enter the formula **=(D3-D2)/D3**, press **ENTER**, click cell **E3**, click the **Percent Style button** in the Number group, then copy the formula to cell **E4** and widen the column as needed

   Total costs for work placements were down 7% in 2026 and then rose by 23% in 2027.

Trouble
If the PowerPoint window minimizes while performing the actions in Step 7, maximize it.

7. Select the range **A1:E4**, click the **Format as Table button** in the Styles group, select **Orange, Table Style Medium 3**, click **OK**, click the **Convert to Range button** in the Tools group, click **Yes**, then click outside the worksheet object

   The embedded worksheet uses the default Office theme, and you want the fonts and colors of the worksheet to use the Retrospect theme you applied to the PowerPoint slide.

8. Double-click the **worksheet object** to display the Excel Ribbon and tabs again, click the **Page Layout tab**, click the **Themes button** in the Themes group, then click **Retrospect**

9. Change the value in cell **C4** to **220**, press **TAB**, click outside the worksheet object, drag the object below the text (refer to **Figure 3-6**), then save the presentation

   The increase in total costs for work placements in 2027 is now 27% over 2026.

Embed an Excel Worksheet in PowerPoint   INT 3-7

Figure 3-4: Resizing the worksheet object

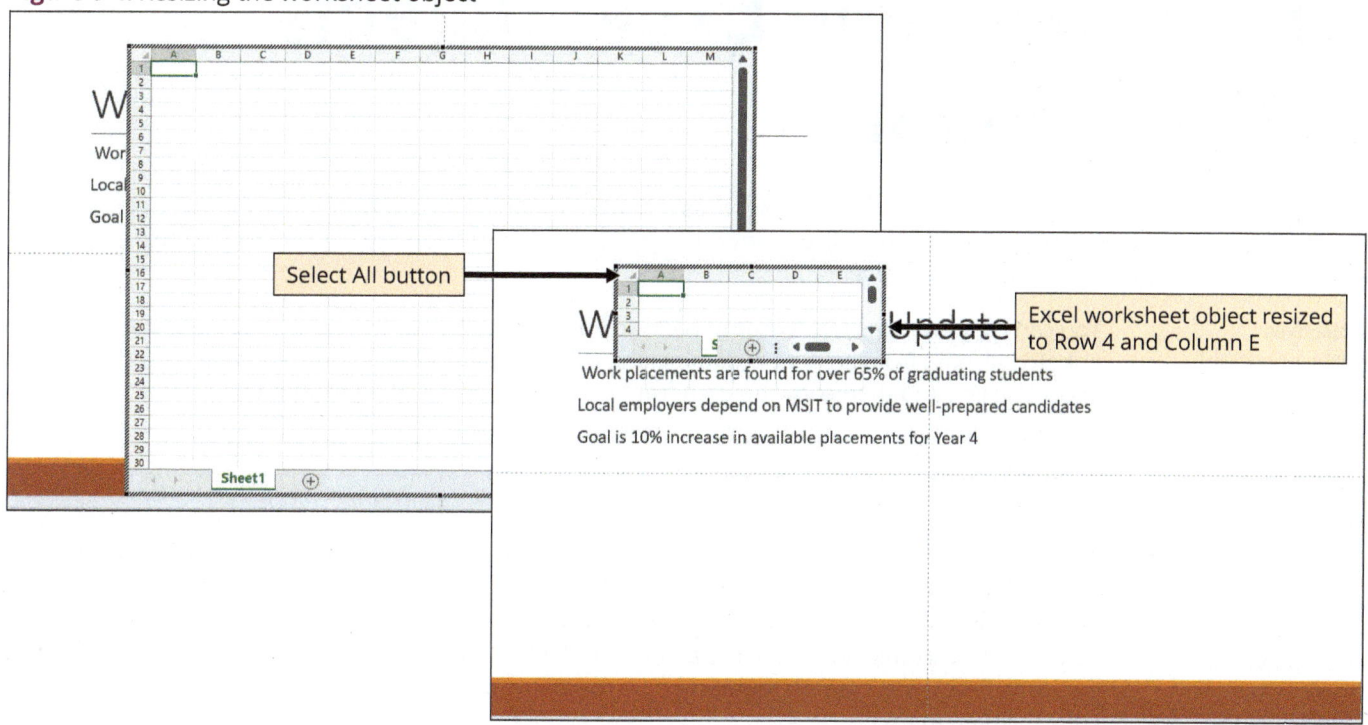

Figure 3-5: Labels and values entered in the Excel worksheet object

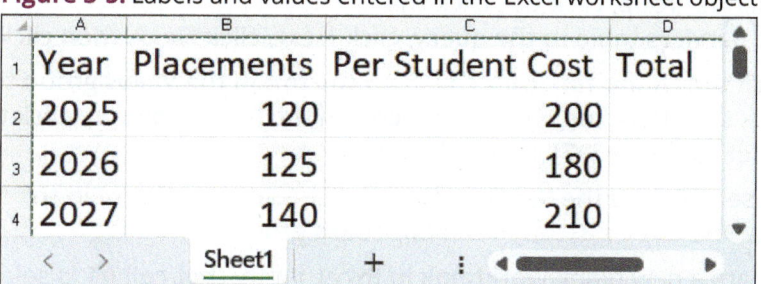

Figure 3-6: Completed Excel worksheet object

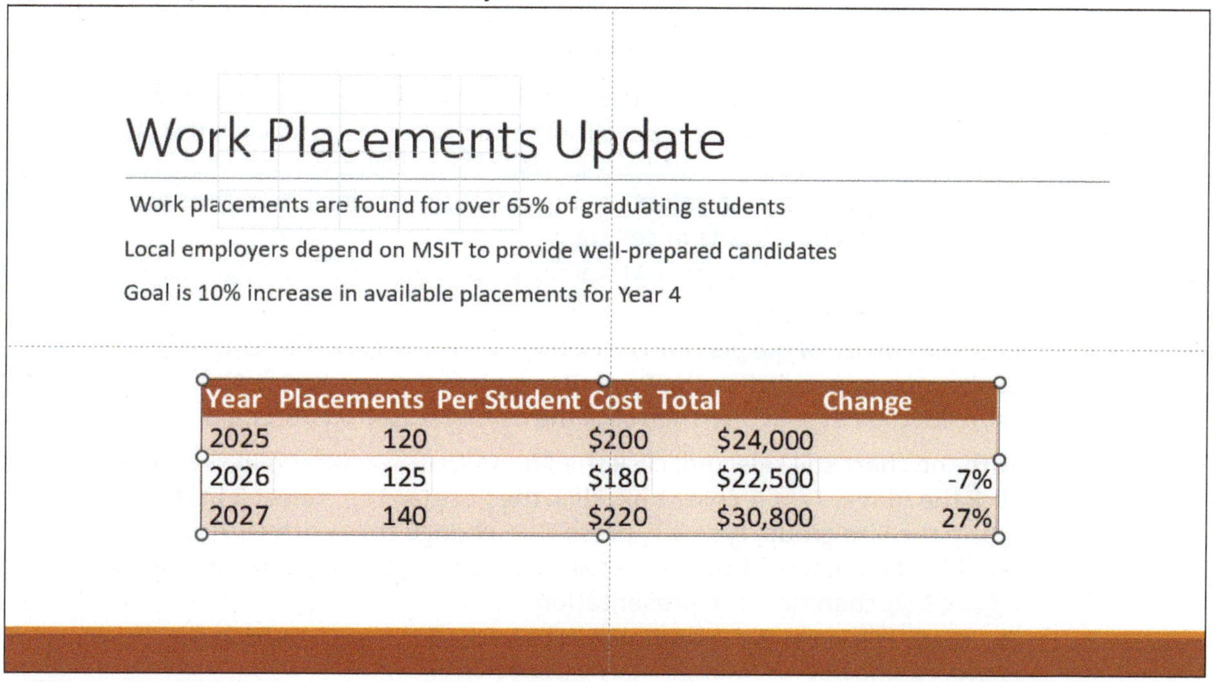

Link Access and Excel Objects to PowerPoint

Case You already have data about which student services are accessed and how often stored in an Access database. You want to include this data in the PowerPoint presentation, and any changes you make to the table in Access also appear in the PowerPoint presentation.

Objectives
- Link an Access table to Excel
- Link an Excel chart to PowerPoint

You can copy an Access table from Access to PowerPoint; however, you cannot paste the table as a link. To link data from an Access database to a PowerPoint presentation, you first copy the data to Excel as a link and then copy the data from Excel and paste it as a link into PowerPoint.

Steps

Quick Tip
To save the database with a new name, click the File tab, click Save As, click the Save As button, navigate to the location where you store your Data Files, type the new filename, then click Save.

1. Start Access, open the file **IL_INT_3-2.accdb** from the location where you store your Data Files, save the database as **IL_INT_3_StudentServices**, click **Enable Content**, double-click the **Services table**, then review the Area field

   You need to sort the Services table alphabetically by Area so you can use the data in a chart you create in Excel. You create a query to sort the data so that the sorting is maintained when you copy the data to Excel.

2. Close the **Services table**, click the **Create tab**, click the **Query Wizard button** in the Queries group, click **OK**, click the **Select All Fields button** >> to add all the fields in the Services table to the query, click **Next**, click **Next**, then click **Finish**

3. Click the **Home tab**, click the **View button** in the Views group to go to Design view, click the blank line below "Services" in the [Area] column, click the **Area Sort arrow** (refer to **Figure 3-7**), then select **Ascending**

4. Close and save the Services query, click **Services Query** in the Navigation pane, then click the **Copy button** in the Clipboard group

5. Create a new blank workbook in Excel, verify that cell **A1** is selected, click the **Paste arrow** in the Clipboard group, click the **Paste Link button**, then widen columns as necessary

6. Save the file as **IL_INT_3_StudentServicesData** in the location where you store your Data Files, click cell **C23**, then refer to **Figure 3-8** to enter the labels and formulas

7. Select the range **C23:F24**, click the **Insert tab**, click the **Insert Pie or Doughnut Chart button** in the Charts group, click the **top-left pie style**, click the **chart title**, type **Most Accessed Student Services**, press **ENTER**, click the **Quick Layout button** in the Chart Layouts group, select **Layout 6** (far right selection in the second row), then move the chart so it starts in cell **G2**

   The total percentage of students who accessed Learning Services is 33%. Health is 26%, Housing is 23% and Financial Aid is 18%.

Quick Tip
The chart you copied from Excel is linked by default to the source file but takes on the theme of the destination file.

8. Click the **border** of the pie chart, click the **Home tab**, click the **Copy button** in the Clipboard group, switch to the PowerPoint presentation, display **Slide 4**, click the **Home tab**, click the **Paste arrow**, then click the **Use Destination Theme & Link Data button**

9. With the chart still selected, click the **Shape Outline button** in the Drawing group, click the **Black, Text 1 color box**, click the **Format tab**, select **3** in the Height text box in the Size group, type **3.7**, press **TAB**, change the width to **7"**, press **ENTER**, click outside of the chart, click a **blank area** of the chart, drag it below the text (refer to **Figure 3-9**), then save the presentation

   The chart is linked to the Excel worksheet and the Services Query datasheet in Access. You will improve the chart's readability in the next lesson.

Link Access and Excel Objects to PowerPoint INT 3-9

Figure 3-7: Sorting the Areas field in Query Design view

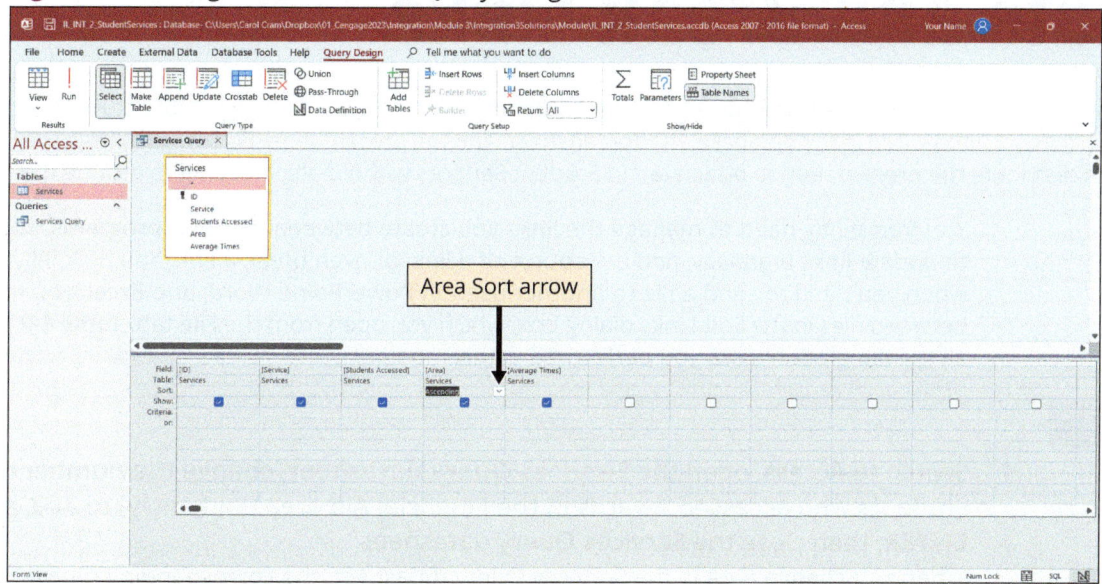

Figure 3-8: Formulas to calculate student access by area

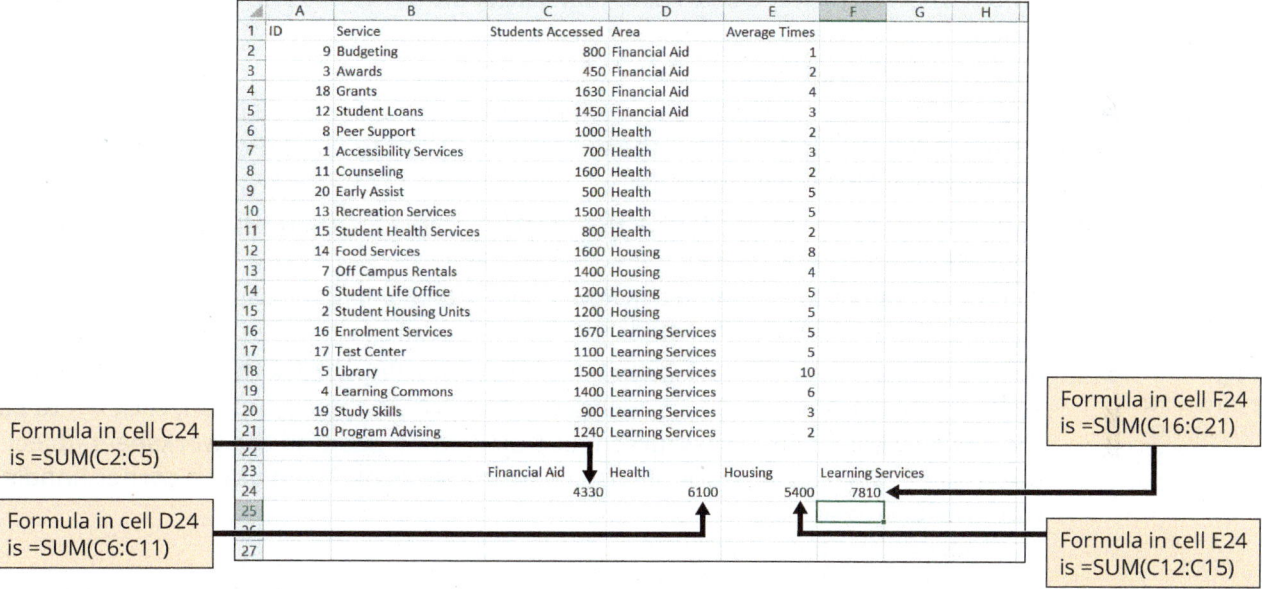

Figure 3-9: Linking a copied chart to PowerPoint

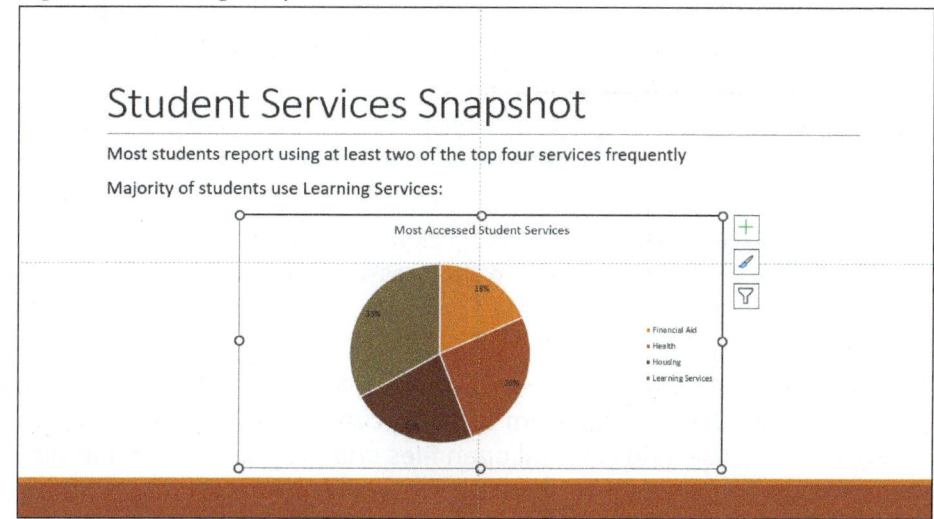

Update and Break Links

Case You want to modify the chart on Slide 4 of the presentation to reflect the addition of more students, then update the links you've created in the database, the spreadsheet, and the presentation. Finally, you break the links so you can distribute the presentation to other staff in Student Services without also needing to include the linked files.

Objectives
- Manually update links
- Break links

You frequently need to manage the links you create between files and programs. You may need to update links manually, find the source of a link, or even break a link. You normally break a link when you need to send a file to another user. In PowerPoint, Word, and Excel, you manage links between files in the Edit Links dialog box, which you open from the File tab. **Table 3-2** summarizes all the integration tasks you performed in this module.

Steps

1. Switch to Access, open the **Services Query datasheet**, change the number of students who accessed Awards in the Financial Aid area (2nd entry) to **700**, press **ENTER**, then close the Services Query datasheet

   When you change data in the Services Query datasheet, the corresponding data in the Services table also changes.

2. Switch to Excel, click the **Data tab**, then click **Edit Links** in the Queries & Connections group

   The Edit Links dialog box opens (refer to **Figure 3-10**).

   Quick Tip
   The linked values will automatically be updated in Excel if you wait a few minutes, but you can speed up the updating process by updating the values manually in the Edit Links dialog box.

▶ 3. Click **Update Values**, click **Close**, verify that the value in cell C3 is **700** and the Financial Aid slice is **19%**, save the workbook, switch to PowerPoint, then verify that the Financial Aid slice is now 19%

4. With the **pie chart** selected, click the **Chart Design tab**, then select **Style 3** in the Chart Styles group

   When you insert an Excel chart into a PowerPoint presentation, you usually need to select a new chart style so the data is easy to read on a slide.

   Quick Tip
   A value you copy from Excel and paste into PowerPoint as a link is formatted as an object that you can move and resize the same as you would any object.

▶ 5. Switch to Excel, copy cell **F24**, switch back to PowerPoint, click the **Home tab**, click the **Paste arrow**, click **Paste Special**, click the **Paste link option button**, click **OK** to paste the link as a Microsoft Excel Worksheet Object, then position the worksheet object to the right of "Majority of students use Learning Services:," and drag a corner handle to increase its size slightly

   The copied object appears as 7810.

6. Switch to Access, open the **Services Query datasheet**, change the number of students who accessed Study Skills to **1100** and the number of students who accessed the Test Center to **1300**, close the query, switch to Excel, and update the link in Excel, switch to PowerPoint, then verify the worksheet object in PowerPoint is now **8210** and the Learning Services pie slice is **34%**

   Trouble
   It is fine if the Links dialog box indicates that the link to the chart is NULL. This link is no longer active after you break the link.

▶ 7. In PowerPoint, click the **File tab**, click **Info**, click **Edit Links to Files**, click the top link, click **Break Link**, click the remaining link, click **Break Link**, click **Close**, then exit Backstage view

8. Switch to Excel, click the **File tab**, click **Info**, click **Edit Links to Files**, click **Break Link**, click **Break Links** in response to the message, click **Close**, then exit Backstage view

   Now when you change data in the Access file, the linked Excel chart in PowerPoint will not be updated.

9. In PowerPoint, click the **View tab**, click the **Slide Sorter button** in the Presentation Views group, change the Zoom to 140%, compare the completed presentation to **Figure 3-11**, save and close all open files and programs, then submit your files to your instructor

Figure 3-10: Edit Links dialog box

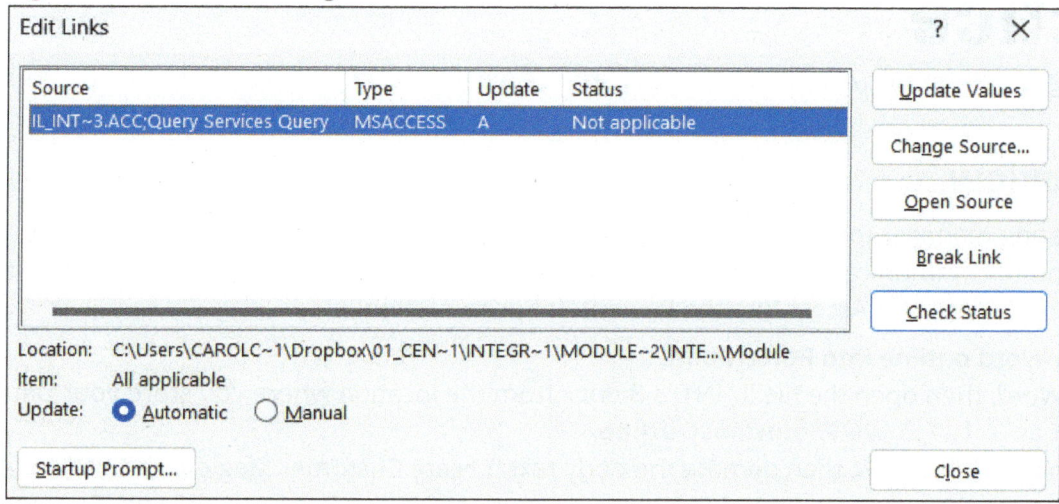

Figure 3-11: Completed presentation in Slide Sorter view

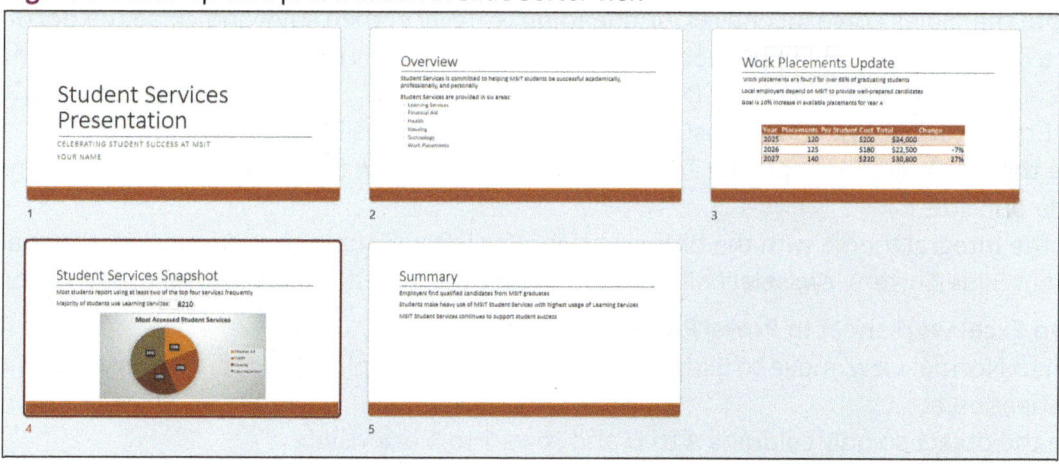

Table 3-2: Module 3 integration tasks

object	commands	source program(s)	destination program	result	connection	page no.
Word outline	In PowerPoint: New Slide/Slides from Outline	Word	PowerPoint	Word outline inserted into PowerPoint; Level 1 headings are slide titles, and Level 2 headings are text items	None	4
Excel worksheet	In PowerPoint: Insert/Object/Create New	Excel	PowerPoint	Excel worksheet created in PowerPoint, then updated by double-clicking and using Excel tools	Embedded	6
Access query	Copy/Paste Link button	Access	Excel	Access query is pasted into Excel as a link; linked data can only be formatted in Excel	Linked	8
Excel chart	Copy/Paste Link using the Use Destination Themes and Link Data button	Access/Excel	PowerPoint	Chart created from linked Access query is pasted into PowerPoint as a link; when Access data changes, Excel and PowerPoint data is updated	Linked	8

Practice

In the exercises that follow, you will practice the skills you have learned in this module.

Skills Review

As the marketing manager for WMP Solutions, a Customer Relationship Management company, you create a presentation to communicate information about the company to potential investors. You will incorporate data from Word, Excel, and Access into the PowerPoint presentation.

1. **Import a Word outline into PowerPoint.**
   a. Start Word, then open the file IL_INT_3-3.docx from the location where you store your Data Files, then save it as **IL_INT_3_WMPSolutionsOutline**.
   b. Switch to Outline view, then demote the body text "Create Customer Magic with CRM" to Level 2.
   c. Demote the three subheadings: "Content Development," "Sales Productivity," and "Service Expansion" to Level 3.
   d. Promote the "Sales Force Incentives" subheading to Level 1, then save and close the document.
   e. Open a blank presentation in PowerPoint, then save it as **IL_INT_3_WMPSolutionsPresentation** in the location where you store your Data Files.
   f. Import the IL_INT_3_WMPSolutionsOutline document as slides into PowerPoint.
   g. Delete the blank Slide 1, apply the Title Slide layout to the new Slide 1, then add your name below the subtitle on Slide 1.
   h. Apply the Integral theme with the brown variant (far left variant in the second row of variants).
   i. Switch to Slide Sorter view, select all the slides, reset the layout, then save the presentation.

2. **Embed an Excel worksheet in PowerPoint.**
   a. Switch to Normal view, move to Slide 4, delete the blank text placeholder, then insert a Microsoft Excel Worksheet object.
   b. Resize the object so only columns A to D and rows 1 to 5 are visible.
   c. Change the font size of all the cells to 28 point, enter labels and values as shown in **Figure 3-12**, then adjust column widths and the size of the worksheet object as needed.
   d. Enter a formula in cell D2 to multiply the number of sales by the average price for the first quarter, then copy the formula to the range D3:D5 and widen columns as needed.
   e. Apply the Integral theme to the embedded workbook, apply the Blue, Table Style Light 10 table style, convert the table to a range, format the dollar values in columns C and D with the Accounting Number format, then widen columns as needed. (**Hint**: To widen column D, resize the object to display column E, widen Column D, then reduce the object size again.)
   f. Move the worksheet object below the slide title.
   g. In the worksheet object, change the number of sales in the third quarter to **40**, then save the presentation.

Figure 3-12

	A	B	C	D
1	QTR	Sales	Average Price	Total
2	Q1	24		980
3	Q2	37		1200
4	Q3	32		1400
5	Q4	51		1300

3. **Link Access and Excel objects to PowerPoint.**
   a. Start Access, open the file IL_INT_3-4.accdb from the location where you store your Data Files, save it as **IL_INT_3_WMPSolutionsData**, then enable the content.
   b. Create a query called **Agents Query** from the Agents table, that contains all fields and that sorts the contents of the Category field in ascending order. (**Hint**: Remember to sort the Category field in Design view.)
   c. Close and save the query, copy it, create a new workbook in Excel, then paste the query datasheet as a link into cell A1.
   d. Format the values in column E using the Accounting Number format and 2 decimal places and the values in column F using the Percent format with 0 decimal places, widen columns as necessary, enter **Total Commission** in cell G1 and widen the column, enter the formula in cell G2 to multiply the Price by the Commission, then copy the formula to the range G3:G16 and widen the column as necessary.
   e. In the range B18:D19, enter labels and formulas to calculate the total sales commissions paid from sales of all products in each of the three categories: Content Development, Sales Productivity, and Service Expansion, widen columns as needed, then save the workbook as **IL_INT_3_WMPSolutionsCommissions**.
   f. Create a pie chart in the first 2D style from the range B18:D19, then apply Quick Layout 1 and move the chart to the right of the data.
   g. Change the chart title to **Sales Commissions by Product Category**, copy the chart, then paste it on Slide 5 in the PowerPoint presentation using the Use Destination Theme & Link Data option.
   h. Move the worksheet object below the bullet point, add a black outline, then save the presentation.

4. **Manage links.**
   a. In the Agents query in Access, change the price of WMP AI Lite sold by Antonia Garza (second entry) to **$4,500.00**, then close the query.
   b. Switch to Excel, then if the value in cell E3 does not automatically update to $4,500.00, update the link in the Edit Links dialog box.
   c. Switch to PowerPoint, then update the link, if necessary, and verify that the Content Development wedge is now 56%.
   d. Change the chart height to 3.7" and the width to 7", center it below the bullet point, then apply Chart Style 9.
   e. In Excel, copy cell B19, then paste it as a linked worksheet object on Slide 5 in PowerPoint.
   f. Position the Excel object after "development tools:" and if necessary, resize it so its font size is comparable to that of the bullet text.
   g. In the Agents Query datasheet in Access, change the price of WMP Sales Pro sold by Adela Jefferson to 2,500, then close the query.
   h. Update the link in Excel, switch to PowerPoint, then, if necessary, update the links to the chart and the worksheet object. The worksheet object is now $2,745.00 and the Content Development slice is 55%.
   i. Break the links to the Excel chart and worksheet, break the link from Excel to Access, view the presentation in Slide Sorter view, increase the zoom to 150%, compare the presentation to **Figure 3-13**, save and close all open files and programs, then submit your files to your instructor.

Skills Review (Continued)

Figure 3-13

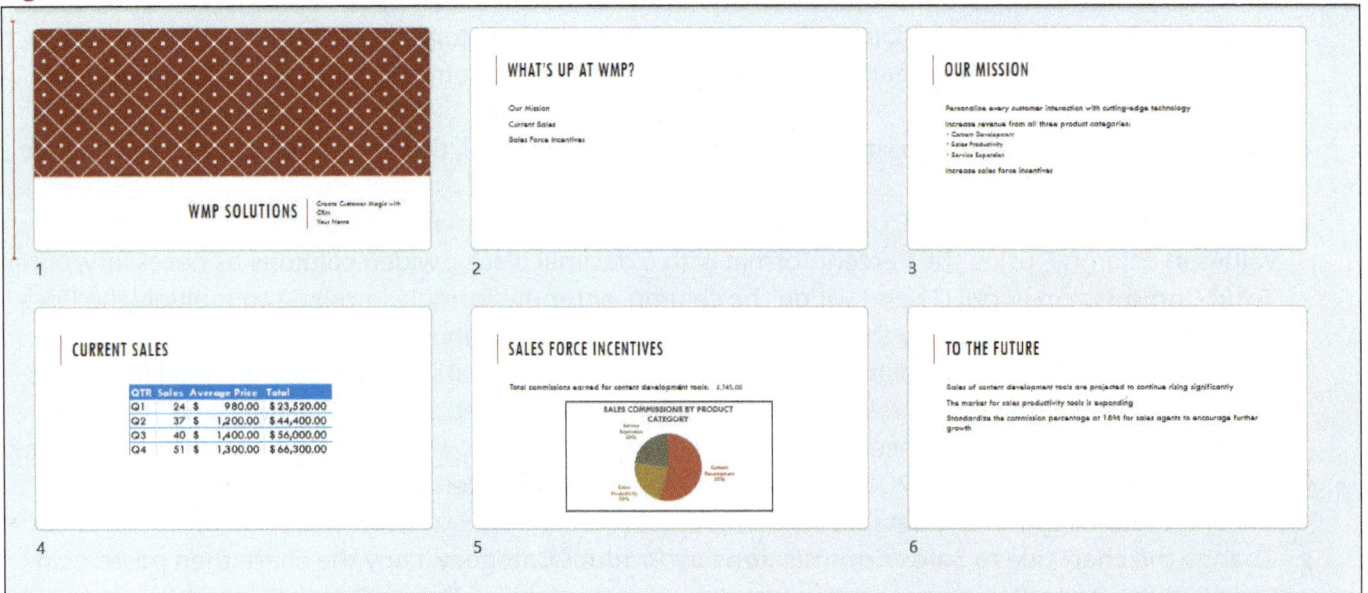

Independent Challenge 1

Coastal Movers in Seattle, Washington, provides comprehensive moving services to residents, companies, and retail operations. You have collected data about recent moving contracts in an Access database, and now you need to create a presentation in PowerPoint to share at a meeting of branch managers. You want the presentation to contain links to the revenue figures. You also need to import some of the slides needed for the presentation from a Word outline.

   a. In Word, open the file IL_INT_3-5.docx from the location where you store your Data Files, then save it as **IL_INT_3_CoastalMoversOutline**.
   b. In Outline view, demote the subtitle text to Level 2, then demote the list of the four target markets (from "Realtors" to "Storage Companies") to Level 3.
   c. Save and close the document.
   d. Start a blank presentation in PowerPoint, then save it as **IL_INT_3_CoastalMoversPresentation** in the location where you store your Data Files.
   e. Insert the CoastalMoversOutline document into PowerPoint, delete Slide 1, apply the Title Slide layout to the new Slide 1, then add your name below the subtitle on Slide 1.
   f. In Slide Sorter view, reset the layout of all the slides, then apply the Wood Type theme with the variant that is second from the left in the selection of variants in the Variants group.
   g. In Normal view on the new Slide 2 (Marketing Overview), embed an Excel Worksheet object resized to column B and row 5 with a 22 pt font size and containing the information as shown in **Figure 3-14**.

Figure 3-14

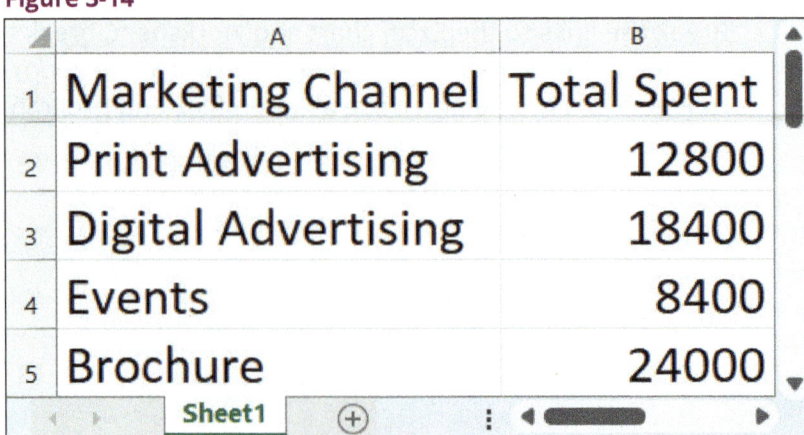

h. Enlarge the worksheet object to include row 6 and calculate the total marketing costs in cell B6, then format the values in column B with the Accounting Number format. Adjust the column width as needed.

i. Apply the Wood Type theme to the Excel worksheet, select the range A1:B6, apply the Dark Red, Table Style Medium 3 style, convert the table to a range, then center the worksheet object below the bulleted item on the slide.

j. Start Access, open the file IL_INT_3-6.accdb the location where you store your Data Files, then save the database as **IL_INT_3_CoastalMoversContracts** and enable content.

k. Create a query called **Contracts Query** from the Contracts table, using all fields, that sorts the contents of the Category field in ascending order. Save and close the query, copy the query, paste it as a link into a new Excel workbook, then save the workbook as **IL_INT_3_CoastalMoversRevenue** in the location where you save your Data Files.

l. Enter **Total Revenue** in cell F1, then calculate the total revenue from moving contracts in column F. Starting in cell B18, enter labels and formulas to calculate the total revenue from each of the four moving categories. (Hint: Enter **Local Household** in cell B18, **Long Distance** in cell C18, **Office** in cell D18, and **Retail** in cell E18, then enter the required calculations in cells B19:E19.)

m. Format all dollar amounts with the Accounting Number format and adjust column widths as needed, then use the data in the range B18:E19 to create a 2D pie chart entitled **Revenue by Category** using Quick Layout 6 and Chart Style 9.

n. Move the chart to the right of the data, copy the pie chart, then paste it on the appropriate slide in the presentation using the Use Destination Theme & Link Data option. Change the height of the pie chart to 3.5" and the width to 6", add a solid black border, then center the pie chart below the text on the slide.

o. In Excel, copy the total revenue received from Long Distance contracts, then paste it as a linked worksheet object in the appropriate location on the slide containing the chart.

p. In Access, change the rate for Edward King's move to **$155.00** and the hours of the move for Nerys O'Brien to **40**, then update the links in Excel and PowerPoint. The slice for Long Distance contracts should be 51% as shown in **Figure 3-15**.

q. Break the links in Excel and PowerPoint, view the presentation in Slide Sorter view, compare it to **Figure 3-15** save and close all open files and programs, then submit your files to your instructor.

Figure 3-15

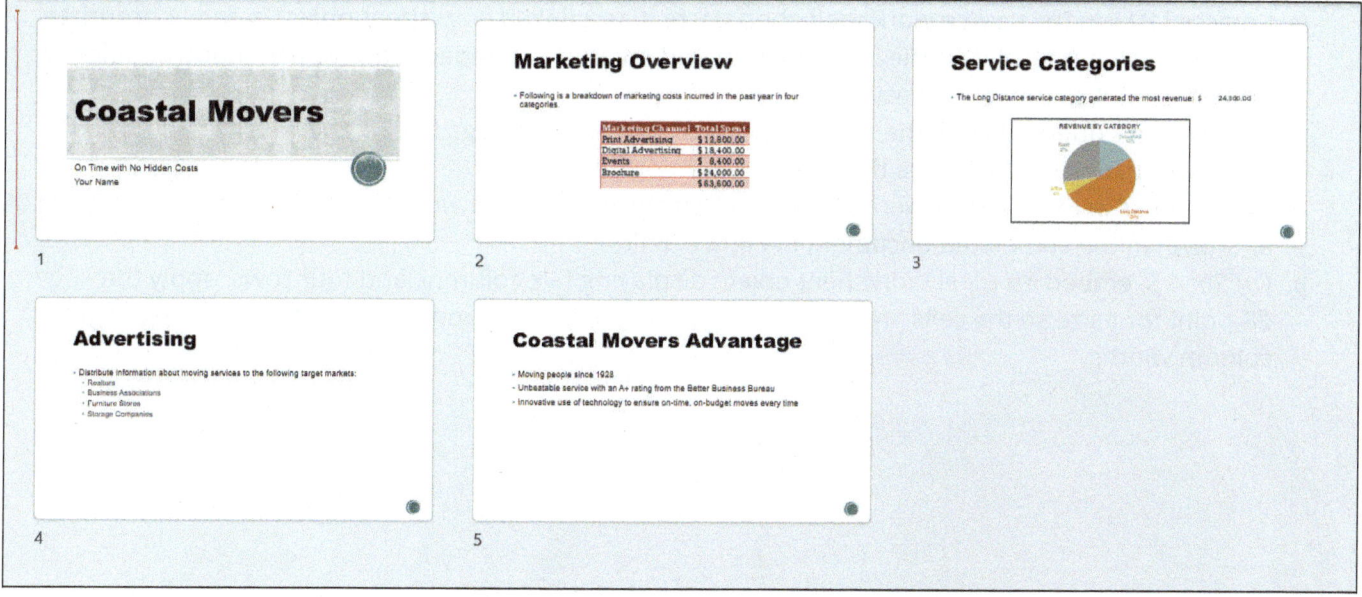

Independent Challenge 2

You work in the Purchasing department at Apex Outdoor Equipment, a retail operation that sells quality outdoor equipment such as camping and climbing gear, footwear, and backpacks. To assist the marketing department in crafting new marketing materials, you have created a database of top-selling products. You have also decided to create a short PowerPoint presentation about the company's top-selling products, new arrivals, and other marketing information for delivery to store managers. The presentation will include text from a Word outline, data from the database, an embedded worksheet, and a linked chart.

a. Start Word, open the file IL_INT_3-7.docx from the location where you store your Data Files, then save the document as **IL_INT_3_ApexOutline**.

b. Switch to Outline view, promote "Our Bestsellers" to Level 1, and demote "K-1 Ultra Sleeping Bags" to Level 3, then save and close the document.

c. Start a new PowerPoint presentation, save it as **IL_INT_3_ApexPresentation**, then import the IL_INT_3_ApexOutline document into the presentation.

d. Delete the blank Slide 1, apply the Title Slide layout to the new Slide 1, add your name below the subtitle on Slide 1, then apply the Ion theme.

e. In Slide Sorter view, reset the layout of all the slides.

f. Start Access, open the file IL_INT_3-8.accdb from the location where you store your Data Files, save the database as **IL_INT_3_TopSellers.accdb**, then enable content.

g. Create a query called **Top Sellers Query** from all the fields in the Top Sellers table that sorts the contents of the Category field in ascending order.

h. Close and save the query, copy it, then paste it as a link into a new Excel workbook saved as **IL_INT_3_ApexTopSellerRevenue** in the location where you store your Data Files. Widen columns as needed. Enter **Total Sales** in cell G1, calculate total sales for each product, then format the values in Columns E, F, and G with the Accounting Numbering format.

i. Starting in cell B15 of the worksheet, enter labels and formulas to calculate the total revenue from each of the four product categories. Widen columns as needed.

j. Create a pie chart of the totals, apply Quick Layout 2, then add a chart title: **Top Selling Product Categories**. Move the chart to the right of the data.

k. Copy the chart, then paste it using the Use Destination Theme & Link Data paste option on slide 3 in the presentation. Add a black border with a width of 3 pt, then change the height to 3.8" and the width to 6" and center the pie chart below the text.

l. Apply Chart Style 12 to the chart.

m. Copy cell B16 in the source workbook, then paste it as a linked worksheet object in the appropriate place following the colon in the bulleted item and enlarge as needed. Change the shape fill color to Gold, Accent 3 so the text is easy to read.

n. In the Access query, change the Average price of the sleeping bags to **300**, the Tents to **900**, and the hiking boots to **220**, then close the query.

o. Update links in Excel and PowerPoint. Verify that the value of the worksheet object is now $262,400.00 as shown in the completed document in **Figure 3-17**.

p. On Slide 5, embed an Excel Worksheet object displaying five columns and four rows, apply the 28-point font size so the cells are visible, then enter the information shown in **Figure 3-16** and adjust column widths.

Figure 3-16

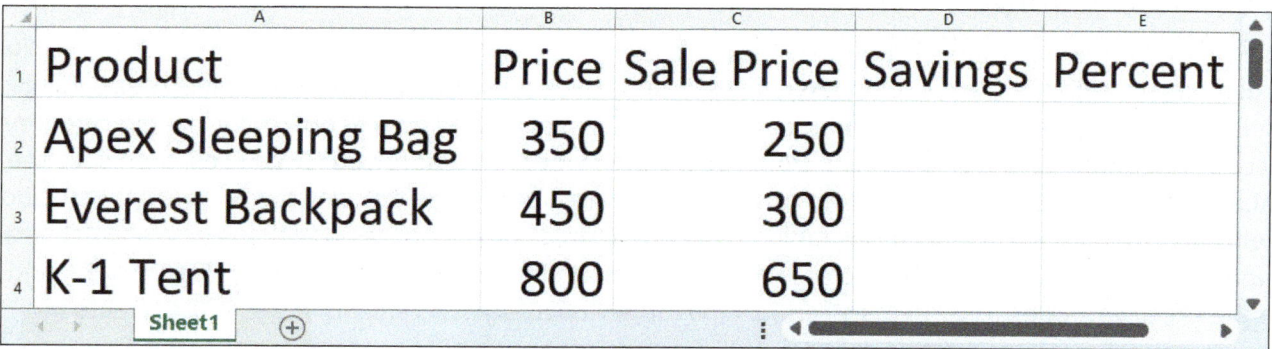

Figure 3-17

q. Calculate the savings per product in cell D2 by subtracting the values in the Sale Price column from the values in the Price column.

r. In cell E2, enter the formula **=D2/B2** to calculate the percent savings.

s. Copy the formulas for the other two product categories, format values with the Accounting Number (with zero decimal points) and Percent formats, then adjust column widths, as necessary.

t. Apply the Ion theme to the workbook, select the range A1:E4, apply Gold, Table Style Medium 11, then convert the table to a range.

u. Make sure the completed table displays all five columns (you may need to readjust the width of the worksheet object).

v. Position the worksheet object so that its left edge is even with the left edge of the slide title.

w. In Excel and PowerPoint, break the links, view the presentation, save and close all open files and programs, then submit your files to your instructor.

Visual Workshop

You work for Premier Learning, a company that sells business skills workshops to local entrepreneurs. For an upcoming meeting of the company executives, you have decided to create a presentation containing one slide displaying a pie chart that indicates the breakdown of workshop revenue by workshop category. In Access, open the file IL_INT_3-9.accdb from the location where you store your Data Files, then save the database as **IL_INT_3_PremierLearningWorkshops**. Create a query called **Workshops Query** that includes all fields and that sorts the Workshops table in ascending order by Category. Copy the query, paste it as a link into a new Excel workbook, then create the 2D pie chart similar to the one shown in **Figure 3-18**, and save the Excel workbook as **IL_INT_3_PremierLearningParticipants**. As shown in the figure, create a one-slide PowerPoint presentation called **IL_INT_3_PremierLearningPresentation**, apply the Title Only slide layout, then copy the pie chart from Excel and paste it onto the slide using the Use Destination Theme & Link Data option. Format the slide as shown: add the slide title, apply the Quotable slide design with the Purple variant (third from the left), format the chart with Quick Layout 6 and Style 8, change the chart height to 4" and the width to 7", and center it on the slide. Switch to Access, open the Workshops query, change the number of participants who attended the Financing for Success workshop to **120**, close the query, update the links in Excel and PowerPoint, then enter your name in the slide footer. Break the link to the Excel workbook and PowerPoint presentation, save and close all open files and programs, then submit your files to your instructor.

Figure 3-18

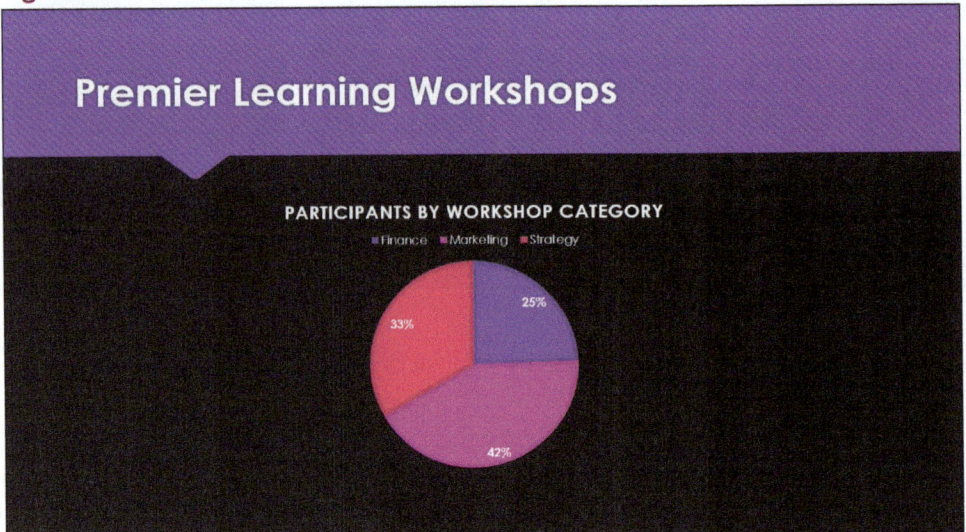

Index

Special Characters

+ (addition), AC 3-21, EX 1-11
^ (caret), EX 1-11
/ (division), AC 3-21, EX 1-11
= (equal to), AC 3-17
^ (exponentiation), AC 3-21
>= (greater than or equal to), AC 3-17
< (less than), AC 3-17
<= (less than or equal to), AC 3-17
* (multiplication), AC 3-21, EX 1-11
<> (not equal to), AC 3-17
% (percent), EX 1-11
− (subtraction), AC 3-21, EX 1-11

A

absolute cell references, EX 3-8 – EX 3-9
Accessibility Checker, WD 3-26
Accessibility pane, EX 4-13
Access objects
 forms and, AC 1-5
 queries and, AC 1-5
 reports and, AC 1-5
 tables and, AC 1-5
Access Options, AC 1-24
action query, AC 3-4
Action Tags, AC 2-11
active cell, PPT 3-6
adding
 title, to chart, EX 4-4 – EX 4-5
 worksheet, EX 2-17
Add-ins, WD 2-11
addition operator (+), AC 3-21
adjusting shapes, WD 3-20 – WD 3-21
adjustment handle, PPT 2-4
aligning
 objects, PPT 2-12 – PPT 2-13
aligning paragraph text, PPT 1-9
alignment, EX 2-6 – EX 2-7
 charts, EX 4-13
 font, EX 2-6 – EX 2-7
Alternative text
 adding to objects, WD 3-26 – WD 3-27
alternative text, EX 4-12
Alt Text
 adding to objects, WD 3-26 – WD 3-27
anchored, WD 3-14
AND criteria, AC 3-16 – AC 3-17
AND function, EX 3-10 – EX 3-11
AND OR SQL keyword, AC 3-18
animated video, PPT 3-18
animation
 attaching sound, PPT 3-17
 objects in presentation, PPT 3-16 – PPT 3-17
 to SmartArt object, PPT 3-17
animation tags, PPT 3-16
append, AC 2-2
application developer, AC 1-16
area chart, EX 4-3, PPT 3-7
arguments, EX 1-10
arithmetic operators, AC 3-21, EX 1-10, EX 1-11
Artistic Effects command, WD 3-19
Attachment data type, AC 1-11
AutoCorrect, WD 1-6, WD 1-7, WD 2-9
 inserting text, WD 2-9
Auto Fill, EX 1-4, EX 1-5
AutoFit, EX 2-8
AutoFit Column Width command, EX 2-9
AutoFit Row Height command, EX 2-9
automatic page break, WD 2-16
AutoNumber, AC 1-6, AC 1-10, AC 1-11
AutoRecover, EX 1-6
AutoSave, WD 1-8
AutoSum, EX 1-10 – EX 1-11
AVERAGE function, EX 1-14
Axis Options, EX 4-11

B

Back button, WD 1-9
Backstage view, WD 1-4
 worksheet in, EX 1-18 – EX 1-19
backup, AC 1-24
bar chart, EX 4-3, PPT 3-7
bar tab, WD 3-5
bibliography, WD 2-24
 creating, WD 2-24 – WD 2-25
bitmap graphics, WD 1-26
blank fields, AC 3-17
blank table, WD 3-9
bookmark, PPT 3-18
borders, WD 3-6 – WD 3-7, WD 3-8
Borders menu, EX 2-13
bound, AC 4-6
bound controls, AC 4-7
brightness, WD 3-19
bullets, WD 1-24
 adding, WD 1-24 – WD 1-25
 adding to paragraphs, PPT 1-13
 applied to list, WD 1-25
button(s)
 Comment, WD 1-4
 control layout, AC 4-11
 Filter, AC 3-13
 Find, AC 3-11
 navigation, AC 4-2
 Save As dialog box, WD 1-9
Byte, in Number Field Size, AC 2-7

C

Calculated data type, AC 1-11, AC 3-20
calculated field
 creating, AC 3-20 – AC 3-21
Caps Lock, AC 2-19
Caption
 Short Text field property, AC 2-9
Cascade Delete Related Records, AC 2-17
Cascade Update Related Fields, AC 2-17
Cascade Windows button, PPT 3-11
category axis, EX 4-2, PPT 3-8
cell(s), PPT 3-6
 active, PPT 3-6
 copying and moving cell data, EX 1-8 – EX 1-9
cell, defined, WD 3-8
cell address, EX 1-2
cell entries, rotating and indenting, EX 2-7
cell pointer, EX 1-2
cells, inserting and deleting, EX 1-5
Cells group, EX 1-5
cell styles, EX 2-4 – EX 2-5
center tab, WD 3-5
Change Chart Type dialog box, EX 4-9
Change your view button, WD 1-9
chart(s), PPT 3-6
 adding hyperlink, PPT 3-9
 aligning, EX 4-13
 axis titles added to, EX 4-11
 combo, EX 4-8
 copying from Excel to Word, INT 1-6 – INT 1-7
 creating, with title, EX 4-4 – EX 4-5
 editing data, PPT 3-8 – PPT 3-9
 elements, EX 4-3
 embedded, EX 4-4
 enhanced, EX 4-11
 features, identifying, EX 4-2 – EX 4-3
 formatted, PPT 3-9
 formatting, EX 4-12 – EX 4-13
 gridlines removal from, EX 4-11
 identifying features, EX 4-2 – EX 4-3
 inserting, PPT 3-6 – PPT 3-7
 inserting WordArt, EX 4-12
 layout, EX 4-10 – EX 4-11
 modifying, EX 4-5 – EX 4-9
 positioning, EX 4-6 – EX 4-7
 in Quick Analysis tool, EX 4-5
 reestablishing links, INT 1-9
 trendlines, EX 4-18 – EX 4-19
 types, EX 4-3
 types of, PPT 3-7
 working with axes, EX 4-11

chart sheet, EX 4-4
Check for Issues, WD 2-27
child records, AC 2-15
child table, AC 2-15
citation, WD 2-22 – WD 2-23
citation dialog box, WD 2-23
Clear All Formatting, WD 3-3
Click and Type pointers, WD 1-5
Clip art, WD 3-14
clipboard. *See* Office clipboard
Clipboard, EX 1-8, WD 1-16
cloud computing, AC 1-20, PPT 1-23
clustered column charts, EX 4-4, EX 4-5
coauthoring a presentation, PPT 3-15
Color command, WD 3-19
color palettes, Office, EX 2-13
color saturation, WD 3-19
color tone, WD 3-19
column(s)
   chart, EX 4-3
   deleting, WD 3-10 – WD 3-11
   deleting and inserting, EX 2-10 – EX 2-11
   hiding and unhiding, EX 2-11
   inserting, WD 3-10 – WD 3-11
column break, WD 2-17
column chart, PPT 3-7
column headings, EX 2-8, PPT 3-6
Column resize pointer, EX 1-7
column width and row height, EX 2-8 – EX 2-9
   changing/adjusting, EX 2-9
   formatting commands, EX 2-9
Column Width command, EX 2-9
combo chart, EX 4-8, PPT 3-7
commands
   formatting, AC 3-23
comment, WD 2-2
   inking, WD 2-5
   inserting, WD 2-2 – WD 2-5
   legacy, WD 2-3
   modern, WD 2-3
Comment button, WD 1-4
compacting, AC 1-24
comparison operators, AC 3-16, AC 3-17, EX 3-7
conditional formatting, AC 4-12 – AC 4-13, EX 2-14 – EX 2-15
Conditional Formatting Rules Manager dialog box, AC 4-13, EX 2-14, EX 2-15
content control, WD 2-18
content placeholder, PPT 1-10
contrast, WD 3-19
control(s), AC 1-16, AC 4-2
control layout buttons, AC 4-11

control worksheet calculations, EX 3-18 – EX 3-19
Convert Text to Table command, WD 3-9
copy, WD 1-18
copying
   Access tables to Word, INT 2-2, INT 2-3, INT 2-10 – INT 2-11
   Word tables to Access, INT 2-2, INT 2-6 – INT 2-7
copying, AC 1-20, WD 1-18 – WD 1-19
   worksheet, EX 2-17
copying and pasting
   data from Clipboard, INT 1-2
   data from Excel to Word, INT 1-4 – INT 1-5
   Excel charts into Word documents, INT 1-2, INT 1-3, INT 1-6 – INT 1-7
Copy pointer, EX 1-7
copyright law, PPT 1-5
Corrections command, WD 3-19
COUNTA function, EX 3-14 – EX 3-15
COUNT function, EX 3-14
creating
   bibliography, WD 2-24 – WD 2-25
   calculated field, AC 3-20 – AC 3-21
   chart, with title, EX 4-4 – EX 4-5
   database, AC 1-22 – AC 1-23
   Date/Time field, AC 2-11
   form, AC 1-16 – AC 1-17
   one-to-many relationships, AC 2-16 – AC 2-17
   pie chart, EX 4-14 – EX 4-15
   primary keys, AC 2-12 – AC 2-13
   query, AC 1-14 – AC 1-15
   reports, AC 1-18 – AC 1-19
   report source, WD 2-23
   table, AC 1-10 – AC 1-11
   table in Datasheet View, AC 1-10
criteria, AC 3-12
   AND, AC 3-16 – AC 3-17
   entering and saving, AC 3-14 – AC 3-15
   entering date, AC 3-15
   entering text, AC 3-15
   OR, AC 3-18 – AC 3-19
criteria syntax, AC 3-14
cropping, PPT 3-4
   pictures, PPT 3-4 – PPT 3-5
CSV (comma-separated value) file, AC 2-2
Currency data type, AC 1-11, AC 2-6
   vs. Number data type, AC 2-5
Currency field
   adding, AC 2-7
   modifying, AC 2-6 – AC 2-7

Current record box, AC 1-6, AC 4-2
custom number format, EX 3-15
cut and paste, WD 1-16 – WD 1-17
cut text, WD 1-16

D

data
   copying and pasting from Excel to Word, INT 1-4 – INT 1-5
   linking, INT 1-2
data
   copying and moving, EX 1-8 – EX 1-9
   editing, EX 1-6 – EX 1-7
   editing existing, AC 1-8 – AC 1-9
   entering, EX 1-4 – EX 1-5
   filtering, AC 3-12 – AC 3-13
   Find and Replace, AC 3-10 – AC 3-11
   importing from Excel, AC 2-2 – AC 2-3
   marker, EX 4-2
   navigating and entering, AC 1-6 – AC 1-7
   point, EX 4-2
   series, EX 4-2
   sorting, AC 3-8 – AC 3-9
   summarizing with sparklines, EX 4-16 – EX 4-17
   table, EX 4-10
   trends, EX 4-18 – EX 4-19
database
   backing up, AC 1-24
   compacting, AC 1-24
   creating, AC 1-22 – AC 1-23
   designer, AC 1-16
   opening and exploring, AC 1-4 – AC 1-5
   relational, AC 1-2 – AC 1-3
   saving and sharing with OneDrive, AC 1-20 – AC 1-21
data cleansing, AC 2-15
data entry
   Excel and Access compared, AC 1-3
data formatting and documentation, modifying, EX 2-12 – EX 2-13
data model
   Excel and Access compared, AC 1-3
data series, PPT 3-6
   labels, PPT 3-6
   markers, PPT 3-6
datasheet
   formatting, AC 3-22 – AC 3-23
datasheet columns
   resizing and moving, AC 1-7
Datasheet View, AC 1-5, AC 2-4
   creating table, AC 1-10

   Employees table in, AC 1-23
   entering new record, AC 1-11
   modifying fields in, AC 2-4 – AC 2-5
   sorting buttons, AC 3-9
data types, AC 1-11
Date and Time functions, EX 3-17
Date function, EX 3-16 – EX 3-17
Date() function, AC 2-10, AC 3-21
Date Picker, AC 2-10
Date/Time data type, AC 1-11
Date/Time field
   creating, AC 2-11
   modifying, AC 2-10 – AC 2-11
DATEVALUE function, EX 3-16
DAY function, EX 3-17
decimal places, EX 2-2
Decimal Places property, AC 2-6
decimal tab, WD 3-5
Default Value
   property, AC 2-6
   Short Text field property, AC 2-9
Default Width command, EX 2-9
DELETE SQL keyword, AC 3-7
deleting
   rows and columns, EX 2-10 – EX 2-11, WD 3-10 – WD 3-11
   worksheet, EX 2-17
delimited text file, AC 2-2
delimiter, AC 2-2
Design Ideas pane, PPT 1-6
Design View, AC 1-10
   creating table in, AC 1-11
   forms, AC 1-16, AC 4-3
   reports, AC 4-9
Design View, tables, AC 2-4
   setting primary key field, AC 2-13
destination file, INT 1-2
destination presentation, PPT 3-10
digital video
digital video
   editing, PPT 3-18 – PPT 3-19
   inserting, PPT 3-18 – PPT 3-19
distributing objects, PPT 2-13
division operator (/), AC 3-21
document(s), WD 1-2
   bibliography field, WD 2-25
   borders and shading, WD 3-7
   copying and moving items between, WD 1-19
   edited document text, WD 1-7
   entering and revising text, WD 1-6 – WD 1-7
   formatted, WD 2-27
   header and footer, WD 2-19
   highlighting in text, WD 1-16
   inspecting, WD 2-26 – WD 2-27
   manual page break, WD 2-17

navigating using Navigation pane and Go to command, WD 2-7
new comment, WD 2-3
page number, WD 2-17
planning, WD 1-3
renumbered footnotes, WD 2-21
resolved comment, WD 2-5
results after inspecting, WD 2-27
saving, WD 1-8 – WD 1-9
setting margins, WD 1-22 – WD 1-23
shape, WD 3-19
splitting to copy and move items in long document, WD 1-18
text highlighted in, WD 2-7
text in document window, WD 1-7
viewing and navigating, WD 1-14 – WD 1-15
document properties, WD 1-14
Backstage view, WD 1-15
document window, WD 1-4
Double, in Number Field Size, AC 2-7
Draft view, WD 1-15
drag and drop, WD 1-16
drawing canvas, WD 3-23
drawing shapes, WD 3-18 – WD 3-19
Draw Table command, WD 3-9
duplicated shapes, PPT 2-11

E

editing
chart data, PPT 3-8 – PPT 3-9
data, EX 1-6 – EX 1-7
digital video, PPT 3-18 – PPT 3-19
existing data, AC 1-8 – AC 1-9
existing record in form, AC 1-17
Edit mode, AC 1-6
keyboard shortcuts, AC 1-9
Editor pane, WD 2-9
edit record symbol, AC 1-6
Effects command, WD 3-21
electronic spreadsheet program, EX 1-2
embedded chart, EX 4-4
embedded objects, PPT 3-6
embedding
Excel worksheets in PowerPoint, INT 3-6 – INT 3-7
linking vs., INT 3-3
objects, INT 3-2
Word files in Excel, INT 1-2, INT 1-3, INT 1-10 – INT 1-11
endnote(s), WD 2-20 – WD 2-21
equal to (=), AC 3-17, EX 3-7
Equal To dialog box, EX 2-15
Error Indicator Action Tag, AC 2-11

Excel Spreadsheet command, WD 3-9
exploding, EX 4-14
exponential operator (^), AC 3-21
exporting
file formats, AC 2-3
expression, AC 3-20
Expression Builder, AC 3-20
Expression property, AC 3-20
Extended Selection, AC 2-19
Extensible Markup Language (XML). See XML (Extensible Markup Language)
Eyedropper, PPT 2-5

F

field(s), AC 1-6, AC 1-7, AC 2-14
modifying, AC 1-12 – AC 1-13
field lists, AC 2-16, AC 3-4, AC 4-6
field properties, AC 1-10, AC 1-12
Field Properties pane, AC 1-12
fields, WD 2-16
field selector, AC 1-12
Field Size
property, AC 2-6
Short Text field property, AC 2-9
Field Size property, AC 1-12
file, WD 1-8
file(s)
destination, INT 1-2
source, INT 1-2
file formats, AC 2-3
filename, WD 1-8
File tab, WD 1-4
Fill handle pointer, EX 1-7
Filter buttons, AC 3-13
Filter By Form, AC 3-12
Filter By Selection, AC 3-12
Filtered status bar indicator, AC 2-19
filtering data, AC 3-12 – AC 3-13
filters vs. queries, AC 3-13
Find and Replace dialog box, AC 3-11, EX 2-19, WD 2-7
Find and Replace text, WD 2-6 – WD 2-7
Find & Select menu, EX 2-19
Find buttons, AC 3-11
first line indent, WD 2-13
floating graphic, WD 1-26, WD 1-27
focus, AC 1-6
font, EX 2-4 – EX 2-5, WD 1-20
document formatted, WD 1-20 – WD 1-21
list, WD 1-21
size, WD 1-20
font alignment, EX 2-6 – EX 2-7
font list, EX 2-5
font size, EX 2-4

font styles, EX 2-6 – EX 2-7
footer, EX 2-12
footer(s), WD 2-18
adding, WD 2-18 – WD 2-19
footers
slide, PPT 2-14 – PPT 2-15
footnotes, WD 2-20 – WD 2-21
foreign key field, AC 2-14, AC 2-15
specifying data type, AC 2-17
form(s), AC 1-4, AC 1-16
Access objects, AC 1-5
creating, AC 1-16 – AC 1-17
editing existing record in, AC 1-17
entering new record, AC 1-17
in Form View, AC 4-3
format, EX 2-2
accounting number, EX 2-3
cells, EX 2-3
conditional, EX 2-14 – EX 2-15
data, EX 2-12 – EX 2-13, EX 2-14
Date/Time field, AC 2-10
number, EX 2-2
Short Text field property, AC 2-9
values, EX 2-2 – EX 2-3
Format Axis pane, EX 4-11
Format Painter, AC 4-15, WD 3-2 – WD 3-3
formatting
chart, EX 4-12 – EX 4-13
clear, from text, WD 3-3
conditional, AC 4-12 – AC 4-13
datasheet, AC 3-22 – AC 3-23
with fonts, WD 1-20 – WD 1-21
shapes, WD 3-18 – WD 3-19
sparklines, EX 4-17
text in presentation, PPT 1-12 – PPT 1-13
text using Mini toolbar and ribbon, WD 1-12 – WD 1-13
using commands, AC 3-23
WordArt, PPT 3-14 – PPT 3-15
formatting marks, WD 1-10
form creation tools, AC 4-3
Form Design View
adding, moving, and aligning controls, AC 4-7
mouse pointer shapes, AC 4-7
use of, AC 4-6 – AC 4-7
Form Layout View
formatting commands, AC 4-5
modifying controls in, AC 4-5
use of, AC 4-4 – AC 4-5
formula(s)
and AutoSum, EX 1-10 – EX 1-11
copying with absolute cell references, EX 3-8 – EX 3-9
copying with relative cell references, EX 3-4 – EX 3-5
entering, EX 1-10 – EX 1-11

entering with multiple operators, EX 1-12 – EX 1-13
Excel, EX 1-13
inserting functions into, EX 3-5
logical formula with AND function, EX 3-10 – EX 3-11
logical formula with IF function, EX 3-6 – EX 3-7
with parentheses, EX 1-13
with percentage increase, EX 1-13
using Quick Analysis tool, EX 3-2 – EX 3-3
Formula AutoComplete, EX 1-14
formula bar, EX 1-2
formula prefix, EX 1-10
Form View, AC 1-16, AC 4-2 – AC 4-3
Form Wizard, AC 1-16
Forward button, WD 1-9
fractional value, AC 2-5
FROM SQL keyword, AC 3-7
function(s), AC 3-20, EX 1-10. See also specific types
AND, EX 3-10 – EX 3-11
COUNT, EX 3-14
COUNTA, EX 3-14 – EX 3-15
DATE, AC 3-21
Date, EX 3-16 – EX 3-17
DATEVALUE, EX 3-16
DAY, EX 3-17
HOUR, EX 3-17
IF, EX 3-6 – EX 3-7
inserting, EX 1-14 – EX 1-15
LEFT, AC 3-21
LEN, AC 3-21
logical, EX 3-6
MINUTE, EX 3-17
MONTH, EX 3-17
MROUND, EX 3-13
nested IF, EX 3-7
NOT logical, EX 3-10
NOW, EX 3-17
OR logical, EX 3-10
PMT, AC 3-21
RIGHT, AC 3-21
ROUND, EX 3-12 – EX 3-13
ROUNDDOWN, EX 3-13
ROUNDUP, EX 3-13
SECOND, EX 3-17
statistical, EX 3-15
SUM, EX 1-11
TIME, EX 3-17
TIMEVALUE, EX 3-17
TODAY, EX 3-16
WEEKDAY, EX 3-17
WORKDAY, EX 3-17
YEAR, EX 3-17
Function Arguments dialog box, EX 3-6, EX 3-7
funnel charts, EX 4-15

G

Get External Data dialog box,
  INT 2-4, INT 2-5
Get External Data - Excel
  Spreadsheet dialog box, AC 2-2,
  AC 2-3
Go to command, WD 2-7
graphic(s)
  arranging objects,
    WD 3-22 – WD 3-23
  bitmap, WD 1-26
  floating, WD 1-26, WD 1-27
  inline, WD 1-26
  inserting, WD 1-26 – WD 1-27
  objects enhancement with style
    and effects, WD 3-21
  sizing and scaling,
    WD 3-16 – WD 3-17
  SmartArt, WD 3-24 – WD 3-25
greater than (>), AC 3-17, EX 3-7
greater than or equal to (>=),
  AC 3-17, EX 3-7
gridline(s), PPT 2-10
gridlines, EX 4-2
grouped shapes, PPT 2-13
groups, PPT 1-6, WD 1-4

H

Hand pointer, WD 1-5
hanging indent, WD 2-13
header, EX 2-12
header(s), WD 2-18
  adding, WD 2-18 – WD 2-19
Header & Footer tab, EX 2-13
Hide & Unhide command, EX 2-9
Hide white space pointer, WD 1-5
Highlighting, WD 1-16
histogram chart, EX 4-15
horizontal axis, EX 4-2
horizontal ruler, AC 4-10, WD 1-4
horizontal scroll bars, WD 1-4
HOUR function, EX 3-17
hyperlink(s), WD 1-10
Hyperlink data type, AC 1-10,
  AC 1-11
hyperlinks, PPT 2-17, PPT 3-9

I

I-beam pointer, EX 1-7, WD 1-5
icon sets, EX 2-14
IF functions, EX 3-6 – EX 3-7
  nesting, EX 3-7
importing, AC 2-2
  Excel worksheets into Access,
    INT 2-2 – INT 2-5
  file formats, AC 2-3
  importing Word outlines into
    PowerPoint, INT 3-2,
    INT 3-4 – INT 3-5

Import Spreadsheet Wizard,
  AC 1-23, AC 2-2, AC 2-3
indent markers, WD 2-12
indents, WD 2-12
  changing, WD 2-12 – WD 2-13
  types, WD 2-13
infinity symbol, AC 2-16
inking, PPT 2-7
inline graphic, WD 1-26, WD 1-27,
  WD 3-15
INNER JOIN ... ON SQL keyword,
  AC 3-7
Input Mask, AC 2-8
  entering data with, AC 2-9
  modifying, AC 2-9
  Short Text field property,
    AC 2-9
  working with, AC 2-9
Insert Chart dialog box, EX 4-3
inserting
  chart, PPT 3-6 – PPT 3-7
  citations, WD 2-22 – WD 2-23
  comment, WD 2-2 – WD 2-5
  digital video,
    PPT 3-18 – PPT 3-19
  function in Excel,
    EX 1-14 – EX 1-15
  functions into formulas, EX 3-5
  graphic, WD 1-26 – WD 1-27
  Online Pictures,
    WD 3-14 – WD 3-15
  page numbers and page breaks,
    WD 2-16 – WD 2-17
  pictures, PPT 1-18 – PPT 1-19
  rows and columns,
    EX 2-10 – EX 2-11,
    WD 3-10 – WD 3-11
  screen recording, PPT 3-5
  slides from other presentations,
    PPT 3-10 – PPT 3-11
  table, WD 3-8 – WD 3-9
  tables, PPT 3-12 – PPT 3-13
  text box, PPT 3-2 – PPT 3-3
  WordArt, PPT 3-14 – PPT 3-15
insertion point, EX 1-6, PPT 1-8,
  WD 1-4
INSERT SQL keyword, AC 3-7
Insert Table command, WD 3-9
integer, AC 2-5, AC 2-7
  integrating Word, Excel, Access,
    and PowerPoint,
    INT 3-1 – INT 3-11
  embedding Excel worksheets
    in PowerPoint,
    INT 3-6 – INT 3-7
  importing Word outlines into
    PowerPoint,
    INT 3-2, INT 3-4 – INT 3-5
  linking Access and Excel
    objects to PowerPoint,
    INT 3-8 – INT 3-9
  methods, INT 3-2, INT 3-11

  updating and breaking,
    INT 3-10 – INT 3-11
  integrating Word, Excel, and
    Access, INT 2-1 – INT 2-11
  copying Access tables
    to Word, INT 2-2 – INT 2-3,
    INT 2-10 – INT 2-11
  copying Word tables to Access,
    INT 2-2, INT 2-6 – INT 2-7
  importing Excel worksheets into
    Access, INT 2-2 – INT 2-5
  linking Access tables to Excel
    and Word, INT 2-2, INT 2-3,
    INT 2-8 – INT 2-9
  methods, INT 2-2,
    INT 2-3, INT 2-11
  integrating Word and Excel,
    INT 1-1 – INT 1-11
  copying charts from Excel to
    Word, INT 1-2, INT 1-3,
    INT 1-6 – INT 1-7
  copying data from Excel to Word,
    INT 1-4 – INT 1-5
  destination file, INT 1-2
  embedding Word files
    in Excel, INT 1-2, INT 1-3,
    INT 1-10 – INT 1-11
  methods, INT 1-2
  object linking and embedding,
    INT 1-3
  source file, INT 1-2
integration, INT 1-2
intellectual property, PPT 1-5
Is Not Null criterion, AC 3-17
Is Null criterion, AC 3-17

J

join line, AC 3-4
junction table, AC 2-15

K

Kana Mode, AC 2-19
keyboard shortcuts, WD 1-22
  Edit mode, AC 1-9
  Navigation mode, AC 1-7
key symbol, AC 2-12, AC 2-16
keyword, WD 3-14

L

label(s), AC 1-16, AC 4-6, EX 1-4,
  PPT 3-2
landscape
  orientation, AC 4-8
  page orientation, AC 1-18
landscape orientation, EX 1-18,
  WD 1-22
Large Number data type, AC 1-11
Layout View
  forms, AC 4-3, AC 1-16

  reports, AC 4-9
LEFT function, AC 3-21
left indent, WD 2-13
left tab, WD 3-5
legend, EX 4-2, PPT 3-6
LEN function, AC 3-21
less than (<), AC 3-17, EX 3-7
less than or equal to (<=), AC 3-17
Like, AC 3-18, AC 3-19, EX 3-7
line chart, EX 4-3, PPT 3-7
line spacings, WD 2-12 – WD 2-13
line with markers chart, EX 4-3
link(s), INT 1-2
  reestablishing links, INT 4-12
link(s), AC 2-2
  file formats, AC 2-3
linked files
  enabling content, INT 2-10
  opening, INT 2-10
linked objects, INT 1-2
  inserting, INT 1-8 – INT 1-9
  opening linked files, INT 1-9
  reestablishing links to charts,
    INT 1-9
linking
  Access and Excel objects to
    PowerPoint,
    INT 3-8 – INT 3-9
  Access tables to Excel and Word,
    INT 2-2 – INT 2-3,
    INT 2-8 – INT 2-9
  data between Word and Excel,
    INT 1-2
  embedding vs., INT 3-3
  objects, INT 3-2
  updating and breaking,
    INT 3-10 – INT 3-11
link line, AC 3-4
Live Preview, PPT 1-14
local application, AC 1-21
logical formula
  with AND function,
    EX 3-10 – EX 3-11
  with IF function,
    EX 3-6 – EX 3-7
logical functions, EX 3-6
logical test, EX 3-6
logical view, AC 1-14
Long Integer, in Number Field Size,
  AC 2-7
Long Text data type, AC 1-11
Lookup Wizard data type, AC 1-11

M

Manage Document, WD 2-27
manual calculation, EX 3-18
manual page break, WD 2-16
many-to-many relationship,
  AC 2-15
margins, WD 1-22
  mirror, WD 1-23

setting document, WD 1-22 – WD 1-23
merging, PPT 2-8
Microsoft Access
　advantages, for database management, AC 1-2
　changing from Navigation mode to Edit mode, AC 1-6
　comparing Excel, AC 1-3
　starting, AC 1-4
Microsoft Excel. *See* Excel
　comparing Access, AC 1-3
　importing Access database, AC 2-2
　importing data from, AC 2-2 – AC 2-3
Microsoft Office
　color palettes, EX 2-13
Microsoft OneDrive, PPT 1-23
Microsoft 2019. *See also* **document(s)**
　adding Alt text, WD 3-26 – WD 3-27
　adding bullets or numbering, WD 1-24 – WD 1-25
　adding footnotes and endnotes, WD 2-20 – WD 2-21
　adding headers and footers, WD 2-18 – WD 2-19
　adjusting and rotating shapes, WD 3-20 – WD 3-21
　applying style to text, WD 2-14 – WD 2-15
　applying table style, WD 3-12 – WD 3-13
　applying theme, WD 1-28 – WD 1-29
　borders, WD 3-6 – WD 3-7
　copying and pasting text, WD 1-18 – WD 1-19
　creating bibliography, WD 2-24 – WD 2-25
　creating SmartArt graphic, WD 3-24 – WD 3-25
　cut and paste text, WD 1-16 – WD 1-17
　drawing and formatting shapes, WD 3-18 – WD 3-19
　entering and revising text, WD 1-6 – WD 1-7
　Find and Replace text, WD 2-6 – WD 2-7
　formatting text using Mini toolbar and ribbon, WD 1-12 – WD 1-13
　formatting with fonts, WD 1-20 – WD 1-21
　graphics objects, WD 3-22 – WD 3-23
　inserting and deleting rows and columns, WD 3-10 – WD 3-11

　inserting citations, WD 2-22 – WD 2-23
　inserting comment, WD 2-2 – WD 2-5
　inserting graphics, WD 1-26 – WD 1-27
　inserting Online Pictures, WD 3-14 – WD 3-15
　inserting page numbers and page breaks, WD 2-16 – WD 2-17
　inserting table, WD 3-8 – WD 3-9
　inspecting document, WD 2-26 – WD 2-27
　line spacings and indents, WD 2-12 – WD 2-13
　mouse pointers, WD 1-5
　proofreading and revising text, WD 2-10 – WD 2-11
　Read Aloud feature, WD 2-10
　report created using, WD 1-3
　saving document, WD 1-8 – WD 1-9
　selecting text, WD 1-10 – WD 1-11
　setting document margins, WD 1-22 – WD 1-23
　shading, WD 3-6 – WD 3-7
　sizing and scaling graphics, WD 3-16 – WD 3-17
　Spelling and Grammar, WD 2-8 – WD 2-9
　starting, WD 1-4 – WD 1-5
　tabs, WD 3-4 – WD 3-5
　using, WD 1-2
　using Format Painter, WD 3-2 – WD 3-3
　viewing and navigating document, WD 1-14 – WD 1-15
Mini toolbar, PPT 1-12, PPT 1-13, WD 1-12
　buttons, WD 1-13
MINUTE function, EX 3-17
mirror margins, WD 1-23
mixed reference, EX 3-9
mode indicator, EX 1-2
modifying
　Date/Time fields, AC 2-10 – AC 2-11
　fields, AC 1-12 – AC 1-13
　Number and Currency fields, AC 2-6 – AC 2-7
　Short Text fields, AC 2-8 – AC 2-9
MONTH function, EX 3-17
mouse pointers, WD 1-5
Move Chart dialog box, EX 4-7
Move Mode, AC 2-19
Move pointer, EX 1-7
MROUND function, EX 3-13
multiple operators
　entering formulas with, EX 1-12 – EX 1-13
multiplication operator (*), AC 3-21

multiuser, AC 1-6
multiuser capabilities, Excel and Access compared, AC 1-3

N

Name box, EX 1-2
navigating
　document, WD 1-14 – WD 1-15
navigation buttons, AC 1-6, AC 4-2
Navigation mode, AC 1-6
　keyboard shortcuts, AC 1-7
Navigation Pane, AC 1-4
Navigation pane, WD 2-7
negative indent, WD 2-13
nested IF function, EX 3-7
New folder button, WD 1-9
Normal pointer, EX 1-7
Normal style, WD 1-6
Normal view, EX 1-16, PPT 1-6, PPT 1-11, PPT 1-17
not equal to (<>), AC 3-17, EX 3-7
note reference mark, WD 2-20
notes
　entering, PPT 2-3
　printing, PPT 2-3
Notes button, PPT 1-6
Notes Page view, PPT 1-17
NOT logical function, EX 3-10
NOW function, EX 3-17
Number data type, AC 1-11, AC 2-6
　vs. Currency data type, AC 2-5
numbered list, WD 1-25
Number field
　adding, AC 2-7
　modifying, AC 2-6 – AC 2-7
Number Field Size property options, AC 2-7
number format, EX 2-2
numbering
　adding, WD 1-24 – WD 1-25
numbering gallery, WD 1-25
Num Lock, AC 2-19

O

object, INT 1-2
object, EX 4-6
object(s), PPT 1-8
　aligning and grouping, PPT 2-12 – PPT 2-13
　animating, PPT 3-16 – PPT 3-17
　distributing, PPT 2-13
　embedded, PPT 3-6
object linking and embedding (OLE), INT 1-3
　copying and pasting, INT 1-2
　embedding, INT 3-2
　linking, INT 3-2
　linking Access and Excel to PowerPoint, INT 3-8 – INT 3-9
objects, AC 1-4, AC 1-7

object views, AC 1-11
Office clipboard
　copying and pasting data from Excel to Word, INT 1-4 – INT 1-5
　copying and pasting objects, INT 1-2
Office Clipboard, WD 1-16
OLE Object data type, AC 1-11
OneDrive, AC 1-20
　creating new folder in, AC 1-21
　saving and sharing database with, AC 1-20 – AC 1-21
one-to-many line, AC 2-16
one-to-many relationship, AC 2-12, AC 2-15
　creating, AC 2-16 – AC 2-17
one-to-one relationship, AC 2-15
Online Picture, EX 2-3
　opening files, linked, INT 2-10
operators, AC 3-20
　arithmetic, AC 3-21
　comparison, AC 3-16, AC 3-17
Options command, WD 3-21
OR criteria, AC 3-18 – AC 3-19
ORDER BY … ASC (DESC) SQL keyword, AC 3-7
order of operations, EX 1-12
Organize button, WD 1-9
OR logical function, EX 3-10
orphan records, AC 2-15
outdent, WD 2-13
outline(s), Word, importing into PowerPoint, INT 3-2, INT 3-4 – INT 3-5
Outline view, PPT 1-17, WD 1-15
Overtype, AC 2-19

P

page break, WD 2-17
　automatic, WD 2-16
　page break inserting, WD 2-16 – WD 2-17
　page break manual, WD 2-16
Page Break Preview, EX 1-17
Page Layout view, EX 1-16, EX 1-17
page numbers
　inserting, WD 2-16 – WD 2-17
page orientation, changing, AC 1-18
Page Setup group, EX 1-19
panes, PPT 1-6
parent records, AC 2-15
parent table, AC 2-15
paste
　text, WD 1-16, WD 1-18 – WD 1-19
Paste command, INT 2-9
　options for copying charts from Excel to Word, INT 1-6 – INT 1-7
Paste Link command, INT 2-9
Paste Options, EX 1-9

Paste Preview, EX 1-9
Paste Special command, INT 2-9
Paste Special dialog box, INT 1-8, INT 1-9
pattern, AC 2-9
permissions, PPT 3-13
Picture(s)
   copying from Excel to Word, INT 1-5
   cropping, PPT 3-4 – PPT 3-5
   defined, PPT 1-18
   inserting, PPT 1-18 – PPT 1-19
   resizing, PPT 1-18 – PPT 1-19
   revising, PPT 3-4 – PPT 3-5
picture sized non-proportionally, PPT 1-19
picture sized proportionally, PPT 1-19
pie chart, EX 4-3, PPT 3-7
   creating, EX 4-14 – EX 4-15
planning
   documents, WD 1-3
   presentation, PPT 1-4 – PPT 1-5
plot area, EX 4-2
PMT function, AC 3-21
point, EX 2-4, WD 1-20
pointers in Excel, EX 1-7
portrait, page orientation, AC 1-18
portrait orientation, AC 4-8, EX 1-18, WD 1-22
PowerPoint
   adding bullets to paragraphs, PPT 1-13
   using on touch screen, PPT 1-3
presentation graphics software, PPT 1-2
presentations
   adding new slides, PPT 1-10 – PPT 1-11
   adding slide footers, PPT 2-14 – PPT 2-15
   animating objects, PPT 3-16 – PPT 3-17
   applying design themes, PPT 1-14 – PPT 1-15
   with Berlin theme applied, PPT 1-15
   coauthoring, PPT 3-15
   comparing presentation views, PPT 1-16 – PPT 1-17
   converting text to SmartArt graphic, PPT 2-2 – PPT 2-3
   entering and editing chart data, PPT 3-8 – PPT 3-9
   entering and printing notes, PPT 2-3
   examining window, PPT 1-6 – PPT 1-7
   formatting text, PPT 1-12 – PPT 1-13
   formatting WordArt, PPT 3-14 – PPT 3-15
   handout, PPT 1-3
   inserting and editing digital video, PPT 3-18 – PPT 3-19
   inserting and resizing pictures, PPT 1-18 – PPT 1-19
   inserting chart, PPT 3-6 – PPT 3-7
   inserting slides from other, PPT 3-10 – PPT 3-11
   inserting tables, PPT 3-12 – PPT 3-13
   inserting text box, PPT 3-2 – PPT 3-3
   inserting WordArt, PPT 3-14 – PPT 3-15
   planning effective, PPT 1-4 – PPT 1-5
   presentation software, PPT 1-2 – PPT 1-3
   printing presentation, PPT 1-22 – PPT 1-23
   revising and cropping picture, PPT 3-4 – PPT 3-5
   saving as video, PPT 3-19
   setting slide transitions and timings, PPT 2-16 – PPT 2-17
   slide text, PPT 1-8 – PPT 1-9
   Spell Checker, PPT 1-20 – PPT 1-21
   start screen, PPT 1-7
   tasks using, PPT 1-2
   on touchscreen, PPT 1-3
   viewing in grayscale or black and white, PPT 1-11
Presenter view, PPT 1-16, PPT 1-17
previewing
   reports, AC 1-19
primary key field, AC 1-7, AC 1-10, AC 2-2, AC 2-12, AC 2-15
   creating, AC 2-12 – AC 2-13
   setting in Design View, AC 2-13
print area, setting, EX 1-19
printing
   presentation, PPT 1-22 – PPT 1-23
print options, customization of, EX 1-18 – EX 1-19
Print Preview, AC 1-18, AC 4-9
properties, AC 1-13
Property Update Options Action Tag, AC 2-11
Protect Document, WD 2-27

Q

queries, AC 1-4, AC 3-2
   Access objects, AC 1-5
   action, AC 3-4
   creating, AC 1-14 – AC 1-15
   filters vs., AC 3-13
   Select, AC 1-14
   sorting datasheet, AC 1-15
query by example (QBE) grid, AC 3-4
Query Datasheet View, AC 3-2
   editing data, AC 3-3
   freezing and hiding columns, AC 3-3
   sorting, AC 3-9
   use of, AC 3-2 – AC 3-3
   viewing Applicants field, AC 3-7
query design grid, AC 3-4
Query Design View, AC 3-4
   adding and deleting table, AC 3-5
   adding and removing fields, AC 3-5
   creating calculated field, AC 3-21
   creating query, AC 3-5
   with AND criteria, AC 3-17
   linking tables, AC 3-5
   with OR criteria, AC 3-19
   with AND and OR criteria, AC 3-19
   sorting, AC 3-9
   use of, AC 3-4 – AC 3-5
query grid. See query by example (QBE) grid
Quick Access toolbar, WD 1-4
Quick Analysis tool
   charts tab in, EX 4-5
   formula using, EX 3-2 – EX 3-3
Quick Style, PPT 2-4
Quick Tables command, WD 3-9

R

radar chart, PPT 3-7
range, EX 1-2
   selecting, EX 1-3
Read Aloud feature, WD 2-10
Reading view, PPT 1-17
Read Mode view, WD 1-15
read-only reports, AC 1-18
record(s), AC 1-6, AC 1-7, AC 2-15
   deleting from table, AC 1-8 – AC 1-9
   editing in table, AC 1-8 – AC 1-9
record source, AC 1-18
Redo command, WD 1-17
referential integrity, AC 2-15
relational database, AC 1-7
   designing, AC 2-14 – AC 2-15
   purpose of, AC 2-14
   software, AC 1-2
   terminologies, AC 2-14 – AC 2-15
Relationship report, AC 2-16
relative cell references, EX 3-4 – EX 3-5
repair, AC 1-24
Repeat command, WD 1-17
report(s), AC 1-4, AC 1-18
   Access objects, AC 1-5
   creating, AC 1-18 – AC 1-19
   Excel and Access compared, AC 1-3
   previewing, AC 1-19
   setting grouping fields, AC 1-19
report creation tools, AC 4-9
Report Design View, AC 4-10 – AC 4-11
Report Layout View
   resizing column, AC 4-9
   use of, AC 4-8 – AC 4-9
report sections, AC 4-11
report source
   creating, WD 2-23
Report View, AC 4-9
report views, AC 4-9
Report Wizard, AC 1-18
Required
   Date/Time field, AC 2-10
   Short Text field property, AC 2-9
resizing
   pictures, PPT 1-18 – PPT 1-19
ribbon, PPT 1-6
   formatting text using, WD 1-12 – WD 1-13
Ribbon Display Options button, WD 1-4
RIGHT function, AC 3-21
right indent, WD 2-13
Right-pointing arrow pointer, WD 1-5
right tab, WD 3-5
rotate handle, PPT 2-4, WD 1-26
rotating
   shapes, WD 3-20 – WD 3-21
ROUNDDOWN function, EX 3-13
ROUND function, EX 3-12 – EX 3-13
ROUNDUP function, EX 3-13
row(s)
   changing height, EX 2-9
   deleting and inserting, EX 2-10 – EX 2-11
   headings, PPT 3-6
   hiding and unhiding, EX 2-11
Row Height command, EX 2-9
rows
   deleting, WD 3-10 – WD3-11
   inserting, WD 3-10 – WD 3-11
run, AC 3-4

S

save, WD 1-8
   documents, WD 1-8 – WD 1-9
Save As command, WD 1-14
Save As dialog box, WD 1-9
Save command, WD 1-14
scale, WD 3-16
scaling to fit, EX 1-18 – EX 1-19

scatter chart, EX 4-15
screen recording, PPT 3-5
ScreenTip, WD 1-4
scroll, WD 1-14
scroll arrows, WD 1-4
scroll boxes, WD 1-4
Scroll Lock, AC 2-19
scrubbing, AC 2-15
Search box, EX 1-2, WD 1-4
SECOND function, EX 3-17
section bars, AC 4-10
sections, AC 4-10
security
    Excel and Access compared, AC 1-3
select, WD 1-10
selection box, PPT 1-8
Selection pointer, WD 1-5
Select query, AC 1-14, AC 3-4
SELECT SQL keyword, AC 3-6, AC 3-7
shading, WD 3-6 – WD 3-7
shapes
    adjusting, WD 3-20 – WD 3-21
    drawing, WD 3-18 – WD 3-19
    editing and duplicating, PPT 2-10 – PPT 2-11
    formatting, WD 3-18 – WD 3-19
    inserting and styling, PPT 2-4 – PPT 2-5
    rearranging and modifying, PPT 2-8 – PPT 2-9
    rotating, WD 3-20 – WD 3-21
    rotating and modifying, PPT 2-6 – PPT 2-7
    size and position of, PPT 2-9
Share button, WD 1-4
sheet tabs, EX 2-16 – EX 2-17
sheet tab scrolling buttons, EX 1-2
Sheet View group, EX 1-17
shortcut key, WD 1-22
Short Text, AC 1-10, AC 2-8
    data type, AC 1-11
    field properties, AC 2-9
    modifying, AC 2-8 – AC 2-9
Show white space pointer, WD 1-5
Simple Query Wizard, AC 1-14
    using, AC 1-15
Single
    in Number Field Size, AC 2-7
sizing handles, EX 4-4, PPT 1-8, WD 1-26
slide footers, PPT 2-14 – PPT 2-15
Slide pane, PPT 1-6
slides
    inking, PPT 2-7
    inserting from other presentation, PPT 3-10 – PPT 3-11
    inserting video clip on, PPT 3-19
    layout, PPT 1-10
    new blank, PPT 1-11
    text, PPT 1-8 – PPT 1-9
    thumbnail pane, PPT 1-6
    thumbnails, PPT 1-6
    two content slide layout, PPT 1-11
Slide Show view, PPT 1-17
Slide Sorter view, PPT 1-17
slide timings, PPT 2-16 – PPT 2-17
slide transitions, PPT 2-16 – PPT 2-17
SmartArt graphic, WD 3-24 – WD 3-25
SmartArt graphics, PPT 2-2 – PPT 2-3
SmartArt Style, PPT 2-2 – PPT 2-3
Smart guides, PPT 2-8
sorting
    data, AC 3-8 – AC 3-9
    query datasheet, AC 1-15
Sort row, AC 3-8
Source Manager dialog box, WD 2-25
source presentation, PPT 3-10 – PPT 3-11
sparklines, EX 4-16 – EX 4-17
Speaker coach, PPT 1-19
speaker notes, PPT 1-16
Spell Checker, PPT 1-20 – PPT 1-21
spelling, PPT 1-20 – PPT 1-21
spelling and finding text, EX 2-18 – EX 2-19
Spelling and Grammar, WD 1-7, WD 2-8 – WD 2-9
Standard Colors, EX 2-13
starting
    Microsoft Access, AC 1-4
starting Excel, EX 1-2 – EX 1-3
stated conditions, EX 3-6
statistical functions, EX 3-15
status bar, PPT 1-6, WD 1-4
status bar indicators, AC 2-19
stock chart, PPT 3-7
storage
    Excel and Access compared, AC 1-3
storyboard, PPT 1-5
Structured Query Language (SQL) View
    adding Applicants field, AC 3-7
    use of, AC 3-6 – AC 3-7
styled triangle shape, PPT 2-5
styles, WD 2-14
    applying to text, WD 2-14 – WD 2-15
style sets, WD 2-14
    changing, WD 2-15
subdatasheets, AC 2-18 – AC 2-19
subscript text, PPT 2-15
subtitle placeholder, PPT 1-8
subtraction operator (-), AC 3-21
SUM function, EX 1-11
sunburst chart, EX 4-15
superscript text, PPT 2-15
surface chart, PPT 3-7
symbol gallery, WD 3-3
symbols, EX 2-3
system clipboard, WD 1-16

T

tab, PPT 1-6, WD 1-4
    setting and modifying, WD 3-4 – WD 3-5
    types, WD 3-5
Tab Color, EX 2-16, EX 2-17
table(s)
    Access, copying to Word, INT 2-2, INT 2-3
    Access, linking to Excel and Word, INT 2-2, INT 2-3, INT 2-8 – INT 2-9
    Word, copying to Access, INT 2-2, INT 2-6 – INT 2-7
table(s), AC 1-4, AC 1-7, AC 2-15, WD 3-8
    Access objects, AC 1-5
    blank, WD 3-9
    creating, AC 1-10 – AC 1-11
    formatted, PPT 3-13
    inserting, PPT 3-12 – PPT 3-13, WD 3-8 – WD 3-9
    menu commands, WD 3-9
    new row, WD 3-9
    text, WD 3-9
tab leaders, WD 3-4, WD 3-5
Table Datasheet View
    calculated field, AC 3-21
Table Design View, AC 2-6
    creating calculated field, AC 3-21
    modifying Number field properties in, AC 2-7
table style, WD 3-12 – WD 3-13
tab stop, WD 3-4 – WD 3-5
template, AC 1-22
    creating presentation using, PPT 1-7
text
    aligning paragraph text, PPT 1-9
    applying shadows, WD 1-21
    applying text effects, WD 1-21
    apply styles, WD 2-14 – WD 2-15
    clear formatting, WD 3-3
    converting to SmartArt graphic, PPT 2-2 – PPT 2-3
    copying and pasting, WD 1-18 – WD 1-19
    cut and paste, WD 1-16 – WD 1-17
    dragging and dropping, WD 1-16, WD 1-17
    Find and Replace, WD 2-6 – WD 2-7
    formatting, PPT 1-12 – PPT 1-13
    formatting using Mini toolbar and ribbon, WD 1-12 – WD 1-13
    methods for selecting, WD 1-11
    moving with Paste option, WD 1-17
    Options button, EX 4-11
    selecting, WD 1-10 – WD 1-11
    slide, PPT 1-8 – PPT 1-9
    subscript, PPT 2-15
    superscript, PPT 2-15
    title slide, PPT 1-9
    translating, EX 2-18
    underlining, WD 3-6
text box
    defaults, PPT 3-3
    inserting in presentation, PPT 3-2 – PPT 3-3
text boxes, AC 1-16, AC 4-6
text placeholders, PPT 1-8
Text predictions, WD 1-6, WD 1-7
text selection, WD 1-10 – WD 1-11
    methods, WD 1-11
text wrapping, WD 2-17
Theme Colors, EX 2-13
themes, AC 4-15 – AC 4-16, EX 2-12
    applying design, PPT 1-14 – PPT 1-15
    colors, PPT 1-14, PPT 1-15
    effects, PPT 1-14
    fonts, PPT 1-14
theme(s), WD 1-20, WD 1-28 – WD 1-29
Thesaurus pane, WD 2-11
TIME function, EX 3-17
TIMEVALUE function, EX 3-17
title bar, WD 1-4
title placeholder, PPT 1-8
TODAY function, EX 3-16
toggle button, WD 1-10
Touch Mode button, PPT 1-3
touchscreen
    using PowerPoint on, PPT 1-3
translating text, EX 2-18
treemap chart, EX 4-15
trendline, EX 4-18
    choosing, for chart, EX 4-19

U

unbound controls, AC 4-7
Undo command, WD 1-17
UPDATE…SET SQL keyword, AC 3-7
updating and breaking links, INT 3-10 – INT 3-11
Up to button, WD 1-9
user, AC 4-2

V

value axis, EX 4-2, PPT 3-8
values, EX 1-4
Version History, WD 2-27
vertical axis, EX 4-2
vertical buttons, WD 1-4
vertical ruler, WD 1-4
View buttons, PPT 1-6
view buttons, WD 1-4
viewing
  document,
    WD 1-14 – WD 1-15
views, PPT 1-6

W

Waterfall chart, EX 4-15
Web Layout view, WD 1-15
webpage
  inserting hyperlink, PPT 2-17
Web publication source,
  WD 2-23
WEEKDAY function, EX 3-17
WHERE SQL keyword, AC 3-7
wildcard characters, AC 3-19

WordArt, EX 4-12, EX 4-15, PPT 3-14,
  WD 1-21
  formatting, PPT 3-14 – PPT 3-15
  inserting, PPT 3-14 – PPT 3-15
Word Count dialog box, WD 2-11
word-processing box, PPT 3-2
word-processing program,
  WD 1-2
Word-program window,
  WD 1-4 – WD 1-5
Word Researcher tool, WD 2-25
word wrap, WD 1-6
workbook(s), EX 1-2, EX 1-3
  AutoRecover, EX 1-6
WORKDAY function, EX 3-17
works cited, WD 2-24
worksheet(s)
  embedding Excel in PowerPoint,
    INT 3-6 – INT 3-7
  importing into Access, INT 2-2,
    INT 2-3, INT 2-4 – INT 2-5
worksheet(s), EX 1-2, PPT 3-6
  adding, EX 2-17
  with annual statistics, EX 1-15
  Backstage view,
    EX 1-18 – EX 1-19

changing views,
  EX 1-16 – EX 1-17
with column widths and row
  height, EX 2-9
with conditional formatting,
  EX 2-15
controlling worksheet
  calculations, EX 3-18 – EX 3-19
copying, EX 2-17
deleting, EX 2-17
edited, EX 1-7
in Edit mode, EX 1-7
fitting content onto a page,
  EX 1-19
font styles and alignment,
  EX 2-7
with formatted headings and
  column labels, EX 2-5
with formatted values, EX 2-3
with AND function, EX 3-11
with IF function, EX 3-7
with inserting and deleting rows
  and columns, EX 2-11
with modified label, EX 4-7
modifying tabs, EX 2-16 – EX 2-17
navigating, EX 1-3

showing and printing formulas,
  EX 3-19
SUM functions in, EX 1-11
translating text, EX 2-18
window, EX 1-2

X

x-axis, EX 4-2
**XML (Extensible Markup
  Language),** AC 2-2
XY (scatter) chart, PPT 3-7
XY scatter chart, EX 4-15

Y

y-axis, EX 4-2
YEAR function, EX 3-17
Yes/No data type, AC 1-11

Z

z-axis, EX 4-2
Zoom level button, WD 1-4
Zoom slider, PPT 1-6, WD 1-4,
  WD 1-15